Introduction to
United States Government
Information Sources

LIBRARY SCIENCE TEXT SERIES

INTRODUCTION TO UNITED STATES GOVERNMENT INFORMATION SOURCES

4th Edition

Joe Morehead
and
Mary Fetzer

1992

LIBRARIES UNLIMITED, INC.
Englewood, Colorado

LIBRARIES UNLIMITED, INC.
P.O. Box 6633
Englewood, CO 80155-6633

Library of Congress Cataloging-in-Publication Data

Morehead, Joe, 1931-
    Introduction to United States government information sources / 4th ed. / Joe Morehead and Mary Fetzer.
    xxxii, 474 p. 17x25 cm. -- (Library science text series)
    Includes indexes.
    ISBN 0-87287-909-7 (cloth) -- ISBN 1-56308-066-4 (paper)
    1. Government publications--United States--Handbooks, manuals, etc. I. Fetzer, Mary K. II. Title. III. Series.
Z1223.Z7M665 1992
[J83]
015.73'053--dc20   92-13251
                                      CIP

Contents

List of Illustrations

Figure

Figure

Preface

The purpose of this text is to provide an introductory account of the general and specialized sources in print and nonprint formats that compose the bibliographic structure of federal government information. Its audiences consist of institutions that acquire government publications and deal with government information, students in schools of library and information studies, and professional librarians and their publics.

Chapters 1 through 3 describe the administrative machinery and the information systems by which both government and libraries transfer and share official and commercial products and services. Chapter 4 introduces the general checklists, indexes, and guides to retrospective and current government information. Chapters 5 through 9 discuss the prominent publications generated by or in support of the activities of the three constitutionally mandated branches, the independent agencies with regulatory powers, and the numerous advisory bodies. The interrelationships among these entities embody the grand dialectic the framers of the Constitution envisioned, the *fons et origo* of our polity. Chapter 10 treats the ubiquitous statistics created by or for the federal establishment, including the products and services generated by the 1990 census. Chapter 11 addresses the several components that constitute the vast research activities commissioned by or directly performed by government in partnership with the private sector. Chapter 12 portrays the consequential role the federal government plays in the creation and distribution of maps, charts, and gazetteers. Chapter 13 alerts the reader to the important reference and research resources that lie within federal serials and periodicals. The appendix provides the text of the "Principles on Government Information" established by the Government Documents Round Table (GODORT). More than 80 figures complement the narrative. Separate title/series, personal name, and subject indexes provide access to the contents.

—JM
—MF

Acknowledgments

Mary Fetzer

My contributions to this work were aided considerably by the forbearance of fine colleagues and staff at the Archibald Stevens Alexander Library, Rutgers University, New Brunswick, New Jersey, and by the generous award of two short research leaves from the Rutgers University Libraries. Special colleague and friend Edward Pason heard my woes, quieted my mind, and pushed me to brisk walks to clear the cobwebs. Two valued associates, Patricia Reeling and Benjamin Weintraub, merit thanks also for introducing me to documents librarianship and for the encouragement each has provided over the years as teacher, professional colleague, and friend. Thanks, too, go to the students, for they have unwittingly nudged, inspired, and fostered a raison d'être. And, finally, my appreciation goes to my husband, Paul Hinsenkamp, who understood the rigors of writing and tolerated domestic benign neglect; to my spirited Springer, Toby, who provided humor; and to two loving parents who have been the best role models life could bestow.

Joe Morehead

Several individuals have contributed to this effort. The small but vital tasks of tracking down correct citations and providing me with illustrations were essential. For these activities I am indebted to Nancy Lenahan of the Schaffer Law Library, Albany Law School; to Otis A. Chadley, Catherine M. Dwyer, Richard D. Irving, and Barbara J. Via of the university library and the Thomas E. Dewey Graduate Library, University of Albany; and to my graduate assistant Paul A. Doty of the School of Information Science and Policy, University at Albany, Albany, New York.

A special measure of gratitude goes to LeRoy C. Schwarzkopf, whose contribution to this work has been of inestimable value. LeRoy's wisdom and humanity have inspired me over the last two decades, and his efforts on behalf of government documents librarianship have been significant indeed.

Introduction

The word *information* in the title of this work and as used throughout is intended to connote, in Peter Hernon's words, "the content of a message or communication conveyed and assimilated by the person receiving that message." In attempting to summarize the salient sources of government information, the authors deliberately eschewed a detailed analysis of information *policy*, defined by Hernon as "a set of laws, regulations, directives, statements, and judicial interpretations that direct and manage the life cycle of information."[1] The policies, or often lack of appropriate doctrines or positions, that the federal government tries to convey relative to information are complex and frequently contradictory. Commentary on information policy forms a large and rapidly expanding body of research and opinion, but that is not addressed here. Accordingly, we have endeavored to delineate the distinctive characteristics of selected information sources, and we encourage readers to consult the many distinguished monographs and articles in the professional literature on the issues surrounding matters of federal information policy. Sources described in this work, of course, are subject to change, as long-established titles can suddenly succumb to or become subsets of databanks spawned by newer technologies. The rapid rate of change effected by policies such as privatization, budgetary cuts, and technological developments made revisions during the writing difficult. Government information products and services and government policies were in flux even as we wrote, and it appears that they will continue to change indefinitely.

The word *information* also permits students of this discipline (studying government information sources) to include without semantic awkwardness the expanding and flourishing sources of bibliographic, numeric, and textual materials transmitted to libraries and to individual users in electronic formats. Of these nonprint forms, CD-ROM (compact disk-read only memory) products appear conspicuously attractive both to the federal establishment and to the community of users. As Sandy Whiteley notes, these puissant carriers of vast amounts of information burst upon the library scene "in the mid-1980s." Their spectacular growth, she remarks, is evidenced by the fact that the

> 1991 edition of Meckler's *CD-ROMs in Print* lists 1,400 products, twice as many as in the previous year.... The median price is now in the hundreds rather than thousands of dollars. Library literature is full of discussions of the implementation of optical discs in libraries, and there are several journals now devoted just to CD-ROM. Once again, we hear the talk about the electronic library that was prevalent when computers were first introduced.[2]

Although we have tried to integrate as many of the useful CD-ROM products as possible into this text, we realize that the field is expanding so rapidly that the only way to keep abreast of new electronic products is, logically but ironically, via electronic bulletin boards. One is tempted to proclaim that all government information is now or shortly will be available in an electronic format of one sort or another and leave it at that. But the crucial issues of ethics, equity, and user empowerment seem to intensify rather than diminish, and these issues also form part of the corpus of information policy research and analysis. As members of the information professions discuss the text of H.R. 2772, the GPO Wide Information Network for Data Online Act of 1991 (known as GPO WINDO), we see merit in the language that "provides that individuals seeking access to ... a wide range of federal electronic databases ... would be charged fees that approximate the incremental cost of dissemination" but that federal "depository libraries would be given free access to the databases."[3]

However, experience tells us to avoid the luxury of unalloyed faith and optimism when confronting government systems that may appear promising for public consumption. As Assistant Comptroller General Lawrence H. Thompson averred in testimony before the House Ways and Means Committee in 1991, the "federal government's acquisition of information technology" has not resulted in the creation of quality service to the public. "The government has reaped a poor return on its multi-billion dollar investment in information systems," Thompson stated.

> Agencies have created tens of thousands of computer systems that resemble mammoth electronic filing cabinets crammed with disconnected data generated by thousands of individual offices. Typically, data are poorly maintained and cannot be accessed by those who need them.... We cannot continue to use automation to make incremental improvements to current operations if we intend to fundamentally change service delivery in the future.[4]

Thompson's remarks constitute a cautionary tale, for the providing of information is a vital service and its accuracy and usability are requisite to all other government services. An organizational chart of the federal establishment, as shown in figure I.1, scarcely reveals the immense amount of information generated in its myriad bureaus.

The pricing of government information, a recurring theme in the draft editions of OMB Circular A-130 during the 1980s, has been challenged by those who envisage public information "as a national resource to be developed and preserved in the public interest."[5] Diane Smith addressed the problem by refuting the formulation that government information is an economic commodity.

> Traditional capitalistic economic theory claims that information is a "free good" and differs from other products in several ways. First, information can never be truly scarce, except through the manipulation of the marketplace. Consequently, the laws of supply and demand and resulting pricing policy are not relevant in any discussion of information as a commodity.... Yet the concept of selling certain types of information runs counter to the social policy of government information as a public good; ... this policy is firmly affixed in the

Fig. I.1. The government of the United States

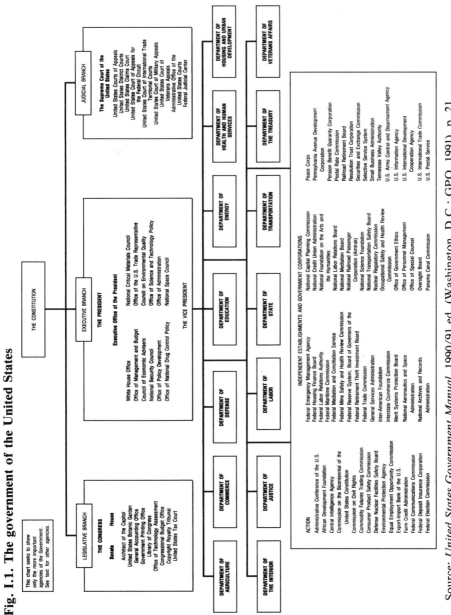

Source: *United States Government Manual*, 1990/91 ed. (Washington, D.C.: GPO, 1991), p. 21.

American free educational system, in the belief in academic freedom
and information exchange, in the First Amendment guarantee of free
speech, and in the Freedom of Information laws dealing with government actions.[6]

Despite Smith's eloquent defense of government information as a public
good, the assumption that access is guaranteed under the First Amendment
merits closer attention. What, for instance, does one make of former Supreme
Court Justice Potter Stewart's assertion that "There exists no constitutional right
to have access to particular government information, or to require openness from
the bureaucracy"?[7] At its June 1990 meeting the National Commission on
Libraries and Information Science (NCLIS) produced a major policy statement
entitled "Principles of Public Information," which was widely disseminated and
eventually published in the *Federal Register*. Preceding the eight principles is a
Preamble, the second paragraph of which "reaffirms that the information policies of the U.S. government are based on the freedoms guaranteed by the Constitution" and "that public information is information owned by the people, held in
trust by their government, and should be available to the people except where
restricted by law."[8]

However, access to public information, similar to penumbras of privacy
secured by the Supreme Court in *Griswold* v. *Connecticut* and extended in *Roe* v.
Wade, is not explicitly enumerated in the Constitution.[9] There may be a *need* to
know, as an informed citizenry is fundamental to a democracy, but government is
not constitutionally obligated to ensure the "right" of access to government information. In the principles proclaimed by NCLIS, words and phrases such as
guarantee, ensure, obligation, and *right of access* are sprinkled throughout. In
other statements asserting an inalienable right to access one finds phrases such as
"inherent in the Bill of Rights" or "embedded in our constitutional freedoms."
Unfortunately, the courts have never dealt with this issue directly.

Eminent constitutional law scholar Thomas I. Emerson has written extensively on the legal foundations of the right to be informed. He avers that the
"most potentially significant application of the right to know lies in the area of
obtaining information" and that "the greatest contribution that could be made in
this whole realm of law would be explicit recognition by the courts that the constitutional right to know embraces the right of the public to obtain information
from the government." Emerson adds that the "public, as sovereign, must have
all information available in order to instruct its servants, the government."
Moreover,

if democracy is to work, there can be no holding back of information;
otherwise ultimate decisionmaking by the people, to whom that function is committed, becomes impossible. Whether or not such a
guarantee of the right to know is the sole purpose of the first amendment, it is surely a main element of that provision and should be
recognized as such.[10]

Even obvious exceptions to full and unfettered access, such as compelling
national security interests, would have to be carefully articulated and justified
and, in Emerson's view, "should be scrupulously limited to those that are
absolutely essential to the effective operation of government institutions."[11]

Citing a small number of cases in which the U.S. Supreme Court has obliquely recognized a constitutional right to government information, Emerson notes in another article that the nation's highest tribunal also has "ignored, or failed to give weight to, the guarantee." The High Court "has never clarified the right or pressed it toward its logical borders. On the contrary, in some cases it has ignored the right to know or severely limited its application."[12] Emerson and other legal scholars have identified dicta in a number of concurring and dissenting opinions on a constitutional right to government information but no *ratio decidendi*. It is one thing to determine that no theoretical barriers or problems preclude recognizing an implicit constitutional guarantee to government information; it is quite another to cite an explicit court ruling.

That government has withheld, eliminated, or otherwise abridged access to information with relative impunity is, regrettably, amply documented in the literature.[13] Since 1981 the Washington, D.C., office of the American Library Association (ALA) has felt it necessary to publish every six months an account of government efforts to restrict access to information. Entitled *Less Access to Less Information by and about the U.S. Government*, the publication continues to be issued semiannually and from time to time has been cumulated (a 1981-1987 chronology has been issued). Widely disseminated and republished in other settings, *Less Access to Less Information* is a month by month chronology culled from newspapers; general and specialized periodicals; and official government issuances such as press releases, the *Congressional Record*, and the *Federal Register*. It documents instances in which government was less than forthcoming in its obligation to inform the public of activities it had undertaken. The January-June 1991 chronology, for example, carried on the first page the same litany reiterated during a decade of government-watching, with the statement that a "combination of specific policy decisions, the administration's interpretations and implementations of the 1980 Paperwork Reduction Act (PL 96-511, as amended by PL 99-500) and agency budget cuts have significantly limited access to public documents and statistics."[14]

Absent an extension of the penumbra doctrine, which could elevate the implied right of access to public information under the First Amendment to that of black letter law, information dissemination by the government is a political decision. Administrations circumvent their implied covenant with the people by invoking spurious exigencies such as the deficit, spies posing as students performing searches on National Technical Information Service (NTIS) databases, waging a "war on waste" that would bring relief to the overburdened taxpayer, attempting to privatize to ensure cost-effective management, and other clever ploys. Unfortunately, the present Freedom of Information Act (FOIA) (5 U.S.C. 552 *et seq.*), weakened by presidential ukases, national security directives, and attorney general guidelines, is not the most effective instrument by which libraries can challenge government's propensity to withhold information.[15] Its several exemptions, its "catch-22" provisions, its ambiguities, and its time-consuming procedures render the act insufficient to the task. Nor are amendments to the FOIA that would expand "citizen access to *electronic* public information" as desirable, in our judgment, as legislative action that would result in a complete revision of Title 44 of the *United States Code*. Veterans of earlier legislative battles will recall an abortive Title 44 revision attempted in the late 1970s. Nevertheless, revision is a desideratum; an incisive analysis of this title and its provisions was assayed by Peter Hernon and Charles R. McClure, and their scrutiny of the issues involved leads us to believe that revision is not a hopeless task.[16]

In any event, given the composition and philosophy of the Supreme Court today, it is unlikely that a First Amendment right of access will be established as a principle of law under the several penumbra precedents cited and summarized by Justice William O. Douglas in *Griswold.* And even strong legislation, if enacted, would mandate many vexing procedural details. Scenarios involving judicial, legislative, or coordinate implementation are capably analyzed by Kathleen Dockry and other scholars.[17] But until statutory construction by the courts holds that access to public information is a constitutional right by virtue of unenumerated and unspecified guarantees that antedate the basic instrument itself — something comparable to the "natural rights" espoused by Montesquieu, John Locke, and Thomas Jefferson — the hopes of documents librarians for "uninhibited access to public information" will probably be dashed again and again.[18]

During the same month and year that NCLIS announced its "Principles of Public Information," the Government Documents Round Table (GODORT) of the American Library Association adopted the "Principles on Government Information" at its business meeting (June 26, 1990) during the association's annual conference in Chicago. As published in *Documents to the People,* the official GODORT periodical, each of the eleven statements of principle is followed by an elaborative annotation. Although the principles "represent official GODORT policy," the annotations do not. "Rather, they are intended to provide language which GODORT members and others can use when corresponding with Congress, the Office of Management and Budget (OMB), and other agencies in all issues regarding government information policy."[19]

GODORT's principles are reproduced with annotations as the appendix in this book. As readers can see, they tend to avoid, unlike the NCLIS declarations, an invocation of constitutional protection. They do, however, contain the standard shibboleths: "unimpeded" or "unrestricted" access as a "public right," "free flow of information" as "essential to maintaining an informed citizenry," access as "essential" to the "health and well-being of society," and so forth. In general, the GODORT principles and annotations are a well-crafted and comprehensive set of precepts, a lucid manifesto that properly places government information in the service of the women and men who comprise the body politic. Sturdy legislation designed to discourage governments from withholding public information for exiguous reasons, legislation that no court could declare ambiguous or unconstitutional, surely would constitute a benefit to all.

Within this context, documents and law librarians would appear to inherit a dual obligation: mastering the apparatus of information that is accessible while seeking diligently to ensure, by suasion or judicial demurrer, that all appropriate government information is made available. The principles that animate both GODORT and NCLIS are worthy testimony of this twofold commitment. Accordingly, those who enjoy positions in these disciplines should not underestimate their luminous role in defending the tenets expressed in these pages. "The knowledgeable documents librarian is a necessity, the highly skilled practitioner an exemplar of virtuosity in the profession."[20]

NOTES

[1]Peter Hernon, "Discussion Forum: National Information Policy," *Government Information Quarterly*, 6 (1989): 229.

[2]Sandy Whiteley, "CD-ROMS—The Wet Carrel of the 1990s?" *Booklist*, 87 (April 1, 1991): 1596.

[3]*Administrative Notes*, 12 (July 31, 1991): 14.

[4]General Accounting Office (GAO), "Service to the Public: How Effective and Responsive Is the Government?" GAO/T-HRD-91-26. May 8, 1991, pp. 8-9 (mimeographed).

[5]55 *Federal Register* (FR) 50899 (December 11, 1990).

[6]Diane Smith, "The Commercialization and Privatization of Government Information," *Government Publications Review*, 12 (January-February 1985): 46-47.

[7]Potter Stewart, "Or of the Press," *Hastings Law Journal*, 26 (1975): 636. See, for example, *Saxbe* v. *Washington Post Co.*, 94 S.Ct. 2811 (1974).

[8]National Commission on Libraries and Information Science, "Adoption of Principles of Public Information," 55 FR 50899 (December 11, 1990).

[9]*Griswold* v. *Connecticut*, 381 U.S. 479 (1965); *Roe* v. *Wade*, 35 L.Ed.2d 147 (1973). Justice William O. Douglas, writing for the majority in *Griswold*, invoked the "penumbra doctrine," in which specific guarantees in the Bill of Rights have penumbras formed by emanations from those guarantees "that help give them life and substance" (@483). In *Roe*, Justice Harry Blackmun, writing for the majority, held that the right to privacy articulated in *Griswold* extended to a woman's decision whether or not to terminate her pregnancy. Detractors of the privacy penumbra, such as Justice William Rehnquist, have termed it a fiction.

[10]Thomas I. Emerson, "Legal Foundations of the Right to Know," *Washington University Law Quarterly*, (1976): 14.

[11]Emerson, "Legal Foundations," p. 16.

[12]Thomas I. Emerson, "Colonial Intentions and Current Realities of the First Amendment," *University of Pennsylvania Law Review*, 125 (1977): 755.

[13]See Joe Morehead, "Federal Government Periodicals: An Endangered Species," *The Serials Librarian*, 8 (Summer 1984): 35-50; "Abridging Government Information: The Reagan Administration's War on Waste," *Dartmouth College Library Bulletin*, 25 (April 1985): 58-71; "Consequences of Federal Government Information Policies, 1981-1986," *The Reference Librarian*, No. 20 (1987): 7-33.

[14]*Less Access to Less Information by and about the U.S. Government: XVI: A 1991 Chronology: January-June* (Washington, DC: American Library Association, June 1991), p. 1.

[15]See J. Norman Baldwin and Dan Siminoski, "Perceptions of the Freedom of Information Act (F.O.I.A.) and Proposed Amendments by the F.O.I.A. Administrators," *Government Information Quarterly*, 2 (1985): 132-33.

[16]Peter Hernon and Charles R. McClure, *Federal Information Policies in the 1980's: Conflicts and Issues* (Norwood, NJ: Ablex, 1987), pp. 141-52.

[17]Kathleen A. Dockry, "The First Amendment Right of Access to Government-Held Information: A Re-Evaluation after *Richmond Newspapers, Inc.* v. *Virginia*," *Rutgers Law Review*, 34 (1982): 339-48.

[18]This language is found in principle 1 of the "Principles of Public Information" adopted by NCLIS and published at 55 FR 50899 (see note 5).

[19]*Documents to the People*, 19 (March 1991): 12-13. The members of the Federal Documents Task Force (FDTF) Work Group were responsible for writing the principles. Their names and those of other GODORT members who commented upon early drafts of the annotations are provided on page 12 of *Documents*.

[20]Joe Morehead, *Introduction to United States Public Documents* (Littleton, CO: Libraries Unlimited, 1975), p. xxiv.

1

Government Publishing and the Government Printing Office

INTRODUCTION

This chapter discusses federal information that is published primarily in printed paper publications. The congressional Office of Technology Assessment (OTA) defines publishing as "the overall process of creating, reproducing, and releasing or issuing information material for sales or distribution."[1] OTA defines printing as the "process of stamping, impressing, or copying information in the form of letters, numbers, or graphics, and the like on some kind of surface, such as paper or microform."[2]

Within the federal government, the publishers are generally considered to be the agencies that originate or create the material for distribution or sale. The name of the publishing or issuing agency is normally found on the title page or cover of the publication. The publishing agency provides the original material (either to be typeset or in camera-ready form) to the printer, specifies the number of copies to be printed, and handles the distribution and sale of copies from the agency.

Section 501, Title 44, *United States Code*, provides as follows:

> All printing, binding, and blank-book work for Congress, the Executive Office, the Judiciary, other than the Supreme Court of the United States, and every executive department, independent office and establishment of the Government, shall be done at the Government Printing Office, except—
>
> (1) classes of work the Joint Committee on Printing considers to be urgent or necessary to have done elsewhere; and
>
> (2) printing in field printing plants operated by an executive department, independent office or establishment, and the procurement of printing by an executive department, independent office or establishment from allotments for contract field printing, if approved by the Joint Committee on Printing.

Thus, the Government Printing Office (GPO) is required by law to provide centralized printing services for the executive, legislative, and judicial branches of the government, with the major exceptions noted above. GPO, the primary printer of federal government publications, may print the materials in its own

1

facilities or contract out to commercial printers. GPO is not the primary *publisher* of federal government publications, as might be indicated by the frequently used collation statement in citations (i.e., Washington, DC: GPO, [date]). GPO is, of course, the publisher of material that it originates or creates, such as the *Monthly Catalog of United States Government Publications* (GP 3.8) and the *GPO Style Manual* (GP 1). GPO performs important publishing functions in the sales and distribution of certain classes of publications and may also distribute publications for the publishing agencies on a reimbursable basis. Figure 1.1 shows a GPO organizational chart as of 1990.

A publishing agency may also print its own publications. These may be printed in field printing plants that have been authorized by the Joint Committee on Printing (JCP) or in agency copying facilities, or they may be contracted out to commercial printers by the agency, rather than by GPO. Such publications are called non-GPO publications. Publications printed by GPO in its own facilities or contracted out by GPO through its regional printing procurement offices to commercial printers are called GPO publications. Generally, if publishing agencies distribute copies to the general public, either through mailing lists or upon request, the publication is free. However, some agencies sell their publications. The Bureau of the Census has an active sales program for its own publications (not sold by GPO) and acts as a consigned agent to the Superintendent of Documents for those that are GPO sales publications. A publishing agency may also furnish copies of its publications to the National Technical Information Services (NTIS) for secondary distribution. The publishing or issuing agency is also generally considered to be the corporate author unless the title page indicates that the publication was prepared by another agency or organization or by an individual(s) as a personal author(s).

HISTORY OF THE GOVERNMENT PRINTING OFFICE

The Printing Act of June 23, 1860 (Joint Resolution No. 25, 12 Stat. 118), provided for the establishment of the Government Printing Office on March 4, 1861.[3] This followed over seventy years of unsatisfactory printing by contract printers, which had been selected each Congress (or session) by both houses of Congress. From 1789-1819 the printing was awarded to the lowest bidder. A joint resolution of March 3, 1819, provided that each house would elect a printer for each session, who would be paid fixed rates established by the resolution. Congress did not anticipate technological advances in printing, and the rates set in 1819 remained unchanged until 1845, when a 20 percent reduction was ordered. These rates proved to be extremely profitable.

A resolution of August 3, 1846 (9 Stat. 113), provided that public printing be given to the lowest bidder instead of each house electing a printer to do work for the whole session at rates prescribed by law. (In August 1842, a similar method had been adopted for departmental printing.) In late 1852 Congress returned to the old practice of electing its own House and Senate printers under rates fixed by law. Although the rates were moderate, profits soon became swollen by the great increase in printing volume. The law of August 26, 1852 (10 Stat. 30), also established the position of Superintendent of Public Printing to supervise the work of the House and Senate printers. The superintendent would also receive matter to

Fig. 1.1. United States Government Printing Office

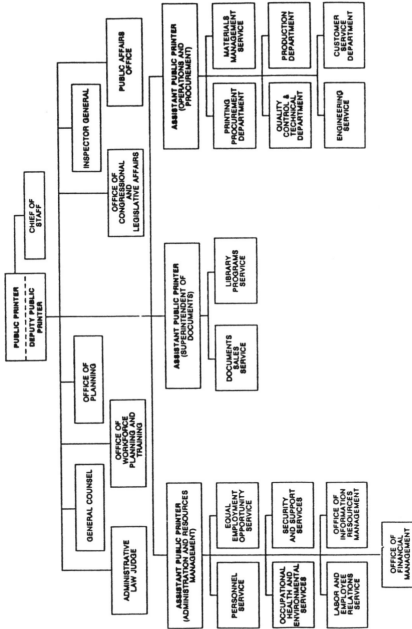

Source: GAO/GGD-90-107 (September 26, 1990): Appendix I, 74.

be printed from executive departments, except for printing required outside of Washington, D.C. that could be printed as cheaply by outside printers.

During this pre-GPO era, the commercial printers were generally newspaper publishers who had printing plants with enough capacity to handle the extra congressional work. Among these printers were Gales and Seaton, Peter Force, Duff Green, and Blair and Rives. The original GPO building, located at North Capitol and H Streets, was a modern printing establishment constructed in 1856 that was formerly owned and occupied by Cornelius Wendell. Wendell was elected House printer from 1855 to 1857. In the late 1850s most of the elected printers subcontracted their printing to Wendell, so that practically all government printing was produced at this plant. The "new" GPO building, which opened in 1940, occupies the site of Wendell's original building. A 1901 GPO building occupies the site immediately adjacent to it on North Capitol.

The Printing Act of June 23, 1860 (12 Stat. 118), provided that the Superintendent of Public Printing (head of the GPO) "is authorized and directed to have executed the printing and binding authorized by the Senate and House of Representatives, the executive and judicial departments, and the Court of Claims." Thus, although GPO was created primarily as a printer for Congress, the principle was established that GPO should provide centralized printing services for the executive and judicial branches as well. By an act of February 22, 1867, the title of the head of GPO was changed from Superintendent of Public Printing to Congressional Printer. By an act of July 31, 1876, the title was changed again to Public Printer, with appointment to be made by the president with the advice and consent of Congress. This is still the current title and practice.

The following language was contained in section 3786 of the 1873 *Revised Statutes*, an earlier codification of the laws of the United States: "All printing, binding, and blank-books for the Senate or House of Representatives, and the Executive and Judicial Departments, shall be done at the Government Printing Office, except in cases otherwise provided by law." This language was repeated in section 87 of the Printing Act of 1895 (28 Stat. 601) and became the basis of section 501, Title 44, *United States Code*, quoted above.

This requirement that executive (and judicial) branch printing be accomplished at GPO has been a cause of controversy, because GPO was established primarily as, and continues to be, a congressional printer and is considered to be a legislative branch agency. Also contributing to the controversy is the role of the Joint Committee on Printing, which serves as a board of directors for GPO and by law exercises approval authority over many GPO actions. The official GPO 1961 centennial history states that "various acts of Congress, Executive orders, Supreme Court decisions, and Attorney General and Comptroller General rulings have placed [GPO] in service for the executive, legislative, and independent branches."[4] It cites various authorities that place GPO in the legislative branch: an 1875 opinion by the chief justice, an 1895 executive order, and a 1932 comptroller general decision. However, it is now generally accepted that GPO is a legislative branch agency. It has for many years been included in legislative branch appropriations and budgets and has also been included with the legislative branch in the *United States Government Manual.*

When GPO was established in 1861, the Congress was the primary branch of government and issued most government publications. Executive branch work was used primarily as a filler when Congress was not in session. The General Accounting Office (GAO) found that in 1861 GPO produced $510,000 worth of printing, of which only $40,000 was for the executive branch.[5] However, the executive branch has since far outstripped the legislative branch in the number of publications issued. The 1988 OTA study found that for fiscal year 1987 GPO workload distribution was $113 million for the legislative branch, $656 million for the executive branch, and $2 million for the judicial branch.[6] These figures represent only GPO billings; it includes practically all legislative branch printing, because most is printed by GPO and there is only a small amount of non-GPO publications. However, not included is a large (and unknown) amount of non-GPO publications produced by executive branch agencies in over 200 field printing plants and a large number of duplicating facilities.

JOINT COMMITTEE ON PRINTING

The Joint Committee on Printing (JCP) was established by section 2, Joint Resolution 16, approved August 3, 1846 (9 Stat. 114). The JCP presently consists of the chairperson and four members of the Senate Committee on Rules and Administration and the chairperson and four members of the Committee on House Administration. The Senate chairperson acts as JCP chairperson during odd-numbered Congresses, and the House chairperson acts as JCP chairperson during even-numbered Congresses. The committee has no legislative powers and rarely meets. Most of the committee's work is performed by the staff, which consists of eighteen persons.

The JCP's jurisdiction, authority, and responsibilities are derived from Title 44, *United States Code*. Section 103 empowers the committee to "use any measures it considers necessary to remedy neglect, delay, duplication, or waste in the public printing and binding and distribution of Government publications." Other sections of the law (particularly section 501) identify specific actions or assignments that are subject to the control of or must be approved by the JCP. The responsibilities of the committee include:

1. Establishment of policy and oversight of the printing, binding, and distribution of federal publications. JCP also promotes cooperation among executive departments in addressing mutual printing, binding, and distribution problems or requirements.

2. Oversight of the Government Printing Office's policies and operations. This includes the committee serving as a final board of appeal in GPO labor/management negotiations pertaining to wage matters.

3. Oversight of the Federal Printing Procurement Program. Through this program approximately 75 percent of the federal government's printing is procured by GPO from the private sector. This program is discussed below.

4. Compilation, publication, and distribution of certain congressional publications, including the *Congressional Directory* (Y 4.P93/1:1) and *Congressional Pictorial Directory* (Y 4.P93/1:1p).

5. Establishment of standards and specifications for printing papers pro-
    cured and used by federal departments. The committee is designated by
    law as the final arbiter for the United States in settling all differences
    between GPO and contractors regarding the quality of paper.

6. Oversight of the public's right of access to government publications. The
    oversight is performed by monitoring the Superintendent of Documents'
    Depository Library Program, general sales program, by-law distribution
    program, and cataloging and indexing programs.

7. Promotion of cooperation between Senate and House of Represen-
    tatives information entities in such areas as automated production of
    congressional publications and automated indexing.[7]

During the abortive attempts by JCP in 1983 and 1984 to revise its *Government Printing and Binding Regulations No. 24*, the Department of Justice (DOJ)
issued memorandum opinions that challenged JCP's authority to issue regulations controlling executive branch printing under authority in section 103, Title
44. DOJ said:

> We believe that the legislative history of section 103 demonstrates
> quite clearly that the purpose of that section was originally—and
> remains—to allow the JCP to take remedial steps with regard only to
> problems that arise in the printing of documents for Congress or in the
> operation of the Government Printing Office, a unit largely within the
> Legislative Branch.... We adhere to our earlier conclusion that section
> 103 does not provide any statutory basis for an attempt by the JCP to
> regulate the operations of the Executive Branch.[8]

DOJ stated that the precursor of present section 103 was section 12, Act of
August 26, 1852 (10 Stat. 35), as follows:

> The Joint Committee on Public Printing shall have power to adopt
> such measures as may be deemed necessary to remedy any neglect or
> delay in the execution of the public printing, (provided that no con-
> tract, agreement, or arrangement entered into by this committee shall
> take effect until the same shall have been approved by *that house of
> Congress to which the printing belongs, and when the printing delayed
> relates to the business of both houses, until both houses shall have
> approved of such contract or arrangement*) [emphasis added].[9]

The language in parentheses above was deleted when this section was continued
as section 2 of the Printing Act of 1895 (28 Stat. 601).

REGIONAL PRINTING PROCUREMENT OFFICES AND FIELD PRINTING PLANTS

In 1965, the Joint Committee on Printing adopted the policy that the federal government, to the greatest practicable extent, should rely on the private sector for its printing requirements. It also adopted the policy that printing should be processed as close to the origin of the order as possible. Accordingly, JCP established the Federal Printing Program with commercially procured printing to be administered by regional offices of the Government Printing Office and for the reduction of in-house field printing by federal departments and agencies.

Increased government reliance on the private sector for commercial printing requirements was first considered in the form of a staff proposal in 1964. At that time, JCP regulations divided all government printing into two major categories: departmental printing, which was done for nationwide use, and field printing, accomplished primarily for regional use. As required under Title 44 and the JCP's *Government Printing and Binding Regulations*, the Public Printer produced or procured all departmental printing unless JCP granted a waiver permitting field production or procurement.[10] In 1968, field printing was produced in one or more of 338 agency field printing plants.

Beginning with Issue No. 20 dated March 1969 of the *Government Printing and Binding Regulations*, JCP regulations used the term *federal printing* to encompass both departmental and field printing. Superintendent of Documents Robert E. Kling, Jr., felt that the new "wording negates the intent of that part of Section 501 [Title 44] dealing with both 'field printing' and 'contract field printing.' [R]edefining 'field' and 'departmental' printing as 'federal' printing makes it possible for much of the work formerly done in field and departmental plants to be bought from private industry."[11] However, the phrase *field printing plants* is still widely used for those federal agency printing plants that JCP has authorized under section 501(2), Title 44.

In 1966 JCP authorized its staff and the Public Printer to move forward to establish regional printing procurement offices. In 1967, the first regional printing procurement office was established at St. Louis. During the 1970s, the regional program was implemented in all ten federal regions in the contiguous United States. Procurement offices have not been established in Alaska (Region 11) or Hawaii (Region 12). Fourteen GPO regional printing procurement offices have been established as follows: Region 1 – Boston; Region 2 – New York City and Philadelphia; Region 3 – Washington, D.C., and Newport News, Virginia; Region 4 – Atlanta; Region 5 – Columbus and Chicago; Region 6 – St. Louis; Region 7 – Dallas; Region 8 – Denver; Region 9 – San Francisco and Lawndale, California; and Region 10 – Seattle. In addition, satellite printing procurement offices have been established in Charleston, South Carolina; Kelly Air Force Base, Texas; Tinker Air Force Base, Oklahoma; and San Diego, California.

Meanwhile, the number of field printing plants has been reduced from 338 in 1968 to 298 in 1978 and to 234 in 1986.[12] Executive departments and agencies are not required by the JCP regulations to go to GPO for printing for less than 5,000 units on a single page or 25,000 units for any number of aggregate pages in an order. They may produce such printing in field printing plants, in agency duplicating and copying centers, or through agency contracts. However, agencies often find it more cost-effective to obtain such printing through the GPO regional printing procurement offices. Reducing the number of field printing plants and channeling more field printing through the GPO regional printing procurement offices has served to significantly decrease the number of non-GPO publications and increase the number of GPO publications. This has the effect of making these publications available for bibliographical control and depository distribution by the Superintendent of Documents.

Of the 234 field printing plants listed in the 1986 edition of the JCP *Government Printing and Binding Regulations No. 24*, 201 were in executive departments, 2 in the legislative branch, 1 in the judicial branch, and 30 in independent agencies. Of the 201 in executive departments the breakdown was as follows: Department of the Army — 70, Department of the Navy — 50, Department of the Air Force — 26, and other Department of Defense activities — 9, for a total of 155 in the Department of Defense; Department of Energy — 19; Department of Justice — 8; Department of the Interior — 7; Department of Commerce — 3; Departments of Agriculture and Treasury — 2 each; and Departments of Health and Human Services, Housing and Urban Development, Labor, State, and Transportation — 1 each. The two legislative branch plants are at the General Accounting Office and the Library of Congress. The judicial branch plant is operated by the Administrative Office of the U.S. Courts. The 30 independent agency plants are as follows: General Services Administration — 11; National Aeronautics and Space Administration — 7; and 1 each for Environmental Protection Agency, Federal Communications Commission, Federal Trade Commission, National Labor Relations Board, Nuclear Regulatory Commission, Office of Personnel Management, Panama Canal Company, Railroad Retirement Board, Securities and Exchange Commission, United States Information Agency, United States International Trade Commission, and United States Postal Service. In addition to its main printing plant at North Capitol and H Streets in Washington, D.C., GPO also operates six regional printing plants at the Washington, D.C., Navy Yard; Chicago; Denver; New York City; San Francisco; and Seattle.

Non-GPO publications may be printed either in agency field printing plants or in agency duplicating facilities. Field printing plants are authorized only by the Joint Committee on Printing; agency duplicating facilities do not require such authorization. In January 1983 the Office of Management and Budget (OMB) began a survey with technical assistance from the Government Printing Office of both field printing plants and duplicating centers. This survey was part of OMB's program (begun in 1981) to eliminate wasteful spending on unnecessary government publications. JCP was not asked to assist in the survey. Cost analyses were performed for 1,021 of the estimated 2,500 printing and duplicating facilities in the executive department.[13]

The results of the survey were announced at an OMB press conference on November 1, 1983, in which the Public Printer participated but not JCP members or staff. Facilities recommended for closing numbered 229 and another 46 were recommended for downgrading, for savings of $51 million in fiscal year (FY) 1985 and elimination of 2,171 positions. The Department of Defense accounted for the largest number of facilities (93), dollar savings ($19 million), and positions (1,063). In December 1985 OMB released the list of the 275 facilities, which included 77 field printing plants; the remainder were duplicating facilities. The downgrading actions included "downgrade to duplicating facility," "increase commercial procurement," "contractor operate," and "consolidate." The reported savings were to be accomplished by contracting printing requirements to the private sector through GPO regional printing procurement offices. The OMB report concluded that "the majority of the presses in use were being operated at around one-third capacity and producing routine printing at a cost of more than three times that charged by commercial printers on contract to GPO."[14]

However, opposition to this executive branch initiative came from the Joint Committee on Printing, other members of Congress sensitive to the idea of eliminating jobs, and the agencies themselves. In March 1987, Public Printer Ralph E. Kennickell, Jr., reported to the Senate Committee on Appropriations that following appeals and challenges by the agencies, the actual number of facilities closed was only 75. He stated that the remaining operating facilities "[account for expenditures] in the hundreds of millions of dollars and support a work force of over 8,000 civilian and military personnel." He urged the committee to "consider appropriate language specifically designed to reduce the Federal Agencies' dependence on in-plant printing and duplicating facilities. Furthermore, they should be encouraged to seek their requirements through the competitive [GPO] printing procurement system already in place."[15]

JCP policy is that all printing suitable for procurement (sufficient leadtime, no security required, etc.) should be procured through the main Government Printing Office or one of its regional printing procurement offices or regional federal printing plants, rather than being printed in-house in field printing plants or duplicating centers. However, JCP helped some agencies retain field printing plants that OMB had earmarked for closing. It felt that OMB did not consider the mission requirements of the agencies carefully enough. "They were looking at bare costs without considering the need for that agency to have that work in-house because it was not procurable through GPO." JCP also furnished the House Committee on Appropriations other reasons to justify printing in-house. "The work can't be procured from the private sector because there are not capable printing companies within a reasonable geographic area that are both willing and able to produce the work, or there are no companies who can and will meet the necessary time schedules at a competitive price. Another factor which necessitates the existence of some of the [field printing] plants is the potential need for mobilization."[16]

The 1988 Office of Technology Assessment (OTA) study provided the following data on GPO billings of $770 million for FY 1987: GPO, main plant printing, $180 million (23.4%); GPO, six regional plants printing, $14 million (1.8%); and procured printing through the GPO central office and regional printing procurement offices, $576 million (74.8%). The breakdown for GPO main plant printing was legislative branch, $90 million (49.7%); executive branch, $90 million (49.7%); and judicial branch, $1 million (0.6%). GPO regional plant printing of $14 million was all executive branch. The breakdown for procured printing was legislative branch, $23 million (4%); executive branch, $552 million (95.8%); and judicial branch, $1 million (0.2%).[17] However, the figure of $23 million for procured printing for the legislative branch is somewhat misleading, as only about $1 million of that was for Congress itself. Most of the amount was for the sales publications program and the depository library program, which are run by the GPO (Superintendent of Documents), a legislative branch agency. Almost all of the titles in these two programs that are procured are executive branch publications. A small number of procured legislative branch publications are for the Library of Congress and other support and related agencies of the legislative branch.

Thus, nearly all congressional publications are printed at the GPO main plant, and this printing accounts for nearly half of the production, with the other half mainly executive branch printing. Congress does not have any field printing plants. Within the legislative branch, the Library of Congress and the General Accounting Office have plants. Executive branch printing serves primarily as filler work at the GPO main plant. Nearly 75 percent of GPO billings for executive branch work are procured from the private sector. The GPO main plant is primarily geared for 24-hour operation to print the *Congressional Record, Federal Register*, and other priority printing requirements. Thus, overhead expenses are high. The executive branch complains that it is forced to pay for much of these overhead expenses in order to provide the legislative branch with its priority printing needs. OTA obtained cost data on twenty sample printing jobs and found that the GPO main plant regular rate was more than double the procured cost rate. Another reason for higher main plant costs is that GPO produces a much more diversified set of printing products than any single private sector printer. Most private firms specialize in a small number of products to keep overhead down and maximize economies of scale.[18]

Most GPO publications—those printed by GPO either at its main printing plant or at its six regional plants or procured through the fourteen GPO regional printing procurement offices—are controlled bibliographically and incorporated into the depository library program. However, there is no agreement on the percent these known titles represent for total U.S. government publications. Percentages are estimates only and range anywhere from 10 percent to 50 percent. Firm expense data are generally not available for non-GPO printing. These costs are frequently lumped in with other general administrative expenses and are not specifically broken out. The number of field printing plants is known, as they are authorized by JCP and can only be established or discontinued with JCP approval. However, the number of agency duplicating centers is unknown. In its 1983 survey OMB identified and obtained cost data from 1,021 duplicating centers, but it is estimated there are over 2,000 such centers.

Another complicating factor is that comparisons are generally made with expenditure data, which can be misleading as they do not relate directly to comparison in the number of titles. GPO printing and procurement are more geared to high-volume printing, with long runs of multiple copies. Field printing and duplicating are geared to low-volume printing, with short runs of few copies of each title. The JCP regulations set a minimum threshold (5,000 units on a single page or 25,000 units for any number of aggregate pages in an order) beyond which agencies are required by JCP regulations to go to GPO for their printing. Also, field printing and duplicating are intended by JCP primarily for work needed in the immediate area, mainly for administrative purposes. Publications determined by the issuing agency to be for "administrative or operational purposes" are exempt from depository distribution under section 1902, Title 44, *United States Code*. Some work in duplicating centers especially may be "record" material to which access is generally available only under the Freedom of Information Act.

The 1988 OTA study found that the billings of the ten largest GPO printing customers for FY 1986 were as follows: Department of the Army, $134.7 million (18.3%); Department of the Navy, $74.6 million (10.1%); Congress, $68.0 million (9.2%); Department of the Treasury, $65.6 million (8.9%); U.S. Postal Service, $53.0 million (7.2%); Department of Health and Human Services, $49.8

million (6.8%); Department of the Air Force, $48.0 million (6.5%); General Services Administration, $23.0 million (3.1%); Department of Agriculture, $21.8 million (3.0%); and Department of Energy, $19.3 million (2.6%). The Department of the Army also has the largest number of field printing plants (70), whereas the Departments of Agriculture and the Treasury have only 2 each.

REVISION OF TITLE 44, *UNITED STATES CODE*

The program to revise Title 44, *United States Code*, began in April 1978 with informal conversations and exchange of memoranda on the subject by JCP staff members. In May 1978, the JCP chairman, Sen. Claiborne Pell (D-RI), announced in the *Congressional Record* (daily edition, p. S10103) that JCP was undertaking such a review and requested comments from the public. In mid-October Chairman Pell announced that an Ad Hoc Advisory Committee on Revision to Title 44 to the JCP would be convened. The following organizations were invited to name a representative: AFL-CIO National Office, American Library Association (ALA), American Paper Institute, Committee on House Administration, Department of Commerce (DOC), Department of Defense (DoD), Federal Library Committee, GPO, Information Industry Association, Joint Bargaining Committee of the GPO Unions, JCP, National Association of Government Communicators, OMB, Printing Industries of America, and Senate Committee on Rules and Administration.[19]

The ad hoc committee held thirteen weekly meetings from November 1978 to January 1979. Six major topics were selected for discussion, with each generally scheduled for two meetings. These topics were administration of policy, federal printing production and procurement, impact of new technology, access to and distribution of government information, depository library program, and pricing of government information. The report of the ad hoc committee, *Federal Government Printing and Publishing: Policy Issues* (Y 4.P93/1:P93/6), was published in May 1979. It is organized into six chapters corresponding to the discussion topics. Each chapter summarizes the discussions of the ad hoc committee, adds significant background information for a consideration of the topics, and lists significant policy questions that arose during the discussions. The report contains six appendixes that correspond directly to the six discussion topics. Each appendix includes the discussion outline, the meeting dates, names of subcommittee members for that topic, and a list of observers. The report also contains an excellent bibliography, with many entries annotated. It is organized by topics that generally correspond to the six discussion topics. The purpose of the committee meetings was not to produce specific legislative recommendations, but to identify key policy issues to assist and guide the JCP in preparing legislation to revise Title 44. Verbatim transcripts of the discussions at the thirteen meetings were not published.[20]

H.R. 4572 (96th Congress), the Public Printing Reorganization Act of 1979, was introduced in the House on June 21, 1970, by Rep. Frank Thompson (D-NJ), JCP chairman and chairman of the Committee on House Administration. An identical companion bill, S. 1436, was introduced in the Senate on June 27 by Sen. Claiborne Pell (D-RI), JCP vice-chairman and chairman of the Senate Committee on Rules and Administration. Four days of joint hearings were held on the bill in late July. Three of these were chaired by Rep. Augustus F. Hawkins

(D-CA), chairman of the Subcommittee on Printing, which was primarily responsible for the bill. The other hearing was chaired by Sen. Pell. The bill amended only those chapters of Title 44 that are under the purview of JCP and the two committees that provide JCP members. These are chapters 1, 3, 5, 7, 9, 11, 13, 17, and 19 (even numbers are reserved for new chapters). Chapters 21 and 37, which deal primarily with archival and records administration, plus chapter 15 are under the purview of the House Committee on Government Operations and the Senate Committee on Governmental Affairs.

The bills would have established the GPO as an "independent establishment." At the head of GPO would be a board of directors composed of seven voting members appointed by the president and three nonvoting members. A full-time board chairman would be appointed for a single, nonrenewable term of five years. Four of the nonvoting members would be chosen from the following sources: printing and reproduction industries, organized labor, library community, and publishing and information industry. These part-time voting members would be appointed for renewable terms of three years. The three nonvoting members would include the chairmen of the Committee on House Administration and the Senate Committee on Rules and Administration and the OMB director (or their representatives). The board of directors would replace the JCP, which would be abolished. JCP management and operational functions would be transferred to GPO, and JCP oversight functions would be transferred to the two respective committees. The board could prescribe regulations as necessary to carry out its duties.

The board would appoint two general managers with equal status and pay: the Public Printer, responsible for "public printing services," and the Superintendent of Documents, responsible for cataloging and distribution of "public documents." The term *public documents* was defined as "a document, publication, form, *machine-readable data file, microform, audio or visual presentation*, or similar matter, reproduced for public use, *wholly or partially at government expense*." The addition of the italicized words greatly expanded the definition of *government publication* as found in section 1901, Title 44, and led to controversy.

The bills directed increased centralized control of government printing. Section 502 provides that "all public printing services for the Government shall be provided through the Government Printing Office in accordance with regulations prescribed by the Board" with several limited exceptions, including the following: "when the interest of the Government so requires, public printing services may be provided other than through the Government Printing Office for a period of limited duration." Field printing plants and direct contracting by agencies were not mentioned.

Among the controversial changes were section 702(a), which directed that "distribution of public documents for the Government shall be through the Government Printing Office in accordance with regulations prescribed by the Board." Waivers to this requirement for centralized distribution might be granted by GPO, but only for "periods of limited duration." Most of the provisions for depository libraries, now in chapter 19, Title 44, were compressed into section 707, which contained all the current congressional and by-law designations but deleted all mention of regional depository libraries.[21]

During the four days of hearings, witnesses included the Public Printer; the Librarian of Congress; representatives from the ALA, the Association of

American Publishers, the American Paper Institute, the Printing Industries of America, the Information Industry Association, the National Association of Government Communicators, the Joint Council of GPO Unions; and other public witnesses. Conspicuous by their absence were representatives of the executive branch. However, the printed hearings, which were published in October, contained copies of written comments by five executive departments (Commerce; Defense; Health, Education, and Welfare; Housing and Urban Development; and Treasury) and ten agencies.[22] No comments were received from OMB. The executive departments expressed strong opposition to the bills, especially those provisions for increased centralization of printing and distribution services at GPO.[23]

On September 27, 1979, Rep. Frank Thompson, Jr. (D-NJ), introduced H.R. 5424, the National Publications Act of 1979. This was a "clean" bill to replace H.R. 4572. Usually a clean bill is introduced after a markup session, but in this case the clean bill was introduced before the markup session began on H.R. 4572. As a result the Senate deferred action on Title 44 revision until the House had passed a bill.

The main differences were name changes. The GPO was changed to the National Publications Agency (NPA), the GPO Board of Directors was changed to the National Publications Commission (NPC), the Public Printer was changed to Director of Production Services, and the Superintendent of Documents was changed to Director of Distribution Services. A third coequal director was added, the Director of Administration. The bill provided that the chairman of the NPC "shall exercise chief executive authority over the National Publications Agency." The terms of service and method of appointment for commission members remained unchanged. The bill also established NPA as an "independent establishment in the executive branch."

There were other significant changes. Section 101 added a definition for *distribution* as follows: "(A) any public documents sales program not specifically established by law; (B) any distribution of public documents required for the depository library program; (C) any distribution of public documents by the National Publications Agency for another Government entity on a reimbursable basis." This watered down the GPO monopoly on distribution implied by section 702. The provision was designed to force agencies that operate sales programs without statutory authority to get a waiver from NPA or discontinue the program. Thompson also said section 702 did not apply to free distribution programs.

The definition of *public document* deleted the words "reproduced wholly or partially at government expense" and substituted the words "reproduced for official use of a Government entity." This was intended to clarify the status of scientific or scholarly works produced under government grants, which are not public documents unless reproduced for official use of a government agency.

Changes to section 502 modified exceptions to centralized printing services through NPA with the following additional conditions. Printing may be done elsewhere "(A) by contract with a private person if such contract: (i) satisfies an urgent requirement that can't be satisfied through NPA; or (ii) results in savings to the government; or (B) in an authorized field printing plant operated by a Government entity if such entity demonstrates that cost savings to the Government will result from the use of such plant or that the interests of national security so require."

Section 707 added a provision that "any public document that is an audio or visual presentation shall be made available ... only on a loan basis." This was in response to executive branch criticism that distributing free audiovisual materials to depository libraries would cost from $2 billion to $5 billion per year.[24]

Hearings on H.R. 5424 were held November 14, 1979, by the Subcommittee on Printing of the Committee on House Administration. The hearings were held primarily at the request of Rep. William L. Dickinson (R-AL), ranking minority member of the Committee on House Administration, to get input from the executive branch. Representatives testified from DoD, the National Archives and Records Service, the National Aeronautics and Space Administration (NASA), and the Office of Personnel Management.[25] The printed hearings contain a copy of H.R. 5424 and two letters from OMB with comments. An addendum organized into three sections contains comments from government departments and agencies, from private organizations and individuals, and from the library and academic communities.[26]

The Committee on House Administration held markup sessions on H.R. 5424 on January 22 and 23 and ordered reported out an amended bill. However, the report (H. Rep. 96-836, pt. I) was not filed until March 19. The delay was caused by the requirement for a Congressional Budget Office estimate. Amended H.R. 5424 had several significant changes. The NPA was made a part of the legislative branch and renamed the National Publications Office (NPO). The term *public document* was changed to *government publication* throughout the bill.

The term *distribution* was amended to add subsection (D): "any free distribution of Government publications to be made by the National Publications Office." A significant change was made in the definition of *government publication* with the deletion of the words "as determined by the issuing Government entity." This deleted language—which is also in present section 1902, Title 44—that the issuing agency (rather than GPO or NPO) shall make the determination on which publications meet one of the exceptions that exempt them from depository distribution. The italicized words (which are also in current section 1902) were deleted in exception (A): "is for administrative and operational purposes only *and is without public interest or educational value.*" The effect of this deletion is less clear. Did this mean that *all* such publications would be exempt, where previously only those that were also without public interest or educational value were exempt?

The report includes the text of amended H.R. 5424 as reported and a detailed section by section explanation of the bill. It includes minority views of six Republican committee members telling why they oppose the bill and additional views by two Republican members, together with supplemental views of ten majority members in rebuttal of the minority views. The section "Amendments to Laws Outside Title 44" contains the language in approximately eighty laws that would be amended by the "technical and conforming amendments" section of the bill. Some of these change the name of the Government Printing Office to National Publications Office. Approximately twenty-eight laws withdrew exemptions from various agencies to obtain printing "without regard to section 501 of Title 44" and required them to obtain printing services from NPO. Approximately eighteen added a requirement, where none existed, that the agency obtain printing services from NPO "in accordance with Title 44."[27]

On March 19, 1980, the House Committee on Government Operations claimed jurisdiction in certain provisions of H.R. 5424. The bill was referred to that committee as well as the Committee on Rules for a period not ending later than June 19. The Committee on Rules claimed jurisdiction on section 307 of revised Title 44, which required that the regulations of the National Publications Commission be submitted to the Committee on House Administration, and on section 10 of H.R. 5424, which terminated the JCP. Despite this limited jurisdiction the committee considered all facets of the bill and invited witnesses from most of the agencies and organizations represented at the initial series of hearings held by the Committee on House Administration. Hearings were held on May 14 and 21, 1980. Witnesses included the acting and former Public Printers; acting Archivist of the United States; Deputy Librarian of Congress; and representatives from the Congressional Budget Office, GAO, OMB, the Office of Personnel Management, ALA, the Joint Council of GPO Unions, and the Printing Industries of America.[28]

The Committee on Rules reported H.R. 5424 on June 18 (H. Rep. 96-836, pt. II) "without recommendation," which effectively killed the legislation. It reported a procedural amendment to section 307 rewarding submission of proposed regulations to Congress. With regard to JCP the committee found that the "ability of a committee of Congress to directly supervise an agency with a budget of about $650 million annually is highly questionable" especially when 83 percent of the budget is for executive branch printing and only 17 percent is for the legislative branch. It found that the legislation fails to resolve "most of the problems of the Government Printing Office and the Joint Committee on Printing, which have prompted this legislation, which stem from the absence of a determination" of the status of GPO as a legislative or executive branch agency.[29] The report also included minority views of five Republican committee members who strongly opposed the bill.

The Committee on Government Operations had on March 11 prepared a draft of a substitute bill, which was eventually reported out. It repeated much of the same text and chapter/section numbering of H.R. 5424 but had major changes that revealed what this committee considered to be basic problems with the legislation. The National Publications Office and National Publications Commission were renamed the Federal Publications Office and the Federal Publications Commission, respectively, and the bill was renamed the Federal Publications Act of 1980. The chief executive officer was no longer chairman of the commission, but rather a separate Director of Federal Publications appointed by the president for an indefinite term. The three directors of administration, production, and distribution services were called assistant directors. The definition of *government publications* deleted the words "machine-readable data file, microform, audio or visual material," which also removed the requirement for these materials to be included in the comprehensive cumulative index, the periodic catalog, and depository library distribution. The amended bill also deleted authority to maintain a complete collection of government publications. The definition of *government publication* was amended to exclude "scientific and technical information if the Government entity is required by law to disseminate information concerning its activities and the results thereof." This amendment applied primarily to NTIS and NASA technical report literature, but other government clearinghouses also could have been involved.[30]

The Committee on Government Operations held hearings on amended H.R. 5424 on June 4, 1980. Only three witnesses appeared, all of whom opposed the bill: the acting Public Printer and representatives from OMB and the Printing Industries of America. On June 19 the committee reported the substitute bill, the Federal Publications Act of 1980, "without recommendation" (H. Rep. 96-836, pt. III). The report contains the text of the amended bill, a section by section analysis, the text of changes made in existing law, and dissenting views of the minority committee members.[31]

After over a decade it is still recognized that those sections of Title 44 dealing with printing and distribution of government publications that were the subject of the revision legislation in the 96th Congress are outdated and need revision. However, no further attempts were made to directly revise Title 44 in the 1980s despite the fact that the administration claimed that those sections that authorize the JCP to micromanage executive branch printing and publishing are unconstitutional under the Supreme Court decision in *INS* v. *Chadha*. However, a review of this revision effort during the 96th Congress helped to identify the players and issues involved and may give a clue as to what revisions are most likely to be successful in the future.

The library community fully supported the Title 44 revision effort, which upgraded distribution and dissemination of government publications to equal status with printing in GPO. It produced greater centralization of printing and distribution of government publications, which has the effect of increasing the number of GPO publications and decreasing the number of non-GPO publications, thereby bringing more government publications under bibliographic control and making them available for distribution to depository libraries. The definition of *government publications* was expanded to include machine-readable data files and audiovisual materials as well as technical report literature, which also results in more informational materials being brought under bibliographic control and depository distribution.

On the other hand the administration and Republican minority members of the three House committees involved claimed that the addition of these materials for depository distribution was prohibitively expensive and would cost an additional $1-$5 billion per year. Most of these costs were attributed to audiovisual materials. No mention was made of the added cost of machine-readable data files at that time, whereas it since has been recognized that providing depositories free access to information in electronic databases would be very expensive.

The executive branch also strongly opposed centralization of printing and distribution services. It argued that most agencies operate under statutes that require them to disseminate information about their programs. Centralized control infringes on agency accountability and inhibits agency flexibility. The executive branch also opposed a centralized printing authority in the legislative branch that would regulate and manage executive branch resources. This conflicts with the constitutional separation of powers among the three branches of government.

The GPO unions strongly supported the legislation because it carried forward their present rights and privileges and, indeed, improved them by placing labor-management relations under the National Labor Relations Act. The commercial printing industries strongly opposed the legislation primarily for this same reason. They claimed that it removed many GPO employees from the protection of the Civil Service Reform Act by placing them along with trade union employees under the National Labor Relations Act. They further claimed that the legislation contained no prohibition against a closed union shop and that as a result of bargaining agreements the GPO unions could dictate wages for contract work and shut off nonunion companies from contracts. The printing industries were also concerned that the legislation encouraged more in-plant work and a consequent decrease in commercial contracts. The Office of Personnel Management also opposed the labor-management relations provisions.

However, it was the opposition of the House Committee on Government Operations that killed the legislation by reporting it "without recommendation." The committee did not give the reasons for its opposition in the report, but they may be deduced from some of the changes the committee incorporated into the amended Federal Publications Act. Apparently JCP had invaded the committee's turf by making the revision not just a "printing" act, but also an "information" act by expanding the definitions of *government publications* and *distribution*. The House Committee on Government Operations has jurisdiction over federal information policy. Also, during the 96th Congress the House Committee on Government Operations had sponsored H.R. 6410, which passed both houses as the Paperwork Reduction Act of 1980. OMB felt that certain provisions of the Title 44 revision legislation conflicted with the Paperwork Reduction Act. Apparently the two committees had not coordinated the two pieces of legislation while they were being prepared and considered during the 96th Congress.

REVISION OF JCP REGULATIONS

Following the unsuccessful attempt to make a major revision of Title 44 in the 96th Congress (1979-1980), no attempts were made for major or minor revisions in the 97th Congress (1981-1982). However, in the 98th Congress, the JCP attempted to revise the printing laws through its regulations, rather than through the legislative process. On November 11, 1983, the JCP chairman, Rep. Augustus Hawkins (D-CA), entered in the *Congressional Record* (daily edition, pp. H9709-H9713) for comments proposed changes to *Government Printing and Binding Regulations No. 24*, dated April 1977. The proposed changes were retitled *Government Printing, Binding, and Distribution Regulations No. 25*. JCP's authority under section 103, Title 44, "to remedy neglect, delay, duplication or waste" includes distribution as well as printing and binding of government publications. Distribution policy had not been included in previous JCP regulations.

Among the reasons Hawkins gave for the revision was that since 1977, "significant technological breakthroughs have made a sharp impact on the ways in which information is captured, edited, formatted, stored, reproduced, and distributed." Thus, the regulations provided "a redefinition of printing that eliminates the distinction between copying, duplicating, and printing, and which include new processes and procedures for electronically capturing, reproducing, and distributing information." Especially significant was the term *printing environment* as used in the regulations to mean "any location where printing is performed including, but not limited to, departmental printing plants, duplicating centers, copier centers, graphic facilities, computer centers, distribution centers and offices." In its *Regulations No. 24* JCP had defined duplicating and copying and had included in its printing equipment lists some duplicating and copying equipment. However, JCP had specifically excluded duplicating and copying from its oversight and management. Likewise, Title 44 revision legislation in its definition of *printing* had excluded "production of multiple copies by office typewriter, office copying machine, duplicator, or other method practical for only limited production."[32]

A major reason for the revision was to introduce a new procedure for JCP to monitor federal printing. Agencies would no longer need to seek JCP approval for individual pieces of printing equipment on an ad hoc basis for their field printing plants. Instead, they would submit to JCP an annual printing and publishing plan for the upcoming fiscal year and projections for the following two years. These annual plans would enumerate equipment, printing environments, planned purchases of equipment, titles and types of publications to be issued, and the means of publication distribution. These plans required approval by JCP before they could be implemented. *Regulations No. 24* had included lists of printing equipment for which an agency must get JCP approval before acquisition. The introduced changes by Hawkins included frequent use of the terms *information* and *publishing*, which indicated JCP had also broadened the term *printing* and its jurisdiction to include those two terms.

Another major revision was the inclusion of policy and regulations regarding distribution of government publications. This was intended to implement the following two chapters of Title 44: chapter 17, "Distribution and Sales of Public Documents," and chapter 19, "Depository Library Program." Among the most controversial proposed regulations was section 3, Title V, which stated: "Departments shall use the services of the Superintendent of Documents, on a reimbursable basis, to initially and subsequently distribute all Government publications outside of a department. Whenever feasible, departments shall use the services of the Superintendent of Documents to distribute all Government publications within a department." The regulations defined *distribution* as the "dissemination of Government publications *or information* [emphasis added] to users (Government and non-Government), through such means as sales, user fees, or free dissemination programs, including the electronic transfer of an original reproducible image." The regulations further stated in section 1, Title III that "the printing *and distribution* [emphasis added] of Government publications shall be accomplished by the Government Printing Office, unless otherwise authorized by the Joint Committee on Printing."

In a letter dated December 12, 1983, OMB Director David A. Stockman stated he had "major reservations" about certain provisions of the proposed regulations. He strongly disagreed "with the need for such a sweeping definition of distribution and the assignment of the distribution to GPO." He said decisions regarding dissemination and use of information were the proper functions of agency program managers. He concluded that "if literally applied, the regulations would not permit the President to issue a press release, or the Supreme Court to issue an opinion, except through GPO and with the approval of JCP."

Stockman said section 6, Title V, which states that "all Government publications shall be distributed to depository libraries," could be read to require executive agencies to supply free copies of computer products to depository libraries, a concept OMB did not support. Further, section 4, Title V, would permit the Superintendent of Documents to sell databases and online access to government information under the same formula as that for printed publications: cost of printing plus 50 percent. Executive agencies were selling such products under OMB Circular A-25, "User Charges," at a price that included the agency's program costs. Further, GPO sales revenues were credited to the GPO revolving fund, "enhancing GPO receipts at the expense of executive agencies." Stockman also wrote that the proposed regulations completely ignored the role of the National Technical Information Service, whose program had concurrent legislative authority to Title 44. Stockman stated that OMB was studying the legal ramifications of the proposed revision and was consulting with the Department of Justice.

On April 11, 1984, the Department of Justice (DOJ) provided a 17-page opinion in response to an OMB letter of December 7, 1983, on the constitutionality of the proposed JCP regulations in light of the Supreme Court's decision in *Buckley* v. *Valeo* (424 U.S. 1, 1976) and *INS* v. *Chadha* (103 S.Ct. 2764, 1983).[33] DOJ concluded that "the regulations are statutorily unsupported and constitutionally impermissible" (p. 1). The opinion addresses three major legal issues: "(1) whether there is statutory authority for the proposed regulations; (2) whether the regulations would involve congressional performance of executive functions; and (3) whether a joint committee of Congress is seeking to exercise legislative power." DOJ concluded that the proposed regulations "fail on three grounds" (p. 2).

The opinion found that JCP relies for statutory authority on three sections of Title 44, *United States Code*: (1) section 103, which allows JCP to "use any measures it considers necessary to remedy neglect, delay, duplication, or waste in the public printing and binding and the distribution of Government publications"; (2) section 501, which provides that all government printing be done at GPO except work that JCP considers "urgent or necessary to be done elsewhere" and in field printing plants authorized by JCP; and (3) section 502, which provides that GPO may contract out printing with JCP approval. The opinion concluded that such "legislative regulations can apply only internally in Congress" to congressional printing (including operations of GPO, a legislative agency) and that Congress never expected "JCP's approval power to be expanded into authority for overseeing, specifying and regulating internal operations of the Executive branch" (p. 7). The opinion further held that the attempt by JCP to redefine *printing* to "control all functions related to the creation [and dissemination] of a printed word or symbol ... strays far from JCP's statutory grant of authority" under sections 103, 501, and 502, Title 44.

As for legislative and executive functions and constitutional principles of the separation of powers, the opinion concluded that the proposed regulations focused primarily on activities outside GPO (a legislative agency) and involved management by JCP of information activities of executive branch agencies. This was illustrated by the annual printing and publishing plan, which required JCP approval prior to implementation.

The Supreme Court in *INS* v. *Chadha* ruled that an action by Congress is "legislative" if it purports to have "the purpose and effect of altering the legal rights, duties, and relations of persons, including ... Executive Branch officials ... outside the legislative branch" (103 S.Ct. 2884). DOJ concluded that Congress improperly delegated legislative power to JCP in section 501 and that JCP use of statutory authority under sections 103 and 502 usurped executive power. Further, the JCP redefinition of *printing* to "encompass virtually all processes by which legible material is created or stored, thus purportedly subject to JCP oversight and control," was a legislative action that required bicameral passage and presentation to the president and that could not be effected unilaterally by a congressional committee.

On June 26, 1984, the JCP chairman, Rep. Augustus Hawkins (D-CA), entered into the *Congressional Record* (pp. H7075-H7078) for comment the revised *Government Printing, Binding, and Distribution Policies and Guidelines No. 25. Regulations* had been changed to *Policies and Guidelines* due to the requirements of *INS* v. *Chadha*, which held that the legislative veto is unconstitutional. The provisions of the guidelines were not mandatory upon the executive branch, except those specified in Title 44, *United States Code*. Thus, twelve actions in the regulations that required prior approval by JCP were deleted. These included three mentions of "waivers": four "with JCP approval," four "unless authorized by JCP," and three "without the prior approval of JCP." The introduction stated that JCP "realizes that circumstances will occur that will necessitate variances from these provisions. When such occasions arise, the Joint Committee should be notified as far in advance as possible." However, the text of the guidelines retained the imperative *shall* in all sections, although some provisions were based on statutory language in Title 44. In addition, some provisions were based on JCP interpretations that are subject to challenge, and these consequently should have been changed to *should*.

A major change was made in the introductory remarks. All references to JCP establishing "information" policy and having oversight over executive agency "publishing" was deleted. The narrow statutory terms *printing* and *distribution* were used. However, this change was not reflected in the provisions of the guidelines, most key sections of which remained unchanged except for deletions requiring JCP approval.

In a letter to the JCP chairman dated August 8, 1984, OMB Director Stockman stated that the "following features to which we previously objected" had not been changed:

1. *Printing* is still defined in a sweeping manner that includes automatic data processing and telecommunications.

2. Although *distribution* is no longer defined to include dissemination of all government information, it still includes electronic dissemination.

3. An annual three-year report on all printing policies, plans, activities, and acquisitions still must be submitted to JCP.

4. GPO can still sell executive agencies' machine-readable data files and online databases. As before, revenues from such sales would remain with GPO.

5. The policies and guidelines are still open to the interpretation that the agencies would be required to give free copies of electronic information products to the Federal Depository Library System and that the agencies would have no control over re-dissemination of such products.

6. There is still no recognition of nor role for the National Technical Information Service, the National Library of Medicine, and the many technical information clearinghouses operated by executive agencies.

Stockman concluded that the policies and guidelines were still "regulations" because they prescribed what executive agencies "shall do and shall not do with respect to printing and distribution of government publications." In a letter dated July 17, 1984, he requested an opinion on the policies and guidelines from the Department of Justice in light of its previous opinion of April 11, 1984.

In an opinion dated August 21, 1984, the Department of Justice made the following conclusions.

> On the assumption that the requirements [of the guidelines] are intended to be binding upon the officials of the Executive branch ... we have been unable to identify any statute which authorizes either the promulgation of mandatory guidelines or the compulsory subordination of executive management discretion to a committee of Congress. For that reason ... we have concluded that the Guidelines, like their predecessor Regulations, are without statutory authority. In addition ... we have concluded that even if the Guidelines were authorized by statute, they would represent a constitutionally impermissible legislative trespass upon the rights, duties, and responsibilities of the Executive Branch. In sum, our analysis leads us to the conclusion that, under either interpretation, the Guidelines would have no binding effect on executive departments.[34]

The JCP did not publish the proposed policies and guidelines as No. 25 in its series of regulations. Instead, in April 1986 it reprinted *Government Printing and Binding Regulations No. 24* "with addenda." The reprint included an updated list of authorized federal printing plants and some corrections of outdated and incorrect material from the 1977 edition. The addenda included six letters, "To the Heads of All Departments and Agencies," that had been issued since No. 24 was published in April 1977. Among these was a letter dated September 23, 1985, from JCP chairman Sen. Charles McC. Mathias, Jr. (R-MD), which began as follows:

> Owing to the many changes in technology, the Joint Committee on Printing requires a broader perspective of agencies' printing and publishing activities in order to perform its oversight mission effectively. For that reason, I am *requesting* [emphasis added] each department and agency to submit a comprehensive printing program plan to the Joint Committee on an annual basis. This plan should include the full range of printing and distribution activities anticipated for the [next] fiscal year and projections for the following two years. Plans should be submitted no later than the date of submission to Congress of requests for authorization and appropriation.[35]

The contents of the report were the same fourteen elements verbatim from the proposed policies and guidelines. These in turn were the same as the original proposed regulations, except for the deletion of two requirements for waivers. The policies and guidelines had also deleted the statement that the plan could be implemented only following JCP approval. One of the elements asked for a description of the numbers and types of "printing environments," but did not define that term, which in the proposed policies and guidelines was broadly defined to include not only field printing plants, but also everything from copier centers to computer centers.

The uneasy truce between the executive and legislative branches was broken when DoD, along with the General Services Administration and NASA, published a final rule in the *Federal Register* on March 20, 1987 (pp. 9036-9039), amending the Federal Acquisition Regulation (FAR). This was a revision to subpart 8.8 of Title 48, *Code of Federal Regulations*, "Acquisition of Printing and Related Supplies." Amended subsection 8.802(a) states that

> the Department of Justice has advised that the requirement in 44 U.S.C. 501(2) for the advance approval of the Congressional Joint Committee on Printing (JCP) prior to conducting field printing operations is unconstitutional under the Supreme Court's decision in *Immigration and Naturalization Service* v. *Chadha*: therefore, that approval requirement neither binds the executive branch nor serves as the basis for any coverage in this subpart.

Subsection 8.802(b) reminds agencies that "Government printing must be done by or through the Government Printing Office (44 U.S.C. 501)" with four specific exceptions authorized by statute. Subsection 8.802(c) states that "each executive agency shall report to the JCP its intention to conduct field printing operations or to acquire printing at least 30 days prior to such action."

The legal opinion relied on was issued by DOJ on March 2, 1984, in response to a DoD request for an opinion on the constitutionality of section 501, Title 44, in view of the *Chadha* decision.[36] The opinion concluded that

> the JCP approval requirement set forth in 44 U.S.C. 501(2) purports to authorize a committee of Congress to take legislative actions; such purported authorization is unconstitutional under the Supreme Court's decision in *Chadha*.... However, we believe the provision allowing executive departments to engage in authorized field-plant printing operations is severable from the invalid approval mechanism, and remains effective.... Therefore, the Department of Defense may conduct its printing activities to the extent permitted by its authorization and appropriations statutes and considerations of efficiency, irrespective of any action of the Joint Committee on Printing.

The Congress interpreted this rule as a challenge to that part of section 501 requiring all executive printing to be done at GPO. In response Congress added section 309 to the Legislative Branch Appropriations Act for FY 1988, which stated that "none of the funds appropriated for fiscal year by this Act or any other law may be obligated or expended by any entity of the executive branch for the procurement from commercial sources of any printing related to the production of Government publications (including forms) unless such procurement is by or through the Government Printing Office." Three exceptions were authorized, and similar language was included in section 309 of the Legislative Branch Appropriations Act for FY 1989.

On August 29, 1988, DoD, the General Services Administration, and NASA published a proposed rule in the *Federal Register* (p. 33017) that the Civilian Agency Acquisition Council and the Defense Acquisition Regulatory Council were considering changes to delete the language in subsection 8.802, Title 48, *Code of Federal Regulations*, regarding advance approval by JCP for acquisition of printing. "Withdrawal of the referenced FAR coverage is intended to be responsive to the fundamental congressional concern that gave rise to enactment of section 309 of the Legislative Branch Appropriations Act, Pub. L. 100-202, Continuing Resolution for FY 1988, as expressed in its accompanying report language." Thus, the uneasy truce was resumed. Neither side seemed willing to mount a challenge in order to get a Supreme Court decision on the matter.

ALTERNATIVE FUTURES FOR THE GOVERNMENT PRINTING OFFICE

In its 1988 study OTA made the following overall projections on the role of paper versus electronic formats for dissemination of government information:

1 to 3 years—steady state in demand for paper formats; rapid growth in electronic formats, but still a very small percentage of total demand;

3 to 5 years—demand for paper formats may start to decline; demand for electronic formats likely to reach critical thresholds for several types of Federal information;

5 to 10 years—demand for paper format likely to decline markedly in some categories, but would still be significant for traditional government books, reports, and publications; electronic formats likely to dominate for many types of information.[37]

OTA discussed three alternative futures for GPO: traditional GPO—centralized, traditional GPO—legislative branch only, and electronic GPO—decentralized. Under the first alternative, GPO would continue to provide centralized conventional printing services, would disseminate paper and microfiche formats through the sales and depository library programs, and would do very little electronic dissemination. Under the second alternative GPO would continue to provide centralized conventional printing services, but only for the legislative branch. The printing procurement program would be transferred to the executive branch, and the sales and depository library programs would probably remain at GPO, but could also be transferred. GPO again would do very little electronic dissemination.[38]

OTA considered the third alternative to be most likely, with GPO continuing to provide centralized conventional printing services. However, OTA did not consider the separation of powers issue or whether GPO should be an independent agency outside or within the legislative or executive branches. In this scenario, GPO would expand the range of electronic publishing services available to agencies and would disseminate selected electronic formats in both the sales and depository library programs. However, dissemination of electronic formats would not be centralized at GPO; agencies could disseminate their own electronic formats, could opt to use the Superintendent of Documents (SuDocs) sales program, or both. Electronic formats selected for depository distribution would be distributed either directly by the agencies or via GPO.[39]

GPO has fully completed the transition from hot type composition to electronic photocomposition at the main plant, most of which took place during the 1970s. In FY 1968 only 40,000 pages of copy were phototypeset. As of FY 1986 about 3.7 million pages per year were being phototypeset. As of FY 1987 about three-quarters of material phototypeset at the GPO main plant was received in electronic form.[40] OTA found that due to widespread use of computer and word processing technologies and the rapid increase in the use of desktop and high-end electronic publishing systems, executive branch agencies were able to capture their own electronic keystrokes and do their own electronic composition. It was estimated that executive branch agencies submitted 39.1 percent of original material to GPO in camera-ready copy; thus, no typesetting or page composition by GPO was required. Executive branch agencies inputted 57.2 percent of their material electronically, primarily on magnetic tape, and provided only 3.1 percent in traditional manuscript form. On the other hand, the legislative branch submitted 47 percent of its material in manuscript and only 1.3 percent in camera-ready copy; 42.6 percent was inputted electronically, primarily by magnetic tape and fiber optic cable. Of critical importance for the future will be the amount of information furnished to GPO that is prepared in electronic format and will no longer be printed on paper for dissemination, but will be disseminated in electronic format only. Such information need no longer be sent to GPO but instead will remain under the control of the agency, which will decide the method of dissemination.[41]

NOTES

[1]Congress, Office of Technology Assessment (OTA), *Informing the Nation: Federal Information Dissemination in an Electronic Age* (Washington, DC: GPO, 1988), p. 332.

[2]OTA, *Informing the Nation*, p. 332.

[3]This history of GPO from 1789 to 1861 is taken from *100 GPO Years, 1861-1961* (Washington, DC: GPO, 1961), pp. 7-33.

[4]*100 GPO Years*, pp. 162-63.

[5]*Documents to the People* (DttP), 7 (September 1975): 195.

[6]OTA, *Informing the Nation*, p. 12.

[7]Congress, House, Committee on Appropriations, *Legislative Branch Appropriations for 1989: Hearings, 100th Congress, 2d Session*, part 1 (Washington, DC: GPO, 1988), pp. 81-82.

[8]Department of Justice, Office of Legal Counsel, "Memorandum for Michael J. Horowitz, Counsel to the Director, Office of Management and Budget, Re: Government Printing, Binding, and Distribution Policies and Guidelines of the Joint Committee on Printing," August 21, 1984, pp. 9-10. See also "Memorandum for Michael J. Horowitz,

Re: Constitutionality of Proposed Regulations of Joint Committee on Printing under *Buckley* v. *Valeo* and *INS* v. *Chadha*," April 11, 1984, pp. 4-6.

[9]This language was edited and codified in the 1873 *Revised Statutes* in section 3757, p. 741. However, the original 1846 act, which created a joint committee on printing and was repealed by the 1852 act, had similar language in section 2, which stated that the committee "shall have power to adopt such measures as may be deemed necessary to remedy any neglect or delay on the part of the contractor to execute the work ordered by the Congress" (9 Stat. 114).

[10]Congress, Joint Committee on Printing, *The Printing Procurement Program of the Federal Government: Report of the Task Force on the Printing Procurement Program*, S. Prt. 99-120, 99th Congress, 1st session (Washington, DC: GPO, 1986), pp. 1-2.

[11]Robert E. Kling, Jr., *The Government Printing Office*, Praeger Library of U.S. Government Departments and Agencies (New York: Praeger Publishers, 1970), p. 49.

[12]Congress, Joint Committee on Printing, *Federal Government Printing and Publishing: Policy Issues: Report of the Ad Hoc Advisory Committee on Revision of Title 44*, committee print, Y 4.P93/1:P93/6 (Washington, DC: GPO, 1979), pp. 16-17. Appendix to JCP *Government Printing and Binding Regulations No. 24*, reprinted April 1986 with addenda, contains a list of the GPO regional printing procurement offices and authorized federal printing plants arranged by agency and by federal region.

[13]Dick Kirschten, "In the Budget Trenches, OMB Takes Aim at Government Printing Cost," *National Journal* (December 3, 1983): 2518.

[14]"OMB/GPO Review of Printing Plants," *Government Publications Review*, 11 (March/April 1984): 189-90.

[15]Congress, Senate, Committee on Appropriations, *Legislative Branch Appropriations for Fiscal Year 1988: Hearings, 100th Congress, 1st Session*, S. Hrg. 100-443 (Washington, DC: GPO, 1988), pp. 300-302.

[16]Congress, House, Committee on Appropriations, *Legislative Branch Appropriations for 1985: Hearings, 98th Congress, 2nd Session,* part 2 (Washington, DC: GPO, 1984), p. 523. This hearing also contains a list of authorized field printing plants showing the agency, location, number of units produced, and cost per thousand units for 1983 (pp. 525-60).

[17]OTA, *Informing the Nation*, p. 75.

[18]OTA, *Informing the Nation*, p. 77.

[19]DttP, 7 (March 1979): 68.

[20]DttP, 7 (July 1979): 156.

[21]DttP, 7 (September 1979): 192-93.

[22]Congress, House, Committee on House Administration, and Senate, Committee on Rules and Administration, *Public Printing Reorganization Act of 1979: Hearings, 96th*

Congress, 1st Session, on H.R. 4572 and S. 1436, July 10, 19, 24, 26, 1979, Y 4.H81/3: P96/3 (Washington, DC: GPO, 1979), pp. 390-452. The printed hearings contain copies of H.R. 4572 and S. 1436.

[23]DttP, 7 (September 1979): 193-96.

[24]DttP, 7 (November 1979): 278-80.

[25]DttP, 8 (January 1980): 32-33.

[26]Congress, Committee on House Administration, *The National Publications Act: Hearings, 96th Congress, 1st Session, on H.R. 5424, November 14, 1979* (Washington, DC: GPO, 1979). See also DttP, 8 (March 1980): 85.

[27]DttP, 8 (March 1980): 85-86; DttP, 8 (May 1980): 126, 128; and DttP, 8 (July 1980): 176.

[28]DttP, 8 (July 1980): 175-76.

[29]H. Rep. 96-836, pt. II, p. 6.

[30]DttP, 8 (September 1980): 228-30.

[31]DttP, 8 (July 1980): 179.

[32]H.R. 5424, 96th Congress, section 101(4)(E).

[33]Department of Justice, Office of Legal Counsel, "Memorandum for Michael J. Horowitz, Counsel to the Director, Office of Management and Budget, Re: Constitutionality of Proposed Regulations of Joint Committee on Printing under *Buckley* v. *Valeo* and *INS* v. *Chadha*," April 11, 1984.

[34]Department of Justice, Office of Legal Counsel, "Memorandum for Michael J. Horowitz, Counsel to the Director, Office of Management and Budget, Re: Government Printing, Binding, and Distribution Policies and Guidelines of the Joint Committee on Printing," August 21, 1984, p. 16.

[35]Joint Committee on Printing, *Government Printing and Binding Regulations No. 24*, reprinted with addenda (April 1986), pp. 58-59.

[36]Department of Justice, Office of Legal Counsel, "Memorandum for William H. Taft, IV, Deputy Secretary of Defense, Re: Effect of *INS* v. *Chadha* on 44 U.S.C. 501, Public Printing and Documents," March 2, 1984.

[37]OTA, *Informing the Nation*, p. 71.

[38]OTA, *Informing the Nation*, pp. 73-85.

[39]OTA, *Informing the Nation*, p. 85.

[40]OTA, *Informing the Nation*, p. 80.

[41]OTA, *Informing the Nation*, pp. 86-87. See also *Strategic Planning, GPO/2001: Vision for a New Millennium*, GP 1.2:V82 (Washington, DC: GPO, December 1991).

Superintendent of Documents

INTRODUCTION

The position of Superintendent of Public Documents was established in the Department of the Interior by an act of March 3, 1869 (15 Stat. 292), with the responsibility of distributing public documents to depository libraries and to the other officials and institutions authorized by law. The position was transferred to the Government Printing Office (GPO) and renamed Superintendent of Documents by the Printing Act of 1895 (28 Stat. 612), which also expanded the superintendent's responsibilities to include bibliographic control and sale of government publications. Sections 62 and 64 required the Superintendent of Documents to prepare three catalogs: a "comprehensive index of public documents," a "consolidated index of Congressional documents," and a "catalog of Government publications ... which shall show the documents printed during the preceding month, where obtainable and the price thereof." The comprehensive index became the *Document Catalogue*, which was published from 1895 to 1947. The consolidated index became the *Documents Index* (1895-1933) and *Numerical Lists and Schedules of Volumes.* The last catalog became the *Monthly Catalog*, which in 1947 was declared by the Joint Committee on Printing (JCP) to also satisfy the statutory requirements of the comprehensive index.

In 1974 the position of Superintendent of Documents was upgraded to Assistant Public Printer who reported directly to the Public Printer. At that time the former Public Documents Department was thoroughly reorganized to create three major service units within the Office of the Superintendent of Documents: Documents Support Service, Documents Sales Service, and Library and Statutory Distribution Service. The Documents Support Service has since been renamed the Documents Technical Support Group. The Documents Sales Service is the largest unit and consists of the Sales Management Division, the Order Division, and the Field Operations Division, which are housed in leased office space in Union Center Plaza, a modern office complex located on North Capitol Street adjacent to the main GPO building. The last division is responsible for the bookstore program and the Pueblo, Colorado, branch, which serves as a distribution point for the Consumer Information Center, a General Service Administration program that GPO operates on a reimbursable basis. Orders are received and processed at the Union Center Plaza location. The sales publications themselves are stored at and mailed from the Laurel, Maryland, complex, where the Retail Distribution and Warehouse Division is located in two large warehouses.

The Library and Statutory Distribution Service was renamed the Library Programs Service (LPS) when the unit moved back to the main GPO building in February 1985. In 1974 the unit had moved from crowded quarters in Washington, D.C., to leased office/warehouse facilities in Alexandria, Virginia. During this same period warehouse facilities had been leased for the Documents Sales Service (DSS) in Laurel, Maryland. With the move in 1985, the statutory distribution function was transferred to the DSS Warehouse Division in Laurel. LPS now occupies space on the sixth floor of the main GPO building, which became available when the GPO hot metal printing operation was phased out and replaced by automated photocomposition equipment.

LPS consists of a Library Division, which is further subdivided into four units: a Cataloging Branch, Information Technology Program, Depository Services Staff Chief, and Depository Administration Branch. The Depository Services Staff Chief includes a depository designation specialist, inspection team, and publications librarian. The inspection team's duties include not only inspections of depository libraries but also workshops and other depository liaison activities. The publications librarian is responsible for preparing and publishing *Administrative Notes: Newsletter of the Federal Depository Library Program, Instructions to Depository Libraries, GPO Cataloging Guidelines*, and related publications.[1] Figure 2.1 shows the current organizational chart of LPS.

Fig. 2.1. LPS organizational chart

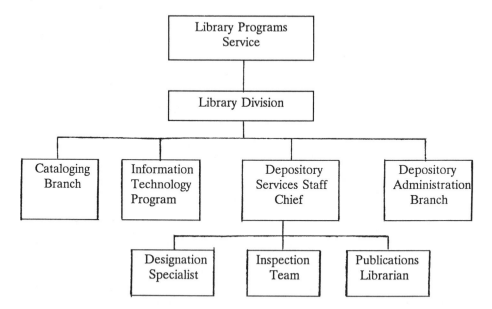

The five major programs of the Superintendent of Documents are the publications sales program, cataloging and indexing of government publications, the depository library program, mailing of certain government publications for Congress and other government agencies in accordance with specific provisions of law ("by-law") or on a reimbursable basis, and the International Exchange Program.

This program, under the provisions of section 1719, Title 44, *United States Code*, authorizes the Library of Congress to conduct official exchanges of government publications with a number of foreign governments "as determined by the Brussels Conventions of 1886, executive agreements, or treaties." The Superintendent of Documents "assembles and distributes the official exchange sets for the United States" and the Library of Congress "receives and houses the official publications of the other nations. The JCP and the Joint Committee on the Library provide oversight."

However, there is a backlog of publications to be distributed. As of October 1990, approximately 7,000 titles were waiting to be microfiched prior to being sent to foreign nations. It has been suggested "that the foreign exchange libraries be added to the domestic depository computerized selection and distribution system" in order for the program to operate with greater efficiency.[2]

PUBLICATIONS SALES PROGRAM

The Documents Sales Service (DSS) operates the publications sales program. Sales are made primarily through mail order, as well as in GPO bookstores. DSS also publishes four catalogs in support of the sales program: *U.S. Government Books, New Books, Price List 36,* and the *Publications Reference File* (PRF). The publications in the program are limited to those printed at or through GPO. However, less than 10 percent of these are sold by GPO. DSS selects for sale those publications that it believes are of public interest and will sell enough copies to cover costs. Although GPO cooperates with the publishing agency on making its decision, the final decision is made by GPO.[3] Thus, the only source of supply for a personal copy of most government publications is the issuing agency. In the past, publications were often available free upon request from the issuing agency. However, with the economic measures introduced by the Reagan administration in 1981, agencies not only were forced to reduce the number of titles they published, but they also were forced to reduce the number of copies of any title published, thus making fewer copies available for distribution to the public.

In 1986, as a result of Gramm-Rudman-Hollings reductions, the JCP instituted several economic measures that reduced or eliminated the availability of free congressional publications for the public. The number of committee prints and hearings allowed to be printed for a committee was reduced from 1,000 to 300. Therefore, GPO established a Congressional Sales Office that now sells hearings and prints. GPO "rides" the print order of all committee prints and hearings for at least 25 extra copies for sale through the Congressional Sales Office only. For those prints and hearings that have wide public interest, GPO obtains a larger number of copies and sells them through the regular sales program, rather than through the Congressional Sales Office.[4]

In 1977, Congress changed the law directing GPO to retain the receipts from the sale of publications and to utilize its revolving fund to cover the cost of the sales program. Previously, the receipts from sales went into the Treasury, and GPO had to request appropriations each year to cover program costs. With the return to profits in the sales program, the congressional appropriations committees have adopted the policy of decreasing by a like amount the appropriations for the other programs of the Office of the Superintendent of Documents.

In 1987, JCP authorized GPO to sell government publications in electronic format in magnetic tape form. These are publishing tapes that are used to print publications. Tapes may be purchased on an individual basis or as a subscription service. Included among the individual tapes available are *Budget of the United States, Congressional Directory, Statistical Abstract, U.S. Government Manual, Congressional Record,* and the *Federal Register.* Subscription services are available for *Congressional Record, Code of Federal Regulations, Federal Communications Commission Record, Federal Register, Monthly Catalog of U.S. Government Publications,* and daily bills and resolutions. Magnetic tapes are standard 16000BPI, 9-track, ASCII, IBM-compatible. They include printing instructions or codes as well as text. However, they do not include illustrations, graphic designs, or documents that were photographed in order to be printed. Ordering instructions are provided in *Price List 36.*

Pricing of Government Publications

The price of government publications is governed by section 1708, Title 44, *United States Code,* which states, "The price at which additional copies of Government publications are offered for sale to the public by the Superintendent of Documents shall be based on the cost as determined by the Public Printer plus 50 percent." The present pricing formula was enacted June 30, 1932, by section 307 of the Legislative Appropriations Act of 1932. The original formula, in section 61 of the Printing Act of 1895 (28 Stat. 610), was as follows: "said cost to be estimated by the Public Printer based upon printing from stereotyped plates." The pricing formula was changed May 11, 1922, by S.J. Res. 132 as follows: "cost of printing and binding, plus 10 per centum."[5]

There is some disagreement on what factors should enter into the cost formula. The legislative history of the 1932 provision is not clear, but it seems to suggest that the cost before the addition of the 50 percent surcharge was only for printing and binding, as provided in the earlier 1922 law. This is the "rider" cost that covers the cost of printing and binding for additional copies from the original press run. From 1932 to 1936, GPO apparently continued to follow the traditional method of limiting the basic cost to printing and binding. However, after 1936, GPO began to add additional costs expressed in percentages of the printing and binding cost, such as "reprint factor," "administrative factor," and postage costs.

Concern over pricing policy arose in the early 1970s due to numerous complaints over the sharp rise in GPO prices. After many years of producing a net income of over 25 percent, the sales program went into a deficit situation in fiscal year (FY) 1972, primarily as a result of greatly increased charges for postal services from $2 million in FY 1971 to $15 million in FY 1972. The Postal Reorganization Act of 1970 (PL 91-375) requires that government agencies pay full unsubsidized rates because the option of receiving additional appropriations to cover such deficiencies was no longer available to the Postal Service, in this case to cover the annual $13 million subsidy for the GPO sales program. During the three-year period 1972-1975 the average cost for a selected group of government periodicals rose nearly 300 percent.

GPO has subsequently refined the cost formula but still includes all operating and overhead costs of the sales program to determine price. However, through the annual appropriations process, the policy has been well established and accepted that the publications sales program should be "self-sustaining," which means it should recover from revenues all costs attributable to the program. The "plus 50 percent" in the price formula has not been interpreted to mean that the program should generate 50 percent profits. Previously, the practice was to return any net income (or profit) to the Treasury. The current practice of the congressional appropriations committees is to use the net income to reduce the amount of appropriations authorized to the nonrevenue-producing programs of the Superintendent of Documents, such as the depository library program.

Mail Orders

GPO prefers that mail orders be submitted on GPO order forms, which may be found in *Price List 36, Monthly Catalog, Subject Bibliographies, U.S. Government Books,* and *New Books.* Ordering instructions are also provided in these catalogs. However, orders may be submitted by letter or local form; sufficient information should be provided to identify the publication(s). Separate publications and subscriptions should be listed or ordered separately. Subscriptions are those titles that are listed in *Price List 36.* For publications, the quantity, stock number, title, unit price, and total price should be provided. For subscriptions, the list identification (ID) code should be shown in lieu of the stock number. Prices listed in the catalogs include domestic postage and handling. However, prices (as well as availability) are subject to change, and the current price will be charged. Therefore, it is advisable to check the latest available *Publications Reference File* for information on price and availability. Price and stock availability information may also be obtained by calling the GPO Order and Information Desk at (202) 783-3238. Charge orders may also be placed at this number, which is open weekdays from 8:00 A.M. to 4:30 P.M. (eastern time). Out-of-town callers should be aware they may be put on hold if no clerk is free.

All orders must be prepaid in the correct amount. Methods of payment include checks drawn in U.S. dollars on a bank located in Canada, the United States, or its possessions; domestic and international money orders; UNESCO coupons; Superintendent of Documents Deposit Accounts; and Visa or Master-Card credit cards. Postage stamps or currency (bills or coins) will not be accepted. Checks should be made payable to the Superintendent of Documents (not to the Government Printing Office). Opening an account requires an initial deposit of $50. It is recommended that a balance sufficient to cover three months' purchases be maintained to avoid the necessity of frequent deposits. Monthly statements are mailed to customers with active accounts. With the use of an account or credit card, an institution or individual can avoid return of an order due to insufficient remittance caused by lack of current price information. Mail orders should be addressed to: Superintendent of Documents, P.O. Box 371954, Pittsburgh, PA 15250-7954. They should include complete name and address and customer's daytime telephone number.

For customers with a Visa or MasterCard credit card or active account, teletype or facsimile (fax) ordering is available. Teletype orders can be placed by dialing TWX 710 822-9413; ANSWERBACK USGPO WSH. Fax orders can be placed by dialing 1-202-512-2233. Customers on the DIALOG system may transfer their orders via DIALORDER. Discounts of 25 percent are allowed to bookdealers and to quantity purchasers (100 or more copies of a single publication, periodical, or subscription service to a single address). Prices for international customers include a surcharge of 25 percent to cover added postage charges and special handling to comply with customs and international mailing regulations. The *Publications Reference File* and *Price List 36* provide both domestic and foreign prices.

GPO Bookstores

The first bookstore was opened in the GPO mail building in 1921. The first out-of-town bookstore was opened in Chicago in 1967. By 1991, there were twenty-three GPO bookstores, two located in the Washington, D.C., area and the remainder in the following cities: Atlanta; Birmingham, Alabama; Boston; Chicago; Cleveland and Columbus, Ohio; Dallas; Denver; Detroit; Houston; Jacksonville; Kansas City, Missouri; Los Angeles; Milwaukee; New York City; Philadelphia; Pittsburgh; Portland, Oregon; Pueblo, Colorado; San Francisco; and Seattle. All are located on federally owned or leased property, except for those in Birmingham, Houston, Kansas City, Los Angeles, Philadelphia, Portland, and Pueblo. These are located in commercial office buildings or shopping centers. One of the Washington, D.C., stores is located in commercial space at 1510 H Street, NW (Farragut West); the other is located in the GPO building at North Capitol and G Streets, NW. A current list of GPO bookstores can be found in the *Monthly Catalog, New Books, Price List 36,* and *U.S. Government Books.*

GPO bookstores are similar to commercial bookstores. Customers may browse and purchase what is available and may also place orders for subscriptions or for publications not in stock. Although the bookstores carry only a small percentage of all titles in the active inventory, they do have those most in demand. A retail sales outlet is operated by the Retail Distribution Division at the Laurel, Maryland, warehouse complex, where customers may order and pick up any title currently in stock.

Current Awareness Sources

The Documents Sales Service publishes five catalogs: *U.S. Government Books, New Books, Price List 36, Subject Bibliographies*, and the *Publications Reference File* (PRF). Although these are designed primarily to support the publications sales program, they are also useful for cataloging, acquisitions, and reference work. It should be remembered that these catalogs list only those government publications available for sale through the Superintendent of Documents.

U.S. Government Books

This quarterly annotated sales catalog began publication with the fall 1982 issue. It describes approximately 1,000 "bestsellers" currently in print and available from the Superintendent of Documents. An introductory section, "Recent Releases," is devoted to new publications. The remaining popular titles are arranged in over twenty subject categories, including agriculture, consumer aids, education, health and physical fitness, housing, and transportation. Entries include title, publication date, pagination, stock number, and price, but the Superintendent of Documents classification notation is not always provided. Most entries are annotated. Many listings include an illustration of the cover. Ordering information and order forms are provided.

U.S. Government Books (GP 3.17/5) replaced *Selected U.S. Government Publications* (GP 3.17), which began as a weekly service in July 1928, changed to semimonthly in 1941, and became a monthly in 1974 until it was discontinued in August 1982. Figure 2.2 (see page 34) is a typical page from an issue of *U.S. Government Books.*

New Books

New Books (GP 3.17/6) began publication with the July/August 1982 issue. This bimonthly unannotated catalog lists all new titles that have entered the GPO general sales publications during the previous two months. It does not include congressional hearings and committee prints that are sold through the GPO Congressional Sales Office. The list is organized into approximately twenty subject areas, including agriculture, business and labor, national topics, public laws, and transportation. Items are listed alphabetically by title under each subject, and each title is listed only once. Entries include title, issuing department or agency, date of publication, pagination, stock number, and price. Ordering information and order forms are included. Figure 2.3 (see page 35) shows a portion of a page from *New Books.*

Price List 36

Price List 36: Government Periodicals and Subscription Services (GP 3.9:36) has had three name changes since it began publication in September 1910. This quarterly catalog lists government publications that are available on subscription from the Superintendent of Documents. These include three categories: (1) basic and supplemental titles (preceded by a dot), which consist of a basic manual or beginning group of materials that are serviced by providing additional material or changes, usually in looseleaf format; (2) dated periodicals issued on a regular basis, such as weekly, monthly, etc.; and (3) irregular periodicals with no fixed rate of issuance. Entries are arranged alphabetically by title in a single list and include frequency of issue; subscription price (usually for one year) and price for single copy, if sold; list identification (ID) code; Superintendent of Documents (SuDocs) class number; stock number; and brief annotation. Introductory pages include a list of changes since the previous edition (such as new subscriptions and discontinued subscriptions) and an agency index by executive departments and independent agencies. Moreover, recent quarterly issues contain a subject index. Ordering information and order forms are included. The Price List series began in 1910; all but *Price List 36* were discontinued in 1975 and replaced with the Subject Bibliography (SB) series. Figure 2.4 (see page 35) shows a portion of a page from *Price List 36.*

Fig. 2.2. Page from *U.S. Government Books*

We the People, 1991 Calendar. A beautiful wall calendar recalling the stirring events of the American Revolution, the era of our Declaration of Independence, and our struggle for freedom and independence. Each day includes a reminder of events that occurred 200 years ago and bore directly upon the forming of our Nation. Each month has a beautiful full-color scene of the Nation's Capital or a memorable sight relating to our seat of Government. Each page allows space to jot down notes. Opens to 11 by 20 inches. 1990. 26 p. il.

S/N 066-001-00010-5
$3.50

Restoring America's Wildlife, 1937-1987. This full-color volume has been produced by the U.S. Department of the Interior as a tribute to the accomplishments of the first 50 years of the Pittman-Robertson Federal Aid in Wildlife Restoration Act. Written by more than 30 recognized authorities from all parts of the country and illustrated with photographs and paintings by nationally known artists, it describes the impact of modern wildlife management on nearly a score of popular species and details the many economic and recreational opportunities created by the Act. 1986. 420 p. il. Cloth.

S/N 024-010-00671-4
$20.00

United States Government Printing Office Style Manual: March 1984. The authority on U.S. Government editorial style. Categories include: guide to compounding, word abbreviations, use of numerals, and more. 1984. 488 p.

Cloth edition.

S/N 021-000-00121-0
$15.00   (GP 1.23/4:St 9/984/cloth)

Paper edition.

S/N 021-000-00120-1
$11.00   (GP 1.23/4:St 9/984/paper)

Word Division. A supplement to the *United States Government Printing Office Style Manual,* which gives the proper line-ending breaks for nearly 20,000 words. 1987. 144 p.

S/N 021-000-00139-2
$1.50

National Topics

Statistical Abstract of the United States, 1990 (110th Edition). The latest of this ever-popular and useful publication. It is the standard summary of statistics on the social, political, and economic status of government and business in the United States. This volume is designed to serve as a convenient reference tool for statistical publications and sources. Provides new tables relating to marital status, health insurance information, government and economic activities, wood energy consumption, and much more. Also includes pocket-size insert "USA Statistics in Brief" summarizing important data for quick and easy reference. 1990. 1017 p. il.

Cloth edition.
S/N 003-024-07096-1
$34.00

Paper edition.
S/N 003-024-07095-2
$28.00

To receive **free** announcements of future editions of the **Statistical Abstract,** please write to: U.S. Government Printing Office, Office of Marketing, Stop: SM, Washington, D.C. 20401.

Use Your MasterCard or VISA.

All prices include postage and handling

You'll find our latest books beginning on page 3.

Order forms missing?
Send orders on plain paper to:
Superintendent of Documents
Dept. 33
Washington, DC 20402

Fig. 2.3. Example from *New Books*

ONE HUNDRED YEARS OF FEDERAL
FORESTRY. (Agriculture) 1976.
199 p. il. 1990-Reprint.
A 1.75:402
S/N 001-000-03668-8 $12.00

★★★★★★★★★★★★★★★

BUSINESS & LABOR

ALCOHOL & DRUG ABUSE PROVISIONS IN
MAJOR COLLECTIVE BARGAINING
AGREEMENTS IN SELECTED INDUSTRIES.
(Labor) 1990. 38 p.
S/N 029-001-03067-3 $2.25

ANNUAL SURVEY OF MANUFACTURES,
1988 --

-- STATISTICS FOR INDUSTRY GROUPS
& INDUSTRIES. (Commerce) 1990.
72 p.
S/N 003-024-07242-4 $3.75

-- VALUE OF PRODUCT SHIPMENTS.
(Commerce) 1990. 44 p.
S/N 003-024-07241-6 $2.50

CITY EMPLOYMENT: 1989. (Commerce)
1990. 40 p.
S/N 003-024-07240-8 $2.25

CLAIM FOR COMPENSATION ON ACCOUNT OF
TRAUMATIC INJURY OR OCCUPATIONAL
DISEASE, FORM CA-7; ATTENDING
PHYSICIAN'S REPORT, FORM CA-20.
(Labor) 1990. 4 p. Revised edition.
L 36.410:CA-7/990
S/N 029-016-00121-2 $27.00

Fig. 2.4. Example from *Price List 36*

CONGRESSIONAL RECORD. (Daily when Congress is in session.) A verbatim report on Congressional debates and other proceedings. Each issue includes a Daily Digest that summarizes the proceedings for that day in each House and before each of their committees and subcommittees. The legislative program for that day is presented, and at the end of the week, the program for the following week. *Discounts are not allowed on the subscription or single copy sales.*

Paperback. Subscription price: Domestic—**$225.00** a year; Foreign—**$281.25** a year. Single copy price: Domestic—$1.50 a copy; Foreign—$1.88 a copy [85].
[CR]   X/a: (Cong.)
(File Code 3A)   S/N 752-002-00000-2

Microfiche (24X). Subscription price: Domestic—**$118.00** a year; Foreign—**$147.50** a year. Single copy price: Domestic—$1.50 a copy; Foreign—$1.88 a copy. [Current calendar year plus previous year.]
[CRM]
(File Code 3A)   S/N 752-029-00000-8

NOTE: A special six-month subscription to the paper edition of the Record is available at Domestic—**$112.50**; Foreign—**$140.65**; the microfiche edition, Domestic—**$59.00**; Foreign—**$73.75**.

CONGRESSIONAL RESEARCH SERVICE REVIEW. (10 Issues.) Subscription price: Domestic—**$9.50** a year; Foreign—**$11.88** a year. Single copy price: Domestic—$1.50 a copy; Foreign—$1.88 a copy [6].
[CRSR]   LC 14.19:
(File Code 2G)   S/N 730-009-00000-3

Contains articles of interest to the United States Congress, legislative staff members, congressional committees, other offices of the legislative branch, others in government, and the general public.

CONSTRUCTION REPORTS. Statistical data compiled into various series covering all areas of construction, such as ownership, location, type of structure, units completed and under construction, sold and for sale prices, contracts and permits, and other useful information.

C20. Housing Starts. (Monthly.) Subscription price: Domestic—**$15.00** a year; Foreign—**$18.75** a year. Single copy price: Domestic—$1.50 a copy; Foreign—$1.88 a copy

Subject Bibliographies

Subject Bibliographies (SB) (GP 3.22/2) provides a list of publications for sale that are in print. They are arranged by topic (e.g., Air Pollution, SB-046), by series (e.g., Agriculture Yearbooks, SB-031), or by agency (e.g., Federal Communications Commission, SB-281). Discontinued SB numbers are not used; over 300 bibliographies have been issued, with about 225 still in print. Titles are arranged alphabetically under topics and subtopics. Many entries are annotated. Bibliographic information includes title, date, pagination, SuDocs class number, stock number, and price. *Subject Bibliography Index* (SB-599) contains a convenient form for ordering individual Subject Bibliographies, which are available free from the Superintendent of Documents. Figure 2.5 is a portion of a page from *Subject Bibliography 150.*

Fig. 2.5. Example from *Subject Bibliography 150*

National Library of Medicine Classification: A Scheme for the Shelf Arrangement of Books in the Field of Medicine and Its Related Sciences 1981: 441 p.; ill. revised ed. Clothbound HE 20.3602:C 56/981	S/N 017-052-00222-8	$16.00
National Library of Medicine, Current Catalog *(Quarterly.) Quarterly listing of citations to publications cataloged by the Library arrnged by subject and name sections. Subscription price: Domestic - $37.00 a year; Foreign - $46.25 a year. Single copy price: Domestic - $27.00 a copy; Foreign - $33.75 a copy. (NLCQ) (File Code 2Q)* HE 20.3609/2:	S/N 717-018-00000-1	
National Library of Medicine Current Catalog, Annual Cumulation:		
1983 1984: 1441 p. Clothbound HE 20.3609/3:983	S/N 017-052-00246-5	$29.00
1984 1985: 1963 p. Clothbound HE 20.3609/3:984	S/N 017-052-00253-8	$39.00
1985 1986: 1711 p. Clothbound HE 20.3609/3:985	S/N 017-052-00262-7	$53.00
1986 1987: 1675 p. Clothbound HE 20.3609/3:986	S/N 017-052-00268-6	$54.00
1987 1988: 1706 p. Clothbound HE 20.3609/3:987	S/N 017-052-00274-1	$68.00
1988 1989: 2 bks. (2088 p.) Clothbound HE 20.3609/3:988/v.1-2	S/N 017-052-00280-5	$52.00
Near East National Union List, Volume 1 *A guide to publications in Near Eastern languages printed before 1979 that have been reported to the National Union Catalog by 240 libraries in the United States and Canada.* 1988: 877 p. Clothbound LC 1.12/2:N 27/v.1	S/N 030-000-00198-2	$47.00

Publications Reference File

The *Publications Reference File* (PRF) was originally developed as an in-house reference tool for filling publications orders and answering inquiries. Following a two-month evaluation period in 1976 by 100 depository libraries, the PRF was made available to depository libraries. An identical edition called the *GPO Sales Publications Reference File* was made available to others as a sales subscriptions service from the Superintendent of Documents in a bimonthly microfiche edition with monthly supplement and a biweekly magnetic tape service.

The PRF is a microfiche catalog of all publications currently in stock for sale by the Superintendent of Documents, plus some forthcoming and recently out-of-stock titles. It is generated by computer output microfiche (COM) weekly for internal use within GPO. Additional copies of the master file (approximately 175 48x microfiche with 270 frames on each fiche) are produced bimonthly (January, March, May, July, September, and November) for distribution to depository libraries and subscribers. Included with each bimonthly mailing of the master file is a monthly supplement, *GPO New Sales Publications*, which also is mailed separately in other months. This supplement consists of one or two fiches listing new publications offered for sale during the past months. Titles are listed alphabetically in one sequence and include forthcoming publications with prices, new publications in stock for the first time, and reprints of older publications that have come back into stock. Following their use at GPO, the discarded weekly PRF microfiche sets are sent to regional depository libraries.

The microfiche file is divided into three sections, with the complete record presented in each section. The first section is arranged by stock number sequence. The second section is arranged by SuDocs class number. The third section is an alphabetical arrangement of subjects, titles, and series. A complete record includes stock number, SuDocs class number, warehouse location, stock status, stock status code and date, title, personal author, issuing agency, imprint statement, description (annotation), SB number, ID list code, type of binding, shipping weight, and domestic and foreign price.

Titles purged from the PRF master file are issued in a companion microfiche publication titled *Out of Print Sales Publications Reference File.* The 1990 edition, which lists all items that went out of stock in the GPO sales program during the years 1985-1988, is a supplement to the *Exhausted GPO Sales Publications Reference File, 1980,* which covers out-of-stock items for the period 1972-1978, and to the *Out of Print GPO Sales Publications Reference File, 1986,* which covers out-of-stock items for 1979-1984. For a complete record of all out-of-stock items, the 1980 and 1986 editions should be retained. No sales copies are available for titles announced in either the 1980 or the 1986 edition.

In 1982, the PRF master file became available online through DIALOG. Customers with Visa or MasterCard credit cards or deposit accounts can order publications directly from GPO via the DIALORDER feature of DIALOG. A commercial edition of the PRF titled *Popular Government Publications File* is available to subscribers from Readex Microprint Corporation on CD-ROM. All entries on the compact disk are available in full text in the Readex microfiche collection. The CD-ROM is updated quarterly.

CATALOGING ACTIVITIES

The principal bibliographic product of the LPS Cataloging Branch is the *Monthly Catalog of United States Government Publications.* Known as the *Monthly Catalog* or just MoCat, this central source is discussed in detail in chapter 4. A *Periodicals Supplement* to the *Monthly Catalog* is published annually, usually as the first catalog issued during the year, beginning with Entry Number 1. From 1977 to 1984 the annual was called the *Serials Supplement.* The *Periodicals Supplement* replaces a comparable listing that was previously published annually in the February issue of the "old" (pre-July 1976) *Monthly Catalog.* It now includes publications that are issued three or more times a year. Figure 2.6 (see page 38) shows a sample entry from the *Periodicals Supplement.*

GPO joined the Online Computer Library Center (OCLC) in order to automate production of MoCat. New publications are cataloged online and such entries are immediately available to OCLC subscribers. At the end of each month OCLC sends GPO a tape of publications cataloged during the period, and from this GPO prepares MoCat. GPO's decision to become an OCLC member has had far-reaching consequences. Since 1895 GPO had employed its own unique system for cataloging government materials involving the use of a locally produced cataloging manual and a locally maintained subject thesaurus. By joining OCLC, GPO was obliged to abandon its former cataloging practices and abide by the Anglo-American Cataloging Rules (AACR) and Library of Congress subject headings. Other OCLC members could now have online access to newly cataloged government publications. They were able to offload catalog cards from

Fig. 2.6. Sample entry from *Periodicals Supplement*

SUPT. OF DOCS. CLASS. NO.—This is the number assigned by the GPO Library to identify the document cataloged.

TITLE PHRASE/STATEMENT OF RESPONSIBILITY—Title phrase and author statement are recorded from the title page or its substitutes. Material in bracket is supplied from other prominent sources.

IMPRINT—Contains place of publication, issuing agency, date of publication (when cataloging from the first or last issue). Includes name of distributors when available.

NOTES—Include additional bibliographic information about the physical makeup of a publication, its issuing corporate authors, or about complex relationships with other publications.

PERIODICITY—Current frequency of publication.

SUBJECT HEADINGS (Arabic numerals)—Headings are selected from the Library of Congress subject headings. Some Natl. Agricultural Library and Natl. Library of Medicine subjects may be used. Natl. Libr. of Med. subjects will be indicated by an asterisk (*). Natl. Agri. Lib. subjects will be indicated by a dagger (†).

ADDED ENTRIES (Roman numerals)—When the government author is not a main entry, it is included with added entries.

OCLC NO.—This is the number assigned by the Ohio College Library Center to identify this record in the data base.

SAMPLE ENTRY

83-125

A 93.10/2:(nos.)

Agricultural outlook (Washington, D.C. : 1975)
Agricultural outlook / United States Department of Agriculture, Economic Research Service.—[Washington, D.C.] : The Service : Supt. of Docs., U.S. G.P.O., [distributor, 1975–. Supt. of Docs., U.S. Govt. Print. Off., Washington, D.C., 20402
v. : ill. ; 30 cm.
$31.00 (U.S.) $38.75 (foreign) no single copies sold
Monthly (except combined Jan./Feb. issue) 1976–
Monthly (except Dec.) 1975
AO–1 (June 1975)– Issues for Jan./Feb., 1978–Oct. 1980–Oct. 1980 classed A 105.27: Indexed by: American statistics index, ISSN 0091-1658 Indexed by: Index to U.S. government periodicals, ISSN 0098-4604 Issued by: United States Dept. of Agriculture, Economic Research Service, June 1975–Dec. 1977; by USDA, Economics, Statistics, and Cooperatives Service, Jan./Feb. 1978–Oct. 1980; by Economics and Statistics Service, United States Department of Agriculture, Nov. 1980–June 1981; by the Economic Research Service, July 1981– Title from cover. Item 42-M, S/N 001-028-80003-7 ISSN 0099-1066
1. Agriculture—Economic aspects—United States—Periodicals. I. United States. Dept. of Agriculture. Economic Research Service. II. United States. Dept. of Agriculture. Economics, Statistics, and Cooperatives Service. III. United States. Dept. of Agriculture. Economics and Statistics Service.
HD 1751.D46a, 75-647210//r81 338.1/0973 OCLC
02243568

MONTHLY CATALOG ENTRY NO.—The entry no. is assigned after the records are arranged alphanumerically by Supt. of Docs. classification no. The first two digits locate the record in the catalog.

MAIN ENTRY—A main entry may be a corporate author, uniform title, or the document title, as established by Anglo-American cataloging rules.

SUBSCRIPTION ADDRESS—Includes street address, city, country, and zip code of sales agent.

COLLATION—Extent of item (including specific material designation), illustrations, and size.

PRICE—GPO sales price.

DATE—Beginning date of publication, and/or volume designation.

ITEM NO.—This document was distributed to depository libraries requesting this item number. Microfiche indicates the document was distributed as such.

ISSN—International standard serial number, assigned or authenticated by the National Serials Data Program. Each number is unique to a title and is part of the international effort for uniform control of serials.

LIBRARY OF CONGRESS CLASS. NO.—This is given when the library of Congress has authenticated the record.

LIBRARY OF CONGRESS CARD NO.—Included when it is available from the Library of Congress.

STOCK NO.—This is a Govt. Print. Off. sales stock no. It is used only in ordering from the Supt. of Docs.

DEWEY CLASS NO.—Given when the record has been authenticated by the Library of Congress.

OCLC. Previously, the main source of standard cataloging was the Library of Congress, which fully cataloged a relatively small percentage of government publications, primarily congressional documents. By 1981 the Library of Congress began accepting GPO as the authoritative source for descriptive cataloging of federal government publications.

However, government documents librarians were slow in reaping the advantages of this new technical development. By the mid-1970s, many large university and research libraries had become OCLC members. Such libraries were generally depository libraries and had large collections of government publications. These large collections were usually shelved separately by SuDocs number under the control of separate documents units. In those early years OCLC was used primarily for cataloging operations by libraries, and OCLC terminals were first installed and used in the technical services units. Gradually, OCLC terminals were installed in general reference departments and, eventually, in separate government documents units. As OCLC grew into a national bibliographic utility, medium and small libraries also became members.

The *Monthly Catalog* computer tapes are sold by both the Library of Congress and the Superintendent of Documents. Some of these tapes have been purchased by individual libraries and then downloaded onto their local online catalogs. Tapes have been purchased by service bureaus, such as Marcive, that make available a variety of services based on cumulative files developed from the tapes. They have also been purchased by information vendors, such as DIALOG, that provide online access to the cumulative *Monthly Catalog* file from July 1976.

SUPERINTENDENT OF DOCUMENTS CLASSIFICATION SYSTEM

This classification, known by its short title "SuDocs class system," was "developed in the Library of the Government Printing Office between 1895 and 1903." Credit for the "foundation of the system (classification by governmental author)" is awarded to Adelaide R. Hasse, a towering historical figure in the discipline of federal and state bibliographic information. Hasse used government organization authorship "to assign classification numbers to a *List of Publications of the U.S. Department of Agriculture from 1841 to June 30, 1895*," and the list was published "by the Department of Agriculture in 1896 as its Library Bulletin No. 9."[6]

The SuDocs class system is an alphanumeric notation based on the principle of provenance, whereby the publications of any government publisher or issuing agency — a department, bureau, agency, or office — are grouped under like notation. It is not a subject classification scheme like the Library of Congress or Dewey decimal systems commonly used in libraries. It has more similarity to systems used in archival administration to file records, which are also based on provenance. The scheme has a fundamental weakness in that an issuing agency's position in the system is determined by the current organizational status (and often the name as well) of that agency. Therefore, the system structure is at the mercy of any governmental reorganization that may be directed by the president, by Congress, or by the head of a department or agency, with the result that the publications of some agencies may be found in as many as eight different places.

For example, publications of the Children's Bureau, established in 1912, can be found at C 19, L 5, FS 3.200, FS 14.100, FS 17.200, HE 21.100, HE 1.450, and HE 23.1200.

When changes in reorganization require changes in classification notation, some librarians have advocated changing the notation assigned by GPO to ensure that all publications are shelved at the same location. Others have advocated changing the new numbers to conform with the old notation, and still others have advocated changing the old numbers to the new notation. However, the practice of changing SuDocs numbers and using numbers other than those assigned by the Superintendent of Documents has many disadvantages. The SuDocs classification number is a nationally recognized standard number used not only in GPO bibliographic tools, primarily the *Monthly Catalog*, but also in commercial catalogs such as those published by the Congressional Information Service. Government publications with the SuDocs classification number assigned by GPO are now also widely found in OCLC online and CD-ROM databases, making it more important than ever to retain the standard SuDocs classification number.[7]

A full SuDocs classification number consists of three major elements: the author symbol, series designation, and book number. The combination of author symbol and series designation (usually found before the colon) is called the "class stem." The book number gives the publication its unique classification identification and completes the notation. No two publications have the same book number. There is even a notation at the end of the SuDocs class number to distinguish each edition or version of a title from all other editions or versions of that same title.

The author symbol consists of a letter (or letters) and a number. For example, TD 4 designates the Federal Aviation Administration within the Department of Transportation. When the system was first established, single letters were used for executive departments (A — Agriculture, T — Treasury) and two letters were used for independent agencies (IC — Interstate Commerce Commission). Now one or two letters may be used for executive agencies, and two or three letters may be used for independent agencies (FHL — Federal Home Loan Bank Board). To set off subordinate bureaus and offices of a department or an independent agency, a number is added, with the digit 1 assigned to the secretary's or administrator's office of the parent organization. When the system was first established, the existing subordinate offices and bureaus were arranged in alphabetical order and assigned sequential numbers. Since then new offices and bureaus have been assigned the next available number.

"Author" symbol is actually a misnomer, as the symbol designates the issuing agency or publisher, which may or may not be also the corporate author. The classification scheme does not necessarily show "authorship" in the sense of an individual or a corporate body responsible for the intellectual content of a publication. Many congressional committee prints are prepared (or authored) by the Congressional Research Service, but they are issued by a congressional committee and the SuDocs class number is assigned to the publications of that committee. However, when the publication is cataloged under AACR, the main entry will show Congressional Research Service (or even an individual) as the author.

The second element is the series designation, which follows the author symbol after the period. A number is assigned to each agency series, and this is followed by a colon. The following numbers are reserved for the most common series issued by most government agencies:

.1   Annual reports

.2   General publications

.3   Bulletins

.4   Circulars

.5   Laws

.6   Regulations, rules, and instructions

.7   Press releases

.8   Handbooks, manuals, and guides

.9   Bibliographies and lists of publications

.10   Directories

.11   Maps and charts

.12   Posters

.13   Forms

.14   Addresses, lectures, etc.

Numbers 1 through 4 were assigned when the system was established, numbers 5 through 8 were assigned in the 1950s, and numbers 9 through 14 were designated in 1985. Older classes will deviate from the current practice of using numbers 5 through 8 and 9 through 14. New series are generally assigned the next open number. However, to get related series to file side by side on the shelf, or adjacent to each other as bibliographic listings, existing series numbers may be extended by the use of a slash and numbers (or letters). After a number has been extended with a slash and number, it may be further extended by the use of a dash and numbers. The use of a slash and/or a dash extends author symbols and book numbers. A theoretical example to tie in related classes is as follows:

.4:   Circulars

.4/a: Separates from circulars (numbered)

.4/b: Separates from circulars (unnumbered)

.4/2:   Administrative circulars (personnel)

.4/2-2:   Administrative circulars (supply)

.4/3:   Technical circulars

A significant weakness of the system is that it is intended to designate only the first two levels of any agency hierarchy. However, modifications have been made to the system to permit designation of agencies at the third and fourth levels, using 100s and 1000s, respectively. Two methods are used to designate third-level agencies: The 100s are placed either in the author symbol or in the series designation. An example of the former is the use of D 100s, D 200s, and D 300s to designate third-level agencies in the Army, Navy, and Air Force Departments, respectively. For example, D 101 designates the Department of the Army (second level in the Department of Defense), and D 103 designates the Army Corps of Engineers (third level in the Department of the Army). An example of the second method is found in the National Oceanic and Atmospheric Administration, C 55 (second level in the Department of Commerce), in which the following designations are made for third-level agencies: C 55.100s — National Weather Service, C 55.300s — National Marine Fisheries Service, and C 55.400s — National Ocean Service. Thus, C 55.304 is the class stem assigned to circulars of the National Marine Fisheries Service.

An example of use of 1000s and 100s in the series designation to designate third- and fourth-level agencies is found in the Public Health Service, HE 20 (second level in the Department of Health and Human Services). The 3000s are assigned to the National Institutes of Health and its subordinate agencies; the 7000s, to the Centers for Disease Control; the 8000s, to the Alcohol, Drug Abuse, and Mental Health Administration; and the 9000s, to the Health Resources and Services Administration. Within the National Institutes of Health, it has been necessary to break some series into 50s due to the large number of subordinate units. Thus, HE 20.3152 designates "general publications" of the National Cancer Institute.

The individual book number follows the colon. In the case of annual reports, the last three digits of the year are used as the book number. For example, A 1.1:992 would indicate a 1992 annual report. For periodicals the volume and issue number, separated by a slash, are the book number: *Social Security Bulletin*, vol. 50, no. 3, is HE 3.3:50/3. Unnumbered periodicals or those without a volume and issue number are identified by the year of issuance and order of issuance throughout the year: the December 1990 issue of *Monthly Product Announcement* is C 3.163/7:990/12. If the December issue were the tenth number issued during 1990, the book number would be 990/10.

Classification librarians at LPS do not always wait for government reorganization to change the SuDocs notation. In the past the book and series numbers assigned to the publications by an agency were the same. However, in the 1980s a new policy of subsuming series was initiated, and the Bureau of Labor Statistics (BLS) Bulletin sequence was the first series to be affected. For example, the well-known biennial *Occupational Outlook Handbook, 1990-1991* edition, was issued as Bulletin 2350. In the past the notation would have been L 2.3:2350. Now the handbook is classed as L 2.3/4:990-91. Similar changes in the classification of the *Industry Wage Survey Bulletins* (L 2.3/3:numbers) were instituted. The *Summaries* are no longer assigned separate class stems. Instead, they are placed in new class stem L 2.3/3-2:(CT). Individual publication numbers after the colon are assigned the most specific designation appearing on the document, as follows: (1) Cuttered by industry, (2) Cuttered by industry and state or region, (3) Cuttered by industry and state with a superior number for cities within the state, and (4) numbered.[8]

Unnumbered publications, or numbered publications for which GPO does not use the publication as a book number, are given a book number based on the principal subject word of the title, using a two-figure Cutter table. For a

Department of the Army publication, *The Old Guard of the Army* is classed D 101.35:G93, with *guard* being the key subject word. Subsequent publications in the same series, which would take the same Cutter number, would be classed as G93/2, G93/3, etc. In some cases the key subject word is not used if it is common to (or is the name of) the agency, such as *energy* for Department of Energy publications. The terms *national, federal, government,* etc., generally are not Cuttered.

Revisions of Cuttered publications are identified by the addition of a slash and the last three digits of the year of revision. For example, if the publication *The Old Guard of the Army* mentioned above was revised in 1991, the class number would be D 101.35:G93/991. Subsequent revisions in 1991 would be identified as 991-2, 991-3, and so on. Previous revisions of numbered publications were identified by the addition of a slash and a number, beginning with 2 for the first revision. However, this policy was changed in the mid-1980s to use the same rule as that for Cuttered publications: Add a slash and the last three digits of year of revision.

Although the system described above governs the classification of the publications of most issuing agencies, special treatments are employed for publications of certain government agencies. These consist of classes assigned to:

1. Some series issued by the Interstate Commerce Commission, such as IC 1 wat. (water carriers) and IC 1 mot. (motor carriers).

2. Boards, commissions, and committees established by an act of Congress or under authority of an act of Congress that are not specifically designated in the executive branch or as completely independent agencies.

3. Congress and its working committees.

4. Multilateral international organizations in which the United States participates, such as S 5.48 (National Commission for UNESCO Publications).

5. Publications of the president, including committees and commissions established by executive order and reporting directly to the president.

Those agencies established by an act of Congress or under authority of an act of Congress that are not specifically designated in the executive branch are grouped under Y 3, one of the agency symbols assigned to congressional publications. The classification numbers of the publications are then pushed over to the right, so that instead of the series designation following the period, the individual agency symbol derived from a two-figure Cutter table follows it. The Cutter number is followed by a colon. For example, Y 3.N88 is the number for the Nuclear Regulatory Commission. Series designations for publications of these agencies then follow the colon instead of preceding it. Book numbers are added to the series designation by the addition of a slash and a number for book numbers with digits (e.g., Y 3.N88:1/988) or by a blank space for Cutters or book numbers starting with letters (e.g., Y 3.N88:2R29).

The class stem for the *Congressional Record* (final edition) is X followed by a period, which is followed by the number of the Congress, a slash, the session number, and a colon. The volume number, the abbreviation *pt.*, and the part number complete the notation (e.g., X.98/2:129/pt.21). The daily *Congressional Record* is treated as a preprint, with */a* as part of the class stem. Then the notation is formed by adding the Congress and session numbers and using the volume and issue numbers as the book number (e.g., X/a.100/2:134/56). The House and Senate journals have been assigned XJH and XJS, respectively. These letters are followed by Congress and session numbers and then the part number, if any (e.g., XJH:98-2/pt.1).

Publications of the Congress as a whole are classed as Y 1.1, House of Representative publications, as Y 1.2; and Senate publications, as Y 1.3. The book number follows the colon. Several exceptions have been made to provide series designation by adding a slash and a number before the colon. For example, Y 1.2/2 is the class stem for *House Calendar*, and Y 1.3/4 is the class stem for the *Senate Executive Journal*.

Numbered House and Senate documents and reports originally were not assigned specific classes but were simply filed by number in individual groups. During the 96th Congress an X preceded the Congress and session numbers to aid in the computer production of the *Monthly Catalog* (e.g., X 96-2:H. Doc. 353). Beginning with the 97th Congress numbered documents and reports were assigned Y 1.1/(nos.) classes. Senate documents and reports were assigned Y 1.1/3 through Y 1.1/6, and House documents and reports were assigned Y 1.1/7 and Y 1.1/8, respectively. The book number following the colon is the report or document number as printed on the publication. For example, Y 1.1/8:100-523 is H. Rep. 100-523.

The working committees of Congress are grouped under one of the agency symbols assigned to Congress, namely Y 4. As in the case of Y 3, an author symbol based on the Cutter number of the name of the committee follows the period and in turn is followed by a colon. For example, Y 4.J89/1 is the House Committee on the Judiciary, and Y 4.J89/2 is the Senate Committee on the Judiciary. With this method of classification, the classes for publications of House, Senate, and joint committees are intermixed. No provision is made for separate classes for subcommittees. After the colon is the individual book number, which is a serial number for those committees that number their hearings and/or committee prints or a Cutter number for unnumbered publications. Prior to the mid-1980s there were only a few separate series designations, which used the same scheme as Y 3 publications: a number immediately after the colon preceding the book number (e.g., Y 4.P93/1:6/24 for JCP *Printing and Binding Regulations*, issue 24). The new series numbers are formed by adding a -(no.) to the class stem (e.g., Y 4.P93/1-10) for the annual *U.S. Government Depository Libraries Directory*.

The agency symbol assigned to the president is Pr followed by the number corresponding to the ordinal number of succession to the presidency, such as Pr 41 for George Bush, forty-first president of the United States. Breakdowns under the agency symbol follow normal methods for series designation and book number, with one exception. In recent years, many presidents have appointed special committees and commissions to study particular problems and report directly to the president. These organizations are usually terminated after they submit their reports. Because their publications are few in number, normal bureau treatment is not warranted. Beginning with those appointed by President Dwight Eisenhower, one series, Pr (no.).8, has been assigned for all such committees and commissions. A Cutter number is then assigned to each based on the principal subject in its name, such as Pr 40.8:Sp3/R29. This notation signifies a study titled *Report of the President's Special Review Board, February 26, 1987*, better known as the *Tower Commission Report*, which initially investigated the scandal surrounding the "Iran-Contra" affair.

The House and Senate documents and reports that appear in the United States Congressional Serial Set are assigned SuDocs class notations. For example, the *Report of the Congressional Committees Investigating the Iran-Contra Affair* was issued as a House report classed as Y 1.1/8:100-433. Serial set classification is further examined in chapter 5.

"Fugitive" Publications

A method for assigning the many "fugitive" or "renegade" publications received by libraries that bypassed the LPS classifiers "builds on the class stem for General Publications, and entails dashing or slashing the numbers 2 through 9 onto the appropriate class stem." This method is most effective when used with publications "for which there is no class listed in the *List of Classes*." LPS points out that "each library should work out a method that suits its own needs, and should feel completely free in assigning these numbers."[9] The system is pragmatic and open-ended. The only inexpiable sin is assigning the *same* complete notation to more than one publication.

Classifying CD-ROM Products

The initial option for classifying CD-ROM products involved the use of the Cutter number. For example, when *Census Test Disc No. 2* was sent to all depository libraries, it was classified as follows:

C 3.275:T28/CD no. 2	The disk itself
C 3.275:T28/Soft.	Software for performing simple data retrieval from the Test Disk on a floppy disk
C 3.275:T28/Doc.	A print product—the technical documentation providing information on the file format

Because *Census Test Disc No. 2* contains agricultural data for counties from the 1982 census of agriculture and also contains retail trade statistics by zip code from the 1982 census of retail trade (part of the 1982 economic censuses), the number 275 (never used in the past) was arbitrarily assigned. The *List of Classes* shows an entry for C 3.275 as "Electronic Products (Irregular) (CD-ROM) 0154-B-01."

When the *Bureau of the Census Electronic County and City Data Book, 1988*, was released, it was listed on Shipping List 90-0057-P (paper) as C 3.134/2:C83/2/988/floppy and C 3.134/2:C83/2/988/floppy-2. Unfortunately, this product was infected with a computer virus; it is announced in the *List of Classes* as C 3.134/2, "County and City Data Book (Irregular) (CD-ROM) 0151-D."

The Interior Department's *Joint Earth Sciences (JES-2) Demonstration Disc* on CD-ROM was assigned the SuDocs notation I 19.119:Si1.[10] And the *1985 Congressional Record on CD-ROM* was classed as X.99/1:131/CD; it appeared on Shipping List 90-0007-E, December 6, 1990.

Guides to the SuDocs Classification System

Issued in looseleaf format and prepared by LPS classification specialist Jorge E. Ponce is a detailed publication titled *GPO Classification Manual: A Practical Guide to the Superintendent of Documents Classification System* (GP 3.29:P88). The looseleaf format permits changes and additions to be inserted into the basic manual. A shorter but useful description of the basic elements of the system is titled *An Explanation of the Superintendent of Documents Classification System* (GP 3.2:C56/8/990). Begun in 1963, this venerable elucidation has gone through several editions and revisions. Together the two sources provide a complete understanding of the many facets in this scheme, a scheme that, despite some inherent problems associated with all provenance classification systems, has for a century proven durable and helpful in organizing separate documents collections.

NOTES

[1]*Administrative Notes*, 11 (March 31, 1990): 1.

[2]U.S. Congress, House, Committee on Appropriations, Subcommittee on Legislative Appropriations, *Legislative Branch Appropriations for Fiscal Year 1992: Hearings, February 7, 1991*, part 1 (Washington, DC: GPO, 1991), pp. 204-05.

[3]U.S. Congress, Joint Committee on Printing, *Federal Government Printing and Publishing: Policy Issues* (Washington, DC: GPO, 1979), p. 51.

[4]*Government Publications Review*, 13 (July/August 1986): 534-35.

[5]LeRoy C. Schwarzkopf, "Pricing Policy of GPO Sales Publications," *Documents to the People* (DttP), 3 (September 1975): 25-30.

[6]U.S. Library Programs Service, *An Explanation of the Superintendent of Documents Classification System, October 1990*, GP 3.2:C56/8/990 (Washington, DC: GPO, 1991), p. iii. The current revision is a useful, 14-page guide to the basic principles and special treatment cases of the system.

[7]For comprehensive summaries of arguments concerning this problem, see Forrest C. Palmer, "Simmons vs. Schwarzkopf: The Great Class(ification) Debate," *Southeastern Librarian* (Fall 1977): 163-66; and Michael Waldo, "An Historical Look at the Debate over How to Organize Federal Government Documents in Depository Libraries," *Government Publications Review*, 4 (1977): 319-29.

[8]*Administrative Notes*, 10 (May 15, 1989): 14-15.

[9]*Administrative Notes*, 5 (January 1, 1984): 2.

[10]*Administrative Notes*, 10 (November 15, 1989): 1.

3

Depository Library System

INTRODUCTION

The purpose of the depository library system is set forth in the legislative history of the Depository Library Act of 1962 in S. Rep. 1587 on H.R. 8141 (87th Congress) as follows:

> The depository library system is a long established cooperative program between the Federal Government and designated major libraries throughout the United States under which certain classes of Government publications are supplied free of cost to those libraries for the purpose of making such publications readily accessible to the American public (p. 3).

This statement is based on language in the 1962 act, which was codified as section 1911, Title 44, *United States Code*, that "depository libraries shall make Government publications available for the free use of the general public." The Senate statement also highlights a key feature of the system: it is a cooperative program between the federal government and the nation's library community. The federal government provides the publications free of charge to libraries, which (except for state appellate court libraries) must make them available free of charge to any member of the general public who wishes to use them. The government also provides an administrative support structure under which it assigns standard Superintendent of Documents (SuDocs) classification numbers for identification, filing, and retrieval purposes, and national bibliographic control is maintained through the *Monthly Catalog*.

The 1991 Legislative Branch Appropriations Act authorized a total of $26,500,000 for the Superintendent of Documents to discharge the several duties assigned by law to that office (104 Stat. 2273). In fiscal year (FY) 1991, $21,693,000 was authorized by the House for depository library distribution costs. Although critics view this as a minuscule amount of money for the major federal program that provides access to government information for the benefit of the citizenry, the number of publications distributed to the almost 1,400 depository institutions in 1990 was 26,934,000. As in years past, the legislative branch appropriations hearings held by the House and Senate provide a wealth of valuable information about all aspects of GPO operations.[1]

Although the depository libraries receive the publications free of charge, they also incur considerable expense in providing staff and facilities to process, maintain, and provide reference service on the collection. The publications remain the property of the federal government. The 1979 Joint Committee on Printing (JCP) Ad Hoc Advisory Committee on Revision of Title 44 reported that one regional depository expends $325,000 annually to maintain its collection.[2] However, depository libraries obtain free many publications that they would want to acquire anyway for their regular clientele, which translates into considerable savings in acquisition costs. In addition, only 10 percent of depository publications are Government Printing Office (GPO) sales publications, so it would be difficult, if not impossible, for libraries to otherwise obtain many of the publications.

HISTORY OF THE DEPOSITORY LIBRARY SYSTEM

The depository library system had its origins in special acts of the first twelve Congresses, which provided for the printing of extra copies of congressional documents outside the federal government to the states and territories. In the 13th Congress, Joint Resolution 1 of December 27, 1813 (3 Stat. 140), provided

> that of the public journals of the Senate and the House of Representatives, of the present and every future congress ... and of the documents published under the orders of the Senate and of the House of Representatives ... there shall be printed two hundred copies beyond the usual number ... and shall be transmitted to the executives of the several states and territories, as shall be sufficient to furnish one copy to each executive, one copy to each branch of every state and territorial legislature, one copy to each university and college in each state, and one copy to the Historical Society ... in each state.

The number of extra copies was increased from 200 to 250 by Joint Resolution 5 of July 20, 1840 (5 Stat. 409), and to 300 by Joint Resolution 5 of April 30, 1844 (5 Stat. 717). The depository library system was formally established by a series of two resolutions in 1857 and 1858 and by an act of 1859. Resolution 5 of January 28, 1857 (11 Stat. 253), transferred responsibility for distributing the congressional journals and documents from the Department of State to the Department of the Interior "to such colleges, public libraries, athenaeums, literary and scientific institutions, boards of trade, or public associations as may be designated by [the Secretary of the Interior]."

The 1857 resolution was amended by Joint Resolution 5 of March 20, 1858 (11 Stat. 368), which provided that the designations would be made by the "representatives in Congress from each congressional district, and by the delegate from each Territory in the United States." The 1858 resolution was in turn amended by section 5 of the Act of February 5, 1859 (11 Stat. 380), which provided that designations would be made by "each of the senators from the several states, respectively, and by the representative in Congress from each congressional district, and by the delegate from each Territory in the United States." Thus, in 1859 the principle of congressional designation was established as the basis for the depository library system, apparently to ensure distribution throughout the country on an equal basis. Another provision of section 5 provided distribution "to the governors of the States and Territories."

Major changes in the depository library system were made by the landmark Printing Act of 1895, approved January 12, 1895 (28 Stat. 601), which had as its main object the consolidation of existing laws on the printing, binding, and distribution of public documents. An act of March 3, 1869 (15 Stat. 292) had established a position of Superintendent of Public Documents in the Department of the Interior. This position was responsible for distributing public documents to depository libraries. The 1895 act transferred the position to the GPO, renamed it Superintendent of Documents, and assigned the additional responsibilities of preparing three catalogs to achieve systematic bibliographical control of government publications, among which was the *Monthly Catalog.* The 1895 act also increased the categories of materials eligible for distribution, established two required-by-law ("by-law") categories of depository libraries, and made other additions and changes.

The 1895 act renewed distribution of congressional reports and documents but decreased the number of journals to three for each state. It added the *Congressional Record* and *Statutes at Large* and, most important, added in section 58 executive department publications "not intended for the especial use, but made for distribution." The act also expanded the system to include other than congressional designations or by-law designations in section 98, which added the libraries of the eight executive departments and of the military and naval academies. It unintentionally established "state and territorial libraries" as by-law depositories by the structure of the language used in the distribution formula.

The 1895 act contained two other additions or changes regarding the inspection program and the free use, or access, clause. Section 70 provides that

> the Superintendent of Documents shall thoroughly investigate the condition of all libraries that are now designated depositories, and whenever he shall ascertain that the number of books in any such library, other than college libraries, is below one thousand, other than Government publications, or it has ceased to be *maintained as a public library* [emphasis added], he shall strike the same from the list.

This section was revised by section 6 of the Depository Library Act of 1962. This revision was codified as section 1909, Title 44, as follows:

> The designated depository libraries shall report to the Superintendent of Documents at least every two years concerning their condition. The Superintendent of Documents shall make first-hand investigation of conditions for which need is indicated.... When he ascertains the number of books in a depository library is below ten thousand, other than Government publications, or it has ceased to be maintained so as to be *accessible to the public* [emphasis added], or that Government publications which have been furnished the library have not been properly maintained, he shall delete the library from the list of depository libraries.

Following the 1895 act, the Superintendent of Documents did not make physical inspections authorized by the act. Instead, in 1950 he inaugurated the familiar "Biennial Survey" conducted by mail, which was written into the 1962 act and is still used. In 1974, the Superintendent of Documents established a formal inspection program by hiring three inspectors. The inspection team has since been increased to four inspectors, an administrative assistant, and a chief inspector who reports to the head of the Library Division. It has a goal of inspecting each depository library at least once every three years, but typically the length of time between inspections is five to six years.

The 1895 act was the first to contain a free public access or use clause, which led to the present language in section 1911, Title 44. Section 74 of the 1895 act stated that "all government publications delivered to designated depositories or other libraries shall be for public use without charge." Section 70, regarding inspections, also stated that a depository shall be "maintained as a public library." The latter section was superseded by section 6 of the Depository Library Act of 1962, which directed that depository libraries shall "be accessible to the public." Section 74 of the 1895 act was superseded by section 8 of the 1962 act, which provided that "government publications which are furnished depository libraries shall be made available for the free use of the general public." Section 8 was codified as section 1911, Title 44, with the language of the 1962 act.

Following the General Printing Act of 1895, the next major revision of the depository library system was made by the Depository Library Act of 1962 (82 Stat. 1282), referred to above. Several significant changes made between 1895 and 1962 were incorporated into the 1962 act. Section 4 of the act of March 1, 1907 (24 Stat. 1014) added a third category of by-law designations by providing for the designation of "all land grant colleges." Section 5 of a lengthy appropriations act approved June 23, 1913 (58 Stat. 75), provided that "libraries heretofore designated by law as depositories ... shall hereafter, during their existence, continue such receipt" of publications. This provision made current and subsequent designations permanent as long as the depository fulfilled the legal requirements. Previously, a designation was subject to removal without cause upon change of a senator or representative. This provision was incorporated in the 1962 act and codified in section 1910, Title 44. The 1962 act further provided that, if following reapportionment the number of congressional designations exceeded the limit, an existing depository would not lose its designation.

The 1923 Legislative Branch Appropriations Act, approved March 20, 1922, contained a provision that no part of appropriated funds "shall be used to supply depository libraries any documents, books, or any printed matter not requested by such libraries" (42 Stat. 436). Thus, all depositories became "selective"; previously they had to accept everything offered. A similar provision was contained in every subsequent legislative branch appropriations act until 1962. The Depository Library Act of 1962 enacted into law this provision as well as the administrative procedures that GPO had adopted to implement the 1922 revision. These are codified in section 1904, Title 44, as follows: "The Superintendent of Documents shall currently issue a classified list of Government publications in suitable form, containing annotations of contents and list by item identification number to facilitate selection of only those publications needed by depository libraries."

Probably the most important amendment between 1895 and 1962 was Public Law (PL) 75-70, approved June 25, 1938 (52 Stat. 1206), which provided that the Public Printer shall furnish to depository libraries "the Journals of the Senate and House of Representatives, all publications not confidential in character, printed upon requisition of any Congressional committee, all Senate and House public bills and resolutions, and all reports on private bills and concurrent or simple resolutions." The 1895 act had reduced the number of journals to three per state;

this act restored full distribution. Reports on public bills previously had been distributed to depositories; this act added reports on private bills, public bills and resolutions, and congressional hearings and committee prints. Although distribution of committee prints was authorized, it was not until the mid-1970s that most prints were distributed to depositories. Previously, committees claimed these prints were "administrative" and exempt from depository distribution.

The Depository Library Act of 1962 incorporated and consolidated many early provisions of law and also made four important revisions in the system: (1) it increased from one to two the number of designations that could be authorized by each representative, delegate, and senator; (2) it increased the number of federal libraries from the executive departments and military academy libraries to provide additional depositories to independent agencies and to each major bureau, office, or division within executive departments and independent agencies; (3) it expanded the categories of depository materials by authorizing the distribution of "non-GPO" publications; and (4) it authorized two regional libraries in each state that could permit selective depositories to discard materials after holding them five years.

One of the major problems and complaints of depository libraries prior to 1962 was that they were required to retain permanently all depository publications. During the 1950s, the Superintendent of Documents authorized the establishment of experimental regional depositories in Wisconsin and New York that could permit selected depositories to discard materials after twenty-five years' retention. The 1962 act reduced the mandatory retention period to five years (for all depositories served by a regional depository), and it required regional depositories to accept all materials, hold them permanently (with limited exceptions), and "within the region served [to] provide interlibrary loan, reference services, and assistance for depository libraries in the disposal of unwanted Government publications." These provisions are codified in section 1912, Title 44.

As of December 1, 1990, there were 51 depository libraries with regional responsibilities. These regionals serve all states, the District of Columbia, and outlying territories. States with two regional depository libraries include Alabama, Colorado, Louisiana, Michigan, New Mexico, Oklahoma, South Carolina, Texas, and Wisconsin. States without regionals are served by libraries in nearby or contiguous states. For example, Alaska is served by Washington State Library; Delaware, by the University of Maryland; and Guam, Micronesia, and the Northern Marianas, by the University of Hawaii. A complete list with directory information is published in *Administrative Notes*, vol. 11, no. 26 (December 30, 1990), pp. 10-17.

Section 4 of the Depository Library Act of 1962 (codified as section 1903, Title 44) repeated all categories of congressional publications from the 1938 act and added non-GPO publications. However, it also included a provision that the publishing agencies would have to pay for the additional copies printed for depository distribution, giving agencies a greater incentive not to comply by declaring such publications to be "administrative" or "operational" and therefore exempt from depository distribution under section 1902, Title 44. However, in 1977, JCP added section 41-2 to its *Government Printing and Binding Regulations No. 24*, which required agencies to supply only two copies of such non-GPO publications to the Superintendent of Documents: one copy for cataloging and bibliographic control in the *Monthly Catalog* and the second copy to prepare a microform master from which additional microfiche could be manufactured for depository distribution, with the added costs paid from congressional appropriations for the depository library program.

Section 7 of the Depository Library Act of 1962 (codified as section 1907, Title 44) renewed the by-law designations of libraries of executive departments and increased the number of military academies to five by adding the U.S. Air Force Academy, the U.S. Coast Guard Academy, and the U.S. Merchant Marine Academy. It also greatly increased the number of federal libraries by authorizing additional depository libraries within executive departments and independent agencies for "major bureaus or divisions" of such departments and agencies.

Another important contribution of the Depository Library Act of 1962 was section 1 (codified as section 1902, Title 44):

> Government publications, except those determined by their issuing components to be required for official use only or those required for strictly administrative or operational purposes which have no public interest or educational value and publications classified for reasons of national security, shall be made available to depository libraries through the facilities of the Superintendent of Documents for public information.

After the landmark 1962 act, two amendments made to the depository library system added two more categories of by-law designations. Public Law 92-368, approved August 10, 1972 (86 Stat. 507), authorized the Public Printer to designate as a depository upon request "the highest appellate court of a State." The law, codified as section 1915, Title 44, exempts such libraries from the section 1911 "free use" clause and from its requirement to retain materials five years before discarding. Public Law 95-261 (92 Stat. 199), approved April 17, 1978, but not effective until October 1, 1978, authorized the Public Printer to designate as depository libraries upon request the library of any accredited law school. The law, codified as section 1916, Title 44, exempts law school libraries from much of section 1909, Title 44, which relates to location of new depositories: "within an area not already adequately served by existing depository libraries."

The depository library system is dominated by academic libraries. In a 1972 study of 1,080 depository libraries, 711 (65.8%) were academic libraries (including 27 law school libraries); 249 (23.1%) were public libraries; 63 (5.8%) were state agency libraries; 41 (3.8%) were federal libraries; and 16 (1.4%) were other types of libraries.[3] In a 1985 study of 1,373 depositories, 765 (55.7%) were academic libraries; 278 (20.2%) were public libraries; 146 (10.6%) were law school libraries; 105 (7.7%) were state agency libraries; 60 (4.4%) were federal libraries; and 19 (1.4%) were other types of libraries. Thus, the percentage of academic libraries (including law school libraries) had increased from 65.8 percent in 1972 to 66.3 percent in 1985. Although the number of public libraries increased from 249 to 278, the percentage decreased from 23.1 percent in 1972 to 20.2 percent in 1985.[4]

A later study by Hernon and Heisser based upon fall 1989 information and covering solely regional depository institutions found that 61.1 percent of all regionals were academic libraries, 27.8 percent were state agencies, public libraries measured 9.3 percent, and one state historical society came to 1.8 percent of the whole. For these and other useful data on regional depositories, see Peter Hernon and David C. Heisser, "GPO Regional Depositories," in Robin Kinder (ed.), *Government Documents and Reference Services* (New York: Haworth Press, 1991), pp. 43-55.

Since 1978, there have been no amendments to the depository library system. Title 44 revision bills proposed significant changes to the depository library system, particularly in expanding the formats of materials available for depository distribution to include machine-readable data files and audiovisual materials and to include any material produced at government expense, such as grant and contract reports. They also proposed that the Superintendent of Documents should maintain a complete collection of government publications and should provide support services (including financial support) to depository libraries. The original bill (H.R. 4572) also had a provision for an additional 100 depository libraries at large to be designated by the Superintendent of Documents. This provision was eliminated in H.R. 5242, the final amended bill, which included no provision for regional libraries. The JCP attempt to revise its *Government Printing and Binding Regulations* in 1983-1984 included a broad definition of the term *printing environment*, which would have allowed free distribution of government publications in electronic formats to depository libraries.

However, there have been (and continue to be) significant changes in the depository library system since the early 1970s that are not the result of legislation. These resulted from the establishment of the Government Documents Round Table (GODORT) of the American Library Association (ALA) and the Depository Library Council to the Public Printer in 1972. As a result, there has been closer cooperation among the library community, GPO, and JCP. In addition, GPO has taken a more active role in the management of the depository library system and has become more receptive to the needs and wishes of depository librarians.

GODORT is, unlike most ALA units, a voluntary rather than an appointed organization. Since its founding, there has been active participation by many depository librarians, rather than by a select, appointed few. GPO also has consistently sent representatives to GODORT meetings to serve as resource persons and to learn about librarians' concerns and needs. A regular feature of the midwinter and annual conference meetings by GODORT's Federal Documents Task Force is an update session with presentations by GPO and JCP representatives, as well as by other federal agencies such as the Bureau of the Census and the National Archives and Records Administration. Resolutions and motions are regularly passed by GODORT at each conference regarding the depository library program and other federal information programs. GODORT resolutions are often adopted by the ALA Council and become ALA policy.

The Depository Library Council to the Public Printer first met following the 1973 ALA midwinter conference in Washington, D.C. During 1973 and 1974, it continued to schedule meetings at the ALA conference sites following the midwinter and annual conferences. In 1975 it adopted its present policy of holding two meetings a year of two-and-a-half days each (Wednesday through Friday noon). A March or April meeting is held in a different city each year, rotating among various regions of the country, and an October meeting is held in the Washington, D.C. area. Spring meetings have been held at St. Paul (1980); San Antonio, Texas (1981); Boston (1982); Seattle (1982); Atlanta (1984); Albuquerque (1985); St. Louis (1986); San Diego (1987); Charleston, South Carolina (1988); and Pittsburgh (1989). The council is composed of fifteen members appointed each year before the fall session. Most of the members are working government documents librarians, with some library administrators, federal government information officials, and representatives from the Information Industry Association (IIA). During the early years, most members were library administrators with a minority of working documents librarians.

Meetings have been open since the January 1974 meeting. Advance notice of time and place is published in the *Federal Register* and announced in the Library Programs Service (LPS) *Administrative Notes*, including schedules and proposed agenda. An unusual aspect is that participation by the audience is not only welcomed but encouraged, the result being that council recommendations often ensue from audience input. Typically, over 100 depository librarians attend each meeting. Usually the first day and a half are devoted to update presentations by GPO, JCP, and other federal agency officials plus the GPO response to the recommendations from the previous meeting. The afternoon of the second day is devoted to an open session for audience input and working sessions by the council to draw up recommendations for action by GPO. During the final morning, the council discusses and adopts its recommendations.

The charter and bylaws of the council, adopted in January 1975, require the submission of an annual report (GP 1.35). The first report covered the years 1972-1975. Since the earliest meetings, a verbatim transcript has been taken and prepared of the proceedings of full council sessions. This document is distributed to depository libraries in microfiche (GP 3.30). Summary reports that include the text of all council recommendations are published in LPS *Administrative Notes*. Immediately prior to the meeting (in addition to the regular agenda), LPS *Administrative Notes* publishes the GPO reply to the council recommendations of the previous meeting, as well as summaries of update presentations to be given by GPO staff.

The Depository Library Council not only has presented recommendations to the Public Printer but also has assisted GPO in other ways, such as preparing or sponsoring proposals for publication and adoption by GPO. In the mid-1970s, council members prepared proposed standards and guidelines primarily as an inspection tool for GPO's newly established inspection program. The standards cover minimum standards for the depository library system, and the guidelines provide direction for the system. They were first published as a *Special Supplement* to the December 1975 issue of *Public Documents Highlights*, and a revised version was published as a *Special Supplement* to the August 1977 issue of *Public Documents Highlights*. A final version was published as an official GPO publication, *Guidelines for the Depository Library System as Adopted by the Depository Library Council to the Public Printer, October 18, 1977* (GP 1.23/4:D44/978). This was superseded by a document published in 1988 by the GPO Inspection Team, *Guidelines for the Depository Library System (revised 1987) with Minimum Standards for the Depository Library System (1976)*.

In 1980 and 1981, the council sponsored the preparation of the "List of Superseded Depository Documents (that may be discarded)" by a group of five volunteers. This was superseded by a revised list prepared by a group of fifteen volunteers recruited by the council. The superseded list is published as appendix C to the *Instructions to Depository Libraries*. The lengthy list, arranged in SuDocs class number order, includes a number of depository items, with discarding instructions pertaining to each item such as "discard if revised," "keep latest edition," "looseleaf—discard revised pages," etc. In 1991, a committee organized to annotate the "List of Superseded Documents" for regional depository libraries completed its work, and the titles, arranged by SuDocs number, item number, and series title, were published in *Administrative Notes*, vol. 12, no. 8 (March 30, 1991), pp. 7-30.

A volunteer group recruited by the council also prepared the *Federal Depository Library Manual*, published by the Superintendent of Documents in 1985. A volunteer was also recruited to compile and prepare the irregular Needs and Offers List (GP 3.31). For this publication, depository libraries submit to the volunteers a list of their "needs" for publications missing from their collections and "offers" of publications that a regional depository has authorized for discarding. The *Instructions for Depository Libraries* advises that "only worthwhile publications should be listed on the Needs and Offers List. These would include long runs of documents and bound sets. The list does not include odd issues of periodicals or dilapidated volumes."

In June 1991, LPS inaugurated the Federal Depository Library Program Bulletin Board System (FDLP/BBS) for the use of the Depository Library Council and depository libraries. The FDLP/BBS is available 24 hours a day, 7 days a week. Access to the bulletin board simply involves dialing 202-275-7923 using one of various telecommunications software packages. The depository library number assigned to all designated depositories is the user ID number. FDLP/BBS contains program operation information. Helpful hints for new users of the system were published in *Administrative Notes*, vol. 12 (June 30, 1991), pp. 3-4.

Another major change that is not the result of legislation has been the GPO microform program for depository publications, begun in the 1970s. Originally, the major purpose was to expand the offerings of non-GPO publications and, by offering certain publications in "dual format" (i.e., both paper and microform), to provide some depositories a means of economizing by reducing storage and handling requirements for less used publications. However, with forced reductions in appropriations in the Gramm-Rudman-Hollings climate, the program has been used as a means for the federal government to economize at the expense of providing information to depository libraries in the most usable format. In 1981, GPO discontinued distribution of bills and resolutions in dual format and only provided them in microfiche, a move approved by the Depository Library Council.

DEPOSITORY DESIGNATION AND TERMINATION

Information on the requirements for designation of a new depository is contained in section 1905, Title 44; in *The Designation Procedures for Federal Depository Libraries*, 1986 (GP 3.2:D44/9); in section 3 of the *Guidelines for the Depository Library System*; and in chapter 14 in *Instructions to Depository Libraries*. The last has separate sections for designations made by a member of Congress and for designation procedures for libraries eligible for by-law status. It, as well as the booklet on designation procedures, has sample letters for the libraries and officials involved in the designation process.

A library seeking a congressional designation should be sure a vacancy exists and should consult with local depositories and/or the regional depository about the benefits, costs, and responsibilities of depository status. A letter must be sent to the State Librarian asking for an evaluation and letter of recommendation. This letter of justification should address the library's eligibility for depository status, its unique qualifications for status, and its commitment to the goals of the depository library system. The State Librarian should consult with the regional depository librarian as well as with other libraries and professional associations. The State Librarian sends a letter of recommendation, along with the library's application, to the appropriate representative or senator. The legislator then sends a letter to the Superintendent of Documents, notifying him or her of the selection. This letter should be accompanied by any letters, especially the State Librarian's, that support the designation. If the selected library is eligible, it is sent "Acceptance of Designation" forms to complete, sign, and return to GPO. GPO then sends notification letters to the library, the designating official, the State Librarian, and the regional depository.

A library seeking a "by-law" designation should send its application directly to the Superintendent of Documents, indicating the section of Title 44 under which it claims eligibility and certification of its eligibility. By-law designations include state libraries; highest state appellate court libraries; land grant college libraries; accredited law school libraries; service academy libraries; libraries of executive departments; and other federal libraries, including those of independent agencies and those of major bureaus or divisions within executive departments or independent agencies. According to section 1907, Title 44, applications from these other federal libraries must be accompanied by certification by the head of each executive department or independent agency as to the justifiable need for additional depository libraries.

A designated depository library has the right to voluntarily relinquish its depository status at any time by sending a letter to the Superintendent of Documents. The regional depository should also be notified of this decision if the library is served by a regional. Depository status can be terminated by the Superintendent of Documents under section 1909, Title 44, if the library fails to meet requirements as set forth in the law or consistently disregards notices, resulting in unnecessary expense to the government in administering the program. A 1985 survey of the 51 libraries that had voluntarily relinquished depository status between 1970 and 1983 gave the following reasons for their action (in order of frequency): publications were seldom used; another library was a better choice for status; severe space limitations; lack of professional staff; lack of support staff to maintain depository status; and participation as a financial burden.[5]

DEPOSITORY ITEM SELECTION

Each new depository library receives one complete set of item cards arranged in item number order. This set consists of a 3"-by-5" card for each item number. Each card gives the item number, issuing agency, series title, SuDocs classification number (i.e., "class stem"), format (paper or microfiche), and description (see fig. 3.1, page 57). As a general rule, an item comprises only one publication series (as represented by the class stem), but some item numbers include more than one series and may include related series. On the other hand, some series are distributed under more than one item number. This is especially true of series that include separate publications for each state, such as the quinquennial and biennial census reports. In this case, a separate item number has been established for each state. Publications distributed in dual format also have separate item numbers for paper and microfiche formats.

Fig. 3.1. Example item card

```
Item No. 422-I

    AIR FORCE DEPARTMENT
    Defense Department

    Studies in Communist          D 301.85
    Affairs (series)




                    Depository Library No._____
```

   Other guides to selection for new (as well as existing) depository libraries are the *List of Classes of U.S. Government Publications Available for Selection by Depository Libraries* (GP 3.24) and the *GPO Depository Union List of Item Selections* (GP 3.32/2). The *List of Classes* is published quarterly and is arranged in SuDocs class number order. Headers are placed at the beginning of each new author symbol to indicate the name of the issuing agency. A header provides, in tabular format, the SuDocs class number (class stem), title of series, format (paper, microfiche, or CD-ROM), and item number. If a series comprises more than one item number, there is a complete entry for each item number. Following the entries is a section titled "List of Items and Class Stems," arranged by item number with reference to the class stem. Appendix I of the *List of Classes* is an alphabetical listing of government authors by name and alphanumeric author symbols, such as "Congressional Budget Office Y 10." Appendix II lists entries by SuDocs notation classes that appeared in previous quarterly editions but have been deleted from the current revision. This section is arranged by class number, item number, and reason for deletion (e.g., "discontinued," "internal use only," etc.). Appendix III lists by item number those categories that are additions to the inactive or discontinued items list revised as of the previous quarterly edition. An annual supplement to the *List of Classes* is *Inactive or Discontinued Items from the 1950 Revision of the Classified List* (GP 3.24/2). This list is arranged in item number order and includes item number, series title, format, SuDocs class number, and issuing agency. The *List of Classes* and its supplement are available for sale as a subscription from the Superintendent of Documents. Figure 3.2 (see page 58) shows a portion of a page from the *List of Classes*.

Fig. 3.2. Example from *List of Classes*

AGRICULTURE DEPARTMENT— CONTINUED

Federal Crop Insurance Corporation

A 62.1:	Annual Report to Congress (MF) 0071-A
A 62.2:	General Publications 0071
A 62.6/2:	Regulations, Rules, Instructions (P) 0072
A 62.15:	Handbooks, Manuals, Guides 0071-C
A 62.16:	A Guide to Crop Insurance Protection (annual) (P) 0071-C

Foreign Agricultural Service

A 67.1/2:	Foreign Agriculture (annual) (P) 0077-A
A 67.2:	General Publications 0077
A 67.7/3:	AgExporter (monthly) (P) 0076
A 67.18:	Circular Series, Various titles (MF) 0076-J
A 67.18/2:	Cocoa, World Cocoa Situation (annual) (MF) 0076-J
A 67.26:	Miscellaneous Series (FAS-M-(nos.) (MF) 0076-G
A 67.40:	U.S. Export Sales (weekly) (MF) 0076-K
A 67.40/2:	Export Briefs (weekly) (MF) 0076-K
A 67.40/4:	U.S. Exports of Reported Agricultural Commodities for Marketing Years (annual) (MF) 0076-K
A 67.40/5:	Trade Policies and Market Opportunities for U. S. Farm Exports, Annual Report (MF) 0076-K-01
A 67.42:	World Production and Trade (MF) 0076-L
A 67.44:	Food for Peace, Annual Report on Public Law 480 (MF) 0024-T
A 67.45:	Agricultural Trade Highlights (monthly) (P) 0076-M

Rural Electrification Administration

A 68.1:	Annual Report of the Administrator (MF) 0115
A 68.1/2:	Annual Statistical Report, Rural Electric Borrowers (MF) 0115-A-01
A 68.1/3:	Annual Statistical Report, Rural Telephone Borrowers (MF) 0115-A-02

The *Union List*, published annually in microfiche, contains a list of all active item numbers in item number order. In addition to all the information on the item cards, it also includes a list of the depository numbers of those libraries selecting the item and the total number of libraries selecting that item. One useful feature about the *Union List* is that item card information is periodically revised to provide current information, whereas the item cards supplied to depositories are not. A depository must enter updated information on its original set of cards from information provided on the Depository Shipping List or in *Administrative Notes.*

Prior to the automation of the item number list, new depositories were furnished two complete sets of 3"-by-5" cards: one set for their files and the other set to pull and submit cards to GPO for those items selected. Current practice is to submit requests for additions or deletions of items on GPO Form 3495 (green postal card), "Amendment Selection." The form allows entry of ten item numbers. New selections are not implemented until the following October. Item deletions may be made at any time; additions may be made only once a year during the annual update cycle.

Notification of new series is made on Depository Shipping Lists by numbered surveys. New items being surveyed are listed in item number order with SuDocs class number and series title. The survey also consists of one set of item cards and an optical character recognition (OCR) scannable form that lists the new item numbers. To select an item, the depository must place an "x" in the box at the left of the item number, using black or blue ink or a no. 2 pencil, and return the completed form by the deadline. Regionals (except "shared" regionals) do not have to complete the form because they automatically receive all items offered. Figure 3.3 shows an annotated item card that accompanied a survey.

Fig. 3.3. Annotated item card that accompanied a survey

```
ITEM NO:   0422-C-01              CARD 01 OF 02

Defense Department

Air Force Department


D 301.26/13-6:

SAM-TR (School of Aerospace Medicine Technical
Report) (series) (MF)



SURVEY:   88-010
```
```
ITEM NO:   0422-C-01              CARD 02 OF 02

Technical reports on miscellaneous topics pertaining
to the mission of the USAF School of Aerospace
Medicine, Brooks AFB, Texas. Frequency and
pagination cannot be predicted.






SURVEY:   88-010
```

Before making their initial selections, it is recommended that new depositories visit the collections of nearby depositories, especially those that select a large percentage of the available items and maintain a separate collection in SuDocs class order. If possible, a visit should be made to the nearest regional depository that receives all items. The item card provides minimum information for selection purposes; therefore, it is advisable to inspect the actual publications covered by an item, not only to judge their value for the collection but also to see the number and types of publications that will be received. Many items, such as general publications, manuals, and bulletins, are open-ended. They may involve as little as one or two publications annually or as many as hundreds of publications of various sizes.

The 1977 edition of *Guidelines for the Depository Library System* contained the following statement in section 4-4: "Selection of at least 25% of the available Item Numbers on the *Classified List* is suggested as the minimum number necessary to undertake the role of depository library. A prospective depository library intending to select fewer than 25% should provide additional justification for its designation as a depository." The 1987 revision changed this section as follows: "Depository libraries, either solely or in conjunction with neighboring depositories, should make demonstrable efforts to identify and meet the Government information needs of the local area."

This language also appears in chapter 5, "Collection Development," of the *Instructions to Depository Libraries.* The guidelines also state in section 4-1 that "each depository library should maintain a basic collection available for immediate use consisting of all titles in Appendix A." The list includes twenty-one titles, among which are the *Congressional Record*, public slip laws, *Statutes at Large, United States Code, Federal Register,* Supreme Court reports, *U.S. Government Manual, Weekly Compilation of Presidential Documents, Budget of the U.S. Government, Monthly Catalog, Publications Reference File,* and *Statistical Abstract.* The *Federal Depository Library Manual* has a section on collection development policy as well as suggested core collection lists for law libraries, small/medium public libraries, and small/medium academic libraries. These detailed lists are arranged in item number order and contain item title, issuing agency, and SuDocs class number.

DEPOSITORY SHIPPING LISTS

The Depository Shipping List is used primarily as an invoice to a complete shipment of publications contained in a standard depository shipping box (dimensions 12-1/2"-by-9-3/16"-by-4-15/16"). In preparing shipments, the Depository Distribution Division gathers one copy each of paper publications to fill completely (or nearly so) one standard box. However, microfiche boxes often contain more than one shipment. Regional depositories receive one paper shipment per box, or a "complete" shipment. But because selective depositories select only a percentage of all items, they receive partial shipments, which are allowed to accumulate to fill a standard box before a shipment is made. Selective depositories receive at least one shipping box each week and also receive a copy of every Depository Shipping List even if none of the items were selected.

Depository Shipping Lists have been used as invoices since August 1, 1951, and each has been numbered, although the numbering system has changed. From

1951 to September 30, 1983, the lists were numbered serially from 1 to 18,430. However, a separate serial sequence for microfiche shipments was begun March 1, 1982, and continued until September 30, 1983, comprising numbers 1-M to 1829-M. From October 1, 1983, to December 31, 1984, the practice of separate numbering sequences for paper and microfiche shipments was continued. Typical numbers might be P840421-4# and M841001-2. The first letter represents paper (P) or microfiche (M). The first two digits represent the year; the next two digits, the month; and the next two digits, the day. The digit after the dash represents the number of the shipment for that day. A major problem with this system was the difficulty in determining whether a shipment was missing, so the symbol # was added after the last shipment for the day. With calendar year 1985, the present system was established, beginning with 85-1-P for paper shipments and 85-1-M for microfiche shipments and numbered sequentially throughout the year. At the beginning of each calendar year, the sequence is repeated: 1986 shipments would begin with 86-1-P and 86-1-M.

In 1990 electronic products mailed to depository libraries were listed on their own separate Shipping Lists. On October 10, 1990, Depository Shipping List 90-0001-E accompanied the distribution of several CD-ROMs, two floppy diskettes, and paper documentation for the disks. For example, the long-awaited 1985 *Congressional Record* on CD-ROM was distributed to *all* federal depositories on Shipping List 90-0007-E, December 6, 1990. Claims for the separate "E" lists for items not received or for defective material follow the normal 60 calendar days from receipt of the Shipping List.

Although Depository Shipping Lists are used primarily as the invoice for a single shipment, they are also used for "separate" shipments, "surveys" of new depository items, and "corrections" to previous lists. The survey was discussed above. "Separates" are materials that are not sent to depositories in regular shipment boxes. They may be too large for the standard boxes or may need special handling before they can be shipped. Separates include maps, charts, and posters (distributed from GPO); prepackaged publications; and oversize publications. These are mailed to depository libraries as they are received by GPO. Special Depository Shipping Lists that list only separates are compiled and sent to depository libraries, usually at least once a week. Depository Shipping Lists that contain only corrections are printed on pink paper. They show the item number and class number under which the title was distributed and the correct number(s), as well as the number of the original Shipping List and the title of the publication.

Certain serial publications that are not listed on the Depository Shipping List for reasons of timeliness are mailed separately as single issues, and thus there is no invoice to any of the issues. Some publications are mailed automatically from another section of GPO or from a printing contractor. These publications are collectively referred to as "direct mail" publications and are listed in Appendix B of the *Instructions to Depository Libraries*. The current list has sixteen titles including the following: *Commerce Business Daily, Federal Register, Weekly Compilation of Presidential Documents, Congressional Record* (daily), *ICC Register,* and *Daily Treasury Statement.*

The Depository Shipping List may also be used as a quick means of informing depository libraries of special publications available upon individual request, changes in the *List of Classes*, additions to item numbers, and other special announcements pertaining to the Depository Library Program. However, *Administrative Notes*, begun in September 1980, has become the main medium for such announcements. The Depository Shipping List, which is now used for this function, is usually mailed between issues of *Administrative Notes* or for more important or timely announcements.

The Depository Shipping List contains columns for the item number, SuDocs class number, and title. Located under the title information is the series number and GPO sales publications information, including stock number and price (if available). The list is arranged in item number order. This closely approximates SuDocs class number order, with the main exceptions being those series that have undergone a change in SuDocs class number due to reorganization. For example, series published by the Federal Aviation Agency (FAA) retained the same item number when the agency transferred to the Department of Transportation as the Federal Aviation Administration (TD 4). Thus, TD 4 entries are found in the middle, rather than near the end, of the listing. The Depository Shipping List is sold as a subscription item by the Superintendent of Documents under the title "Daily Depository Shipping List." It is useful to nondepository libraries as an announcement tool for newly published U.S. government publications. Figures 3.4, 3.5, and 3.6 show Shipping Lists for paper copy (P), microfiche (M), and electronic (E) items, respectively.

Claims

Several "complete" shipments are mailed each working day from GPO. Upon receipt of a shipment box (which for a selective library may contain several partial shipments), the Shipping List numbers should be checked or logged in on a register to ensure that all Shipping Lists have been received. In the event a shipment does not contain a particular Shipping List, a nearby depository or the regional depository should be contacted for a photocopy of the list. A copy may also be obtained from GPO using the "Depository Inquiry Form" (GPO Form 3794). The contents of the shipment box should immediately be checked against the Shipping List(s) and the item numbers selected. A claim should be made for any item that was selected but is not in the shipment box. However, it must be remembered that new item selections from the annual selection update only take effect after October 1. Libraries cannot claim new selections before that time, and such requests will be rejected.

All claims for nonreceipt of publications must be postmarked within 60 days from receipt of the Shipping List. However, it is advisable to submit claims as quickly as possible, as GPO usually has only twenty extra copies of a publication to fulfill claim requests and these may be quickly exhausted. Once the supply is exhausted, GPO will return the claim unfilled. The claim should be submitted using the Shipping List (previously, a separate claim form was used). A circle should be drawn around the entry for the missing publication; the Shipping List should be stamped with the depository's number/date stamp; and the bottom of the list, which includes a certification statement and mailing label, should be completely filled in. A photocopy should be made of the Shipping List claim for the library's records until the claim has been acted upon by GPO and returned.

(Text continues on page 64.)

Fig. 3.4. Paper copy (P) Shipping List

GPO Form 3452
(R 7-86)
Box Number
91-527

Depository Shipping List No. 91-0471-P

Date ___July 8, 1991___ Page ___1___ Of ___

Claims for nonreceipt of publications on this list under item numbers previously selected by a library must be post-marked within 60 calendar days of receipt of this shipment. When filing a claim for missing publications, please return a copy of the list on which they appear and circle the item numbers that are missing.

ITEM NUMBER	CLASSIFICATION NUMBER	TITLE
		DISTRIBUTION IS BEING MADE ACCORDING TO THE 1990 ANNUAL UPDATE (i.e., RETURNED BY JULY 3, 1990).
0002	A 1.58/a:990-2/v.49/pt.2	Agriculture Decisions, Vol. 49, Part 2, (P&S), July - December 1990
0002	A 1.58/a:990-2/v.49/pt.3	Agriculture Decisions, Vol. 49, Part 3, (PACA), July - December 1990
0019	A 93.33/2:12/6	Farmline, Vol. 12, No. 6, June 1991, * $1.25
0126-E-02	C 60.8:R 11/989/rev.3	Manual of Regulations and Procedures for Federal Radio Freguency Management, May 1989 Edition, [Revision 3]
0133-A-07	C 3.204/3-8:989	County Business Patterns, 1989, Connecticut, CBP-89-8, *
0133-A-29	C 3.204/3-31:989	County Business Patterns, 1989, New Hampshire, CBP-8-9-31, *
0133-A-39	C 3.204/3-41:989	County Business Patterns, 1989, Rhode Island, CBP-89--41, *
0245-A	C 13.6/2:Ad 9	Advanced Technology Program, Proposal Preparation Guidelines, Proposal Solicitation - ATP 91-01
0375	D 202.9:73/5	Naval Aviation, Vol. 73, No. 5, July-August 1991, * $1.75
0508-F-02	HE 20.3615/3:4/4	Aids Bibliography, Vol. 4, No. 4, April 1991, S/N 717-128-00004-4, * $5.00
0516-S	HE 3.6/504/125/trans.19	Program Operations Manual System, Part 04 - Disabili-ty, Chapter 125, Transmittal No. 19, July 1991
0516-S	HE 3.6/5:01/002/05/basic/TN 16	Programs Operations Manual System, Part 01 Records Maintenance, Chapter 002, Subchapter 05, Basic, TN 16, May 1991
0740-A	Ju 6.8/b:990/89-1905	Supreme Court of the United States, (Slip Opinion), No. 89-1905, June 21, 1991, * on sub.
0740-A	Ju 6.8/b:990/90-26	Supreme Court of the United States, (Slip Opinion), No. 90-26, June 21, 1991, * on sub.
0740-A	Ju 6.8/b:990/90-50	Supreme Court of the United States, (Slip Opinion), No. 90-50, June 20, 1991, * on sub.
0740-A	Ju 6.8/b:990/90-333	Supreme Court of the United States, (Slip Opinion), No. 90-333, June 20, 1991, S/N 828-004-00098-1, * $1.25
0740-A	Ju 6.8/b:990/90-634	Supreme Court of the United States, (Slip Opinion), No. 90-634, June 24, 1991, * on sub.
0740-A	Ju 6.8/b:990/90-5551	Supreme Court of the United States, (Slip Opinion), No. 90-5551, June 21, 1991, * on sub.
0769-P	L 2.120/2-13:991	News, Employer Costs for Employee Compensation - March 1991

Number of Titles: 28

Mail Claims To:

U.S. GOVERNMENT PRINTING OFFICE
LIBRARY PROGRAMS SERVICE (SLDM)
PAPER CLAIMS
WASHINGTON, D.C. 20401

Signature of librarian authorized to make claim_____ LIB #_____

CLEARLY PRINT OR TYPE ADDRESS AND INFORMATION ON MAILING LABEL

U.S. GOVERNMENT PRINTING OFFICE
LIBRARY PROGRAMS SERVICES (SLDM)
WASHINGTON, D.C. 20401

OFFICIAL BUSINESS

LIB #_____ SL #_____

Institution_____

Address_____

City_____ State_____ Zip_____

Fig. 3.5. Microfiche (M) Shipping List

GPO Form 3452A
(R 12-88) P.51596-5

Depository Shipping List No. ___91-0636-M___

Date ___July 2, 1991___ Page ___1 of 1___

> Claims for nonreceipt of publications on this list under item numbers previously selected by a library must be post-marked within 60 calendar days of receipt of this shipment. When filing a claim for missing publications, please return a copy of the list on which they appear and circle the item numbers that are missing.

ITEM NUMBER	CLASSIFICATION NUMBER	Microfiche# 2714 TITLE
		DISTRIBUTION IS BEING MADE ACCORDING TO THE 1990 ANNUAL UPDATE. (i.e. RECEIVED BY JULY 3, 1990).
		THIS PACKAGE IS MAILED AS A SEPARATE PACKAGE
1024-B	Y 4.P 96/11:100-24	Use of Foreign Repair Stations by U.S. Airlines, No. 100-24, Hearing 100-1
	Y 4.P 96/11:100-75	Implementation of the Water Resources Development Act of 1986..., No. 100-75, Hearing 100-2
	Y 4.P 96/11:100-77	Oversight of the Department of Transportation's Commercial Air Carrier Fitness..., No. 100-77, Hearing 100-2

Fig. 3.6. Electronic (E) Shipping List

GPO Form 3452
(R 7-86)

Depository Shipping List No. ___91-0038-E___

Date ___July 10, 1991___ Page ___1___ Of ___1___

> Claims for nonreceipt of publications on this list under item numbers previously selected by a library must be post-marked within 60 calendar days of receipt of this shipment. When filing a claim for missing publications, please return a copy of the list on which they appear and circle the item numbers that are missing.

ITEM NUMBER	CLASSIFICATION NUMBER	TITLE
		DISTRIBUTION IS NOW BEING MADE ACCORDING TO THE 1990 ANNUAL UPDATE. (i.e. RETURNED BY JULY 3, 1990).
154-E	C 3.279:Al 1 b/990/CD	TIGER/Line Census Files, 1990, Alabama (Compact Disc)
	C 3.279:Io 9/990/CD	TIGER/Line Census Files, 1990, Iowa (Compact Disc)

The claim should be sent to the address listed on the bottom of the Shipping List. On claims for separate shipments, depositories should wait at least 7 working days after receipt of the Shipping List to allow time for all shipments to be received. The Shipping List number is stamped on the outer container of each separate shipment. Claims for "direct mail" serial publications should be made on a "Depository Library Inquiry Form" (GPO Form 3794). Only one title request (multiple issues accepted) should be listed on each form, because claims for four of the titles are handled through the printing contractors and must be forwarded by the GPO Claims Section after receipt.

Depositories have at times through claims tried to obtain copies of desirable publications that they had not previously selected, especially titles in "general publications" or "bulletin" series. However, GPO processes each claim and rejects those for which the depository did not select the item. Depositories have also used the claims procedures to obtain extra copies of publications. Due to the limited number of claims copies available, this deprives other libraries with a legitimate claim. Claims may be made for incomplete copies or those damaged in shipment but should not be used to replace lost copies.

In a system under which millions of copies of publications are distributed annually, some mistakes are bound to occur. GPO's batting average has been exceptionally good. This was improved considerably by the "lighted bin" system installed shortly after the Library Programs Service returned to the main GPO building in 1985. In the GPO sorting and shipping area are bins with numbered compartments, one bin for each depository library. Previously, under a manual system, separate books were maintained for each item showing which depositories had selected the item. It was easy to miss a library number or throw a publication in the wrong compartment. As part of the automation of the system, a light was installed above each compartment. When publications for an item are picked, the lights above the compartments of those libraries that selected the item are lit, thus greatly reducing the chance for error. The National Technical Information Service had for years used a similar computer-operated lighted bin system for distribution of technical reports under its Selected Research in Microfiche (SRIM) program.

Shipment Processing

Initial processing of regular shipments, as well as direct-mail shipments, should begin as soon as possible after receipt. Initial processing for separate shipments should normally begin as soon as possible after the Shipping List is received. After the boxes or containers are opened, the Superintendent of Documents requires that "all depository materials regardless of format must be marked, in some manner, by the library to distinguish these items from non-depository materials."[6] This is usually done with a library property date stamp. The stamp should contain the word *depository* or *document*. The date stamped should be either the date of receipt or the date of the Shipping List. In either case, the same date should be used consistently, and the Shipping List should likewise be stamped so that, if necessary later, the Shipping List on which the publication was received can be traced. The publication should usually be stamped in the upper right corner on the cover of a paper publication, on the flyleaf of a bound publication, and on the envelope of a microfiche. Non-acidic ink should be used.

It is recommended that the Superintendent of Documents class number as found on the Shipping List be placed on all publications. The number should be entered even if the publication will eventually be cataloged with a Library of Congress or Dewey decimal class number for integration into a library's regular collections or if it is planned to use another SuDocs class number for filing and record purposes. This facilitates identification of materials from standard citations, as well as assists in updating and formal discard procedures. The number is usually placed in the upper left-hand corner on the cover of a paper or glossy. A label should be placed on the document and the class number entered on it.

Following this initial processing, publications should be sorted in the order of the library's holdings records for checking in. The Superintendent of Documents states that "a comprehensive shelflist is the preferred holdings record."[7] A depository shelflist can be in either paper or electronic format. However, the normal holding records are 3"-by-5" catalog cards arranged in shelflist (i.e., SuDocs class number) order. Usually, plain cards are used for Cuttered monographs. For serials, a year card is usually used for publications issued annually or less frequently; a month/year card is used for periodicals issued weekly through semiannually; a numbered card is normally used to check in publications issued in numbered series, such as a bulletin series; and a daily card is used for the *Commerce Business Daily* and other serials issued daily. Separate cards have to be prepared for each new Cuttered monograph, whereas cards already in the file are used to check in serials.

The minimum amount of information on a card is SuDocs class number, issuing agency, title, pagination, and date. The holdings record should also contain cross references, either on separate cards or record cards, for changes in SuDocs class number, changes in issuing agency, and changes in title. Records should also contain information, as appropriate, about format and/or location for materials not filed in the regular separate depository collection, such as maps, posters, microfiche, CD-ROM, and oversize. If an item is filed in another collection by other than a SuDocs class number, the file number should be listed. The record should also contain, as appropriate, any notes on retention requirements, such as "keep latest edition only" or "discard after six months."

With GPO joining OCLC in 1974 and the advances in computer technology during the 1980s, a number of electronic record-keeping options have presented themselves. OCLC members may have online access to U.S. government publications in the OCLC file. The *Monthly Catalog* tapes are available from the Library of Congress and GPO, and these may be downloaded into the library's files. Various options for access to the *Monthly Catalog* tapes are provided by commercial vendors such as Marcive. Cumulative *Monthly Catalog* entries from July 1976 are available on CD-ROM from several vendors. Thus, full AACR/MARC entries are available either online or printed as catalog cards. Libraries can obtain electronic catalog cards not only for separate Cuttered monographs but also for monographs within numbered series, such as Bureau of Labor Statistics or Geological Survey bulletin series. In a manual system, such numbered bulletins are usually checked in only by number on a numbered card, and separate cards are not prepared for each title. However, it will still be necessary to prepare holding records and manually check in periodicals and other serials issued at least three times a year. Such periodicals and serials are announced in the *Periodicals Supplement* to the *Monthly Catalog*, which is updated annually. The electronic record does not provide a record of individual issues.

Computer technology advances in the 1980s have made it feasible for documents units to have their own personal computer. Prices have come down dramatically, and with advances in hard disk and chip technology there is adequate low-cost storage and memory and fast execution. A number of commercial flat-file and relational database software programs can be readily adapted to a library's requirements for holding records, so that it is no longer necessary for the librarian to be a computer programmer.

DISPOSAL OF DEPOSITORY MATERIALS

Publications distributed through the depository library program are, and remain, federal government property. Depository libraries can only dispose of these materials in the manner prescribed in the *Instructions to Depository Libraries* or at the direction of a GPO official. Libraries cannot materially benefit from the disposal of depository materials. If, after following prescribed procedures, the materials are sold as publications or as waste paper, the proceeds with a letter of explanation must be sent to the Superintendent of Documents.

Only the first copy of a particular publication is considered the "depository" copy and must be discarded in accordance with procedures in the *Instructions*. Any copies that are duplicates (including preprints or reprints), superseded (including preprints), and unrequested publications sent from GPO by mistake are collectively referred to as "secondary" copies.

Federal libraries, highest state appellate court libraries, and regionals must permanently retain one copy of all government publications received through depository distribution, except for superseded publications or those issued later in bound form or microfiche. Selective depositories served by a regional may dispose of any depository publication that has been held for at least five years after obtaining permission and receiving instructions from the designated regional depository. Regional depositories must require such selectives as a minimum to offer those publications to "other depository libraries within their area, then to other libraries" in accordance with section 1912, Title 44. If the depository is unable to find a receipt for the materials after reasonable effort, the publications become "secondary" copies and may be disposed of at the library's discretion. In accordance with section 1907, Title 44, federal libraries "may dispose of unwanted Government publications after first offering them to the Library of Congress and the Archivist of the United States."

In accordance with section 1915, Title 44, the highest state appellate court libraries that have been designated under this provision are exempt from the provisions of section 1911, Title 44. Thus, they do not have to retain depository materials for five years before discarding, and they do not have to discard materials through a regional depository. All their materials are considered to be "secondary" copies and may be disposed of at the library's discretion. However, this does not preclude them from offering their discards to the regional depository, state discard lists, or the national Needs and Offers List.

In chapter 10, section G, of *Instructions to Depository Libraries*, the Superintendent of Documents authorizes all depositories (including regionals) to dispose of "publications, maps, and other depository materials which are superseded ... as soon as the update or final version of the publication is received in the library." Fifteen examples are given of types of materials that may be disposed of by all libraries, not all of which are strictly "superseded" materials. Among the superseded materials are preliminary paper editions superseded by final bound volumes such as the daily *Congressional Record*, slip laws (by the *Statutes at Large*), and Senate and House numbered reports and documents (by *Serial Set* volumes). *House Calendars* may be discarded upon receipt of a new issue; the *Senate Calendar* must be held for at least one year following the adjournment of the Congress. *Commerce Business Daily* may be discarded 90 days after receipt. Materials that are cumulated in later issues may be discarded after the cumulation is received. Only the latest issues of materials that have an expiring effect date need be kept. A more complete list of superseded items may be found in the "List of Superseded Depository Documents" (Appendix C to the *Instructions to Depository Libraries*). However, although all depositories (including regionals) are authorized to discard such superseded materials, they should not automatically do so. They should seriously evaluate each title for its historical value to the collection. Care should especially be taken in discarding superseded materials with legal value, because court cases are based on the law in effect at the time rather than the current law.

In chapter 11 of the *Instructions to Depository Libraries*, the Superintendent of Documents authorizes depositories to substitute micrographic copies for any depository materials, provided that the copies are properly referenced, can be readily located, and are accessible to users and that proper reading equipment is provided. The substitute copies are treated as depository materials and are subject to the same rules and regulations that govern the care and treatment of depository materials. Depository materials that are replaced by micrographic copies must be offered to the regional libraries or other libraries, as appropriate, before they can be discarded.

ORGANIZATION OF UNIT AND DOCUMENTS COLLECTION

The type of personnel or unit organization for documents service and the type of physical organization of the collection are interrelated and depend on a number of factors. These include the size and type of library; the organization of the library; the size and type of its general collection; the size and type of the library's parent unit; responsibility for other government documents (international, state, local); responsibility for other depository formats (CD-ROM, microforms, maps); the number or type of clientele that the library serves; and the number, size, and location of other depositories within the area or congressional district. No single organization is right for every depository. What may work well for one library may be entirely wrong for another. However, "the Government Printing Office insists that the maintenance accorded to depository materials be no less than that given to commercially purchased publications. Every effort should be made to ensure that the depository collection is used, and that publications are not merely stored or placed in inaccessible locations."[8]

A unique feature of complete depository service is that it includes both traditional library technical services and readers or public services. At some depositories, these services may be separated, with one person or unit responsible for technical services such as acquisition, cataloging, processing, and record keeping and another person or unit responsible for reader services such as providing reference, circulation, and stack maintenance of the collection. However, technical services and reader services responsibilities are usually combined within one person or unit, and this person or unit is generally located in reader services, either as a separate unit or as part of a reference services unit. Usually, a separate government documents unit is found only in a large library that selects a sizeable percentage of the available depository items.

The physical organization of the collection is an important determination of the unit organization. If the collection is maintained primarily as a separate special collection shelved by SuDocs class numbers, this promotes the establishment of a separate documents unit. A separate documents unit is also appropriate if the unit or personnel responsible for the depository collection and federal documents are also responsible for other government publications, including international, state, and local, and if these documents also are organized as a special collection with a unique numbering system and not integrated into the library's general collection. Also influencing the establishment of a separate unit is responsibility for other formats such as CD-ROM, microform, and maps. A library may have a centralized microform unit, which may or may not include depository microfiche. The library may have a separate map collection and unit, or there may be on a university campus a separate map library (usually in the Geography or Geology Department). Another influence may be whether the library has a centralized reference service or is decentralized into separate rooms by topic (such as Social Sciences, Business, Science and Technology, etc.); likewise, whether the university library services are primarily centralized or decentralized into a number of branch libraries by discipline. Other libraries may bibliographically and physically integrate most of their depository publications into the library's regular collections. This is generally true for small libraries or those that select relatively few items.

GPO MICROFORM PROGRAM

The first regular shipment of GPO microfiche was made on November 3, 1977 (Depository Shipping List 10,301). It included 355 non-GPO General Accounting Office reports sent to depository libraries that had previously selected Item 546-D. By the mid-1980s, microfiche titles constituted over 60 percent of those shipped in the depository library program. The GPO Microform Program is primarily concerned with those printed publications that have been converted by GPO to microfiche format. However, it may also include microforms that agencies have produced and have furnished copies to GPO for depository distribution. These microfiche may have been produced from reproduction of printed publications or may have been produced only in microfiche, particularly COM (computer-output-microfiche).

The GPO Microform Program had its origins in a letter of August 4, 1970, from the Public Printer, A. N. Spence, to the JCP chairman. Spence asked for approval for GPO to enter the field of micropublishing and to offer filmed documents both in the sales program and in the depository library program. JCP authorized the Public Printer to establish a Micropublishing Advisory Committee. As part of its study, this committee developed a questionnaire that was sent to all depository libraries in mid-1971 to learn their "needs and desires" for microforms. Over 75 percent of the depositories indicated a preference for some documents in microforms. Based on these results and its technical studies, the committee recommended that GPO enter the micropublishing field. In a letter of October 12, 1971, to the JCP chairman, Spence requested approval to proceed.[9]

However, following Spence's untimely death in January 1972, the program remained inactive until after the appointment of Thomas J. McCormick as Public Printer in March 1973. In a letter of August 17, 1973, to the JCP chairman, McCormick proposed another survey of depository libraries followed by a pilot project. A survey questionnaire was mailed to all depositories in February 1974 as an attachment to the biennial survey. The survey consisted of 102 pages with line entries for the then current 2,812 depository items. Depositories were directed to indicate their preference in either paper or film for each item. Preliminary results showed that 731 libraries out of 931 responding indicated a preference for microfiche in at least one category of material. Based on these positive results, McCormick, on June 29, 1974, requested permission to undertake a four-month pilot project involving eighteen depositories that would be furnished approximately 300 titles.[10]

In another letter to JCP on November 14, 1975, McCormick requested authority to undertake a four-month pilot project using the *Code of Federal Regulations* (CFR) as the test vehicle. Twenty-one libraries participated, mostly academic and/or regional libraries. JCP authorized the four-month pilot project on January 9, 1975. Bids were let out to commercial contractors, and the first microfiche were distributed in October 1975. The final report of test results was submitted to JCP on July 7, 1976. McCormick requested continued distribution of the CFR and further requested authorization for the "selected conversion of that category of publications known as 'non-GPO' documentation." Thus, a significant new element had entered not only the GPO Microform Program but the depository library program as well.

Although the Depository Library Act of 1962 authorized the distribution of non-GPO publications, it also required the issuing agencies to pay for the extra depository publications. This placed a damper on their efforts to comply with the law. The suggestion for solving this dilemma of distributing non-GPO publications in microform was first advanced in 1965 by Clifton Brock.[11] JCP *Printing and Binding Regulations No. 24*, April 1977, added section 41-2, which requires each agency printing officer to forward to the Superintendent of Documents two copies of non-GPO publications qualifying for depository distribution under section 1902, Title 44. GPO uses one of these copies to prepare an entry for the *Monthly Catalog* and the second copy for filming a microform master from which additional distribution copies of microfiche can be produced.

In a letter of October 13, 1977, the JCP authorized GPO to continue distributing the CFR on a request basis. In a letter of March 23, 1977, JCP authorized GPO to convert to microfiche non-GPO publications and, "when savings in costs are clearly demonstrable, that category of publications identified as 'GPO-documentation.'" However, permission was not granted at this time to include such microfiche in the sales publications program.

The GPO Microform Program began with distribution primarily of non-GPO titles, which previously had not been available to depository libraries. These included many Department of Energy technical reports, Joint Publications Research Service (JPRS) translations, and Foreign Broadcast Information Service (FBIS) daily broadcast reports. The "GPO documentation" phase was slower getting off the ground. In most cases, GPO had to perform cost-analysis studies to demonstrate savings due to conversion. GPO worked closely with the Depository Library Council in developing lists of titles for conversion. It either asked for lists of suggested titles from the council or presented to the council its own lists for consideration. GPO materials may be furnished in microfiche only or they may be distributed in "dual format" – in both microfiche and paper – in which case regionals receive the publications in both formats (but are required to keep only one format), whereas selectives must choose to receive either microfiche or paper, but not both. Appendix B in the *Instructions to Depository*

Libraries contains a list of items available in dual format, including all congressional materials except bills and resolutions, *Federal Register, Code of Federal Regulations, Official Gazette of the U.S. Patent and Trademark Office*, and *Congressional Record*. Titles furnished in dual format have separate item numbers for each format.

One of the early controversies over the microform program was second-generation silver halide versus third-generation diazo. At the beginning of the program, regional depositories received two sets of microfiche: silver halide and diazo. Selective depositories received diazo, and many requested to also receive silver halide. Silver halide of archival quality costs three times as much as diazo. Silver halide tends to scratch more readily under use than does diazo, whereas diazo products tend to fade under continued exposure to light. In April 1978, the manager of the GPO Control and Technical Department, following tests of the two types, concluded that "furnishing all silver halide fiche would not be cost effective since mechanical stresses encountered in handling the film could well cause it to deteriorate much faster than any density changes occurring in storage."[12] As a result of the report, not only was silver halide fiche not furnished to selective depositories, but also distribution of silver halide fiche to regional depositories was discontinued.

GPO policy regarding conversion of materials to microfiche can be found in Superintendent of Documents Policy Statement SOD 13, August 22, 1983. General policy is stated as follows:

> Distribution will be made in microfiche rather than paper format, when appropriate, to minimize the cost of printing and binding and to help alleviate space problems in depository libraries. Some series and types may be distributed in both formats when it is cost effective for the Federal Government and beneficial to the library community.... Primary considerations [for conversion to microfiche] will be physical characteristics of the publication, the nature of its content, and its relationship to other publications.

Types of publications that are distributed in paper and are not normally converted to microfiche include materials with physical characteristics that make them unusable in microform (e.g., publications that are oversize, use color or half-tone illustrations or photographs, use small type or other than white paper, or looseleaf services); popular and consumer-oriented publications; standard reference works; law reference works except bills and resolutions; posters, maps, charts, and pictures; publications not cost-effective to convert, such as publications less than 14 pages; dated periodicals in a magazine or newsletter format; annual reports of major federal agencies; documents classified as addresses (typically speeches); and publications for the visually impaired.

Types of publications that are converted to microfiche (unless they meet criteria above) include annual reports of small or subordinate organizations and programs; proceedings and papers from symposia, conferences, or meetings; scientific, technical, and research publications; and documents that are primarily compilations of statistics compiled from surveys on specialized topics.

The question of dual format became an issue during FY 1987. On September 9, 1986, the Public Printer, Ralph E. Kennickell, Jr., sent a letter to the JCP chairman requesting authority to discontinue dual format distribution and to distribute those items in microfiche only as of October 1, 1986 (beginning of FY 1987), in order to keep within reduced appropriations authorized by Congress in the Gramm-Rudman-Hollings climate. The proposal would save $3,132,000 if implemented October 1. In a letter of October 2, 1986, the JCP chairman, Sen. Charles McC. Mathias (D-MD), rejected the request, saying it is JCP policy to allow depositories a choice for format when multiple formats are available. On November 9, the Public Printer offered a modified proposal to discontinue dual format distribution except for seven major items: daily *Congressional Record* including the biweekly *Index, Federal Register, Code of Federal Regulations, Monthly Catalog,* and *Official Gazette of the U.S. Patent and Trademark Office: Patents and Trademarks.* The discontinued paper items were primarily congressional hearings and committee prints and numbered reports and documents.[13] The modified proposal would save $1,647,000 if implemented by January 1, 1987. This request was also subsequently rejected. At the hearings on FY 1988 appropriations, GPO did not ask for a supplemental appropriation to make up for the predicted shortfall. GPO witnesses testified that current appropriations for FY 1987 were adequate, saying that reductions in agency printing requirements had abridged the number of depository publications distributed to libraries. In mid-1981, dual format distribution of bills and resolutions had been discontinued as an economy measure. Bills and resolutions are filmed in chronological order as they are issued, the result being that they are not arranged on the fiche in numerical order or by category (e.g., House bills, resolutions, concurrent resolutions, joint resolutions). In addition, amendments to bills and to later amended or reported versions are scattered. A finding aid is issued at irregular intervals throughout each session of Congress.

By the early 1980s, over half of depository titles were furnished to libraries in microfiche format. By the mid-1980s, the number of titles furnished in microfiche had stabilized in the low 60 percent range. However, this statistic must be read with caution considering the type of material that can be found in microfiche. Much of the materials are "non-GPO documentation" that would not otherwise have been made available to depository libraries. By its very definition, non-GPO publications are those for which an agency requires only a limited number of copies, primarily for internal agency use or for a limited regional area, and thus the agency was not required to submit the print order to GPO under Title 44. Of the GPO documentation items, most that qualify for microfiche format are technical in content and have a limited audience. Thus, although microfiche materials account for the majority of current depository publications, they have only a very small percentage of usage.

During 1987, there was a noticeable decrease in distribution of microfiche to depository libraries due to quality control problems with the single contractor and the eventual default of the single contract for GPO microfiche on August 27, 1987. To prevent a reoccurrence of this situation, GPO broke down the single contract into eight separate microfiche contracts. However, it was not until the early summer of 1988 that microfiche production and distribution were resumed on a steady basis, following a series of appeals by the defaulting contractor and delays in awarding the new multiple contracts.

CD-ROM DISTRIBUTION

The Depository Library Program "entered the age of electronic information dissemination" on September 6, 1988, with the issuance of the first CD-ROM to selected depository libraries. Called *Census Test Disc No. 2*, it contained data from the 1982 censuses of agriculture and retail trade.[14] Having proved cost-effective, especially in comparison to print materials, the CD-ROM distribution program has grown steadily. The decade of the 1990s and beyond will show a dramatic increase in the free distribution of CD-ROMs to depository institutions. The immediate future will show that the Census Bureau is the leader in CD-ROM statistical products owing to the widespread use of that format, as well as print and microfiche products, to store and deliver detailed data from the 1990 decennial census. Despite initial problems of inadequate technical documentation and general user-unfriendliness, the rapid growth in the distribution of government information in a CD-ROM format is assured.

As noted previously in figure 3.6, the increased number of CD-ROM products made available to depository libraries required a separate Shipping List designated by the suffix "E" following the year and shipping list number. Disposal of superseded CD-ROMs follows the same pattern as that described above for paper and microfiche products. Similarly, responsibility for adequate storage and access of CD-ROM information remains the same as that for other formats, and certain aspects of the handling of these materials are necessarily different from other formats. The *Federal Depository Library Manual* contains a section devoted to the handling and storage of CD-ROMs.

Cataloging practices for CD-ROM products, an evolving process, are illustrated in *Administrative Notes*, vol. 12 (July 15, 1991), pp. 4-8. The records on OCLC are organized by title and *Monthly Catalog* month, year, and entry number, with reference to the OCLC number, depository item number, and SuDocs class notation. Examples and their format are arranged as follows:

Title	OCLC #	Item #	SuDocs #
National Health Interview Survey MoCat 91-11401, 5/91	23062568	0500-E-1	HE 20.6209/4-3:10/
Congressional Record Serial 1990-9999 MoCat 91-10318, 4/91	22840665	0556-C	X:

Moreover, the Library Programs Service supplies in a recurring table in *Administrative Notes* information about the status and availability of electronic products of agencies, such as Census Bureau TIGER/Line files on CD-ROM. The feature is called *The E-Report: Status of Federal Electronic Information* and first appeared in *Administrative Notes*, vol. 12 (July 15, 1991), p. 3.

TYPES OF DEPOSITORY PUBLICATIONS

Administrative Notes, vol. 14 (June 30, 1990), pp. 3-8, lists seventeen types of publications for inclusion in the Depository Library Program and gives some examples of each category. The selections available within each category are considered to be of "public interest" and/or "educational value," thus falling within the provisions of chapter 19 of Title 44 of the *United States Code*. The seventeen types are as follows:

1. Public Notices, Information Memos, News (Press) Releases, Bulletins, and Newsletters published on a recurring basis;

2. Handbooks, Manuals, Guides, including Technical, Procedural, Administrative, and Training publications;

3. Circulars advisory in nature, warning the public or segments of the public about dangers, proper conditions for safety, etc.;

4. Directories that list staff, office and agency locations, services, and so forth;

5. Proceedings of symposia, public meetings, workshops, conferences, hearings, etc.;

6. Forms, including surveys, applications for services, grants, admission to programs, jobs, etc.;

7. Maps, Atlases, Charts (geographical, topographical, climatological, nautical, economic, etc.);

8. Posters (lithographs, photographs, pictures, etc.);

9. Catalogs, bibliographies, abstracts, and indexes which identify and describe publications, educational courses, activities, events, etc.;

10. Reports, including one-time and recurring reports, which generally describe the status of organizations and/or results of research, investigations, studies, surveys, etc.

11. Journals, Periodicals, Newspapers (published on a periodic basis and considered more substantial than Newsletters and Bulletins, identified in category No. 1);

12. Environmental Impact Statements and Assessments, both in draft form and final;

13. Legal Materials, including Laws, Decisions issued by regulatory agencies, Legal Opinions, Regulations and Rules, Legislative Histories, and Treaties and International Agreements;

14. Flyers, Brochures, Booklets, Pamphlets designed to explain government services and activities to the public;

15. Statistics (broadly defined as publications of any nature that report statistics);

16. Marketing, Promotional Flyers & Pamphlets (such as *U.S. Government Books, New Books*, etc.);

17. Monographs (defined as substantial publications complete in one part or a finite number of parts).

Concerning the above categories, depository libraries were asked to complete a survey form indicating the types that are essential for long-term retention "based on observed use patterns." Based upon the responses received, the JCP and the GPO are prepared to issue guidelines on printing "long-term retention" publications on alkaline paper to avert the threat of deterioration of materials printed on acid paper. For further reading, see *Administrative Notes*, vol. 11 (June 15, 1990), pp. 2-5, and H. Rep. 101-179 (July 26, 1989), pp. 34-35.

"FUGITIVE" PUBLICATIONS

As noted above, the distribution of non-GPO publications in a microfiche format was intended to increase the amount of information from agencies required under Title 44. However, this has not solved the problem of agency noncompliance. LPS officials define "fugitive" or "renegade" publications as all government information products "produced in any format which is within the scope of the Federal Depository Library Program (FDLP) but which is not distributed to depository libraries for whatever reason." No entity, including GPO, JCP, and the Office of Management and Budget (OMB), knows exactly how many of these agency-produced materials escape the FDLP, but the number is alarmingly substantial. Moreover, often "agency printing officers do not know the scope of renegade publications in their own organizations especially with desk-top publishing, photocopy machines, and now electronic deliverables." Some strategies for reducing the magnitude of this problem were presented by LPS officers before the Depository Library Council to the Public Printer in a meeting held in Boston on April 18, 1991. The suggestions were sound but admittedly only a stopgap measure "of a very complex set of issues and problems."[15]

Public Printer Robert W. Houk addressed this problem a week after the council's Boston meeting in a prepared statement before the JCP. In his remarks, Houk noted that GPO's Inspector General (IG) issued a report in which he made several recommendations "to minimize the occurrence of fugitive documents." Pledging his personal commitment to this task, Houk averred that the "most effective way to increase the number of publications disseminated to the American public through the FDLP is through educating the Federal publishing community to enhance their knowledge of the advantages of the FDLP, and in so doing make participation a matter of self-interest." He said that the common objectives of all of our educational activities are to make the publishing agencies aware of the FDLP, to establish its relevance to agency information dissemination programs and responsibilities, to insure that they understand the benefits of participation in the FDLP, and to inform agencies of their obligations under Title 44.[16]

The outlook for significant increases in agency compliance with sections 1902 and 1903 of Title 44 is not auspicious when one reviews the history of earlier attempts to corral renegade publications. Nevertheless, it is hoped that current efforts, resourcefully and relentlessly pursued, will effect improvement in compliance with the law.

SUMMARY

On April 25, 1991, the JCP conducted an oversight hearing, "Government Information as a Public Asset: A Review of the Role and Importance of the Depository Library Program." One of the witnesses, Ridley Kessler, documents librarian at the University of North Carolina-Chapel Hill, spoke of "the time and money spent in obtaining fugitive documents from other sources including private vendors." Kessler also enunciated a credo well worth repeating here.

Documents librarians believe in two things. One is that there should be a public bibliographic record of every document produced whether it be paper, microfiche, CD-ROM, or electronic data base except for those publications that can clearly be shown to be secret or limited to official use only. The second thing we believe in is cost free public access to this material by the general public through the Depository Library Program. That is the sum total for our reason of being, it is the core of our professional creed, it is our political commitment, and last but not least it is our passion.

Addressing the members of the JCP, Kessler concluded, "We hope that you will join us in trying to find solutions to this problem and that you will help us protect and defend the Depository Library Program and the public's right to free access to government information."[17]

NOTES

[1]See Congress, House, Committee on Appropriations, Subcommittee on Legislative Branch Appropriations, *Legislative Branch Appropriations for Fiscal Year 1992: Hearings, February 7, 1991,* part 1 (Washington, DC: GPO, 1991), pp. 195-211, 1236-42.

[2]Congress, Joint Committee on Printing, *Federal Government Printing and Publishing: Policy Issues: Report of the Ad Hoc Advisory Committee on Revision of Title 44* (Washington, DC: GPO, 1979), p. 45.

[3]LeRoy C. Schwarzkopf, *Regional Libraries and the Depository Library Act of 1962* (College Park, MD: LeRoy C. Schwarzkopf, 1972), pp. 1-6 (available from ERIC Documents Reproduction Service as ED 066 177).

[4]Hernon, Peter, Charles R. McClure, and Gary R. Purcell, *GPO's Depository Library Program: A Descriptive Analysis* (Norwood, NJ: Ablex, 1985), p. 59.

[5]Hernon, McClure, and Purcell, *GPO's Depository Library Program*, p. 136.

[6]*Instructions to Depository Libraries*, chapter 1, p. 3.

[7]*Instructions to Depository Libraries*, chapter 1, p. 3.

[8]*Instructions to Depository Libraries*, chapter 1, p. 2.

[9]LeRoy C. Schwarzkopf, "The GPO Microform Program: Its History and Status," *Documents to the People* (DttP), 6, 4 (June 1978): 163-66.

[10]Schwarzkopf, "GPO Microform Program," p. 164.

[11]Clifton Brock, "Implementing the Depository Law: A Proposal for Distribution of 'Non-GPO' Publications to Depository Libraries, as Required by the 1962 Statute," *Library Journal*, 90 (April 15, 1965): 1825-33.

[12]Albert E. Materazzi, *Archival Stability of Microfilm* (Washington, DC: GPO, 1978), p. 11.

[13]*Government Publications Review*, 14 (March/April 1987): 259-60.

[14]*Administrative Notes*, 9 (October 1988): 11-24. *Census Test Disc No. 2* became the first machine-readable data file ever cataloged by GPO when record number 18482139 was entered into OCLC.

[15]*Administrative Notes*, 12 (May 15, 1991): 11-19.

[16]Statement by Robert W. Houk before the Joint Committee on Printing on Public Access to Government Information through the Depository Library Program, April 25, 1991, pp. 1-9 (mimeographed).

[17]DttP, 19 (September 1991): 181-82.

4

General Catalogs, Indexes, Bibliographies, and Selected Reference Sources

INTRODUCTION

The bibliographic apparatus of U.S. public documents is as complex and variegated as the unwieldy body of materials it attempts to encompass. Indexes, lists, guides, bibliographies, whatever the name assigned to them, exhibit—like the materials they enumerate—a pattern that is irregular and often confusing. Attempts to achieve the bibliographic ideal challenge the ingenuity of publisher and librarian.

Traditionally, most libraries with large depository collections have opted not to catalog their federal documents. Instead, librarians and patrons alike have needed to know how to use a variety of tools and techniques to access government information. Only recently have some libraries attempted to facilitate access to their public documents (in particular those issued after 1976) by including them in online public access catalogs. This approach holds great promise for the future.[1] Gary Cornwell, federal documents librarian at the University of Florida, attributes the tremendous increase in patron use of federal documents at his institution to the GOVDOC cataloging service recently provided by OCLC. Since OCLC began this service in 1990, 130 federal depository libraries have signed up for it.[2]

Developments in micropublishing and computer-generated information have created a contemporary revolution in bibliographic control and retrieval. Yet there is often a feeling of helplessness in the face of the huge amount of government information that must be brought swiftly and accurately under control. Distribution of government materials in different formats—audiovisual, paper, microfiche, CD-ROM, electronic, etc.—has also exacerbated the problem of information management, as users are confronted with an overwhelming array of tools, equipment, and software to access government information. This chapter surveys some of the more important retrospective and current reference sources (general guides, catalogs, indexes, and bibliographies) that purport to organize the vast and sometimes bewildering mass of federal government information. Understanding how to use these sources effectively is the key to unlocking government information.

BACKGROUND SOURCES

Consistent with the growth of government information, there has been a steady increase in the size and variety of guides to the literature reporting and commenting on the federal publishing enterprise. Currently, a number of useful publications assist researchers in their quest for U.S. government information. Some are old and therefore, perforce, of limited value, except to those seeking historical documents. In this category, two textbooks stand out as classics: Anne M. Boyd, *United States Government Publications*, 3d ed. rev. by Rae E. Rips (New York: Wilson, 1949); and Laurence F. Schmeckebier and Roy B. Eastin, *Government Publications and Their Use*, 2d rev. ed. (Washington, DC: Brookings, 1969). The latter source is particularly useful for its detailed descriptions of the idiosyncrasies that characterize some of the pre-1969 bibliographic tools still in use.

The late James Bennett Childs, noted documents bibliographer, included federal documents in his comprehensive survey of the bibliographic structure of worldwide government publishing.[3] While at the Library of Congress, Childs was also responsible for initiating *Government Publications: A Guide to Bibliographic Tools*. The fourth edition of this guide, prepared by Vladimir M. Palic (Washington, DC: Library of Congress, 1975), covers official publications worldwide. A compilation of catalogs, checklists, indexes, accession lists, and bibliographies issued by federal agencies is found on pages 11-80.[4] Another useful guide is Yuri Nakata's *From Press to People: Collecting and Using U.S. Government Publications* (Chicago: American Library Association, 1979). Nakata concentrated her practical advice on the organization and arrangement of documents, collection development, cataloging and classification, record keeping, etc.

Of more recent vintage are the following selected guides (in chronological order):

Jean L. Sears and Marilyn K. Moody, *Using Government Publications* (Phoenix, AZ: Oryx Press, 1985/1986), presents a step-by-step search strategy for accessing government publications. Volume 1, *Searching by Subjects and Agencies*, provides guidance for known item, subject, and agency searches; volume 2, *Finding Statistics and Using Special Techniques,* covers patents, legislative histories, and technical reports in addition to statistical sources.

Julia Schwartz, *Easy Access to Information in United States Government Documents* (Chicago: American Library Association, 1986), is a tutorial book that teaches how to use basic documents access tools.

Judith Schiek Robinson, *Tapping the Government Grapevine: The User-Friendly Guide to U.S. Government Information Sources* (Phoenix, AZ: Oryx Press, 1988), is a practical reference guide of use to the beginning searcher. One chapter is devoted to foreign and international documents.

Peter Hernon and Charles R. McClure, *Public Access to Government Information: Issues, Trends and Strategies*, 2d ed. (Norwood, NJ: Ablex,

1988), addresses information policy and managerial issues rather than enumerating specific sources of information. Together and individually, Hernon and McClure have produced a number of distinguished documents-related studies, some of which are cited in other chapters of this book.

Frederick J. O'Hara (ed.), *Informing the Nation: A Handbook of Government Information for Librarians* (Westport, CT: Greenwood Press, 1990), reprints introductory and promotional material from the Government Printing Office and other selected federal and international agencies that disseminate government information. As most depository libraries will have these materials in their collection, its value is limited primarily to the convenience factor provided by a compilation.

ACCESS TO PROFESSIONAL LITERATURE

The literature of librarianship is replete with numerous articles and studies (both published and unpublished) about government information. Many of the journals regularly feature columns, bibliographic roundups, annual updates, reviews, general commentary, news notes, and specialized articles on topics of interest to the profession. For a full range of secondary source materials, such index/abstracting services as *Library Literature, Resources in Education* (RIE), LISA, and *Current Index to Journals in Education* (CIJE) must be consulted.

Another very useful bibliographic tool providing access to that body of professional literature dealing specifically with U.S. government documents is Alan E. Schorr's *Federal Documents Librarianship, 1879-1987* (Juneau, AK: Denali Press, 1988). Schorr cites more than 2,000 articles, monographs, chapters, theses, and dissertations dealing with substantive issues, trends, problems, and accomplishments. Appropriately, one section of his classified bibliography is titled "Bibliographies, Guides, Indexes, and Abstracts." Other sections include "General Publications," "Administration," "Collection Development," "Depository Library Programs," "Government Information Policy," "Microform," "Public Services," "Teaching," and "Technical Services."

Currently, three professional journals are devoted entirely to the publications and activities of governments at all levels. Two are research-oriented and one is a professional newsletter. The last, *Documents to the People* (DttP), is the oldest of the three, having begun publication in 1972. It is the official quarterly publication of ALA's Government Documents Round Table and provides a wealth of practical information and tips for the documents librarian wanting to keep up-to-date. Its issues feature new publications, columns, current activities, and periodic bibliographies of materials relating to government publications and documents librarianship. DttP irregularly produces its own index.

Government Publications Review: An International Journal of Issues and Information Resources (GPR) is published bimonthly by Pergamon Press. Current editors of this refereed journal are Steven D. Zink and Bruce Morton, both practicing librarians and authorities in the field. Founded in 1973, GPR "provides a forum for the publication of articles that provide insight into the history, current practice, national policies, and new developments in the production, distribution, processing, and use of information in all formats and at all levels of government."[5] The last issue of each year is devoted entirely to columns identifying notable documents of the year. Other regular features include book reviews; "News from Washington," a column written by LeRoy C. Schwarzkopf, author and compiler of numerous documents guides; and an annual bibliography of primary and secondary sources.

The third periodical, *Government Information Quarterly: An International Journal of Resources, Services, Policies, and Practices* (GIQ), was established in 1984. Well-known library educators Peter Hernon and Charles R. McClure edit this refereed journal published by JAI Press, Inc. GIQ "is a cross-disciplinary journal that provides a forum for theoretical and philosophical analyses, the presentation of research findings and their practical applications, and a discussion of current policies and practices, as well as new developments at all levels of government."[6]

Filling a need for an analysis of government information research conducted at library schools by master's and doctoral candidates is John Richardson, Jr.'s *Government Information: Education and Research, 1928-1986* (Westport, CT: Greenwood Press, 1987). After discussing the nature of education and research and identifying major centers for research and influential faculty advisers, Richardson provides a comprehensive list of 317 master's theses and doctoral dissertations written on aspects of government information at library schools in the United States and Canada from 1928 through 1986. Abstracts of the research studies are provided.

REFERENCE GUIDES

Omnibus guides to reference sources inevitably list many government publications and works about them. Standard classics, such as Eugene P. Sheehy's *Guide to Reference Books* and its *Supplements* and Bohdan S. Wynar's *American Reference Books Annual*, include government publications. Guides to the literature of a specific discipline such as social sciences, political science, or education frequently list numerous governmental reference sources. Also, official government issuances such as the *National Union Catalog* and *New Serial Titles* should not be overlooked when searching for government documents.

Consistent with the growth of government information, there has been a steady increase in the size and variety of information sources reporting and commenting exclusively on the federal publishing enterprise. The following titles represent a selection of basic sources that have withstood the test of time and more recent contributions that attempt to classify and evaluate government materials.

The late John L. Andriot began publishing guides to federal statistics (McLean, VA: Documents Index) and to major U.S. government series in the 1950s. These guides have been widely used and provide a good overview of agency publishing. Of Andriot's several efforts, his *Guide to U.S. Government Publications* is the most prominent and consistently updated. Andriot's guide underwent multiple title and format changes, from looseleaf to hardcover to microfiche and back to hardcover, representing a cataloger's nightmare. However, the guide, issued as a one-volume work since 1986, is of considerable practical value, particularly for the librarian who is attempting to trace a serial title. The 1990 guide, which unfortunately lacks a table of contents, provides a listing in Superintendent of Documents (SuDocs) number order of important series and periodicals currently being published by the various government agencies. The guide also includes significant reference works issued within each series. Each entry provides a brief, handy note on the agency's creation and history. The main portion of the guide is followed by an "Agency Class Chronology" in which, for example, one can quickly trace the transition from Education Department (I 16) to Education Bureau (FS 5, HE 5, HE 19.10) back to Education Department (ED 1). The guide is indexed by both agency and title.

Government Reference Books 88/89: A Biennial Guide to U.S. Government Publications, compiled by LeRoy C. Schwarzkopf (Englewood, CO: Libraries Unlimited, 1990), is the eleventh volume in a series that began in 1970. Arranged in four main sections—"General Reference," "Social Sciences," "Science and Technology," and "Humanities"—the guide includes atlases, bibliographies, catalogs, dictionaries, directories, handbooks, guides, indexes, and other reference aids issued by federal agencies during 1988 and 1989. Entries are annotated.

Subject Guide to U.S. Government Reference Sources, by Judith Schiek Robinson (Littleton, CO: Libraries Unlimited, 1985), is a revision of Sally Wynkoop's 1972 *Subject Guide to Government Reference Books*. The title change reflects a broadening of the definition of a government publication to include both bibliographic and numeric databases. The 1,324 entries are annotated. About 275 entries are new, and Robinson has revised or expanded upon three-fourths of the earlier annotations to historical, seminal, and other key works.

Subject Guide to Major United States Government Publications, 2d ed., by Wiley J. Williams (Chicago: American Library Association, 1987), focuses on the period since 1968, when Ellen Jackson's earlier edition of this work was published. However, works dating from the inception of the federal government are included. Entries are organized under some 250 subject headings with annotations calling attention to related publications. One of the appendixes lists and annotates guides, catalogs, and indexes to government publications.

Guide to Popular U.S. Government Publications, 2d ed., by William G. Bailey (Englewood, CO: Libraries Unlimited, 1990), describes some 1,500 federal publications of popular interest in various topics. The latest edition covers the period from June 1985 to June 1989 but extends back to 1980 to include popular serials and best-selling titles.

United States Government Publications Catalogs, 2d ed., by Steven D. Zink (Washington, DC: Special Libraries Association, 1987), contains over 350 annotated selections of the current publication lists of federal agencies. Included are descriptions of agency catalogs of audiovisuals, machine-readable data files, and microforms.

U.S. Government Publications for the School Library Media Center, 2d ed., by Leticia T. Ekhaml and Alice J. Wittig (Englewood, CO: Libraries Unlimited, 1991), provides an annotated description of over 500 government publications chosen for their potential usefulness to school libraries and classrooms. Part 1 includes introductory material on the history of government printing, the SuDocs class system, and the depository library program; a list of suggested basic reference sources; and a bibliography of professional books on government information. Part 2 is the annotated bibliography, including grade-level suitability and ordering information.

DIRECTORIES

Directories can connect the user with other people or collections that can get one started when floundering in new territory or can provide contacts of a last resort where difficult queries are involved. An important title is the *Directory of Government Documents Collections & Librarians*, 6th ed., 1992. The current edition profiles thousands of institutions with substantial holdings of federal, state, local, international, and foreign government publications and lists over 4,000 professional librarians in the field. The main entry section lists institutions arranged alphabetically by city within each state, with summaries of salient facts about holdings, special collections, staff, and access policies. Indexes are provided by name, subject specialty, collection type, and institution. As in past editions, the *Directory* is published under the auspices of GODORT and is available for sale through the Congressional Information Service, Bethesda, Maryland. The editor is Judy Horn, Head of Government Publications and Microforms at the University of California, Irvine.

Although some of the same information is provided under the "District of Columbia" listing in the above directory, a more comprehensive list of libraries of the federal government may be found in William R. Evinger's *Directory of Federal Libraries* (Phoenix, AZ: Oryx Press, 1987). This directory identifies over 2,400 libraries serving the federal government. Arrangement follows the order of departments and agencies listed in the *United States Government Manual 1986/87*. In addition to providing official library name, address, and telephone number, entries show names of the library's administrator and persons in charge of acquisitions, reference, and interlibrary loan; type of library (e.g., Presidential, law, penal, etc.); major focus of the collection; depository status; information retrieval, shared cataloging, and other networks used; and the extent of any restrictions on each library's services.

A useful bibliography of directories that picks up where Sally Wynkoop and David W. Parish's *Directories of Government Agencies* (Rochester, NY: Libraries Unlimited, 1969) leaves off is Donna Rae Larson's *Guide to U.S. Government Directories* (Phoenix, AZ: Oryx Press, 1981-1985). Volume 1 covers 1970-1980; volume 2, 1980-1984. The combined set includes over 1,600 entries arranged by SuDocs class number and provides information on each directory's coverage, arrangement, and indexing. Each volume contains its own subject index. An alternate source is *U.S. Government Directories, 1970-1981* (Littleton, CO: Libraries Unlimited, 1984) by Constance Staten Gray.

CITATION MANUALS

There is no single uniform way to cite federal government material. Citations should, however, contain sufficient bibliographic information to lead the reader to the source, and similar material should be consistent in format. General citation manuals such as Kate L. Turabian's *A Manual for Writers of Term Papers,*

Theses, and Dissertations, 5th ed., revised (Chicago: University of Chicago Press, 1987), provide limited assistance with federal government sources. Another source, *The Bluebook: A Uniform System of Citation*, 15th ed. (Cambridge, MA: Harvard Law Review Association, 1991), is intended for the legal community.

Two manuals devoted exclusively to government publications are available. George D. Brightbill and Wayne C. Maxson's *Citation Manual for United States Government Publications* (Philadelphia: Temple University, Center for the Study of Federalism, 1974) provides generous sample citations. The compilers operate on the theory that the fuller the citation, the easier it is to identify and locate a document, but at the same time there should be a rationale for every part of the citation.

The *Complete Guide to Citing Government Documents: A Manual for Writers and Librarians* (Bethesda, MD: Congressional Information Service, 1984) by Diane L. Garner and Diane H. Smith includes 63 pages on federal documents alone. The authors instruct and explain various series along the way and offer pertinent suggestions for citing difficult items such as translations, microform editions of government documents, and other thorny materials.

BIBLIOGRAPHIES OF BIBLIOGRAPHIES

An anomaly that sometimes escapes student and practitioner alike is that a bibliography of government bibliographies may itself be a commercially published tool; on the other hand, governmentally published bibliographies may cite privately published sources. A master guide that continues to be updated is Alexander C. Body's *Annotated Bibliography of Bibliographies on Selected Government Publications and Supplementary Guides to the Superintendent of Documents Classification System* (Kalamazoo: Western Michigan University), first published in 1967. Five supplements were issued by Body through 1977; beginning with the sixth supplement in 1980, the bibliography has been supplemented biennially by Gabor Kovacs. The tenth edition (Greeley, CO: Gabor Kovacs, 1988) contains 96 pages of thoroughly annotated citations as well as a cumulative index (in microfiche) to the previous editions.

Several other bibliographic guides cover significant periods of time but have not been updated recently. One is the seven-volume *Cumulative Subject Guide to U.S. Government Bibliographies 1924-1973*, compiled by Edna A. Kanely (Arlington, VA and Inverness, Scotland: Carrollton Press, 1976-1977), which extracts and arranges by subject the 112 pages of bibliographies found under each heading in the fifteen-volume *Cumulative Subject Index to the Monthly Catalog ... 1900-1971*, as well as all entries from the *Monthly Catalog* in which the phrase *with bibliography* or *with list of references* appeared. The Kanely set identifies 40,000 bibliographies in all. Some libraries may own *U.S. Government Bibliography Masterfile 1924-1973*, a corresponding microfiche package that Carrollton Press originally compiled.

Two other guides are Roberta A. Scull's *A Bibliography of United States Government Bibliographies, Vol. 1: 1968-1973* (Ann Arbor, MI: Pierian Press, 1974), which was updated in a second volume covering 1974-1976 and subsequently updated through 1979 in *Reference Services Review*. The set covers over 2,600 bibliographies grouped within broad subject categories, with both subject and title indexes. Most entries are annotated and include full bibliographic information.

Noted in chapter 2 is GPO's own *Subject Bibliography Index* (SB-599), which lists almost 300 individual Subject Bibliographies that readers can request free of charge from the GPO. These brief (usually 2-8 pages) guides cover topics ranging from "Accidents and Accident Prevention" to "Zoning" and touch on almost every aspect of life. The SBs cite federal publications currently available and include the SuDocs number for anyone wishing to locate one in a depository collection, as well as the Stock Number (S/N) and price for order purposes. The SB series often fills the need of the user who wants a quick overview of what is currently available from the government on a specific topic.

ACRONYMS

William R. Evinger (ed.), *Guide to Federal Government Acronyms* (Phoenix, AZ: Oryx Press, 1989), includes almost 20,000 abbreviations, acronyms, and initialisms relating to federal government entities, programs, projects, statutes, agency products and services, automated information systems, and the like. The preface notes that some agencies, such as EPA, NASA, NOAA, NUREG, and the Army Department, "are more thoroughly covered due to the existence of acronym compilations available for those agencies." Although many of these ubiquitous subspecies of the language are duplicated in other works—including the *United States Government Manual* and the massive *Acronyms, Initialisms, and Abbreviations Dictionary* volume and supplements by Gale Research Company—the major advantage of Evinger's guide is its scope and specialized attention to the multitude of acronyms and related word-condensation forms spawned by the activities of the federal establishment. The first section gives the short form followed by its title and, in most cases, the federal department or agency associated with the abbreviation. In the second section the user can proceed from the full name or title to the acronym. Examples include PURPA (Public Utilities Regulatory Policies Act), PLO (Passenger Liaison Office(r) [Army]), SPACETRACK (National Space Surveillance Control Center), and Amtrak (National Railroad Passenger Corporation).

AUDIOVISUAL MATERIALS

Audiovisual (AV) materials are not considered "publications" under the provisions of chapter 19 of Title 44, *United States Code*, and therefore are not distributed to depository libraries. Neither are they listed individually by title in the *Monthly Catalog* or standard bibliographic sources for government information. The National Audiovisual Center (NAC), a unit within the National Archives and Records Administration (NARA), acts as a clearinghouse to collect copies of federally produced audiovisual products and to make them available to other agencies and the public for sale or rent. Agencies are not required to deposit their AV materials with NAC; thus, the collection housed at NAC is not comprehensive. The NAC provides information on the availability of federal AV materials from agencies and other sources if the materials are not in the NAC collections.

In the past NAC published irregularly a comprehensive catalog of its collections. However, its most recent detailed listing, the *1986 Media Resource Catalog* (AE 1.110:M46), announced only 2,700 of the newest and best titles from a NAC collection of over 8,000 programs. NAC publishes a series of individual pamphlets on selected subjects in its collections: *A List of Audiovisual Materials Produced by the United States Government for [subject]* (AE 1.110/2). NAC also issues *Quarterly Update* (AE 1.109), which lists AV materials and services that have been added to the collection and are available for sale or rent.

The Library of Congress publishes two serials that provide bibliographic coverage of currently produced AV materials. The *National Union Catalog: Audiovisual Materials* (LC 30.8/4) contains information on motion pictures, filmstrips, transparency and slide sets, videorecordings, and kits currently cataloged by LC. The *Catalog of Copyright Entries, 4th Series* (LC 3.6/6), includes motion pictures in part 4 and sound recordings in part 7.

The *Department of Defense Catalog of Audiovisual Productions* (D 1.33:Au2) was published in looseleaf format in 1984 in four volumes: *Army Productions, Navy and Marine Corps Productions, Air Force and Miscellaneous DoD Productions,* and *DoD Productions Cleared for Public Release.*

The National Library of Medicine (NLM) has a bibliographic database called AVLINE (AudioVisuals onLINE) that provides information on clinical medicine AV materials including films, filmstrips, and videocassettes. Printed products include the quarterly *Health Sciences Audiovisuals Catalog* (HE 20.3614/5) on microfiche. This catalog contains citations to all audiovisuals cataloged by NLM, except Cataloging-in-Publication (CIP) titles and those that have been withdrawn from the NLM collection. Issued on computer-output-microform (COM), each issue supersedes the preceding one. The *National Library of Medicine Audiovisuals Catalog* (HE 20.3609/4) is also published quarterly, with the fourth issue being the annual cumulation. It lists serials and monographs and both publicly and privately produced materials.

In general there are two types of audiovisual catalogs: those that list or announce AV materials produced by the agency and those that list collections of AV materials in a library or media center as a guide to authorized users of those facilities. An example of the former is *National Science Foundation Films* (NS 1.2:F43/yr.), which lists films produced by the National Science Foundation (NSF). An example of the latter (and more common of the two) is the Army National Training Center's *Audiovisual Catalog: Photo Devices, Graphics, Audiovisuals* (D 101.56:Au2/2), which lists materials available for loan only to authorized military personnel of the Training and Audiovisual Support Center, Fort Irwin, California. Audiovisual catalogs are indexed in the *Monthly Catalog* under the heading "Audio-visual Materials—Catalogs," and the biennial *Government Reference Books* published by Libraries Unlimited has a section called "Audiovisual Materials Catalogs."

COMPUTER REFERENCE PROGRAM

Karen F. Smith, documents librarian at the State University of New York at Buffalo, developed a microcomputer reference program for identifying the sources of government information in order to direct users to the text of the documents themselves. In this system, called POINTER, the search can be made by title (monograph, periodical or serial, numbered series, or public law); by bill, PL, House or Senate document/report, technical report, or presidential executive order number; by subject, including biographical information and numeric data; by directory information; by grants, fellowships, or employment opportunities; by executive branch information; by documents produced in the legislative process; by judiciary information; and by general indexes for subject searching in time frames (e.g., 1789-1892, 1957-1966, and so forth). This system is capably described by the creator of POINTER in an essay in *The Reference Librarian*, no. 23 (1989), pages 191-205. Smith compares the usefulness and limitations of POINTER with the benefits and shortcomings of *Using Government Publications*, the two-volume reference guide by Jean L. Sears and Marilyn K. Moody.

CATALOGS, INDEXES, AND CHECKLISTS:
Official Sources

Recent bibliographic accomplishments at GPO provide some cause for optimism, especially when viewed in light of governmental endeavors of the nineteenth and early twentieth centuries. Although the need for a catalog of official U.S. publications was first publicly discussed in 1845, Congress waited until 1883 before charging Benjamin Perley Poore with the unenviable task of finding and cataloging all U.S. government publications produced since the beginning of the republic. We have indeed come a long way since Poore compared his task to that of "Christopher Columbus when he steered westward on his voyage of discovery, confident that a new world existed, but having no knowledge of its distance or the direction in which it lay. No one could estimate how many publications were to be cataloged, where they were to be found, how long it would take to perform the work, or what would be the probable cost."[7]

The official sources that follow in this section include Poore's *Descriptive Catalogue of the Government Publications of the United States*, as well as four other key bibliographical tools produced under the aegis of the federal government that continue to remain in use in depository libraries. (As federal documents customarily are not copyrighted, reprints of these heavily used nineteenth and early twentieth century bibliographical catalogs usually can be obtained from commercial publishers.) Both the *Document Catalog* and the *Monthly Catalog* were mandated by the Printing Act of 1895 and merit especially close attention.

Sources are listed chronologically, with the dates that appear after the popular name heading intended to assist the searcher by indicating scope of coverage. Although all tools purport to include federal documents from each branch of the government, as will be shown, access to pre-twentieth century executive branch (i.e., departmental) documents can be difficult when relying solely upon official sources. Those official sources intended to index only congressional reports and documents (i.e., the Serial Set) are discussed in a later section of this chapter.

Poore
(1774-1881)

More than 100 years had passed since the birth of our nation when Benjamin Perley Poore, Clerk of the Senate's Committee on Printing, and his fourteen equally inexperienced helpers undertook the monumental bibliographic task of compiling all federal government publications—executive, legislative, and judicial. After scouring the contents of the major federal libraries, as well as other appropriate public and private libraries, they were able to identify 63,063 documents. The result was Poore's *Descriptive Catalogue of the Government Publications of the United States, September 5, 1774-March 4, 1881*, issued as Senate Miscellaneous Document 67, 48th Congress, second session.

To use a "poore" pun, no doubt some researchers would agree that the author's name accurately describes the quality of his bibliography. The chronological listing of documents lacks an effective index, is riddled with errors, omits many early documents, and is particularly weak in its coverage of departmental (executive) documents. Nonetheless, for many documents librarians unable to afford one of the newer commercially produced tools (see below), Poore's *Descriptive Catalogue* is the mainstay for identifying early government publications from the first century of our existence. Because Poore does not provide serial volume numbers for congressional documents, the *Checklist* or *Tables and Index* (these are discussed in upcoming sections) may need to be used in conjunction with Poore's *Descriptive Catalogue*.

Ames
(1881-1893)

In his capacity as Superintendent of Documents, Dr. John Griffith Ames began an official enumeration of documents in 1881, at the point where Poore's *Descriptive Catalogue* left off. Ames' *Comprehensive Index to the Publications of the United States Government, 1881-1893*, was issued in two volumes as H. Doc. 754, 58th Congress, second session. Although coverage of departmental publications still showed some neglect, Ames' *Comprehensive Index* was a manifest improvement over Poore's *Descriptive Catalogue*. Arrangement is alphabetical by subject (key word in the title) with a personal name index. Serial volume numbers are given in tables under the subject heading "Congressional Documents."

Checklist
(1789-1909)

Not only did Ames produce the *Comprehensive Index*, but he also developed the concept of serial set numbering (see next section) and was responsible for the issuance of the *Checklist of United States Public Documents, 1789-1909*. This *Checklist* reproduced the shelflist of the Public Documents Library. It is arranged by classification number in three sections: congressional edition by serial number, departmental edition by SuDocs classification number, and miscellaneous publications of Congress. The *Checklist*'s inclusion of departmental publications marks a significant improvement over the *Descriptive Catalogue* and the *Comprehensive Index*. Hence it is a handy tool to see the scope of a particular agency's publishing from the time of its establishment through 1909, as well as the evolution of editions of a particular document. Unfortunately, the projected index volume – which would have provided author, subject, and title access to the documents – was never published, thereby making it difficult for the neophyte documents searcher to use the *Checklist*.

Document Catalog
(1893-1940)

The Printing Act of 1895 provided that "the Superintendent of Documents shall, at the close of each regular session of Congress, prepare and publish a comprehensive index of public documents beginning with the 53rd Congress." The resulting biennial work is highly praised by librarians for its bibliographic thoroughness and accuracy. Such high standards of cataloging no doubt contributed to the fact that the *Document Catalog* was continually behind schedule. Finally, in 1947, as the cost of compiling and printing the retrospective work grew ever more burdensome, the Superintendent of Documents recommended to the Joint Committee on Printing that it be discontinued after being brought up to date to 1940.

The official title of this analytic dictionary catalog, with entries for personal and government author, subject, and frequently title, is *Catalogue of the Public Documents of the* [Fifty-third-Seventy-sixth] *Congress and of All Departments of the Government of the United States.* Proclamations and executive orders are indexed, as are periodicals that were issued regularly. A list of government offices appears at the end of each catalog to serve as a guide to government organization. Beginning with the 56th Congress, the serial volume number is also included in brackets to permit easy access to the bound volumes of the Congressional Serial Set. The *Document Catalog* is the most accurate and most comprehensive official bibliographic source for the time period 1893-1940, thereby making the *Monthly Catalog* a less reliable source for the pre-World War II era.

Monthly Catalog
(1895-)

The *Monthly Catalog of United States Government Publications* is the most comprehensive ongoing source for federal publications, including both depository and nondepository documents. Because it fulfills so many functions in libraries, including reference, cataloging, and acquisitions, it is an indispensable source.

Known as the *Monthly Catalog* or MoCat, this work also had its origin in the Printing Act of 1895, which directed the Superintendent of Documents "to prepare and publish a Monthly Catalog of Government Publications, which shall show the publications printed during a month, where obtainable, and the price thereof." Thus, it began as little more than an in-print list, designed to remedy the haphazard system of distribution and sales of public documents. It was only after the *Document Catalog* ceased publication that the *Monthly Catalog* was required by law to expand its coverage and improve its bibliographic accuracy. Therefore, from 1940 until the advent of the *Publications Reference File* (PRF), the *Monthly Catalog* served as the single official source of publications, fulfilling both statutory requirements of the 1895 law: that there be a "comprehensive index" and also a "Monthly [sales] Catalog."

Since it was first issued in 1895, the *Monthly Catalog* has changed its name seven times and has undergone numerous other changes, some minor and others major, the most monumental occurring with the issuance of the July 1976 *Monthly Catalog*, the Superintendent of Documents' proud contribution to the U.S. bicentennial celebration. Prior to July 1976 the *Monthly Catalog* was arranged alphabetically, either by department or by issuing agency, with the exception of the publications of the Congress, which were subdivided both by form and by issuing entity. Entries were brief; subject access was via catchwords or selected keywords.

Monthly and annual indexes to the "old" MoCat were organized in an inter-filed author-title-subject format. Decennial indexes (1941-1950 and 1951-1960), quinquennial cumulations (1961-1965 and 1966-1970), and a cumulation covering the period 1971 through June 1976 made searching somewhat easier. These indexes were notoriously slow to appear in print, thereby making the search process especially tedious. Because most libraries used the *Monthly Catalog* as a substitute for their card catalog, users needed to consult multiple volumes (both monthlies and annuals) to locate a specific document if the date of publication was unknown or to develop a bibliography of documents on a particular subject. Commercial products have eased the retrospective search process considerably.

Relatively simple and unsophisticated, the earlier *Monthly Catalog*'s format was as familiar to users as an old but comfortable shoe. But that relative stability ended with the appearance of the July 1976 issue. Not only was there a visible change in its size and appearance, but also, for the first time, the *Monthly Catalog* used Library of Congress subject headings, followed Anglo-American Cataloging Rules, incorporated MARC format, and participated in the OCLC cataloging network. GPO had entered the electronic age; it now would be possible to have online and, later, CD-ROM access to the *Monthly Catalog*.

INDEXES TO THE U.S. CONGRESSIONAL SERIAL SET

Researchers working with congressional materials will rapidly become familiar with those publications constituting the U.S. Congressional Serial Set, which contains reports and documents issued by the House and the Senate. (See chapter 5 for a detailed discussion of the contents and organization of the serial set.) The serial set was established in 1817 to provide a uniform system of congressional publishing. A serial number, or accession number, is assigned to the spine of each bound volume, with the first volume assigned the number 1 in 1817 right on through the latest serial numbering. The serial number itself is a locational device intended for convenience in shelving.

Specialized GPO-produced indexes to the serial set include the titles listed below in chronological order. Although serial set numbering did not begin until the 15th Congress, Adolphus Washington Greely's catalog is included here to provide coverage for earlier Congresses. Likewise, a description of the commercially produced *CIS US Serial Set Index, 1789-1969*, concludes the section because this source is so vital. Although the tools described below purport to include only congressional publications, they also can be of use in accessing executive publications, because many such departmental publications transmitted to Congress were later ordered to be issued in a "Congressional edition."

Greely
(1789-1817)

Adolphus Washington Greely was a soldier, scientist, and Arctic explorer who supervised a compilation of congressional publications for the early Congresses. His *Public Documents of the First Fourteen Congresses, 1789-1817—Papers Relating to Early Congressional Documents*, issued as Senate Document 428, Fifty-sixth Congress, first session, overlaps somewhat with Poore, although Greely made no attempt to include departmental publications as such. The arrangement is chronological by Congress, followed by a name index. A supplement was published in volume 1 of the 1903 *Annual Report* of the American Historical Association.

Tables and Index
(1817-1893)

Continuing Greely's work, the *Tables of and Annotated Index to the Congressional Series of United States Public Documents* lists publications of the 15th to the 52nd Congresses, 1817-1893. The first section of the book, the "Tables," replicates the first section of the *Checklist* (pp. 5-169) and gives congressional series information, with notes on contents and on omission or duplication in the Congressional Serial Set. The second section, the "Index," which the *Checklist* lacks, is a useful reference by subject and name, with the accompanying serial number of the bound congressional set. However, as the *Tables and Index* includes little more than half of the congressional documents and reports issued during the time period covered, the researcher must turn to the commercially produced *CIS US Serial Set Index, 1789-1969* (see below), for comprehensive coverage.

Document Index
(1895-1933)

The Printing Act of 1895 also provided that the Superintendent of Documents should "prepare and print in one volume a consolidated index of congressional documents." The resulting *Index to the Reports and Documents of the [Fifty-fourth-Seventy-second] Congress, with Numerical Lists and Schedule of Volumes, 1895-1933*, is an alphabetical subject (or inverted title) listing for congressional documents and reports contained in the serial set. Libraries with the *Document Catalog* will rarely need to use the *Document Index* (its short title) unless the client has only the number of the document or report. The *Document Index* was superseded by *Numerical Lists and Schedule of Volumes*.

Numerical Lists
(1933-1980)

The *Numerical Lists and Schedule of Volumes* continues those sections of the *Document Index* listing the congressional reports and documents in numbered sequence (the "Lists") and showing the arrangement of the reports and documents by volumes (the "Schedule") of the serial set. There is no subject access. With the discontinuance of the *Document Catalog*, the *Numerical Lists* assumed a more important role in accessing the bound serial set volumes. Because of its essential value in this respect, the *Numerical Lists* is considered in more detail in chapter 5.

Monthly Catalog – U.S. Congressional Serial Set Supplement, 97th Congress, 1981-1982

For the 97th Congress only (1981-1982), the *Numerical Lists* was renamed, reformatted, and issued as part of the *Monthly Catalog*, utilizing the same format and indexing as the MoCat. Figure 4.1 shows a sample entry from this source.

U.S. Congressional Serial Set Catalog: Numerical Lists and Schedule of Volumes, 98th Congress, 1983-1984

Commencing with the 98th Congress, yet another change in format and title was made. Following the "Numerical Lists" and "Schedule of Volumes," full bibliographic records for the reports and documents are arranged by SuDocs classification number. Author, title, subject, series/report, and bill number indexes are provided. In a survey conducted by the GPO in 1989, librarians expressed some concern over the many changes occurring in this product in recent years and urged that the catalog's format be stabilized. Reported usage was low with many librarians still unfamiliar with the new publication. More than half reported using commercial sources (CIS and/or Autographics products) in lieu of the official *Serial Set Catalog*.[8]

CIS US Serial Set Index, 1789-1969

This massive undertaking permits users to bypass the earlier, flawed bibliographic guides described above and provides access through 1969. From 1970, coverage of serial set publications, as well as other congressional materials, is provided by *CIS/Index*. Thus, the *CIS US Serial Set Index* is the definitive retrospective tool, encompassing some 330,000 publications issued over a 180-year period. The indexes consist of twelve parts totaling thirty-six volumes. Access is provided by subjects and keywords, private relief and related actions (private legislation affecting persons or organizations), numerical lists of report

(Text continues on page 94.)

Fig. 4.1. Sample entry from MoCat serial set, 97th Congress

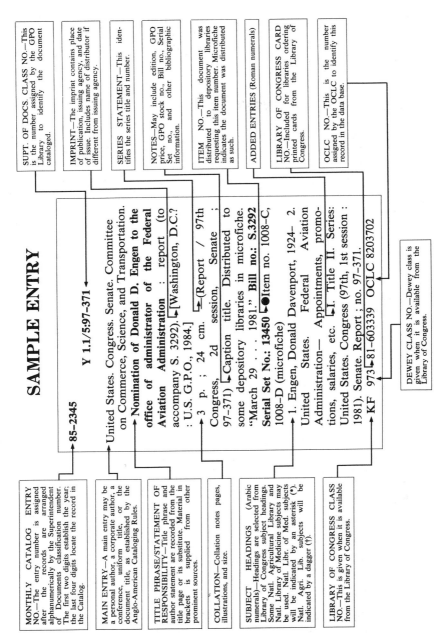

SAMPLE ENTRY

85-2345   Y 1.1/5:97-371

United States. Congress. Senate. Committee on Commerce, Science, and Transportation. **Nomination of Donald D. Engen to the office of administrator of the Federal Aviation Administration :** report (to accompany S. 3292). [Washington, D.C.? : U.S. G.P.O., 1984.]

3 p. ; 24 cm. (Report / 97th Congress, 2d session ; Senate 97-371) Caption title. Distributed to some depository libraries in microfiche. "March 29 . . . 1981." **Bill no.: S.3292** **Serial Set No.: 13450** Item no. 1008-C, 1008-D (microfiche)

1. Engen, Donald Davenport, 1924- 2. United States. Federal Aviation Administration— Appointments, promotions, salaries, etc. I. Title II. Series: United States. Congress (97th, 1st session : 1981). Senate. Report ; no. 97-371.

KF 973 81-603339 OCLC 8203702

SUPT. OF DOCS. CLASS NO.—This is the number assigned by the GPO Library to identify the document cataloged.

IMPRINT—The imprint contains place of publication, issuing agency, and date of issue. Includes name of distributor if different from issuing agency.

SERIES STATEMENT—This identifies the series title and number.

NOTES—May include edition, GPO price, GPO stock no., Bill no., Serial Set no., and other bibliographic information.

ITEM NO.—This document was distributed to depository libraries requesting this item number. Microfiche indicates the document was distributed as such.

ADDED ENTRIES (Roman numerals)

LIBRARY OF CONGRESS CARD NO.—Included for libraries ordering printed cards from the Library of Congress.

OCLC NO.—This is the number assigned by the OCLC to identify this record in the data base.

MONTHLY CATALOG ENTRY NO.—The entry number is assigned after the records are arranged alphanumerically by the Superintendent of Documents classification number. The first two digits establish the year; the last four digits locate the record in the Catalog.

MAIN ENTRY—A main entry may be a personal author, a corporate author, a conference, uniform title, or the document title, as established by the Anglo-American Cataloging Rules.

TITLE PHRASE/STATEMENT OF RESPONSIBILITY—Title phrase and author statement are recorded from the title page or its substitute. Material in brackets is supplied from other prominent sources.

COLLATION—Collation notes pages, illustrations, and size.

SUBJECT HEADINGS (Arabic numerals)—Headings are selected from Library of Congress subject headings. Some Natl. Agricultural Library and Natl. Library of Medicine subjects may be used. Natl. Libr. of Med. subjects will be indicated by an asterisk (*), Natl. Agri. Lib. subjects will be indicated by a dagger (†).

LIBRARY OF CONGRESS CLASS NO.—This is given when it is available from the Library of Congress.

DEWEY CLASS NO.—Dewey class is given when it is available from the Library of Congress.

and document numbers, and a schedule of serial volumes. The bibliographic information thus gained can be effectively used to access a library's collection of the volumes, or the full text is available for purchase by subscribing to the *CIS US Serial Set on Microfiche.*

SEARCHING THE *MONTHLY CATALOG*

It is as easy to search the post-July 1976 *Monthly Catalog* as it is to use the typical catalog found in a large research library. After all, its entries resemble a catalog record. When searching manually, it is especially important to keep in mind that the date of the *Monthly Catalog* reflects the month in which the documents were cataloged, which is not always identical to the year in which the document was published. When conducting a subject search, one may consult *Library of Congress Subject Headings* for appropriate subject terminology.

Bibliographic entries in the *Monthly Catalog* are arranged in SuDocs classification number order. Each record is also assigned a unique catalog number, which consists of a two-digit prefix representing the catalog year followed by a sequential number beginning with 1 in the first issue of each year. Within this arrangement, the publications of each government author are further identified by the name of the issuing agency.

Salient features of the bibliographic record that should be noted include the following:

1. Black dot depository item number: This symbol and number indicate that the document was automatically distributed to regional depositories and to those selective depository libraries choosing it. If the document is not a depository item, there is no black dot.

2. SuDocs classification number: This number is used in many libraries to shelve or file the document. The entries indicate whether the document was issued in microfiche, in paper, or on CD-ROM.

3. Series title and number: Because so many documents are issued in series format, this information can be especially helpful in locating and citing a document. Catalog entries may be accessed manually via eight indexes. Use the margin index on the back cover to locate them. Cumulative indexes are published semiannually, annually, and quinquennially and, in addition to the indexes listed below, include a classification number index for all the publications listed during the period of cumulation.

4. Author index: An alphabetical list of personal authors, editors, co-authors, corporate authors, and conferences.

5. Title index: An alphabetical list of titles proper, subtitles, and alternate titles.

6. Subject index: An alphabetical list of subjects derived from the *Library of Congress Subject Headings.*

7. Series/Report index: An alphabetical listing of series statements and tracings, series numbers, and report numbers.

8. Contract number index: An alphanumeric list of contract, grant, and project numbers associated with technical report publications. Abridged cataloging records are not accessible by contract number.

9. Stock number index: An alphanumeric list of SuDocs sales stock numbers.

10. Title keyword index: An alphabetical list of truncated titles, arranged by important words selected from publication titles.

Figures 4.2, 4.3, and 4.4 (see pages 96, 97, and 98) show, respectively, a *Monthly Catalog* sample entry, a main entry page, and a page from the Subject Index referencing that main entry.

COMMERCIAL SOURCES TO AID USE OF THE *MONTHLY CATALOG*

That the federal government itself does not always provide the best indexing for its own publications comes as no surprise to frequent users of government material. Publication time frames lag, index language often eludes common terminology, and format leaves much to be desired. Although variant editions provided by legal publishers were commonplace, the role of commercial publishers became increasingly evident in the field of government publications around 1970, perhaps due to the proactive stance often taken by Government Documents Round Table (GODORT) members.

As a remedy to the limitations of the government's own index tools, most specifically the *Monthly Catalog*, a number of commercial sources were published to enhance MoCat's utility. Performing a general subject search or a search on a specific topic, date unknown, was a tedious undertaking prior to the advent of the *Cumulative Subject Index to the Monthly Catalog of United States Government Publications 1900-1971*, a fifteen-volume, single-alphabet index advertised by Carrollton Press almost concurrently with the publication of an article by Robert Simmons lamenting that "locating United States government documents on a given subject is a task which many librarians no doubt like to avoid."[9] The *Cumulative Subject Index*, compiled by Edna A. Kanely and William Buchanan, conveniently merged the indexing from forty-eight annual indexes, the 1941-1950 and 1951-1960 decennial indexes, and one six-month index. It also added original indexing for thirty issues of the MoCat that were never indexed by subject.

Publication of the *Cumulative Subject Index* and other indexes enhanced the value of the *Monthly Catalog* and spurred the availability of reprint and microcopy editions of the venerable but flawed set. One reprint edition, the *Classes Added Reprint Edition of the Monthly Catalog of U.S. Government Publications, 1895-1924*, compiled by Mary Elizabeth Poole and published by

(Text continues on page 99.)

Fig. 4.2. Sample entry from *Monthly Catalog*

SAMPLE ENTRY

SUPT. OF DOCS. CLASS NO.—This is the number assigned by the GPO Library to identify the document cataloged.

EDITION—The edition is recorded from information in the document.

SERIES STATEMENT—This identifies the series title and number.

NOTES—Notes include additional bibliographic information about the publication, including funding information for technical reports.

ITEM NO.—This document was distributed to depository libraries requesting this item number. Microfiche indicates the document was distributed as such.

STOCK NO.—This is a Government Printing Office sales stock number. It is used only in ordering from the Superintendent of Documents.

PRICE—GPO sales price.

ADDED ENTRIES (Roman numerals)—When the Government publisher is not a main entry, it is included with added entries.

83-0123

A 1.9:2271

Creighton, C. S. (Charles S.), 1926–
   Control of caterpillars on cabbage / [prepared by Science and Education Administration.] —1981 ed.—Washington, D.C.? : The Administration : For sale by the Supt. of Docs., U.S. G.P.O., 1980 i.e. 1981.
   23 p. : 23 cm. — (Farmers' bulletin (United States, Dept. of Agriculture) ; no. 2271) This bulletin supersedes Farmers' bulletin no. 2099, Control of Caterpillars on commercial cabbage." Item 9 (microfiche) S/N 001-000-04185-1 $1.50
   1. Cabbage—Diseases and pests—United States. 2. Caterpillars—Control—United States. I. United States. Science and Education Administration. II. Title. III. Series : Farmers' bulletin (United States. Dept. of Agriculture) ; no. 2271.
   SB   762.U55a   1981   80-603339
   334.76/0664 OCLC 8203702

LIBRARY OF CONGRESS CARD NO.—Included when it is available from the Library of Congress.

OCLC NO.—This is the number assigned by the OCLC to identify this record in the data base.

MONTHLY CATALOG ENTRY NO.—The entry number is assigned after the records are arranged alphanumerically by the Superintendent of Documents classification number. The first two digits establish the year; the last four digits locate the record in the Catalog.

MAIN ENTRY—A main entry may be a personal author, a corporate author, a conference, uniform title, or the document title, as established by the Anglo-American Cataloging Rules.

TITLE PHRASE/STATEMENT OF RESPONSIBILITY—Title phrase and author statement are recorded from the title page or its substitutes. Material in brackets is supplied from other prominent sources.

IMPRINT—The imprint contains place of publication, issuing agency, and date of issue. Includes name of distributor if different from issuing agency.

COLLATION—Collation notes pages, illustrations, and size.

SUBJECT HEADINGS (Arabic numerals)—Headings are selected from the Library of Congress subject headings. Some Natl. Agricultural Library and Natl. Libr. of Medicine subjects may be used. Natl. Libr. of Med. subjects will be indicated by an asterisk (*). Natl. Agri. Lib. subjects will be indicated by a dagger (†).

LIBRARY OF CONGRESS CLASS NO.—This is given when it is available from the Library of Congress.

DEWEY CLASS NO.—Dewey class is given when it is available from the Library of Congress.

PRELIM. 13

Fig. 4.3. Main entry page from *Monthly Catalog*

CENTERS FOR DISEASE CONTROL
Health and Human Services Dept.
Atlanta, GA 30333

87-16834

HE 20.7026:P 95

Pseudomembraneous colitis in hospitalized patients : New Jersey.
— Atlanta : Public Health Service, CDC, 1987.
14 p. : ill. ; 28 cm. Caption title. For administrative use.
"May 5, 1987." Bibliography: p. 7-8. "EPI-85-44-2."
1. Colitis. 2. Epidemiology — Research — New Jersey. I.
Centers for Disease Control (U.S.) OCLC 16403444

87-16835

HE 20.7026:Sa 3

Food-borne outbreak of salmonellosis, Lynchburg, Virginia. —
Atlanta : Public Health Service, CDC, 1987.
11 p. : 1 ill. ; 28 cm. — (Field epidemiology report ; 87-01)
Caption title. For administrative use. "June 4, 1987."
1. Salmonellosis — Virginia. I. Centers for Disease Control
(U.S.) II. Series. OCLC 16393343

87-16836

HE 20.7026:Sm 7/2

Assessment of smoking control measures : New York City. —
Atlanta : Public Health Service, CDC, 1987.
[8] p. ; 28 cm. Caption title. For official use only. "May
28, 1987." Includes bibliographies. "EPI-86-41-2."
1. Smoking — Law and legislation — New York (N.Y.) I.
Centers for Disease Control (U.S.) OCLC 16409323

NATIONAL INSTITUTE FOR OCCUPATIONAL
SAFETY AND HEALTH
Health and Human Services Dept.
Rockville, MD 20857

87-16837

HE 20.7102:In 2/10

Advanced industrial hygiene engineering (552). — Rev. June
1986. — Cincinnati, Ohio : U.S. Dept. of Health and Human
Services, Public Health Service, Centers for Disease Control,
National Institute for Occupational Safety and Health, Division
of Training and Manpaower Development, 1986.
viii, [922] p. : ill., forms ; 28 cm. Distributed to depository
libraries in microfiche. "November 1978." Includes bibliographies. ●Item 499-F-2 (microfiche).
1. Industrial hygiene. 2. Human engineering. I. National
Institute for Occupational Safety and Health. Division of Training & Manpower Development. OCLC 16505479

CENTER FOR PREVENTION SERVICES
Health and Human Services Dept.
Atlanta, GA 30333

87-16838

HE 20.7312:Se 9/987

Survey of research on sexually transmitted diseases / [prepared by
Centers for Disease Control, Center for Prevention Services,
Technical Information Services ; editor, Sherrie L. Deyette]. —
Atlanta, Ga. : U.S. Dept. of Health and Human Services,
Public Health Service, Centers for Disease Control, Center for
Prevention Services, Division of Sexually Transmitted Diseases,
[1987]
vi, 133 p. ; 28 cm. Shipping list no.: 87-423-P. "May 1987."
Includes bibliographies. ●Item 494-K-7
1. Sexually transmitted diseases — Abstracts. I. Deyette,
Sherrie. II Center for Prevention Services (U.S.). Division of
Sexually Transmitted Diseases. III. Center for Prevention
Services (U.S.). Technical Information Services. OCLC
16318274

NATIONAL INSTITUTE OF MENTAL HEALTH
Health and Human Services Dept.
Rockville, MD 20857

87-16839

HE 20.8102:D 63/6

Human problems in major disasters : a training curriculum for
emergency medical personnel / prepared by Division of Education and Service Systems Liaison, Emergency Services
Branch. — Rockville, Md. : U.S. Dept. of Health and Human
Services, Public Health Service, Alcohol, Drug Abuse, and
Mental Health Administration, National Institute of Mental
Health, [1987]
23 p. ; 18 cm. — (DHHS publication ; no. (ADM) 87-1505)
Shipping list no. 87-463-P. Bibliography: p. 23. ●Item 507-B-
5
1. Stress (Psychology) 2. Emergency medical personnel —
United States. 3. Disasters — United States — Psychological
aspects. I. National Institute of Mental Health (U.S.). Division
of Education and Service Systems Liaison. Emergency Services
Branch. II. Series. OCLC 16505534

87-16840 ←

HE 20.8102:St 8/4

Prevention and control of stress among emergency workers : a
pamphlet for workers / prepared by Division of Education and
Service Systems Liaison, Emergency Services Branch. — Rock-
ville, Md. : U.S. Dept. of Health and Human Services, Public
Health Service, Alcohol, Drug Abuse, and Mental Health Administration, National Institute of Mental Health, 1987.
9 p. ; 18 cm. — (DHHS publication ; no. (ADM) 87-1497)
Shipping list no. 87-460-P. Bibliography: p. 9. ●Item 507-B-5
1. Stress (Psychology) 2. Job stress — United States. 3.
Emergency medical personnel — United States. 4. Disasters —
United States — Psychological aspects. I. National Institute of
Mental Health (U.S.). Division of Education and Service Systems Liaison. Emergency Services Branch. II. Series. OCLC
16447976

87-16841

HE 20.8110/2:DN/6

Campbell, Thomas L., 1952-
Family's impact on health : a critical review and annotated
bibliography / Thomas L. Campbell. — Rockville, Md. : U.S.
Dept. of Health and Human Services, Public Health Service,
Alcohol, Drug Abuse, and Mental Health Administration, National Institute of Mental Health, Division of Biometry and
Applied Sciences, Biometric and Clinical Applications Branch,
1986.
vii, 242 p. ; 23 cm. — (Mental health service system reports,
Series DN, Health/mental health research ; Series DN no. 6)
(DHHS publication ; no. (ADM) 86-1461) Includes bibliographies and indexes. ●Item 491-A (microfiche)
1. Health. 2. Family — Health and hygiene — Bibliography.
3. *Family 4. *Health I. National Institute of Mental Health
(U.S.). Division of Biometry and Applied Sciences. Biometric
and Clinical Applications Branch. II. Title. III. Series. IV.
Series: Mental health service system reports. Series DN,
Health/mental health research ; no. 6. OCLC 14641762

Fig. 4.4. Page from Subject Index referencing main entry in fig. 4.3

Landslides Wyoming.

Jewish religious education — United States — Curricula — Bibliography.
Resource guide, update 1986 / (D 1.6/2:J 53/4), 87-16579

Jews — Bibliography.
Resource guide, update 1986 / (D 1.6/2:J 53/4), 87-16579

Job stress — United States.
Prevention and control of stress among emergency workers : a pamphlet for workers / (HE 20.8102:St 8/4), 87-16840

Judges — United States — Selection and appointment.
Administrative law judge : opportunities in the federal government as an administrative law judge. (PM 1.21/2:318/984), 87-17172

Judicial discretion — United States.
Sentencing guidelines : preliminary draft / United States Sentencing Commission. (Y 3.Se 5:8 G 94/draft), 87-17432

Junior colleges — United States.
What statistical information is available on two-year colleges : a summary of research findings. (ED 1.310/2:261759), 87-16667

Juniper Dunes Wilderness — Washington (State)
Wilderness management plan for the Juniper Dunes Wilderness, Washington. United States. Bureau of Land Management. Spokane District Office. (I 53.2:J 95), 87-17083

Justice, Administration of — United States.
The federal civil justice system. McGillis, Daniel. (J 29.11:C 49), 87-17109

K

Korea (North) — Foreign relations — Korea (South)
Korea, new beginnings / Sigur, Gaston Joseph. (S 1.71/4:989), 87-17193

Korea (South) — Foreign relations — Korea (North)
Korea, new beginnings / Sigur, Gaston Joseph. (S 1.71/4:989), 87-17193

L

Labor and laboring classes — Arizona.
An Act to Amend Title 5, United States Code, to Extend the Pay Retention Provisions of Such Title to Certain Prevailing Rate Employees in the Tucson Wage Area Whose Basic Pay Would Otherwise Be Subject to Reduction Pursuant to a Wage Survey. United States. (AE 2.110:100-47), 87-16535

Labor laws and legislation — United States.
An Act to Amend Title 5, United States Code, to Extend the Pay Retention Provisions of Such Title to Certain Prevailing Rate Employees in the Tucson Wage Area Whose Basic Pay Would Otherwise Be Subject to Reduction Pursuant to a Wage Survey. United States. (AE 2.110:100-47), 87-16535

Labor productivity — United States.
Productivity improvement : your guide to today's resources. (C 1.8/3:P 94), 87-16546

Technology and its impact on labor in four industries : lumber and wood products, footwear, hydraulic cement, wholesale trade. (L 2.3:2263), 87-17115

Laboratories.
Interlaboratory comparability, bias, and precision for four laboratories measuring analytes in wet deposition, October 1983-December 1984 / Brooks, Myron H. (I 19.42/4:87-4067), 87-16906

Laboratories — United States — Furniture, equipment, etc.
So you are going to move your laboratory? : a guide to better moving. (HE 20.3008:L 11/3), 87-16799

Laboratories — United States — Location.
So you are going to move your laboratory? : a guide to better moving. (HE 20.3008:L 11/3), 87-16799

Ladders — Safety measures.
Some baby gates are dangerous, others are safer ; Pool ladder step safety replacement program ; Safety recall of shoulder harness on Championship brand bicycle child carrier sold by Sears ; Lowe's recalls electric bug killers ; CPSC warns parents about child accidents in recliner chairs. (Y 3.C 76/3:11-3 B 11/987) (Y 3.C 76/3:11-3 P 78/2) (Y 3.C 76/3:11-3 H 22) (Y 3.C 76/3:11-3 L 95) (Y 3.C 76/3:11-3 C 34/987), 87-17372

Lakes.
Near-real-time forecasting of large-lake water supplies : a user's manual / Croley, Thomas E. (C 55.13/2:ERL GLERL-61), 87-16569

Land capability for agriculture — Indiana — Scott County — Maps.
Important farmlands, Scott County, Indiana / United States. Soil Conservation Service. (A 57.69:Sco 8/3), 87-16518

Land settlement — West Bank — Maps.
Israeli settlements in the West Bank, October, 1986. United States. Central Intelligence Agency. (PrEx 3.10/4:Is 7/4/986), 87-17177

Land tenure — Alaska — Maps.
Alaska, land status map, June, 1986 / United States. Bureau of Land Management. Alaska State Office. (I 53.11:Al 1 s/9), 87-17086

Land use — Arizona — Coconino National Forest.
Environmental impact statement for the Coconino National Forest plan. (A 13.92:C 64/plan), 87-16500

Land use — Colorado — Uncompahgre River Watershed — Planning.
Draft Uncompahgre Basin planning area wilderness technical supplement : June 1987 / (I 1.98:Un 1/2/draft/supp.), 87-16861

Draft Uncompahgre Basin resource management plan and environmental impact statement June 1987 / (I 1.98:Un 1/2/draft/plan), 87-16860

Land use — Government policy — Alaska.
Availability of land for mineral exploration and development in northern Alaska, 1986 / Maas, Kenneth M. (I 28.151:Al 1 s/4) (I 28.151:Al 1 s/4/maps), 87-17063

Land use — Idaho.
Final environmental impact statement : eastern Idaho wilderness study / (I 1.98:Id 1/3/prop./amdt.), 87-16858

Land use — Ohio — Columbiana County.
Columbiana Soil and Water Conservation District resources inventory. (A 57.38/2:C 72), 87-16517

Land use — Wyoming.
Wyoming BLM : Operation Respect. (I 53.2:W 99/3), 87-17085

Land use — Wyoming — Planning.
Record of decision for the Lander resource management plan / United States. Bureau of Land Management. Lander Resource Area. (I 1.98:L 23/record), 87-16859

Landslides — Montana.
Landslide deposits in the Lodge Grass 30' x 60' quadrangle, Montana and Wyoming / Geological Survey (U.S.) (I 19.113:MF-1928), 87-17046

Landslides — Puerto Rico — Ponce.
Preliminary response activities and recommendations of the USGS Landslide Hazard Research Team to the Puerto Rico landslide disaster of October 7, 1985 [microform] / USGS Landslide Hazard Research Team. (I 19.76:85-719), 87-16919

Landslides — Wyoming.
Landslide deposits in the Lodge Grass 30' x 60' quadrangle, Montana and Wyo-

Do not order from index; see indicated entry

Carrollton, added SuDocs class numbers, which were absent from the original edition, to this thirty-year run of the MoCat. As availability of reprint and micro-copy editions is subject to constant change, one seeking up-to-date information should consult the annual *Guide to Reprints* (Kent, CT: Guide to Reprints) or the *Guide to Microforms in Print* (Westport, CT: Meckler Corporation).

Further enhancing access to the historical period is Edna A. Kanely (comp.), *Cumulative Index to Hickcox's Monthly Catalog of U.S. Government Publica-tions, 1885-1894.* Kanely's three-volume decennial index provides cumulative sub-ject and author entry to Hickcox's ten annual catalogs, which were compiled and published privately by John H. Hickcox. In addition, Mary Elizabeth Poole pro-duced a six-volume *"Classes Added" Reprint Edition of Hickcox's Monthly Catalog of U.S. Government Publications, 1895-1899* (Washington, DC: Carroll-ton Press, 1977).

Although personal authorship is not as pervasive a concept in relation to government publications (note, for instance, the infrequency with which newspaper articles cite personal authorship when citing government reports) as it is to privately published sources, personal authors are sometimes known or cited. Just as Carrollton Press enhanced the use of the official *Monthly Catalog* by pro-viding a cumulative subject approach, Pierian Press (Ann Arbor, Michigan) was the frontrunner in providing cumulative indexing for personal authors. Edited by Edward Przebienda, the volumes include two decennial and three quinquennial indexes. They consist of alphabetical lists of all personal names that have appeared in the entries of the *Monthly Catalog* for the years 1941-1975 under the series title *Cumulative Personal Author Indexes to the Monthly Catalog.* Names provided include virtually every relationship of author to cited publica-tion—editor, compiler, translator, researcher, lecturer, joint author(s), or illus-trator—including a systematic author approach to Joint Publications Research Service (JPRS) translations.

These author indexes are invaluable because from September 1946 to December 1962 personal authors were omitted from the *Monthly Catalog* in-dexes, including the two decennial cumulative indexes (1941-1950 and 1951-1960). In other years the *Monthly Catalog* indexed by first author only. The *Document Catalog* (1893-1940) includes personal authors, and since July 1976 the *Monthly Catalog* has been thoroughly indexing personal authors, editors, illus-trators, and others. However, despite the additional aid of bibliographic utilities such as OCLC and RLIN, Pierian Press's contribution to *Monthly Catalog* access remains indispensable.

Another commercial venture in support of *Monthly Catalog* access is the full-text edition of entries filmed by Readex Microprint Corporation (New Canaan, CT). In 1953 the company began filming and selling nondepository titles and in 1956 began offering the depository series of *Monthly Catalog* titles. The SuDocs notation and *Monthly Catalog* entry number are displayed on the micro-fiche title stripes since 1981, thus giving libraries the choice of either sequence to organize their collections. Before 1981, Readex subscribers received microprint cards, a format that was unacceptable to user and librarian alike. Acceding to the wishes of documents librarians, Readex began to offer the series on microfiche.

Readex introduced a "documents-on-demand" service, extending to the pub-lications of individual departments and agencies and even to individual titles that have been announced in MoCat. Separate sets available for purchase include the Congressional Serial Set, the *Congressional Record*, the *Federal Register*, and other series, which are noted in the chapters covering those specialized information sources.

AUTOMATED VERSIONS OF THE *MONTHLY CATALOG*

The decision to automate the *Monthly Catalog*, to make it available in machine-readable form, paved the way for new approaches to the bibliographic data contained therein. By 1990, the three common avenues of accessing this cumulative database in electronic format were to subscribe directly to the GPO tapes from the government, to use dial-up access through a vendor of online services, or to purchase or lease a CD-ROM version. With the advent of database searching services in libraries in the 1970s, several commercial vendors began to provide online access to the *Monthly Catalog*, such as DIALOG (File 66) and BRS (GPOM).

For a relatively short time, the *Monthly Catalog* was also offered by commercial publishers in an automated, cumulative microform version. Brodart, Auto-Graphics, and Information Access Corporation, for instance, offered the *Monthly Catalog* from 1976 on in a self-contained, motorized microfilm reader. These automated versions, although having the advantage of continuous cumulation, also had numerous disadvantages. Subscriptions (microfilm plus equipment) were costly, few librarians were able to support the purchase of more than one reader, queues to use the reader were common, and equipment was frequently inadequate. Furthermore, the readers were not ordinarily equipped with printers. The technology was an intermediate one.

By the late 1980s, online searching, as well as the roll-film versions of *Monthly Catalog*, began to take a back seat to various CD-ROM versions. CD-ROM, which stands for Compact Disk-Read Only Memory, is an optical technology in which lasers are used to read high-density optical disks. A CD-ROM workstation normally consists of a microcomputer, with keyboard and monitor, a disk drive (or player), and a printer (optional). The disk itself can carry at least 550 megabytes, or the equivalent of about 250,000 printed pages.

The rapid popularity of CD-ROM began to place fewer demands on librarians for mediated online searches, and vendors who had been successfully marketing the automated roll-film packages of *Monthly Catalog* were quick to convert their products to the new technology. The *Monthly Catalog*—from July 1976 forward—is now sold or leased under a variety of labels and with a variety of search enhancements. Searches on CD-ROM products generally can be done by author, title, subject/keyword, and series, as well as by SuDocs, item, MoCat report, and stock numbers. Most offer boolean search capability.

Marketing under the name Government Documents Catalog Service (GDCS), Auto-Graphics, Inc. (Pomona, California), made available one of the more user-friendly products, advertising that "Each month, the Cataloging Distribution Service of the Library of Congress provides us with machine readable cataloging for new publications and corrections to previously cataloged records." Auto-Graphics processes these tapes to update the GPO database, generates name and subject cross-references from the LC authorities, and produces a new CD-ROM catalog each month for automatic distribution to GDCS subscribers.

Presumably, the scenario is similar to that of other vendors. GPO SilverPlatter, a bimonthly service that introduced boolean search capability early and required a greater degree of initial sophistication to search, advertised

"300,000 citations to books, reports, audiovisual materials, and other documents" and "14 years of information on one CD-ROM." SilverPlatter Information, Inc. (Wellesley Hills, Massachusetts), was, in fact, probably the first to offer a solution to a major drawback of early CD-ROM products—the limitation of one user at a workstation at any given time—through the introduction of their MultiPlatter local area network (LAN) concept.

Other versions of MoCat to be offered include Brodart Automation's (Williamsport, Pennsylvania) Le Pac and an OCLC (Dublin, Ohio) bimonthly version that beginning in 1990 offers an optional feature of daily updates. Another service, Marcive's GPO CAT/PAC (San Antonio, Texas), advertised- that their product had already "cleaned up" the GPO tapes and offered the most accurate database. The H. W. Wilson Company also offers a CD-ROM version.

Reviews of multimedia products and services cannot adequately keep pace with the fast-changing technologies. For example, a useful essay discussing and summarizing the several versions of the *Monthly Catalog* was published in a 1990 issue of *Government Information Quarterly* (GIQ). In addition to the official paper version, the authors identified two microform versions, three online versions, a magnetic tape product distributed by the Library of Congress, and six CD-ROM versions, all of the last conforming to the High Sierra/ISO 9660 standards.[10] Ongoing reviews of competing nonprint products that enjoy heavy use in libraries (compare the ERIC CD-ROM products noted in chapter 11) are necessary for current awareness. Unfortunately, these commentaries become rapidly dated as vendors react to competitors, use and user studies, and subscriber comments and refine their products. Moreover, prices (which were provided in the GIQ article) are important for acquisitions decisions in a climate where budgets are tight, but these too change at least annually.

BIBLIOGRAPHIC UTILITIES

From the standpoint of the information provider, the availability of two national bibliographic utilities, the Online Computer Library Center and the Research Libraries Information Network, paved the way for easier and far greater bibliographic access to the nation's governmental resources. With *Monthly Catalog* tapes available in the OCLC Online Union Catalog from July 1976 on and GPO tapes mounted in RLIN (the bibliographic database of the Research Libraries Group) since 1983, librarians have two powerful tools at their command.

The OCLC system allows for searching by title, personal name (or a name/ title combination), corporate name, Library of Congress card number, ISBN, ISSN, and OCLC control number. In 1980, a government document search key was added; the key consists of one or two alphabetic characters and one to ten numeric characters. The prefix "gn" is used to initiate a search by the SuDocs number. For instance, "gn: ga11376109" would retrieve the record for a General Accounting Office document classified as GA 1.13:MWD-76-109, assuming that the SuDocs number was present in the 0086 field of the catalog record.[11] Although many libraries use OCLC for the technical service function, it is used by public service librarians as well.

With the addition of the EPIC service to the existing OCLC capabilities, subject keyword and phrase searching is possible. OCLC also has been adding other databases, such as ERIC to EPIC, and these enhancements provide a greater dimension in the service of access to information. The Holdings information for the OCLC database in the form of the three-character OCLC symbol permits the user to consult the resources of nearly 10,000 libraries worldwide for research and interlibrary loan purposes. The early availability of serial records makes OCLC an attractive database to search. Although not all libraries that catalog their documents do so through OCLC, holdings are generally available for enough institutions to expedite referral and interlibrary loans.

Whereas the OCLC database is widely used by smaller academic and by public libraries and is often the best source to determine holdings within one's own state, the RLIN database is an excellent source for verifying government publications from any jurisdiction and provides information obtained from the many institutions that are members of the Research Libraries Group. RLIN offers a wider variety of access points than OCLC. The database can be searched-by the same access positions as OCLC, and in addition searchers can use title phrase, title word, corporate name phrase, corporate name word, subject phrase, and other avenues. RLIN searches may also be limited by publication date.

Sample descriptions of government records at the municipal, state, and federal levels are set forth in a free brochure titled "Government Records in the RLIN Database: An Introduction and Guide" (June 1990). This useful pamphlet is available from the Research Libraries Group, Inc., 1200 Villa St., Mountain View, CA 94041-1100.

SUPPLEMENTAL SOURCES

Not to be overlooked in retrospective bibliographic searching is that portion of the Library of Congress's *National Union Catalog, Pre-1956 Imprints* (NUC), that deals with the corporate author heading "United States" and its subdivisions. This section of NUC was reprinted separately as *United States Government Publications* (London: Mansell Publishing, 1981, 16 vols.) and consists of almost 229,000 entries, thereby forming the largest single segment of the total 755-volume printed catalog. Government publications of all kinds are listed and represent the holdings of approximately 900 North American research libraries.

Another useful source prepared by the Library of Congress is *Popular Names of U.S. Government Reports: A Catalog*, now in its fourth edition (1987). The list includes reports, cited by their commonly used name as well as by the official titles used in library catalogs and bibliographies. Coverage dates back to the nineteenth century and includes not only advisory bodies but also selected congressional committee reports, committee prints, or hearings that have come to be known by the name of the chairperson or chief investigative office. Although the media often refer to newsworthy reports by the name of the chairperson, indexing tools such as the *Monthly Catalog* are not likely to include popular names of reports.

Other omnibus guides useful in the quest to identify federal as well as other government publications are based on the fine collections of the New York Public Library, whose Documents Division was formally established in 1897. The forty-volume *Catalog of Government Publications in the Research Libraries: The New York Public Library, Astor, Lenox, and Tilden Foundations* (Boston: G. K. Hall, 1972) includes nearly eight volumes of main and added entries of U.S.

government material. Entries are broken down by political unit and agency; the listings for each agency are then divided into serial publications arranged alphabetically by title, followed by monographs arranged by date of publication. G. K. Hall also publishes *Bibliographic Guide to Government Publications – U.S.*, an annual subject bibliography that brings together publications cataloged by the Research Libraries of the New York Public Library with additional entries from Library of Congress MARC tapes.

As an extension to the historical search that the *Catalog* and *Bibliographic Guides* permit, one might also pursue more recent citations through the familiar *PAIS International in Print* (New York: Public Affairs Information Service) in its paper, online, or CD-ROM version.

OTHER COMMERCIALLY PRODUCED SOURCES

Several related commercial projects merit attention in that they supplement official tools for accessing older materials. The shelflist of the old Public Documents Library of the Government Printing Office, which in 1972 became part of the Printed Archives Branch of the National Archives and Records Administration, was microfilmed, and a dual-media edition of 118 microfilm reels and 5 paper copy indexes called *Checklist of United States Public Documents, 1789-1976*, was marketed by U.S. Historical Documents Institute, Inc. (Washington, DC). *Checklist '76*, as it is commonly called, contains some 1.3 million bibliographic entries for over 2 million publications and represents all the information found in the official 1909 *Checklist,* the *Document Catalog* (1893-1940), and the *Monthly Catalog* (1895-1976), as well as shelflist entries that were never listed in any catalog either because supply of the publication was limited and the issuing agency did not want it advertised or because of security classification.

A spinoff of *Checklist '76* was the useful *Cumulative Title Index to United States Public Documents, 1789-1976*, compiled by Daniel Lester, Marilyn Lester, and Sandra Faull. This sixteen-volume hardcover listing of all titles in the above microfilm set provides, in addition to title, the SuDocs classification, date, and corresponding microfilm reel section wherein the full description can be found in *Checklist '76*. Excluded are those publications that are part of the U.S. Serial Set, as such publications were not classified in the SuDocs system at that time.

Two projects that relate to the 1909 *Checklist* merit notice. A small but utilitarian supplement to the early *Checklist* is Mary Elizabeth Poole's *1909 Checklist, Correlation Index* (Millwood, NY: Kraus-Thomson Organization, Limited, 1976), which provides a quick method for determining the SuDocs number for a departmental edition when the user already knows the serial number of the equivalent congressional document.

The Congressional Information Service is in the process of issuing, in a six-part series, an ambitious project titled *CIS Index to U.S. Executive Branch Documents, 1789-1909*. Based upon the listings in the *Checklist, 1789-1909* (noted above), the CIS version provides a detailed index lacking in the *1909 Checklist* and a separately published microfiche collection of most of the documents listed in the index. Part 1 covers the Departments of Commerce, Labor, and Treasury, and part 2 covers tens of thousands of documents issued by the old War Department; both parts were available for purchase as of 1991.

Parts 3 through 6 are scheduled for publication on an annual basis, and the entire indexing and microfiche collections are projected for release by 1995. Part 3 will include titles issued by the Labor, Interior, and Justice Departments; the Library of Congress; and the independent Interstate Commerce Commission (ICC). Part 4 comprises publications of the Department of Agriculture and the United States Civil Service Commission. Part 5 is devoted to titles and series issued by the Navy Department. Part 6 will cover documents issued by the Department of State, the National Academy of Sciences, the Post Office Department, the Office of the President, the National Home for Disabled Volunteer Soldiers, and the Smithsonian Institution. Access to the microfiche text through the index is by subject and name, SuDocs class number, agency report number, title, and a "Reference Bibliography" by CIS accession number in an arrangement corresponding to the order of the *1909 Checklist.*

Without going into detail, it is important to point out that these other CIS indexes and companion microfiche collections represent a formidable contribution to documents bibliography. The CIS products have become synonymous with quality and in-depth indexing and include the following titles: *CIS US Serial Set Index, CIS US Congressional Committee Hearings Index, CIS US Congressional Committee Prints Index, Index to US Senate Executive Documents and Reports, CIS Index to Unpublished U.S. Senate Committee Hearings, CIS Index to Unpublished U.S. House of Representative Hearings,* and *CIS Index to Presidential Executive Orders and Proclamations.* No discussion of commercially produced catalogs and indexes for locating government publications would be complete without considerable attention to these CIS products. Most of this attention is reserved, however, to appropriate chapters on congressional and presidential materials.

SUMMARY

This chapter offers a selection of guides to federal government materials. Other lists, indexes, and finding aids are discussed in the chapters that follow. Moreover, new products or updated editions of existing sources will appear at a steady rate, for the production of bibliographic services in this field has become a growth industry. Owing to technological advances, bibliographic control has traveled great distances since the heroic but inadequate efforts of individuals such as Poore and Ames. Yet as microform collections and electronic services expand the scope and enhance the quality control of government information, the result seems only to reveal the need for more and better systems. Indeed, the sheer amount of information continually threatens to overwhelm the bibliographic apparatus that seeks to contain it and render it manageable.

NOTES

[1]For a directory of thirty-five depository libraries with online documents catalogs, see *Administrative Notes*, 12 (February 22, 1991): 16-21.

[2]*College and Research Libraries News*, 52 (February 1991): 121.

[3]James Bennett Childs, "Government Publications Documents," in Allen Kent et al. (eds.), *Encyclopedia of Library and Information Science*, vol. 10 (New York: Marcel Dekker, 1973).

[4]This guide was combined with another work by Palic and republished in one volume. See Vladimir M. Palic, *Government Publications: A Guide to Bibliographic Tools Incorporating Government Organization Manuals: A Bibliography* (New York: Pergamon, 1977).

[5]*Government Publications Review*, 17 (1990): 6.

[6]*Government Information Quarterly*, 7 (1990): 1.

[7]Benjamin Perley Poore, *Descriptive Catalogue of the Government Publications of the United States, September 5, 1774-March 4, 1881*, Senate Miscellaneous Document 67, 48th Congress, 2d session, 1885, p. iii.

[8]*Administrative Notes*, 10 (September 29, 1989): 11.

[9]Robert M. Simmons, "Finding That Government Document," *RQ*, 12 (Winter 1971): 167.

[10]Jim Walsh and Mallory Stark, "The *Monthly Catalog of United States Government Publications*: One Title, Many Versions," *Government Information Quarterly*, 7 (1990): 359-70.

[11]The system does not index any alpha characters that follow the first numeric character, nor will it index blank spaces or punctuation.

5

Legislative Branch
Information Sources

INTRODUCTION

The three branches of the federal government were established by the Constitution of the United States, approved September 17, 1787: the legislative branch in Article I, the executive branch in Article II, and the judicial branch in Article III. It is evident that the framers regarded the legislative branch as *primus inter pares*. Article I, Section 1, of that basic instrument bears the statement, "All legislative powers herein granted shall be vested in a Congress of the United States, which shall consist of a Senate and House of Representatives." In historical fact Congress antedates both the presidency and the judicial branch. The 1st Congress made the arrangements for counting the ballots of the first electoral college and for inaugurating George Washington and John Adams as the first executive officers. The office of Attorney General and the Departments of War, Foreign Affairs, and Treasury were established by acts of the 1st Congress. Moreover, this proto-assembly established the judicial system of the United States and enacted bills on tariffs, appropriations, patents and copyrights, the punishment of crimes, uniform militia, succession to the presidency, reduction of the public debt, rates of foreign exchange, naturalization, harbors, the establishment of hospitals, and the progress of the useful arts. The crown jewel in the diadem of the 1st Congress was the submission of the first ten amendments to the Constitution, the Bill of Rights.

The word *congress* was taken from the Articles of Confederation, whereas the words *house of representatives* and *senate* emerged from the Constitutional Convention of 1787. In addition to the committee structure of Congress, from which emanates most of the significant information available to the public, Congress established agencies specifically designed to support congressional operations. These "support" entities include the Congressional Budget Office, Office of Technology Assessment, Congressional Research Service, and the Architect of the Capitol. It also created units that form part of the legislative branch, among them the United States Botanic Garden, Library of Congress (in which the Congressional Research Service resides), Government Printing Office, Copyright Royalty Tribunal, and General Accounting Office. These "support" and "related" agencies are provided with funds to carry out their duties, and these monies are detailed in legislative branch authorization and appropriations measures.

It has been noted that "there are really two Congresses, not just one." These represent (1) the "lawmaking" or "institutional" duties and (2) the "representing," "constituent," or "individual" responsibilities.[1] The "representing" role forms the dialectic between the members of the House and Senate and their constituencies. In general, records pertaining to "constituent" services are not what we define as "government information," save in instances in which members introduce or support legislation designed to aid their constituencies.

This chapter is concerned with the institutional role of the Congress as a lawmaking body. Over the last century the number of introduced bills and joint resolutions has exceeded the number of laws approved in each Congress by a ratio of eight to one or greater. According to the authoritative "Final Edition" of the *Calendars of the United States House of Representatives and History of Legislation* for the 100th Congress, the House and Senate introduced 9,588 bills and joint resolutions. Of these only 1,736 were reported out of committee. Floor action in both chambers and failure to reconcile differing measures in both houses effected a further reduction, so that the end result of the legislative process produced 713 public laws and 48 private laws. Moreover, there were 19 presidential vetoes (11 "pocket vetoes" and 8 regular vetoes), only 3 of which became law by congressional override (pp. 19-64). Out of this process numerous publications are generated. The reader will discover that the multiplicity of textual and bibliographic sources, in various print and nonprint formats both official and commercial, permits access to the information fashioned by the legislative branch of the federal establishment.

THE LEGISLATIVE PROCESS

A knowledge of the process by which a bill becomes a law is a prerequisite to an understanding of the publications generated by that process. Useful guides to both process and content include Walter J. Oleszek's *Congressional Procedures and the Policy Process*, 3d ed. (Washington, DC: Congressional Quarterly Books, 1988); *Guide to Congress*, 4th ed. (Washington, DC: Congressional Quarterly Books, 1991); Robert Goehlert's *Congress and Law-Making: Researching the Legislative Process* (Santa Barbara, CA: Clio Press, 1979); and certain official publications. The best known official issuance is *How Our Laws Are Made*, first published in 1953 and frequently revised and updated, which is issued as a House document. *How Our Laws Are Made* is prepared by the Law Revision Counsel of the House of Representatives pursuant to a House Congressional Resolution. A companion publication, *Enactment of a Law: Procedural Steps in the Legislative Process*, is revised periodically and issued as a Senate document. The latter illustrates the progress of legislation originating in the Senate. The chart "How a Bill Becomes Law" is shown in figure 5.1 (see page 108). Published by Congressional Quarterly, Inc., the chart traces the passage of legislation in both houses of Congress and provides a graphical account of the process from introduction to enactment or veto.

(Text continues on page 109.)

Fig. 5.1. How a bill becomes law

This graphic shows the most typical way in which proposed legislation is enacted into law. There are more complicated, as well as simpler, routes, and most bills fall by the wayside and never become law. The process is illustrated with two hypothetical bills, House bill No. 1 (HR 1) and Senate bill No. 2 (S 2). Each bill must be passed by both houses of Congress in identical form before it can become law. The path of HR 1 is traced by a solid line, that of S 2 by a broken line. However, in practice most legislation begins as similar proposals in both houses.

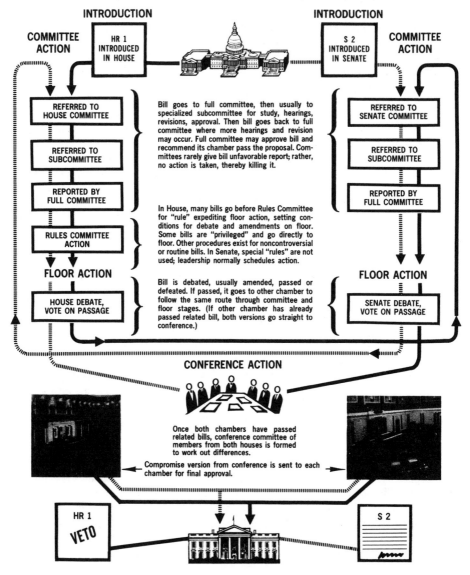

Compromise version approved by both houses is sent to President who can either sign it into law or veto it and return it to Congress. Congress may override veto by a two-thirds majority vote in both houses; bill then becomes law without President's signature.

Reprinted with permission from *Congressional Quarterly*.

Introduction of Legislation

Legislation may originate in many ways. In the twentieth century the "executive communication" has become an abundant source of legislative proposals. Article II, Section 3, of the Constitution obliges the president to report to the Congress from time to time on the state of the Union and to recommend for consideration such measures as he deems necessary and expedient. In addition, legislation may be conceived and drafted by interest groups such as labor unions, chambers of commerce, professional societies like the American Library Association, and even by individuals. Legislative ideas may come from senators and representatives, of course; these initiatives arise from campaign pledges, pressure by constituents, or, after the member has taken office, from experience gained concerning the need for changes to or repeal of existing laws.

Whatever the origin, only a member of Congress can *introduce* legislation. Bills and resolutions are the forms of legislation, and they may be introduced in either chamber. Most bills and resolutions introduced never become law. Those that do not complete the legislative process automatically die at the conclusion of a two-year Congress and must be introduced in a subsequent Congress. Both House and Senate permit multiple sponsorship of a bill. Although multiple sponsorship is indeed allowed by House rules, the names of only twenty-five members are permitted on one bill, and additional identical bill(s) must be introduced to accommodate any remaining sponsors. In the House a bill is introduced by placing it in the "hopper" provided for that purpose at the side of the clerk's desk in the House chamber. It is no longer a custom in the House to read bills, even by title, at the time of introduction. In the more formal Senate procedure, a senator may introduce a bill or resolution by presenting it to the clerks at the desk of the presiding officer without commenting on it from the floor, or the senator may rise and introduce the measure from the floor.

Introduced measures take four principal forms: bills, joint resolutions, concurrent resolutions, and simple resolutions. These may be grouped into two categories. Joint resolutions are considered in a category with bills because they must be passed by both chambers and signed by the president into law or vetoed. Concurrent and simple resolutions must be passed by one or both houses, but they are used either for general housekeeping purposes or to express the "sense" of the Congress and do not require presidential approval.

Bills (H.R.; S.)

The term *bill* is used for most legislative proposals that involve the appropriation of monies. Bills may originate in either chamber, except for measures raising revenue, which, according to Article I, Section 7, of the Constitution, shall originate in the House. It is also customary, but not required, that general appropriations measures originate in the House. Bills are assigned a number in the order in which they are introduced during the two-year congressional term. The number is retained throughout the parliamentary stages with the exception of a "clean bill."[2] "Be it enacted" is the formal beginning phrase in the language of a bill.

Joint Resolutions (H.J.Res.; S.J.Res.)

Joint resolutions are generally used for incidental or subordinate purposes of legislation, but there are exceptions to this practice. Like bills, they are assigned a sequential number upon introduction; "resolved" is used as the opening word. Joint resolutions are traditionally the vehicle for at least two singular kinds of legislative initiatives: proclaiming commemorative days, weeks, or months and introducing constitutional amendments. When the Congress wants to sanction and draw attention to occasions such as Older Americans Month, World Trade Week, or Veterans Day, it passes a joint resolution "authorizing" and "requesting" the president to designate the period of time by issuing a proclamation. The joint resolution actually becomes a public law, and at some time thereafter the president issues the proclamation pursuant to (and citing) the congressional authority. Proclamations are discussed in chapter 6.

Numerous constitutional amendments never get out of committee. Indeed, over 10,000 proposed constitutional amendments have been introduced in the Congress since 1789. The vast majority of these amendments, with little or no chance of passage, are introduced regularly as a matter of political expediency. They are routinely referred to the House or Senate Judiciary Committee, where they expire with little or no fanfare. A cursory glance at constitutional amendments introduced in the past reveals perennial issues: guaranteeing full employment; limiting the tenure of Supreme Court justices; allowing voluntary school prayer; and abolishing the electoral college, bilingual education, or busing. With inexorable consistency at least one member introduces in every Congress a constitutional amendment to repeal the Sixteenth Amendment (federal income tax). This amendment usually carries a number of cosponsors and has undeniable appeal to taxpayers around April 15.

Even serious constitutional amendments face a formidable challenge, as seen in the struggle for passage of the Equal Rights Amendment and the amendment calling for a Constitutional Convention. Constitutional amendments approved by two-thirds of both chambers are sent directly to the Archivist of the United States for submission to the state legislatures for ratification. If three-fourths of the states ratify, the amendment is filed and need not be presented to the president for approval.

Figures 5.2 and 5.3 (see page 112) show a House introduced print and the introduced print of a Senate companion bill, a bill that is similar or identical to a bill introduced in the other chamber. Figure 5.4 (see page 113) shows a constitutional amendment introduced as a House joint resolution.

Billcast, a database available on LEXIS and WESTLAW, contains summary information on public bills introduced in the Congress, excluding bills introduced in the appropriations committees. In addition to bill summaries, the database contains predictions of a bill's chance of surviving each stage of the legislative process. This forecasting is based upon a statistical analysis developed by the Center for Public Choice at George Mason University and boasts a high accuracy rate in predicting the fate of analyzed bills. Billcast is updated weekly with revised odds for existing bills and predictions for newly introduced measures.

(Text continues on page 114.)

Fig. 5.2. House introduced print

101st CONGRESS
1st SESSION

H. R. 1722

To amend the Natural Gas Policy Act of 1978 to eliminate wellhead price controls on the first sale of natural gas, and to make technical and conforming amendments to such Act.

IN THE HOUSE OF REPRESENTATIVES

APRIL 6, 1989

Mr. SHARP (for himself, Mr. MOORHEAD, Mr. TAUZIN, Mr. DANNEMEYER, Mr. LELAND, Mr. FIELDS, Mr. SYNAR, Mr. OXLEY, Mr. RICHARDSON, Mr. NIELSON of Utah, Mr. BRYANT, Mr. BILIRAKIS, Mr. HALL of Texas, Mr. BARTON of Texas, Mr. WALGREN, Mr. CALLAHAN, Mr. SWIFT, Mr. BATES, Mr. COOPER, Mr. BRUCE, Mr. THOMAS A. LUKEN, Mr. WHITTAKER, Mr. SLATTERY, Mr. BLILEY, Mr. WYDEN, Mr. SCHAEFER, Mr. MCMILLAN of North Carolina, Mr. WAXMAN, Mr. LENT, and Mr. DINGELL) introduced the following bill; which was referred to the Committee on Energy and Commerce

A BILL

To amend the Natural Gas Policy Act of 1978 to eliminate wellhead price controls on the first sale of natural gas, and to make technical and conforming amendments to such Act.

1   *Be it enacted by the Senate and House of Representa-*

2   *tives of the United States of America in Congress assembled,*

3   **SECTION 1. SHORT TITLE.**

4   This Act may be cited as the "Natural Gas Decontrol

5   Act of 1989".

*   *   *   *   *   *   *

(Sample copy of first page and end of last page of this 3-page introduced bill)

*   *   *   *   *   *   *

21   (b) PERMANENT ELIMINATION OF WELLHEAD PRICE

22   CONTROLS.—Title I of the Natural Gas Act of 1978 (15

23   U.S.C. 3311–3333) is repealed, effective on January 1,

24   1993.

Fig. 5.3. Senate introduced print

101ST CONGRESS
1ST SESSION

S. 783

To amend the Natural Gas Policy Act of 1978 to eliminate wellhead price and nonprice controls on the first sale of natural gas, and to make technical and conforming amendments to such Act.

IN THE SENATE OF THE UNITED STATES

APRIL 13 (legislative day, JANUARY 3), 1989

Mr. JOHNSTON (for himself, Mr. McCLURE, Mr. NICKLES, Mr. FORD, Mr. BINGAMAN, Mr. WALLOP, Mr. BREAUX, Mr. WIRTH, Mr. BOREN, Mr. SIMPSON, Mr. GARN, Mr. COATS, and Mr. GRAMM) introduced the following bill; which was read twice and referred to the Committee on Energy and Natural Resources.

A BILL

To amend the Natural Gas Policy Act of 1978 to eliminate wellhead price and nonprice controls on the first sale of natural gas, and to make technical and conforming amendments to such Act.

1   *Be it enacted by the Senate and House of Representa-*

2 *tives of the United States of America in Congress assembled,*

3   SECTION 1. SHORT TITLE.

4   This Act may be referred to as the "Natural Gas Well-

5 head Decontrol Act of 1989".

Fig. 5.4. House joint resolution

97TH CONGRESS
1ST SESSION

H. J. RES. 16

Proposing an amendment to the Constitution of the United States relative to freedom from forced assignment to schools or jobs because of race, creed, or color.

IN THE HOUSE OF REPRESENTATIVES

JANUARY 5, 1981

Mr. ASHBROOK introduced the following joint resolution; which was referred to the Committee on the Judiciary

---

JOINT RESOLUTION

Proposing an amendment to the Constitution of the United States relative to freedom from forced assignment to schools or jobs because of race, creed, or color.

1 *Resolved by the Senate and House of Representatives of*

2 *the United States of America in Congress assembled (two-*

3 *thirds of each House concurring therein),* That the following

4 article is proposed as an amendment to the Constitution of

5 the United States, which shall be valid to all intents and

6 purposes as part of the Constitution when ratified by the leg-

7 islatures of three-fourths of the several States:

Washington Alert, an online service provided by Congressional Quarterly, Inc., offers customized bill service for measures relevant to a subscriber's interests and needs. An exclusive feature of this service is SmartRank, which places the "most relevant" bills in order of importance. If desired, the subscriber may ask Washington Alert for all *CQ Weekly Report* articles on the issue, and again SmartRank offers a listing accompanying the text of the bills and articles in order of relevance.

LEGI-SLATE (Legi-Slate, Inc., Washington, DC) is an outstanding online service and, unfortunately, a very expensive one. Among its many features are bill status, digests, and full-text capabilities. Bill tracking can be accomplished daily. Digests prepared by the Congressional Research Service of the Library of Congress are provided online, and all parliamentary versions of all bills introduced since the beginning of the 99th Congress (1985) are online where one can retrieve the full text of the measure, an outline, or any portion of a bill that mentions a specific word or phrase.[3] LEXIS, too, has the full text of introduced measures.

Concurrent Resolutions
(H.Con.Res.; S.Con.Res.)

The term *concurrent* does not necessarily signify simultaneous introduction and consideration in both chambers. Concurrent resolutions are not normally legislative in character and do not require the president's signature. They may be introduced in either chamber, are numbered sequentially, and are used to express an opinion, purpose, fact, principle, or "sense" of the Congress. Figure 5.5 shows a typical House concurrent resolution.

Resolutions (H.Res.; S.Res.)

Known as "simple" resolutions, these govern the action of the body in which they originate and are for the concern only of the chamber passing them. They are used to initiate administrative or housekeeping procedures, such as adoption of rules, assignment of committee members, and the like. The House initiates a greater number of simple resolutions than the Senate, because the House Committee on Rules uses this form to issue "special orders," which regulate the flow of reported bills onto the floor and prescribe rules governing the number and type of amendments allowed and the time allotted for debate on the measures. They require no presidential signature and, like the forms above, are numbered in sequence throughout the two-year term of a Congress. Figure 5.6 (see page 116) is an example of a House resolution.

(Text continues on page 116.)

Fig. 5.5. House concurrent resolution

House Concurrent Resolution

97TH CONGRESS
1ST SESSION

H. CON. RES. 131

To express the sorrow of the Congress upon the death of former world heavyweight boxing champion Joe Louis.

IN THE HOUSE OF REPRESENTATIVES

MAY 12, 1981

Mr. SAVAGE submitted the following concurrent resolution; which was referred to the Committee on Post Office and Civil Service

---

CONCURRENT RESOLUTION

To express the sorrow of the Congress upon the death of former world heavyweight boxing champion Joe Louis.

Whereas Joe Louis, who was born the son of a black sharecropper, overcame the barriers of racial bigotry to become the longest reigning world heavyweight boxing champion in history;

Whereas Joe Louis was a man of exceptional talent, pride, and determination, both inside and outside of the boxing ring;

Whereas the life and career of Joe Louis continue to serve as inspirations for people of all races throughout the world and as models of courage and achievement for all Americans; and

Fig. 5.6. House resolution

House Resolution

97TH CONGRESS
1ST SESSION

H. RES. 16

To reaffirm the use of our national motto on currency.

IN THE HOUSE OF REPRESENTATIVES

JANUARY 5, 1981

Mr. GUYER submitted the following resolution; which was referred to the Committee on Banking, Finance and Urban Affairs

---

RESOLUTION

To reaffirm the use of our national motto on currency.

1   *Resolved,* That it is the sense of the House that the

2   national motto, "In God We Trust", shall be reaffirmed and

3   shall continue to be engraved and printed on our currency.

Printings of a Bill

The first printing is known as the introduced print, but when legislation is reported from committee there is a reported print (see figure 5.7) bearing a calendar number and report number. "Engrossed bills" are printed on blue paper. When passed by one chamber and sent to the other body, the bill becomes known as a referred (Act) print (see figures 5.8, page 118, and 5.9, page 119). When reported out of a Senate committee, the bill is called a Senate reported print and carries a calendar and report number for that chamber (see figure 5.10, page 120). A bill that contains an error is designated a "star print"; the corrected bill has a small star in its lower left-hand corner. A detailed description of these parliamentary stages, with illustrations, is found in the current edition of *How Our Laws Are Made* and in a number of commercial publications.

(Text continues on page 121.)

Fig. 5.7. Reported print

Union Calendar No. 17

101st CONGRESS
1st SESSION

H. R. 1722

[Report No. 101–29]

To amend the Natural Gas Policy Act of 1978 to eliminate wellhead price controls on the first sale of natural gas, and to make technical and conforming amendments to such Act.

IN THE HOUSE OF REPRESENTATIVES

APRIL 6, 1989

Mr. SHARP (for himself, Mr. MOORHEAD, Mr. TAUZIN, Mr. DANNEMEYER, Mr. LELAND, Mr. FIELDS, Mr. SYNAR, Mr. OXLEY, Mr. RICHARDSON, Mr. NIELSON of Utah, Mr. BRYANT, Mr. BILIRAKIS, Mr. HALL of Texas, Mr. BARTON of Texas, Mr. WALGREN, Mr. CALLAHAN, Mr. SWIFT, Mr. BATES, Mr. COOPER, Mr. BRUCE, Mr. THOMAS A. LUKEN, Mr. WHITTAKER, Mr. SLATTERY, Mr. BLILEY, Mr. WYDEN, Mr. SCHAEFER, Mr. McMILLAN of North Carolina, Mr. WAXMAN, Mr. LENT, and Mr. DINGELL) introduced the following bill; which was referred to the Committee on Energy and Commerce

APRIL 17, 1989

Additional sponsors: Mr. ARCHER, Mr. BARTLETT, Mr. SMITH of Texas, Mr. COMBEST, Mr. DeLAY, and Mr. ARMEY

APRIL 17, 1989

Committed to the Committee of the Whole House on the State of the Union and ordered to be printed

A BILL

To amend the Natural Gas Policy Act of 1978 to eliminate wellhead price controls on the first sale of natural gas, and to make technical and conforming amendments to such Act.

1   *Be it enacted by the Senate and House of Representa-*

2 *tives of the United States of America in Congress assembled,*

*   *   *   *   *   *   *

(Sample copy of beginning and end of this 4-page reported bill)

*   *   *   *   *   *   *

6   (b) PERMANENT ELIMINATION OF WELLHEAD PRICE

7 CONTROLS.—Title I of the Natural Gas Act of 1978 (15

8 U.S.C. 3311–3333) is repealed, effective on January 1,

9 1993.

Fig. 5.8. Engrossed bill

101ST CONGRESS
1ST SESSION

H. R. 1722

AN ACT

To amend the Natural Gas Policy Act of 1978 to eliminate wellhead price and nonprice controls on the first sale of natural gas, and to make technical and conforming amendments to such Act.

1   *Be it enacted by the Senate and House of Representa-*

2 *tives of the United States of America in Congress assembled,*

3 **SECTION 1. SHORT TITLE.**

4   This Act may be cited as the "Natural Gas Wellhead

5 Decontrol Act of 1989".

*   *   *   *   *   *   *

(Sample copy of part of first page and last page of this 8-page bill)

*   *   *   *   *   *   *

1   (A) by striking "AUTHORITY TO PRESCRIBE

2   LOWER" and inserting in lieu thereof "AUTHOR-

3   ITY TO PRESCRIBE"; and

4   (B) by striking "which does not exceed the

5   applicable maximum lawful price, if any, under

6   title I of this Act".

Passed the House of Representatives April 17, 1989.

Attest: DONNALD K. ANDERSON,

Clerk.

Fig. 5.9. Referred (Act) print

101ST CONGRESS
1ST SESSION

H.R. 1722

IN THE SENATE OF THE UNITED STATES

APRIL 18 (legislative day, JANUARY 3), 1989

Received; read twice and referred to the Committee on Energy and Natural Resources

AN ACT

To amend the Natural Gas Policy Act of 1978 to eliminate wellhead price and nonprice controls on the first sale of natural gas, and to make technical and conforming amendments to such Act.

1   *Be it enacted by the Senate and House of Representa-*

2   *tives of the United States of America in Congress assembled,*

3   SECTION 1. SHORT TITLE.

4   This Act may be cited as the "Natural Gas Wellhead

5   Decontrol Act of 1989".

*   *   *   *   *   *   *

(Sample copy of part of first page and last page of this 8-page bill)

*   *   *   *   *   *   *

1   (A) by striking "AUTHORITY TO PRESCRIBE

2   LOWER" and inserting in lieu thereof "AUTHOR-

3   ITY TO PRESCRIBE"; and

4   (B) by striking "which does not exceed the

5   applicable maximum lawful price, if any, under

6   title I of this Act".

Passed the House of Representatives April 17, 1989.

Attest: DONNALD K. ANDERSON,

Clerk.

Fig. 5.10. Senate reported print

Calendar No. 77

101st CONGRESS
1st Session
H.R. 1722

[Report No. 101–39]

IN THE SENATE OF THE UNITED STATES

APRIL 18 (legislative day, JANUARY 3), 1989
Received; read twice and referred to the Committee on Energy and Natural Resources

MAY 31 (legislative day, JANUARY 3), 1989
Reported by Mr. JOHNSTON, with amendments
[Omit the part struck through and insert the part printed in italic]

AN ACT

To amend the Natural Gas Policy Act of 1978 to eliminate wellhead price and nonprice controls on the first sale of natural gas, and to make technical and conforming amendments to such Act.

1   *Be it enacted by the Senate and House of Representa-*

2   *tives of the United States of America in Congress assembled,*

3   **SECTION 1. SHORT TITLE.**

4   This Act may be cited as the "Natural Gas Wellhead

5   Decontrol Act of 1989".

*   *   *   *   *   *   *

(Sample copy of first page and end of last page of this 8-page bill)

*   *   *   *   *   *   *

5   (A) by striking "AUTHORITY TO PRESCRIBE

6   LOWER" and inserting in lieu thereof "AUTHOR-

7   ITY TO PRESCRIBE"; and

8   (B) by striking "which does not exceed the

9   applicable maximum lawful price, if any, under

10   title I of this Act".

Passed the House of Representatives April 17, 1989.

Attest: DONNALD K. ANDERSON,

Clerk.

Depository Distribution

Before 1979, bills, resolutions, and amendments were sent to depository libraries in paper copy. Beginning with the 96th Congress, a microfiche-only distribution policy was promulgated. Bills are filmed chronologically as issued instead of from a merged file at the end of the Congress. Thus, different versions of the same bill or resolution and its amendments are scattered over a number of fiche (some complex and/or controversial bills have hundreds of amendments). A *Microfiche Users Guide* (sometimes called the *Bill Finding Aid*) is provided in paper copy to facilitate retrieval. There is a time lag between filming the fiche from the printed version, production, and distribution.

Beginning with the bills and resolutions of the 101st Congress, 2d Session, the Library Programs Service (LPS) discontinued the sequential numbering of the microfiche on which these publications are distributed. Because sequential numbering required that second session bills be held until the last number for the first session had been located, there was an inevitable delay in filming and distributing. Complaints by a number of librarians resulted in a policy change that was not so much an improvement as the lesser of two evils. Under the old system the requirements of compiling the *Cumulative Finding Aid for Congressional Bills and Resolutions* included locating amendments and motions in their various parliamentary stages that proved to be "fugitive" from the first session, and this search delayed the issuing of fiche for the second session. Librarians suggested starting the numbering system anew with number 1 for second session bills and resolutions, a process wholly inconsistent with all the bibliographic sources in which the bill's "real" number is shown. Although this spurious numbering managed to reduce the delay in filming and distributing bill shipments, LPS agreed with disaffected librarians that timely issuance transcended bibliographic inaccuracy. The 1979 policy of offering these seminal documents to depository libraries on microfiche only typifies the government's myopic interest in saving minuscule amounts of money at the expense of accurate access to government information. Many younger documents librarians will never realize that bills with all their amendments shipped in paper copy did not occupy that much file-cabinet space in the first place.

Advantages of the microfiche-only procedure include economies for the government in the lower cost of production and mailing and the putative saving of storage space and staff time in filing for libraries. Private bills, public bills, resolutions, and amendments are listed in *Price List 36* and sold by subscription per session of Congress. In 1991 the subscription price for public bills was almost $5,000 per session.[4]

The Superintendent of Documents (SuDocs) class notation for House and Senate bills, resolutions, and amendments is as follows:

Y 1.4/1:(Cong.-no.)	Senate Bills
Y 1.4/2:(Cong.-no.)	Senate Resolutions
Y 1.4/3:(Cong.-no.)	Senate Joint Resolutions
Y 1.4/4:(Cong.-no.)	Senate Concurrent Resolutions
Y 1.4/5:(Cong.-no.)	Senate Printed Amendments
Y 1.4/6:(Cong.-no.)	House Bills
Y 1.4/7:(Cong.-no.)	House Resolutions
Y 1.4/8:(Cong.-no.)	House Joint Resolutions
Y 1.4/9:(Cong.-no.)	House Concurrent Resolutions

All of these measures may be received by subscribing to Depository Item Number 1006-A.

Commercial Products and Services

As noted, LEGI-SLATE offers bibliographic and textual service for bills and resolutions. The Electronic Legislative Search System (ELSS) of Commerce Clearing House (CCH) furnishes online descriptions of bills and resolutions and full-text distribution. WESTLAW and LEXIS carry the Billcast system (mentioned above), and LEGISLEX (Legislex Associates, Columbus, Indiana) contains federal bill and resolution information online. The LEGIS (Legislative Information and Status System) in-house system used by Congress permits bill tracking and printed status reports on measures. LEGIS is capable of computerized retrieval of over 250 possible steps identified in the legislative process.

CIS/Congressional Bills, Resolutions & Laws on Microfiche offers the most complete full-text collection of these forms. Because CIS waits until the end of a Congress, the bills in their parliamentary stages, including amendments, are arranged by number behind the introduced print, thus avoiding the scattering effect of the GPO's microfiche edition. Both a current and a retrospective project, *CIS/Congressional Bills* as of 1991 provided sets from the 74th (1935-1936) through the 101st (1989-1990) Congresses.

Committee Action

After introduction, a bill is referred to the appropriate committee of the House or Senate. Both chambers practice multiple referral of complex legislation to two or more committees. There are three categories of multiple referral: "[J]oint referral of a bill concurrently to two or more committees; sequential referral of a bill successively to one committee, then a second, and so on; and split referral of parts of a bill to several committees for consideration of each part."[5] Within a committee, the bill is normally referred directly to a subcommittee. Internal committee reforms of the 1970s and 1980s increased the power of the subcommittees and reduced that of the committee chairperson, who may no longer "pocket," or kill, a bill by refusing to act on it promptly. Of course, many bills die in subcommittee, a phenomenon discussed later in this chapter.

Hearings

If a bill warrants consideration, the subcommittee will usually schedule public hearings. However, a subcommittee may choose not to hold hearings if that body held extensive hearings on similar legislation in a previous Congress and the measure failed to complete the legislative cycle. After hearings are held, the subcommittee engages in the "marking-up" process, a section by section analysis of the measure, at which stage major or minor revisions may be effected. If the bill is extensively revised, it will be rewritten and reintroduced as a "clean bill" with a new bill number (see note 2).

Although hearings pursuant to legislation are perhaps the most familiar category, they are held by committees and subcommittees for other purposes. Hearings may be exploratory, providing testimony and data about general topics. Evaluative hearings provide information about the economy and efficiency of program operations. Appropriations hearings provide testimony and information about department or agency operations, oversight activities, and comparative fiscal information. Investigatory hearings explore the need for legislation, inform public opinion, or uncover scandal.

Televised Hearings

The first reported instance of a televised congressional hearing "occurred in 1948 when the Senate Armed Services Committee allowed coverage of its March 30 and April 2 hearings on universal military training." In that same year, the House Committee on Un-American Activities (HUAC) "allowed telecasting of its hearings regarding claims of communist infiltration of the U.S. Government." Popularly known as the Hiss-Chamber hearings, the televised portion "of these hearings lasted for twenty-one days, running from late July through early September 1948."[6] From the Kefauver Committee hearings on organized crime to the Watergate hearings, this kind of congressional committee activity represents a powerful and visible forum.

Commercial Sources

Congressional Information Service has provided us with the definitive bibliographic and full-text record for hearings. *CIS/Index* indexes and abstracts hearings and provides a microfiche edition from 1970 to date. *CIS US Congressional Committee Hearings Index* and its microfiche text cover published titles from 1833 through 1969. Two separate series, *CIS Index to Unpublished U.S. Senate Committee Hearings* and *CIS Index to Unpublished U.S. House of Representative Committee Hearings*, with companion microfiche, are major retrospective sources. Senate coverage extends from 1823 through 1964 and House coverage dates from 1833 through 1946. The finding aids and other editorial enhancements for these sets reflect the meticulous care that has come to be associated with the company's many products and services.

Numbered Hearings

In recent years the Senate has adopted a policy of serially numbering hearings chronologically and in sequential order within a Congress, irrespective of committee. For example, Senate hearing (S.Hrg.) 100-439 is an Appropriations Committee hearing, and S.Hrg. 100-500 is an Indian Affairs Committee hearing. Senate hearings in parts retain the same basic number. By contrast the House has no standard policy on numbering hearings; some committees assign a number whereas others do not. The Superintendent of Documents assigns a Y 4 class notation to hearings.

Electronic Products

LEGI-SLATE provides all committee and subcommittee hearings schedules and witness lists — sometimes months in advance — and updates the schedules and lists daily. Schedules can be retrieved by date, committee, or subject and by the legislation on the agenda for a hearing or a mark-up session.

Congressional Information Service's *Congressional Masterfile 1* includes on CD-ROM a number of its retrospective indexes, including the *Committee Hearings Index* itself and the unpublished House and Senate hearings set. The *CIS Index to Unpublished U.S. Senate Committee Hearings, 1965-1968*, was made available as an upgrade to *Congressional Masterfile 1* in 1990.

Committee Prints

Committee prints are publications prepared for the use and reference of committees and their staffs. They are frequently composed by the Congressional Research Service of the Library of Congress; they may also be researched and written by independent consultants or by the committee staffs. They consist of a number of diverse materials, from legislative histories to bibliographies. Studies on topics of public concern, investigative reports, confidential staff reports and memoranda, analyses of similar bills on a subject, and excerpts from hearings constitute some of the information that may be contained in committee prints.

Although more committee prints have been made available to depository institutions in recent years, the series is not automatically distributed. Under the "administrative or operational" exemption provision of Title 44, *United States Code*, section 1902, a committee chairperson is not obliged to authorize all committee prints for distribution or sale. The Documents Expediting Project (DocEx) has been able to obtain a number of prints and send them to its subscribers. In addition, *CIS/Index* indexes and abstracts committee prints and makes them available on microfiche. In yet another retrospective collection, *CIS US Congressional Committee Prints Index* and its full-text microfiche and CD-ROM services cover the period from 1830 (when the first known print was issued) through 1969.

Senate committee prints (S.prt.) are issued in a separate series and numbered in the same way as Senate hearings. The House has no standard system of numbering prints. Some committees of the House number their prints, with the Congress number as a prefix followed serially by letters. Prints, like hearings, are classed in Y 4 by SuDocs.

Committee Reports

Committee reports on public bills are significant documents generated in the legislative process. They describe the purpose and scope of a bill and the reasons for approval of the measure. Few bills are reported unfavorably. In some instances, a committee may report a measure "without recommendation," which has the chilling effect of an unfavorable report. When a committee declines to report a bill, that measure is effectively killed. Most bills do not survive committee scrutiny, and this winnowing process has been a function of committees for generations. Woodrow Wilson in 1885 commented upon this role of committees when he wrote, "As a rule, a bill committed [referred to committee] is a bill doomed. When it goes from the Clerk's desk to a committee room, it crosses a parliamentary bridge of sighs to dim dungeons of silence whence it will never return."[7]

House and Senate reports are assigned a report number and include that indispensable piece of bibliographic information, the bill or resolution number. Issued initially in slip (pamphlet) form, they are later gathered into the bound volumes of the Congressional Serial Set. Figure 5.11 (see page 126) shows an example of a House committee report, and figure 5.12 (see page 127) shows an example of a Senate committee report.

Reports are indexed and abstracted in *CIS/Index* from 1970 to date. The *CIS US Serial Set Index, 1789-1969*, includes reports on both public and private legislation as well as other materials that constitute the historical serial set. This retrospective definitive index is accompanied by the full-text CIS microfiche companion series. The *United States Code Congressional and Administrative News* (U.S.C.C.A.N.), published by the West Publishing Company, expanded its coverage beginning with the 99th Congress (1985-1986) to include the text of both House and Senate reports along with the text of each statute. It also includes any statement the president makes upon signing a law (see chapter 6).

LEGI-SLATE offers the full text of committee reports online shortly after they are printed by GPO. Information in U.S.C.C.A.N. is found in WESTLAW's U.S. Code Legislative History (LH). The *CIS US Serial Set Index* is one of the databases available on its CD-ROM *Congressional Masterfile 1*.

Floor Action

After a bill is reported, it is placed on a calendar and may be called to the floor of the originating chamber for consideration. The scheduling of bills for floor debate is controlled by the policy committee of the majority party. Action on pro forma legislation is typically characterized by no debate and passage by unrecorded voice vote. Because of its larger membership, House procedures on floor action are more formal than those of the Senate. Amendments are usually permitted on the floor of both houses. They consist of the parliamentary motions to insert, strike out and insert, strike out, and substitute. A strategy not infrequently practiced in Congress is the introduction on the floor of a "rider," a provision not germane to the subject matter of the bill. As noted, for controversial or complex legislation hundreds of amendments may be introduced as motions.

(Text continues on page 128.)

Fig. 5.11. House committee report

| 101st Congress
1st Session | HOUSE OF REPRESENTATIVES | Report
101-29 |

NATURAL GAS DECONTROL ACT OF 1989

April 17, 1989.—Committed to the Committee of the Whole House on the State of the Union and ordered to be printed

Mr. Dingell, from the Committee on Energy and Commerce, submitted the following

REPORT

together with

DISSENTING VIEWS

[To accompany H.R. 1722]

[Including cost estimate of the Congressional Budget Office]

The Committee on Energy and Commerce, to whom was referred the bill (H.R. 1722) to amend the Natural Gas Policy Act of 1978 to eliminate wellhead price controls on the first sale of natural gas, and to make technical and conforming amendments to such Act, having considered the same, report favorably thereon without amendment and recommend that the bill do pass.

CONTENTS

Fig. 5.12. Senate committee report

Calendar No. 77

| 101st Congress | | SENATE | | Report |
| 1st Session | | | | 101-39 |

NATURAL GAS WELLHEAD DECONTROL ACT OF 1989

MAY 31 (legislative day, JANUARY 3), 1989.—Ordered to be printed

---

Mr. JOHNSTON, from the Committee on Energy and Natural Resources, submitted the following

REPORT

together with

MINORITY VIEWS

[To accompany H.R. 1722]

The Committee on Energy and Natural Resources, to which was referred the Act (H.R. 1722) to amend the Natural Gas Policy Act of 1978 to eliminate wellhead price and nonprice controls on the first sale of natural gas, and to make technical and conforming amendments to such Act, having considered the same, reports favorably thereon with amendments and recommends that the Act, as amended, do pass.

The amendments are as follows:

1. On page 2, line 6, strike "(2), (3), and (4)," and insert "(2), and (3),".

2. On page 3, strike lines 10 through 15.

PURPOSE OF THE MEASURE

The purpose of H.R. 1722 is to promote competition for natural gas at the wellhead in order to ensure consumers an adequate and reliable supply of natural gas at the lowest reasonable price. H.R. 1722 does so by amending the Natural Gas Policy Act of 1978 (NGPA) to repeal on January 1, 1993, all remaining price and nonprice controls on the first sale (generally, the wellhead or producing field sale) of natural gas.

In certain circumstances, H.R. 1722 also decontrols first sale transactions earlier than January 1, 1993. The bill would decontrol

These are serially numbered for each chamber during a Congress, are usually printed, and, if introduced at least one day before debate, are published in the *Congressional Record* (CR). This renowned (and often disparaged) publication is the principal vehicle in which consideration (debate) and passage of legislation are recorded.

Congressional Record

In the beginnings of the republic there was little interest in transcribing the deliberations of the members of the Congress. Thomas Lloyd of New York recorded many of the debates in the 1st Congress in shorthand and published them in a commercial edition called *The Congressional Register*. Indeed, from 1789 to 1873 there was no official record of debates, and commercial ventures were haphazard and often biased. Their "accuracy and comprehensiveness" were "limited by such factors as the column space available in newspapers, the political leanings of the editors and reporters, the ability of a reporter to actually hear the debates when his assigned seat may have been far from the speakers, and the inadequacy of existing longhand and shorthand methods for recording the debates." That the textual record is so abysmal is not surprising. No precedent existed; the "English Parliament did not report its debates, though the House of Lords and House of Commons did keep journals of their proceedings, as did colonial American assemblies."[8] It should be noted that the only reference to a government publication in the Constitution is found in Article I, Section 5, Clause 3, which states that "Each House shall keep a Journal of its Proceedings, and from time to time publish the same." Accordingly, the *proceedings* (not the transcription of debates) are recorded in the *House Journal* (XJH) and in the *Senate Journal* (XJS), which are issued annually. *CIS US Congressional Journals* on microfiche spans the years 1789 to 1978.

For the proceedings *and* debates, the first formal, sustained effort was the *Annals of Congress* (1789-1824). Compiled by Joseph Gales and William Seaton "over a period of 22 years, from 1834-1856," this retrospective effort relied upon "old press accounts and other published sources ... and only included summaries of House and Senate activities and debates deemed most important by its compilers." Neither chamber was fully covered, the Senate less so. In fact, it was not until 1802 that the Senate "voted to admit reporters to the floor."[9]

The *Register of Debates* (1824-1837) "was contemporaneously published and so actually was printed before the *Annals* ... appeared in print." Like the *Annals*, the *Register* was not a "verbatim account but rather a compilation of summaries of the debates.... Since the speeches were not recorded verbatim, Members of Congress were welcomed by Gales and Seaton to revise their speeches before they were printed."[10] This practice continues to this day, and although substantive alterations are prohibited by House and Senate rules, the potential for mischief is established by law. Title 44, *United States Code*, section 901, states that the *Congressional Record* "shall be substantially a verbatim report of proceedings." Eliminate the qualifying adverb and the statutory authority for an untarnished *Record* would at least be codified.

The *Congressional Globe* competed with the *Register* from 1833 to 1837 and continued "after the *Register*'s demise until the birth" of the present *Congressional Record* on March 5, 1873. By the mid-nineteenth century the *Globe* succeeded in becoming a "more verbatim account of Congressional debates" owing to "improvements in shorthand" and a "new Congressional willingness to pay the salaries of the [official floor] reporters and to purchase copies of the reports."[11]

The *Congressional Record* Today

The daily *Congressional Record* (X/a) is available for sale by the Superintendent of Documents and to depository libraries in either hard copy or microfiche. The quotidian *Record* has four sections: the proceedings of the House and Senate, arrangement of which may alternate with issues; the Extensions of Remarks; and the Daily Digest. Each section is paged continuously and separately during a session, and each page in each section has a letter prefix as follows: S (Senate), H (House), E (Extensions of Remarks), and D (Daily Digest).

A permanent bound edition of the *Record* (X:) is available to depository libraries in hard copy or on microfiche. This edition is suffering a time lag of some years. Due to revision and rearrangement, the pagination of the final bound edition differs from that of the daily CR. The permanent edition eliminates the H, S, and E prefix designations and is numbered consecutively. CIS films the bound edition and makes it available for purchase. The company also filmed, as separate collections, all the predecessors of the current CR, which are sold individually or as a complete set. Readex too sells the full text of the CR on microfiche.

Congressional Privileges

Members of Congress used to be permitted to insert "speeches" into the *Record* that were not actually delivered on the floor in such a manner that the reader had no way of determining that the member was absent. On March 1, 1978, the Joint Committee on Printing (JCP) regulations were amended to identify statements or insertions in the *Record* where no part of them was spoken. The ruling was severely qualified as follows:

(a) When, upon unanimous consent or by motion, a prepared statement is ordered to be printed in the Record and no part of it is spoken, the entire statement will be "bulleted."

(b) If a Member verbally delivers the first portion of the statement (such as the first sentence or paragraph), then the entire statement will appear without the "bullet" symbol.

(c) Extemporaneous speeches supplemented by prepared statements will not be "bulleted."[12]

The bullet device is, of course, no stranger to librarians. It is the symbol used to signify a depository title in a *Monthly Catalog* entry and a basic loose-leaf manual in a subscription service announced in *Price List 36*. Paragraph (b) of the JCP amendments so vitiated the intent to bring integrity to the *Record* that the news media, as well as a number of senators and representatives, ridiculed the qualified amendment as constituting "not a wholehearted embrace of truth and accuracy, but more a flirtation."[13] In fact, members of Congress brought action in the United States District Court, District of Columbia, for declaratory and injunctive relief against then acting Public Printer William J. Barrett et al., asking the court to order the GPO, the official reporters, and the JCP to "stop printing a corrupt *Congressional Record*." The district court dismissed the suit, whereupon plaintiffs Gregg et al. appealed. The United States Court of Appeals, District of Columbia Circuit, upheld the lower court's decision. Although the lower court and the appeals court arrived at their findings "on different but related grounds," in effect both tribunals told the Congress to clean up its own act. The concluding paragraph of the court of appeals' opinion is a paradigm of discretion: "Notwithstanding the deference and esteem that is properly tendered to individual congressional actors, our deference and esteem for the institution [Congress] as a whole and for the constitutional command that the institution be allowed to manage its own affairs precludes us from even attempting a diagnosis of the problem."[14] Political questions are not properly subject to judicial determination, and the federal courts have amassed a large body of precedent with respect to squabbles in a coequal branch of government for which a clear remedy can be found within that branch.

The "bullet" rule existed for several years in the House, but disaffection with the application of its provisions mounted. Members complained that too many instances occurred wherein the "bullet" symbol did not set off a Member's remarks which did not appear to have been spoken on the floor of the House, while in the same colloquy, another Member's remarks had the "bullet" symbol correctly preceding and following non-spoken remarks. Heated debate resulted in House Resolution 230 (July 23, 1985), in which nonspeeches in their entirety were required to be printed in bold type, providing a clear and dramatic visual contrast to the paler serif typeface used for speeches delivered in person and for other proceedings. The typeface distinction became effective September 1, 1985, on a trial basis for the remainder of the 99th Congress, 1st Session. It proved not to be a success. With the start of the 99th Congress, 2d Session, a less prominent typeface known as Helvetica was employed to indicate nonspeeches, making a far weaker visual impact than had the earlier boldface.[15] It may have been that the substitution of the bullet symbol for bold type led readers to believe that the darker format actually indicated speeches, thus giving the opposite impression desired by the reformers. Moreover, GPO printers said that "frequent production problems resulted from the heavier ink required for the boldface segments."[16] Throughout all of this foolishness the Senate continued to use the bullet symbol to set off "unspoken" speeches. Episodes like this, although little publicized and quickly forgotten, hardly inspire faith in the House of Representatives as an institution.

Meanwhile, the members of Congress continue to pursue the traditional perquisites of revising and editing their remarks. Studies have shown that the editing privilege is not abused; the great majority of revisions concern syntactical or related infelicities and are within the bounds of propriety. However, one study concluded that "until Congress takes action to either prohibit the practices of revision and insertion, or clearly identify them when and where they occur, the *Record* will continue to be a less desirable source of speech texts than it might otherwise be."[17] But that assessment was made before television found its way into the chambers of the House and Senate.

Televising the Debates

In 1989 Cable-Satellite Public Affairs Network (C-SPAN) celebrated its tenth anniversary. On March 19, 1979, representative Albert Gore (D-TN) read a brief one-minute speech welcoming TV cameras into the House of Representatives, and with that short introduction the marriage of television and open debate was consummated. On June 2, 1986, Senate majority leader Robert Dole (R-KS) said in the glare of the Senate's TV cameras, "I think that today we catch up with the 20th century." It had taken the Senate over seven years to catch up with the House. Both chambers expressed strong opposition to the televising of floor proceedings. They would not allow the major networks to do the job; rather, they purchased their own equipment, at considerable cost to taxpayers, and they exercise control over where the camera roams. C-SPAN, a nonprofit cooperative of the cable television industry, was created in 1977 to provide public affairs programming from the nation's capital to a national cable TV audience. The network's debut in 1979 coincided with the inauguration of live telecasts from the House floor. On April 3, 1979, the House officially began televised proceedings, and C-SPAN became the carrier.

C-SPAN II covers Senate floor action on a different cable TV channel. Both channels have gone beyond the basic coverage of House and Senate proceedings and debates to include public policy conferences, viewer call-in programs, bar association meetings, addresses by government officials and private sector poobahs, a roundup of "events of the day," roundtable discussion by journalists, National Press Club luncheon addresses, high school students discussing "current issues," foundation teleconferences where groups such as the League of Women Voters respond to questions about reforming election laws, political party conventions, and so on. Every hour on the hour C-SPAN updates its schedule for the next few hours with program information that appears along the bottom line of the TV screen. In short, C-SPAN operates around the clock and has expanded its coverage to include the strident debates in the British House of Commons.

The centerpiece of C-SPAN coverage remains the House (C-SPAN I) and Senate (C-SPAN II) deliberations. The camera provides a wholly faithful transcription of floor debates. It has been stated that "courts rely on floor debates only when the legislation or [committee] reports are ambiguous." The audiotapes "might eventually supersede [the *Congressional Record*] for the courts." Moreover, the House and Senate will be virtually forced to adopt a truly verbatim *Record*. Otherwise, "the press will highlight instances of discrepancies between the audiotapes and the printed version whenever anything significant is involved to the discomfiture of the Members.... The dignity of Congress will suffer when invidious comparisons are made between the printed and taped record."[18]

Electronic Products

LEGI-SLATE provides the full text of the *Record* online, as do LEXIS, WESTLAW, and DIALOG. The 1985 *Record* on CD-ROM was distributed to all federal depository libraries with Shipping List 90-0007-E (December 6, 1990). This effort represents the permanent bound edition for the first session of the 99th Congress, including retrieval software on the CD-ROM disks and documentation. A reference manual accompanied the shipment for user convenience. The manual provides examples of screens, diagrams, and indexes contained in the database as well as supplemental appendixes. Moreover, the manual includes user software support information. The sessional publication is also available for sale (S/N 052-000-00800-8) from the Superintendent of Documents.[19] Although this product may be justly heralded, the bound CR volumes to be issued to depository libraries in either paper copy or microfiche experience a time lag of several years, obliging libraries to retain the daily *Record*, a massive "space invader," for an unreasonable period of time.[20]

By contrast with the dilatory official *Record* on CD-ROM, a commercial publisher, FD Inc., Washington, D.C., has made available the 1991 *Congressional Record* on CD-ROM. Moreover, the publisher offers a current monthly service on compact disk that contains the full text of the *Congressional Record* accessed by word and phrase search terms.

CR Finding Aids

The daily *Record* has a fortnightly index composed of two parts: an index by subject and individual name to the proceedings and debates, including material in the Extensions of Remarks, and a History of Bills and Resolutions. The history is arranged by chamber and within chamber by bill and resolution number. Bill and resolution information cumulates every two weeks, so that the most recent index can be used to trace current legislation with page references to the measure's introduction, referral to committee, consideration and passage, and enactment or veto. Presidential veto messages are published in the CR (as well as in many other sources) and are issued as House or Senate documents as part of the Congressional Serial Set.

Action in the Other Chamber

When the House passes a bill, an enrolling clerk in that chamber prepares an "engrossed bill" containing all the amendments agreed to; it is delivered to the Senate, referred to the appropriate committee or committees, reprinted, and called an "Act print." The bill then follows the same process as described in the House: subcommittee action, hearings if necessary, a committee report, floor action, and vote. However, there are exceptions to this process. An "Act print" is omitted in the Senate when one of its committees has reported a bill identical to or substantially the same as the one received from the House. In this case, the Senate may substitute the text of its bill for that of the House but retain that body's bill number. Either chamber may consider bills passed by the other without referring them to committee. In this case, there will not be a reported print in the second chamber, although the bill will be printed with a calendar number.[21] If the bill is passed in the second chamber without amendment, it is then sent to the president.

The Conference Committee

Differing versions of a measure must be resolved before the bill can be sent to the president. Resolution may be accomplished without a conference, but the formal machinery for reconciling differences involves the conference committee, a strategy adopted by the 1st Congress and used ever since.

Conference committees have been referred to as the "Third House of Congress." Managers, or conferees, are appointed from each body; they attempt to effect a compromise satisfactory to both chambers. When the conferees reach agreement, a conference report is prepared. Beginning with the 92d Congress in 1971, the conference report was required to be printed in both houses, but that duplication can be waived. In conference committee no further amendments are allowed, and when the report is published, no floor action is permitted. If one or both chambers reject the report, the measure reverts to the pre-conference stage.

Conference reports are classed in the same notation as House reports (Y 1.1/8) and Senate reports (Y 1.1/5) and are sent in slip form to depository libraries in paper copy or on microfiche. They are also sold by the Superintendent of Documents on subscription as announced in *Price List 36*. Later they are incorporated into the bound volumes or microfiche edition of the Congressional Serial Set. Figure 5.13 (see page 134) shows a conference report issued by the House.

Presidential Action

After approval by both houses, a copy of the bill is enrolled for presentation to the president. Prepared by the enrolling clerk of the chamber that originated the measure and signed by the Speaker of the House and the President of the Senate, it is sent to the chief executive for veto or signature into law. A bill may become law without the president's signature if he does not veto it within ten days (excluding Sundays) after it was presented to him. However, if the Congress adjourns before that ten-day period ends, a "pocket veto" takes place and the bill does not become law. In a regular veto, the president returns the bill to the originating chamber with a message stating his objections. To override a veto requires a two-thirds vote in both chambers. Veto messages are published either as House documents (Y 1.1/7) or Senate documents (Y 1.1/3) depending upon the bill's origin. *Presidential Vetoes, 1789-* , cumulated every few years, lists vetoes from the 1st Congress and is accessed by subject and name indexes, with citations to the *Congressional Record*. Figure 5.14 (see pages 135 and 136) shows an enrolled bill approved by President George Bush.

(Text continues on page 137.)

Fig. 5.13. Conference report

101ST CONGRESS	HOUSE OF REPRESENTATIVES	REPORT
1st Session		101-100

NATURAL GAS WELLHEAD DECONTROL ACT OF 1989

JUNE 22, 1989.—Ordered to be printed

Mr. DINGELL, from the committee of conference,
submitted the following

CONFERENCE REPORT

[To accompany H.R. 1722]

The committee of conference on the disagreeing votes of the two Houses on the amendments of the Senate to the bill (H.R. 1722) to amend the Natural Gas Policy Act of 1978 to eliminate wellhead price and nonprice controls on the first sale of natural gas, and to make technical and conforming amendments to such Act, having met, after full and free conference, have agreed to recommend and do recommend to their respective Houses as follows:

That the Senate recede from its amendment numbered 1.

That the House recede from its disagreement to the amendment of the Senate numbered 2, and agree to the same with amendments as follows:

* * * * * * *

(Sample copy of part of first page and page 2 of conference report)

* * * * * * *

And the Senate agree to the same.

> JOHN D. DINGELL,
> PHILIP R. SHARP,
> BILLY TAUZIN,
> NORMAN F. LENT,
> CARLOS MOORHEAD,
> *Managers on the Part of the House.*

> J. BENNETT JOHNSTON,
> DALE BUMPERS,
> WENDELL H. FORD,
> JAMES A. MCCLURE,
> PETE DOMENICI,
> *Managers on the Part of the Senate.*

Fig. 5.14. Enrolled bill

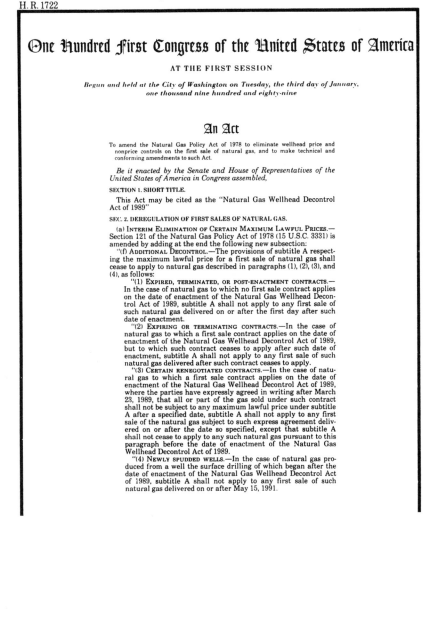

PUBLIC LAW 101-60

H. R. 1722

One Hundred First Congress of the United States of America

AT THE FIRST SESSION

Begun and held at the City of Washington on Tuesday, the third day of January, one thousand nine hundred and eighty-nine

An Act

To amend the Natural Gas Policy Act of 1978 to eliminate wellhead price and nonprice controls on the first sale of natural gas, and to make technical and conforming amendments to such Act.

Be it enacted by the Senate and House of Representatives of the United States of America in Congress assembled,

SECTION 1. SHORT TITLE.

This Act may be cited as the "Natural Gas Wellhead Decontrol Act of 1989"

SEC. 2. DEREGULATION OF FIRST SALES OF NATURAL GAS.

(a) INTERIM ELIMINATION OF CERTAIN MAXIMUM LAWFUL PRICES.—Section 121 of the Natural Gas Policy Act of 1978 (15 U.S.C. 3331) is amended by adding at the end the following new subsection:

"(f) ADDITIONAL DECONTROL.—The provisions of subtitle A respecting the maximum lawful price for a first sale of natural gas shall cease to apply to natural gas described in paragraphs (1), (2), (3), and (4), as follows:

"(1) EXPIRED, TERMINATED, OR POST-ENACTMENT CONTRACTS.—In the case of natural gas to which no first sale contract applies on the date of enactment of the Natural Gas Wellhead Decontrol Act of 1989, subtitle A shall not apply to any first sale of such natural gas delivered on or after the first day after such date of enactment.

"(2) EXPIRING OR TERMINATING CONTRACTS.—In the case of natural gas to which a first sale contract applies on the date of enactment of the Natural Gas Wellhead Decontrol Act of 1989, but to which such contract ceases to apply after such date of enactment, subtitle A shall not apply to any first sale of such natural gas delivered after such contract ceases to apply.

"(3) CERTAIN RENEGOTIATED CONTRACTS.—In the case of natural gas to which a first sale contract applies on the date of enactment of the Natural Gas Wellhead Decontrol Act of 1989, where the parties have expressly agreed in writing after March 23, 1989, that all or part of the gas sold under such contract shall not be subject to any maximum lawful price under subtitle A after a specified date, subtitle A shall not apply to any first sale of the natural gas subject to such express agreement delivered on or after the date so specified, except that subtitle A shall not cease to apply to any such natural gas pursuant to this paragraph before the date of enactment of the Natural Gas Wellhead Decontrol Act of 1989.

"(4) NEWLY SPUDDED WELLS.—In the case of natural gas produced from a well the surface drilling of which began after the date of enactment of the Natural Gas Wellhead Decontrol Act of 1989, subtitle A shall not apply to any first sale of such natural gas delivered on or after May 15, 1991.

(Figure 5.14 continues on page 136.)

Fig. 5.14 *(cont.)*

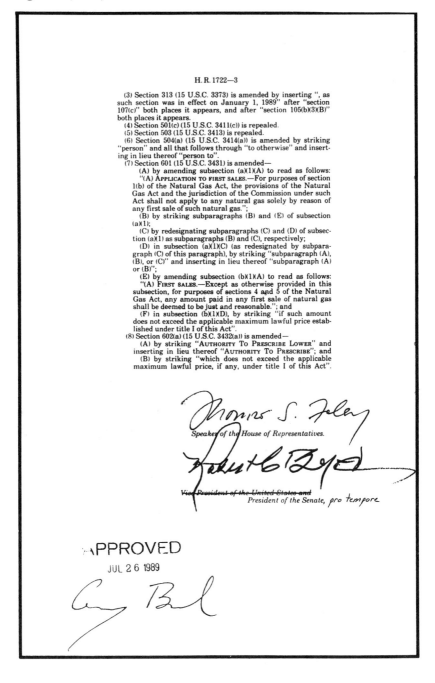

H. R. 1722—3

(3) Section 313 (15 U.S.C. 3373) is amended by inserting ", as such section was in effect on January 1, 1989" after "section 107(c)" both places it appears, and after "section 105(b)(3)(B)" both places it appears.

(4) Section 501(c) (15 U.S.C. 3411(c)) is repealed.

(5) Section 503 (15 U.S.C. 3413) is repealed.

(6) Section 504(a) (15 U.S.C. 3414(a)) is amended by striking "person" and all that follows through "to otherwise" and inserting in lieu thereof "person to".

(7) Section 601 (15 U.S.C. 3431) is amended—

(A) by amending subsection (a)(1)(A) to read as follows:

"(A) APPLICATION TO FIRST SALES.—For purposes of section 1(b) of the Natural Gas Act, the provisions of the Natural Gas Act and the jurisdiction of the Commission under such Act shall not apply to any natural gas solely by reason of any first sale of such natural gas.";

(B) by striking subparagraphs (B) and (E) of subsection (a)(1);

(C) by redesignating subparagraphs (C) and (D) of subsection (a)(1) as subparagraphs (B) and (C), respectively;

(D) in subsection (a)(1)(C) (as redesignated by subparagraph (C) of this paragraph), by striking "subparagraph (A), (B), or (C)" and inserting in lieu thereof "subparagraph (A) or (B)";

(E) by amending subsection (b)(1)(A) to read as follows:

"(A) FIRST SALES.—Except as otherwise provided in this subsection, for purposes of sections 4 and 5 of the Natural Gas Act, any amount paid in any first sale of natural gas shall be deemed to be just and reasonable."; and

(F) in subsection (b)(1)(D), by striking "if such amount does not exceed the applicable maximum lawful price established under title I of this Act".

(8) Section 602(a) (15 U.S.C. 3432(a)) is amended—

(A) by striking "AUTHORITY TO PRESCRIBE LOWER" and inserting in lieu thereof "AUTHORITY TO PRESCRIBE"; and

(B) by striking "which does not exceed the applicable maximum lawful price, if any, under title I of this Act".

Speaker of the House of Representatives.

~~Vice President of the United States and~~
President of the Senate, pro tempore

APPROVED

JUL 2 6 1989

PUBLICATION OF LAWS

When a bill becomes law either by presidential inaction or approval or by congressional override, it is sent to the Office of the Federal Register for publication. Technically speaking, upon enactment the legislative process ends, but this oversimplifies a dialectic involving administrative entities and the federal judiciary. Questions of "legislative intent" may arise, and the several documents described above may be examined to determine the "meaning" of a statute. But before any other activities involving the executive or the courts take place, laws appear in several forms; it is important to understand the publishing process and the sources, official and commercial, print and nonprint, in which the public may access these statutes.

Slip Laws

The first official appearance of a law is in "slip" (pamphlet) form. Assigned a public law number, the slip law references the *Statutes at Large* citation and the bill number and contains marginal notes that may include, if applicable, citations to prior statutes, treaties, and provisions of the *United States Code.* At the end of the slip law is a "Legislative History" that provides citations to the important publications generated in the legislative process, including any presidential statement made upon approval of the legislation. The public and private law numbers run in sequence starting anew at the beginning of each Congress and, since 1957, are prefixed for ready identification by the number of the Congress. For example, the first public law of the 102d Congress is designated Public Law (PL) 102-1, and the first private law is designated Private Law 102-1. Figure 5.15 (see page 138) shows a public (slip) law.

As slip laws (and almost all other federal issuances) are not subject to copyright restrictions, commercial firms publish current laws, and these editions, with editorial enhancements, often reach subscribers before the official slip laws are received by depository libraries or by subscription as a sales item from the Superintendent of Documents.[22] *United States Law Week* (USLW), published by the Bureau of National Affairs, provides the text of selected laws passed for that period. *United States Code Congressional and Administrative News* (U.S.C.C.A.N.), issued monthly, includes the full text of all public laws. The *United States Code Service* (Lawyers Cooperative Publishing) issues *Advance Sheets* that provide the same information offered by West's U.S.C.C.A.N.

Because public laws are the provenance of the Office of the Federal Register, they are assigned the SuDocs class notation AE 2.110. Private laws are designated AE 2.110/2.

United States Statutes at Large

A chronological arrangement of the slip laws in bound sessional volumes is published as the *Statutes at Large* (Stat.). These volumes, which unfortunately experience a distinct time lag, include in chronological or numerical order in *separate series* public laws, private laws, joint resolutions, concurrent

(Text continues on page 139.)

Fig. 5.15. Public (slip) law

PUBLIC LAW 101-60—JULY 26, 1989   103 STAT. 157

Public Law 101-60
101st Congress

An Act

To amend the Natural Gas Policy Act of 1978 to eliminate wellhead price and nonprice controls on the first sale of natural gas, and to make technical and conforming amendments to such Act.

> July 26, 1989
> [H.R. 1722]

Be it enacted by the Senate and House of Representatives of the United States of America in Congress assembled,

SECTION 1. SHORT TITLE.

This Act may be cited as the "Natural Gas Wellhead Decontrol Act of 1989"

> Natural Gas
> Wellhead
> Decontrol
> Act of 1989.
> 15 USC 3301
> note.

SEC. 2. DEREGULATION OF FIRST SALES OF NATURAL GAS.

(a) INTERIM ELIMINATION OF CERTAIN MAXIMUM LAWFUL PRICES.—Section 121 of the Natural Gas Policy Act of 1978 (15 U.S.C. 3331) is amended by adding at the end the following new subsection:

"(f) ADDITIONAL DECONTROL.—The provisions of subtitle A respecting the maximum lawful price for a first sale of natural gas shall cease to apply to natural gas described in paragraphs (1), (2), (3), and (4), as follows:

"(1) EXPIRED, TERMINATED, OR POST-ENACTMENT CONTRACTS.—In the case of natural gas to which no first sale contract applies on the date of enactment of the Natural Gas Wellhead Decontrol Act of 1989, subtitle A shall not apply to any first sale of such natural gas delivered on or after the first day after such date of enactment.

"(2) EXPIRING OR TERMINATING CONTRACTS.—In the case of natural gas to which a first sale contract applies on the date of enactment of the Natural Gas Wellhead Decontrol Act of 1989, but to which such contract ceases to apply after such date of enactment, subtitle A shall not apply to any first sale of such natural gas delivered after such contract ceases to apply.

"(3) CERTAIN RENEGOTIATED CONTRACTS.—In the case of natural gas to which a first sale contract applies on the date of enactment of the Natural Gas Wellhead Decontrol Act of 1989, where the parties have expressly agreed in writing after March 23, 1989, that all or part of the gas sold under such contract shall not be subject to any maximum lawful price under subtitle A after a specified date, subtitle A shall not apply to any first sale of the natural gas subject to such express agreement delivered on or after the date so specified, except that subtitle A shall not cease to apply to any such natural gas pursuant to this paragraph before the date of enactment of the Natural Gas Wellhead Decontrol Act of 1989.

"(4) NEWLY SPUDDED WELLS.—In the case of natural gas produced from a well the surface drilling of which began after the date of enactment of the Natural Gas Wellhead Decontrol Act of 1989, subtitle A shall not apply to any first sale of such natural gas delivered on or after May 15, 1991.

Approved July 26, 1989.

LEGISLATIVE HISTORY—H.R. 1722 (S. 783):

HOUSE REPORTS: No. 101-29 (Comm. on Energy and Commerce) and No. 101-100 (Comm. of Conference).
SENATE REPORTS: No. 101-38 accompanying S. 783 (Comm. on Energy and Natural Resources) and No. 101-39 (Comm. on Energy and Natural Resources).
CONGRESSIONAL RECORD, Vol. 135 (1989):
    Apr. 17, considered and passed House.
    June 8, 9, 13, 14, considered and passed Senate, amended.
    June 15, House disagreed to Senate amendments.
    June 22, Senate agreed to conference report.
    July 12, House agreed to conference report.
WEEKLY COMPILATION OF PRESIDENTIAL DOCUMENTS, Vol. 25 (1989):
    July 26, Presidential statement.

resolutions, and some presidential materials (see chapter 6 for more information about presidential materials). The *Statutes at Large* has a subject index and an individual (name) index for access to private laws. The *Statutes* constitute legal evidence of the laws contained in them, acceptable as proof of those laws in the courts. They bear the SuDocs class number AE 2.111.

Researchers generally prefer to consult the text of public laws in the cumulated volumes of U.S.C.C.A.N. because this service also publishes the text of committee reports and presidential statements. Private legislation, however, cannot be found in U.S.C.C.A.N. CIS offers a comprehensive microfiche collection of the *Statutes at Large*.

United States Code

The *United States Code* (U.S.C.) consists of a consolidation and codification of the general and permanent laws. Arranged under titles, the *United States Code* provides subject access, collates the initial law with subsequent amendments, and excludes statutory provisions that over time have been repealed or superseded. Prepared by the Law Revision Counsel of the House of Representatives, *United States Code* is published every six years in a new edition with cumulative annual supplements.

About one-half of the titles of the *United States Code* have been "revised and enacted into positive law, and 2 have been eliminated by consolidation with other titles. Titles that have been revised and enacted into positive law are legal evidence of the law and the courts will receive them as proof of those laws. Eventually all the titles will be revised and enacted into positive law, and thereafter they will be kept up to date by direct amendment."[23] A list of current enacted titles is found following Section 204(e) of Title 1 in the *United States Code Annotated*, on the inside front cover of the volumes of the *United States Code Service*, and in the *United States Code*.[24]

In addition to the codified laws, the *United States Code* includes tables covering presidential documents, conversion tables from the *Statutes at Large* to the *Code, District of Columbia Code* sections classified to the *United States Code*, an "Index of Acts Cited by Popular Name," and a general subject index. Currently, the SuDocs class notation assigned to this source is Y 1.2/5.

Commercial editions of the *United States Code*, with their value-added enhancements and sophisticated indexing, provide timely, in-depth research capabilities. The *United States Code Annotated* (U.S.C.A.), a West Publishing Company product, presents the identical wording and language of the official *Code*, but it also includes "Notes of Decisions" (digest paragraphs followed by citations to cases construing provisions of the *Code*); "Historical and Revision Notes" (indicating the derivation of various sections, amendments, citations to earlier committee reports, public law numbers and dates of enactment, and other useful references); cross-references; and "Library References" (citing appropriate sections of the *Code of Federal Regulations*, West's legal encyclopedia, *American Digest System* topics and key numbers, and selected legal periodical articles on the topic).

The *United States Code Service* (U.S.C.S.), published by Lawyers Cooperative Publishing and the Bancroft-Whitney Company, follows the language of the *Statutes at Large.* When clarification is needed, bracketed words or references in text notes are inserted.[25] Like U.S.C.A., the *United States Code Service* contains editorial features that facilitate research. Although it cites fewer cases than U.S.C.A. construing provisions of the *Code*, it provides extensive cross-references to the "sister publications" of Lawyers Cooperative Publishing (formerly called the Lawyers Co-operative Publishing Company) such as the *A.L.R. Annotations* series and to external sources such as the *Code of Federal Regulations* and selected legal periodical articles. The several legal materials that are referenced in both of these annotated codes are discussed in greater detail in chapter 9.

Both commercial sets include in unnumbered volumes the Constitution of the United States with citations to court cases construing the Articles and Amendments. Both sources are kept up to date by annual pocket supplements, monthly pamphlets, and replacement volumes as needed. In general, both U.S.C.A. and U.S.C.S. are preferable to the official edition of the *Code* for their currency and editorial finding aids.

Electronic Products

LEXIS and WESTLAW have databases for the public laws series and for the *United States Code.* In addition, units of *Shepard's Citations* are online with both electronic services. LEXIS features *USLW Daily Edition.*

Shepard's Citations

To trace the history and treatment of federal statutes that have been cited by various citing sources, use a Shepard's unit titled *Shepard's United States Citations: Statute Edition.* These volumes include all recorded cases and other citing sources that have cited the U.S. Constitution, the *United States Code, Statutes at Large*, rules of the U.S. Supreme Court, and treaties.

Popular Name Indexes

Shepard's Acts and Cases by Popular Names, Federal and State (Colorado Springs, CO: Shepard's/McGraw-Hill) lists federal acts by their popular names with citations to the public law number, *Statutes at Large*, and *United States Code.* Other popular name tables are found in the *United States Code* itself, as noted, and in U.S.C.C.A.N., U.S.C.A., and U.S.C.S.

PRIVATE LEGISLATION

The framers of the U.S. Constitution adopted the concept of private legislation from the British Parliament, but the venerable practice dates at least from Roman times. Based on the principle of equity, the introduction of a private bill is intended to exempt "specific individuals, groups, or localities from the application of a [public] law that was not intended to apply to them."[26]

Renowned House parliamentarian Asher C. Hinds, in his *Precedents of the House of Representatives of the United States* (1907), proposed this definition: "A private bill is a bill for the relief of one or several specified persons, corporations, institutions, etc., and is distinguished from a public bill, which relates to public matters and deals with individuals only by classes." And he added this caveat, published in the *House Manual*: "The line of distinction between public and private bills is so difficult to be defined in many cases that it must rest on the opinion of the Speaker and the details of the bill."[27] Despite this difficulty, when a private bill becomes law, it is routinely assigned a separate slip law number and grouped in a separate section in the *Statutes at Large*.

The number of private bills over the past century has decreased dramatically, with a corresponding attrition in the number of private laws enacted. This reduction has been achieved through case law and by a series of "public laws delegating to executive agencies the authority to act on cases previously handled by Congress."[28] However, the Congress remains involved in private legislation. Two main categories predominate: claims and immigration cases. "Bills for the relief of individuals in those two fields have been introduced in large numbers in every session of Congress for many years."[29] The former category includes moral and legal obligations of the federal government and is anchored in Article I, Section 8, Clause 1, of the Constitution. The latter is based on the fact that public laws on the admission of aliens into this country do not cover all hardship cases. Private measures on other matters constitute a miscellany. Private laws have been passed permitting a person awarded a foreign decoration to accept the honor and wear it in public. Inventors have been awarded monetary sums where they were not justly protected by patents. Land claims, military justice, and pensions have also been the subject of private legislation.[30] Other examples in the miscellaneous category include authorizing the secretary of the interior to exchange federal lands for lands owned by an individual, exempting from taxation certain property belonging to a religious foundation, authorizing the secretary of agriculture to grant easement over certain forest lands to a railroad company, and authorizing documentation of a vessel owned by a private party for coastal transportation and fishing despite lack of full compliance with merchant marine laws.[31]

Legislative Procedure

The steps by which a private bill becomes a private law are similar in their general lineaments to those of a public measure. Individuals or institutions initiate the process directly or through an intermediary, such as an attorney or a lobbyist, by contacting the representative or senator in the appropriate jurisdiction. In virtually all instances, the introduced measure is referred to the House or Senate Judiciary Committee, which in turn delegates the bill to the relevant subcommittee or to the individual sponsoring member. If the bill is reported favorably out of committee, it is placed on the Senate's Calendar of Business or the Private Calendar of the House, where floor action takes place on certain predetermined days of the month.[32] Figure 5.16 (see page 142) shows a House reported print on a private bill.

(Text continues on page 143.)

Fig. 5.16. House reported print on private bill

Private Calendar No. 47

100TH CONGRESS
2D SESSION

H. R. 3439

[Report No. 100–552]

For the relief of Marisela, Felix, and William [Doe].

IN THE HOUSE OF REPRESENTATIVES

OCTOBER 6, 1987

Mr. FUSTER introduced the following bill; which was referred to the Committee on the Judiciary

MARCH 31, 1988

Committed to the Committee of the Whole House and ordered to be printed

---

A BILL

For the relief of Marisela, Felix, and William [Doe].

1   *Be it enacted by the Senate and House of Representa-*

2 *tives of the United States of America in Congress assembled,*

3 That Marisela, Felix, and William [Doe], the children of

4 Manual [Doe], a Secret Service agent who was killed in a

5 fire while on duty in the Dupont Plaza Hotel in Puerto Rico,

6 shall for the purposes of section 6(c) of the Act of Sep-

7 tember 30, 1950 (20 U.S.C. 241(c)), be considered to be chil-

8 dren residing with a parent employed by the United States

9 and thus be eligible to receive free public education arranged

10 by the Secretary of Education under such section.

Both chambers use a group of "objectors" to screen private bills for possible disapproval. The system of objectors, which has no counterpart in the passage of public legislation, is designed in part to reduce the possibility that the merits of the measure will be overruled by political pressures. If a private bill has strong support in the House or Senate Judiciary Committees, passage is likely. Floor action on favorable committee reports typically is routine. But before final passage, the House and Senate may refer a claim "involving determination of facts" to the United States Claims Court for guidance. Usually the court's report is included in the committee report, but only a small number of private bills during a session are referred to the claims court.[33] Figure 5.17 (see page 144) shows a House Judiciary Committee report accompanying a private bill.

Presidential approval or veto completes the process. A veto message is returned to the chamber in which the bill originated. As in public legislation, a two-thirds vote is necessary by both House and Senate to override a president's objections. *Congressional Quarterly* points out that "two-thirds of all vetoed bills since 1789 [through the mid-1970s] have been private bills." However, of those private measures that the claims court determines to have merit, the judiciary committees report favorably, and the plenary chambers pass, very few are vetoed by a president.[34] Figure 5.18 (see page 145) shows a private (slip) law, which is later incorporated into the *Statutes at Large*.

Bibliographic Finding Aids

The "Private Calendar" section of the *Calendars of the United States House of Representatives and History of Legislation*, formerly published daily but currently published weekly, has parallel tables showing date and bill number with reference to sponsoring member, committee, title, report number, and calendar number. A cumulative table called "Private Laws" provides private law number with reference to bill number. The status table, "Numerical Order of Bills and Resolutions Which Have Passed Either or Both Houses, and Bills Now Pending on the Calendars," includes private legislation by bill number with all relevant citations through private law number and date of approval. Moreover, the subject index in the Monday *Calendars* provides access to individuals and institutions alphabetically by name under the heading "Private Relief." The *House Calendars* includes Senate action and covers all legislative activity. This source is assigned SuDocs class notation Y 1.2/2.

From July 1976 to date, the *Monthly Catalog* provides entries for reports on private bills and private laws. These can be accessed through the subject index by name of person or institution, through the title keyword index under the word "relief," and through the series/report index by House or Senate committee report number.

The fortnightly index to the daily *Congressional Record* includes private measures arranged by bill number in the "History of Bills and Resolutions" section, with page references to the legislative process. In addition, both the *House Journal* and *Senate Journal* have in their sessional volumes a "History of Bills and Resolutions" section organized by private bill number.

(Text continues on page 145.)

Fig. 5.17. Committee report on private bill

100TH CONGRESS 2d Session	HOUSE OF REPRESENTATIVES	REPORT 100-552

MARISELA, FELIX, AND WILLIAM [DOE]

MARCH 31, 1988.—Committed to the Committee of the Whole House and ordered to be printed

Mr. FRANK, from the Committee on the Judiciary, submitted the following

REPORT

[To accompany H.R. 3439]

The Committee on the Judiciary, to whom was referred the bill (H.R. 3439), for the relief of Marisela, Felix, and William [Doe], having considered the same, report favorably thereon without amendment and recommend that the bill do pass.

PURPOSE

H.R. 3439 authorizes the Secretary of Defense to allow the children of a secret service agent killed while on duty to attend school at a military facility in Puerto Rico.

BACKGROUND

On December 31, 1986, Special Agent Manual [Doe], who was assigned to the San Juan Office of the U.S. Secret Service, was killed in the line of duty at the Dupont Plaza Hotel fire in San Juan. At the time of his death, Mr. [Doe] was conducting an investigation in the manager's office when fire and explosions broke out. The fire quickly engulfed the lower level of the hotel, and Special Agent [Doe] died of smoke inhalation. He was killed in the line of duty and was survived by a wife and three children.

Following his death, the family was notified by the Defense Department that his three children were no longer eligible to attend the Antilles Consolidated Military School System due to the fact that the children were no longer dependents of a federally employed person in Puerto Rico.

* * * * * * *

(Sample copy of part of first and second pages of this 4-page House report)

* * * * * * *

COMMITTEE ACTION

The Committee on the Judiciary on March 15, favorably reported by voice vote H.R. 3439 to the House. The Committee concluded that the children of Special Agent Manual [Doe] should be authorized to continue attending school in a military facility operated by the Department of Defense. Therefore, the Committee recommends that the House favorably consider H.R. 3439.

Fig. 5.18. Private (slip) law

[Figure 16—Slip law of a Private Law]

PRIVATE LAW 100-11—MAY 5, 1988

Private Law 100-11
100th Congress

An Act

For the relief of Marisela, Felix, and William [Doe].

May 5, 1988
[H.R. 3439]

Be it enacted by the Senate and House of Representatives of the United States of America in Congress assembled, That Marisela, Felix, and William [Doe], the children of Manual [Doe], a Secret Service agent who was killed in a fire while on duty in the Dupont Plaza Hotel in Puerto Rico, shall for the purposes of section 6(c) of the Act of September 30, 1950 (20 U.S.C. 241(c)), be considered to be children residing with a parent employed by the United States and thus be eligible to receive free public education arranged by the Secretary of Education under such section.

Manual [Doe].

Approved May 5, 1988.

Reported private bills bear an individual report number and are later incorporated into the Congressional Serial Set. The *Numerical Lists and Schedule of Volumes* (GP 3.7/2) covering the period 1933-1980 bridges the gap between the numerical designation of individual reports on private bills (and reports on public measures as well) and their subsequent appearance in numbered serial set volumes. For example, the *Numerical Lists* show that 96-1: H. Rep. 387, Relief of City of Nenana, Alaska, was republished in Serial Set Volume 13299.[35]

Commercial sources include *CIS/Index* and *CIS US Serial Set Index, 1789-1969.* The former has annual and cumulative four-year indexes. Unfortunately, only public bills are listed in the "Index of Bill Numbers." However, the "Index of Report Numbers" section notes reports on private measures (for example, H. Rep. 96-1249......Private) but provides no corresponding abstract for those reports in the issues of *CIS/Index.* The retrospective CIS product has become the definitive source for locating citations to reports on private bills. The multi-volume index provides useful finding aids. The "Numerical List of Reports and Documents" section contains tables showing, for example, that S. Rep. 1247, 89th Congress, 2d Session (1966), Relief of Abraham Presser, is found in Serial Set Volume 12711-1. In addition, the "Private Relief and Related Actions: Index of Names of Individuals and Organizations" section provides a list of the proper names of persons and organizations referencing the individual House or Senate report number, Congress and session in parentheses, and serial set volume number. The retrospective *CIS US Serial Set Index* is available on *Congressional Masterfile 1* (CD-ROM) and the current *CIS/Index* is available on *Congressional Masterfile 2*, a companion CD-ROM product.

Textual Sources

Depository libraries receive the text of private bills and committee reports, the former on microfiche and the latter in paper copy or on microfiche. Private bills are available on subscription from the Superintendent of Documents, but reports on private bills and private laws are not a SuDocs sales category.

The full text of private laws is published in the sessional volumes of the *Statutes at Large*. Private laws were assigned chapter numbers through volume 69, but this practice ceased with the 84th Congress (volume 70, 1956). For example, Private Law 40 (May 13, 1949), "For the Relief of Stone and Cooper Coal Company, Incorporated," was assigned Chapter 102 and is published at 63 Stat. 1090. The "Individual Index" in each sessional volume of the *Statutes at Large* provides an alphabetical list of individuals and institutions that have been the recipient of private legislation; the list references the page number in the *Statutes* where the text of the private law is published. In addition, two tables in the *Statutes at Large* afford access to the texts. A "List of Private Laws Contained in This Volume" is arranged by private law number with reference to the name of the recipient, title of the act, date of enactment, and page. A "List of Bills Enacted into Private Law" is organized by bill number referencing the private law number. Because the focus of private legislation is, by definition, on the person or institution, the "Individual Index" is the search strategy most frequently employed.

When dealing with private measures, Congress "resembles an ancient court of equity," and the passage of private legislation "may be said without distortion to represent an exercise of congressional conscience."[36]

THE UNITED STATES CONGRESSIONAL SERIAL SET

The United States Congressional Serial Set has been known by different short or popular names including the serial number set, congressional edition, congressional set, congressional series, and sheep set (owing to its distinctive sheepskin binding). Throughout its illustrious history it has included a wide variety of titles and series. A partial list would include the House and Senate *Journals*, reports from agencies in the executive branch, annual or fiscal audits of federally chartered private organizations, investigative and background studies, directories, manuals, research and statistical studies, and reports on public and private bills. Thorough accounts of the historical set are presented in Schmeckebier and Eastin and in the "User Guide" section found in the several volumes of the *CIS US Serial Set Index*.[37]

The serial numbering system was developed by Dr. John G. Ames (see chapter 4) in the late nineteenth century. A reprint of records covering the early Congresses not part of Ames' numbering scheme was privately published by authority of Congress between 1832 and 1861. This reprint, known as the *American State Papers*, includes records previously available only in manuscript as well as printed legislative and executive materials. The *State Papers* are generally considered a part of the set and were numbered 001 through 038 when shelved in the old Public Documents Division, which housed a collection that was called a "Library."[38]

Some significant changes occurred in the format and distribution of the serial set beginning with the 96th Congress, and the following account addresses the series as it exists today. The current set consists of three categories of congressional publications issued in six distinct parts: House reports, Senate reports, House documents, Senate documents, Senate treaty documents, and Senate executive reports.

House and Senate Reports

House and Senate reports on public and private measures have been described in this chapter in some detail. Pursuant to legislation, they constitute the majority of the reports series. In addition, "special reports" include investigative activities of committees, summaries of committee oversight functions, studies of matters relating to public policy, and the like.[39] From the 84th through the 95th Congresses, House and Senate reports on public and private bills were bound separately in serial set volumes entitled "Miscellaneous Reports on Public Bills" and "Miscellaneous Reports on Private Bills." Beginning with the 88th Congress, 2d Session, special reports were also bound separately. With the 96th Congress, all House and Senate materials are bound in numerical sequence because of the exigencies of issuing the serial set in a microfiche format.

House and Senate Documents

Throughout this text, the word *documents* has been used largely in a generic sense, synonymous with "publications," "materials," or "sources." For serial set publications in this series, however, the word assumes a specificity not encountered elsewhere.

The kinds of materials ordered to be published as House or Senate documents are many and varied. Prior to the 96th Congress, documents labeled "miscellaneous" were bound in serial volumes bearing the same base serial number with individual volumes designated by a numerical suffix (e.g., 13145-1, 13145-2, 13145-3, etc.). In these volumes one finds presidential messages, including vetoes; reports on rescissions and deferrals of budget authority; budget amendments; the president's annual State of the Union Address; and the like. Reports on audits of government corporations such as the Federal Home Loan Bank Board and the Tennessee Valley Authority were usually grouped into another serial volume with numbered parts. Other titles issued in the House and Senate document series include annual reports of federal agencies and important reference works such as *How Our Laws Are Made*; the *Biographical Directory of the United States Congress*; the *Constitution of the United States of America, Analysis and Interpretation* and its biennial supplements; the House and Senate *Manuals*; and the *Budget of the United States Government*. An unusual category of documents includes the annual reports of nongovernmental organizations such as the Boy Scouts and Girl Scouts of America; Veterans of World War I of the United States, Inc.; proceedings of the National Encampment, United Spanish War Veterans; and National Convention of Disabled American Veterans. These are submitted to Congress pursuant to statutory authority.[40] They are listed in an annual pamphlet entitled *Reports to Be Made to Congress* (itself issued as a

House document). The annual and fiscal reports of these societies, associations, and other nongovernmental bodies provide a lively mix to the series.

The latitude that inheres in this form results in something that falls short of bibliographic precision. For example, committee prints have been published as House or Senate documents and in the *Congressional Record*. Some "special reports" in the House and Senate reports series could just as easily have been issued as "documents." In general this series consists of a potpourri of information designated as not appropriate for inclusion in the other components of the serial set. Figure 5.19 shows the title page of a publication in the House document series.

Fig. 5.19. Title page of House document

100th Congress, 1st Session - - - - - - - - - House Document 100-23

DISABLED AMERICAN VETERANS
65th NATIONAL CONVENTION

COMMUNICATION

FROM

THE NATIONAL ADJUTANT, DISABLED AMERICAN VETERANS

TRANSMITTING

THE REPORT OF THE PROCEEDINGS OF THE ORGANIZATIONS 65TH NATIONAL CONVENTION, INCLUDING A REPORT OF RE-CEIPTS AND EXPENDITURES AS OF DECEMBER 31, 1985, PURSU-ANT TO TITLE 44, UNITED STATES CODE, SECTION 1332, AND SECTION 3 OF PUBLIC LAW 88-504

JANUARY 21, 1987.—Referred to the Committee on Veterans' Affairs and ordered to be printed, with illustrations

---

U.S. GOVERNMENT PRINTING OFFICE

65-458 O   WASHINGTON : 1987

Senate Treaty Documents

Senate treaty documents, formerly called Senate executive documents, were issued in a lettered series. In 1977 this series was made available to depository libraries, and it became part of the serial set beginning with the 96th Congress (1979). Prior to this availability, the Documents Expediting Project was the principal source for obtaining treaty documents. In the 97th Congress the title change became effective and the treaty documents became a numbered series throughout a Congress. The series is issued pursuant to the president's requirement to submit all treaties to the Senate for their advice and consent under Article II, Section 2, Clause 2, of the Constitution.

A Senate treaty document consists of messages from the president to the Senate Foreign Relations Committee transmitting the text of treaties. The INF treaty signed by Ronald Reagan and Mikhail Gorbachev was transmitted as Senate Treaty Doc. 100-11 (see chapter 6). An example of an earlier treaty in the lettered series was the unratified Salt II treaty, which was issued as 96-1: Senate Executive Document Y and bound with other executive documents in Serial Set Volume 13235.

Senate Executive Reports

Like treaty documents, Senate executive reports were first made available to depository institutions in 1977 and became part of the serial set beginning in 1979. They, too, are a numbered series and serve two purposes: (1) when issued by the Senate Foreign Relations Committee, they recommend to the plenary Senate that a treaty proposed by the president (in a Senate treaty document) be approved and (2) when issued by *any* Senate committee with the appropriate oversight function, they recommend confirmation of nominations of high officials in the executive and judiciary. Thus, the INF treaty was reported favorably out of the Foreign Relations Committee as Executive Report 100-15. But Executive Report 97-1 was reported out of the Senate Armed Services Committee pursuant to the nomination of Caspar W. Weinberger to be secretary of defense. Similarly, the Senate Judiciary Committee issued Executive Report 97-22 on the president's nomination of Sandra Day O'Connor for the position of associate justice of the Supreme Court. For executive reports on nominations there is no prior "executive document" series, but nominations are noted in the *Weekly Compilation of Presidential Documents* (WCPD).

The *CIS Index to US Senate Executive Documents & Reports, 1818-1969*, provides a comprehensive means of accessing these important series. From 1970 to date, selective Senate executive reports and all Senate treaty documents are indexed and abstracted in *CIS/Index*. The CIS retrospective microfiche collection and the current microfiche for *CIS/Index* provide full-text capability.[41] Moreover, treaty documents and executive reports are indexed in the *Monthly Catalog* from the time they became depository items in 1977.

Numerical Lists and
Schedule of Volumes

Known by its short title, the *Numerical Lists* (GP 3.7/2) was a handy, user-friendly guide to the bound volumes of the serial set. In existence from 1933 to 1980, it bridged the gap between the numerical designation of individual reports and documents and their subsequent appearance in serial set binding. The *Numerical Lists* was issued sessionally and compiled in the Office of the Superintendent of Documents.

The title of the publication identifies its two-part arrangement. The first part, the "Numerical Lists," arranges the categories by individual number, title, and serial volume designation. The second part, the "Schedule of Volumes," shows the same categories grouped by inclusive numbers within a volume with reference to the serial volume number. Users will discover that the "Schedule of Volumes" section of the *Numerical Lists* before the 96th Congress reflected the grouping of like reports and documents in the bound serial volumes and, of course, did not include treaty documents and executive reports. Moreover, the bound set in its entirety as indicated in the "Schedule of Volumes" was sent *only* to the Senate and House libraries, the Library of Congress, the National Archives, and the office of the Superintendent of Documents. This practice of providing two "editions" of the Congressional Serial Set was confusing to librarians and users alike, but starting with the 96th Congress all congressional materials listed in the "Schedule of Volumes" are sent to depository libraries that subscribe to the appropriate depository items.

Monthly Catalog Editions
of the Serial Set

Beginning with the 97th Congress (1981-1982) the user-friendly *Numerical Lists* was terminated and was replaced by the *Monthly Catalog of United States Government Publications: United States Congressional Serial Set Supplement, 97th Congress: 1981-1982: Entries and Indexes.* Classed in GP 3.34:981-82, the cumbersome title mirrors the size of the volume. Entries are organized in SuDocs class notation order and contain full bibliographic information like the entries in the regular issues of the *Monthly Catalog.* There are seven indexes: author, title, subject, series/report, bill number, stock number (S/N), and title keyword. Preceding the main entry section is a "List of Serial Set Volumes, 97th Congress," which is roughly analogous to (with a slightly different arrangement) the "Schedule of Volumes" section of the *Numerical Lists.* The "Numerical Lists" section is embedded in the series/report index but in an awkward manner.

Whereas the *Numerical Lists and Schedule of Volumes* was issued sessionally in a reasonably timely fashion, this product and its successor suffered a time lag of unconscionable proportions. The unsatisfactory tradeoff represents a step backward in timely, reliable access to the serial set volumes when one knows only the individual document or report number.

Compounding this ill-advised change, the Library Programs Service issued a new edition of serial set categories and bibliographic data but changed the title. The *United States Congressional Serial Set Catalog: Numerical Lists and Schedule of Volumes, 98th Congress: 1983-1984: Entries and Indexes*

(GP 3.34:983-84) contains the same main entry arrangement and information but introduces some changes from the 97th Congress edition. A positive change is the *inclusion* of the "Numerical Lists" and the retention of the "Schedule of Volumes." The stock number and title keyword indexes were eliminated from the 98th Congress publication. In the preliminary pages, a sample entry, which did not appear for the 97th Congress, was included. The task of compiling these two-year serial set entries and indexes was apparently so time-consuming that the "Schedule of Volumes" for future sessions of Congress has been published in various issues of *Administrative Notes*.[42]

Figures 5.20 and 5.21 (see pages 152 and 153) show, respectively, a page from the "Numerical Lists" and a page from the "Schedule of Volumes" of the 1933-1980 *Numerical Lists and Schedule of Volumes*. Figure 5.22 (see page 154) shows a main entry page in the *Monthly Catalog* serial set supplement for the 97th Congress. Fortunately for researchers, the *CIS US Serial Set Index, 1789-1969*, is available in its multivolume print edition and on *Congressional Master-file 1* (CD-ROM). Figure 5-23 (see page 155) shows a page from this retrospective index that comprises subjects and keywords.

Departmental and Congressional "Editions"

As indicated above, the House and Senate *documents* series included a number of executive branch publications. Congressional policy was never consistent regarding this practice. In some nineteenth-century Congresses, executive materials comprised over one-half of the serial set. These publications were required to be sent to Congress and included annual reports of departments and agencies, several series publications such as the *Geological Survey Bulletins*, a few periodicals, and reports and bulletins issued by the Bureau of Labor Statistics and the Smithsonian Institution. Notification of these kinds of non-congressional materials was given in every sessional issue of the *Numerical Lists*. In the "Schedule of Volumes" section preceding the titles of these "departmental" editions, there is this explanatory statement:

> Note. — The documents listed below originated in executive departments and agencies. They were or will be furnished to depository libraries and international exchanges at the time of printing in the format used by the departments and agencies. They will not be furnished as Congressional documents nor in the volumes as indicated hereby.

The result was that two editions of the same publication were often printed: the "departmental" edition and the "congressional" edition. But depository libraries received those publications only in the "departmental" edition with the SuDocs class notation and *only* if the library subscribed to the appropriate depository item number. This practice resulted in apparent gaps in the serial set, unless a cross-reference was made to the departmental edition.

(Text continues on page 156.)

Fig. 5.20. Page from "Numerical Lists"

34   NUMERICAL LISTS

No.	HOUSE REPORTS	Vol.; serial

537. Earnings test for social security beneficiaries. 2 pts _ _ _ _   15; 13302
538. Reduce unemployment compensation by retirement benefits _   15; 13302
539. Unemployment compensation, employees of National Oceanic and Atmospheric Administration. 3 pts _ _ _ _   15; 13302
540. Civil Service authorization act of 1979 _ _ _ _ _ _ _ _ _ _ _   15; 13302
541. 2d concurrent resolution on budget, fiscal 1980 _ _ _ _ _ _   15; 13302
542. Appropriations for Department of Housing and Urban Development _   15; 13302
543. Designate birthday of Martin Luther King, Jr., as legal holiday _   15; 13302
544. Amend act of Dec. 22, 1974, 88 Stat. 1712_ _ _ _ _ _ _ _ _ _   15; 13302
545. Tax administration provisions revision act of 1979 _ _ _ _   15; 13302
546. Department of Defense authorization act, fiscal 1980 _ _ _   15; 13302
547. Consideration of H.J. Res. 430 _ _ _ _ _ _ _ _ _ _ _ _ _ _ _   15; 13302
548. Civil suits for violations of civil rights _ _ _ _ _ _ _ _ _ _ _ _   15; 13302
549. Amend District of Columbia redevelopment act of 1945 _ _·   15; 13302
550. Extend borrowing authority for District of Columbia _ _ _   15; 13302
551. Conveyance to Little Sisters of the Poor _ _ _ _ _ _ _ _ _ _ _   15; 13302
552. Low-income energy assistance supplemental appropriation. 2 pts _   15; 13302
553. Appropriations for Agriculture, Rural Development, and related agencies programs, fiscal 1980_ _ _ _ _ _ _ _ _ _   15; 13302
554. Consideration of H.R. 4904 _ _ _ _ _ _ _ _ _ _ _ _ _ _ _ _ _ _   15; 13302
555. Consideration of H.R. 5192 _ _ _ _ _ _ _ _ _ _ _ _ _ _ _ _ _ _   15; 13302
556. Maritime appropriation authorization act, fiscal 1980 _ _ _   15; 13302
557. Indiana Dunes National Lakeshore _ _ _ _ _ _ _ _ _ _ _ _ _ _   15; 13302
558. Report by Permanent Select Committee on Intelligence pursuant to sec. 108(b), Foreign intelligence surveillance act _   15; 13302
559. Revitalize passenger ship industry _ _ _ _ _ _ _ _ _ _ _ _ _   15; 13302
560. Relief of Ohio Wesleyan University, Delaware, Ohio _ _ _ _   15; 13302
561. Relief of St. Paul's Episcopal Church, Riverside, Conn. 2 pts _   15; 13302
562. Temporary duty suspension on certain alloy steels used for making chipper knives _ _ _ _ _ _ _ _ _ _ _ _ _ _ _ _ _   15; 13302
563. Temporary reduction of duty on strontium nitrate _ _ _ _ _   15; 13302
564. Temporary suspension of duty on fluorspar _ _ _ _ _ _ _ _ _   15; 13302
565. Temporary duty reduction on titanium sponge _ _ _ _ _ _ _   15; 13302
566. Tariff classification of cold finished steel bars _ _ _ _ _ _ _   15; 13302
567. Temporary suspension of duty on pillow blanks of latex foam rubber_   15; 13302
568. Child health assurance act of 1979_ _ _ _ _ _ _ _ _ _ _ _ _ _ _   15; 13302
569. Miscellaneous tariff schedules amendments_ _ _ _ _ _ _ _ _ _   15; 13302
570. Establish Legionville National Historic Site in Pennsylvania _   15; 13302
571. Consideration of H.R. 4985 _ _ _ _ _ _ _ _ _ _ _ _ _ _ _ _ _ _   15; 13302
572. Term of Federal Reserve Board Chairman _ _ _ _ _ _ _ _ _ _   15; 13302
573. Further expenses of investigations, etc., by Permanent Select Committee on Intelligence _ _ _ _ _ _ _ _ _ _ _ _ _   15; 13302
574. National Archives film-vault fire, Suitland, Maryland, Dec. 7, 1978 _   15; 13302
575. Express sense of Congress with respect to Baltic States and Soviet claims of citizenship over U.S. citizens _ _   15; 13302
576. Consideration of H.R. 2603 _ _ _ _ _ _ _ _ _ _ _ _ _ _ _ _ _ _   15; 13302
577. Consideration of H.R. 2608 _ _ _ _ _ _ _ _ _ _ _ _ _ _ _ _ _ _   15; 13302
578. Consideration of H.R. 3994 _ _ _ _ _ _ _ _ _ _ _ _ _ _ _ _ _ _   15; 13302
579. Consideration of H.R. 2063 _ _ _ _ _ _ _ _ _ _ _ _ _ _ _ _ _ _   15; 13302

Fig. 5.21. Page from "Schedule of Volumes"

40   SCHEDULE OF VOLUMES

SENATE EXECUTIVE DOCUMENTS—SENATE REPORTS SENATE EXECUTIVE REPORTS—HOUSE DOCUMENTS	Serial no.	Date of receipt
SENATE EXECUTIVE DOCUMENTS		
Letters A–II: Senate executive documents	13235	
SENATE REPORTS		
Vol. 1. Nos. 1–47: Senate miscellaneous reports _	13236	
Vol. 2. Nos. 48–65: Senate miscellaneous reports_	13237	
Vol. 3. Nos. 66–104: Senate miscellaneous reports	13238	
Vol. 4. Nos. 105–155: Senate miscellaneous reports _ _ _ _ _ _ _ _ _ _ _ _ _ _ _ _ _ _ _	13239	
Vol. 5. Nos. 156–195: Senate miscellaneous reports _ _ _ _ _ _ _ _ _ _ _ _ _ _ _ _ _ _ _	13240	
Vol. 6. Nos. 196–237: Senate miscellaneous reports _ _ _ _ _ _ _ _ _ _ _ _ _ _ _ _ _ _ _	13241	
Vol. 7. Nos. 238–250: Senate miscellaneous reports _ _ _ _ _ _ _ _ _ _ _ _ _ _ _ _ _ _ _	13242	
Vol. 8. Nos. 251–299: Senate miscellaneous reports _ _ _ _ _ _ _ _ _ _ _ _ _ _ _ _ _ _ _	13243	
Vol. 9. Nos. 300–330: Senate miscellaneous reports _ _ _ _ _ _ _ _ _ _ _ _ _ _ _ _ _ _ _	13244	
Vol. 10. Nos. 331–374: Senate miscellaneous reports _ _ _ _ _ _ _ _ _ _ _ _ _ _ _ _ _ _ _	13245	
Vol. 11. Nos. 375–394: Senate miscellaneous reports _ _ _ _ _ _ _ _ _ _ _ _ _ _ _ _ _ _ _	13246	
Vol. 12. Nos. 395–423: Senate miscellaneous reports _ _ _ _ _ _ _ _ _ _ _ _ _ _ _ _ _ _ _	13247	
Vol. 13. Nos.424–471: Senate miscellaneous reports _ _ _ _ _ _ _ _ _ _ _ _ _ _ _ _ _ _ _	13248	
Vol. 14. Nos. 472–547: Senate miscellaneous reports _ _ _ _ _ _ _ _ _ _ _ _ _ _ _ _ _ _ _	13249	
SENATE EXECUTIVE REPORTS		
Nos. 1–26: Senate executive reports _ _ _ _	13250	
HOUSE DOCUMENTS		
Vol. 1. Nos. 1–15: Miscellaneous documents _ _ _	13251	
Vol. 2. Nos. 16–20: Examinations of rivers and harbors _ _ _ _ _ _ _ _ _ _ _ _ _ _ _ _ _ _	13252	
Vol. 3. Nos. 21–23: Examinations of rivers and harbors _ _ _ _ _ _ _ _ _ _ _ _ _ _ _ _ _	13253	
Vol. 4. Nos. 24–26: Examinations of rivers and harbors _ _ _ _ _ _ _ _ _ _ _ _ _ _ _ _ _	13254	
Vol. 5. Nos. 27–39: Miscellaneous documents_ _ _	13255	

Fig. 5.22. Page from MoCat Serial Set, 97th Congress

MONTHLY CATALOG

UNITED STATES CONGRESSIONAL SERIAL SET SUPPLEMENT

SENATE DOCUMENTS

Senate documents are available from the Senate Document Room unless otherwise indicated.

85-5762

Y 1.1/3:97-1

Sapp, Jack L.
  Senate manual containing the standing rules, orders, laws, and resolutions affecting the business of the United States Senate : Articles of Confederation and the Constitution of the United States / prepared by Jack L. Sapp, Committee on Rules and Administration, United States Senate, Ninety-seventh Congress. — Rev. ed. — Washington : U.S. G.P.O. : For sale by the Supt. of Docs., U.S. G.P.O., 1981 [i.e. 1982]
  v, 843 p. ; 24 cm. — (Senate document ; no. 97-1) **Serial Set No.: 13385** GPO stock number noted in publication. Includes bibliographical references and indexes. ●Item 996-A, 996-B (microfiche) S/N 052-071-00641-9 @ GPO $8.50
  1. United States. Congress. Senate I. United States. Congress. Senate. Committee on Rules and Administration. II. Title. III. Series: Senate document (United States. Congress (97th, 1st session : 1981). Senate) ; no. 97-1. OCLC 08741655

85-5763

Y 1.1/3:97-2

Riddick, Floyd Millard, 1908-
  Senate procedure : precedents and practices / by Floyd M. Riddick, Parliamentarian Emeritus, United States Senate. — Washington : U.S. G.P.O. : For sale by the Supt. of Docs., U.S. G.P.O., 1981.
  xiv, 1325 p. ; 24 cm. — (Senate document ; no. 97-2) **Serial Set No.: 13386** Includes bibliographical references and index. ●Item 996-A, 996-B (microfiche) S/N 052-071-00623-1 @ GPO $15.00
  1. United States. Congress. Senate I. United States. Congress. Senate. II. Title. III. Series: Senate document (United States. Congress (97th, 1st session : 1981). Senate) ; no. 97-2. OCLC 08584659

85-5764

Y 1.1/3:97-3

How can the U.S. elementary and secondary education systems best be improved? : national debate topic for high schools, 1981-1982, pursuant to Public law 88-246 / compiled by the Congressional Research Service, Library of Congress. — Washington : U.S. G.P.O., 1981.
  vii, 724 p. : ill. ; 24 cm. — (Senate / 97th Congress, 1st session, document ; no. 97-3) **Serial Set No.: 13387** Includes bibliographies. ●Item 996-A, 996-B (microfiche) S/N 052-071-00631-1 @ GPO $8.00
  1. Educational planning — United States. 2. Education, Elementary — United States. 3. Education, Secondary — United States. 4. Debates and debating — United States. I. Library of Congress. Congressional Research Service. II. Series: Senate document (United States. Congress (97th, 1st session : 1981). Senate) ; no. 97-3. 81-603645 OCLC 07970538

85-5765

Y 1.1/3:97-4/pt.1-2

United States. Congress. Senate.
  Report of the Secretary of the Senate from ... Washington : U.S. G.P.O.,
  v. ; 24 cm. (Senate document ; no. 97-4/pt.1-2)
  Semiannual
  Began with 1954. **Serial Set No.: 13388** Oct. 1, 1980-Mar. 31, 1981, pts. 1-2. Description based on: Apr. 1, 1980 to Sept. 30, 1980. Vols. for Apr.1-Sept. 30, 1979- issued in 2 pts. ●Item 996-A, 996-B (microfiche) Main series: Senate document (United States. Congress. Senate)
  1. United States. Congress. Senate — Appropriations and expenditures — Periodicals. I. Title. II. Series: Senate document (United States. Congress (97th, 1st session : 1981). Senate) ; no. 97-4/pt.1-2. OCLC 02944567

85-5766

Y 1.1/3:97-5

History of the Committee on Finance, United States Senate. — [4th ed.] — Washington : U.S. G.P.O., 1981.
  ix, 138 p. : ill., ports ; 24 cm. — (Senate document ; no. 97-5) **Serial Set No.: 13389** "May 12, 1981." ●Item 996-A, 996-B (microfiche)
  1. United States. Congress. Senate. Committee on Finance 2. United States — History. I. Series: Senate document (United States. Congress (97th, 1st session : 1981). Senate) ; no. 97-5. OCLC 11194877

85-5767

Y 1.1/3:97-6

United States. President (1981- : Reagan)
  Amendments to the supplemental appropriations for fiscal year 1981 (EC 1189) : communication from the president of the United States transmitting amendment to the request for supplemental appropriations for fiscal year 1981 in the amount of $2,379,000 and an amendment to the appropriations for fiscal year 1982 in the amount of $1,670,000. — Washington : U.S. G.P.O., 1981.
  3 p. ; 24 cm. — (Senate document ; no. 97-6) **Serial Set No.: 13389** "Referred to the Committee on Appropriations and ordered to be printed." "May 14, 1981." ●Item 996-A, 996-B (microfiche)
  1. Expenditures, Public. I. United States. Congress. House. Committee on Appropriations. II. Title. III. Series: Senate document (United States. Congress (97th, 2nd session : 1981). Senate) ; no. 97-6. OCLC 08403485

85-5768

Y 1.1/3:97-7

United States. President (1981- : Reagan)
  Supplement budget of District of Columbia : communicaton from the president of the United States transmitting proposed supplemental for fiscal year 1981 of $17 million from District of Columbia's own revenues. — Washington : U.S. G.P.O., 1981.

Fig. 5.23. Page from *CIS US Serial Set Index*

A. A. RAVEN (SHIP)
Relief of owners of steamship A. A. Raven
S.rp. 127 (69-1) 8527
ABANDONED
see also Abandonment
Disposal of abandoned military reservations in Alaska
S.rp. 526 (70-1) 8830; H.rp. 331 (70-1) 8835
Sale of abandoned tract of land in Florida
S.rp. 1062 (69-1) 8526
Sale of certain abandoned land and buildings
H.rp. 372 (69-1) 8532
Set aside lands around abandoned well, Bowdoin, Mont.
H.rp. 1269 (72-1) 9493
Setting aside lands around abandoned well, Bowdoin, Mont.
S.rp. 862 (72-1) 9488
Transfer of abandoned Indian-school site at Zeba, Mich.
S.rp. 620 (72-1) 9488; H.rp. 945 (72-1) 9492
ABANDONMENT
see also Desertion
see also Nonsupport
Abandonment and non-support of wife or children in D.C.
S.rp. 895 (69-1) 8526
Abandonment or curtailment of river and harbor projects
H.doc. 467 (69-1) 8579
ABERDEEN
Bridge across Ohio River, Maysville, Ky., and Aberdeen, Ohio
H.rp. 1651 (69-2) 8688; H.rp. 1654 (69-2) 8688;
S.rp. 292 (70-1) 8829; S.rp. 301 (70-1) 8829; H.rp. 415 (70-1) 8835;
H.rp. 416 (70-1) 8835; S.rp. 1749 (70-2) 8977;
H.rp. 2197 (70-2) 8979; H.rp. 2198 (70-2) 8979
Bridge across Tombigbee River near Aberdeen, Miss.
S.rp. 151 (70-1) 8829; H.rp. 197 (70-1) 8835
Dredging and filling near Proving Ground, Aberdeen, Md.
H.rp. 1277 (69-1) 8534
Making available to Aberdeen, Wash., U.S.S. Newport
S.rp. 603 (73-2) 9769
To make available to Aberdeen, Wash., U.S.S. Newport
S.rp. 1097 (72-2) 9647; H.rp. 1197 (73-2) 9775
ABILENE
American Legion memorial building at Abilene, Tex.
S.rp. 487 (72-1) 9487; H.rp. 255 (72-1) 9491
ABOLITION
Abolish criers and bailiffs in courts of United States
H.rp. 1016 (70-1) 8836
Abolish Papago Saguaro National Monument, Ariz.
H.rp. 260 (71-2) 9190
Abolish statute permitting renewal of patent applications
H.rp. 1198 (72-1) 9492

Abolishing certain office in Library of Congress
S.rp. 908 (70-1) 8831
Abolishing Papago Saguaro National Monument, Ariz.
S.rp. 128 (71-2) 9185
Abolishing term of district court at Portsmouth, N.H.
H.rp. 200 (69-1) 8531
Abolition of office in Library of Congress, etc.
H.rp. 806 (70-1) 8836
Amendment to Constitution abolishing electoral college
H.rp. 262 (73-1) 9774
Executive order abolishing Geographic Board
H.doc. 308 (73-2) 9821
Executive order abolishing Indian Commissioners Board
H.doc. 57 (73-1) 9751
Executive order abolishing Office of Alien Property Custodian and
transferring functions to Justice Dept.
H.doc. 337 (73-2) 9821
Executive order for consolidation, transfers, and abolition of
Executive agencies
H.doc. 69 (73-1) 9751
To abolish capital punishment in District of Columbia
H.rp. 876 (69-1) 8533
To abolish Personnel Classification Board
H.rp. 960 (71-2) 9193
Transfer to States of records of abolished land offices
S.rp. 794 (69-1) 8526; H.rp. 870 (69-1) 8533
ABRASIVE
Labor Statistics Bur. bull. 436; Safety code for protection of abrasive
wheels
H.doc. 638 (69-2) 8795
Labor Statistics Bur. bull. 527; Safety code for protection of abrasive
wheels
H.doc. 583 (71-3) 9446
ABROAD
see also Overseas
Amend Public act 141 rel. to pensions to veterans who enlisted after
Aug. 12, 1898, and served outside of U.S.
H.rp. 1770 (73-2) 9776
American branch factories abroad
S.doc. 120 (73-2) 9800
Conservation of estates of citizens of U.S. dying abroad
H.rp. 1334 (71-2) 9192
Encourage sale of American agricultural surplus products abroad,
provide for payment therefore in silver, etc.
S.rp. 697 (73-2) 9770
Equalizing annual leave of employees of Agriculture Department
stationed outside of United States
S.rp. 544 (73-2) 9769

The number of such "duplicate" printings was gradually reduced. The changes effected in the serial set beginning with the 96th Congress included a reduction of duplicate publications to a small number of titles and series. However, the occasional exception persisted. For example, a General Accounting Office (GAO) study titled *Audit of the Rural Telephone Bank* was issued as 96-2: H. Doc. 297 but in its "departmental" edition was titled *Examination of the Rural Telephone Bank's Financial Statements*. The main entries in the *Monthly Catalog* provide bibliographic information for serial set publications and include the availability of other editions.[43]

The reduction in duplication was designed to decrease costs. By eliminating the so-called posterity edition (one with red, green, and black ink labels, stamped with imitation gold), the traditional, less elaborate edition is sent to depository institutions and all other authorized recipients of the serial set. But librarians need to be aware that certain serial set volumes are important reference sources. Because of their size, they are not issued in slip form but are sent directly in bound volumes with a serial volume number on the spine. They are, however, assigned an individual House or Senate document number for bibliographic consistency. These volumes include the *Constitution of the United States, Analysis and Interpretation*, and its supplements; investigative studies such as the Iran-Contra reports; the quarterly *Report of the Clerk of the House of Representatives*; financial disclosure reports of members of both chambers; appropriations and budget estimate statements; the *Biographical Directory of the United States Congress* cumulative editions; and the *Guide to the Records of the United States Senate at the National Archives, 1789-1989*, and its companion volume, *Guide to the Records of the United States House of Representatives at the National Archives, 1789-1989*.[44]

The last publications provide an illustration of this practice. The *Guide to the Records of the United States Senate* was assigned S. Doc. 100-42 but was sent to depository libraries as Serial Set Volume 13853. Similarly, the *Guide to the Records of the United States House of Representatives* was designated H. Doc. 100-245 but was received by depository institutions as Serial Set Volume 13886. Reference sources of this nature should be removed from their numerical sequence in the serial set shelves and assigned to the reference collection in the classification system used by the library.

The Serial Set on Microfiche

The largest cost-saving measure adopted in 1979 was the production of the serial set in a microfiche edition. In December of that year depository libraries were offered the choice of microfiche or paper copy distribution. Those libraries opting for the serial set on microfiche are provided with dividers indicating the serial volume number and the number of reports and documents included in that volume. Accordingly, the initial sequence of materials issued in fact becomes the "bound" serial volume. Libraries choosing paper copy distribution receive the series in slip form and later in bound volumes. That all printed materials are bound in numerical order is clearly an accommodation to the decision to issue a microfiche edition, a policy based on economics rather than user convenience. It forced the elimination of the earlier policy of grouping House and Senate reports into logical categories and assigning a numbered suffix to the base serial volume number. Because of the various sizes and shapes of publications issued in the serial set, the present arrangement is awkward for those libraries still receiving the serial set in hard copy.

Moreover, users in those depository institutions that had accepted the serial set on fiche were intolerably inconvenienced when, in the late 1980s, a series of problems with the contractors responsible for filming the set resulted in an egregious time lag receipt of these materials. Although the problem was eventually resolved, the possibility of contractor default or "quality problems" with the fiche once a contract has been awarded is a factor to bear in mind when libraries are offered a choice between fiche and hard copy in receiving series as important as the Congressional Serial Set.[45] Readex Microprint Corporation offers subscribers the full text of the serial set for individual Congresses on microcard and more recently on either diazo negative or silver halide microfiche.

Serial Set Classification

Prior to the 96th Congress, the serial set was simply *designated*, without a SuDocs classification symbol. Thus, a committee report for the Extension of the Library Services and Construction Act was designated 95-1: H. Rep. 97. After an abortive attempt to use the alpha "X" as an author symbol, a letter that had been used earlier for the *Annals of Congress, Register of Debates,* and *Congressional Globe*, the present class notation was devised to comprise both paper copy and microfiche distribution and bibliographic control.[46] As shown in the current edition of the *List of Classes*, the serial set is organized in the manner described in figure 5.24 (see page 158).

LEGISLATIVE HISTORIES

Legislative histories comprise citations to and the text of those internal documents generated in the legislative process and any comments by the president upon signing the legislation or issuing a veto message. Some or all of these texts have been consulted by the courts in an attempt to determine "legislative intent" if the meaning or purpose of a statute is ambiguous. "Over the past six decades the courts have increasingly relied on legislative history when faced with interpretation of Federal statutes." At one time committee reports were considered the most reliable source for finding congressional intent. As Justice John Marshall Harlan noted in 1969, committee reports "have this status because they represent the 'considered and collective understanding of those Congressmen involved in drafting and studying proposed legislation.'"[47] But Supreme Court Justice Antonin Scalia and other prominent jurists question that assumption. "Because reports are prepared by committee staff and not necessarily even read by committee members, let alone by the vast majority of voting members not on the recommending committee," Scalia and like-minded judges and justices find committee reports ineffective instruments for ascertaining intent.[48]

(Text continues on page 159.)

Fig. 5.24. Serial set classification

SuDocs Class Number	Category	Depository Item Number
Y 1.1/2: (Serial Volume Number)	Serial Set Volumes, H & S rpts., S. Exec. rpts.	1008-E
Y 1.1/2: (Serial Volume Number)	Serial Set Volumes, H & S docs., S. Treaty docs.	996-C
Y 1.1/3: (Cong.-no.)	S. docs.	996-A
Y 1.1/4: (Cong.-no.)	S. Treaty docs.	996-A
Y 1.1/5: (Cong.-no.)	S. rpts.	1008-C
Y 1.1/6: (Cong.-no.)	S. Exec. rpts.	1008-C
Y 1.1/7: (Cong.-no.)	H. docs.	996-A
Y 1.1/8: (Cong.-no.)	H. rpts.	1008-C

MICROFICHE DISTRIBUTION

SuDocs Class Number	Category	Depository Item Number
Y 1.1/2: (Serial Volume Number)	Serial Set Volumes, H & S rpts., S. Exec. rpts.	1008-D
Y 1.1/2: (Serial Volume Number)	Serial Set Volumes, H & S docs., S. Treaty docs.	996-B
Y 1.1/3: (Cong.-no.)	S. docs.	996-B
Y 1.1/4: (Cong.-no.)	S. Treaty docs.	996-B
Y 1.1/5: (Cong.-no.)	S. rpts.	1008-D
Y 1.1/6: (Cong.-no.)	S. Exec. rpts.	1008-D
Y 1.1/7: (Cong.-no.)	H. docs.	996-B
Y 1.1/8: (Cong.-no.)	H. rpts.	1008-D

There has never been a clear consensus on the Supreme Court regarding the usefulness of the several texts generated in the legislative process. In recent years the High Court

> is resorting less readily to legislative history, and is reemphasizing statutory text. This trend, begun well before Justice Scalia's arrival on the Court, appears not only from cases in which statutory language is deemed plain and unambiguous ... but also from other cases in which legislative history is consulted only to determine if there is a "clear statement" of congressional intent contrary to the Court's reading of the statute's meaning ... or in which legislative history is not consulted at all despite disputed meaning.[49]

Moreover, interpreting the "meaning" of a statute or an administrative regulation pursuant to statutory authority depends in large part upon jurisprudential proclivities. In his insightful essay on theories of statutory construction, Peter Schanck demonstrates that the relative emphasis (or lack thereof) on certain legislative publications in the complex process by which a bill becomes a law varies according to whether one has embraced deconstructionism, public choice theory, conventionalism, or evolutionary constructivism. In the opinion of one legal scholiast, interpretation "is an ongoing process of creating new and evolving meaning from text.... Judges are at once constrained by their community's legal and political history and free to interpret it so that it will reflect their own vision of the community's political morality."[50] And if the courts, including the U.S. Supreme Court, have difficulty construing the intent of legislation Congress enacted a decade or a generation ago, consider the problems they face when trying to determine "original intent." In a concurring opinion in *Youngstown Sheet and Tube Co.* v. *Sawyer* (1952), Supreme Court Justice Robert H. Jackson, reflecting upon the extent of presidential authority implicit in the Constitution, said:

> Just what our forefathers did envision, or would have envisioned had they foreseen modern conditions, must be divined from materials almost as enigmatic as the dreams Joseph was called upon to interpret for Pharaoh. A century and a half of partisan debate and scholarly speculation yields no net result but only supplies more or less apt quotations from respected sources on each side of the question. They largely cancel each other. (72 S.Ct. 863, 870)

It is impossible to summarize the amount of casuistry, verbiage, informed opinion, and common sense surrounding this topic. Fortunately, the sources that constitute legislative histories are relatively easy to collect and collate, and it is an undertaking that documents and law librarians are frequently asked to perform.

Basic Textual Materials

The sources cited at the end of each slip law (see figure 5.15) constitute a minimal legislative history: the bill number; House and Senate reports, including a conference report if appropriate; dates of consideration and passage in the

Congressional Record; and a presidential statement published in the *Weekly Compilation of Presidential Documents.* Beyond that, legislative histories may include all the parliamentary stages of related bills, hearings, and committee prints.

Electronic Services

WESTLAW, LEXIS, and LEGI-SLATE all provide bibliographic access to the texts that constitute legislative histories. The last makes available these documents for all bills and resolutions introduced since the start of the 96th Congress.

Microfiche Services

Commerce Clearing House (CCH) publishes a service called *Public Laws — Legislative Histories on Microfiche,* in which the documentation for laws are sent to subscribers shortly after enactment. The package usually includes the text of House or Senate bills as introduced or reported, committee reports (including the conference report), debates and voting information in the *Congressional Record,* and the slip law.

Information Handling Services (IHS) offers an *IHS Legislative Histories Program,* in which the filming of important general legislation for current Congresses and retrospective sessions is accomplished. The documentation on fiche includes the text of the public law, bills, reports, hearings, committee prints, *Congressional Record* debates, and relevant presidential statements.

Congressional Information Service offered a *Basic Legislative History Service* and a *Comprehensive Legislative History Service.* The latter included the standard textual information plus a number of related publications. Although this service was discontinued, selected microfiche histories were made available for the years 1909 through 1952.

REMAC (McLean, Virginia) offers the full text of legislative histories on fiche from the 67th Congress and as an ongoing subscription. This compilation is filmed from the collection maintained by the GAO.

Sources for Compiling Legislative Histories

A number of government publications and commercial guides provide citations to the several congressional forms that constitute a legislative history. A useful starting point is Nancy P. Johnson (comp.), *Sources of Compiled Legislative Histories: A Bibliography of Government Documents, Periodical Articles, and Books* (AALL Pub. Ser. No. 14). Issued in looseleaf binder, the basic volume with periodic supplements covers selective compilations of legislative histories from the 1st Congress. The contents include citations to looseleaf, microfiche, and electronic services; collections dealing with specific subjects arranged by topic; and parallel tables. The tables are helpful in that if one knows the public law number, references are made to the bill number, *Statutes at Large* citation, title of act, sources such as the *CCH Public Laws — Legislative Histories on Microfiche*, law review articles that discuss the statute, and "contents" information. Figure 5.25 shows a page from a 1988 supplement to Johnson's *Sources*.

Fig. 5.25. Page from *Sources of Compiled Legislative Histories*

98-499 S. 1146	98 Stat. 2312	AVIATION DRUG-TRAFFICKING CONTROL ACT CCH Public Laws-Legislative Histories on Microfiche.
98-501 S. 1330	98 Stat. 2320	PUBLIC WORKS IMPROVEMENT ACT OF 1984 CCH Public Laws-Legislative Histories on Microfiche.
98-502 S. 1510	98 Stat. 2327	SINGLE AUDIT ACT OF 1984 CCH Public Laws-Legislative Histories on Microfiche.
98-507 S. 2048	98 Stat. 2339	NATIONAL ORGAN TRANSPLANT ACT CCH Public Laws-Legislative Histories on Microfiche. Denise, Susan Hankin. "Regulating the Sale of Human Organs." 71 Virginia Law Review 1015 (1985). X X Johnson, Karen L. "The Sale of Human Organs: Implicating a Privacy Right." 21 Valparaiso University Law Review 741 (1987). X X
98-524 H.R. 4164	98 Stat. 2435	CARL D. PERKINS VOCATIONAL EDUCATION ACT CCH Public Laws-Legislative Histories on Microfiche.
98-528 H.R. 5618	98 Stat. 2686	VETERANS HEALTH CARE ACT OF 1984 CCH Public Laws-Legislative Histories on Microfiche.

CIS/Annual from 1970 to 1983 includes legislative history citations as a section of the *Abstracts* volume. Beginning with 1984, detailed legislative histories are published in a separate volume entitled *CIS/Annual: Legislative Histories of U.S. Public Laws*. The format is large and user-friendly and includes information on all pertinent documents for every law enacted during a session of Congress. As is typical of CIS's publishing schedule, the user can go directly from these citations to the full text on microfiche. One can gain access in the same way using *Congressional Masterfile 2* on CD-ROM.

United States Code Congressional and Administrative News in its annual volumes contains a number of features, among them a "Legislative History" table arranged by public law number referencing the date approved, *Statutes at Large* citation, bill number, House and Senate report numbers, abbreviations for the names of the House and Senate committees reporting, and dates of consideration and passage in the *Congressional Record*.

CCH Congressional Index contains "Status of House Bills" and "Status of Senate Bills" divisions that show, in tabular form, the current status of legislation. The cumulative features of these divisions, published weekly, provide an ongoing legislative history and can be used as a retrospective finding aid for bills that eventually become law. Completed legislation can be located in the "Enactments – Vetoes" division by public law number, original bill number, subject, and sponsor. Because of its timeliness, cumulative features, and detailed subject index, *CCH Congressional Index* is perhaps the most useful print source for ascertaining the current status of federal legislation.

Certain government publications also provide citations for tracking legislation and compiling legislative history documents. The biweekly *Congressional Record Index* contains a cumulative "History of Bills and Resolutions" section. Organized by bill number, information with references to the pages of the daily *Record* includes co-sponsors added, reported with amendments, amended and passed Senate, amended and passed House, conference reports submitted and agreed to, and presentation to and approval by the president. Moreover, the annual cumulation of the "Daily Digest" section of the CR features a *History of Bills Enacted into Public Law* arranged by public (slip) law number.

The *House Calendars*, which include Senate action, is sent to depository institutions weekly. A section titled "Numerical Order of Bills and Resolutions Which Have Passed Either or Both Houses, and Bills Now Pending on the Calendars" provides by chamber and within chamber by form of measure the current status and legislative history of all actions on each bill. It is arranged by bill or resolution number, with similar or identical bills and bills having reference to one another indicated by number in parentheses. Tables of public and private laws are organized by public law number referencing the bill number. A "Status of Major Bills" table is arranged by bill number with reference to title, committee report numbers, reported dates, dates of passage in both chambers, conference report dates, and public law numbers.

Moreover, tables of "Bills in Conference" and "Bills through Conference" provide number and date, brief title of measure, names of House and Senate conferees, and report numbers with dates. The several "calendars" of the House are arranged by date with bill or report number, sponsor and committee, title of measure, and calendar number. Unlike the Senate, which has a *Calendar of Business*, the House has a Union Calendar, House Calendar, Private Calendar, Consent Calendar, and Calendar of Motions to Discharge Committees. The functions of these calendars are discussed in the current edition of *How Our Laws Are Made*.

The *House Calendars* cumulate bill status information. At the end of a Congress, the *Final Edition* should be permanently retained. It becomes a most valuable retrospective source for the information noted above as well as providing numerous tables and summary pages of bills and resolutions introduced, committee reports, public and private laws, presidential vetoes, vetoes overridden, constitutional amendments submitted to the states for ratification, and comparative statistics for previous Congresses. In ascertaining current legislative progress the *House Calendars* can most profitably be used after a bill has been reported out of committee. This publication has been designated Y 1.2/2 in the SuDocs class notation.

The Senate *Calendar of Business* is far less useful because it does not cumulate and has no index. However, it has a "Bills in Conference" section arranged by date sent to conference, with bill number, brief title, Senate and House conferees, Senate report number, and current status. A separate table, "Status of Appropriations Bills," is arranged by bill number with brief title and legislative history to date. The *Calendar of Business* (Y 1.3/3) is available to depository libraries, but the *House Calendars* should be used to access current status information for both chambers.

The *Digest of Public General Bills and Resolutions* (LC 14.6) has been issued since 1936 and is prepared by the Congressional Research Service of the Library of Congress. Formerly sent to depository libraries in several cumulative issues during a session, it is currently distributed only in an annual edition. Its unique feature, as the title of the publication suggests, is the provision of digests or summaries of every public measure, with legislative history information included. The annotations can be brief or protracted depending upon the length of the actual measure. Useful indexes by sponsor and co-sponsors, identical bills, short titles, and subjects provide access to the main contents.

The *House Calendars* until recent times was issued daily and, as noted, the *Digest* appeared in depository Shipping Lists about every two months. These significant congressional guides were reduced in frequency as a consequence of the Gramm-Rudman-Hollings Act of 1985 (PL 99-177), which mandated that all branches of government assay cost reductions (sequestrations) in the never-ending attempts to bring the huge federal deficit under control.[51]

The *United States Statutes at Large* from 1963 through 1974 contained a handy "Guide to Legislative History of Bills Enacted into Public Law," which provides tabular data by public law number referencing date, volume and page of the *Statutes*, bill number, House and Senate report number and name of committee, and CR dates of consideration and passage. Although this table was discontinued, U.S.C.C.A.N. and other sources mentioned above provide this information. In 1975 the public laws began to provide citations to legislative history and, of course, these appear in the bound volumes of the *Statutes at Large*. Upon receipt of the volumes, depository libraries may discard the slip laws covering that session.

Voluminous legislative histories are issued on a selective basis by a House or Senate committee. Usually prepared by the Congressional Research Service and issued as committee prints, they are indexed in the *Monthly Catalog* and indexed and abstracted in *CIS/Index* and *CIS/Annual*. Citations to these legislative histories are provided in Johnson's *Sources of Compiled Legislative Histories*, and users fortunate enough to locate a "ready made" legislative history on a law germane to their interests will probably encounter more information than they can assimilate.

Other official sources for legislative histories include the annual House *Journal* and Senate *Journal* and to a limited extent the *Journal of the Executive Proceedings of the Senate of the United States of America*, which is useful for information on nominations and treaties. With this range of sources the librarian should have no trouble directing users to legislative history citations and texts. The recondite mysteries of legislative "intent" are the province of the historian or political scientist and the legal profession.

OTHER LEGISLATIVE SOURCE MATERIALS

Publications issued by the Congress and its committees, by other federal entities, and by commercial publishers not discussed in the preceding pages provide supporting documentation for the legislative process. A selective account of these several sources follows.

House and Senate Manuals

The full title of the House *Manual* is *Constitution, Jefferson's Manual, and Rules of the House of Representatives of the United States.* It is published biennially during the first session of each Congress as a House document and contains the fundamental source material for parliamentary procedures used in that chamber. The full title of the Senate *Manual* is *Senate Manual, Containing the Standing Rules, Orders, Laws and Resolutions Affecting the Business of the United States Senate, Articles of Confederation and the Constitution of the United States.* Also published biennially in the Senate document series, it consists of three parts: rules, laws, procedures; historical documents; and statistical data. The last part contains information on electoral votes for president and vice-president, 1789 to date; lists of presidents pro tempore of the Senate; Supreme Court justices; cabinet officers; and the like. As part of the Congressional Serial Set, both *Manuals* are available to depository libraries in hard copy or on microfiche.

House and Senate Procedure

Deschler's Precedents of the United States House of Representatives is a series of volumes analyzing the precedents of the House. It is updated biennially as required by law and issued as a House document. The early precedents of the House, dating from the 1st Congress, are found in *Hinds' Precedents of the House of Representatives* (1907) and *Cannon's Precedents of the House of Representatives* (1936). The author of the current set, Lewis Deschler, was Parliamentarian of the House from 1928 to 1974.

Senate Procedure: Precedents and Practices was prepared by Floyd M. Riddick, parliamentarian emeritus of the Senate, and is issued as a Senate document. It is a large compilation of the rules of that chamber, portions of laws affecting Senate procedure, rulings by the presiding officer, and established Senate practices. The author was granted copyright under the provisions of 91 Stat. 115.

Memorial Addresses

Eulogies delivered in the House or Senate upon the death of a current or former member are classed in Y 7.1. Depository libraries subscribing to item 1005 used to receive these addresses in a series of bound volumes with a black cover, but this series is currently available on microfiche only. But when presidents, vice-presidents, or presidential appointees who have held high office in the executive or judiciary are memorialized, the compilation of tributes is issued in the serial set as House or Senate documents. Memorial issuances in the case of persons who have enjoyed careers in both the Congress and other government positions may be found in both series, for issuing patterns have not always been consistent. Tributes memorializing John F. Kennedy, who served in the Congress before becoming president, for example, appeared as 88-2: S. Doc. 59 (Serial Set Volume 12624). Senator Edward Kennedy's tribute to his brother Robert, which was delivered not in the Congress but at St. Patrick's Cathedral on June 8, 1968, was issued as 90-2: S. Doc. 86 (Serial Set Volume 12798-2). Clarification of the distinction between the "departmental" and "congressional" editions of memorial addresses was noted in *Administrative Notes*, vol. 12 (June 15, 1991), p. 1.

Constitution Annotated

The Congressional Research Service of the Library of Congress is required by law (2 U.S.C. 168) to issue a new edition of the *Constitution of the United States of America, Analysis and Interpretation*, every ten years with biennial supplements between editions. Known by its short title, the *Constitution Annotated* provides commentary on every article, section, and clause, with citations to important decisions of the U.S. Supreme Court appearing as footnotes. High Court decisions cited construing these provisions are not as numerous as those appearing in the unnumbered volumes of the Constitution found in the *United States Code Service* and the *United States Code Annotated* (both discussed above). Nevertheless, this volume and its supplements provide source materials for the beginning researcher.

The basic volume and the two-year supplements contain tables that include constitutional amendments pending and unratified, acts of Congress held unconstitutional wholly or in part by the High Court, state and local laws held unconstitutional, Supreme Court decisions subsequently overruled, a table of cases, and an adequate index.

The current base volume fell behind its decennial publishing schedule and was finally issued as 99-1: S. Doc. 16 (Serial Set Volume 13611); the first supplement in this new series was issued as 100-1: S. Doc. 9 (Serial Set Volume 13721). The series is also available for sale from the Superintendent of Documents.

An 81-page brochure titled *The Constitution of the United States of America as Amended* was issued in its bicentennial edition as 100-1: H. Doc. 94 (August 5, 1987). The text is not annotated but contains footnotes on ratification dates and states and on clauses superseded or affected by constitutional amendments. The section on Amendments following the Articles contains historical information on the proposals and ratification by the states. A section titled "Proposed Amendments to the Constitution Not Ratified by the States" is followed by an analytical index referencing the Articles and Amendments. Prepared under the direction of the House Judiciary Committee, this pamphlet is a starting point for further research. Like the *Constitution Annotated*, this House document is available for sale by the Superintendent of Documents.

Directories

The *Biographical Directory of the United States Congress, 1774-1989*, represents the latest edition in an irregularly updated series that was first published privately as the *Dictionary of Congress* (J. B. Lippincott & Co., 1859). After several privately published editions, the Joint Committee on Printing was authorized to compile updates of the *Biographical Directory* that were published in 1950, 1961, and 1971. The creation of the Senate Historical Office in 1975 and the Office for the Bicentennial in the House provided the first opportunity for professional historians to revise and update this series. A review of existing entries made manifest the need "for substantial revisions and additions" to bring the current work "into line with ... historical scholarship and accepted standards of accuracy and consistency."[52] Improvements include, *inter alia*, noting all standing committee chairpersons and all major, formal leadership positions; standardizing all political party designations to reflect contemporary electoral labels; providing bibliographic citations for all members "who have been the subject of scholarly publications"; verifying information by comparison with other standard reference works and primary sources; devising more nearly uniform categories of information in the entries; and revising the several reference tables that precede the biographies.

Consisting of over 11,000 entries, the "bicentennial edition" of the *Directory* involved a massive amount of scholarly research. Accordingly, this version is more accurate than previous editions, although the editors recognize that the "volume is and will always be a work in progress."[53] The *Directory* is a SuDocs sales item.

The *Official Congressional Directory*, published privately prior to 1848, was assigned to the Joint Committee on Printing in 1865. Published annually through 1974, it is currently issued biennially (Y 4.P93/1:1). Its main entries update the *Biographical Directory* for current members, and it contains several reference features, including a list of state delegations, lists of congressional committees with names of staff personnel as well as members, statistical data on sessions of Congress and congressional elections, lists of House and Senate officers, directories of legislative agencies such as the Government Printing Office, floor plans of the capitol, authorized members of the press covering Congress, and maps of congressional districts. Also included are lists of foreign diplomatic representatives and foreign consular offices in the United States and directory information on principal executive and judicial units. Like the *Biographical Directory*, the *Official Congressional Directory* is sold by the Superintendent of Documents.

A commercial publication, the *Congressional Yellow Book* (New York: Monitor Publishing Co.) is updated quarterly and includes biographical information for members of Congress, membership rosters and key staff aides for all committees and subcommittees, district maps and zip codes by district, and important staff members for congressional agencies.

CRS Serials

Three serials prepared by staff members of the Congressional Research Service (CRS) of the Library of Congress offer commentaries on current issues facing the Congress. *Major Legislation of the Congress* (MLC) (LC 14.18), published irregularly, provides summaries of topical issues and major legislation introduced in response thereto. MLC is an automated byproduct of the CRS Major Issues System, a special online program that extracts selected background material on key legislation.

Congressional Research Service Review (CRSR) (LC 14.19) is issued nine times during the year. Most issues feature a "Major Issue Forum" section in which a specific topic is discussed. In addition, each issue contains a number of other articles of current interest to Congress and its staff, congressional committees, other governmental units, and the general public. Both MLC and CRSR are announced in the current edition of *Price List 36* and sold as SuDocs subscription items.

Major Studies and Issue Briefs of the Congressional Research Service is not available to depository libraries but is sold commercially by University Publications of America (Bethesda, Maryland). A retrospective compilation of these valuable studies covers the period 1916-1974 with supplements through 1990; these collections are available on 35mm microfilm. In 1991 the publisher began a quarterly index and microfiche service on standing order. The indexes are accompanied by detailed abstracts and provide easy retrieval of the text from the microfiche file. The *Cumulative Index* covering the period 1916-1989 consists of two parts. Volume 1 is the "Bibliography of Documents and Supplementary Indexes" and volume 2 is the "Index by Names and Subjects." The companion microfilm collection for this period reproduces the 5,000 documents listed in the *Cumulative Index*.

Commercial Reference Sources

Congressional Quarterly, Inc., a commercial publisher located in Washington, D.C., enjoys a deserved reputation for the quality of its many publications. Some of its sources that provide access to congressional activities are enumerated here.

CQ Weekly Report, perhaps the best known specialized periodical that tracks the workings of Congress, contains essays on major legislation and related activities of the legislative branch. Its recurring features include a "Status of Major Legislation" table; House and Senate recorded voting charts with annotations covering each motion, names of members, and party affiliation (including a breakdown into "Northern Democrats" and "Southern Democrats"); members' committee assignments; bill sponsorship; transcripts of remarks by congressional leaders and the president; summaries of major Supreme Court decisions; and discursive accounts of ongoing legislation. The last contain citations to the important publications in the legislative process. Quarterly indexes by subjects and names cumulate throughout the year. The voting tables are organized in such a way that they are far easier to access than the comparable information in the *Congressional Record*. Figure 5.26 (see page 168) shows a typical voting chart in an issue of *CQ Weekly Report*.

LEGI-SLATE provides an online "Voting Analysis Service" including committee and subcommittee votes. It also indexes each article in *CQ Weekly Report* by subject, member of Congress, bill number, committee, vote, or public law; this service covers the period 1985 to date.[54]

(Text continues on page 169.)

Fig. 5.26. Voting chart from *CQ Weekly Report*

HOUSE VOTES 82, 83, 84, 85, 86

KEY

Y	Voted for (yea).
#	Paired for.
+	Announced for.
N	Voted against (nay).
X	Paired against.
-	Announced against.
P	Voted "present."
C	Voted "present" to avoid possible conflict of interest.
?	Did not vote or otherwise make a position known.

Democrats **Republicans**

82. HR 1502. District of Columbia Police Expansion/Passage. Dellums, D-Calif., motion to suspend the rules and pass the bill to authorize $127.3 million through fiscal year 1994 for the hiring of 700 additional police officers for the District of Columbia and to allow for the construction of a new 800-bed prison. Motion agreed to 289-105: R 59-100; D 230-5 (ND 158-3, SD 72-2), June 13, 1989. A two-thirds majority of those present and voting (263 in this case) is required for passage under suspension of the rules. A "nay" was a vote supporting the president's position. *(Story, p. 1469)*

83. HR 2072. Fiscal 1989 Supplemental Appropriations/Instruction of Conferees. Conte, R-Mass., motion to instruct the House conferees on the fiscal 1989 supplemental appropriations bill not to meet with Senate conferees on any issue in disagreement until resolution of supplemental funding for the Department of Veterans Affairs medical care programs. Motion agreed to 395-0: R 157-0; D 238-0 (ND 162-0, SD 76-0), June 13, 1989. *(Story, p. 1453)*

84. Procedural Motion. Solomon, R-N.Y., motion to approve the House *Journal* of Tuesday, June 13. Motion agreed to 303-104: R 66-97; D 237-7 (ND 156-7, SD 81-0), June 14, 1989.

85. HR 1278. Savings and Loan Restructuring/Rule. Adoption of the rule (H Res 173) to provide for House floor consideration of the bill to raise $50 billion to close and liquidate insolvent savings and loan associations and to restructure the thrift industry. Adopted 330-95: R 93-78; D 237-17 (ND 162-12, SD 75-5), June 14, 1989. *(Story, p. 1449)*

86. HR 2. Minimum-Wage Increase/Veto Override. Passage, over President Bush's June 13 veto, of the bill to raise the minimum wage from $3.35 an hour to $4.55 over three years, and to provide for a 60-day training wage — equal to 85 percent of the minimum — for workers who have not worked a total of 60 days. Rejected 247-178: R 20-150; D 227-28 (ND 171-3, SD 56-25), June 14, 1989. A two-thirds majority of those present and voting (284 in this case) of both houses is required to override a veto. A "nay" was a vote supporting the president's position. *(Story, p. 1465)*

	82	83	84	85	86
ALABAMA					
1 *Callahan*	?	?	Y	Y	N
2 *Dickinson*	?	?	N	Y	N
3 Browder	?	Y	Y	Y	Y
4 Bevill	Y	Y	Y	Y	Y
5 Flippo	Y	Y	Y	Y	Y
6 Erdreich	Y	Y	Y	Y	Y
7 Harris	Y	Y	Y	Y	Y
ALASKA					
AL *Young*	N	Y	N	N	N
ARIZONA					
1 *Rhodes*	N	Y	N	Y	N
2 Udall	Y	Y	?	Y	Y
3 *Stump*	N	Y	N	N	N
4 *Kyl*	N	Y	N	N	N
5 *Kolbe*	N	Y	N	Y	N
ARKANSAS					
1 Alexander	?	Y	Y	Y	Y
2 Robinson	Y	Y	Y	Y	Y
3 *Hammerschmidt*	N	Y	Y	Y	N
4 Anthony	Y	Y	Y	Y	Y
CALIFORNIA					
1 Bosco	?	?	Y	Y	Y
2 *Herger*	N	?	N	Y	N
3 Matsui	Y	Y	Y	Y	Y
4 Fazio	Y	Y	Y	Y	Y
5 Pelosi	Y	Y	Y	Y	Y
6 Boxer	Y	Y	Y	Y	Y
7 Miller	Y	Y	Y	Y	Y
8 Dellums	Y	Y	Y	Y	Y
9 Stark	Y	Y	Y	Y	Y
10 Edwards	Y	Y	Y	Y	Y
11 Lantos	Y	Y	Y	Y	Y
12 *Campbell*	N	Y	Y	Y	N
13 Mineta	Y	Y	Y	Y	Y
14 *Shumway*	N	Y	Y	Y	N
15 Coelho	Y	Y	Y	Y	Y
16 Panetta	Y	Y	Y	Y	Y
17 *Pashayan*	Y	Y	N	Y	N
18 Lehman	Y	Y	Y	Y	Y
19 *Lagomarsino*	N	Y	N	N	N
20 *Thomas*	Y	Y	N	Y	N
21 *Gallegly*	N	Y	N	N	N
22 *Moorhead*	N	Y	N	Y	N
23 Beilenson	Y	Y	Y	Y	Y
24 Waxman	Y	Y	?	Y	Y
25 Roybal	Y	Y	Y	Y	Y
26 Berman	Y	Y	Y	Y	Y
27 Levine	Y	Y	Y	Y	Y
28 Dixon	Y	Y	Y	Y	Y
29 Hawkins	Y	Y	Y	Y	Y
30 Martinez	Y	Y	Y	Y	Y
31 Dymally	Y	Y	Y	Y	Y
32 Anderson	Y	Y	Y	Y	Y
33 *Dreier*	N	Y	N	Y	N
34 Torres	Y	Y	?	Y	Y
35 *Lewis*	N	Y	N	N	N
36 Brown	Y	Y	Y	Y	Y
37 *McCandless*	N	Y	N	Y	N
38 *Dornan*	?	?	?	?	?
39 *Dannemeyer*	?	?	N	N	N
40 *Cox*	?	?	Y	N	N
41 *Lowery*	?	?	N	Y	N

	82	83	84	85	86
42 *Rohrabacher*	N	Y	Y	N	N
43 *Packard*	N	Y	Y	N	N
44 Bates	Y	Y	Y	Y	Y
45 *Hunter*	N	Y	?	N	N
COLORADO					
1 Schroeder	Y	Y	N	Y	Y
2 Skaggs	Y	Y	Y	Y	Y
3 Campbell	Y	Y	Y	Y	N
4 *Brown*	N	Y	N	N	N
5 *Hefley*	N	Y	N	N	N
6 *Schaefer*	N	Y	N	N	N
CONNECTICUT					
1 Kennelly	Y	Y	Y	Y	Y
2 Gejdenson	Y	Y	Y	Y	Y
3 Morrison	Y	Y	Y	Y	Y
4 *Shays*	Y	Y	N	Y	Y
5 *Rowland*	Y	Y	Y	Y	Y
6 *Johnson*	Y	Y	Y	Y	Y
DELAWARE					
AL Carper	Y	Y	Y	Y	Y
FLORIDA					
1 Hutto	Y	Y	Y	Y	N
2 *Grant*	N	Y	Y	Y	N
3 Bennett	Y	Y	N	Y	N
4 *James*	N	Y	N	N	N
5 *McCollum*	Y	Y	Y	N	N
6 *Stearns*	N	Y	N	N	N
7 Gibbons	Y	Y	Y	Y	Y
8 *Young*	Y	Y	Y	N	N
9 *Bilirakis*	Y	Y	N	N	N
10 *Ireland*	Y	Y	N	N	N
11 Nelson	Y	Y	Y	Y	Y
12 *Lewis*	Y	Y	N	N	N
13 *Goss*	N	Y	N	N	N
14 Johnston	Y	Y	Y	Y	Y
15 *Shaw*	N	Y	Y	Y	N
16 Smith	Y	Y	Y	Y	Y
17 Lehman	Y	Y	Y	Y	Y
18 Vacancy					
19 Fascell	Y	Y	Y	Y	Y
GEORGIA					
1 Thomas	Y	Y	Y	Y	N
2 Hatcher	Y	Y	Y	Y	Y
3 Ray	Y	Y	Y	Y	Y
4 Jones	Y	Y	Y	Y	Y
5 Lewis	Y	Y	Y	Y	Y
6 *Gingrich*	N	Y	?	Y	N
7 Darden	Y	Y	Y	Y	Y
8 Rowland	Y	Y	Y	Y	N
9 Jenkins	Y	Y	Y	Y	Y
10 Barnard	?	Y	Y	Y	N
HAWAII					
1 *Saiki*	Y	Y	Y	Y	N
2 Akaka	Y	Y	Y	Y	Y
IDAHO					
1 *Craig*	N	Y	N	N	N
2 *Stallings*	Y	Y	Y	Y	Y
ILLINOIS					
1 Hayes	Y	Y	Y	Y	Y
2 Savage	?	?	Y	Y	Y
3 Russo	Y	Y	Y	Y	Y
4 Sangmeister	Y	Y	Y	Y	Y
5 Lipinski	Y	Y	Y	Y	Y
6 *Hyde*	Y	Y	N	Y	N
7 Collins	?	?	?	?	?
8 Rostenkowski	Y	Y	Y	Y	Y
9 Yates	Y	Y	Y	Y	Y
10 *Porter*	N	Y	N	Y	N
11 Annunzio	Y	Y	Y	Y	Y
12 *Crane*	N	Y	N	N	N
13 *Fawell*	N	Y	N	N	N
14 *Hastert*	N	Y	N	N	N
15 *Madigan*	N	Y	N	Y	N
16 *Martin*	N	Y	N	N	Y
17 Evans	Y	Y	Y	Y	Y
18 *Michel*	N	Y	N	Y	N
19 Bruce	Y	Y	Y	Y	Y
20 Durbin	Y	Y	Y	Y	Y
21 Costello	Y	Y	Y	Y	Y
22 Poshard	Y	Y	Y	Y	Y
INDIANA					
1 Visclosky	Y	Y	Y	Y	Y
2 Sharp	Y	Y	Y	N	Y
3 *Hiler*	N	Y	N	Y	N

ND Northern Democrats   SD Southern Democrats

CQ Almanac is a voluminous hardbound volume published annually. It distills, reorganizes, and cross-indexes the information reported in the *CQ Weekly Report*. Features include coverage of every bill reported out of committee and useful charts of all recorded votes. Congressional action is summarized in major policy areas, following the arrangement in the *Weekly Report*, such as economic affairs, defense, agriculture, etc. For legislation that has been enacted into public law, this source can be a valuable entry point for an overview and for citations to specific publications generated in the legislative process.

For example, if one is researching the National Archives and Records Administration Act of 1984, the index in *CQ Almanac* would direct the user to page 191 of the text. On that page a concise summary of the process, with citations to the bill number, public law number, House and Senate report numbers, *Congressional Record* dates, and background information referencing earlier *CQ Almanac* issues and pagination, is epitomized. With the citations the researcher can access primary source materials to the extent desired.

Other Congressional Quarterly, Inc., reference sources of value include *Congress and the Nation*, which is published about every four years. A substantive review of government and politics, the current volume (VII) covers the period 1985-1988. *Congressional Roll Call*, published annually, examines key votes on the major issues of the session; the second section of the book is a complete compilation of the roll call votes in both chambers. CQ's *Guide to Congress*, now in its fourth edition (1991), is over 1,000 pages and arguably is the best reference source on that institution in print. Meticulously detailed and replete with tables, charts, and summaries, it also contains numerous appendixes, a glossary of congressional terms, and authoritative bibliographies. The current edition has been extensively revised to reflect changes over the 1980s. It includes sections on congressional pay and perquisites, ethics investigations, campaign financing, and the like. Although retaining its historical summaries, it includes a great deal of timely information. In Congressional Quarterly's stable of thoroughbred monographs and series are excellent sources on the presidency and the courts, but the focus remains on Congress in all of its substantive and procedural manifestations.

SUMMARY

The complexity of Congress as an institution, the intricacy of its procedures, and the sheer amount and kinds of information engendered by or on behalf of its official duties cannot be adequately encompassed in a chapter. Numerous jokes about the Congress have found their way into books and anthologies. Mark Twain observed that "there is no distinctly native American criminal class except Congress." Dr. Raymond Smock, Historian of the House of Representatives, noted that ridiculing Congress "is as American as apple pie."[55]

To be sure, there have been, are, and will be knaves and fools representing the nation, roughly in direct proportion to the rascals and buffoons among the populace. But the framers of the Constitution knew that if "angels were to govern men, neither external nor internal controls on government would be necessary."[56] Yet some declarations of virtue provide a glimpse of what it can mean to serve in this body composed of fallible creatures. When Sam Rayburn first entered Congress as a member of the House of Representatives in 1913, he proclaimed his fealty to the ideals that occasionally animate the institution. In his maiden speech before his colleagues, he said, "I have always dreamed of a country ... inhabited by a people liberty loving, patriotic, happy, and prosperous, with its lawmakers having no other purpose than to write such just laws as shall in the years to come be of service to human kind yet unborn."[57]

NOTES

[1]Roger H. Davidson and Walter J. Oleszek, *Congress and Its Members*, 3d ed. (Washington, DC: Congressional Quarterly Books, 1989), p. 7.

[2]If a bill has been amended extensively in committee, the committee may decide to report a new bill incorporating these amendments, which is commonly known as a "clean bill." See *How Our Laws Are Made* (101-2: H. Doc. 139), p. 13.

[3]For a detailed review of LEGI-SLATE see *Government Publications Review*, 16 (May/June 1989): 304-06.

[4]See *Price List 36*, Spring 1991, pp. 28, 39. Far fewer private bills are published, and the subscription price as of 1991 for a session was $169.

[5]Walter J. Oleszek, *Congressional Procedures and the Policy Process* (Washington, DC: Congressional Quarterly Press, 1978), p. 57.

[6]Ronald Garay, *Congressional Television: A Legislative History* (Westport, CT: Greenwood Press, 1984), pp. 36-37. Garay's monograph is an excellent summary of this topic.

[7]Cited in *Guide to the Congress of the United States: Origins, History and Procedure* (Washington, DC: Congressional Quarterly Service, 1971), p. 41.

[8]Peggy Garvin, "Before the *Record*," *Law Library Lights*, 32 (January/February 1989): 1. Garvin's article is a splendid, succinct account of the shenanigans surrounding the predecessors of today's *Congressional Record*.

[9]Garvin, "Before the *Record*," pp. 1, 4.

[10]Garvin, "Before the *Record*," p. 4.

[11]Garvin, "Before the *Record*," p. 4. See also Robert E. Kling, Jr., *The Government Printing Office* (New York: Praeger Publishers, 1970), pp. 98-109.

[12]*Congressional Record*, daily edition, February 20, 1978, p. H1193.

[13]*Congressional Record*, daily edition, March 2, 1978, p. H1638.

[14]*Gregg* v. *Barrett*, 771 F.Supp. 108 (1984), 109, 110; 771 F.2d 539 (1985), 540. The suit was brought by then Representative Judd Gregg (R-NH), two of his House colleagues, three practicing lawyers, a law school librarian, and a second-year law school student.

[15]*Accuracy in House Proceedings Resolution*, 99-1: H. Rep. 228, July 25, 1985. Helvetica type is characterized by the absence of serifs (sans serif), whereas the actual speeches employed serifs, which are small lines used to finish off the main strokes of letters.

[16]Syndicated columnist Jack Anderson in the *Albany* [New York] *Times Union*, February 6, 1986, p. A-11.

[17]Alan Green, *Gavel to Gavel: A Guide to the Televised Proceedings of Congress* (Washington, DC: Benton Foundation, 1986), pp. 6-7.

[18]*Congressional Record*, daily edition, January 19, 1978, pp. E47, E48. For detailed analyses of televising the proceedings of the Congress, see Joe Morehead, "Congress and the *Congressional Record*: A Magical Mystery Tour," *The Serials Librarian*, 13, 1 (1987): 66-69; and Joe Morehead, "Ariadne's Thread: The United States Congress Celebrates Its Bicentennial—Part One," *The Serials Librarian*, 18, 3/4 (1990): 88-93.

[19]*Administrative Notes*, 12 (March 15, 1991): 13. See also *Administrative Notes*, 12 (January 15, 1991): 1.

[20]See *Administrative Notes*, 10 (January 1989): 7.

[21]Jerrold Zwirn, "Congressional Bills," *Government Publications Review*, 7A (1980): 19, 23.

[22]Public laws, like private bills, public bills, resolutions, amendments, and reports on public bills, are announced in the current quarterly edition of *Price List 36*. However, private laws are not available for sale from the Superintendent of Documents.

[23]*How Our Laws Are Made* (101-2: H. Doc. 139), p. 47.

[24]This distinction is summarized in J. Myron Jacobstein and Roy M. Mersky, *Legal Research Illustrated*, 5th ed. (Westbury, NY: Foundation Press, 1990), pp. 145-47.

[25]This feature makes U.S.C.S. technically more accurate when consulting the language of titles not yet enacted into positive law. See Jacobstein and Mersky, *Legal Research*, p. 148.

[26]*Guide to the Congress of the United States: Origins, History and Procedure* (Washington, DC: Congressional Quarterly Service, 1971), p. 329.

[27]Asher C. Hinds, *Hinds' Precedents of the House of Representatives of the United States* (Washington, DC: GPO, 1907), vol. 4, p. 247.

[28]*Guide to the Congress*, p. 329.

[29]*Guide to the Congress*, p. 303.

[30]*Guide to the Congress*, pp. 339-40.

[31]*Guide to the Congress*, p. 329.

[32]*How Our Laws Are Made* (101-2: H. Doc. 139), p. 18.

[33]*Congressional Quarterly's Guide to Congress*, 2d ed. (Washington, DC: Congressional Quarterly Service, 1976), pp. 306-07.

[34]*Congressional Quarterly's Guide to Congress*, p. 307.

[35]The *Monthly Catalog – U.S. Congressional Serial Set Supplement* for the 97th Congress and the *U.S. Congressional Serial Set Catalog: Numerical Lists and Schedule of Volumes* for the 98th Congrress are separate editions that also provide access to private reports.

[36]"Private Bills in Congress," *Harvard Law Review*, 79 (June 1966): 1686. See also Joe Morehead, "Private Bills and Private Laws: A Guide to the Legislative Process," *The Serials Librarian*, 9 (Spring 1985): 115-25.

[37]Laurence F. Schmeckebier and Roy B. Eastin, *Government Publications and Their Use*, 2d rev. ed. (Washington, DC: Brookings Institution, 1969), pp. 109-16, 124-29, 150-66.

[38]The "Library" was a collection developed in the Public Documents Division because of the requirements under the Printing Act of 1895 to prepare the *Document Catalog* and the *Monthly Catalog*. Closed to the general public, the "Library" was strictly "functional." See Joseph A. King, "The United States Government Printing Office Library," *D.C. Libraries*, 22 (January 1951): 2-4.

[39]For example, 101-1: S. Rep. 216, on the Iran-Contra brouhaha along with its source documents, depositions, and testimonial chronology, comprises Serial Set Volumes 13739-13774. Similarly, 101-1: H. Rep. 433 consists of much the same material. Comprising Serial Set Volumes 13811-13840, the material is *identical* to that issued in [Senate] Serial Set Volumes 13740-13769.

[40]For example, the annual report, *Girl Scouts of the U.S.A.*, is required to be printed as a House document by Act of April 16, 1951 (65 Stat. 32).

[41]Congressional Information Service's *Congressional Masterfile 1* on CD-ROM includes the *CIS Index to US Senate Executive Documents & Reports*, and *Congressional Masterfile 2* on CD-ROM is the compact disk edition of *CIS/Index*.

[42]The "Schedule of Volumes," but *not* the "Numerical Lists," was published for the 99th Congress in *Administrative Notes*, 9 (October 1988): 18-25, and for the 100th Congress in *Administrative Notes*, 11 (November 15, 1990): 3-14.

[43]*Monthly Catalog*, July 1980, Entry No. 80-15307, p. 310. See also *Documents to the People*, 9 (January 1981): 42.

[44]See Joe Morehead, "Ariadne's Thread: The United States Congress Celebrates Its Bicentennial – Part Two," *The Serials Librarian*, 18 (1990): 110-12.

[45]*Administrative Notes*, 10 (October 16, 1989): 15-20; 11 (April 25, 1990): 11, 13-14; 11 (May 15, 1990): 1. See also U.S. General Accounting Office, *Government Printing Office Supply of Microfiche to Libraries Disrupted* (GGD-89-44), February 1989.

[46]Issues of the *Monthly Catalog* used the incorrect notation during this period until the reports and documents of the 97th Congress began to appear.

[47]George A. Costello, "Reliance on Legislative History in Interpreting Statutes," *CRS Review*, 11 (January/February 1990): 30.

[48]Costello, "Reliance on Legislative History," p. 11.

[49]Costello, "Reliance on Legislative History," p. 11.

[50]Peter C. Schanck, "The Only Game in Town: Contemporary Interpretive Theory, Statutory Construction, and Legislative Histories," *Law Library Journal*, 82 (1990): 453.

[51]See Joe Morehead, "Consequences of Federal Government Information Policies, 1981-1986," in Richard D. Irving and Bill Katz (eds.), *Reference Services and Public Policy* (New York: Haworth Press, 1987), pp. 7-13. This collection of essays was also published under the Haworth imprint as volume 20 of *The Reference Librarian*.

[52]*Biographical Directory of the United States Congress, 1774-1989* (Washington, DC: GPO, 1989), pp. 1-7.

[53]*Biographical Directory*, p. 7. The *Biographical Directory* was issued as 100-2: S. Doc. 34 (Serial Volume 13849).

[54]The "Voting Analysis Service" in LEGI-SLATE also contains biographies of members and their congressional districts. Moreover, an online cross-reference between zip codes and congressional districts is provided.

[55]"Congress Turns 200: A Special Section of the Bicentennial," *Roll Call: The Newspaper of Congress*, vol. 34, section 3 (February 27–March 5, 1989): 1.

[56]"The Federalist No. 51" (Madison), in *The Federalist Papers* (New York: New American Library, 1961), p. 322.

[57]*Congressional Record*, vol. 50, p. 1249. Cited in Suzy Platt (ed.), *Respectfully Quoted: A Dictionary of Quotations Requested from the Congressional Research Service* (Washington, DC: Library of Congress, 1989), pp. 55-56.

6

The Presidency

INTRODUCTION

Article II, Section 1, of the Constitution provides that the "executive power shall be vested in a President of the United States of America." The pertinent sections of Article II for our purposes cover those powers and responsibilities that the president shares with the Congress, specifically the Senate. These include the making of treaties and agreements; the nomination of officials to serve in high positions in the executive departments and agencies, including the independent agencies; and the transmission of the budget to the Congress. In all of these activities, significant government publications are generated. The content, indexing, and bibliographic control of these important documents constitutes the focus of this chapter.

THE WHITE HOUSE OFFICE

The immediate staff of the president is located in the White House Office, which includes the president's press secretary. Information regarding the activities of the president is furnished to the print and broadcast media through press releases and briefings. Publications of the "President of the United States" have been assigned Superintendent of Documents (SuDocs) author symbol "Pr [no.]." The number indicates the chronology of the persons who have held the office; for example, Ronald Reagan (Pr 40), George Bush (Pr 41), and so forth.[1] Issued under the Pr class are several annual reports of the president, most of which are prepared by other executive agencies. One of the more important publications is the *Economic Report of the President* (Pr [no.].9), which is prepared by the president's Council of Economic Advisers; the major part of this publication is the *Annual Report of the Council of Economic Advisers*. Also assigned Pr author symbols are the *Federal Advisory Committee Annual Report of the President* (Pr [no.].10) and the *Annual Report of the President on the Trade Agreements Program* (Pr [no.].11). Pr [no.].8 class stems are used to designate special committees and commissions appointed by the president, with a Cutter symbol following the colon to indicate the name of the body. For example, Pr 40.8:Sp1 was the notation assigned to the Presidential Commission on the Space Shuttle *Challenger* Accident.

In addition, several publications issued by the Office of the Federal Register constitute a rich source of presidential actions. These include the *Federal Register* (AE 2.106), *Code of Federal Regulations* (AE 2.106/3), *Weekly Compilation of*

Presidential Documents (AE 2.109), *Public Papers of the Presidents of the United States* (AE 2.114), and *Codification of Presidential Proclamations and Executive Orders* (AE 2.113). Presidential materials are also found in House and Senate documents, the *Congressional Record*, and the House and Senate *Journals* when they represent messages or communications transmitted to the Congress by the president.

EXECUTIVE ORDERS AND PROCLAMATIONS

At the beginning of the daily *Federal Register* is a section titled "Presidential Documents," when an issue contains such materials. The most commonly published types of these documents are executive orders (EOs) and proclamations (Proc.). EOs and proclamations

> are the formal mechanism through which the president ... prescribes the conduct of business in the executive branch. Scholars and government officials widely regard executive orders and proclamations as "presidential legislation"—a form of executive lawmaking used in instances in which the Constitution or Congress directly or indirectly permits or mandates the president to take action.[2]

According to Laurence Schmeckebier and Roy Eastin, executive orders generally relate to the conduct of government business or to the organization of government agencies. They have "never been defined by law or regulation"; thus, "in a general sense every act of the President authorizing or directing that an act be performed is an executive order."[3] Most executive orders have the force of law, and some proclamations have effective legal status, such as those granting pardons. In practice it is customary to issue celebratory days, months, and years in the form of proclamations. Thus, EO 12667 (January 18, 1989) is titled "Access to Presidential Records," whereas Proc. 6008 (August 14, 1989) is called "National Library Card Sign-Up Month."

In 1907 the Department of State began numbering executive orders that it had on file and later received. Beginning March 14, 1936, all executive orders "except such as have no general applicability and legal effect" were published in the *Federal Register* (FR). In the mid-1980s, Congressional Information Service (CIS) published an invaluable research source, *Presidential Executive Orders and Proclamations, 1789-1983*, with a companion microfiche text collection, *Presidential Executive Orders and Proclamations on Microfiche*. The task of locating and organizing these EOs and proclamations is ably detailed by Gary Hoag, collections development specialist for CIS, in an article in the Fall 1989 issue of *Microform Review*.[4] Figures 6.1 (see page 176) and 6.2 (see page 177) show an executive order and proclamation, respectively.

Rulings other than EOs and proclamations published in the *Federal Register* (and the *Code of Federal Regulations*) include memorandums, usually to heads of departments and agencies; directives, designating matters such as assignments for officials of agencies; presidential determinations resolving that certain provisions of law are or are not in the national interest; letters, such as instructions

(Text continues on page 178.)

Fig. 6.1. Executive order

Executive Order 12765 of June 11, 1991

Delegation of Certain Defense Related Authorities of the President to the Secretary of Defense

By the authority vested in me as President by the Constitution and the laws of the United States of America, including section 301 of title 3 of the United States Code, and my authority as Commander in Chief of the Armed Forces of the United States, it is hereby ordered as follows:

Section 1. The Secretary of Defense is hereby designated and empowered, without the approval, ratification, or other action by the President, to exercise the authority vested in the President by section 749 of title 10 of the United States Code to assign the command without regard to rank in grade to any commissioned officer otherwise eligible to command when two or more commissioned officers of the same grade or corresponding grades are assigned to the same area, field command, or organization.

Sec. 2. The Secretary of Defense is hereby designated and empowered, without the approval, ratification, or other action by the President, to exercise the authority vested in the President by section 7299a(a) of title 10 of the United States Code to direct that combatant vessels and escort vessels be constructed in a Navy or private yard, as the case may be, if the requirement of the Act of March 27, 1934 (ch. 95, 48 Stat. 503) that the first and each succeeding alternate vessel of the same class be constructed in a Navy yard is inconsistent with the public interest.

Sec. 3. For vessels, and for any major component of the hull or superstructure of vessels to be constructed or repaired for any of the armed forces, the Secretary of Defense is hereby designated and empowered, without the approval, ratification, or other action by the President, to exercise the authority vested in the President by section 7309(b) of title 10 of the United States Code to authorize exceptions to the prohibition in section 7309(a) of title 10 of the United States Code. Such exceptions shall be based on a determination that it is in the national security interest of the United States to authorize an exception. The Secretary of Defense shall transmit notice of any such determination to the Congress, as required by section 7309(b).

Sec. 4. The Secretary of Defense may redelegate the authority delegated to him by this order, in accordance with applicable law.

Sec. 5. This order shall be effective immediately.

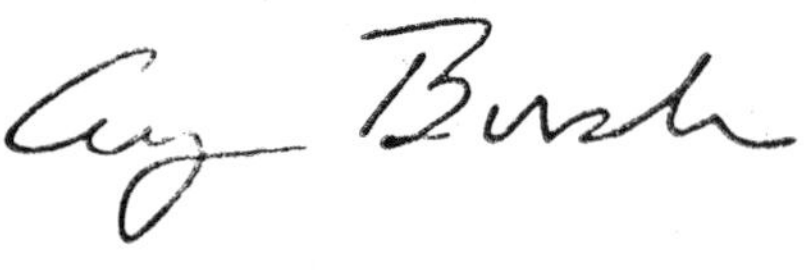

Ay Bush

THE WHITE HOUSE,
June 11, 1991.

Fig. 6.2. Proclamation

Proclamation 6303 of June 11, 1991

National Scleroderma Awareness Week, 1991
By the President of the United States of America

A Proclamation

Scleroderma, which literally means "hard skin," is a connective tissue disorder in which excessive amounts of the protein collagen accumulate in the skin. In addition to the skin, scleroderma affects small blood vessels, muscles, and joints. It may also damage internal organs such as the esophagus, lungs, kidneys, and heart.

Although scleroderma can strike men and women of any age, it occurs most often in women during their childbearing years. The disease is often painful, and it may cause disfigurement, disability, and even death. The impact on victims and their families—in terms of both physical and emotional suffering—is enormous.

Fortunately, progress is being made in determining the cause of scleroderma and in developing more effective treatments for the disease. Researchers have developed an animal model that will help them to understand more about the nature and the progression of scleroderma. They have also made an important finding in the discovery of abnormalities in collagen-producing cells, known as fibroblasts, among scleroderma victims. Furthermore, they have found that treatment with specific agents, such as d-penicillamine, may retard the hardening of collagen in the skin.

As is the case with any other disease, it is very important to diagnose scleroderma in its early stages. Timely intervention, coupled with sound treatment, can improve the quality of life enjoyed by people with scleroderma until research yields a cure.

To enhance public awareness of scleroderma, the Congress, by House Joint Resolution 219, has designated the week beginning June 9, 1991, as "National Scleroderma Awareness Week" and has authorized and requested the President to issue a proclamation in observance of this week.

NOW, THEREFORE, I, GEORGE BUSH, President of the United States of America, do hereby proclaim the week beginning June 9, 1991, as National Scleroderma Awarness Week. I encourage the people of the United States to observe this week with appropriate programs and activities that will enhance their understanding of scleroderma and the need for continued research.

IN WITNESS WHEREOF, I have hereunto set my hand this eleventh day of June, in the year of our Lord nineteen hundred and ninety-one, and of the Independence of the United States of America the two hundred and fifteenth.

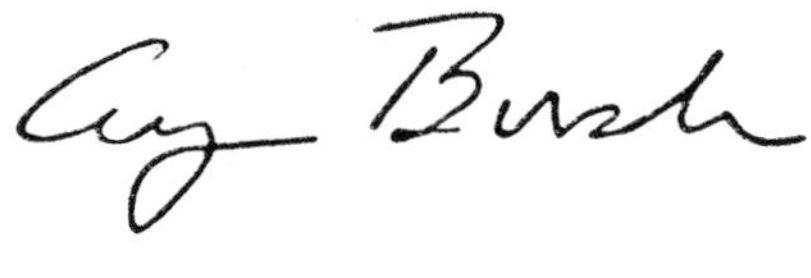

GW Bush

to chiefs of diplomatic missions; and reorganization plans. The last are instruments by which the president proposes changes in the structure of agencies below the departmental or independent agency level. They take effect automatically unless disapproved by Congress within a specified period of time. Access to these presidential initiatives published in the FR can be made by using the *Federal Register Index*, which cumulates monthly into an annual issue. A more thoroughly indexed commercial publication, the *CIS Federal Register Index*, is issued weekly.

Title 3, *Code of Federal Regulations*

Title 3 of the *Code of Federal Regulations* (CFR) is called *The President* and contains the full text of documents signed by the president during a calendar year. Periodic cumulations of Title 3 include 1936-1938, 1938-1942, 1943-1948, 1949-1953, 1954-1958, 1959-1963, 1964-1965, 1966-1970, and 1971-1975. The Title 3 series began with Proc. 2161 (March 19, 1936) and EO 7316 (March 13, 1936).

An annual issue of Title 3 typically contains EOs and proclamations in separate numbered sequence, other presidential documents arranged by date, and regulations of the Executive Office of the President. Various tables and finding aids are also included, as is an index at the end of the issues. For user convenience, *Title 3, 1936-1965 — Consolidated Indexes* and *Title 3, 1936-1965 — Consolidated Tables* are available. The former consists of a consolidated subject index covering the period; the latter contains tables and finding aids to facilitate searching presidential documents during this period.

Duplication of the text of EOs and proclamations in several places constitutes an embarrassment of riches. These directives can be found not only in the FR and Title 3, CFR, but also in the *Weekly Compilation of Presidential Documents, Public Papers of the Presidents*, the West Publishing Company's *United States Code Congressional and Administrative News* (U.S.C.C.A.N.), and the advance pamphlets of Lawyers Cooperative Publishing [Company's] *United States Code Service*. In addition, proclamations are published in the *Statutes at Large*.

The *Federal Register* is online with WESTLAW and LEXIS, with the latter's database called FEDREG. In addition LEXIS has a database (PRESDC) that provides the text of presidential documents from January 1981. Commercial printed sources include access to presidential actions published in the FR and in Title 3. The *Code of Federal Regulations Index* (New York: R. R. Bowker) is an annual with quarterly cumulative supplements. The *Index to the Code of Federal Regulations* (Bethesda, MD: Congressional Information Service) is published annually with the full text of all CFR titles on microfiche since 1938. Readex Microprint Corporation offers separate series on microfiche of the *Federal Register* and, indeed, the full text of all publications listed in the "PrEx" SuDocs class number series in its "Agency Collection" series and individually in its "Documents on Demand" service.

Weekly Compilation of
Presidential Documents

The *Weekly Compilation of Presidential Documents* (WCPD) began on August 2, 1965, and is the single most accessible compilation of presidential activities in the public record. It includes the text of proclamations and executive orders, addresses and remarks, communications to Congress, letters, messages, telegrams, news conferences, reorganization plans, resignations, swearing-in ceremonies, retirements, and White House Office news releases. In addition, it cites laws approved by the president and lists nominations sent to the Senate. Each issue carries an index of contents that cumulates. Separate cumulative indexes are published quarterly, semiannually, and annually.

Communications scholars such as Donald C. Smith, concerned with the construct of "source credibility," have called into question the accuracy of some statements found in WCPD, especially remarks by a president's press secretary. WCPD is putatively governed "in terms of style and distribution" by regulations, but "there are no regulations governing content." Smith points out that on more than one occasion, Ronald Reagan's press secretary "admitted to fabricating presidential comments." It is likely, Smith avers, "that for over 20 years now academicians and politicians have been using a source of information that they do not fully understand.... The WCPD is supposed to be a source of 'public and official discourse', however, there is no public or official regulation of the discourse itself, or its presentation to the public."[5]

Public Papers of the Presidents

In response to a recommendation of the National Historical Publications Commission, an annual series of *Public Papers of the Presidents* was begun with the 1957 volume covering the fifth year of the Eisenhower administration. Provision was also made for retrospective collections, and volumes were subsequently published for the earlier years of the presidencies of Dwight Eisenhower (1953-1956), Harry Truman (1945-1952), and Herbert Hoover (1929-1933). Compilations for President Franklin D. Roosevelt and earlier chief executives have been published commercially. Kraus International has issued *The Cumulative Indexes to the Public Papers of the Presidents of the United States* (1977-1983).[6]

Prior to the 1977 volume, the *Public Papers* was an edited version of WCPD. Beginning with the Carter administration, the *Public Papers* were expanded to include virtually all materials published in the *Weekly Compilation*. Current volumes in this series arrange presidential materials in chronological order within each week. Textnotes, footnotes, and cross-references are provided by the editors for purposes of identification and clarity. All information is fully indexed by subject entries and by categories reflecting the type of presidential activity or document.

The public record, however voluminous, reveals little of the complexity and moil of momentous decisions that presidents must execute. Theodore C. Sorensen, speech writer and confidant of President John F. Kennedy, stated as much when he wrote in the foreword to volume III of the Kennedy *Papers*, "The public papers of a president cannot capture the full flavor of the man and his philosophy—for there is much that is not said or written publicly, and much that is not said or written at all, only felt and observed."[7]

Codification of Presidential Proclamations and Executive Orders

Begun in 1979, the *Codification* is updated periodically and is arranged in titles like the CFR. The current edition covers the period April 13, 1945— January 20, 1989. As a retrospective and ongoing cumulation, the *Codification* is the best source for proclamations and EOs for the period indicated because it provides in one volume the text of all EOs and proclamations, with amendments, in effect as of January 20, 1989. If an executive order or proclamation relates to more than one subject area, the most appropriate title/chapter is chosen. More- over, the *Codification* includes a comprehensive index and a "Disposition Table." The latter lists, by number, EOs and proclamations referencing all amendments regardless of current status, and a "disposition" column indicates documents that were revoked, superseded, temporary, or hortatory. Figure 6.3 shows a page from the "Disposition Table" section of the *Codification*.

Shepard's CFR Citations provides citations to the CFR, including proclama- tions, executive orders, and reorganization plans published in Title 3. The citing sources include federal and state cases reported in units of the National Reporter System, *A.L.R. Annotations*, and selected legal periodicals.

EXECUTIVE OFFICE OF THE PRESIDENT

Under authority of the Reorganization Act of 1939 (53 Stat. 561), various agencies were transferred to the Executive Office of the President by Reorganiza- tion Plans 1 and 2 of 1939, effective July 1, 1939. EO 8248 (September 8, 1939) established the divisions of the Executive Office and defined their functions. Sub- sequently, presidents have used EOs, reorganization plans, and legislative initia- tives to reorganize the Executive Office in an attempt to further the goals of their administrations. In terms of public policy, some of these agencies within the Executive Office exercise substantial power and influence. Beginning with the administration of President Kennedy, the Superintendent of Documents assigned a "PrEx" author symbol to these agencies.

Office of Management and Budget

The Office of Management and Budget (OMB) was originally established as the Bureau of the Budget by an Act of June 10, 1921 (42 Stat. 20). Pursuant to Reorganization Plan No. 2 of 1970 (EO 11541, July 1, 1970), the agency was transferred to the Executive Office of the President and given its present name. OMB wields substantial power in formulating federal information policies. Its various edicts in this area are revised and refined over time, typically in the form of numbered bulletins and circulars. For example, OMB's "Advance Notice of

(Text continues on page 182.)

Fig. 6.3. "Disposition Table" from *Codification*

Proclamations

Number	Amendments	Disposition
4457		Hortatory.
4458		Hortatory.
4459		Hortatory.
4460		Hortatory.
4461		Hortatory.
4462		Hortatory.
4463	Amended by Proc. 4466	Tariff.
4464		Hortatory.
4465		Hortatory.
4466		Tariff.
4467		Hortatory.
4468		Hortatory.
4469		Tariff.
4470		Hortatory.
4471		Hortatory.
4472		Hortatory.
4473		Hortatory.
4474		Hortatory.
4475		Hortatory.
4476		Hortatory.
4477		Tariff.
4478	Amended by Proc. 4480	Tariff.
4479		Hortatory.
4480		Tariff.
4481		Hortatory.
4482		Tariff.

EXECUTIVE ORDERS

Number	Amendments	Disposition
8684	Amended by EO 11673	Revoked by EO 11886.
9066		Terminated by Proc. 2714; termination confirmed by Proc. 4417.
9586	Amended by EO 10336, 11085, 11515.	Codified at Chapter III.
9698		See note at Chapter XXII.
9708	Amended by EO 10532, 11070	Codified at Chapter XLII.
9751	Amended by EO 10083, 10864	See note at EO 9698, Chapter XXII.
9823		See note at EO 9698, Chapter XXII.
9863		See note at EO 9698, Chapter XXII.
9911		See note at EO 9698, Chapter XXII.
9972		See note at EO 9698, Chapter XXII.
10000	Amended by EO 10261, 10623, 10636, 10903, 11938.	Codified at Chapter XXII.
10016		Revoked by EO 10903.
10025	Amended by EO 10983	See note at EO 9698, Chapter XXII.
10086		See note at EO 9698, Chapter XXII.
10096	Amended by EO 10695, 10930	Codified at Chapter XXXVII.
10122	Amended by EO 10400, 11733	Codified at Chapter XXXII.
10228		See note at EO 9698, Chapter XXII.
10242	Amended by EO 10773, 11051. See EO 11725.	Codified at Chapter XXXII.
10261		Revoked by EO 10903.

Plans for Revision of OMB Circular No. A-130, Management of Federal Information Resources," was published in the "Notices" section of the *Federal Register* on March 4, 1991 (56 FR 9026). This circular, first promulgated in December 1985, has undergone revisions and has generated considerable controversy within the community of documents librarians and related interest groups. Circular A-130's continuing purpose has been to articulate "a general framework for the management of federal information resources."

Useful current information about OMB activities and related information policy issues is found in the quarterly *Coalition on Government Information Newsletter*, which serves in part "as an exchange of publications and papers relating to public access to U.S. government information."[8] Another timely source of information and analysis of key issues involving fundamental questions about public access to federal government information is the periodical *Government Information Insider*, published by OMB Watch, a private institution based in Washington, D.C.

The Budget of the United States Government

The fundamental act of governance is budgeting—choosing how much, and on what, to spend. The federal budget is arguably the nation's most important public document. It represents a continuous process involving analysis and discussion among the president, the Director of OMB, the Comptroller General, the Board of Governors of the Federal Reserve System, the General Accounting Office, the Congressional Budget Office, and, of course, the several committees of Congress that must authorize and appropriate monies for the programmatic activities of the entire federal establishment.

A complex process under any circumstances, the shaping of the budget was made more difficult by the enactment of the Public Debt Limit—Balanced Budget and Emergency Deficit Control Act of 1985 (PL 99-177). Known as Gramm-Rudman-Hollings (G-R-H), after the three senators who sponsored the legislation, the law mandates automatic cuts in spending over a period of time for the unlikely purpose of achieving at some point a balanced budget, one in which expenditures and revenues would reach a rough equality. Incremental reductions, called "sequestrations," and the mechanisms for compliance are based on deficit projections assayed by the Congressional Budget Office (CBO) and the OMB, forecasts contingent upon a number of complex economic and political variables with a wide margin of error.

Eric Hansen has authored an important account of the steps in the process, including sources of background information, major budget documents, and other publications relating to the budget, with useful appendixes. Titled "Introduction to the U.S. Congressional Budget Process," the essay was published in *Government Publications Review*, vol. 16 (May/June 1989), pp. 219-37. As Hansen notes (pp. 225-26), in past years the "budget" as submitted by the president to Congress was actually a series of related, separately published documents. However, the *Budget of the United States Government, Fiscal Year 1991* (Y 1.1/7:101-122) was issued in its congressional edition as a single document. This fiscal year (FY) 1991 publication includes the *United States Budget in Brief*; *Budget of the United States Government—Appendix*; *Special Analyses, Budget of the United States Government; Historical Tables, Budget of the United States Government; Management of the United States Government;* and *Major Policy Initiatives.*

The *United States Budget in Brief,* designed for use by the general public, is less technical than the other series and contains summary and historical information with graphic displays. *Special Analyses* highlights specific program areas with alternate views of the budget. The *Historical Tables* provides budget data covering longer time frames than those in the basic budget document, in many cases from 1940. The *Budget—Appendix* is the largest of the series, containing detailed information on the various appropriations and funds that comprise the budget. The information includes the proposed text of appropriations language, budget schedules for each account, new legislative proposals, explanations of the work to be performed and the funds needed, proposed general provisions applicable to the appropriations of entire agencies or groups of agencies, and schedules of permanent positions. The departmental edition of the *Budget* with its related documents is classed in PrEx 2.8.

As the executive's "wish list," the budget occupies a great deal of time in the Congress and its appropriate committees. When profound philosophical differences over revenues and expenditures divide the executive and the legislature, the "battle of the budget" consumes immense amounts of time, frequently to the detriment of other legislative matters.

Article I, Section 9, Clause 7, of the U.S. Constitution states in part that "a regular statement and account of the receipts and expenditures of all public money shall be published from time to time"; this is, of course, part of the budget process in which monies are authorized and appropriated by Congress. Despite that constitutional requirement, the intelligence agencies of the United States are allowed to spend money in secret without any public accounting.

In addition to the Central Intelligence Agency, eleven other intelligence units exist within the federal establishment: the National Security Agency, which specializes in electronic reconnaissance and code breaking; the supersecret National Reconnaissance Office, which runs the U.S. satellite surveillance program; the Defense Intelligence Agency (DIA); the four intelligence arms of the Navy, Air Force, Army, and Marines; the Federal Bureau of Investigation (FBI); and the intelligence branches of the Departments of State, Energy, and Treasury. Altogether these entities are believed to spend close to $30 billion a year, and these covert billions are called the nation's "black budget."

These expenditures are concealed within the *Budget of the United States Government,* primarily in the Department of Defense (DoD) segment of that document, in a variety of ways. For instance, blank spaces appear where dollar figures normally belong; code words shield the identity of secret programs; covert projects are buried within allotments for seemingly unclassified items; and meaningless descriptions, such as "special activities," may shield large sums in line items.

A more detailed analysis of the budget process and the data generated by the several studies and documents produced are assayed in chapter 10, "Statistical Sources."

Catalog of Federal Domestic Assistance

The *Catalog of Federal Domestic Assistance* (PrEx 2.20) is a standard reference source issued by OMB. Published in looseleaf format, the *Catalog* is a compendium of over 1,000 programs, projects, services, and activities that provide assistance or benefits (financial and nonfinancial) to state and local governments, public and private institutions, and specialized groups and individuals. Program descriptions are indexed by department and agency name, applicant eligibility, functional classification, subject, and deadlines. Entries are classified by type of assistance, such as formula grants, direct payments, loans, scholarships and fellowships, exchange programs such as Fulbright-Hays, and other forms. Program information is also available from the National Technical Information Service (NTIS) on magnetic tape, microfiche, and paper copy. Entries are often extracted and reprinted in other documents, and references to program entries are frequently made elsewhere to the *Catalog*'s five-digit program numbers. The responsibility for preparation and updating of the *Catalog* was assigned to the General Services Administration (GSA), although the issuing agency continues to be OMB; consequently, the *Catalog* has retained its SuDocs class number in the PrEx series. Because it is a subscription service, it is announced in *Price List 36*; it is also available to depository libraries.

As librarians and users know, the *Catalog* is not the easiest source from which to extract appropriation information. A commercial publication, J. Robert Dumouchel's *Government Assistance Almanac, 1991-1992* (Detroit, MI: Omnigraphics, 1991), now in its fifth edition, attempts to rectify this difficulty by condensing the information in the official *Catalog*. Thus, although *Government Assistance Almanac* is indeed easier to use, the *Catalog* provides more comprehensive information on assistance or benefits to the public.

Standard Industrial Classification Manual

The *Manual* (PrEx 2.6/2:In27/year) provides the standardized codes used by the federal government to classify businesses by type of activity. These codes facilitate the collection, tabulation, presentation, and analysis of data relating to establishments. The Standard Industrial Classification (SIC) for establishments differs from classifications used for enterprises (companies), commodities or products, and occupations (as found in the *Dictionary of Occupational Titles*). The *Manual* is available to depository libraries and is also sold through NTIS in microcomputer versions with ASCII formats. Prices and ordering information for the electronic versions are provided in the current edition of the *NTIS Catalog of Products & Services*.

A related document is *Concordance between the Standard Industrial Classifications of the United States and Canada*, a joint project between the Census Bureau and Statistics Canada linking the 1987 U.S. SIC and the 1980 Canadian SIC codes. The *Concordance* was developed to help users compare industrial data between the two countries by identifying the differences in the national SICs. The explanatory notes assist users in understanding the relationship between the classes of the U.S. and the Canadian systems by divisions (letters), major groups (two-digit), industry groups (three-digit), and industries (four-digit). The *Concordance* is a SuDocs sales item (S/N 003-024-07264-5).

Other Executive Office Agencies

The Council of Economic Advisers, mentioned above, was established to provide economic analysis and advice to the chief executive. It assists in the preparation of the annual *Economic Report of the President*, the major part of which includes its annual report. It also assists in the preparation of the monthly *Economic Indicators* (Y 4.Ec7:Ec7), the provenance of the Joint Economic Committee of the Congress. This periodical provides relevant economic information on wages, production, purchasing power, prices, credit, money, and federal finance.

The Council on Environmental Quality was established by the National Environmental Policy Act of 1969 to formulate and recommend policies to promote improvement of environmental quality. Its annual report, *Environmental Quality* (PrEx 14.1), gives a thorough summary of federal actions related to control of air and water pollution and solid waste management. The Office of Science and Technology Policy (PrEx 23) was established in 1976. Its *Biennial Science and Technology Report to Congress* is issued by the National Science Foundation (NS 1.40).

Other entities within the Executive Office include the Office of the United States Trade Representative (PrEx 9), the Office of Telecommunications Policy, and the National Security Council. Units such as the Central Intelligence Agency, the Foreign Broadcast Information Service, and the Joint Publications Research Service, although still possessing a SuDocs class notation of PrEx, are no longer part of the Executive Office and are discussed in chapter 11.

PRESIDENTIAL ADVISORY COMMITTEES AND COMMISSIONS

A president has the authority to appoint special committees and commissions to study specific problems and to report their findings directly to the chief executive. At the time the Federal Advisory Committee Act (FACA) of 1972 was passed (86 Stat. 770), over 1,400 federal advisory committees were in existence. Frequently, the news media will use the name of the chairperson of an advisory committee, and it becomes known to the public by that popular title. For example, the *Tower Commission Report* that investigated the "Iran-Contra" scandal was titled *Report of the President's Special Review Board* (Pr 40.8:Sp3/R29). Convened by the president, this three-member panel submitted its report to the president; hence, the SuDocs class provenance. A president may authorize or amend an advisory body by promulgating an executive order citing FACA as authority. The Serial and Government Publications Division of the Library of Congress has issued a useful publication titled *Popular Names of U.S. Government Reports: A Catalog* (LC 6.2:G74/984), but this compilation, now in its fourth edition, suffers a time lag and is not comprehensive.

Several commercial sources may be used to supplement and augment the *Popular Names Catalog*. T. R. Wolanin, *Presidential Advisory Commissions: Truman to Nixon* (Madison: University of Wisconsin Press, 1975), includes these ad hoc advisory bodies through 1972. Steven D. Zink, *Guide to the Presidential Advisory Commissions, 1973-84* (Alexandria, VA: Chadwyck-Healey, 1987), contains detailed information on seventy-four commissions and committees during this period. Replete with accurate information and citations to the genesis, termination, composition, functions, and summary of each panel's activities, including its popular name and appropriate directory information, Zink's compilation includes an annotated bibliography of reports published pursuant to the mandate of the committee or commission. Moreover, Zink provides citations to privately published reports as well as the Government Printing Office (GPO) edition. With separate personal name, title, and subject indexes, this work is of greater value to users than the minimal bibliographic data contained in the *Popular Names Catalog.*

The *Encyclopedia of Governmental Advisory Organizations* is a comprehensive guide to permanent, continuing, terminated, and authorized but never funded advisory bodies reporting not only to the president but also to Congress and to executive departments and agencies. The 1992-1993 edition, edited by Donna Batten (Detroit, MI: Gale Research), contains over 6,000 entries and is organized by general subject chapters. Entry information includes addresses, contact persons' names, telephone and fax numbers, history and authority, programmatic mandates, and publications issued. Following the descriptive listings are two appendixes: a directory of committee management officers and the full text of the Federal Advisory Committee Act. Five indexes provide access to the entries by staff or contact name, publication or report name, presidential administration, federal department or agency, and organization name by keyword. The basic volume is updated by periodic supplements titled *New Governmental Advisory Organizations.*

Advisory bodies have existed since George Washington's presidency. Although their recommendations are not binding, they have been extensively used by the three branches, especially in recent decades. It is not unusual for a president, Congress, or the judiciary to ignore the recommendations of an advisory committee. When a controversy erupts, the announcement of a "blue ribbon panel" to study or investigate an issue may simply constitute a ploy to mollify public reaction. Nevertheless, advisory bodies have played an important role in prompting presidential actions or congressional initiatives. Their proliferation and occasional persuasive authority led a House Government Operations Committee to call them the "fifth arm of the Federal establishment" (91-2: H. Rep. 1731, p. 5) alongside the constitutionally created three branches and the independent regulatory entities.

TREATIES AND AGREEMENTS

Nowhere in the constitutional mandate is the "shared powers, separation of functions" doctrine more evident than in the forging of treaties and other international compacts. Article II, Section 2, of the Constitution states that the president "shall have power, by and with the advice and consent of the Senate, to make treaties, provided two thirds of the Senators present concur." The making of treaties involves a series of steps that generally include negotiation, signing, approval by the Senate, ratification by the president, deposit or exchange of ratification with the other party or parties to the treaty, and proclamation. "Contrary to popular impression, the Senate does not ratify treaties; the President ratifies treaties upon receiving the advice and consent of the Senate to this act."[9]

The framers of the Constitution were sharply divided on the issue of allowing the president such a central role in treaty making. By and large, the delegates to the Constitutional Convention expected the Senate to dominate the making of foreign policy, certainly to the extent that the Congress controlled, in Article I, the sole right "to declare war." James Madison felt a president "should be an agent in treaties," where the word *agent* meant a "deputy," one who represents another.[10] John Jay, however, highly approved of the joint responsibility of the Senate and the president in the treaty process.[11] Alexander Hamilton asserted that "if we attend carefully to its operation, [treaty making] will be found to partake more of the legislative than of the executive character, though it does not seem strictly to fall within the definition of either of them."[12] Whatever the framers' original intent, historian Leonard W. Levy notes that "Hamilton's position was destined for acceptance by presidents in the twentieth century."[13]

Executive agreements, on the other hand, are not specifically mentioned in the Constitution; "yet the executive agreement has been used since 1817 when the Rush-Bagot Agreement was reached with Great Britain, limiting naval forces to be kept on the Great Lakes."[14] In recent decades the number of executive agreements concluded has far exceeded that of formal treaties. The distinction between treaty and agreement in practice is the

> submission or nonsubmission of an international instrument to the Senate.... Any international agreement which is not submitted to the Senate for its advice and consent is not considered a treaty, even though it may have legislative sanction, whereas any agreement which is submitted to the Senate, be it called a protocol, convention, treaty, agreement, articles, or by some other name, is considered a treaty.[15]

Thus, for treaties the Senate's shared partnership in the process

> is a central constitutional provision. As such it represents a principal means by which the Senate participates in the shaping of American foreign policy.... It is fundamental to the logic of the Treaty Clause [in the Constitution] that it does *not* envisage that the President may unilaterally remake a treaty. If he could, the Senate's portion of the shared power inherent in the Treaty Clause would be nullified.[16]

The bibliographic apparatus of the president's role in the treaty and agreement process is largely structured in certain publications of the Department of State. The following is a selection of the more useful publications that provide information on treaties and other international agreements.

US Department of State Dispatch (USDSD)

The *Dispatch* is the latest series in a periodical formerly called the *Department of State Bulletin* that began in 1939 and was published weekly until January 1978, when it became a monthly. This arrangement lasted until December 1989, when the *Bulletin* abruptly ceased publication. Its demise shocked the library community, as the *Bulletin* was widely consulted by all kinds of users for its important textual as well as bibliographic information.

State Department officials, in trying to justify the *Bulletin*'s termination, stated that its many addresses, news conferences, statements, press releases, presidential proclamations, treaty and agreement information, and other features could be easily found in other sources. This absurdity was refuted by Lucy DeLuca and David W. Lewis in a closely reasoned content analysis that appeared in the September 1990 issue of *Documents to the People* (DttP). The authors found that in the penultimate issue of the *Bulletin*, fourteen of the twenty-six articles could "not be located in the Homer Babbidge Library" of the University of Connecticut, a federal depository "which receives approximately 90% of the items distributed in the Depository Library Program of the Government Printing Office."[17]

After funding was restored for the periodical in S. Rep. 101-334 (June 18, 1990), the *Bulletin* became the *US Department of State Dispatch* (S 1.3/5) and was issued weekly, an improvement in terms of currency.[18] The important update service, "Treaty Actions," was also reinstated, which provides bibliographic information on current slip treaties (Treaties and International Acts Series [TIAS]) as deposited, entered into force, amended, signed, withdrawn, and the like. *Dispatch* was reborn as volume 1, number 1, September 3, 1990, and in that issue "Treaty Actions" covered the period January-July 1990. Although this section does not appear in every issue of *Dispatch*, it is presumably complete and current. Moreover, *Dispatch* provides the text of the various speeches, ambassadorial appointments, essays, news conferences, etc., mentioned above. Figure 6.4 shows a page from *Dispatch* announcing "Treaty Actions," which includes both bilateral and multilateral pacts. The InfoTrac database on CD-ROM provides access to the contents of *Dispatch*. Moreover, *Dispatch* is online with LEXIS/NEXIS.

In 1990 the Bureau of Public Affairs, Office of Public Communication, Department of State, announced that the department joined the Computer Information Delivery Service (CIDS), which provides the following information in electronic format:

Official transcripts of the daily State Department press briefing;

Full text of the *Dispatch*;

Major speeches and congressional testimony by senior State Department officials;

Travel advisories, in which the State Department warns of places abroad that would be harmful or potentially harmful to visit;

Foreign policy summaries and updates on world events;

Chronologies, Facts Sheets, and *Country Profiles*;

Full text of *Background Notes*, detailed profiles by country or international organization; and

U.S. treaty actions.

(Text continues on page 190.)

Fig. 6.4. Page from *Dispatch*, "Treaty Actions" section

Treaty Actions

Treaty Actions
January–July 1990

Multilateral

Agriculture—Diseases
International agreement for the creation at Paris of an International Office of an International Office for Epizootics, with annex. Done at Paris Jan. 25, 1924. Entered into force Jan. 17, 1925; for the US July 29, 1975. TIAS 8141.
Accession deposited: Burma, Aug. 24, 1989.

Atomic Energy
Amendment of Article VI.A.1 of the Statute of the International Atomic Energy Agency of Oct. 26, 1956, as amended (TIAS 3873, 5284, 7668). Done at Vienna Sept. 27, 1984. [Senate] Treaty Doc. 99-7.
Acceptances deposited: Cote d'Ivoire, Oct. 27, 1989; Jamaica, Dec. 28, 1989; Luxembourg, Jan. 11, 1990.
Entered into force: Dec. 28, 1989.

Amendment of Article VI.A.1 of the Statute of the International Atomic Energy Agency of Oct. 26, 1956, as amended (TIAS 3873, 5284, 7668). Done at Vienna Sept. 27, 1984. Entered into force Dec. 28, 1989. [Senate] Treaty Doc. 99-7.
Acceptances deposited: Mali, Mar. 13, 1990; South Africa, May 25, 1990.

Agreement regarding protection of information transferred into the United States in connection with the initial phase of a project for the establishment of a uranium enrichment installation in the United States based upon the gas centrifuge process developed within the three European countries [Fed. Rep. of Germany, Netherlands, UK]. Signed at Washington Apr. 11, 1990. Entered into force Apr. 11, 1990.
Parties: Germany, Fed. Rep., Netherlands, UK, US.

Aviation
Convention on offenses and certain other acts committed on board aircraft. Done at Tokyo Sept. 14, 1963. Entered into force Dec. 4, 1969. TIAS 6768.
Accession deposited: German Democratic Republic, Jan. 10, 1989;[1] Marshall Islands, May 15, 1989; Zimbabwe, Mar. 8, 1989.

Convention for the suppression of unlawful acts against the safety of civil aviation. Done at Montreal Sept. 23, 1971. Entered into force Jan. 26, 1973. TIAS 7570.
Accession deposited: Vanuatu, Nov. 6, 1989.

Protocol for the suppression of unlawful acts of violence at airports serving international civil aviation. Done at Montreal Feb. 24, 1988. Entered into force Aug. 6, 1989.[2] [Senate] Treaty Doc. 100-19.
Senate advice and consent to ratification: Nov. 22, 1989.

Protocol relating to an amendment (Article 56) to the convention on international civil aviation (TIAS 1591). Done at Montreal Oct. 6, 1989. Enters into force on the date on which the 108th instrument of ratification is deposited.
Protocol for the suppression of unlawful acts of violence at airports serving international civil aviation, supplementary to the convention of Sept. 23, 1971 (TIAS 7570). Done at Montreal Feb. 24, 1988. Entered into force Aug. 6, 1989.[2]
Ratifications deposited: Austria, Dec. 28, 1989; Chile, Aug. 15, 1989; Denmark, Nov. 23, 1989;[3] France, Sept. 6, 1989.[1]

International air services transit agreement. Done at Chicago Dec. 7, 1944. Entered into force Jan. 20, 1945; for the US Feb. 8, 1945. EAS 487.
Acceptance deposited: German Dem. Rep., Apr. 2, 1990.

Convention on international civil aviation. Done at Chicago Dec. 7, 1944. Entered into force Apr. 4, 1947. TIAS 1591.
Adherence deposited: German Dem. Rep., Apr. 2, 1990.

Coffee
Extension of the international coffee agreement, 1983.[4] Done at London July 3, 1989. Entered into force Oct. 1, 1989.
Acceptances deposited prior to Oct. 1, 1989: Angola, Benin, Bolivia, Burundi, Cameroon, Canada, Colombia, Costa Rica, Cote d'Ivoire, Dominican Republic, El Salvador, Equatorial Guinea, Fiji, Finland, France, Gabon, Fed. Rep. of Germany,

Ghana, Guatemala, Guinea, Haiti, Honduras, India, Indonesia, Kenya, Liberia, Madagascar, Malawi, Mexico, Nicaragua, Norway, Panama, Papua New Guinea, Paraguay, Philippines, Portugal, Rwanda, Sri Lanka, Sweden, Switzerland, Tanzania, Thailand, Togo, Uganda, US, Zaire, Zambia, Zimbabwe.
Notifications of provisional application deposited prior to Oct. 1, 1989: Belgium, Brazil, Central African Rep., Cuba, Denmark, Ecuador, Ethiopia, European Economic Community, Greece, Ireland, Italy, Japan, Luxembourg, Netherlands, Nigeria, Peru, Spain, UK, Venezuela.
Accessions deposited: Trinidad and Tobago, Nov. 13, 1989; Singapore, Nov. 28, 1989; Sierra Leone, Nov. 29, 1989.

International coffee agreement, 1983, with annexes, done at London Sept. 16, 1982, as extended July 3, 1989.[4] Entered into force Oct. 1, 1989.
Acceptances deposited: Ethiopia, Mar. 26, 1990; Japan, July 17, 1990; Peru, Mar. 14, 1990; Venezuela, Mar. 2, 1990.
Accession deposited: Jamaica, Mar. 22, 1990.

Conservation
Convention on international trade in endangered species of wild fauna and flora, with appendices. Done at Washington Mar. 3, 1973. Entered into force July 1, 1975. TIAS 8249.
Ratification deposited: Poland, Dec. 12, 1989.
Accession deposited: Burkina Faso, Oct. 13, 1989.

Consular Relations
Optional protocol to the Vienna convention on consular relations, concerning the compulsory settlement of disputes. Done at Vienna Apr. 24, 1963. Entered into force Mar. 19, 1967; for the US Dec. 24, 1969. TIAS 6820.
Accessions deposited: Hungary, Dec. 8, 1989; Nicaragua, Jan. 9, 1990.

Containers
International convention for safe containers, with annexes, as amended. Done at Geneva Dec. 2, 1972. Entered into force Sept. 6, 1977; for the US Jan. 3, 1979. TIAS 9037, 10220, 10914.
Accession deposited: Dem. People's Rep. of Korea, Oct. 18, 1989; Indonesia, Sept. 25, 1989.

Copyright
Berne convention for the protection of literary and artistic works of Sept. 9, 1886, as revised at Paris July 24, 1971, and amended on Oct. 2, 1979. Entered into force for the US Mar. 1, 1989. [Senate] Treaty Doc. 99-27.
Accession deposited: Honduras, Oct. 24, 1989.
Ratification deposited: UK, Sept. 29, 1989.

Cultural Property
Statutes of the International Centre for the Study of the Preservation and Restoration of Cultural Property. Adopted at New Delhi Nov.-Dec. 1956, as amended at Rome Apr. 24, 1963, and Apr. 14-17, 1969. TIAS 7038.
Accession deposited: Mali, Oct. 9, 1989.

Convention on the means of prohibiting and preventing the illicit import, export, and transfer of ownership of cultural property. Done at Paris Nov. 14, 1970. Entered into force Apr. 24, 1972; for the US Dec. 2, 1983.
Acceptance deposited: Australia, Oct. 30, 1989.[12]
Ratifications deposited: Belize, Jan. 26, 1990; Madagascar, June 21, 1989.

Customs
Customs convention on containers, 1972, with annexes and protocol. Done at Geneva Dec. 2, 1972. Entered into force Dec. 6, 1975; for the US May 12, 1985.
Accession deposited: Trinidad and Tobago, Mar. 23, 1990.

Convention establishing a Customs Cooperation Council, with annex. Done at Brussels Dec. 15, 1950. Entered into force Nov. 4, 1952; for the US Nov. 5, 1970. TIAS 7063.
Accessions deposited: German Dem. Rep., Mar. 27, 1990; Iraq, June 6, 1990; Togo, Feb. 12, 1990.

Diplomatic Relations
Optional protocol to the Vienna convention on diplomatic relations concerning the compulsory settlement of disputes. Done at Vienna Apr. 18, 1961. Entered into force Apr. 24, 1964; for the US Dec. 13, 1972. TIAS 7502.
Accession deposited: Hungary, Dec. 8, 1989; Nicaragua, Jan. 9, 1990.

CIDS information resides on a mainframe computer system at the Martin Marietta Data Center in Orlando, Florida, and can be accessed by Telenet and other commercial services using a PC and modem or via a dedicated line to the nearest node. CIDS makes it possible for State Department information to reach a global audience within minutes of release and at a fraction of the cost for current printing and distribution methods. However, it will complement, not take the place of, traditional methods of printing and disseminating information.[19]

Treaties in Force (TIF)

Treaties in Force (TIF) (S 9.14) is an annual volume that contains a bibliographic record of all bilateral and multilateral treaties and agreements in force as of the date of issuance (January 1, [year]). Its index is not satisfactory, but the bibliographic information for each compact is updated to include any modifications, additional members joining or leaving multilateral pacts, and citations to the location of the full texts as they have been published in the *Statutes at Large* (prior to 1950), United States Treaties (UST), TIAS, *United Nations Treaty Series, League of Nations Treaty Series, Treaties and Other International Agreements of the United States of America, 1776-1949* (Bevans), and earlier series.

TIF is arranged in two parts followed by an appendix. Part 1 includes bilateral treaties and agreements listed by country or other political entity. Part 2 includes multilateral treaties and agreements, arranged by subject, together with a list of nations that are signatories to each pact. The appendix contains a consolidated tabulation of documents affecting international copyright relations of the United States. The latest edition of TIF is updated and supplemented by the information formerly published in "TREATIES: Current Actions" in the *Bulletin* and "Treaty Actions" currently published in the *Dispatch*.

Treaties and Other International Acts Series (TIAS)

Pursuant to PL 89-479, July 8, 1966 (80 Stat. 271; 1 U.S.C. 113),

> the Treaties and Other International Acts Series issued under the authority of the Secretary of State shall be competent evidence ... of the treaties, international agreements other than treaties, and proclamations by the President of such treaties ... in all the courts of law and equity and of maritime jurisdiction, and in all the tribunals and public offices of the United States, and of the several States, without any further proof or authentication thereof.

This Department of State "Note" is published on the verso of the title page of every TIAS numbered pamphlet. The slip treaties in their current form replaced an earlier Treaty Series (TS) and Executive Agreement Series (EAS) in 1945, both of which are still cited, as appropriate, in TIF. The numbering system continued when the earlier series were merged into the TIAS pamphlets; thus, TIAS begins with Treaty 1501 and Executive Agreement 506.

Because of the importance of the TIAS text pursuant to PL 89-479, it is regrettable indeed that the State Department has allowed this series to suffer a time lag of several years. Figure 6.5 shows a multilateral treaty (TIAS 10561) in pamphlet form. Note that the legislative chronology includes the role of the Senate. Figure 6.6 (see page 192) shows a typical presidential proclamation for a multilateral treaty (TIAS 10350). Figure 6.7 (see page 193) shows a typical legislative chronology of an executive agreement (TIAS 10558). Note the absence of any mention of Senate advice and consent to ratification.

Fig. 6.5. Legislative chronology of a multilateral treaty

MULTILATERAL

Marine Pollution: Intervention on the High Seas in Cases of Pollution by Substances Other Than Oil

Protocol done at London November 2, 1973, as rectified by the proces-verbal of October 14, 1977;[1]
Transmitted by the President of the United States of America to the Senate July 25, 1977 (S. Ex. L, 95th Cong., 1st Sess.);
Reported favorably by the Senate Committee on Foreign Relations June 26, 1978 (S. Ex. Rept. No. 95–24, 95th Cong., 2d Sess.);
Advice and consent to ratification by the Senate July 12, 1978;
Ratified by the President August 3, 1978;
Ratification of the United States of America deposited with the Secretary General of the Inter-Governmental Maritime Consultative Organization September 7, 1978;
Proclaimed by the President April 11, 1983;
Entered into force March 30, 1983.

---

[1] The text of the protocol which appears herein incorporates the corrections set forth in the proces-verbal.

(1)   TIAS 10561

(Text continues on page 193.)

Fig. 6.6. Presidential proclamation in a TIAS pamphlet

BY THE PRESIDENT OF THE UNITED STATES OF AMERICA

A PROCLAMATION

CONSIDERING THAT:

The 1981 Protocol for the Sixth Extension of the Wheat Trade Convention, 1971, was open for signature in Washington from March 24 through May 15, 1981, and the Protocol was signed during that period by the respective plenipotentiaries of the Government of the United States of America and certain other Governments;

The text of the Protocol, in the English, French, Russian, and Spanish languages, is hereto annexed;

The Senate of the United States of America by its resolution of December 16, 1981, two-thirds of the Senators present concurring therein, gave its advice and consent to ratification of the Protocol;

The President of the United States of America ratified the Protocol on January 12, 1982, in pursuance of the advice and consent of the Senate;

The Government of the United States of America deposited a declaration of provisional application of the Protocol on June 23, 1981, and deposited its instrument of ratification on January 12, 1982;

Pursuant to the provisions of Article 9 of the Protocol, the Protocol entered into force provisionally for the United States of America on June 23, 1981;

Pursuant to the provisions of Article 9 of the Protocol, the Protocol entered into force definitively for the United States of America on January 12, 1982;

Now, THEREFORE, I, Ronald Reagan, President of the United States of America, proclaim and make public the Protocol, to the end that it be observed and fulfilled with good faith on and after January 12, 1982, by the United States of America and by the citizens of the United States of America and all other persons subject to the jurisdiction thereof.

IN TESTIMONY WHEREOF, I have signed this proclamation and caused the Seal of the United States of America to be affixed.

[SEAL]   DONE at the city of Washington this first day of February in the year of our Lord one thousand nine hundred eighty-two and of the Independence of the United States of America the two hundred sixth.

RONALD REAGAN

By the President:
ALEXANDER M. HAIG JR
Secretary of State

TIAS 10350

Fig. 6.7. Legislative chronology for an executive agreement

ISRAEL

Peacekeeping: Multinational Force and Observers— Privileges and Immunities

Agreement effected by exchange of notes
Signed at Jerusalem and Tel Aviv September 28 and October 1,
* 1982;*
Entered into force October 1, 1982.

TIAS 10558

United States Treaties
and Other International Agreements

Just as public laws are bound together chronologically in the *Statutes at Large*, so the TIAS pamphlets are collected into *United States Treaties* (S 9.12). UST volumes, published on a calendar year basis beginning January 1, 1950, are accessed by a subject and country index. Before 1950, the full text of treaties and agreements was published in the *Statutes at Large*. The time lag that afflicts the issuance of TIAS pamphlets causes UST volumes to fall behind several years.

Treaties and Other International Agreements
of the United States of America,
1776-1949 (Bevans)

Earlier collections of treaties have been issued in separate sets known by the names of their compilers—Miller, Malloy, Redmond, Trenwith. With the definitive edition of *Treaties, 1776-1949*, compiled under the direction of Charles I. Bevans, the text of treaties and agreements for those years is easily accessed in one twelve-volume set. Each volume has an index, and volume 13 serves as an index to the entire set. Bevans was assigned the SuDocs notation S 9.12/2.

COMMERCIAL SOURCES FOR TREATIES AND AGREEMENTS

Unperfected Treaties of the United States, 1776-1976, edited by Christian L. Wiktor (Dobbs Ferry, NY: Oceana, 1976), is an annotated, multivolume set of treaties that did not receive Senate approval or were not ratified by the president.

William S. Hein & Company (Buffalo, New York), a commercial publisher, issues a series of products and services designed to reduce the time lag of the official treaty and agreement publishing pattern. Igor I. Kavass (ed.), *United States Treaty Index: 1776-1990 Consolidation*, provides a more comprehensive access to international acts than its official GPO predecessor sets. Treaties and agreements may be accessed by TIAS number, country or countries, subject, and time frame (chronology). The guide includes unpublished acts from 1776-1950, and current treaties and agreements *not yet published* in the TIAS pamphlets from 1950-1990.

Igor I. Kavass and Adolph Sprudzs (eds.), *United States Current Treaty Index*, is an annual updating the bound *Consolidation* by providing a cumulative index to acts not yet published in TIAS or UST. Information for accessing this update is by subject, type of agreement, dates of entry into force or legislative chronology, etc. To compile this information, the editors utilize the *Dispatch*, TIF, *Federal Register*, Senate legislative calendars, and secondary sources such as newspapers and journals.

A Guide to United States Treaties in Force consists of two parts. Part I is a "Numerical List and Subject Reference Index," and part II contains a numerical guide, chronological index, and a directory of countries and international organizations (IGOs).

Hein also produces two nonprint services. *Hein's United States Treaties and Other International Agreements — Current Microfiche Service* offers the full text of treaties that have not yet been published in the TIAS pamphlets with index and other finding aids. Updated bimonthly, this work provides access to the text of treaties and agreements within eight weeks of receipt by Congress. Begun in 1990, segments are now offered for full-text treaties covering the period 1984-1989. *Hein's United States Treaty Index on CD-ROM* provides access to treaties and other international pacts from 1776 through January 1, 1990, using the West Publishing Company's PREMISE software. Future updates will include the full text of agreements and treaties listed in the annual TIF.

Oceana Publications, Inc. (Dobbs Ferry, New York) issues a three-part treaty reference service designed, like the products noted above, to rectify the dilatory State Department schedule. Edited by Erwin C. Surrency, *Consolidated Treaties and International Agreements* (CTIA) consists of *CTIA: Current Document Service — United States* which contains the text of unreleased international compacts, *Index: CTIA*, and CTIA: CD-ROM. Of undeniable value, the Hein and Oceana products, like those of other commercial firms, are likely to be purchased by libraries solely because the federal government appears apathetic about providing timely information to the public.

OTHER SOURCES OF TREATY ACTIONS

In addition to the above, several official and commercial finding aids may be used for researching treaty and agreement materials. Because of the doctrine of shared powers, many of these sources are mentioned in chapter 5, on the legislative process.

CIS/Index

CIS/Index indexes and abstracts Senate Treaty Documents and Senate Executive Reports, which became part of the United States Congressional Serial Set beginning with the 96th Congress. Treaty Documents consist of presidential messages transmitting the text of treaties to the Senate Foreign Relations Committee. The Treaty Documents may also contain letters of submittal by the secretary of state followed by an article by article analysis of the treaty as signed, including any memorandums of understanding, procedural protocols, annexes, notes, and the like. A Treaty Document is merely the text of the treaty *before* Senate committee mark-up and should not be confused with the final version of the treaty as it eventually is issued in the TIAS pamphlets.

Senate Executive Reports are reports out of the Senate Foreign Relations Committee and, in the absence of the official TIAS slip treaty, are the closest equivalent to the treaty itself. Often other congressional committees are involved in hearings and reports if the treaty crosses jurisdictional lines and is of grave importance. For example, the Treaty between the United States of America and the Union of Soviet Socialist Republics on the Elimination of Their Intermediate-Range and Shorter-Range Missiles (the INF treaty), signed by Ronald Reagan and Mikhail Gorbachev in December 1987, was duly transmitted to the Senate Foreign Relations Committee. However, this committee received reports from Senate Majority Leader Robert C. Byrd, the Senate Armed Services Committee, and the Senate Select Committee on Intelligence.[20] The hearings, the Treaty Documents, and the Executive Reports are indexed and abstracted in *CIS/Index* and *CIS/Annual.* Figures 6.8 (see page 196) and 6.9 (see page 197) show the title page of a Treaty Document and an Executive Report, respectively.

CCH Congressional Index

Like *CIS/Index, CCH Congressional Index* is preeminent in its bibliographic coverage of congressional activities and presidential actions in which Congress participates within the framework of the Constitution. Volume 1 of *Congressional Index* has a section called "Reorganization Plans — Treaties — Nominations," which tracks current treaty action. For Senate treaty documents, *Congressional Index* shows a cumulative legislative chronology including dates of removal from the injunction of secrecy, referral to the Senate Foreign Relations Committee, reference to the Senate Executive Reports, ratification, etc. With its currency and cumulative features, *Congressional Index* provides a retrospective capability with the passage of time.

(Text continues on page 198.)

Fig. 6.8. Title page of a Senate treaty document

100TH CONGRESS 2d Session	SENATE	TREATY DOC. 100–11

TREATY BETWEEN THE UNITED STATES OF AMER-
ICA AND THE UNION OF SOVIET SOCIALIST REPUB-
LICS ON THE ELIMINATION OF THEIR INTERMEDI-
ATE-RANGE AND SHORTER-RANGE MISSILES

MESSAGE

FROM

THE PRESIDENT OF THE UNITED STATES

TRANSMITTING

THE TREATY BETWEEN THE UNITED STATES OF AMERICA AND
THE UNION OF SOVIET SOCIALIST REPUBLICS ON THE ELIMINA-
TION OF THEIR INTERMEDIATE-RANGE AND SHORTER-RANGE
MISSILES, TOGETHER WITH THE MEMORANDUM OF UNDER-
STANDING AND TWO PROTOCOLS, SIGNED AT WASHINGTON ON
DECEMBER 8, 1987

JANUARY 25, 1988.—Treaty was read the first time, and together with the
accompanying papers, referred to the Committee on Foreign Relations
and ordered to be printed for the use of the Senate.

U.S. GOVERNMENT PRINTING OFFICE

81–428   WASHINGTON : 1988

Fig. 6.9. Title page of a Senate executive report

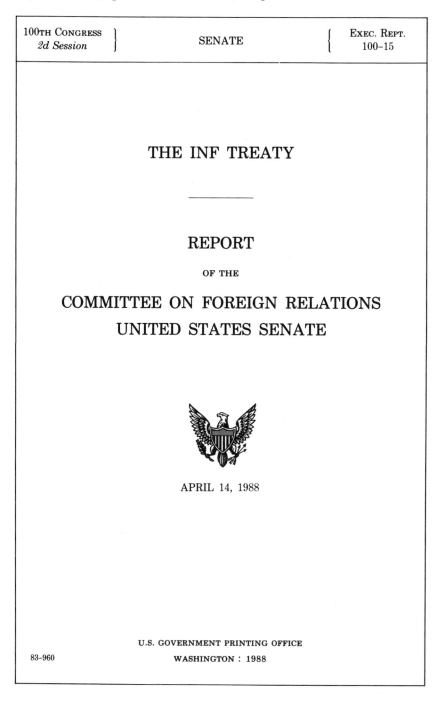

100TH CONGRESS 2d Session	SENATE	EXEC. REPT. 100-15

THE INF TREATY

REPORT

OF THE

COMMITTEE ON FOREIGN RELATIONS
UNITED STATES SENATE

APRIL 14, 1988

U.S. GOVERNMENT PRINTING OFFICE
WASHINGTON : 1988

83-960

Congressional Quarterly Weekly Report

CQ Weekly Report provides a lucid explanation of treaty and agreement actions, transforming the often stylized language found in official documents into readable prose. With its indexes and detailed table of contents, *CQ Weekly Report* establishes not only narrative but bibliographic superiority over prestigious newspapers such as *The New York Times* or *The Washington Post*. This is manifested in its accurate *citations* to the official documents and its detailed voting charts. Its companion volume, the annual *CQ Almanac*, although condensed from the weekly issues, is organized in such a way that the information on treaties is easy to access through its detailed index.

Shepard's United States Citations: Statute Edition

This unit of Shepard's Citations may be used to update a treaty by history and treatment. The history function complements the bibliographic information provided in the "Treaty Actions" section of the *Dispatch*. Treatment offers citations to case law and other citing sources that have cited the treaty. Although Shepard's *Statute Edition* does not yet have online capability with LEXIS or WESTLAW, one can Shepardize treaty information manually.

Popular Names of Treaties

Shepard's Acts and Cases by Popular Names, Federal and State, is best known for providing citations to federal and state statutes and case law when only the popular name is known. This service also includes the popular names given to treaties. For example, the Kellogg-Briand Pact [War Renunciation] of August 27, 1928, which ironically is still in force, is shown to be at 46 Stat. 2343; and the Rio de Janeiro Pact [Reciprocal Assistance] of September 2, 1947, is cited at 62 Stat. 1681.

AMERICAN INDIAN LAWS AND TREATIES

There are several useful sources for the specialist in Indian laws, treaties, and other presidential and congressional actions. Because the Congressional Serial Set contains a wealth of information on American Indian affairs, the *CIS US Serial Set Index, 1789-1969*, is a valuable guide. The Institute for the Development of Indian Law issued *A Chronological List of Treaties and Agreements Made by Indian Tribes with the United States*, which provides a list of all treaties and agreements, ratified or unratified, covering the period 1778-1909. Volume 7 of the *United States Statutes at Large* contains the text of Indian treaties from 1778 to 1842, and thereafter treaties and agreements with Indian tribes appear in regular chronological order in the *Statutes*. Current law is codified in Title 25 of the *United States Code*, and the regulations of agencies such as the Bureau of Indian Affairs (BIA) and the Indian Claims Commission are found in Title 25 of the *Code of Federal Regulations* (CFR).

Charles J. Kappler's *Indian Affairs: Laws and Treaties* (Y 4.In2/2:L44/ v. 1-5) was first published by GPO. Additional volumes list "all ratified and unratified treaties, all executive agreements, major federal court decisions relating to Indians, and tribal cases considered by the U.S. Court of Claims."[21] Frances Paul Prucha (ed.), *Documents of United States Indian Policy*, 2d ed. (Lincoln: University of Nebraska Press, 1990), is a single-volume work that includes almost 200 documents — statutes, Supreme Court decisions, treaties and agreements, and various reports relevant to government policies, past and present, toward Native Americans. Prucha's compilation is a good introduction to this topic. Other contemporary sources on legislative and executive actions include *CIS/Index*, the *Monthly Catalog*, and the *Congressional Record*.[22]

NOMINATIONS

Article II, Section 2, of the Constitution gives the president the power to nominate principal officers of the executive branch and the judiciary, but their *appointment* is subject to the advice and consent of the Senate. Most presidential nominees are confirmed by the Senate. For example, in the 91st Congress, 133,797 presidential nominations were confirmed by the Senate, 487 were withdrawn, and only 2 were rejected. This staggering number is not a misprint. In the vast majority of nominations, Senate action is a formality. Appointments and promotions of military officers, lower federal court judges, postmasters, and officials in various specialized services are almost automatically given Senate approval. Cabinet positions, sensitive or controversial appointments such as those of the directors of the FBI and the CIA, and nominations to the Supreme Court receive varying degrees of Senate scrutiny.[23]

The legislative path built into the Congress's LEGIS computer system consists of a series of steps in which the Executive Clerk of the Senate receives from the president the nomination and refers the name to the appropriate Senate committee. For example, nominees for the federal courts are referred to the Senate Judiciary Committee. There is no prior "executive document" series like the Senate Treaty Documents for international law, but the appropriate Senate committee does issue a Senate Executive Report. In most cases the committee report is favorable and only a simple majority of the plenary Senate is necessary for confirmation.

Senate Executive Reports are indexed and abstracted in *CIS/Index* and *CIS/ Annual*. For example, in S. Exec. Rep. 97-22 (Serial Volume 13406), the nomination of Sandra Day O'Connor to be the first woman to hold the office of associate justice of the Supreme Court was reported out of the Senate Judiciary Committee. Other sources providing information on nominations include the *Congressional Record, Journal of the Executive Proceedings of the Senate of the United States*, the *Monthly Catalog*, WCPD, and the *Public Papers* series. *CIS Index to US Senate Executive Documents and Reports, 1818-1969*, and companion text on microfiche provide a definitive retrospective source for research.

REORGANIZATION PLANS

Reorganization Plans are presidential directives submitted to both chambers of Congress. Under this format, the president may merge, abolish, or transfer functions of designated agencies of the executive branch below the rank of department or independent agency. Following the Supreme Court decision in *Immigration and Naturalization Service* v. *Chadha*, 77 L.Ed.2d 317, 103 S.Ct. 2764 (1983), which held that the "legislative veto" is unconstitutional, Congress decided to replace the one-House veto in the executive reorganization statute with a joint resolution of approval. Thus, the president must obtain the approval of both chambers within a fixed number of days to implement a reorganization schedule, as authorized under the provisions of Title 5, *United States Code*, section 901-912.

Plans carry a consecutive number and the year in which they became effective. They are usually accompanied by executive orders. For example, the Federal Emergency Management Agency (FEMA) was established by *Reorganization Plan No. 3* of 1978 and Executive Orders 12127 and 12148. Minor internal reorganization within existing agencies may be accomplished at the direction of the head of the unit and is frequently announced in the "Notices" section of the *Federal Register*.

The text of *Reorganization Plans* is duplicated in numerous sources, but they are collected in Title 5 of the *United States Code, Appendix*, which gathers together all pertinent documents such as executive orders implementing them, any presidential messages pertaining to the *Plans*, historical and revision notes, and cross-references. Other locations in which *Reorganization Plans* are published are listed in the tabular summary at the end of this chapter.

It should be noted that the *United States Government Manual* provides citations to reorganization plans, proclamations, executive orders, statutes, and the *United States Code* in its main section and in an appendix entitled "Executive Agencies and Functions of the Federal Government Abolished, Transferred, Terminated, or Changed in Name Subsequent to March 4, 1933." Figure 6.10 shows a page from the *Manual* in which presidential edicts are cited in this appendix.

SUMMARY

The foregoing has been an attempt to categorize the various publications that are generated by or for the presidency through official provenances or under commercial imprints. Although the duplication of materials that carry the public record of presidential activity may seem wasteful, such duplication does provide one clear advantage to libraries and other institutions that require this information. By this duplication, libraries large and small, nondepository and depository, may participate in the acquisition of at least some of these publications.

It is within the budget of a small library, for example, to subscribe to the *Department of State Dispatch, Weekly Compilation of Presidential Documents, Monthly Catalog,* or *Public Papers of the Presidents* series. All depository libraries should select the full range of these materials according to their several item categories. Moreover, commercial products and services in support of official documentation are usually available in the larger research libraries.

Fig. 6.10. Page from *U.S. Government Manual, Appendix*

conformity in U.S. coins as to fineness and weight. Terminated and functions transferred to Secretary of the Treasury (*see* text) by an act of Mar. 14, 1980 (94 Stat. 98; 31 U.S.C. 363).

Apprenticeship Section, Division of Labor Standards (Labor) Transferred to Federal Security Agency by EO 9139 of Apr. 18, 1942, where it functioned as Apprentice Training Service. Its organizational entity preserved by section 6 of the order. Transferred to War Manpower Commission by EO 9247 of Sept. 17, 1942, where it functioned within Bureau of Training. Returned to Department of Labor by EO 9617 of Sept. 19, 1945. (*See* Bureau of Apprenticeship and Training, text.)

Archive of Folksong (Library of Congress) Renamed Archive of Folk Culture by administrative order of the Deputy Librarian, effective Sept. 21, 1981 (*see* text).

Area Redevelopment Administration Established May 8, 1961, by Secretary of Commerce pursuant to Area Redevelopment Act (75 Stat. 47; 42 U.S.C. 2501) and Reorg. Plan No. 5 of 1950, effective May 24, 1950. Terminated Aug. 31, 1965, pursuant to terms of the act, as amended (79 Stat. 195; 42 U.S.C. 2525). Functions, personnel, and property transferred to Economic Development Administration in Department of Commerce (*see* text) by Department Order 4–A, effective Sept. 1, 1965.

Arlington Memorial Amphitheater Commission Established by act of Mar. 4, 1921 (41 Stat. 1440; 24 U.S.C. 291–295), to report annually to Congress, through the President of the United States, on memorials to be erected and bodies of certain deceased members of Armed Forces to be entombed during next ensuing year within Amphitheater in Arlington National Cemetery in Virginia. Abolished by act approved Sept. 2, 1960 (74 Stat. 739), and functions transferred to Secretary of Defense.

Arlington Memorial Bridge Commission Established by act of Mar. 4, 1913 (37 Stat. 885; D.C. Code (1951 ed.) 8–158), to report to Congress a suitable design for a memorial bridge across the Potomac River from the city of Washington to the Arlington estate. Abolished by EO 6166 of June 10, 1933, and functions transferred to Office of National Parks, Buildings, and Reservations (*see* appendix A).

Armed Forces Medical Library Originally founded in 1836 as Library of the Surgeon General's Office, U.S. Army, and later known as Army Medical Library, it was given title of Armed Forces Medical Library in 1952. The National Library of Medicine Act, approved Aug. 3, 1956 (70 Stat. 960; 42 U.S.C. 275), established the National Library of Medicine in Public Health Service (*see* appendix A) and transferred to it all civilian personnel, property, and funds of Armed Forces Medical Library.

Armed Services Renegotiation Board Established by directive of Secretary of Defense on July 19, 1948, to conduct contract renegotiation with contractors and subcontractors assigned. Board abolished by letter of Secretary of Defense dated Jan. 18, 1952, and functions transferred to Renogotiation Board (*see* appendix A).

Army, Department of the Functions, powers, and duties relating generally to water vessel anchorages, draw-bridge operating regulations, obstructive bridges, tolls, pollution of the sea by oil, and location and clearance of bridges and causeways in navigable waters of the U.S. transferred to Secretary of Transportation by Department of Transportation Act of Oct. 15, 1966 (80 Stat. 931; 49 U.S.C. 1651 note).

Army and Navy Staff College Established Apr. 23, 1943, and operated under Joint Chiefs of Staff. Wartime mission was to train specially selected Army, Navy, and Marine Corps officers for command and staff duties in point operations. Redesignated National War College (*see* text), effective July 1, 1946.

Army Specialist Corps Established in War Department by EO 9078 of Feb. 26, 1942, to marshal outstanding scientific, technical, labor, and business skills directly into the Army in positions where it was not necessary to employ military personnel. Abolished as a separate organization by Secretary of War on Oct. 31, 1942, and functions merged into a central Officer Procurement Service.

Ash Council *See* President's Advisory Council on Executive Organization, appendix A.

Assistance Payments Administration (HEW) Established by Secretary's reorganization of Aug. 15, 1967, to administer assistance programs of certain State grants, Work Incentive Program, and for U.S. citizens returning from abroad and refugees. Transferred by

Figure 6.11 provides a tabular summary of a *selective* list of official and commercial sources containing the *text* of major presidential activities.

Fig. 6.11. Selective summary of official and commercial sources

Type of Activity	Sources
Addresses and remarks	*Congressional Record* Congressional Serial Set *Dispatch*[24] House and Senate *Journals* *Public Papers* WCPD
Executive orders	*CIS Presidential Executive Orders and Proclamations on Microfiche* *Codification of Presidential Proclamations and EOs* *Dispatch* *Federal Register* LEGI-SLATE LEXIS *Public Papers* Title 3, CFR U.S.C.C.A.N. USCS Advance Pamphlets WCPD WESTLAW
Messages	*Congressional Record* Congressional Serial Set *Dispatch* House and Senate *Journals* *Public Papers* U.S.C.C.A.N. WCPD
Nominations	*Congressional Record* Congressional Serial Set *Journal of the Executive Proceedings of the Senate* *Public Papers* Senate *Journal* WCPD
Proclamations	*CIS Presidential Executive Orders and Proclamations on Microfiche* *Codification of Presidential Proclamations and EOs* *Dispatch* *Federal Register*

Type of Activity	Sources
Proclamations *(continued)*	LEGI-SLATE
	LEXIS
	Public Papers
	Statutes at Large
	Title 3, CFR
	U.S.C.C.A.N.
	USCS Advance Pamphlets
	WCPD
	WESTLAW
Reorganization plans	*Congressional Record*
	Congressional Serial Set
	Federal Register
	LEGI-SLATE
	LEXIS
	Public Papers
	Statutes at Large
	Title 3, CFR
	Title 5, *United States Code*
	WCPD
	WESTLAW
Treaties and agreements	Bevans
	Congressional Record
	Congressional Serial Set
	CTIA
	Dispatch
	Hein's United States Treaties
	Journal of the Executive Proceedings of the Senate
	Public Papers
	Statutes at Large
	TIAS
	UNTS
	UST
	WCPD

NOTES

[1]According to a Department of State ruling Grover Cleveland is counted twice, as the twenty-second and twenty-fourth president, because his two terms were not consecutive.

[2]Nancy P. Johnson, "Presidential Legislation," *Legal Reference Services Quarterly*, 2 (Spring 1982): 1.

[3]Laurence F. Schmeckebier and Roy B. Eastin, *Government Publications and Their Use*, 2d rev. ed. (Washington, DC: Brookings Institution, 1969), p. 341.

[4]Gary Hoag, "The Search for Orders: CIS Presidential Executive Orders and Proclamations, 1789-1983," *Microform Review*, 18 (Fall 1989): 222-34. This dual-media publication consists of a 22-volume index that includes over 75,000 presidential documents issued during those years. See also Mary Woodward, "Executive Orders: A Journey," *Legal Reference Services Quarterly*, 10 (1990): 125-34.

[5]Donald C. Smith, "The Rhetoric of the *Weekly Compilation of Presidential Documents*," *Government Publications Review*, 16 (May/June 1989): 213, 215-16.

[6]For earlier official and privately published compilations of presidential materials, see Schmeckebier and Eastin, *Government Publications*, pp. 330-47. Unpublished presidential materials before the advent of the presidential libraries program have been collected by the Manuscript Division of the Library of Congress (LC) and are available on microfilm from the LC Photoduplication Division. Printed finding aids to these collections, from Washington to Coolidge, have been published by LC.

[7]Statement by Theodore C. Sorensen, December 1963, in Foreword to volume III of the *Public Papers of the Presidents: Kennedy* [1963], p. v.

[8]*Coalition on Government Information Newsletter*, 5 (April 1991): 1, 13.

[9]*The Role of the Senate in Treaty Ratification*, a committee print prepared for the use of the Senate Foreign Relations Committee (Washington, DC: GPO, 1974).

[10]Leonard W. Levy, *Original Intent and the Framers' Constitution* (New York: Macmillan, 1988), pp. 38, 41-42.

[11]Jacob E. Cooke (ed.), *The Federalist* (New York: Meridian Books, 1961), pp. 432-36.

[12]Cooke, *Federalist*, pp. 503-06.

[13]Levy, *Original Intent*, p. 52.

[14]Margaret A. Leary, "International Executive Agreements: A Guide to the Legal Issues and Research Sources," *Law Library Journal*, 72 (Winter 1979): 1.

[15]*The Role of the Senate in Treaty Ratification*, p. 27.

[16]*Senate Executive Report 100-15* (April 14, 1988), pp. 87-88.

[17]*Documents to the People* (DttP), 16 (September 1990): 170-71.

[18]Section 113 of the "Supplemental Foreign Relations Authorization Act of 1990" (S. Rep. 101-334, June 18, 1990) restored the *Bulletin/Dispatch*, and Section 114 dealt with the *Foreign Relations of the United States* historical series.

[19]Department of State, Office of Public Communication, press release, "Computerized News and Information Service Begins in February [1991]," pp. 1-2 (mimeographed). The print edition of *Dispatch* is indexed in *Readers' Guide to Periodical Literature.*

[20]*Senate Executive Report 100-15* (April 14, 1988), pp. 74-79.

[21]Michael L. Tate, "Studying the American Indian through Government Documents and the National Archives," *Government Publications Review*, 5 (1978): 289.

[22]Michael L. Tate, "Red Power: Government Publications and the Rising Indian Activism of the 1970s," *Government Publications Review*, 8A (1981): 499-518.

[23]Congressional Quarterly Service, *Congressional Quarterly's Guide to the Congress of the United States* (Washington, DC: Congressional Quarterly, 1971), p. 228.

[24]The *Department of State Dispatch* publishes virtually all presidential messages, executive orders, proclamations, and other official statements as they pertain to the duties of the president as commander-in-chief of the armed forces and head of the diplomatic machinery of the government.

7

Administrative Law: Regulations and Decisions

INTRODUCTION

The rulemaking process is a set of formal procedures through which a statute adopted by the Congress and signed by the president is translated into specific written requirements to be carried out and enforced by executive branch and independent agencies. These regulations are far more detailed and precise than the statutory provisions to which they are pursuant. The major instruments of rulemaking are the *Federal Register* (FR) and the *Code of Federal Regulations* (CFR). Insofar as the president is an active agent in this process, his actions, as we noted in chapter 6, are promulgated in the FR and in Title 3 of the CFR.

BACKGROUND

The Federal Register Act of 1935 (49 Stat. 500; 44 U.S.C. Chapter 15) established for the first time in the nation's history a systematic and bibliographically consistent process for government regulations. Before 1935 there was no central system; each agency did little more than type, sign, and file regulations in agency cabinets. Frequently one had to search out a regulation by going to the agency and tracking it down. This ineffective practice led the government in a series of miscalculations to become embarrassed by what is known as the "Hot Oil Case," which was based upon a provision that had been nullified by a later rule.[1] The government's case was dismissed and the Supreme Court denounced all parties for their ignorance of the law. The failure to publicize adequately executive orders and other agency regulations came to be known as "hip pocket" law, and its proven lack of effectiveness resulted in a bibliographic structure that was called the *Federal Register*, the first issue of which was published March 14, 1936.

ADMINISTRATIVE RULES AND REGULATIONS

The Federal Register Act provides that, in addition to presidential documents, the kinds of information to be published include "documents or classes of documents that may be required so to be published by Act of Congress." At present the FR includes the following sections: presidential documents, rules and regulations (including interim rules), proposed rules, and notices (including meetings required to be announced in the FR pursuant to the 1976 Government in the Sunshine Act). Various finding aids link the FR with the CFR and provide a bibliographic mechanism that, refined over the years, reveals a symmetry not always found in other federal government records.

Section 1510 of Title 44 of the *United States Code* calls for "the preparation and publication ... of complete codification of the documents of each agency," and this is accomplished in the *Code of Federal Regulations.* Just as the *United States Statutes at Large* are codified in the *United States Code,* so the daily issues of the FR are codified in the CFR. Divided into fifty Titles, not all of which parallel the *United States Code* upon which the structure was based, the CFR is revised each calendar year on a quarterly schedule as follows:

Titles 1-16. . . . . as of January 1
Titles 17-27. . . . . as of April 1
Titles 28-41. . . . . as of July 1
Titles 42-50. . . . . as of October 1

When no amendments or other changes are promulgated in a volume during a quarter, a reprint of the cover of the volume with the new date and a new color is sent to subscribers and depository libraries. This cover can be stapled to the volume and serves to direct that the unrevised issue be retained. With the exception of Title 3, the pamphlet volumes of the CFR are coded by different colors every year.

Online Products

The *Federal Register* and the CFR are online with WESTLAW, LEXIS, and LEGI-SLATE. The last, best known for its comprehensive coverage of congressional activities, is a Washington, D.C.-based commercial service that indexes every announcement in each day's FR. Access to the contents of the FR is by issuing agency, docket number, CFR part, and enabling statute cited in the regulation. Within 24 to 48 hours, LEGI-SLATE provides the full text of the daily *Register* in such a way that, in effect, the CFR is being updated on a daily schedule. Online indexing searches have been available since 1981 and full text capability, since January 1985.

CD-ROM Product

The *Compact Disc Federal Register* (Wellesley Hills, MA: Counterpoint Publishing) provides the full text of the past six months of the *Federal Register.* Issued weekly, this service can be searched by agency provenance, words and phrases, page number citation, and table of contents.

CFR Finding Aids

All CFR titles have a "Finding Aids" section that includes a Table of CFR Titles and Chapters; an Alphabetical List of Agencies appearing in the CFR; and a List of CFR Sections Affected, divided into yearly units. A Parallel Table of Authorities and Rules appears in the *CFR Index and Finding Aids* volume, providing references to the *United States Code, Statutes at Large,* public (slip) law number, and presidential documents to CFR parts construed or applied. Earlier separately published tables include the *Code of Federal Regulations List of Sections Affected, 1949-1963*; a two-volume *List of CFR Sections Affected, 1964-1972*; and a four-volume *List of CFR Sections Affected, 1973-1985.*

RULEMAKING PROCEDURES

With the advent of the CFR in 1939, systematic bibliographic linkage between the FR and its codified companion was effected. The FR is keyed to the CFR, enabling the user to know in advance of issuance the title and part of the *Code of Federal Regulations* in which the final rule promulgated in the FR will be published. The Administrative Procedure Act of 1946 (60 Stat. 237) clarified the public's role in the rulemaking process. Under normal circumstances agencies are obliged to publish "proposed rules" so interested parties have the opportunity to respond either in writing or in person at administrative hearings. However, this procedure may be waived under extraordinary circumstances. The most dramatic example in recent years of the authority to waive the proposed rule process occurred following the deaths of seven Chicago-area residents from cyanide-laced Tylenol in 1982.

Shortly after the deaths generated something approximating a national wave of terror, the Food and Drug Administration (FDA) invoked a subsection of the Administrative Procedure Act providing that a general notice of proposed rulemaking need not be published in the *Federal Register* when the agency for good cause finds that "notice and public procedure ... are impracticable, unnecessary or contrary to the public interest" (5 U.S.C. 553[b][B]). FDA noted that the Tylenol killings received wide exposure in the news media and therefore "it is clearly in the public interest to move quickly to establish uniform Federal regulatory standards that will enable manufacturers to implement tamper-resistant packaging and labeling requirements as efficiently and expeditiously as possible" (47 FR 50448). The action appeared as a *final rule* in the November 5, 1982, issue of the FR and was codified at Title 21, CFR, Parts 211, 314, and 700.

Updating the CFR

To update the CFR, some or all of the following steps may be taken:

1. To locate the title and part one is searching, consult the unnumbered *CFR Index and Finding Aids* volume. Revised annually as of January 1, it provides subject access to the CFR volumes. Some CFR titles have their own index, and these titles are referenced in the contents page of the *Finding Aids.*

2. Because of the quarterly publishing schedule of titles, references in the *CFR Index and Finding Aids* include material in the basic CFR volumes as well as amendatory information promulgated in the FR through January 1 but not yet incorporated into the CFR issues. Therefore, users should consult separate pamphlets entitled *LSA — List of CFR Sections Affected*. Issued monthly and cumulated, the December, March, June, and September *LSA — Lists* provide an annual cross-reference for those CFR titles listed on the covers, and these issues must be saved. Organized by titles and appropriate subdivisions, the *LSA — List* references the page numbers of the FR where amendatory information is announced. The absence of any reference to a title and part indicates that the rule published in the CFR has not been changed.

3. To complete the updating of the most current issue of the FR, consult:

    a. "CFR Parts Affected during [Month]." Located in the back of each daily FR, this cumulative table also provides references from the CFR titles and subdivisions to *Federal Register* page numbers.

    b. "CFR Parts Affected in This Issue" appears in the front of each daily FR and completes the updating information. This parallel table is similarly arranged.

Figure 7.1 (see page 210) provides a typical *LSA — List*, an illustration of "CFR Parts Affected during [Month]" is shown in figure 7.2 (see page 211), and "CFR Parts Affected in This Issue" appears in figure 7.3 (see page 212).

Page/Date Guide to the FR

Beginning in 1970 the *Federal Register Index* included at the end of each cumulative monthly issue a useful parallel table referencing the inclusive page numbers to the date of the daily issue.

(Text continues on page 213.)

Fig. 7.1. Page from an *LSA — List of CFR Sections Affected*

TITLE 21—FOOD AND DRUGS

Chapter I—Food and Drug Administration, Department of Health, Education, and Welfare

2.125 (e)(6) added	30334
5.30 (d) revised	62281

List of CFR Sections Affected

Page

882 Added	51730–51778
895 Added	29221
1000.16 (c) and (d) suspended	44844
Redesignated as 1020.30 (p) and revised	49670, 49671
1002.61 (a)(4) revised; eff. 5–7–80	65357
Technical correction	67655
1010.4 (c) revised	48191
1020.30 (a)(1)(i), (h)(2)(i), (4) introductory text and (i) and (k) revised; (b)(21) amended; (b)(55) added	29654
(b)(3), (d) introductory text, and (e)(2) revised; (p) redesignated from 1000.16 and revised; (b)(56), (57), (d)(3), (e)(3), and (q) added	49671
(m)(1) revised; eff. 12–1–80	68822
1020.31 (g)(1) revised	29654
1020.32 (b)(2)(iv) revised	29654
1040.20 Added; eff. 5–7–80	65357
Technical correction	67655
1040.30 Added; eff. in part 9–7–81	52195
1220.40 (a) revised	30335

Chapter II—Drug Enforcement Administration, Department of Justice

1308.13 (e) introductory text revised	40888
1308.14 (b) introductory text revised	40888
1308.15 (b) introductory text revised	40888
1308.24 (i) table amended	27981
1316.65 (b) revised	42179
(b) and (c) revised	55332
1316.66 Redesignated as 1316.67 and revised; new 1316.66 added	42179
Revised	55332
1316.67 Redesignated as 1316.68; new 1316.67 redesignated from 1316.66 and revised	42179
Amended	55332
1316.68 Redesignated from 1316.67	42179
1316.75 Nomenclature change	

Fig. 7.2. Page from "CFR Parts Affected during [Month]"

CFR PARTS AFFECTED DURING DECEMBER

At the end of each month, the Office of the Federal Register publishes separately a list of CFR Sections Affected (LSA), which lists parts and sections affected by documents published since the revision date of each title.

1 CFR

445	77127
480	74791
490	75392

3 CFR

Administrative Orders:

Memorandums:

December 11, 1979	71809
December 14, 1979	74781

Executive Orders:

11223 (Amended by EO 12178)	71807
11322 (Revoked by EO 12183)	74787
11419 (Revoked by EO 12183)	74787
11888 (Amended by EO 12180, 12181)	72077, 72083
11978 (Revoked by EO 12183)	74787
12103 (Amended by EO 12176)	70705
12153 (Amended by EO 12186)	76477
12173	69271
12174	69609
12175	70703
12176	70705
12177	71805
12178	71807
12179	71811
12180	72077
12181	72083
12182	74785
12183	74787
12184	75091
12185	75093
12186	76477

Proclamations:

4705	70701
4706	71399
4707	72348
4708	72069
4709	74789

Reorganization Plans:

No. 3 of 1979	69273

Presidential Determinations:

No. 80–8 of December 18, 1979	77125

4 CFR

6	70115
420	73001

5 CFR

Ch. I	76747
212	75615
213	69611, 70449, 72569, 75615, 77127
214	75615
315	72569
317	75615
737	72570
771	77127
831	76748
870	76748
871	70449, 76748
890	76748
891	76748
1250	75914
1251	75914
1252	75914
1253	75914
1254	75914
1255	75914
1256	75914
1257	75914
1258	75914
1259	75914
1260	75914
1261	75914
1262	75914
1263	75914
1264	75914

★ ★ ★ ★ ★

Proposed Rules:

Ch. I	69304
229	75399
230	70349
231	72604
239	75399
240	75399
241	70189, 72604
249	75399

18 CFR

1	69284, 77155
2	69935, 71821, 75383, 76482
4	75383
271	69642, 69935, 76482, 76778
274	69642, 76778
284	75383
701	72583
707	69921
713	72892

Proposed Rules:

Ch. I	70752
35	70752
46	71428
271	70189
280	73121
282	77198
284	73121
292	69978

19 CFR

4	70458
159	70138, 75135
171	70459
201	76458
207	76458

Proposed Rules:

4	75685
6	73122
144	75685
151	75685
159	75685

20 CFR

404	73018
676	72584

Proposed Rules:

Ch. III	72728

21 CFR

Ch. I	72585

5	75626
10	70459
12	70459
13	70459
14	70459
15	70459
16	70459
176	75627
177	74816
178	69649
201	74816
202	74817
510	71412, 74818, 76779
520	71412, 72586, 74818
522	71412, 76780
526	71412
529	72587
548	69650
558	71412, 74819, 76779
701	75627
820	75627
1000	71728
1308	71822

Proposed Rules:

Ch. I	71428, 72728, 75990
25	71742
58	69666
70	75659
131	69668, 69669, 72613
170	75662
182	74845
184	74845
320	69669
333	71428
357	75666
438	69768
452	69670
660	76811
868	69673, 70486

22 CFR

42	72108

23 CFR

170	75552
172	75552
420	75552
620	75552
650	72109
713	73018

Proposed Rules:

630	70191
656	70753

Fig. 7.3. Page from "CFR Parts Affected in This Issue"

CFR PARTS AFFECTED IN THIS ISSUE

A cumulative list of the parts affected this month can be found in the Reader Aids section at the end of this issue.

7 CFR
53.. 45320
1464.. 45115
1806.. 45115

10 CFR
212.. 45352

Proposed Rules:
903.. 45141

12 CFR
201.. 45115
545.. 45116

Proposed Rules:
226.. 45141
509.. 45175
509a.. 45175
550.. 45175
566.. 45175

13 CFR
107.. 45120
108.. 45123

16 CFR
Proposed Rules:
Ch. I....................................... 45178
13.. 45181

17 CFR
Proposed Rules:
1.. 45192

19 CFR
Proposed Rules:
Ch. I....................................... 45333

24 CFR
Proposed Rules:
Subtitle A.............................. 45342
Subtitle B.............................. 45342

26 CFR
Proposed Rules:
1.. 45192
601.. 45192

27 CFR
Proposed Rules:
Ch. I....................................... 45326
6.. 45298
8.. 45298
10.. 45298
11.. 45298

81.. 45210
162.. 45218

43 CFR
Public Land Orders:
5675.. 45133
5676.. 45133

44 CFR
64.. 45133
65 (2 documents)........... 45136,
                                                45137

Proposed Rules:
67 (6 documents).......... 45225–
                                                45227

45 CFR
302.. 45137

47 CFR
Proposed Rules:
15.. 45227

50 CFR
32.. 45137
Proposed Rules:
652.. 45227

COMMERCIAL AND OFFICIAL FINDING AIDS

As noted in chapter 6, the *CIS Federal Register Index*, issued weekly, provides a sophisticated, detailed index to the FR. CIS also publishes an annual *Index to the Code of Federal Regulations*. R. R. Bowker's *Code of Federal Regulations Index* issues quarterly supplements that cumulate into an annual issue. Certain looseleaf services published by Commerce Clearing House, Prentice Hall, the Bureau of National Affairs, and other reporters provide the full text of administrative regulations published in the FR and CFR. Combined with other features such as relevant statutes, agency administrative decisions, and case law, a topical reporter on a particular subject is a more appropriate source to use than the official FR/CFR if the user is interested in a specific topic such as taxation, insurance, collective bargaining, labor law, etc.

In addition, a number of regulations are published on a selective basis in the advance sheets of the *United States Code Service* (Lawyers Cooperative Publishing) and *U.S. Code Congressional and Administrative News* (West). Readex provides full text of the FR and the CFR on microfiche.

Shepard's CFR Citations

Shepard's Code of Federal Regulations Citations provides citations to the CFR. The citing sources include the U.S. Supreme Court, the lower federal courts, state courts in cases reported in units of the National Reporter System, *A.L.R. Annotations*, and selected legal periodicals. As noted in chapter 6, this source can also be used to Shepardize presidential actions.

User Guide

An official publication, *The Federal Register: What It Is and How to Use It* (AE 2.108:F31), is a handbook with many illustrations of pages taken from sections of the FR and CFR. Also explained, with appropriate examples, are the *LSA – List* and the two "CFR Sections Affected" appearing in each daily issue of the *Federal Register*. For the reference librarian unfamiliar with the components of the FR and CFR and their bibliographic interrelationship, this guide is a useful reference source.

Directory Information

The *Federal Regulatory Directory*, a publication of Congressional Quarterly, Inc., is now in its sixth edition (1990). Almost 1,000 pages of text describe in detail over 100 agencies that have regulatory functions. Profiles summarize the functions and statutes the agencies enforce; identify the private sector entities responsible for complying with the regulations; and discuss procedures for exceptions, appeals, and oversight. Standard directory information such as names, telephone numbers, and even some photographs of personnel in Washington and in the regional offices of decentralized agencies is included. The directory also includes organization charts, explanations of hearings procedures, and lists of congressional committees with jurisdiction over regulatory matters. A brief, accurate section on how to use the FR and CFR, an appendix that incorporates the text of important regulatory acts and executive orders, and subject and name indexes make this a valuable ready-reference source.

The *Federal Yellow Book* (New York: Monitor Publishing Company), issued quarterly, contains directory information for over 35,000 key members of departments, agencies (including independent regulatory entities), regional offices, and Federal Information Centers in over 70 cities.

SPECIFICITY AND READABILITY

The ferocious specificity of administrative regulations, proposed rules, and notices requires a clarity and precision of language not always found in the pages of the FR and CFR. The attention to detail in promulgating rules comes as a surprise when students first encounter the prose of these famous publications. For example, the Agricultural Marketing Service of the Department of Agriculture stipulates that

> no handler shall handle any navel oranges grown in District 1 or District 3 which are of a size smaller than 2.20 inches in diameter, which shall be the largest measurement at a right angle to a straight line running from the stem to the blossom end of the fruit; provided, that not to exceed 5 percent, by count, of the navel oranges contained in any type of container may measure smaller than 2.20 inches in diameter.[2]

Specificity runs rampant in the regulations promulgated by the Food and Drug Administration covering the preparation of food for human consumption. For example, a portion of the requirements for sweet chocolate, found at 21 CFR 163.123(a), stipulates that the finished product contain

> not less than 15 percent by weight of chocolate liquor calculated by subtracting from the weight of chocolate liquor used the weight of cacao fat therein and the weights therein of alkali and seasoning ingredients, if any, multiplying the remainder by 2.2, dividing the result by the weight of the finished sweet chocolate, and multiplying the quotient by 100.

Former director of the Office of the Federal Register Fred Emery issued in 1975 a *Document Drafting Handbook* in a somewhat futile attempt to assist agencies in improving the linguistic quality of regulatory documents. Appendix B of the *Handbook* provides a list of eschewed words and phrases: *aforementioned, hereby, provided that, wheresoever, to wit, shall be deemed to be, sole and exclusive, unless and until, null and void, authorized and empowered, may be treated as, hereinafter,* and so on.[3] Three years later President Jimmy Carter issued EO 12044 (March 23, 1978), which established in Section 1 a policy that "Regulations shall be as simple and clear as possible." Section 2(a) of EO 12044 requires all federal agencies to publish in the FR twice a year "an agenda of significant regulations under development or review." During the Reagan administration the rush to deregulate reduced the thousands of rules deemed burdensome to the private sector. The *Federal Register* for 1981 totalled 63,553 pages, a 25 percent reduction from the 1980 *Register*. For the remaining years of President Ronald Reagan's tenure, the total annual pages of the FR hovered around the 50,000 mark. However, since George Bush became president, "the number of rules ... developed by federal agencies has grown about 17 percent," from approximately 4,000 during the period 1983 through 1988 to almost 4,700. Officials in the Bush administration said "new rules were proliferating because they were required by new laws dealing with, among other things, immigration, federal grants to child care centers, restrictions on lobbying, food product labeling, aircraft noise and the rights of disabled people."[4]

Any increase in statutory enactments inevitably results in more administrative regulations written pursuant to statutory authority. And the specificity of rulemaking language becomes evident when one notes that the volumes of the official (unannotated) *United States Code* occupy less than one-third of the shelving space required for the CFR volumes. Moreover, one common rule promulgated in the *Federal Register* affecting several executive branch and independent entities adds to the quantity of verbiage when carried over into the CFR. For example, the Federal Policy for the Protection of Human Subjects was published as a final rule at 56 FR 28003-28032 (June 18, 1991), but this information was promulgated in various titles and parts of the CFR as appropriate departments and agencies were required to comply: Agriculture (7 CFR [1c]); Commerce (15 CFR 27); Energy (10 CFR 745); Housing and Urban Development (24 CFR 60); Defense (32 CFR 219); Education (34 CFR 97); Health and Human Services, including the CIA pursuant to EO 12333 (45 CFR 46); Transportation (49 CFR 11); Veterans Affairs (38 CFR 16); as well as the National Aeronautics and Space Administration (NASA), the Consumer Product Safety Commission, the Environmental Protection Agency (EPA), the National Science Foundation, and others.

The Privacy Act (5 U.S.C. 552[a]) alone added over 5,000 pages to the FR in 1975, a sum greater than the total number of pages published in 1936. Concerning the abundance of statutes, administrative regulations, agency tribunal decisions, and cases, a comment by James Webb, former assistant secretary of defense, is apposite:

> Washington is a town whose only industry is the making, shaping, processing, and marketing of words. Words to define how citizens should conduct themselves. Words to direct and limit industry. Words to throw at one another in the halls of Congress, or in front of devouring cameras. Words that in the end can kill, impoverish, or imprison, or empower.... Words without poetry or music, whose mastery brings money and authority.[5]

Despite criticism of the FR and CFR for their allegedly oppressive paperwork requirements, enforcement of rules that appear trivial, and tortuous prose, regulatory activity is probably necessary to restrain the excesses of private sector free-wheeling activities. Whatever the merits of the perennial controversy in which words such as *overregulation* and *deregulation* are bandied, the entities that promulgate administrative rules, created by Congress, have indeed become a "veritable fourth branch of the Government."[6]

ADMINISTRATIVE DECISIONS

Rulings, decisions, orders, and advisory opinions of agencies with quasi-judicial authority are published in sources other than the *Federal Register* and the CFR. Tribunals within the agencies, generally presided over by administrative law judges, interpret and enforce administrative rules. Decisions rendered in this context are subject to review by the courts. The publications of these rulings are found in official GPO documents and in commercial sources including online services such as WESTLAW and LEXIS.[7] "Because the official government publications are often poorly indexed and not published in a timely manner, the commercial looseleaf services are generally more helpful and are more frequently relied on by legal researchers."[8]

In her excellent guide to selected sources of agency decisions and opinions, Veronica Maclay cites and annotates both official (GPO) and commercial publications to assist documents librarians in locating these scattered sources, which, unfortunately, lack the systematic linkage capabilities found in the FR and CFR. Governmental units covered in her essay include the Atomic Energy Commission, Benefits Review Board, Civil Aeronautics Board, Commodity Futures Trading Commission, Comptroller General, Consumer Product Safety Commission, EPA, and several other units with regulatory functions.[9]

Compilations or series of decisions rendered by agencies and published in the official GPO documents are available to federal depository libraries. A few examples suffice: the monthly *Agriculture Decisions* (A 1.58/a); the *Rulings* series issued by the Social Security Administration (HE 3.44) covering old age, survivors, disability, supplemental security income, and black lung benefits; the *Rulings* on Medicare, Medicaid, professional standards review, and related matters published by the Health Care Financing Administration (HE 22.15); Internal Revenue Service's *Regulations, Rules, and Instructions* (T 22.19); the quarterly decisions and rulings of the Customs Service (T 17.6/3); and the *Official Opinions of the Attorneys General* issued in slip form (J 1.5/a) and later in bound volumes (J 1.5). However, as noted, these official sources are issued irregularly in many instances, are not timely, and lack the value-added editorial enhancements provided by commercial publishers.

The advent of computer-assisted legal research (CALR) has made the quest for administrative decisions and opinions more manageable. Both WESTLAW and LEXIS produce hundreds of general and specialized databases, adding new material—bibliographic and textual—at a sprightly rate. These specialized databases provide, to name but a handful, the opinions of the General Counsel of the Department of Veterans Affairs, labor arbitration reports, Treasury Department decisions on international trade, Federal Deposit Insurance Corporation decisions and interpretive letters, and many other quasi-judicial pronouncements.

THE RESEARCH CONNECTION

The bibliographic apparatus that unites the activities of the executive branch, the independent agencies, the Congress, and the federal courts "is a complex web—perhaps not always seamless, but often ingenious in its inter-relationships and sometimes even beautiful in its harmony."[10] The paradigm of functional unity is found in thousands of sources; one example serves to illustrate its presence in the intricate workings of the law.

A provision of the Government in the Sunshine Act of 1976 (90 Stat. 1241) directs that "every portion of every meeting" of a multimember agency must "be open to public observation," with, of course, certain exceptions closely parallel to and based upon the exceptions from disclosure in the Freedom of Information Act (5 U.S.C. 552[b]). Notice of meetings under the Sunshine Act is required to be published in a special division of the *Federal Register*. Each Tuesday's FR contains a unit entitled "Sunshine Act Meetings" located at the end of the "Notices" section. These notifications are accessed in the *Federal Register Index* under the heading "Meeting: Sunshine Act," and the contents of this special section are organized alphabetically by name of agency.

The Sunshine Act gives the courts jurisdiction to review those regulations governing open meetings published by agencies to determine whether they are consonant with the act's requirements. Private sector organizations affected by the regulations governing meetings may challenge the requirements if they are deemed inconsistent, ambiguous, or incorrect in construing the statute's mandate. If the agency's administrative tribunal, acting as a quasi-judicial body, rules against the organization's complaint, that party may seek relief in federal district court. In January 1979 the Pacific Legal Foundation, a nonprofit, tax-exempt, public interest group, challenged the regulations of the Council on Environmental Quality, an agency in the Executive Office of the President, on the grounds that a subsection of the council's open meeting regulations permitted executive sessions (closed-door deliberations) when discussing advice to be presented to the president on matters of environmental policy. The foundation's appeal to the agency was dismissed, so the organization filed suit in the District Court of the District of Columbia against the council, its members, and its general counsel, seeking declaratory and injunctive relief.

In June 1979 the district court granted the council's motion for summary judgment and dismissed the suit. However, on appeal to the Court of Appeals, District of Columbia Circuit, the lower court's decision was reversed. In reviewing the language of the disputed provision and the legislative history of the Sunshine Act, the appellate court held that the council's procedures were indeed inconsistent with the open meetings requirements under the statute. The offending regulations were set aside and the judgment of the district court was vacated.[11]

The council had promulgated its original Sunshine Act regulations at 42 FR 20818 (1977). Under the court's direction, the council proceeded to amend its rules in the prescribed manner. In the "Proposed Rules" section of the *Federal Register* of July 27, 1981 (46 FR 38390), the deficient provision contained new language, and within thirty days persons were invited to comment on the proposed changes. On February 11, 1982, a final rule was published in the "Rules and Regulations" section of the *Register* (47 FR 6276). The final action involved an amendment to Title 40 (Protection of Environment) of the *Code of Federal Regulations*, wherein Part 1517, Sections 1517.1 *et seq.*, governs "Public Meeting Procedures of the Council on Environmental Quality."

In this example the system worked, the renowned "checks and balances" concept that James Madison so eloquently articulated in *The Federalist No. 48* prevailed.[12] Yet the process was leisurely. The appellate court rendered its decision October 27, 1980. The council's proposed rule change was promulgated

July 27, 1981. The final rule amending the regulation was published February 11, 1982. The mills of government like those of God, grind slowly.

NOTES

[1]*Panama Refining Company* v. *Ryan*, 293 U.S. 388 (1935). See also E. Gellhorn, *Administrative Law and Process in a Nutshell* (St. Paul, MN: West Publishing Company, 1972), pp. 16-18.

[2]*The New York Times*, February 19, 1977, p. 12. The regulations of the Agricultural Marketing Service are published in Title 7 of the *Code of Federal Regulations*.

[3]U.S. Office of the Federal Register, *Document Drafting Handbook* (Washington, DC: GPO, 1975), p. 26.

[4]Reported by Robert Pear of *The New York Times* and published in the *Albany* [New York] *Times Union*, April 28, 1991, p. B-5.

[5]James Webb, *Something to Die For* (New York: William Morrow, 1991), p. 15.

[6]Supreme Court Justice Robert H. Jackson, *FTC* v. *Ruberoid*, 343 U.S. 470 (1952).

[7]J. Myron Jacobstein and Roy M. Mersky, *Legal Research Illustrated*, 5th ed. (Westbury, NY: Foundation Press, 1990), pp. 228-30.

[8]Christopher G. Wren and Jill Robinson Wren, *The Legal Research Manual: A Game Plan for Legal Research and Analysis*, 2d ed. (Madison, WI: A-R Editions, 1986), p. 136.

[9]Veronica Maclay, "Selected Sources of United States Agency Decisions," *Government Publications Review*, 16 (May/June 1989): 271-301.

[10]Morris L. Cohen (ed.), *How to Find the Law*, 7th ed. (St. Paul, MN: West Publishing Company, 1976), p. xvi.

[11]*Pacific Legal Foundation* v. *The Council on Environmental Policy*, 636 F.2d 1259, 1262 (1981). The complaint alleged "that since June 8, 1977 the Council had not complied with the Sunshine Act ... because it had acted in proceedings that constituted 'meetings' under the Act but had neither made the meetings public nor closed the meetings in accordance with the statutory requirements for such action."

[12]*The Federalist Papers* (New York: New American Library, 1961), pp. 308-13. Madison argued the proposition that "unless [the legislative, executive, and judiciary departments] be so far connected and blended as to give to each a constitutional control over the others, the degree of separation which the maxim requires, as essential to a free government, can never in practice be duly maintained."

8

Executive Departments
and Independent Agencies

INTRODUCTION

The president, as administrative head of the executive branch of government, must delegate to the departments and their many subordinate agencies his mandate under the Constitution to ensure that "the laws be faithfully executed." As noted in chapter 6, strong entities within the Executive Office of the President, such as the Office of Management and Budget, assist the president in accomplishing this task. In addition to this "staff" organization, the "line" organization is made up of the president's cabinet and the much maligned "bureaucracy." Although the cabinet has existed since the administration of George Washington, it is not mentioned by name in the Constitution. The various departments and agencies have been established by congressional action. By controlling the purse strings through its appropriations powers, Congress has a major impact on the size, functions, and scope of operations of executive branch departments and subordinate units. By failing to provide funds, Congress can force the president to suspend operations of, or discontinue, an agency or other executive unit.

To understand the information dissemination and publications practices of the executive branch, it is helpful if not necessary to understand its organization. A major reference source for this understanding is the annual *United States Government Manual* (AE 2.108/2). The Library Programs Service's bibliographic control of government publications through the Superintendent of Documents (SuDocs) classification system is based on the archival principle of provenance, and assignment of classification letters and numbers is based upon the current status of the issuing (publishing) agency within the federal organization. Accordingly, publications are grouped together by issuing agency in the *Monthly Catalog*, which is arranged in SuDocs class order. As a general rule, depository libraries with large federal documents collections maintain them in a separate collection shelved in SuDocs class notation.

Congress not only has created cabinet departments within the executive branch, it also has created specific agencies within those departments, independent agencies within the executive branch, and independent entities as well as independent boards and commissions that are not part of any of the three branches. Moreover, the president has under his constitutional or statutory authority created agencies within executive departments as well as independent agencies and independent temporary boards and commissions. Indeed, the heads of departments and agencies have under statutory authority created units within their purview. In this large system of hierarchical units a multitude of publications has issued forth. This chapter discusses the genesis and organization of executive departments, independent agencies, and boards and commissions both inside and outside the executive branch. Selected publications of these entities are noted within the provenances of the units under discussion. The arrangement that follows is based on the conviction that knowledge of the structure, history, organization, and hierarchical relationships among government entities markedly improves the ability of documents librarians to serve their clientele.

EXECUTIVE DEPARTMENTS

Department of Agriculture

The Department of Agriculture (USDA) was created by an act of May 15, 1862 (7 U.S.C. 2201), and was administered by a commissioner of agriculture until 1889, when, by an act of February 9, 1889 (25 Stat. 659), its powers and duties were enlarged. It then became the eighth executive department in the federal government, and the commissioner became the secretary of agriculture.

The major operating bureaus and offices are organizationally placed under the supervision of various undersecretaries and assistant secretaries as follows: undersecretary, international affairs and commodity programs (Agricultural Stabilization and Conservation Service and Foreign Agricultural Service); undersecretary, small community and rural development (Farmers Home Administration, Federal Crop Insurance Corporations, and Rural Electrification Administration); assistant secretary, economic (Economic Research Service, National Agricultural Statistics Service, and World Agricultural Outlook Board); assistant secretary, food and consumer services (Food and Nutrition Service, Human Nutrition Information Service); assistant secretary, marketing and inspection services (Agricultural Cooperative Service, Agricultural Marketing Service, Animal and Plant Health Inspection Service, Federal Grain Inspection Service, Food Safety and Inspection Service, Office of Transportation, and Packers and Stockyards Administration); assistant secretary, national resources and environment (Forest Service and Soil Conservation Service); and assistant secretary, science and education (Agricultural Research Service, Cooperative State Research Service, Extension Service, and National Agricultural Library).

Unlike most executive departments, the Department of Agriculture has several numbered departmental series in which publications prepared by the various bureaus and offices of the department are incorporated. These include Farmers' Bulletins (A 1.9); Statistical Bulletins (A 1.34); Technical Bulletins (A 1.36); Miscellaneous Publications (A 1.38); Bibliographies and Literature of Agriculture (A 1.60/3); Program Aids (A 1.68); Agriculture Information Bulletins (A 1.75); Agriculture Handbooks (A 1.76); and Home and Garden Bulletins (A 1.77). Several significant annual departmental serials are jointly prepared by several offices or services, such as *Yearbooks of Agriculture* (A 1.10) and *Agricultural Statistics* (A 1.47). The monthly *Agriculture Decisions* (A 1.58/a) makes available in an orderly and accessible form administrative decisions issued under regulatory laws administered in the Department of Agriculture. The grouping of agencies below is that used by the *United States Government Manual.*

Small Community and Rural Development

The Farmers Home Administration (A 84) provides credit to those in the rural United States who are unable to get credit from other sources at reasonable rates and terms. It was established by act of August 14, 1946 (Public Law 79-731), which abolished the Farm Security Administration, whose functions it absorbed. The Farm Security Administration (A 61) superseded the Resettlement Administration, which was established by Executive Order (EO) 7020 on April 30, 1934, as an independent agency (Y 3.R31). The administration was transferred to the Department of Agriculture by EO 7530 on December 31, 1936, effective January 1, 1937, and renamed the Farm Security Administration.

The Rural Electrification Administration (REA) (A 68) is a credit agency that assists rural electric and telephone utilities to obtain financing. It was established as an independent emergency agency (Y 3.R88) by EO 7073 on May 11, 1935; became a permanent agency by the Rural Electrification Act of 1936 (49 Stat. 1363); and was transferred to the Department of Agriculture by Reorganization Plan No. 2 of 1939, effective July 1, 1939. REA publishes three detailed annual reports on its operations: *Annual Statistical Report: Rural Electric Borrowers* (A 68.1/2), *Annual Statistical Report: Rural Telephone Borrowers* (A 68.1/3), and *Annual Report of Energy Purchased by REA Borrowers* (A 68.1/4).

The Federal Crop Insurance Corporation (FCIC) seeks to improve the economic stability of agriculture through a sound system of crop insurance. All capital stock of FCIC is owned by the United States. Management is vested in a board of directors under the supervision of the secretary of agriculture. FCIC was established by the Federal Crop Insurance Act of February 16, 1938 (52 Stat. 72). During the period 1942-1947, it was placed under other agencies, including the Agricultural Conservation and Adjustment Administration (1941) (A 76.100), Food Production Administration (1942-1943) (A 79.300), War Food Administration (1943-1945) (A 80.900), and Production and Marketing Administration (1945-1947) (A 82.200). Effective July 1, 1947, FCIC again became an independent agency within the Department of Agriculture (A 62).

Marketing and Inspection Services

The Agricultural Cooperative Service (A 109) helps farmers to help themselves through cooperative organizations. It was established by Departmental Memorandum 1320, Supplement 4, November 2, 1953, as the Farmer Cooperative Service (A 89). It was consolidated with other organizations to form the Economics, Statistics and Cooperative Service (A 105) by Secretary's Memorandum 1927, Supplement 1, of December 19, 1977, effective January 1, 1978. It was reestablished as the Agricultural Cooperative Service by Secretary's Memorandum 2025 of September 17, 1980, when its functions were transferred to the redesignated agency. Its monthly periodical, *Farmer Cooperatives* (A 109.11), reports current developments and research for cooperative management.

The Agricultural Marketing Service (AMS) (A 88) administers standardization, grading, inspection, market news, marketing orders, and research and regulatory programs of the Department of Agriculture. It was established as the Agricultural Marketing Service (A 66) by Secretary's Memorandum 830 of July 7,

1939, pursuant to Act of June 30, 1939 (53 Stat. 939). It was consolidated with the Surplus Marketing Administration (A 73) and the Commodity Exchange Administration (A 59) to form the Agricultural Marketing Administration (A 75) by EO 9069 of February 23, 1942. During the period 1942-1945, it was part of the Food Distribution Administration (A 78), the Administration of Food Production and Distribution (A 80.100), and the Office of Distribution. From 1945-1953, it was part of the Production and Marketing Administration. It was reestablished as an independent agency by Secretary's Memorandum 1320, Supplement 4, November 2, 1953, pursuant to Reorganization Plan No. 2 of 1953. The agency's name was changed to Consumer and Marketing Service by Secretary's Memorandum 1567, Supplement 1, of February 8, 1965, and changed back to Agricultural Marketing Service effective April 2, 1972. It publishes a quarterly list, *Dairy Plants Surveyed and Approved for USDA Grading Service* (A 88.14/12).

The Animal and Plant Health Inspection Service (APHIS) (A 101), in cooperation with state governments, administers federal laws and regulations pertaining to animal and plant health and quarantine, humane treatment of animals, and the control and eradication of pests and diseases. It was established by Secretary's Memorandum 1744, Supplement 1, October 29, 1971, as the Animal and Plant Health Service and given its present name in April 1972.

The Federal Grain Inspection Service (FGIS) (A 104) is responsible for establishing official U.S. standards for grain and other assigned commodities and for administering a nationwide system of official inspection and weighing. It was established November 20, 1976, to carry out the provisions of the U.S. Grain Standards Act (7 U.S.C. 71).

The Office of Transportation (A 108) was established in 1980 to formulate agricultural policy and promote an efficient transportation system that improves farm income, expands farm exports, and meets the needs of the rural United States.

The Packers and Stockyards Administration (A 96) administers provisions of the Packers and Stockyards Act of 1921, the Truth in Lending and Fair Credit Billing Act, and the Equal Credit Opportunity Act with respect to firms subject to the act. The Packers and Stockyards Act is an antitrust, trade practice, and financial protection law, whose principal purpose is to maintain effective competition and fair trade practices in the livestock, meat, and poultry industries. A Packers and Stockyards Administration (A 39) was originally established in 1921 but was abolished in July 1927. Its functions were subsequently transferred to the Bureau of Animal Industry (A 4, 1927-1953; A 77.200, 1953-1967) until 1967, when the agency was reestablished by Secretary's Memorandum 1613, Supplement 1, May 8, 1967.

Food and Consumer Services

The Food and Nutrition Service (FNS) (A 98) administers food assistance programs in cooperation with state and local governments. These include the Food Stamp Program; National School Lunch Program; School Breakfast Program; Summer Food Service Program; Food Distribution Program; Special Supplemental Food Program for Women, Infants, and Children (WIC); and the Commodity Supplemental Food Program. FNS was established August 8, 1969, by Secretary's Memorandum 1659, Supplement 1. It publishes a quarterly periodical, *Food and Nutrition* (A 98.11), as well as nutrition guides dealing with its food assistance programs.

The Human Nutrition Information Service (HNIS) (A 111), established in 1981, performs research, analysis, and technical assistance in regard to human nutrition. It also collects and disseminates information regarding nutrition and diets. HNIS maintains a Nutrient Data Bank that compiles information on the nutritive value of foods and publishes representative values in Agriculture Handbook No. 8, *Composition of Foods* (A 1.76:8). This handbook is undergoing extensive revision and is being published in parts in looseleaf format.

International Affairs and Commodity Programs

The Agricultural Stabilization and Conservation Service (ASCS) (A 82) administers commodity and related land use programs designed for voluntary production adjustment; resource protection; and price, market, and farm income stabilization. ASCS was established by Secretary's Memorandum 1458 of June 14, 1961. It continues functions previously performed by other agencies including the Agricultural Adjustment Agency, the Office of Marketing Services, the Commodity Stabilization Service, and the Production and Marketing Administration.

The Commodity Credit Corporation (CCC) (A 82.300) seeks to stabilize, support, and protect farm income and prices; to assist in maintaining balanced and adequate supplies of agriculture commodities and their products; and to facilitate the orderly distribution of commodities. The corporation is capitalized at $100 million and has statutory authority to borrow up to $25 billion from the U.S. Treasury. CCC was established as an independent agency (Y 3.C73) October 17, 1933, under the laws of Delaware pursuant to EO 6340 of October 16, 1933. It was transferred to the Department of Agriculture by Reorganization Plan No. 1 of 1939 (A 71), effective July 12, 1939. By EO 9322 of March 20, 1943, it was placed in the Food Production and Distribution Administration (A 80), later redesignated the War Food Administration (1943-1945). The Commodity Credit Corporation Charter Act of 1948 established CCC as an agency and instrumentality of the United States under a permanent federal charter.

The Foreign Agricultural Service (FAS) (A 67) seeks to stimulate overseas markets for U.S. agricultural products. FAS maintains a worldwide agricultural intelligence and reporting system through its attaché service, consisting of over 100 specialists posted at 70 U.S. embassies and consulates around the world. The service was established by act of June 5, 1930 (46 Stat. 497), with economic research and agricultural attaché activities administered by the Foreign Agricultural Service, Bureau of Agricultural Economics, until June 29, 1939. Reorganization Plan No. 2 of 1939, effective July 1, 1939, transferred attaché functions to the State Department. Economic research functions were transferred to the Office of Foreign Agricultural Relations (A 64), renamed Foreign Agricultural Service, March 10, 1953. Agricultural attachés were returned to the Department of Agriculture by act of August 28, 1954 (68 Stat. 908). FAS issues a monthly periodical, *AgExporter* (A 67.7/3), that contains information useful to business firms selling U.S. farm products overseas.

Science and Education Agencies

The Agricultural Research Service (ARS) (A 77) was established as the Agricultural Research Administration by EO 9060 of February 23, 1942, to which were transferred the Bureau of Agricultural Chemistry and Engineering (A 70), Bureau of Animal Industry (A 4), Bureau of Dairy Engineering (A 44), Bureau of Home Economics (A 42), and Bureau of Plant Industry (A 19). The agency was reorganized by Departmental Memorandum 1320, Supplement 4, November 2, 1953, and redesignated the Agricultural Research Service. Effective January 1, 1978, it was consolidated with other agencies to form the Science and Education Administration, which was abolished June 17, 1981, when ARS was reestablished as an independent agency. ARS administers fundamental and applied research in many areas and disciplines related to animal and plant protection and production; conservation and improvement of soil, water, and air; the processing, storage, and distribution of farm products; and human nutrition. ARS publishes a monthly periodical, *Agricultural Research* (A 77.12).

The Cooperative State Research Service (CSRS) (A 94) has as its primary function the administration of federal programs that authorize funds for agricultural research carried on by Agricultural Experiment Stations of the fifty states and outlying territories, by approved schools of forestry, by land grant universities, by colleges of veterinary medicine, and by other eligible institutions. CSRS was established as the Cooperative State Experiment Station Service by Secretary's Memorandum 1462, Supplement 1, August 30, 1961. It was consolidated along with other agencies to form the Science and Education Administration (A 106) by Secretary's Memorandum 1927, Supplement 1, December 19, 1977, effective January 28, 1978. The administration was abolished June 17, 1981, and the Cooperative State Research Service was reestablished. CSRS publishes an annual *Directory of Professional Workers in State Agricultural Experiment Stations and Other Cooperating State Institutions*, which is issued as Agricultural Handbook 305 (A 1.76:305).

The Extension Service (A 43) is the federal partner in the Cooperative Extension System, which consists of the land grant universities as the state partner and more than 3,150 county offices representing local governments as the third partner. All three partners share in financing, planning, and conducting education programs. The Extension Service was created by the Smith-Lever Act of 1914 (35 Stat. 372) and established within the Department of Agriculture on July 1, 1923, pursuant to the Agricultural Appropriations Act of 1924 (42 Stat. 1289). During the period 1943-1945, it was consolidated with other agencies in the Administration of Food Production and Distribution and War Food Administration (A 80.300). From 1953 to 1970, it was called the Federal Extension Service. During the period 1978-1981, it was consolidated with other agencies in the Science and Education Administration. The Extension Service published a quarterly periodical, *Extension Review* (A 43.7).

The National Agricultural Library (NAL) (A 17) is the largest agricultural library in the United States. In commemoration of its 100th anniversary on May 15, 1962, the Library of the Department of Agriculture was renamed the National Agricultural Library pursuant to Secretary's Memorandum 1496 of March 23, 1962. During the period 1978-1981, it was consolidated with other agencies in the Science and Education Administration and renamed Technical Information Systems. NAL stores bibliographic data in the AGRICOLA

(Agricultural Online Access) system, a group of databases that consist of indexes to general agriculture, food and nutrition, and agricultural economics. Its Current Awareness Literature Service (CALS) provides selective dissemination of information from twelve multidisciplinary bibliographic databases, including AGRICOLA, to USDA scientists. NAL publishes major bibliographies in the departmental series *Bibliographies and Literature of Agriculture* (A 1.60/3). It also publishes a monthly newsletter, *Agricultural Libraries Information Notes* (A 17.23). NAL's monumental *Bibliography of Agriculture*, formerly a depository item, is now published commercially by Oryx Press.

Natural Resources and Environment

The Forest Service (A 13) was created by the Transfer Act of February 1, 1905 (33 Stat. 628), which transferred the federal forest reserves and the responsibility for their management from the Department of the Interior to the Department of Agriculture. There previously existed in the department a Division of Forestry (1880-1901), superseded by a Bureau of Forestry (1901-1905). The Forest Service manages 156 national forests, 19 national grasslands, and 17 land utilization projects on 191 million acres in 44 states, the Virgin Islands, and Puerto Rico. Many of the Forest Service publications available to depository libraries are published by its ten regional offices and nine forest and range experiment stations in three Forest Service numbered series: Research Papers (A 13.78), Research Notes (A 13.79), and Resource Bulletins (A 13.80). The Forest Service annually publishes an *Organizational Directory* (A 13.36/2-2).

The Soil Conservation Service (SCS) (A 57) was established under authority of the Soil Conservation Act of 1935 (49 Stat. 163), superseding the Soil Erosion Service (I 30), which had been transferred from the Department of the Interior by Secretary's Administrative Order of March 25, 1935. During the period 1942-1945 it was consolidated with other agencies in the Agricultural Conservation and Adjustment Administration (A 76.200), Food Agricultural Conservation and Adjustment Administration (A 76.200), Food Production Administration (A 79.200), and War Food Administration (A 80.200 and A 80.500). SCS is responsible for administering a national soil and conservation program in cooperation with other federal, state, and local government agencies as well as with private landowners, operators, and users. Its principal publications are detailed *Soil Surveys* (A 57.38), which have been prepared in cooperation with state Agricultural Experiment Stations for most counties in the fifty states and outlying areas. It publishes an annual list (A 57.38:list) of all completed surveys, both current and out-of-print.

Economics Agencies

The Economic Research Service (ERS) (A 93) monitors economic activity, makes short-term forecasts of key economic indicators, and develops long-range projections of U.S. and world agricultural resources (land, water, and manufactured inputs) and demand for agricultural commodities and food products. ERS was established by Secretary's Memorandum 1446, Supplement 1, April 3, 1961. From 1978 to 1981, it was consolidated with other agencies to form the

Economics, Statistics, and Cooperatives Service (A 106), later redesignated the Economics and Statistics Service. ERS publishes several periodicals: *Agriculture Outlook* (A 93.10/2, 11 times a year); *Food Review* (A 93.16/3, quarterly); and *Journal of Agricultural Economic Research* (A 93.26, quarterly). ERS also issues a series of outlook and situation reports on agricultural crops and dairy products.

The National Agricultural Statistics Service (NASS) (A 92) prepares estimates and reports on production, supply, and prices of field crops, fruits and vegetables, cattle, hogs, sheep, poultry, and related commodities or processed products. The *Agricultural Statistics Board Catalog* (A 92.35/2) provides a detailed listing of the many estimates and reports published by NASS, including periods covered and dates on which reports are released. The National Agricultural Statistics Service was established as the Statistical Reporting Service by Secretary's Memorandum 1446, Supplement 1, April 3, 1961. From 1978 to 1981 it was consolidated with the Economic Research Service and the Cooperative State Research Service to form the Economics, Statistics, and Cooperatives Service, later redesignated the Economics and Statistics Service. In 1986 it was renamed the National Agricultural Statistics Service, and its Crop Reporting Board was renamed the Agricultural Statistics Board.

Department of Commerce

The Department of Commerce was established as the Department of Commerce and Labor by act of February 14, 1903 (32 Stat. 826), deriving most of its functions from the Department of the Treasury. It was redesignated the Department of Commerce when its Bureau of Labor (C 8) and Bureau of Immigration and Naturalization (C 7) were transferred to the newly created Department of Labor by act of June 29, 1913 (37 Stat. 737). The department is characterized as a conglomerate, a "crazy quilt" of government agencies. A former assistant secretary called the department "a backwater of the federal bureaucracy. It has been a place where you put things when you didn't know what else to do with them."[1] From its initial days in 1903, the department "has been a launching pad for important tasks — only to have those which became glamorous taken away."[2] A number of agencies have been transferred to and from the department. In 1915, the Bureau of Corporations (C 5) was merged with the Federal Trade Commission. In 1925, the Patent Office and Bureau of Mines were transferred to the Department of the Interior. In 1932, Commerce's Radio Division was transferred to the Federal Radio Commission (which became the Federal Communications Commission). In 1939, the Bureau of Lighthouses (C 9) was transferred to the Department of the Treasury, and the Bureau of Fisheries (C 6), to the Interior Department. In 1940, the Weather Bureau was added from the Department of Agriculture. In 1958, the Civil Aeronautics Administration was transferred to the Federal Aviation Agency. In 1966, the Community Relations Service (C 50) was transferred to the Department of Justice, and the new Department of Transportation acquired the Bureau of Public Roads (C 37). In 1979, the United States Fire Administration (C 58) was transferred to the Federal Emergency Management Agency. In 1981, the Maritime Administration (C 29.200) was transferred to the Department of Transportation.

The administrations of Jimmy Carter and Ronald Reagan considered proposals to abolish or reorganize the department. The Carter administration considered proposals to split up most of the department's functions between a new Department of Economic Development and an expanded Department of the Interior (renamed Department of Natural Resources). The Reagan administration considered proposals to retain the department's economic and trade functions in a Department of Trade and transfer its other functions to a new Department of Science and Technology. A 1988 official history groups the department's agencies under the following categories: trade (International Trade Administration, Bureau of Export Administration, and U.S. Travel and Tourism Administration); economics (Bureau of Economic Analysis, Bureau of the Census, and National Technical Information Service); science (National Oceanic and Atmospheric Administration, National Bureau of Standards, National Telecommunications and Information Administration, and Patent and Trademark Office); and development (Economic Development Administration and Minority Business Development Agency).[3] The department publishes a monthly *Commerce Publications Update* (C 1.24/3) and the *Commerce Business Daily* (C 1.76). The former consists of a listing of all publications and press releases issued by the Commerce Department. The latter is the vehicle by which government agencies notify the public of proposed U.S. government procurements, contract awards, sources sought, surplus property sales, and related notices.

Trade Agencies

The International Trade Administration (ITA) (C 61) was established in 1980 to succeed the Industry and Trade Administration (C 57) (1977-1980), formerly the Domestic and International Business Administration (1972-1977). In 1984, ITA absorbed the functions of the Bureau of Industrial Economics (C 62), which was abolished. However, ITA has absorbed the functions of a number of other predecessor Commerce Department agencies, the most important of which were the Bureau of Foreign and Domestic Commerce (C 18) (1912-1953), Business and Defense Services Administration (C 41) (1953-1970), and Bureau of Foreign Commerce (C 42) (1953-1961).[4] ITA publishes a monthly periodical, *Commercial News USA* (C 61.10), and a companion volume, *Commercial News USA: New Products Annual Directory* (C 61.10/2). Within its Overseas Business Reports series (C 61.12) is included the subseries *Marketing in ...*, which provides useful information about various countries. Among its significant reference works are the annual *Franchise Opportunities Handbook* (C 61.31) and *U.S. Industrial Outlook* (C 61.34).

The U.S. Travel and Tourism Administration (USTTA) (C 47) was created by the National Tourism Policy Act of 1981 (96 Stat. 1014) to replace the U.S. Travel Service, which had been established by the International Travel Act of 1961 (75 Stat. 129). Its mission is to expand export earnings and job opportunities by promoting in foreign countries business and pleasure travel to the United States.

Economics Agencies

The Bureau of Economic Analysis (BEA) (C 59) attempts to provide a clear picture of the U.S. economy through preparation, development, and interpretation of the national income and product accounts, summarized by the gross national product; the wealth accounts; the income-output accounts; personal income and related economic series by geographic area; and the U.S. balance of payments accounts and associated foreign investment accounts. BEA was established as the Office of Business Economics (C 43) by a Departmental Order of December 1, 1953. It was transferred to the Economic Statistics Administration (ESA), effective January 1, 1972, and renamed Office of Economic Analysis (C 56.100). When ESA was abolished by Department Organization Orders 35-1A and 2A, effective August 4, 1975, it was reestablished as an independent agency and renamed the Bureau of Economic Analysis. The bureau publishes the monthly *Survey of Current Business* (C 59.11), which is supplemented biennially by *Business Statistics* (C 59.11/3). The useful *Business Conditions Digest* (C 59.9) was discontinued in March 1990, and its information on business cycle indicators was transferred as a separate section to the *Survey of Current Business*.

The Bureau of the Census was established as a permanent office within the Department of the Interior by act of March 6, 1902 (32 Stat. 51), and was transferred to the newly established Department of Commerce and Labor on July 1, 1903. Previously, a temporary office had been established every ten years to conduct the decennial census required by the Constitution. During the period 1972-1975, it was part of the Economics Statistics Administration (C 56.200). The bureau publishes a *Monthly Product Announcement* (C 3.163/7) and an annual *Census Catalog and Guide* (C 3.163/3) that provides annotations and detailed bibliographic information about the bureau's publications, products, and services. The bureau has become the federal government's general purpose statistical agency, and its publications are discussed in greater detail in chapter 10.

The National Technical Information Service (NTIS) (C 51) was established in 1970, but it has its origins in offices created in 1945 to handle the release of thousands of technical reports (both captured German documents and other classified materials) to U.S. industry following World War II. In 1945, the Publications Board (PB) was created by EO 9568. Also in 1945, the secretary of commerce established an Office of Declassification and Technical Services, which was redesignated the Office of Technical Services the following year and absorbed the functions of the Publications Board and the Director of War Mobilization. The Office of Technical Services was superseded in 1965 by the Clearinghouse for Federal Scientific and Technical Information, which in turn was superseded by NTIS. NTIS is the central source for the public sale of U.S. government sponsored research, development, and engineering reports, as well as foreign technical reports and other analyses prepared by national and local government agencies, their contractors, or their grantees. It is the central source for federally generated machine-readable data files and manages the Federal Software Center for intragovernmental distribution. NTIS products and services are discussed in greater detail in chapter 11.

Science Agencies

The National Oceanic and Atmospheric Administration (NOAA) (C 55) was established on October 3, 1970, by Reorganization Plan No. 4 of 1970, succeeding the Environmental Science Services Administration (ESSA) (1965-1970) (C 52). NOAA includes the National Ocean Service, National Weather Service, National Marine Fisheries Service, and several other entities.

The National Ocean Service (NOS) (C 55.400) was formerly the Coast and Geodetic Survey (C&GS) within ESSA. The Coast and Geodetic Survey traces its origins to the Survey of the Coast (T 11), which was established in the Treasury Department in 1811. In 1836, the name was changed to Coast Survey, and again to Coast and Geodetic Survey by act of June 20, 1878 (20 Stat. 206). On July 1, 1903, C&GS was transferred to the newly established Department of Commerce and Labor (C 4). On July 13, 1965, it became part of ESSA by Reorganization Plan No. 2, then it was transferred to NOAA in 1970 and the name was changed to National Ocean Survey. The change to the present name was made in 1984. NOS's mission is to explore, map, and chart the global ocean and its living resources; to describe, monitor, and predict conditions in the atmosphere, ocean, sun, and space environment; to manage and disseminate long-term environmental information; and to prepare aeronautical charts. It prepares annual *Tide Tables* for the coasts of all continents (C 55.421) and *United States Coast Pilots* for U.S. coastal waters. Its map and chart products are discussed in chapter 12.

The National Weather Service (C 55.100) traces its origins to the Weather Bureau (A 29), which was established within the Department of Agriculture by act of October 1, 1890 (26 Stat. 653). The Weather Bureau was transferred to the Department of Commerce by Reorganization Plan No. 4, effective June 30, 1940 (C 30). It was later transferred to ESSA by Reorganization Plan No. 2 of 1965, effective July 13, 1965, and in 1970 it was transferred to NOAA by Department Organization Order 25-5A, effective October 9, 1970, and renamed National Weather Service. The original government weather service had been established in the War Department in 1870, and the first daily weather maps appeared in January 1871 with weather predictions beginning the following month.[5] The National Weather Service reports the weather of the United States and possessions and provides weather forecasts to the general public; issues warnings against destructive natural events; and provides services in support of weather-sensitive activities such as aviation, marine activities, agriculture and forestry, and urban air-quality control. The National Weather Service issues a *Weekly Climate Bulletin* (C 55.129/2), and the National Meteorological Center issues a weekly series of *Daily Weather Maps* (C 55.195).

The National Marine Fisheries Services (C 55.300) by that name came into being with the establishment of NOAA in 1970, but it traces its origins to the Fish Commission (FC) established by Congressional Joint Resolution of February 9, 1871. When the commission was transferred to the Department of Commerce and Labor upon its establishment in 1903, it was renamed the Bureau of Fisheries (C 6). The bureau was transferred to the Department of the Interior by Reorganization Plan No. 2 of 1939, effective July 1, 1939 (I 45). In 1956, the Bureau of Fisheries was combined with the Bureau of Biological Survey (I 47) to form the Fish and Wildlife Service (I 49). In 1970, that part of the Fish and Wildlife Service known as the Bureau of Commercial Fisheries was transferred to NOAA and renamed the National Marine Fisheries Service. In addition to promoting commercial fisheries of the United States, the responsibilities of the service also include protection of marine mammals and endangered marine species. The service publishes an annual statistical compilation, *Fisheries of the United States* (C 55.309/2-2), in the Current Fisheries Statistics (CFS) series.

The National Institute of Standards and Technology (C 13) traces its origins to the establishment of the National Bureau of Standards by act of March 3, 1901. Its present name was conferred under the National Science Foundation Authorization Act of 1988 (102 Stat. 2865). The responsibilities of the institute consist of aiding U.S. companies in adopting new technologies and scientific advances to enhance their international competitiveness. Among the many publications of the institute is the important bimonthly *Journal of Research of the National Institute of Standards and Technology* (C 13.22).

The National Telecommunications and Information Administration (NTIA) (C 60) was established by EO 12046 of March 27, 1978, which merged the Office of Telecommunications in the Department of Commerce and the Office of Telecommunications Policy in the Executive Office of the President. NTIA is responsible for developing policy on the advancement and use of new technologies in common carrier, telephone, and broadcast and satellite communications systems.

The Patent and Trademark Office (PTO) (C 21) traces its origins to the Patent Office, which was established within the Department of State in 1802. The first patent had been issued in 1790 by an ad hoc Patent Board. An act of February 21, 1793 (1 Stat. 318), created a patent registration system in the State Department. Upon the creation of the Department of the Interior in 1849, the Patent Office was transferred to that department (I 23), where it remained until 1925, when it was transferred to the Department of Commerce by EO 4175 of March 17, 1925. The name was changed to Patent and Trademark Office by act of January 2, 1975 (88 Stat. 1949). PTO registers three types of patentable subjects, beginning in the year indicated: inventions (1790), designs (1842), and plants (1930). The Patent Office began registering trademarks in 1870.[6] The publications of the Patent and Trademark Office are discussed in chapter 11.

Development Agencies

The Economic Development Administration (EDA) (C 46) was established under the Public Works and Economic Development Act of 1965 (70 Stat. 552). It seeks to generate and preserve private sector jobs through the use of public works funds, business loans, loan guarantees, technical assistance, long-range economic planning, and economic research. It had been a prime candidate for abolishment during the Reagan administration.

The Minority Business Development Agency (MBDA) was established by the secretary of commerce on November 1, 1979. It continues the Office of Minority Business Enterprise, which operated under authority of EO 11458 of March 5, 1969, and EO 11625 of October 13, 1971. MBDA promotes and coordinates the efforts of other federal agencies in assisting or providing market opportunities for minority business, primarily through its affiliate network of Minority Business Development Centers. It publishes the monthly periodical *Access* (C 1.57/4).

Electronic Products and Services

One hundred depository libraries were selected to participate in the Commerce Department's Economic Bulletin Board (EBB), a pilot project that provided free online access to current economic and statistical information generated by a variety of federal agencies. The project ended December 31, 1990, whereupon the participating libraries were asked to submit staffing and cost data for the project in a survey instrument mailed to them by the Library Programs Service (LPS). All libraries can access the EBB by registering with the department and paying the standard subscription fee and connect charges.[7]

In addition, the National Trade Data Bank (NTDB) on CD-ROM is a compilation of trade promotion and international economic data from fourteen federal agencies, including spot exchange rates, agricultural commodities futures, and balance of payments information.

Department of Defense

The Department of Defense (DoD) is the successor agency to the National Military Establishment, created as an executive department by the National Security Act of 1947 (61 Stat. 495). It was established by the National Security Act Amendments of 1949 (63 Stat. 578) with the secretary of defense as its head. The Department of Defense is composed of the Office of the Secretary of Defense (OSD); the Organization of the Joint Chiefs of Staff (OJCS); the Defense agencies and joint service schools; DoD field activities; the military departments and the military services within those departments (air force, army, navy); and other such offices, agencies, activities, and commands as may be designated by law or executive authority.

The principles of the SuDocs classification scheme have been ignored or violated more often for Department of Defense agencies and publications than for any other executive department. This is understandable due to the complexity, frequent organization changes, and levels represented in the DoD hierarchy. For example, three defense agencies have been assigned D 5 numbers, which incorrectly indicate that they are under the supervision of the Joint Chiefs of Staff. The Defense Technical Information Center (D 10) is assigned a SuDocs author symbol on the same level as the agency to which it is subordinate, the Defense Logistics Agency (D 7). Within the Department of the Air Force, a number of subordinate commands and field activities have been given D 301 numbers, which is the same level as the department itself.

Office of the Secretary of Defense

The Office of the Secretary of Defense includes the offices of civilian undersecretaries and assistant secretaries of defense. Among these are the undersecretary for acquisition, who exercises authority over the Defense Advanced Research Project, Defense Communications Agency, Defense Logistics Agency, Defense Mapping Agency, Defense Nuclear Agency, and Defense Systems Management College; the assistant secretary for command, control, communications, and intelligence, who has primary staff responsibility over the Defense Intelligence

Agency and the National Security Agency/Central Security Service; the assistant secretary (comptroller), who exercises authority over the Defense Contract Audit Agency and the Washington Headquarters Services; the assistant secretary for health affairs, who exercises authority over the Office of the Civilian Health and Medical Program of the Uniformed Services (OCHAmPUS) and is director of the Defense Medical Facilities Office; the assistant secretary for force management and personnel, who exercises authority over the Armed Forces Chaplains Board, Office of Economic Adjustment, DoD Explosive Safety Board, Equal Opportunity Management Institute, Defense Advisory Committee on Women in the Services, Defense Manpower Data Center, and the Training Data and Analysis Center; assistant secretary for public affairs, who exercises authority over the Defense Information Services Activity and American Forces Information Service; and the general counsel, who serves as director of the Defense Legal Services Agency. DoD departmental directives are often published by one of these OSD offices. Probably the best known OSD publication was *Soviet Military Power* (D 1.74), which was discontinued after the dissolution of the former Union of Soviet Socialist Republics.

DoD Field Activities

Under this category are included the American Forces Information Service (D 2), Defense Information Services Activity, Department of Defense Dependent Schools, Office of Civilian Health and Medical Program of the Uniformed Services, Defense Medical Support Activity, Defense Technology Security Administration, Office of Economic Adjustment, and Washington Headquarters Services. Publications of these agencies are distributed under the D 1 SuDocs classification except for the American Forces Information Service, which publishes DoD pamphlets including pocket guides to various countries (D 2.14) and a bimonthly periodical, *Defense* (D 2.15/3). Washington Headquarters Services prepares a number of statistical reports dealing with defense contracts (D 1.57).

Department of Defense Agencies and Joint Service Schools

The Department of Defense agencies include the Armed Services Board of Contract Appeals, Defense Advanced Research Projects Agency, Defense Communications Agency, Defense Contract Audit Agency, Defense Intelligence Agency (D 5.200), Defense Investigative Service, Defense Legal Services Agency, Defense Logistics Agency (D 7), Defense Mapping Agency (D 5.300), Defense Nuclear Agency (D 15), Defense Security Assistance Agency, National Security Agency/Central Security Service, and the Strategic Defense Initiative ("Star Wars") Organization.

The Joint Service Schools include the Defense Intelligence College, Defense Institute of Security Assistance Management, Defense Systems Management College, National Defense University (D 5.400), and the Uniformed Services University of the Health Sciences. Most of the depository publications of these agencies come from the Defense Logistics Agency, Defense Mapping Agency, and the National Defense University. The Defense Investigative Service prepares the

Industrial Security Manual for Safeguarding Classified Information (D 1.6/2:Se2/4). A number of student guides and manuals prepared by the Defense Systems Management College have been classified in the D 1 series.

The Defense Logistics Agency (DLA) (D 7), which continues the Defense Supply Agency, was given its present name by DoD Directive 5105.22 of January 22, 1977. Its mission is to provide support to the military services, other DoD components, federal civil agencies, foreign governments, and other authorized agencies for assigned material commodities and items of supply, logistics services directly associated with the supply management function, contract administration services, and other support services. The DLA primary field activities include six supply centers, six service centers, four depots, and nine defense contract administration services regions (DCASRs). The service centers include the Defense Technical Information Center (D 10) and the Defense Reutilization and Marketing Service (formerly Defense Property Disposal Service, renamed by DLA General Order 10-85, effective July 1, 1985). Most DLA publications distributed to depository libraries are issued by the DLA headquarters offices, with some prepared or issued by the supply centers or service centers.

The Defense Mapping Agency (DMA) (D 5.300) was established as an entity within DoD on January 1, 1972, under the provisions of the National Security Act of 1947, as amended (50 U.S.C. 401). Its mapping, charting, and geodesy functions are largely conducted by its two major production centers: the Aerospace Center (DMAAC) in St. Louis, Missouri, and the Hydrographic/Topographic Center (DMAHTC) in Brookmont, Maryland. The mapping and charting activities of this agency are discussed in chapter 12.

The National Defense University (NDU) (D 5.400) was established January 16, 1976, by merging the Industrial College of the Armed Forces and the National War College, both located at Fort Leslie J. McNair, Washington, D.C. The Armed Forces Staff College, located at Norfolk, Virginia, was added in 1981. Other agencies subsequently incorporated into NDU include Strategic Concepts Development Center, Mobilization Concepts Development Center, War Gaming and Simulation Center, Institute for Higher Defense Study, and the Department of Defense Computer Institute. Several NDU series of research studies on defense and security policy are distributed to depository libraries, including National Security Affairs Monographs (D 5.409), National Affairs Issue Papers (D 5.409/2), and National Security Essays (D 5.413).

Joint Chiefs of Staff

The Organization of the Joint Chiefs of Staff was established by act of August 10, 1949 (Public Law 81-216) to advise the president, the National Security Council, and the secretary of defense on military and security matters. The Joint Chiefs of Staff (JCS) consists of the JCS chairman, the chief of staff, U.S. Army; the chief of Naval Operations; the chief of staff, U.S. Air Force; and the commandant of the Marine Corps. The JCS staff includes military members from all the armed services as well as civilian employees and is limited to 1,627 military and civilian personnel. The JCS publishes *United States Military Posture* (D 5.19) for the annual Department of Defense appropriations and authorization hearings. It also publishes *Department of Defense Dictionary of Military and Associated Terms* (D 5.12:1).

Department of the Army

The Department of the Army was established as the War Department by act of August 7, 1789. It was merged with the Navy Department and the newly established Department of the Air Force to create the National Military Establishment by the National Security Act of 1947 (61 Stat. 495) and was redesignated Department of the Army. The National Security Act Amendments of 1949 established the Department of Defense as an executive department and provided that the Departments of the Army, Navy, and Air Force be military departments within DoD.

The Department of the Army is headed by the secretary of the army. Headquarters consists of a small civilian staff composed of undersecretaries, assistant secretaries, and other officials, who are primarily responsible for policy direction, and a much larger military staff headed by the chief of staff. The major army field commands include the U.S. Army Forces Command (consisting of the six continental U.S. Armies); U.S. Army Training and Doctrine Command (which includes the army military school and training installations); U.S. Army Materiel Command (which is responsible for research, development, production, procurement, and supply of military equipment and supplies); U.S. Army Information Systems Command; U.S. Army Intelligence and Security Command; U.S. Army Health Services Command; U.S. Army Criminal Investigation Command; Military Traffic Management Command (a joint defense agency responsible for land transportation, common-user ocean terminal service, and movement and storage of household goods); U.S. Army Military District of Columbia; U.S. Army Corps of Engineers; and the army components of the unified and specified combatant commands (for Europe, Japan, and Korea, and the Eastern, Western, and Southern Commands).

The Department of the Army issues a number of publications in departmental series as Army Regulations (D 101.9), Department of the Army Pamphlets (D 101.22), and technical manuals (D 101.11). These publications are prepared by headquarter staff offices, military schools, and field agencies of the U.S. Army Materiel Command (particularly technical manuals), but they are issued as departmental publications by Department of the Army headquarters. The Country Studies series, formerly called the [Army] Area Handbooks, is issued within the Department of the Army Pamphlet 550 series.

The Army Corps of Engineers (D 103) was established by an act of March 16, 1802. It is responsible for the civil works program of the army, including water resources development, flood control, and protection of the inland navigable waters. Its Water Resources Support Center publishes the Port Series (D 103.8), which provides detailed information about U.S. coastal, Great Lakes, and inland ports. Moreover, the Support Center issues on a state-by-state basis the important Water Resources Development series by the Corps of Engineers on an annual, biennial, quadrennial, or irregular schedule (D 103.35), including United States Summary (D 103.35/52) and Outlying Areas (D 103.35/53) as separate depository items.

The Army Center of Military History (D 114) continues the Historical Division (M 103) established in 1947. In 1950, the division was redesignated the Office of the Chief of Military History (D 114), and it got its present name in 1974. The center has published a number of detailed operational histories such as the *U.S. Army in World War II* (D 114.7). It is currently in the process of issuing the

United States Army in Vietnam series (D 114.7/3), and the center also publishes an Army Lineage series (D 114.11) as well as separate monographs and special studies. On an irregular schedule it issues an annotated catalog, *Publications of the U.S. Army Center of Military History* (D 114.10).

Department of the Navy

The Department of the Navy was established by act of April 30, 1798, as an executive department. From 1789 to 1798, the conduct of naval affairs was under the War Department. The Department of the Navy was merged with the War Department and Department of the Air Force to form the National Military Establishment in 1947. National Security Act Amendments of 1949 established the Department of Defense as an executive department and provided that the Department of the Navy be a military department within DoD. The department is organized into three main elements: headquarters, Navy Department; the Shore Establishment; and the operating forces. Headquarters, Navy Department, includes the secretary of the navy and his or her civilian staff, including assistant secretaries and other civilian officials, and the office of the chief of Naval Operations and his or her military staff. The Shore Establishment includes the following major commands (formerly called bureaus): Naval Sea Systems Command, Naval Air Systems Command, Space and Naval Warfare Systems Command, Naval Supply Systems Command, Naval Facilities Engineering Command, Strategic Systems Program Office, Naval Military Personnel Command, Naval Medical Command, Naval Oceanographic Command, Naval Space Command, Naval Legal Service Command, Naval Telecommunications Command, Naval Security Group Command, Naval Intelligence Command, Naval Security and Investigative Command, Naval Education and Training Command, and Naval Data Automation Command. The operating forces of the navy include the Pacific Fleet; Atlantic Fleet; Naval Forces, Europe; Military Sealift Command (a joint defense command); Fleet Marine Forces; and other seagoing forces and elements. The Marine Corps is also a part of the Department of the Navy.

Unlike the army (and air force), the Navy Department does not have departmental series for its directives (called "instructions") and manuals that have applicability throughout the department. Although the preparation of publications is decentralized, as it is in the army, the publication (and printing) is also decentralized, rather than centralized as in the army. Most directives and manuals are prepared and published by the various commands of the Shore Establishment (and in some cases by the headquarter military staff offices). Thus, many such publications are not published through GPO and, as "non-GPO" publications, are not distributed to depository libraries. Decentralized publications are not distributed to depository libraries. Decentralized publications also present problems for comprehensive departmental bibliographies and catalogs. The Navy Department publishes a general interest monthly periodical, *All Hands* (D 207.17).

The Naval Air Systems Command (D 202) was established in 1966. It continues the Bureau of Aeronautics, which was established by act of July 12, 1921 (42 Stat. 140), was abolished by act of August 18, 1959 (73 Stat. 395), and finally had its functions transferred to the Bureau of Naval Weapons (abolished in 1966). The command provides material support to the navy and Marine Corps for aircraft, airborne weapons systems, avionics, related photographic and support equipment, ranges, and targets. It publishes three periodicals: *Naval Aviation News* (D 202.9), *Approach* (D 202.13), and *Mech* (D 202.19).

The Naval Medical Command (D 206) continues the Bureau of Medicine and Surgery, which was established by act of August 13, 1842 (5 Stat. 579). It provides comprehensive medical and dental services for navy and Marine Corps personnel.

The Naval Historical Center is compiling the multivolume set *Naval Documents of the American Revolution* (D 207.12), the three-volume set *The Naval War of 1812: A Documentary History* (D 207.10/2:H62), and the United States Navy and the Vietnam Conflict series (D 207.10/3).

The Naval Education and Training Command (D 207.200) provides assigned shore-based education and training for navy and certain Marine Corps personnel. It publishes rate training manuals (D 207.208/2) and nonresident career courses, which are used by naval enlisted personnel to fulfill requirements for promotion. Most of these manuals are distributed to depository libraries.

The Naval Military Personnel Command (D 208) continues the Bureau of Naval Personnel and the earlier Bureau of Navigation, which was established by act of July 5, 1862 (12 Stat. 51). It publishes the *Manual of Navy Enlisted Manpower and Personnel Classifications and Occupational Standards* (D 208.6/3-4) and the *Register of Commissioned and Warrant Officers of the U.S. Navy and Reserve Officers on the Active Duty List (Navy Register)* (D 208.12).

The Naval Facilities Engineering Command (D 209) was established in 1966. It continues the Bureau of Yards and Docks, which was established by act of August 13, 1842 (5 Stat. 579). The command provides for material and technical support to the navy and Marine Corps for shore facilities; real property and utilities; fixed ocean systems and structures; transportation and construction equipment; energy, environmental, and natural resources management; and support of the Naval Construction Forces. It publishes a series of *Design Manuals* (D 209.13/2) for construction and maintenance of buildings and facilities.

The Naval Sea Systems Command (D 211), established in 1966, continues the Bureau of Ships (N 29), which was established in 1940 by a consolidation of the Bureau of Construction and Repair (1862-1940) and the Bureau of Engineering (1920-1940). The Naval Supply Systems Command (D 212), established in 1966, continues the Bureau of Supplies and Accounts (1892-1966) and the Bureau of Provisions and Clothing (1842-1892).

The Naval Observatory (D 213) is the provenance of the well-known annual reference source *Astronomical Almanac* (D 213.8:). Formerly titled *American Ephemeris and Nautical Almanac*, this is the standard compilation of ephemerides and other astronomical data. Interestingly, in public libraries *Astronomical Almanac*'s main clientele consists of astrology aficionados.

The United States Marine Corps (USMC) was initially established on November 10, 1775. The National Security Act Amendments of 1978 reaffirmed the Marine Corps as a separate service within the Department of the Navy and placed the commandant of the Marine Corps on the Joint Chiefs of Staff as a full member. The Marine Corps consists of the headquarters, Supporting Establishment, and operating forces. The Supporting Establishment recruits and trains Marines, provides supply and equipment support to the operating forces, and maintains permanent bases and installations. The principal elements of the operating forces are Fleet Marine Force, Pacific (FMFPAC), and Fleet Marine

Force, Atlantic. Most Marine Corps publications distributed to depository libraries are issued by USMC headquarters. The corps operates an active historical program through its History and Museums Division. It prepared a number of monographs on Marine Corps operations in World War II and is issuing a multivolume U.S. Marines in Vietnam series (D 214.13:V67). The Marine Corps publishes the monthly general interest periodical *Marines* (D 214.24).

Department of the Air Force

The Department of the Air Force was established as a separate military department and service by the National Security Act of 1947. The U.S. Air Force continues the Army Air Forces and Army Air Corps and predecessor activities in the Army Signal Corps. The department consists of the Office of the Secretary of the Air Force, the Air Staff, and the field organization. The Office of the Secretary of the Air Force is essentially the civilian staff responsible for policy direction, consisting of the assistant secretaries and supporting offices. The Air Staff is headed by the chief of staff and represents the military staff at headquarters, U.S. Air Force.

The field organization consists of the major commands, separate operating agencies, and direct reporting units. The major commands include both support and operating commands as follows: Air Force Logistics Command (AFLC); Air Force Systems Command (AFSC); Air Training Command (ATC); Air University (AU); Military Airlift Command (MAC); a JCS-specified command responsible for providing transportation for all military services worldwide; Strategic Air Command (SAC); a JCS-specified command responsible for conducting strategic air combat operations; Electronic Security Command; U.S. Air Forces in Europe; Pacific Air Forces; Alaskan Air Command; and Air Force Space Command.

The separate operating agencies include the Air Force Accounting and Finance Center, Air Force Audit Agency, Air Force Inspection and Safety Center, Air Force Office of Special Investigations, Air Force Military Personnel Center, Air Force Intelligence Service, Air Force Commissary Service, Air Force Legal Service Center, Air Force Service Information and News Center, Air Force Office of Medical Support, and Air Force Office of Security Police. Among the direct report units are the USAF Historical Research Center and the U.S. Air Force Academy.

Despite this large number of air force agencies and activities, the Superintendent of Documents has established only four additional author symbols in the D 300 series: Judge Advocate General of the Air Force (D 302), Administrative Services (D 303), Air Force Medical Service (D 304), and Air Force Academy (D 305). Most air force publications distributed to depository libraries are prepared or published by the headquarters, Air Force Systems Command, Air Training Command, Air University, and Office of Air Force History. The air force has adopted the army system of departmental publications series and has centralized publication (and decentralized preparation) of Air Force Regulations (AFRs) (D 302.6), Air Force Manuals (AFMs) (D 301.7), Air Force Pamphlets (AFPs) (D 301.35), and technical orders (TOs). These are comparable to Army Regulations (ARs), Department of the Army Pamphlets (PAMs), field manuals (FMs), and technical manuals (TMs), respectively. However, only a few AFRs,

AFMs, and AFPs are printed through GPO and distributed to depository libraries. Technical orders are not distributed to depositories and a SuDocs class has not been assigned to them. Among the few AFRs distributed to depository libraries are the several indexes and catalogs of the "0" series: for example, *Numerical Index of Specialty Training Standards*, issued quarterly (D 301.6:0-8). The air force publishes the general interest monthly periodical *Airman* (D 301.60).

Indeed, the large number of dated periodicals and subscription services (those publications issued irregularly in looseleaf formats), such as *Department of Defense Index of Specifications and Standards* (D 1.76:year), issued by components of the Department of Defense and sold by the Superintendent of Documents may surprise the reader unfamiliar with DoD's publishing empire. The winter 1992 edition of *Price List 36* announced over seventy, including the obvious (*Recruiter Journal*, a monthly) and perhaps not so obvious (*Fortitudine*, a quarterly intended to educate and train Marines on active duty in the uses of military and Marine Corps history).[8]

Department of Education

The Department of Education (ED) was created as an executive department by the Department of Education Organization Act, approved October 17, 1979 (93 Stat. 668). It traces its origins to the Bureau of Education, which was created as an independent agency by act of March 2, 1867 (14 Stat. 434), and transferred to the Department of the Interior on July 1, 1869 (I 16), by an act of July 20, 1868 (15 Stat. 106). In 1929, it was renamed the Office of Education and transferred to the Federal Security Agency (FS 5) by Reorganization Plan No. 1 of 1939, effective July 1, 1939. On April 11, 1953, the Office of Education became part of the newly created Department of Health, Education, and Welfare, which replaced the Federal Security Agency (HE 5).[9] The Education Amendments of 1972 (86 Stat. 327) created within the Department of Health, Education, and Welfare an Education Division (HE 19), under which was placed an Office of Education (HE 19.100),[10] National Institute of Education (HE 19.200),[11] and National Center for Education Statistics (HE 19.200).[12] The Education Division was transferred to the Department of Education in 1979.

During the Reagan administration, the Department of Education underwent various internal reorganizations under two secretaries of education. However, GPO failed to establish new SuDocs author symbols for subordinate agencies that were created or reorganized. Most publications issued by these subordinate agencies were given ED 1 class numbers. The Office of Educational Research and Improvement (OERI) absorbed the functions of the National Institute of Education (ED 1.300) and the National Center for Education Statistics (ED 1.100). The latter was first renamed Center for Statistics and, in 1987, Center for Education Statistics within the OERI. The Elementary and Secondary School Improvements Amendments of 1988 (Public Law 100-297) revitalized and restored its name and established the National Center for Education Statistics as a semi-independent agency within the department. The National Institute of Education was transferred to OERI by act of October 17, 1979 (93 Stat. 678). The Office of Special Education and Rehabilitative Services absorbed the functions of the Rehabilitation Services Administration (HE 1.200), which had been transferred from the Department of Health, Education, and Welfare by the Department of Education

Organization Act of 1979 (HE 23.4100). Publications of the Office of Financial Assistance are assigned ED 1 SuDocs class numbers.

The Department of Education sponsors the Educational Resources Information Center (ERIC), which publishes *Resources in Education* (ED 1.310). This source is described in more detail in chapter 11. The National Center for Education Statistics publishes annually *The Condition of Education* (ED 1.109), *Education Directory: Colleges and Universities* (ED 1.111), and *Projections of Education Statistics* (ED 1.120).

Department of Energy

The Department of Energy (DOE) was established by the Department of Energy Organization Act of August 4, 1977 (91 Stat. 569), effective October 1, 1977, pursuant to EO 12009 of September 13, 1977. The act consolidated major federal energy functions in one executive department by transferring to DOE all responsibilities of the Energy Research and Development Administration (ER 1); the Federal Energy Administration (FE 1); the Federal Power Commission (FO 1); and the Alaska, Bonneville, Southeastern, and Southwestern Power Administrations, formerly components of the Department of the Interior, as well as the power-marketing functions of the Bureau of Reclamation. Also transferred to DOE were certain functions of the Interstate Commerce Commission and the Departments of Housing and Urban Development, the Navy, and the Interior.

The Department of Energy was primarily the direct successor to the Energy Research and Development Administration (ERDA) and the Federal Energy Administration (FEA). ERDA was established by the Energy Reorganization Act, approved October 11, 1974 (88 Stat. 1234), which abolished the Atomic Energy Commission (AEC) (Y 3.At7) and transferred AEC research and development and production functions to ERDA and its regulatory functions to the Nuclear Regulatory Commission (NRC) (Y 3.N88). AEC had been established by the Atomic Energy Act of 1946 (60 Stat. 755). The Federal Energy Administration had been established by the Federal Energy Administration Act of 1974 (88 Stat. 96), effective June 28, 1974, in response to the energy crisis of the early 1970s caused by the embargo of petroleum by the Organization of Petroleum Exporting Countries (OPEC) in 1973. FEA replaced the Federal Energy Office (PrEx 21), which had been established by EO 11748 of December 4, 1973.

The principal subordinate agencies of DOE located in the Washington, D.C., area are the Economic Regulatory Administration (E 4), Energy Information Administration (E 3), Office of Civilian Radioactive Waste Management, and Office of Energy Research. The Federal Energy Regulatory Commission (FERC) (E 2) is an independent regulatory agency within DOE that continues the Federal Power Commission, which was established by act of June 10, 1920 (41 Stat. 1063). The Economic Regulatory Administration administers DOE regulatory programs other than those assigned to FERC.

The DOE field structure includes the operations offices and government-owned, contractor-operated field installations as well as the five power administrations (Bonneville [E 5], Southeastern, Alaska, Southwestern, and Western Area [E 6]). The vast majority of DOE's research and development and testing are carried out by contractors who operate government-owned facilities. The management and administration of the contracts are the responsibility of eight

DOE operations offices located in Albuquerque, New Mexico; Idaho Falls, Idaho; Chicago; Las Vegas, Nevada; Oak Ridge, Tennessee; Richland, Washington; San Francisco/Oakland; and Savannah River/Aiken, South Carolina. These operations offices also provide a formal link between DOE headquarters and its field laboratories and other operating facilities.

The Department of Energy sponsors a number of technical reports that are announced in the monthly *Energy Research Abstracts* (E 1.17), published by its Scientific and Technical Information Office located in Oak Ridge, Tennessee. These are discussed in greater detail in chapter 11. The Energy Information Administration (EIA) publishes a number of statistical reports and periodicals covering all forms of energy and those devoted to specific types, such as petroleum. Among the former are the *Annual Energy Review* (E 3.1/2) and *Monthly Energy Review* (E 3.9). EIA has separate Offices of Oil and Gas; Energy Markets and End Use; and Coal, Nuclear, Electric, and Alternate Fuels.

A GPO/DOE pilot project involving a selected number of federal depository libraries with electronic access to the Energy Department's Integrated Technical System (ITS) began in October 1990. Evaluation of this project by LPS staff was scheduled to be completed during fiscal year 1991. Those depository institutions chosen for the project currently select all or a portion of DOE's important Contractor Reports and Publications series (E 1.99) under Item Nos. 0430-M-01 through 0430-M-40, distributed on microfiche.

Department of Health and Human Services

The Department of Health and Human Services (DHHS) (HE 1) continues the Department of Health, Education, and Welfare (DHEW), which was created pursuant to the Reorganization Act of 1949 (63 Stat. 206). The department was redesignated by the Department of Education Organization Act of 1979 (93 Stat. 695). DHEW had superseded the Federal Security Agency (FS), which was established by Reorganization Plan No. 1 of 1939. The Department of Health and Human Services is the executive department most involved with the nation's human concerns—whether it is mailing Social Security checks or making health services more widely available. The department administers its functions through the Office of the Secretary and five operating bureaus: Social Security Administration, Health Care Financing Administration, Office of Human Development Services, Family Support Administration, and the Public Health Service.

Social Security Administration

The Social Security Administration (SSA) (HE 3) was established by Federal Security Agency Reorganization Plan No. 2 of 1946, effective July 16, 1946. It superseded the Social Security Board (SS 1), which was established as an independent agency by the Social Security Act, approved August 14, 1935 (49 Stat. 620). By Reorganization Plan No. 1 of 1939, effective July 1, 1939, the board became part of the newly established Federal Security Agency (FS 3). The Social Security Administration administers the Social Security program, which is a national program of contributory social insurance providing benefits to retired and disabled workers, their spouses, and their children and to survivors of insured workers.

SSA also administers the Supplemental Security Income (SSI) program, which is a joint federal/state welfare program for the aged, blind, and disabled.

The Social Security Administration issues the monthly *Social Security Bulletin* (HE 3.3), which has an annual *Statistical Supplement* (HE 3.3/3). It also publishes a number of pamphlets describing benefits available under the Social Security and Supplemental Security Income programs, as well as the comprehensive *Social Security Handbook* (HE 3.6/8).

Health Care Financing Administration

The Health Care Financing Administration (HCFA) (HE 22) was established by the Secretary's Reorganization Order of March 8, 1977 (42 FR 13262), as a principal operating component of the department for the oversight of the Medicare and Medicaid programs and related federal medical care quality control staffs. It continues in part the functions of the Medical Service Administration (HE 17.500), which was a part of the Social and Rehabilitation Service (HE 17) that was abolished in the 1977 reorganization. HCFA issues a quarterly periodical, *Health Care Financing Review* (HE 22.18), as well as annual statistical reports on the Medicare and Medicaid programs.

Office of Human Development Services

The Office of Human Development Services (OHDS) (HE 23) was established by the Secretary's Reorganization Order of July 26, 1977, to replace the Office of Human Development (HE 1.700) established in 1976. OHDS includes the Administration on Aging (AoA); Administration for Children, Youth, and Families (ACYF); Administration for Native Americans; and Administration for Developmental Disabilities (ADD). The important bimonthly *Children Today* (HE 23.12) is issued by OHDS.

The Administration on Aging (HE 23.3000) was established as an independent agency on October 1, 1965 (HE 15), to carry out the provisions of the Older Americans Act of 1965 (79 Stat. 218). The administration was assigned to the Social and Rehabilitation Service by Department Reorganization Order of August 15, 1967 (HE 17.300), and in 1977 was reassigned to the newly established Office of Human Development Services when the Social and Rehabilitation Service was abolished. A useful publication issued by this entity is the quarterly periodical *Aging* (HE 23.3015).

The Administration for Children, Youth, and Families (HE 23.1000) was established by the Secretary's Reorganization Order of July 26, 1977, to replace the Office of Child Development (HE 21, 1970-1975; HE 1.400, 1975-1977). It absorbed the functions of the venerable Children's Bureau, which was established in 1912; the Head Start Bureau; and the Youth Development and Delinquency Prevention Administration. Among its present units is the National Center on Child Abuse and Neglect (HE 23.1200), which continues many of the functions of the Children's Bureau.

The Administration for Native Americans (HE 23.5000) represents the concerns of American Indians, Alaska Natives, and Native Hawaiians in all matters relating to the mission of the department and serves as department liaison with other agencies on Native American affairs.

The Administration on Developmental Disabilities (HE 23.6000) assists states to increase the provision of quality services to persons with developmental disabilities. It administers formula grants programs and grants for projects that assist persons with developmental disabilities.

Family Support Administration

The Family Support Administration (HE 25) administers family support programs within the department. It includes the Office of the Administrator, the Office of Child Support Enforcement, the Office of Family Assistance, the Office of Community Services, and the Office of Refugee Resettlement.

The Office of the Administrator jointly administers the Work Incentive Program (WIN) nationwide and is the director of the Office of Child Support Enforcement (OCSE). The Office of Child Support Enforcement (HE 24) was established within the Social Security Administration pursuant to an act of January 4, 1975 (88 Stat. 2351). It was continued as a separate organization under the Secretary's Reorganization Order of March 8, 1977, and was transferred to the Family Support Administration in 1986. OCSE administers programs that require states to enforce support obligations owed by absent parents to their children by locating absent parents, establishing paternity, and obtaining child support.

The Office of Family Assistance is the principal agency designated to administer the Aid to Families with Dependent Children (AFDC) Program (Title VI-A of the Social Security Act) (49 Stat. 627). This was previously a responsibility of the Social Security Administration. The office also administers the Low Income Home Energy Assistance Program.

The Office of Community Services was established by section 676 of the Omnibus Budget Reconciliation Act of 1981 (95 Stat. 516). It administers the Community Services Block Grant and Discretionary Grant programs established by the act. It also manages the programmatic closeout functions related to funds awarded by the Community Services Administration (CSA 1) in fiscal year (FY) 1981 and prior years. CSA was established by the Community Partnership Act of 1974 and approved January 4, 1975 (88 Stat. 2291), as the successor to the Office of Economic Opportunity (PrEx 10), which was the lead agency in the Johnson administration's "war on poverty." CSA was abolished by act of August 13, 1981 (95 Stat. 519).

The Office of Refugee Settlement administers the Refugee Assistance Program, which provides cash, medical assistance, and social services to refugees as well as to Cuban and Haitian entrants under provisions of Title IV of the Immigration and Nationality Act (8 U.S.C. 1521) and section 501 of the Refugee Education Assistance Act of 1980.

Public Health Service

The Public Health Service (PHS) (HE 20) has the largest number of publishing/issuing agencies (corporate authors) of any bureau-level agency in the federal government. PHS has its origins in an act of July 16, 1798 (Ch. 77, 1 Stat. 605), which authorized marine hospitals for the care of U.S. merchant seamen. Subsequent legislation has vastly broadened the scope of its activities. The Public Health Service Act of July 1, 1944 (58 Stat. 682), consolidated and revised substantially all existing legislation relating to the service. Major organization transfers to PHS since 1944 have included vital statistics (1946), health services for Native Americans (1955), the National Library of Medicine (1956), and the Food and Drug Administration (1968).

The major units within PHS include the Alcohol, Drug Abuse, and Mental Health Administration; Centers for Disease Control; Food and Drug Administration; Health Resources and Services Administration; and the National Institutes of Health. The Agency for Toxic Substances and Disease Registry was established as a separate operating agency within PHS by Secretary's Order of April 19, 1983. The National Center for Health Services Research (HE 20.6500), formerly a part of the Health Resources Administration, was combined with the National Center for Health Care Technology (HE 20.200) and is now part of the Office of the Assistant Secretary for Health as the National Center for Health Services Research and Health Care Technology. On September 1, 1982, the Health Resources Administration was merged with the Health Services Administration (HE 20.5000) to form the Health Resources and Services Administration (HE 20.9000) pursuant to Secretary's Reorganization Order of August 20, 1982 (47 FR 38409).[13]

Alcohol, Drug Abuse, and Mental Health Administration. The Alcohol, Drug Abuse, and Mental Health Administration (ADAMHA) (HE 20.8000) was established in 1973 by a spinoff of two new, separate institutes from the National Institute of Mental Health: the National Institute on Drug Abuse (HE 20.8200) and the National Institute on Alcohol Abuse and Alcoholism (HE 20.8300). The National Institute of Mental Health was formerly part of the Health Services and Mental Health Administration (HE 20.2000), which was established April 1, 1968, and abolished by Secretary's Reorganization Order, effective July 1, 1973. Most of its functions and agencies were transferred to the Centers for Disease Control (HE 20.7000), the Health Resources Administration (HE 20.6000), and the Health Services Administration (HE 20.5000).

The National Institute of Mental Health publishes the annual status report *Mental Health, United States* (HE 20.8137), and the quarterly *Psychopharmacology Bulletin* (HE 20.8109) and *Schizophrenia Bulletin* (HE 20.8115). The National Institute on Drug Abuse publishes the annual *Drug Use among American High School Students* (HE 20.8219). The National Institute on Alcohol Abuse and Alcoholism publishes the irregular *Special Report to the U.S. Congress on Alcohol and Health* (HE 20.8313).

Centers for Disease Control. The Centers for Disease Control (CDC) (HE 20.7000) was established by Secretary's Order effective July 1, 1973, with most of its functions transferred from the Health Services and Mental Health Administration, which was abolished. It was known as the Center for Disease Control until the present name was assigned by Secretary's Notice of October 1, 1980 (45 FR 67772). The Centers for Disease Control continues the Center for Disease Control (1971-1973) (HE 20.2300) and the National Communicable Disease Center (1951-1969). CDC is presently composed of nine major operating components: Epidemiology Program Office, International Health Program Office, Training and Laboratory Program Office, Center for Prevention Services (HE 20.7300), Center for Environmental Health (HE 20.7500), Center for Health Promotion and Education (HE 20.7600), Center for Infectious Diseases (HE 20.7800), National Institute for Occupational Safety and Health (NIOSH) (HE 20.7100), and National Center for Health Statistics (HE 201.6200). CDC publishes the *Morbidity and Mortality Weekly Report* (HE 20.7009) and the annual *Health Information for International Travel* (HE 20.7315).[14]

The National Center for Health Statistics (NCHS) (HE 20.6200) was established under Reorganization Plan No. 2, effective July 16, 1946, as the National Office of Vital Statistics (FS 2.100) when functions of the Bureau of the Census relative to vital statistics were transferred to the Federal Security Agency for administration by the Public Health Service. It was placed under the Health Services and Mental Health Administration in 1970 (HE 20.2200) and was reassigned to the Health Resources Administration by Secretary's Reorganization Order of July 1, 1973. It was transferred from the Health Resources Administration to the Office of the Assistant Secretary of Health by departmental reorganization effective December 2, 1977, and was later transferred to the Centers for Disease Control.

Food and Drug Administration. The Food and Drug Administration (FDA) (HE 20.4000) traces its origins to the Food, Drug, and Insecticide Administration (A 46), which was established by the Agricultural Appropriation Act of 1928 (44 Stat. 1002). The name was changed to Food and Drug Administration by the Agriculture Appropriation Act of 1931 (46 Stat. 422). FDA was transferred to the Federal Security Agency by Reorganization Plan No. 4, effective June 30, 1940 (FS 7), and was transferred to the newly established Department of Health, Education, and Welfare in 1953. FDA activities are directed toward protecting the nation's health against impure and unsafe foods, drugs, cosmetics, and other potential hazards.

The Food and Drug Administration includes the Center for Drugs and Biologics (HE 20.4200), Center for Food Safety and Applied Nutrition (formerly Bureau of Foods) (HE 20.4500), Center for Veterinary Medicine (HE 20.4400), National Center for Toxicological Research, and Center for Devices and Radiological Health (HE 20.4600), which was formed on March 9, 1984, by a merger of the Bureau of Radiological Health (HE 20.4100) and the Bureau of Medical Devices (HE 20.4300). The Food and Drug Administration publishes the *National Drug Code Directory* (HE 20.4012) and the popular periodical *FDA Consumer* (HE 20.4010), which contains information written for consumers about FDA scientific and regulatory decisions and about the safe use of products regulated by the FDA.

Health Resources and Services Administration. The Health Resources and Services Administration (HRSA) (HE 20.9000) was created by a merger on September 1, 1982, of the Health Resources Administration (HE 20.6000) and the Health Services Administration (HSA) (HE 20.5000). Its major operating components are the Bureau of Health Care Delivery and Assistance (HE 20.9100), Bureau of Health Professions (HE 20.9300), Bureau of Resources Development, and the Indian Health Service (HE 20.9400).

The Bureau of Health Care Delivery and Assistance was established by Secretary's Reorganization Order, effective July 1, 1973 (HE 20.5100). It serves as a national focus for efforts to ensure the availability and delivery of health care services to medically underserved areas and to special services populations. The Bureau of Health Professions was established in 1975 as the Bureau of Health Manpower within the Health Resources Administration (HE 20.6600) and was transferred to the Health Resources and Services Administration in 1982. Its name was changed to Bureau of Health Professions by Secretary's Order of March 12, 1980 (45 FR 71207). The bureau provides national leadership in coordinating, evaluating, and supporting the development and utilization of the nation's health personnel.

The Bureau of Resources Development administers grant, loan, loan guarantee, and interest subsidy programs under Titles VI, VII, VIII, and XVI of the Public Service Act relating to construction, modernization, conversion, or closure of health care facilities, including facilities for health professions education and nurses training. The Indian Health Service provides comprehensive health care services for American Indians and Alaska Natives, including hospital and ambulatory medical care, preventive and rehabilitative services, and development of community sanitation facilities.

National Institutes of Health. The National Institutes of Health (NIH) (HE 20.3000) conducts and supports biomedical research into the causes, prevention, and cure of diseases; supports research training and the development of research resources; and makes use of modern methods to communicate biomedical information. The National Institutes of Health includes twelve affiliated institutes, the Clinical Center, the Fogarty International Center, the National Library of Medicine, the National Center for Nursing Research, the Division of Computer Research and Technology, the Division of Research Resources, the Division of Research Services, and the Division of Research Grants.

The Clinical Center brings together scientists working in the center's research laboratories and clinicians caring for patients. The research institutes select patients referred to NIH by physicians nationwide for clinical studies of specific diseases and disorders. The Fogarty International Center (HE 20.3700) promotes discussion, study, and research on the development of science internationally as it relates to health and administers a number of international programs for advanced study in the health sciences.

The National Library of Medicine (HE 20.3600) was established by the Public Health Service Amendments of August 3, 1956 (60 Stat. 960). It has its origins in 1838 as the Library of the Surgeon General's Office, which later became known as the Army Medical Library. The library was redesignated as the Armed Forces Medical Library in 1952 (D 8) and in 1956 was transferred to the Department of Health, Education, and Welfare and renamed the National Library of Medicine (NLM). NLM was a pioneer in the development of online bibliographic databases in the MEDLARS systems. It publishes *Index Medicus* (HE 20.3612), *Abridged Index Medicus* (HE 20.3612/2), and the *National Library of Medicine Current Catalog* (HE 20.3609/3). MEDLARS (MEDical Literature Analysis and Retrieval System) consists of some thirty-two databases offered by the National

Library of Medicine, available through NTIS or commercial vendors such as SilverPlatter. GRATEFUL MED 5.0, released in 1990, is an example of a software package that first appeared in 1986 designed to provide a user-friendly program for searching the MEDLARS system.

Department of Housing and Urban Development

The Department of Housing and Urban Development (HUD) (HH 1) was established as an executive department by the Department of Housing and Urban Development Act of September 9, 1965 (79 Stat. 667), effective November 9, 1965. It continues the Housing and Home Finance Agency, which had been established by Reorganization Plan No. 3 of 1947, effective July 27, 1947. The Department of Housing and Urban Development is principally responsible for programs concerned with the nation's housing needs, the development and preservation of the nation's communities, and the provision of equal housing opportunity for all Americans. The department administers a wide variety of programs including Federal Housing Administration (FHA) mortgage insurance programs; rental assistance programs for low-income families; the Government National Mortgage Association, mortgage securities programs that help ensure an adequate supply of mortgage credit; programs to combat housing discrimination and to affirmatively further fair housing; programs that aid the community and neighborhood development and preservation; and programs to help the homebuyer in the marketplace. Most HUD publications distributed to depository libraries are departmental publications. The main subordinate issuing agencies within the department are the Office of Community Planning and Development and Office of Housing. However, SuDocs author symbols have not been assigned for these offices, and their publications are assigned HH 1 class numbers.[15]

HUD joined forces with the Bureau of the Census to produce the *1985 American Housing Survey* on CD-ROM. Interagency cooperation to make available large amounts of numeric data (microdata) is becoming more frequent as the potential for storing vast amounts of information on CD-ROM makes such cooperative ventures feasible.

Department of the Interior

The Department of the Interior (I 1) was created by act of March 3, 1849 (9 Stat. 395), which transferred to it the General Land Office (I 21), the Office of Indian Affairs (I 20), the Pension Office (I 24), and the Patent Office (I 23). The department also was responsible for supervising the Commissioner of Public Buildings, the Board of Inspectors and the Warden of the Penitentiary of the District of Columbia, the census of the United States, the accounts of Marshals and other officers of the U.S. courts, and the accounts of lead and other mines in the United States. Over its many years of existence, other functions have been added and/or removed; its role has changed from that of general housekeeper to that of custodian of the nation's natural resources. The principal operating bureaus and offices of the department are National Park Service, U.S. Fish and Wildlife Service, Bureau of Indian Affairs, Bureau of Land Management,

Minerals Management Service, Office of Surface Mining Reclamation and Enforcement, U.S. Geological Survey, Bureau of Mines, and Bureau of Reclamation. Among the departmental offices are the Office of the Solicitor and the Office of Hearings and Appeals.

National Park Service

The National Park Service (NPS) (I 29) was established by an act of August 25, 1916 (39 Stat. 535). It administers more than 337 units in the national park system, including national parks and monuments; scenic parkways, riverways, seashores, lakeshores, recreation areas, and reservoirs; and historic sites. NPS also administers the following programs: state portion of the Land and Water Conservation Fund, the Nationwide Outdoor Recreation Plan, the Urban Park and Recreation Program, park and recreation technical services, planning for the National Wild and Scenic Rivers System and the National Trails System, the National Register of Historic Places, national historic landmarks and preservation, Historic American Buildings Survey, Historic American Engineer Record, and interagency archaeological services.

The National Park Service publishes visitor guides for units in the national park system, as well as a Handbook series (I 29.9/5) that provides greater detail on major sites and an annual *National Parks: Camping Guide* (I 29.71).

Fish and Wildlife Service

The Fish and Wildlife Service (FWS) (I 49) traces its origins to the U.S. Fish Commission, which was established as an independent agency by Joint Resolution of February 9, 1871 (16 Stat. 594). The commission became part of the newly established Department of Commerce and Labor in 1903 and was renamed the Bureau of Fisheries (C 6). The Bureau of Fisheries was transferred to the Department of the Interior by Reorganization Plan No. 2 of 1939 (I 45) and was merged with the Bureau of Biological Survey (I 47) by Reorganization Plan No. 3 of 1940 to form the Fish and Wildlife Service (I 49). The Fish and Wildlife Act of 1956 (70 Stat. 1119) created the U.S. Fish and Wildlife Service to replace the former Fish and Wildlife Service and established two bureaus within the new service: Bureau of Commercial Fisheries and Bureau of Sport Fisheries and Wildlife. Under Reorganization Plans No. 3 and No. 4 of 1970, the Bureau of Commercial Fisheries was transferred to the Department of Commerce and renamed the National Marine Fisheries Service (C 55.300). The Bureau of Sport Fisheries and Wildlife, which remained in the department, was renamed the U.S. Fish and Wildlife Service by act of April 1974 (88 Stat. 92).

The service is composed of headquarters, 7 regional offices, and a variety of field units and installations that include 437 national wildlife refuges and 150 waterfowl production areas. Its mission is to conserve and protect migratory birds, endangered species, certain marine mammals, and inland sport fisheries. It issues a bimonthly periodical, *Fish and Wildlife News* (I 49.88), a bimonthly abstract review, *Wildlife Review* (I 49.17) and a quarterly, *Fisheries Review* (I 49.40/2), and conducts the quinquennial *National Survey of Fishing, Hunting, and Wildlife* (I 49.98). In addition, for the philatelic buff there is the *Duck Stamp*

Collection subscription service (I 49.93), consisting of a basic manual and supplementary material issued periodically. Each stamp is represented with a photograph, an enlargement of the art, and data on the designer, engraver, plates issued, first day of sale, and quantity sold.

Bureau of Indian Affairs

The Bureau of Indian Affairs (BIA) (I 20) was created as part of the War Department in 1824 and was transferred to the Department of the Interior upon that department's establishment in 1849. The principal objectives of the bureau are to actively encourage and train Indian and Alaska Native peoples to manage their own affairs under the trust relationship to the federal government. The bureau acts as trustee for Indian lands and monies held in trust by the United States. The bureau seeks for Indians adequate educational opportunities in public education systems, assists them in creating their own systems, or provides from federal sources the educational systems needed. The bureau has field offices in Alaska, Arizona, California, Minnesota, Montana, Oklahoma, Oregon, and Washington, D.C. About seventeen series of BIA items are available to depository libraries.

Bureau of Land Management

The Bureau of Land Management (BLM) (I 53) was established July 16, 1946, by the consolidation of the General Land Office (I 21) and the Grazing Service (formed in 1934) in accordance with sections 402 and 403 of Reorganization Plan No. 3 of 1946. The General Land Office had been established within the Treasury Department by act of April 25, 1812, and transferred to the Department of the Interior upon the department's establishment in 1849. The bureau's basic organization consists of a headquarters in Washington, D.C., a Denver Service Center, a Boise [Idaho] Interagency Fire Center, and a field organization of twelve state offices (in ten western states, Alaska, and an Eastern States Office) together with their district and resource area offices. BLM is responsible for the total management of 270 million acres of public lands, plus subsurface resource management of an additional 300 million acres where mineral rights are owned by the federal government. The bureau publishes the annual *Public Land Statistics* (I 53.1/2) and *Managing the Nation's Public Lands* (I 53.12/2).

Minerals Management Service

The Minerals Management Service (MMS) (I 72) was established January 19, 1982, by Secretarial Order 3071. All Outer Continental Shelf (OCS) leasing responsibilities of the Department of the Interior were consolidated within MMS on May 10, 1982, by Amendment 1 to Secretarial Order 3071. Secretarial Order 3087 of December 3, 1982, with Amendment 1 dated February 7, 1983, transferred royalty and minerals revenue management functions to MMS and transferred all onshore minerals management functions on federal Indian lands to the Bureau of Land Management. The basic organization of MMS consists of a headquarters in Washington, D.C., with program components in Reston and Herndon, Virginia; the Royalty Management Program Accounting Center in Lakewood, Colorado; four OCS regional offices (Atlantic, Gulf of Mexico, Pacific, and Alaska regions); and three administrative centers. The revenues generated by minerals leasing are one of the largest nontax sources of income to the federal government. About thirty MMS series are available to depository libraries.

Geological Survey

The Geological Survey (I 19) was established by act of March 3, 1879 (20 Stat. 394), to continue the functions of the Geographical and Geological Survey of the Rocky Mountain Region (I 17) (1874-1879) and the Geological and Geographical Survey of the Territories (I 18) (1872-1879). The primary responsibilities of the Geological Survey are identifying the nation's land, water, energy, and mineral resources; classifying federally owned lands for minerals and energy resources and water power potential; investigating natural hazards such as earthquakes, volcanoes, and landslides; and conducting the National Mapping Program. The survey's mapping activities are discussed in chapter 12.

The Geological Survey announces extensive series of numbered bulletins (I 19.3), circulars (I 19.4/2), water-supply papers (I 19.13), and professional publications and maps through its monthly *New Publications of the U.S. Geological Survey* (I 19.14/4) and annual *Publications of the Geological Survey* (I 19.14). The Geological Survey's *National Gazetteer of the United States* (Professional Paper No. 1200) is accessed by depository libraries under a separate item number (0624-A-01) from the other Professional Papers series, although the class stem remains I 19.16. The Bureau of Land Management and the Geological Survey produced a CD-ROM containing Side-Looking Airborne Radar (SLAR) image files. Titled "Joint Earth Science (JES-2) Demonstration Disc," this product was offered to depository libraries on a first-come, first-serve basis. The disk was cataloged by LPS under OCLC number 20444603 and carries the SuDocs class notation I 19.119:Si1.

Bureau of Mines

The Bureau of Mines (I 28) was established by the Organic Act of May 16, 1910 (36 Stat. 369), effective July 1, 1910. It was transferred to the Department of Commerce by EO 4239 of June 4, 1925, effective July 1, 1925 (C 22), and was returned to the Department of the Interior by EO 6611 of February 22, 1934, effective April 23, 1934. The bureau is primarily a research and fact-finding agency. Research is conducted to provide the technology for the extracting, processing, use, and recycling of the nation's nonfuel mineral resources at reasonable cost. The bureau also collects, compiles, and publishes statistical and economic information on all phases of nonfuel mineral resource development, including exploration, production, shipments, demand, stocks, prices, imports, and exports.

The Bureau of Mines publishes the multivolume *Minerals Yearbook* (I 28.37) and the annual *Bureau of Mines Research: A Summary of Significant Results in Mineral Technology and Economics* (I 28.115). The results of its research and fact-finding are published in two numbered series: Reports of Investigations (I 28.23) and Information Circulars (I 28.27). It maintains comprehensive bibliographic control of its publications through its monthly *New Publications of the Bureau of Mines* (I 28.5/2) and *List of Bureau of Mines Publications and Articles with Subject and Author Index* (I 28.5), published annually with quinquennial cumulations.

Bureau of Reclamation

The Bureau of Reclamation (I 27) has its origins in the Reclamation Act of 1902 (32 Stat. 388), which authorized the secretary of the interior to administer a reclamation program that would provide the arid and semiarid lands of the seventeen contiguous western states a secure, year-round water supply for irrigation. To perform this mission, the Reclamation Service was created within the Geological Survey. In March 1907, the Reclamation Service was separated from the survey, and in June 1923, the name was changed to Bureau of Reclamation. Power-marketing functions were transferred to the Department of Energy by act of August 4, 1977 (91 Stat. 565), effective October 1, 1977. The bureau was renamed the Water and Power Resources Service by Secretarial Order 3042 of November 6, 1979; the name was changed back to Bureau of Reclamation by Secretarial Order 3064 of May 18, 1981. The bureau now provides water for farms, towns, and industries and is responsible for generating hydroelectric power, river regulation and flood control, outdoor recreation opportunities, and enhancing and protecting fish and wildlife habitats. Present bureau project facilities in operation include 355 storage reservoirs; 360 diversion dams; 51 hydroelectric power plants; and thousands of miles of connecting canals, pipelines, and project drains. In addition to headquarters in Washington, D.C., the bureau operates an Engineering and Research Center in Denver, Colorado, and has six operating regions. Over thirty series from the bureau are available to depository libraries.

Department of Justice

The Department of Justice was established by act of June 22, 1870 (16 Stat. 162), with the attorney general at its head. Prior to 1870, the attorney general was a member of the president's cabinet but not head of an executive department, the office having been created by act of September 24, 1789 (1 Stat. 92). The department represents the federal government in enforcing the law in the public interest. It plays a key role in protection against criminals and subversion, in ensuring healthy business competition in our free enterprise system, and in enforcing drug, immigration, and naturalization laws.

The Department of Justice organization consists of headquarters offices, divisions, and operating bureaus. Among the offices are solicitor general, Office of Legal Counsel, and the Community Relations Service. The divisions include the Antitrust Division, Civil Division, Civil Rights Division, Criminal Division, and Tax Division. The operating bureaus include the Federal Bureau of Investigation; Bureau of Prisons; United States Marshals Service; Immigration and Naturalization Service; Drug Enforcement Administration; and Office of Justice

Programs, which coordinates the activities of the National Institute of Justice, Bureau of Justice Statistics, Office of Juvenile Justice and Delinquency Prevention, and Bureau of Justice Assistance.

Federal Bureau of Investigation

The Federal Bureau of Investigation (FBI) (J 1.14) was established in 1908 by the attorney general, who directed that the department's investigations be handled by its own staff. The FBI is charged with investigating all violations of federal law except those assigned by law or executive order to other federal agencies. Its present priorities are investigation of organized crime, terrorism, white-collar crime, and foreign counterintelligence. The FBI's investigations are conducted through fifty-nine field offices. Perhaps the most consulted reference publication issued by the FBI is the annual *Crime in the United States* (J 1.14/7) in the Uniform Crime Reports series.

Immigration and Naturalization Service

The Immigration and Naturalization Service (INS) (J 21) was established as the Bureau of Immigration within the Treasury Department on July 12, 1891 (T 21), pursuant to the act of March 3, 1891 (26 Stat. 1085). On July 1, 1903, the bureau was transferred to the newly established Department of Commerce and Labor (C 7). On July 14, 1906, its name was changed to Bureau of Immigration and Naturalization under an act of June 29, 1906, and functions pertaining to naturalization were added. By act of March 4, 1913 (37 Stat. 736), the bureau was transferred to the Department of Labor and separated into the Bureau of Immigration (L 3) and Bureau of Naturalization (L 6). EO 6166 of June 10, 1933, consolidated the two bureaus into the Immigration and Naturalization Service (L 15). INS was transferred to the Department of Justice by Reorganization Plan No. 5 of 1940, effective June 14, 1940.

INS's mission is divided into four major areas of responsibilities, with respect to aliens entering the United States, aliens within the United States, naturalization and certification of citizenship, and undocumented aliens. INS publishes a series of *Federal Textbooks on Citizenship* (J 21.9) and a *Statistical Yearbook* (J21.2/10).

Drug Enforcement Administration

The Drug Enforcement Administration (DEA) (J 24) is the lead agency in enforcing narcotics and controlled substances laws and regulations. It traces its origins to the Federal Narcotics Control Board, which was established by an act of May 26, 1922, in the Treasury Department (T 53). The functions of the board were transferred to the Bureau of Narcotics (T 56), which was established by an act of June 14, 1930 (46 Stat. 585). The bureau was abolished by Reorganization Plan No. 1 of 1968, effective February 7, 1968, which transferred its functions along with those of the Bureau of Drug Abuse Control in the Food and Drug Administration to the Bureau of Narcotics and Dangerous Drugs. The Bureau of

Narcotics and Dangerous Drugs was established within the Department of Justice (J 24) by the same order. The bureau was abolished by Reorganization Plan No. 2 of 1973, which established the Drug Enforcement Administration to supersede it. DEA also chairs the eleven-agency National Narcotics Intelligence Consumers Committee, which publishes the annual *Narcotics Intelligence Estimate* (J 24.22) on drug production, trafficking, and abuse trends.

Department of Labor

The Department of Labor was created by act of March 4, 1913 (37 Stat. 736). A Bureau of Labor (La 1) was first organized in January 1885, under act of June 27, 1884, as part of the Department of the Interior. By an act of June 13, 1888, it became an independent agency called Department of Labor, but without executive rank. It returned to a bureau status and was transferred to the newly created Department of Commerce and Labor (C 8) by an act of February 14, 1903 (32 Stat. 825). The department administers various federal labor laws guaranteeing workers' rights to safe and healthful working conditions; a minimum hourly wage and overtime pay; freedom from employment discrimination; unemployment insurance and workers' compensation; protection of workers' pension rights; assistance in finding jobs; the provision of job training programs; and keeping track of changes in employment, prices, and other national economic measures.

Employment and Training Administration

The Employment and Training Administration (ETA) (L 37) was established by Secretary's Order 14-75 of November 12, 1975, to succeed the now abolished Manpower Administration. Its principal programs deal with employment security and job training. Employment security programs are supervised by the Office of Employment Security and administered by the Unemployment Insurance Service, the United States Employment Service, and the Office of Trade Adjustment Assistance. Job training programs are administered by the Office of Job Training Programs and the Bureau of Apprenticeship and Training.

The United States Employment Service (L 37.300) assists states, under the provisions of the Wagner-Peyser Act (48 Stat. 113), in establishing and maintaining a system of local public employment offices in the states and territories and interstate clearance of labor. It is the provenance of a significant reference source, the *Dictionary of Occupational Titles* (L 37.302:Oc1). It is now in its fourth edition (1977), and a new edition is being prepared for publication in 1992. Since its first appearance in 1939, the *Dictionary of Occupational Titles* (DOT) has provided the service with detailed standardized occupational information essential to the effective classification and placement of job seekers. The fourth edition of DOT is based on over 75,000 onsite analyses conducted from 1965 to the early and mid-1970s and on extensive contacts with professional and trade associations. Consequently, over 2,100 new occupational definitions were added and some 3,500 were deleted from the third edition. The present edition contains descriptions of about 20,000 jobs. Volume I, "Occupational Definitions," indicates a revision date of 1991.

The DOT groups jobs into "occupations" based on their similarities and defines the structure and content of all listed occupations. The term *occupation* as used in the DOT refers to a collective description of a number of individual jobs performed, with minor variations, in many establishments. An occupational definition has six basic parts: (1) the occupational code number; (2) the occupational title; (3) the industry designation; (4) alternate titles, if any; (5) the body of the definition, which includes the lead statement, task element statements, and "may" items; and (6) undefined related titles, if any. A nine-digit occupational code is used to define occupations. The first three digits identify a particular group, the middle three digits signify the worker functions ratings of the tasks performed, and the last three digits indicate the alphabetical order of titles within six-digit code groups, serving to differentiate a particular occupation from all others. Thus, a "cloth printer" is assigned the numerical sequence 652.382-010. This digitized code system allows for an extraordinarily precise description of occupations, but care is required in interpreting the information provided.

DOT provides *composite* descriptions of occupations as they typically occur and therefore may not coincide with a specific job as actually performed in a particular establishment or a given industry. A supplement to DOT titled *Selected Characteristics of Occupations Defined in the Dictionary of Occupational Titles* (L 37.302:Oc1/supp.) meets the needs of job seekers who require more detailed information, such as physical demands, environmental conditions, and training time ratings. Part A of *Selected Characteristics* clusters occupational titles using the special coding system explained in the *Guide for Occupational Exploration* (GOE), thus helping the user to see relationships among requirements of jobs characterized by a predominant worker interest factor. Part B lists occupational titles in order of the nine-digit DOT code and specifies the physical strength required for each listed occupation. For example, a "snag grinder" (705.684-074) requires medium strength output (exertion) during job performance, thus precluding persons with cardiac or respiratory impairments from engaging in this occupation. But occupations that require knowledge and abilities similar to those of a snag grinder may involve different physical demands and environmental conditions. Thus, *Selected Characteristics* is most effective when used with the DOT and the GOE, assisting the user in deciding the suitability of jobs for employment training and rehabilitation considerations.

Office of Labor-Management Standards

The Office of Labor-Management Standards (OLMS), formerly the Office of Labor-Management Standards Enforcement within the Management Service Administration, was created by Secretary's Order 3-84 of May 3, 1984. OLMS administers provisions of the Labor-Management Reporting and Disclosure Act (LMRDA) of 1959 (73 Stat. 519); section 1209 of the Postal Reorganization Act; section 701 of the Civil Service Reform Act (CSRA) (92 Stat. 1210); and section 1017 of the Foreign Service Act (FSA), which regulates certain internal union procedures and protects the rights of members in approximately 48,000 unions. OLMS publishes the biennial *Register of Reporting Employers* (L 1.81), biennial *Register of Reporting Surety Companies* (L 1.82), and triennial *Register of Reporting Labor Organizations* (L 1.84).

Bureau of Labor Statistics

The Bureau of Labor Statistics (BLS) (L 2) traces its origins to the Bureau of Labor, which was first organized in January 1885, under an act of June 27, 1884, as part of the Department of the Interior. In 1888, the Bureau of Labor became an independent agency called Department of Labor, but without executive rank. It returned to bureau status upon transfer in 1903 to the newly established Department of Commerce and Labor. With the establishment of the Department of Labor in 1913, the Bureau of Labor Statistics became a separate unit in the Department of Labor. BLS is one of the principal data-gathering agencies of the federal government in the broad field of labor economics. Its statistical publications are discussed in chapter 10. BLS has no enforcement or regulatory functions.

Women's Bureau

The Women's Bureau (L 36.100) was established by an act of June 5, 1920 (41 Stat. 987). It is responsible for formulating standards and policies that promote the welfare of wage-earning women, improve their working conditions, advance their opportunities for profitable employment, and investigate and report on all matters pertinent to the welfare of women in industry. The bureau publishes a statistical compilation, *Handbook of Women Workers* (L 36.103: no.), in its bulletin series.

Department of State

The Department of State (S 1), the senior executive department, was established by an act of July 27, 1789 (1 Stat. 28), as the Department of Foreign Affairs and was renamed Department of State by an act of September 15, 1789 (1 Stat. 68). During the first few decades of the Republic, the department had been assigned a number of domestic duties that eventually were transferred to other departments as the federal government grew in size and complexity. The duties of the Department of State in the field of foreign affairs have not changed significantly in scope since 1789.

The main organizational elements of the department are the Office of the Secretary, the five regional bureaus, the functional areas, and the Foreign Service. Included in the Office of the Secretary of State are the undersecretaries for political affairs; economic and agricultural affairs; security assistance, science, and technology; management; and the Office of the Inspector General and Counselor. Five assistant secretaries direct the activities of the geographic bureaus, which are responsible for foreign affairs activities in the major regions of the world. These are the Bureaus of African Affairs, European and Canadian Affairs, East Asian and Pacific Affairs, Inter-American Affairs, and Near Eastern and South Asian Affairs.

The functional areas that are part of the headquarters organization include the Bureaus of Economic and Business Affairs, Intelligence and Research, International Organization Affairs, Public Affairs, Consular Affairs, Politico-Military Affairs, Oceans and International Environmental and Scientific Affairs, and Human Rights and Humanitarian Affairs; the Bureau for Refugee Programs; and the Office of the Chief of Protocol. The functional units generally prepare many of the Department of State publications available to depository libraries and the general public, but these are usually issued as departmental publications.

The United States' relations with other countries overseas are conducted principally by the U.S. Foreign Service. The service provides representatives at 141 embassies, 11 missions, 73 consulates general, 29 consulates, 1 branch office, and 4 consular agencies worldwide. A listing of Foreign Service posts appears in *Key Officers of Foreign Service Posts—Guide for Business Representatives* (S 1.40/5), published three times a year.[16] The department publishes two quarterly directories, *Diplomatic List* (S 1.8) and *Employees of Diplomatic Missions* (S 1.8/2), and the annual *Foreign Consular Offices in the United States* (S 1.69/2).

The venerable Foreign Relations of the United States historical series (S 1.1) was threatened with termination until funds were restored in the Supplemental Foreign Relations Authorization Act of 1990. Section 114 of S. Rep. 101-334 (June 18, 1990) established a system for "review of documents to ensure that the Foreign Relations Historical Series constitutes an authoritative and complete diplomatic record." Section 114 also established a "Historians Advisory Committee to review documents that may be withheld" within national security and protection of living persons limitations. However, all other documents are "subject to public access after 40 years."[17] Historians had complained that certain deletions in the series were arbitrary and had not been declassified correctly.[18] Published since 1861 through 1951 on an annual basis and thereafter on a triennial schedule, *Foreign Relations* experiences a time lag of some thirty years between date of publication and the period covered.

American Foreign Policy Current Documents (S 1.71/2) was issued annually from 1956 to 1967 and resumed in 1981. It is a compilation of major official messages, addresses, statements, interviews, press conference and briefing reports, congressional testimonies, and communications by the White House, the Department of State, and other federal agencies or officials involved in the foreign policy process. To cover the intervening years, a cumulation for 1977-1980 was published in 1983, and separate volumes covering the periods 1968-1972 and 1973-1976 are planned. A cumulation for 1941-1949 was published in 1950 as *A Decade of Foreign Policy: Basic Documents, 1941-1949* (S. Doc. 81-123). A revised edition was published in 1985 (S. 1.69:415). Since 1981, an annual microfiche supplement has been published that includes important documents that for reasons of space could not be included in the book edition.[19]

Other significant State Department series involving the constitutional duties of the president and the Senate are discussed in chapter 6.

Department of Transportation

The Department of Transportation (DOT) (TD 1) was established by an act of October 15, 1966 (80 Stat. 931), and became operational in April 1967. It was comprised of elements transferred from eight other major departments and agencies. It consists of the Office of the Secretary and nine operating administrations, whose heads report directly to the secretary and who have highly decentralized authority. Within the Office of the Secretary are the assistant secretaries and the general counsel, who are generally staff officers having one or more functional areas in which they assist the secretary in matters of department-wide scope. These officials do not exercise line control over the operating administrations, unlike the case in most of the other departments, where the undersecretaries have line control over the operating bureaus. The nine administrations are the U.S. Coast Guard, Federal Aviation Administration, Federal Highway Administration, Federal Railway Administration, National Highway Traffic Safety Administration, Urban Mass Transportation Administration, St. Lawrence Seaway Development Corporation, Maritime Administration, and Research and Special Programs Administration.

Coast Guard

The Coast Guard (TD 5) traces its origins to the Revenue Marine Division in the Treasury Department (T 33), which was established by an act of August 4, 1790. On July 31, 1894, the division was renamed the Revenue-Cutter Service, which merged with the Life-Saving Service (T 24) under an act of January 28, 1915, to form the Coast Guard (T 47). The Life-Saving Service had been established by an act of June 18, 1878 (20 Stat. 164). The Coast Guard was transferred to the Department of Transportation by an act approved October 15, 1966 (80 Stat. 931). The Coast Guard is a branch of the Armed Forces of the United States at all times and is a service within the Department of Transportation except when operating as part of the navy in time of war or when the president so directs. The Coast Guard was part of the navy during World War I and World War II. It was transferred to the Navy Department by EO 2587 of April 7, 1917, and returned by EO 3160 of August 28, 1919; likewise, it was transferred by EO 8929 of November 1, 1941, and again returned by EO 9666 of December 25, 1945, effective January 1, 1946.

The functions and activities of the Coast Guard cover a number of areas: search and rescue (SAR); maritime law enforcement; inspection of commercial vessels and offshore structures on the outer continental shelf (OCS); licensing of U.S. Merchant Marine personnel; regulation of pilotage services on the Great Lakes; enforcing the Federal Water Pollution Control Act and other laws related to protection of the marine environment; port safety and security; management of traffic on inland waterways; maintaining aids to navigation; regulating the construction, maintenance, and operation of bridges over navigable waters; ice operations; licensing and regulatory programs for deepwater ports; and boat safety for small craft in U.S. waters. The Coast Guard updates annually in seven volumes the *Light Lists* (TD 5.9), which are aids to navigation along the Atlantic, Pacific, and Gulf of Mexico coasts; the Great Lakes; and the Mississippi River system.

Federal Aviation Administration

The Federal Aviation Administration (FAA) (TD 4) traces its origins to the Aeronautics Branch (C 23), which was established in the Department of Commerce by the Air Commerce Act of 1926, approved May 20, 1926 (44 Stat. 568).

The name was changed to Bureau of Air Commerce by Secretary's Administrative Order of July 1, 1934. EO 7959 of August 22, 1938, transferred the functions of the bureau to the Civil Aeronautics Authority (CA 1), an independent agency established by the Civil Aeronautics Act of 1938 (52 Stat. 973). Reorganization Plans No. 3 and No. 4 of 1940, effective June 30, 1940, placed within the Department of Commerce the Civil Aeronautics Administration (C 31.100) and the Civil Aeronautics Board (CAB) (C 31.200). Pursuant to the Federal Aviation Act of 1958, approved August 23, 1958 (72 Stat. 731), the functions and personnel of the Civil Aeronautics Administration were transferred to the newly established Federal Aviation Agency on January 1, 1959, and the Civil Aeronautics Board became an independent agency. The Federal Aviation Agency was transferred to the Department of Transportation in 1966 and renamed Federal Aviation Administration. The Civil Aeronautics Board was abolished pursuant to act of October 4, 1984 (98 Stat. 1703). Most of its remaining functions were transferred to the Federal Aviation Administration, and the remainder went to the U.S. Postal Service.

The Federal Aviation Administration is charged with regulating air commerce; controlling the use of navigable airspace of the United States; promoting, encouraging, and developing civil aeronautics; consolidating research and development and installing and operating air navigation facilities; developing and operating a common system of air traffic control and navigation for both civil and military aircraft; and developing and implementing programs and regulations to control aircraft noise, sonic boom, and other environmental effects of civil aviation. FAA publishes various manuals and guides related to flight safety and navigation including *International Notices to Airmen* (TD 4.11), *Notices to Airmen* (TD 4.12/2), *Airman's Information Manual* (TD 4.12/3), and *International Flight Information Manual* (TD 4.309).

Federal Highway Administration

The Federal Highway Administration (FHWA) (TD 2) traces its origins to the Bureau of Public Roads (A 22), which was established in the Department of Agriculture in 1918. The bureau was, in turn, a continuation of the Office of Road Inquiry, which was established on October 3, 1893, under authority of the Agricultural Appropriation Act for fiscal year 1894 (28 Stat. 264). The Bureau of Public Roads was transferred to the Federal Works Agency by Reorganization Plan No. 1 of 1939, effective July 1, 1939, and renamed Public Roads Administration (FW 2). The Public Roads Administration was transferred to the newly created General Services Administration by the Federal Property and Administrative Services Act of 1949, effective July 1, 1949 (63 Stat. 3800), and its name was changed to Bureau of Public Roads. Under Reorganization Plan No. 7 of 1949, effective August 20, 1949, the bureau was transferred to the Department of Commerce (C 39). It was again transferred in 1966 to the newly established Federal Highway Administration (TD 2.100). In 1969 the bureau was abolished and its functions were absorbed by FHWA.

The Federal Highway Administration functions and activities involve the federal-aid highway program, which provides for the construction and maintenance of over 42,000 miles of interstate highways and for the improvement of over 800,000 miles of other federal-aid urban roads and streets; highway safety programs through the promulgation of safety standards and matching grants to states; motor carrier programs related to truck size and maximum weight and regulatory jurisdiction over safety performance of carriers engaged in interstate commerce; the federal lands program, related to highways on public lands; and research and development activities. FHWA annually publishes *Highway Statistics* (TD 2.23) and a quarterly periodical, *Public Roads* (TD 2.19).

National Highway Traffic Safety Administration

The National Highway Traffic Safety Administration (NHTSA) (TD 8) continues the National Highway Safety Agency, which had been established in the Department of Commerce by act of September 9, 1966 (80 Stat. 731). The agency's functions were transferred to the Department of Transportation by act of October 15, 1966 (80 Stat. 931), and in turn were transferred to the National Highway Traffic Safety Bureau (TD 2.200) by EO 11357 of June 1967. The bureau was renamed National Highway Traffic Safety Administration by act of December 31, 1970 (84 Stat. 1739). It carries out a congressional mandate to reduce the number of deaths and injuries and the economic losses resulting from traffic accidents on the nation's highways; to provide motor vehicle damage susceptibility and ease of repair information, motor vehicle inspection demonstrations, and protection of purchases of motor vehicles with altered odometers; and to provide average standards for greater vehicle mileage per gallon of fuel for vehicles under 10,000 pounds. NHTSA publishes the *Federal Motor Vehicle Safety Standards and Regulations* (TD 8.6/2).

Maritime Administration

The Maritime Administration (TD 11) was transferred from the Department of Commerce (C 39.200) by the Maritime Act of 1981 (95 Stat. 151), effective August 6, 1981. The administration had been established by Reorganization Plan No. 21 of 1950, effective May 24, 1950. It has its origins in the U.S. Shipping Board (SB 1), which was established by an act of September 7, 1916 (39 Stat. 729), and organized on January 30, 1917. The Shipping Board was abolished by EO 6166 of June 10, 1933, which transferred its functions to the U.S. Shipping Board Bureau in the Department of Commerce (C 27), effective March 2, 1934. The bureau was abolished by act of June 29, 1936 (49 Stat. 1985), which transferred its functions to the U.S. Maritime Commission (MC 1). The commission was abolished by Reorganization Plan No. 21 of 1950, and its functions were transferred to the Maritime Administration in the Department of Commerce.

The Maritime Administration administers programs to aid in the development, promotion, and operation of the U.S. Merchant Marine; constructs or supervises the construction of merchant type ships for the federal government; administers a War Risk Insurance Program; conducts research and development activities to improve the efficiency and economy of the Merchant Marine; maintains the National Defense Reserve Fleet for government-owned ships; operates the U.S. Merchant Marine Academy at Kings Point, New York; and administers a federal assistance program for six state-operated maritime academies. It publishes the annual *United States Oceanborne Foreign Trade Routes* (TD 11.13).

Department of the Treasury

The Department of the Treasury was created by an act of September 2, 1789 (1 Stat. 65). The department performs four basic types of functions: formulating and recommending economic, financial, tax, and fiscal policies; serving as financial agent for the U.S. government; enforcing the law; and manufacturing coins and currency. The headquarters organization of the department includes the Office of the Secretary with its general counsel; inspector general; assistant secretaries for tax policy, international affairs, legislative affairs, public affairs and public liaison, management, domestic policy, economic policy, and enforcement; the Treasurer of the United States; and the fiscal assistant secretary. The operating bureaus of the department include the U.S. Savings Bonds Division, United States Mint, and Bureau of Engraving under line authority of the Treasurer of the United States; the Financial Management Service and Bureau of the Public Debt under line authority of the fiscal assistant secretary; the Bureau of Alcohol, Tobacco, and Firearms, U.S. Customs Service, U.S. Secret Service, and Federal Law Enforcement Training Center under the line authority of the undersecretary for enforcement; the Office of the Comptroller of the Currency; and the Internal Revenue Service.

Financial Management Service

The Financial Management Service (T 63.100) continues the Bureau of Government Financial Operations, which was established by Treasury Order 229 of January 24, 1974; it replaced the Bureau of Accounts, which had been established as part of the Fiscal Service by Reorganization Plan No. 3 of 1940, effective June 30, 1940. The name was changed to Financial Management Service by Secretary's Order 145-21, effective October 10, 1984.

The Financial Management Service is responsible for the federal government's cash management, credit management, and debt collections programs, payments, and collections; the investment of Social Security and other trust funds; and the government's central accounting and reporting system. The service issues approximately 500 million treasury checks and 250 million electronic fund transfer (EFT) payments annually for federal salaries and wages, payments to contractors, income tax refunds, and payment of Social Security and veterans' benefits. The service maintains a central system that accounts for the monetary assets and liabilities of the treasury and tracks government collection and payment operations. Periodic reports are prepared to show budget results, the government's financial position, and other financial operations. These reports include the *Daily Treasury Statement* (T 63.113/2-2), *Monthly Treasury Statement* (T 63.113/2), the quarterly *Treasury Bulletin* (T 63.103/2), and several annual reports.

Bureau of Alcohol, Tobacco, and Firearms

The Bureau of Alcohol, Tobacco, and Firearms (BATF) (T 70) was established by Treasury Department Order 221, effective July 1, 1972. The order transferred the functions, powers, and duties arising under laws relating to alcohol, tobacco, firearms, and explosives from the Internal Revenue Service to the bureau. BATF is responsible for enforcing and administering firearms and explosives federal laws, as well as laws covering the production, use, and distribution of alcohol and tobacco products. The bureau's functions include law enforcement and compliance operations. It annually publishes *Explosive Incidents Report* (T 70.11), *States Laws and Published Ordinances — Firearms* (T 70.14), and *Firearms Curios and Relics List* (T 70.15).

United States Customs Service

The United States Customs Service (T 17) traces its origins to the fifth act of the 1st Congress, passed on July 31, 1789 (1 Stat. 29), which established customs districts and authorized customs officers to collect duties on goods, wares, and merchandise. The Bureau of Customs was established as a separate agency in the Department of the Treasury by an act of March 3, 1927 (44 Stat. 1381). It was redesignated the United States Customs Service by Treasury Department Order 165-23 of April 4, 1973, effective August 1, 1973. The service collects the revenue from imports and enforces customs and related laws. It also administers the Tariff Act of 1930, as amended, and other customs laws. It publishes advance weekly issues (T 17.6/3-4) and bound volumes (T 17.6/3-5) of the *Customs Bulletin.*

United States Secret Service

The United States Secret Service (T 34), formerly the Secret Service Division, was established July 5, 1865. It derives its authority from acts of June 23, 1860 (12 Stat. 102) and July 11, 1862 (12 Stat. 533). The service was reorganized by an act of August 5, 1882 (22 Stat. 230). The Secret Service protects the president and vice-president and their immediate families, as well as former presidents, major presidential candidates, visiting heads of foreign governments, and other distinguished foreign visitors and provides security at the White House Complex, buildings that house presidential offices, the vice-president's residence, and various foreign diplomatic missions in the Washington, D.C., area. Other functions include detecting and arresting offenders for counterfeiting coins, currency, stamps, and other obligations or securities of the United States. Perhaps the best known publication of the Secret Service is the brochure *Know Your Money* (T 34.2), which is revised periodically.

Internal Revenue Service

The Internal Revenue Service (IRS) (T 22) traces its origins to an act of July 1, 1862 (12 Stat. 432), which established the Office of the Commissioner of Internal Revenue in the Treasury Department. The name was changed to Internal Revenue Service in 1953 from Bureau of Internal Revenue. The IRS is responsible for administering and enforcing the internal revenue laws and related statutes except those relating to alcohol, tobacco, firearms, and explosives. The IRS organization is designed for maximum decentralization with a national office, seven regional offices, sixty-two district offices, and ten service centers. IRS annually publishes the familiar *Your Federal Income Tax* [for Individuals] (T 22.44), as well as a number of publications on specific subjects dealing with the individual income tax. It also publishes annual reports for *Individual Income Tax Returns* (T 22.35/8) and *Corporation Income Tax Returns* (T 22.35/5-2).

Department of Veterans Affairs

The Department of Veterans Affairs (DVA) was awarded departmental status by the Department of Veterans Affairs Act of 1988 (102 Stat. 2635; 38 U.S.C. 201 note). Earlier it was established as an independent agency in the executive branch by EO 5398, July 21, 1930, pursuant to an act of July 3, 1930 (46 Stat. 1016). The DVA operates the nation's largest medical system, with 172 hospitals, 233 outpatient clinics, 119 nursing homes, and 28 domiciliaries. In addition, it provides direct monetary benefits including compensation to service-disabled veterans, pensions for low-income veterans and survivors, educational assistance, and vocational rehabilitation. It also has guaranteed over 12 million home loans and operates the nation's eighth largest life insurance program. Moreover, the DVA operates and maintains 113 national cemeteries; provides cemetery headstones and markers; and awards matching funds grants to states to build, improve, or expand state veterans cemeteries.

The department publishes a number of relevant series, including Fact Sheets; for example, VA IS-1 fact sheet, titled *Federal Benefits for Veterans and Their Dependents* (VA 1.34:IS-1), is widely circulated.

INDEPENDENT AGENCIES

This section covers those independent agencies, government corporations, boards, committees, and commissions that are not part of the executive, legislative, or judicial branches. It is limited to those entities that are currently active and that are considered significant in publishing and disseminating government information. Most of the agencies discussed issue publications that have been distributed to depository libraries or furnish publications to LPS for cataloging and assignment of SuDocs classification author symbols. Federal advisory committees, as defined by the Federal Advisory Committee Act (FACA) as amended (86 Stat. 770), are discussed in chapter 6.

These independent agencies are grouped into the following categories: major independent agencies of the executive branch; other major independent agencies, corporations, and quasi-official agencies; major independent regulatory agencies; other regulatory and quasi-judicial agencies; financial regulatory agencies and corporations; independent agencies whose functions deal primarily with foreign affairs; and other independent entities, corporations, committees, and commissions.

Independent Agencies: Executive Branch

The major independent agencies of the executive branch are the Central Intelligence Agency, Environmental Protection Agency, General Services Administration, National Aeronautics and Space Administration, National Archives and Records Administration, Office of Personnel Management, Small Business Administration, and United States Postal Service.

Central Intelligence Agency

The Central Intelligence Agency (CIA) (PrEx 3) was established under the National Security Council by the National Security Act of 1947 (61 Stat. 495).[20] It now functions under that statute as amended; EO 12333 of December 4, 1981; and other edicts. The CIA collects, produces, and disseminates counterintelligence and foreign intelligence; conducts counterintelligence activities outside the United States and within the United States in coordination with the FBI; coordinates counterintelligence activities and the collection of information when conducted outside the United States by other departments and agencies; and conducts special operations approved by the president.

As the foregoing suggests, the CIA is but one of several intelligence-gathering agencies within the federal establishment, although the media attention the CIA is given obscures that fact. The CIA, however, publishes a number of useful unclassified reference works that are available through the depository library system, the sales program of the Superintendent of Documents, NTIS, and the Documents Expediting Project (DocEx). These include annual directories of officials of communist governments, the bimonthly *Chiefs of State and Cabinet Members of Foreign Governments* (PrEx 3.11/2), the highly regarded Maps and Atlases series (PrEx 3.10/4), and the annual *World Factbook* (PrEx 3.15). The last has been incorporated virtually word for word in a commercial publication titles *Nations of the World: A Factbook* (McLean, VA: Documents Index), a cautionary tale advising librarians to check carefully to ensure that they do not purchase materials already received free of charge through the depository system.

Environmental Protection Agency

The Environmental Protection Agency (EPA) (EP 1) was established in the executive branch as an independent agency pursuant to Reorganization Plan No. 3 of 1970, effective December 2, 1970. EPA endeavors to abate and control pollution systematically by properly integrating a variety of research, monitoring, standard setting, and enforcement activities in the areas of air, water, solid waste, pesticides, radiation, and toxic substances. EPA continues the functions formerly assigned to other agencies, primarily in the Department of Health, Education, and Welfare and the Department of the Interior. At headquarters, EPA has assistant administrators for administration and resources management; enforcement and compliance monitoring; policy, planning, and evaluation; external affairs; water; solid waste and emergency response; air and radiation; pesticides and toxic substances; and research and development, plus a general counsel and an inspection unit.

Under the assistant administrator for water are the Offices of Enforcement and Permits, Water Regulations and Standards, Municipal Pollution, Drinking Water, Marine and Estuarine Protection, Ground-Water Protection, and Wetlands Protection. The publications of offices under this assistant administrator are generally classed as EP 2. These offices continue the functions of the Federal Water Pollution Control Administration (FS 16), which was established in the Department of Health, Education, and Welfare by section 2 of the Water Quality Act of 1965 (70 Stat. 903). The administration was transferred to the Department of the Interior by Reorganization Plan No. 2 of February 18, 1966, effective May 1966. The name was changed to Federal Water Quality Administration pursuant to the Water Quality Improvement Act of 1970 (84 Stat. 113), effective April 3, 1970. The administration was transferred to EPA in December 1970 and renamed Office of Water Programs Operations.

Under the assistant administrator for solid waste and emergency response are the Offices of Solid Waste, Emergency and Remedial Response, Waste Programs Enforcement, and Underground Storage Tanks. The publications of offices under this assistant administrator are generally classed as EP 3. These offices continue the functions of the Bureau of Solid Waste Management (HE 20.1400) in DHEW.

Under the assistant administrator for air and radiation are the Offices of Air Quality Planning and Standards, Mobile Sources, and Radiation Programs. The publications of offices under this assistant administrator are generally classed as EP 4 (air) or EP 6 (radiation). These offices continue the functions of the National Air Pollution Control Administration (HE 20.1300) in DHEW and in part the functions of the Bureau of Radiological Health (HE 20.1400).

Under the assistant administrator for pesticides and toxic substances are the Office of Pesticide Programs, Toxic Substances, and Compliance Monitoring. The publications of offices under this assistant administrator are generally classed as EP 5. The Toxic Release Inventory (TRI) annual on CD-ROM was announced by LPS as ready for distribution in 1989, but delays were encountered. TRI annual issuances by state are sent to depository institutions on microfiche (EP 5.22). Problems bedeviled the microfiche distribution, however. The set of 1,038 second-generation silver reproducible fiche was sent to LPS in January 1990, but the quality was so poor that LPS was obliged to submit a "Notice of Quality Defect" and order the contractor to remedy the product. TRI's database is also available online via the National Library of Medicine's TOXNET system. An explanation of how to use the TRI on CD-ROM was published in *Administrative Notes*, vol. 12 (May 31, 1991), pp. 24-31.

General Services Administration

The General Services Administration (GSA) was established by section 101 of the Federal Property and Administrative Services Act of 1949 (63 Stat. 379), effective July 1, 1949, in response to the recommendations of the Committee on Organization of the Executive Branch of the Government ("first Hoover Commission"). The act transferred to the administration the functions of the following agencies: Office of Contract Settlement (T 67), including the Contract Settlement Act Advisory Board and the Contract Settlement Appeals Boards; Bureau of Federal Supply (T 58); Federal Works Agency (FW 1), including Bureau of Community Facilities (FW 7) and Public Roads Administration (FW 2); National Archives Establishment (AE 1); and War Assets Administration (Y 3.W19/8). The Bureau of Public Roads was transferred to the Department of Commerce by Reorganization Plan No. 7 of 1949, effective August 20, 1949, and was later transferred to the newly established Department of Transportation in 1966. The National Archives Establishment (later redesignated National Archives and Records Service) was reestablished as an independent agency in 1985 and renamed the National Archives and Records Administration.

The General Services Administration establishes policy and provides for the federal government a system for the management of its property and records, including construction and operation of buildings; procurement and distribution of supplies; utilization and disposal of property; transportation, traffic, and communications management; stockpiling of strategic materials; and the management of the government-wide automated data processing resources program. GSA consists of supporting staff offices and operating services. The support staff offices include the Office of Acquisition Policy, Office of Small and Disadvantaged Business Utilization, and GSA Board of Contract Appeals. The four GSA operating services are the Information Resources Management Service, Federal Supply Service, Public Buildings Service, and Federal Property Resource Services.

Information Resources Management Service. The Information Resources Management Service (IRMS) (GS 12) continues the Automated Data and Telecommunications Service, which was established in 1972 and renamed Office of Information Resources Management by GSA Order of August 17, 1982. IRMS is responsible for coordinating and directing a government-wide program for the management, procurement, and utilization of automated data processing (ADP) and telecommunications equipment and services; planning and directing programs for improving federal records and information management practices; and managing and operating the Federal Information Centers. IRMS administers major provisions of the Paperwork Reduction Act of 1980 regarding information resources management policy and the Brooks Act of 1965 regarding acquisition and use of ADP equipment. IRMS operates the Federal Telecommunications System (FTS), a comprehensive voice and low-speed data system. IRMS operates the seventy-two Federal Information Centers located in thirty-five states, which answer telephone calls or letters regarding federal government programs or agencies. Toll-free (800) service is provided in four states: Iowa, Kansas, Missouri, and Nebraska. IRMS publishes the *Federal Information Resources Management Regulations* (FIRMR) (GS 12.15:In3).

Office of Federal Supply and Services. The Federal Supply Services Office (FSS) (GS 2) continues the Bureau of Federal Supply (T 58), which was transferred from the Department of the Treasury upon the establishment of the General Services Administration. The bureau in turn traces its origins to the General Supply Committee (GS 1), which was established as an independent agency by EO 1071 of May 13, 1909, pursuant to an act of January 27, 1894 (28 Stat. 33). The committee was abolished when a new General Supply Committee (T 45) was established in the Treasury Department by an act of June 17, 1920 (36 Stat. 531).[21] The committee was abolished by EO 6166 of June 10, 1933, and its functions transferred to the Procurement Division (T 58). The name was changed to Bureau of Federal Supply by Departmental Order 73 of November 19, 1946, effective January 1, 1947.

The Federal Supply Services Office operates a worldwide supply system to contract for and distribute supplies, services, and personal property to federal civilian agencies. It had been named Office of Personal Property by GSA Order effective September 28, 1982, and later renamed Office of Federal Supply and Services by GSA Order of January 22, 1983. The service manages government-wide transportation and travel services and regulations, including transportation audits; operates a vehicle fleet program; and administers a government-wide property management program for the utilization of excess personal property and the donation and/or sale of surplus property. Its services are generally supplied only to federal civilian agencies and, with some exceptions, to the Department of Defense. FSS publishes *Federal Specifications* (GS 2.8), *Federal Standards* (GS 2.8/3), and the *GSA Supply Catalog* (GS 2.10/6).

National Aeronautics and Space Administration

The National Aeronautics and Space Administration (NASA) (NAS 1) was established by the National Aeronautics and Space Act of 1958 (72 Stat. 426). It continues the functions of the National Advisory Committee for Aeronautics (NACA) (Y 3.N21/5), which was established by an act of March 3, 1915 (38 Stat. 930), as well as some of the space activities of the Department of Defense. The principal statutory functions of NASA are to conduct research to solve problems of light within and outside the Earth's atmosphere and to develop, construct, test, and operate aeronautical and space vehicles; to conduct activities required for the exploration of space with manned and unmanned vehicles; and to arrange for the most effective utilization of the scientific and engineering resources of the United States in concert with other nations engaged in aeronautics and space activities for peaceful purposes.

NASA's principal field installations are Ames Research Center, Moffett Field, California; Goddard Space Flight Center, Greenbelt, Maryland; Jet Propulsion Laboratory, Pasadena, California; Lyndon B. Johnson Space Flight Center, Houston, Texas; John F. Kennedy Space Center, Cape Canaveral, Florida; Langley Research Center, Hampton, Virginia; Lewis Research Center, Cleveland, Ohio; George C. Marshall Space Flight Center, Huntsville, Alabama; and National Space Technology Laboratories, Bay St. Louis, Missouri. NASA technical publications are discussed in chapter 11.

National Archives and Records Administration

The National Archives and Records Administration (NARA) (AE 1) was established by an act of October 19, 1984 (98 Stat. 2280), effective April 1, 1985, as an independent agency in the executive branch. It continues the National Archives Establishment, which was created by an act of June 19, 1934 (48 Stat. 1122), and subsequently incorporated into the General Services Administration as the National Archives and Records Service (NARS) by section 104 of the Federal Property and Administrative Services Act of June 10, 1949. The major operating units of NARA are the Office of the National Archives, Office of Federal Record Centers, Office of Presidential Libraries, Office of Records Administration, and Office of the Federal Register. NARA also supports the National Archives Trust Fund Board and the National Historical Publications and Records Commission (NHPRC).

Office of the National Archives. The National Archives maintains the historically valuable records of the federal government. It arranges and preserves records and prepares inventories, guides, and other finding aids to facilitate their use. NARA makes original records available for use in research rooms in all of its facilities, answers oral and written requests for information, and, for a fee, provides copies of documents. Many important records are available through a microfilm publications program. Most records in NARA's custody are maintained in the National Archives Building and other facilities in the Washington, D.C., area. Records that are primarily of regional or local interest are maintained in eleven National Archives field branches located in Waltham, Massachusetts; Bayonne, New Jersey; Philadelphia; East Point, Georgia; Chicago; Kansas City, Missouri; Fort Worth, Texas; Denver, Colorado; San Bruno, California; Laguna Niguel, California; and Seattle, Washington.

Office of Presidential Libraries. Through the Presidential Libraries, which are located on sites selected by the presidents and built with private funds, NARA preserves and makes available for use the presidential records and personal papers of each president since Herbert Hoover. Presidential Libraries are located at West Branch, Iowa (Herbert Hoover); Hyde Park, New York (Franklin Roosevelt); Independence, Missouri (Harry Truman); Abilene, Kansas (Dwight Eisenhower); Boston (John Kennedy); Austin, Texas (Lyndon Johnson); Ann Arbor, Michigan (Gerald Ford); Atlanta, Georgia (Jimmy Carter); and Simi Valley, California (Ronald Reagan). The presidential records of Richard M. Nixon are being held at the NARA Pickett Street Annex in Alexandria, Virginia. Each library prepares documentary and descriptive publications and operates a museum (except that the Gerald R. Ford Museum is located in Grand Rapids, Michigan). Once considered personal papers, all presidential records created on or after January 20, 1981, are declared by law to be owned and controlled by the United States and are required to be transferred to NARA at the end of the administration pursuant to the Presidential Records Act of 1978 (92 Stat. 2423).

Office of Federal Records Centers. Federal agencies transfer their non-current records to thirteen Federal Records Centers in accordance with established disposition schedules. In addition to the eleven locations indicated above for National Archives field branches, records centers are also located at St. Louis, Missouri (National Personnel Records Center), and Suitland, Maryland (Washington National Records Center). The centers provide reference services on the materials and are responsible for disposing of records of transitory value and transferring those with enduring value to the National Archives.

Office of the Federal Register. The Office of the Federal Register (AE 2.100) was established within the National Archives by an act of July 26, 1935. When the independent National Archives and Records Administration was created in 1985, the publications of the Federal Register Office fell within its provenance. Important public documents and information sources prepared by the office include the public slip laws (AE 2.110), private slip laws (AE 2.110/2), *United States Statutes at Large* (AE 2.111);[22] the *Federal Register* (AE 2.106) and *Code of Federal Regulations* (AE 2.106/3); the *Weekly Compilation of Presidential Documents* (AE 2.109) and annual *Public Papers of the Presidents of the United States* (AE 2.114);[23] the *Codification of Presidential Proclamations and Executive Orders* (AE 2.113); and the *United States Government Manual* (AE 2.108/2). These publications are discussed elsewhere in this text.

National Historical Publications and Records Commission (NHPRC). NARA supports the initiatives of this statutory commission in making plans, estimates, and recommendations for historical works and in cooperating with and encouraging various nonfederal agencies and institutions in gathering and publishing papers and other documents important for the study of U.S. history. The commission awards grants to promote a variety of historically oriented projects, such as archival programs, documentary publications projects, and archival and editorial education. The name of the commission was changed from National Historical Publications Commission by an act of December 22, 1974 (88 Stat. 1734). NHPRC publishes *Historical Documentary Editions* (AE 1.110:H62), a catalog that lists publications that have been supported by the commission with funds or by formal endorsement.

Office of Personnel Management

The Office of Personnel Management (OPM) (PM 1) was created as an independent agency by Reorganization Plan No. 2 of 1978, effective January 1, 1979, pursuant to EO 12107 of December 28, 1978. Transferred to OPM were many functions of the former Civil Service Commission (CS 1), which had been created by an act of January 16, 1883. OPM's duties and authority are specified in the Civil Service Reform Act of 1978 (92 Stat. 1111), approved October 13, 1978. The Office of Personnel Management administers a merit system for federal civilian employment, which includes recruiting, training, and promoting people on the basis of their knowledge, skills, and training without regard to their race, religion, sex, political influence, or other nonmerit factors. OPM publishes the *Federal Personnel Manual* (PM 1.14), which is kept up-to-date by looseleaf page changes, bulletins, and circulars. It publishes the monthly *Personnel Literature* (PM 1.16) and *Index to Information* (PM 1.44), the latter designed to satisfy many Freedom of Information Act inquiries.

Small Business Administration

The Small Business Administration (SBA) (SBA 1) was created by the Small Business Act of 1953 (67 Stat. 232) and derives its present authority from the Small Business Act (15 U.S.C. 631). The fundamental purposes of the SBA are to aid, counsel, assist, and protect the interests of small businesses; to ensure that small business concerns receive a fair portion of government purchases, contracts, and subcontracts, as well as of the sales of government property; to make loans to small business concerns, state and local development companies, and the victims of floods or other catastrophes or of certain types of economic injury; and to license, regulate, and make loans to small business investment companies. Attempts were made—unsuccessively—during the Reagan administration to abolish the Small Business Administration. Series such as Small Business Management (SBA 1.12), Management Aids for Small Manufacturers (SBA 1.10), Starting and Managing (SBA 1.15), and Starting Out (SBA 1.35) are heavily used publications in public and other types of libraries.

United States Postal Service

The United States Postal Service (USPS) (P 1) was created as an independent establishment of the executive branch by the Postal Reorganization Act approved August 12, 1970 (84 Stat. 719), with its operations commencing July 1, 1971. It traces its origins to the Office of the Postmaster General, created by an act of September 22, 1789, which continued the Postal Service created by the Continental Congress on July 26, 1775. The Post Office Department was established as an executive department by an act of June 8, 1972 (17 Stat. 283), and was replaced by the United States Postal Service in 1971. USPS provides mail processing and delivery services to individuals and businesses within the United States. It has more than 780,000 employees and handles more than 147 billion pieces of mail annually. In addition to the national headquarters, there are regional and field division offices supervising almost 40,000 post office branches, stations, and community post offices throughout the United States. USPS annually publishes the *National Zip Code and Post Office Directory* (P 1.10/8).

Other Independent Agencies and Corporations

National Foundation on the Arts
and the Humanities

The National Foundation (NF 1) was created as an independent agency by an act of 1965 (79 Stat. 845). The foundation consists of a National Endowment for the Arts, a National Endowment for the Humanities, a Federal Council on the Arts and the Humanities, and an Institute of Museum Services. Each endowment has its own council, composed of the endowment chairperson and twenty-six other members appointed by the president. The Federal Council on the Arts and Humanities consists of twenty members, including the two endowment chairpersons and the director of the Institute of Museum Services, and is designed to coordinate the activities of the two endowments and related programs of other federal agencies.

The National Endowment for the Arts (NF 2) awards grants to individuals, state and regional arts agencies, and nonprofit organizations representing the highest quality in the fields of design arts, dance, expansion arts, folk arts, literature, media arts (film, radio, and television), museums, music, opera-musical theater, theater, and the visual arts. Its *Annual Report* (NF 2.1) contains a comprehensive list of grants that were awarded during the year. It also publishes the monthly periodical *Artifacts* (NF 2.14).

The National Endowment for the Humanities (NF 3) makes grants to individuals, groups, and institutions to increase understanding and appreciation of the humanities including the following areas: language, both modern and classical; linguistics; literature; history; jurisprudence; philosophy; archaeology; comparative religion; ethics; the history, criticism, and theory of the arts; and those aspects of the social sciences that have humanistic content and employ humanistic methods. Its *Annual Report* (NF 3.1) contains a comprehensive list of grants that were awarded during the year. It also publishes the bimonthly periodical *Humanities* (NF 3.11).

The Institute of Museum Services (NF 4) was established by an act of June 23, 1972 (86 Stat. 327). It was transferred to the Office of Educational Research and Improvement within the Department of Education by an act of October 17, 1979 (93 Stat. 678), effective May 4, 1980. By an act of December 23, 1981 (95 Stat. 1414), the institute was established as an independent agency within the National Foundation on the Arts and the Humanities. The institute awards grants to support the efforts of museums to conserve the nation's heritage, to maintain and expand their educational programs, and to ease their financial burdens.

National Science Foundation

The National Science Foundation (NSF) (NS 1) was established by the National Science Foundation Act of 1950 (64 Stat. 149) and was given additional authority by the Science and Engineering Equal Opportunities Act (94 Stat. 3010) and Title I of the Education for Economic Security Act (99 Stat. 893). NSF initiates and supports fundamental, long-term research in all the scientific and engineering disciplines through grants, contracts, and other agreements to universities and to nonprofit and other research organizations. It supports major national and international science and engineering activities, including the U.S. Antarctic Program and the Ocean Drilling Programs. It assesses the status and health of science and its various disciplines on such matters as national resources and manpower. It publishes a bimonthly periodical, *Mosaic* (NS 1.29), and the quarterly *Antarctic Journal of the United States* (NS 1.26). It also publishes statistical reports in the Surveys of Science Resources series (NS 1.22) and the annual *Federal Funds for Research, Development, and Other Scientific Activities* (NS 1.18).

Smithsonian Institution

The Smithsonian Institution (SI 1) was created by an act of August 10, 1846 (9 Stat. 102), under the terms of the will of James Smithson of London, England, who in 1829 bequeathed his fortune to the United States to found, at Washington, D.C., under the name of the "Smithsonian Institution," an establishment for the "increase and diffusion of knowledge among men." The institution, an independent trust establishment, performs fundamental research; publishes the results of studies, explorations, and investigations; preserves for study and reference over 100 million items of scientific, cultural, and historical interest; and maintains exhibits representative of the arts, U.S. history, technology, aeronautics and space exploration, and natural history. It is administered by a Board of Regents under the executive direction of the secretary. The Secretary's Management Committee includes assistant secretaries for research, museums, public service, and administration.

Under the secretary for museums are the major museums of the institution, including the Anacostia Museum; Arthur M. Sackler Museum (Near Eastern and Asian Art); Cooper-Hewitt Museum, the Smithsonian Institution's National Museum of Design located in New York City; Freer Gallery of Art (collections of oriental art) (SI 7); Hirschhorn Museum and Sculpture Garden (collections of modern art and sculpture) (SI 13); National Museum of African Art (SI 14); National Air and Space Museum (SI 9); National Museum of American Art (SI 6); National Museum of American History (SI 3); National Museum of Natural History (SI 3); and National Portrait Gallery (SI 11). Catalogs of major exhibitions by these museums are usually distributed to depository libraries.

The National Zoological Park is under the supervision of the assistant secretary for research. Three independent bureaus of the Smithsonian Institution operate under separate boards of directors: the John F. Kennedy Center for the Performing Arts (SI 10), the National Gallery of Art (SI 8), and the Woodrow Wilson International Center for Scholars (SI 12).

The Smithsonian Institution publishes several numbered series of research publications, including Smithsonian Contributions to the Earth Sciences (SI 1.26), Smithsonian Contributions to Zoology (SI 1.27), Smithsonian Studies in History and Technology (SI 1.28), and Smithsonian Contributions to Anthropology (SI 1.33). The institution also is publishing a twenty-volume set, *Handbook of North American Indians* (SI 1.20/2).

United States International Trade Commission

The United States International Trade Commission (USITC) (ITC 1) is an independent agency created by an act of September 9, 1916 (39 Stat. 795), and originally named the United States Tariff Commission (TC 1). The name was changed by section 171 of the Trade Act of 1974, approved January 3, 1975 (88 Stat. 2009).[24] The commission's present powers and duties are provided largely by the Tariff Act of 1930, the Trade Expansion Act of 1962, the Trade Act of 1974, and the Trade Agreements Act of 1979. The commission furnishes studies, reports, and recommendations involving international trade and tariffs to the president, the Congress, and other government agencies. It annually publishes the *Tariff Schedules of the United States Annotated* (ITC 1.10).

Independent Regulatory Agencies

In this section are the major independent regulatory agencies of the federal government: Consumer Product Safety Commission (CPSC), Federal Communications Commission (FCC), Federal Trade Commission (FTC), Interstate Commerce Commission (ICC), Nuclear Regulatory Commission (NRC), and the Securities and Exchange Commission (SEC). They all issue regulations in the *Federal Register* with which industries and companies affected must comply. Most of them require a company to register with the agency before that company can operate in the industries that the agency regulates (FCC, ICC, NRC, and SEC). Most of them also have quasi-judicial powers by which they hold hearings on violations of their regulations and issue decisions that legally affect the parties involved (FCC, FTC, ICC, NRC, and SEC).

Consumer Product Safety Commission

The Consumer Product Safety Commission (CPSC) (Y 3.C76/3) was established as an independent regulatory agency by the Consumer Product Safety Act, approved October 27, 1972 (86 Stat. 1207). The commission also administers the Flammable Fabrics Act (67 Stat. 111); Poison Prevention Packaging Act of 1970 (84 Stat. 1670); Federal Hazardous Substances Act (74 Stat. 372); and Act of August 2, 1956 (70 Stat. 953), which prohibits the transportation of refrigerators without door safety devices. The commission develops uniform safety standards for consumer products and promotes research and investigation into the causes and prevention of product-related deaths, illnesses, and injuries. CPSC publishes various pamphlets dealing with unsafe products and operates a toll-free Consumer Product Safety Hotline, 800-638-CPSC.

Federal Communications Commission

The Federal Communications Commission (FCC) (CC 1) was created by the Communications Act of 1934 (48 Stat. 1064) to regulate interstate and foreign communications by wire and radio in the public interest. It was assigned additional regulatory jurisdiction under the Communications Satellite Act of 1962 (76 Stat. 419). The scope of its regulation includes radio and television broadcasting; telephone, telegraph, and cable television operation; two-way radio and radio operators; and satellite communications. The FCC continues the Federal Radio Commission, which was established by act of February 23, 1927 (44 Stat. 1162). The commission was abolished by act of June 19, 1934 (48 Stat. 1102), and its functions transferred to the FCC. In 1987, the Federal Communications Commission discontinued the *FCC Reports* (CC 1.12) as the commission's official published record of decisions and replaced it with the biweekly *FCC Record* (CC 1.12/3).

Federal Trade Commission

The Federal Trade Commission (FTC) (FT 1) was established by the Federal Trade Commission Act of September 26, 1914 (38 Stat. 717). The principal functions of the commission are to promote competition in or affecting commerce through the prevention of trade restraints and other unfair methods of competition; to safeguard the public by preventing the dissemination of false or deceptive advertising of consumer products; to promote truthful labeling of textile and fur products; to regulate packaging and labeling of certain consumer commodities; to achieve true credit cost disclosure; and to protect consumers against circulation of inaccurate or obsolete credit reports.

Interstate Commerce Commission

The Interstate Commerce Commission (ICC) (IC 1) was created as an independent regulatory agency by the Act to Regulate Commerce of February 4, 1887 (24 Stat. 379), now known as the Interstate Commerce Act. The commission's authority has been strengthened and its jurisdiction broadened by subsequent legislation, such as the Hepburn Act, the Panama Canal Act, the Motor Carrier Act of 1935, and the Transportation Acts of 1920, 1940, and 1958. ICC's responsibilities include regulating carriers engaged in surface transportation in interstate commerce and in foreign commerce to the extent that such transportation takes place within the United States. Affected areas include railroads, trucking companies, bus lines, freight forwarders, water carriers, transportation brokers, and a coal slurry pipeline.

With the enactment of the Railroad Revitalization and Regulatory Reform Act of 1976 (90 Stat. 31), the commission's statutory mandate was altered to provide for less regulation of freight rates and practices. This fundamental shift in transportation policy was reinforced by enactment of the Motor Carrier Act of 1980 (94 Stat. 793), the Staggers Rail Act of 1980 (94 Stat. 1895), the Household Goods Transportation Act of 1980 (94 Stat. 2011), and the Bus Regulatory Reform Act of 1982 (96 Stat. 1102). These measures provided for a sharply reduced federal role in regulating the trucking, railroad, and bus industries. ICC publishes the annual *Transportation Statistics in the United States* (IC 1.25) and the *Interstate Commerce Commission Reports*, 2d series (IC 1.6/10).

Nuclear Regulatory Commission

The Nuclear Regulatory Commission (NRC) (Y 3.N88) was established as an independent regulatory agency under the provisions of the Emergency Reorganization Act of 1974 (88 Stat. 1242) and EO 11834 of January 15, 1975, effective January 19, 1975. Transferred to NRC were all licensing and related regulatory functions formerly assigned to the Atomic Energy Commission (AEC), which was established by the Atomic Energy Act of 1946 (60 Stat. 755). Major NRC components are the Office of Nuclear Reactor Regulation, Office of Nuclear Material Safety and Standards, and Office of Nuclear Regulatory Research. NRC licenses persons and companies to build and operate nuclear reactors and other facilities and to own and use nuclear materials. It makes rules and sets standards for these types of licenses. The commission also inspects the activities of the licensees to ensure that they do not violate the safety rules of the commission. NRC maintains approximately 100 Local Public Document Rooms around the country, which are usually located in cities and towns near proposed or actual nuclear plant sites. It publishes the monthly *Title List of Documents Made Publicly Available* (Y 3.N88:21-2).

Securities and Exchange Commission

The Securities and Exchange Commission (SEC) (SE 1) was created under authority of the Securities Exchange Act of 1934 (48 Stat. 881) and was organized on July 2, 1934. The commission is vested with quasi-judicial powers. The act requires issuers of securities making public offerings to register them with the SEC. The act assigns to the SEC broad regulatory responsibilities over the security markets, the self-regulatory organizations within the securities industry, and persons conducting a business in securities. The SEC also regulates mutual funds and other investment companies, investment counselors and advisors, and the securities of companies controlling electric or gas utilities. The commission publishes the weekly *SEC Docket* (SE 1.29), the daily *SEC News Digest* (SE 1.25/12), the *SEC Monthly Statistical Review* (SE 1.20), and the monthly *Official Summary of Security Transactions and Holdings* (SE 1.9). The Electronic Data Gathering, Analysis, and Retrieval (EDGAR) disclosure system of the SEC provides access to information filed by registrants whose activities fall under the regulatory authority of the commission.

Other Regulatory and Quasi-Judicial Agencies

In this section are discussed other independent regulatory agencies that in most cases also have quasi-judicial powers and issue decisions. These include the Equal Employment Opportunity Commission, Federal Labor Relations Authority, Federal Maritime Commission, National Labor Relations Board, and Occupational Safety and Health Review Commission. Most of these agencies issue regulations implementing legislation dealing with labor-management relations, in both the private and public sectors, and with conditions of employment and work, both broadly in all industries and in specific industry groups.

Equal Employment Opportunity Commission

The Equal Employment Opportunity Commission (EEOC) (Y 3.Eq2) was created by Title VII of the Civil Rights Act of 1964 (78 Stat. 253) and became operational July 2, 1965. The purposes of the EEOC are to eliminate discrimination based on race, color, religion, sex, national origin, or age in hiring, promoting, firing, wages, testing, training, apprenticeship, and all other terms of employment. EEOC also has oversight responsibility for all compliance and enforcement activities relating to equal employment opportunity among federal employees and applicants, including handicap discrimination. The commission receives charges or complaints, makes investigations, and may bring suit in federal district courts. The EEOC is also a major publisher of data on the employment status of minorities and women, based on information obtained in six ongoing employment surveys.

Federal Labor Relations Authority

The Federal Labor Relations Authority (FLRA) (Y 3.F31/21-3) was established as an independent agency by Reorganization Plan No. 2 of 1978, effective January 1, 1979, pursuant to EO 12107 of December 28, 1978, to supersede the Federal Labor Relations Council (Y 3.F31/21), which was established by EO 10491 of October 29, 1969. FLRA administers Title VII of the Civil Service Reform Act of 1978 (92 Stat. 1191), which protects the right of federal government civilian employees to organize, bargain collectively, and participate in labor organizations. The FLRA includes the Federal Services Impasses Panel, which provides assistance in resolving negotiation impasses between federal agencies and unions.

Federal Maritime Commission

The Federal Maritime Commission (FMC) (FMC 1) was established by Reorganization Plan No. 7 of 1961, effective August 12, 1961, as an independent agency. It administers functions and discharges regulatory authorities under the following statutes: Shipping Act of 1984 (98 Stat. 67), Shipping Act of 1916 (39 Stat. 728), Merchant Marine Act of 1920 (41 Stat. 988), Intercoastal Shipping Act of 1933 (47 Stat. 1425), and Merchant Marine Act of 1936 (49 Stat. 1985). The FMC regulates the waterborne foreign and domestic offshore commerce of the United States, assures that U.S. international trade is open to all nations on fair and equitable terms, and protects against unauthorized, concerted activity in the waterborne commerce of the United States.

National Labor Relations Board

The National Labor Relations Board (NLRB) (LR 1) is an independent agency created by the National Labor Relations Act of 1935 (Wagner Act) (49 Stat. 449), as amended by an act of June 23, 1947 (Taft-Hartley Act) (61 Stat. 136), and an act of September 14, 1959 (Landrum-Griffin Act). The NLRB has two principal functions: (1) preventing and remedying unfair labor practices by employers and labor organizations or their agents and (2) conducting secret ballot elections among employees in appropriate collective-bargaining units to decide whether or not they desire to be represented by a labor organization. In unfair labor practice cases, the general counsel has final authority to investigate charges, issue complaints, and prosecute such complaints before the NLRB. The NLRB publishes a *Weekly Summary of N.L.R.B. Cases* (LR 1.15/2), the monthly *N.L.R.B. Election Reports* (LR 1.16), *Decisions and Orders of the National Labor Relations Board* (LR 1.8), and *Court Decisions Relating to the National Labor Relations Act* (LR 1.14).

Occupational Safety and
Health Review Commission

The Occupational Safety and Health Review Commission (OSHRC) (Y 3.Oc1) is an independent quasi-judicial agency established by the Occupational Safety and Health Act of 1970 (84 Stat. 1590). The OSHRC is charged with ruling on cases forwarded to it by the Department of Labor when disagreements arise over the results of safety and health inspections performed by the Occupational Safety and Health Administration (OSHA). The OSHRC publishes its *Decisions* (Y 3.Oc1:10-2), which are subject to review by the United States Courts of Appeal.

Financial Regulatory Agencies
and Corporations

Commodity Futures Trading Commission

The Commodity Futures Trading Commission (CFTC) (Y 3.C73/5) was established as an independent agency by the Commodity Futures Trading Commission Act of 1974 (88 Stat. 1389), superseding the Commodity Exchange Authority in the Department of Agriculture (A 85), which was abolished. The CFTC regulates trading on the eleven U.S. futures exchanges that offer futures and options contracts. It also regulates the activities of numerous commodity exchange members, public brokerage houses, commission-registered futures industry salespeople and associated persons, commodity trading advisors, and commodity pool operators. Futures contracts for agricultural commodities were traded in the United States for more than 100 years before futures trading was diversified to include trading in contracts for precious metals, raw materials, foreign currencies, commercial interest rates, and securities.

Federal Deposit Insurance Corporation

The Federal Deposit Insurance Corporation (FDIC) (Y 3.F31/8) was organized under authority of section 12B of the Federal Reserve Act of June 16, 1933 (48 Stat. 162). By act of September 21, 1950 (64 Stat. 873), section 12B of the Federal Reserve Act, as amended, was withdrawn and made a separate law known as the Federal Depository Insurance Act. The act also made numerous amendments to the former deposit insurance statutes. The FDIC insures, up to the statutory limit ($100,000 per depositor), the deposits in national banks, in state banks that are members of the Federal Reserve System, and in state banks that apply for Federal Deposit Insurance and meet certain prescribed qualifications.

Federal Home Loan Bank Board

The Federal Home Loan Bank Board (FHLB) (FHL 1) was established by the acts of July 22, 1932 (47 Stat. 725), June 13, 1933 (48 Stat. 128), and June 27, 1934 (48 Stat. 1246). Under Reorganization Plan No. 1 of 1939, effective July 1, 1939, the board was transferred to the Federal Loan Agency (FL 3). Under EO 9070 of February 24, 1942, the board was transferred to the National Housing Agency and redesignated the Federal Home Loan Bank Administration (NHA 3). The administration was abolished by Reorganization Plan No. 3 of 1947, effective July 27, 1947, and its functions transferred to the Home Loan Bank Board (HH 4) within the Housing and Home Finance Agency. Under the Housing Amendments of 1955 (69 Stat. 640), the board was made an independent agency and redesignated the Federal Home Loan Bank Board. The FHLB supervises and regulates savings institutions that specialize in the financing of residential real estate. It operates the Federal Savings and Loan Insurance Corporation (FSLIC) and directs the Federal Home Loan Bank System.

Federal Reserve System

The Federal Reserve System (FR 1) was established by the Federal Reserve Act of December 3, 1913 (38 Stat. 251). The system consists of six parts: the Board of Governors in Washington, D.C.; the twelve Federal Reserve Banks and their twenty-five branches and other facilities located throughout the country; the Federal Open Market Committee; the Federal Advisory Council; the Consumer Advisory Council; and the nation's financial institutions, including commercial banks, savings and loan associations, mutual savings banks, and credit unions. Federal Reserve System publications that are generally available are those published by the Board of Governors, including the *Federal Reserve Bulletin* (FR 1.3) and a number of periodical statistical releases. Unfortunately, some of these publications, such as the *Savings and Loan Financial Source Book* and the *Federal Reserve Bulletin*, are no longer available to depository libraries, according to the September 1991 edition of the *List of Classes*.

National Credit Union Administration

The National Credit Union Administration (NCUA) (NCU 1) was established by an act of March 10, 1970 (85 Stat. 49), and reorganized by an act of November 19, 1978 (92 Stat. 3641), as an independent agency in the executive branch. The Federal Credit Union System was established by an act of June 26, 1934 (48 Stat. 1216), to be administered by the Farm Credit Administration. It was transferred to the Federal Deposit Insurance Corporation by EO 9148 of April 27, 1942, and Reorganization Plan No. 1 of 1947, effective July 1, 1947. The functions were transferred to the Bureau of Federal Credit Unions (FS 3.300; HE 3.300), which was established within the Federal Security Agency by act of June 29, 1948, and placed within the Social Security Administration by agency order. The bureau was abolished and its functions transferred to NCUA in 1970. NCUA grants federal credit union charters to eligible groups. It conducts annual examinations of federal credit unions (FCUs) to determine their solvency and their compliance with laws and regulations. It operates the National Credit Union Share Insurance Fund (NCUSIF), in which individual accounts are insured up to $100,000 in FCUs, as well as in state-chartered credit unions that apply and qualify for insurance. NCUA issues an annual *Credit Union Directory* (NCU 1.16) listing all federal credit unions.

Independent Agencies — Foreign Affairs

This category includes the following independent agencies whose functions deal primarily with foreign affairs: Board for International Broadcasting, National Advisory Council on International Monetary and Financial Policies, Peace Corps, U.S. Arms Control and Disarmament Agency, U.S. Information Agency, and the U.S. International Development Cooperation Agency.

Board for International Broadcasting

The Board for International Broadcasting (Y 3.B78) was established as an independent federal agency by the International Broadcasting Act of 1973 (87 Stat. 456). The board consists of nine private sector members distinguished in the field of foreign policy or mass communications and is served by a permanent executive staff. The board oversees the operations of Radio Liberty, which broadcasts to the former Soviet Union, and Radio Free Europe, which broadcasts to Poland, Romania, Czechoslovakia, Hungary, Bulgaria, and the Baltic States.

National Advisory Council on International Monetary and Financial Policies

The National Advisory Council on International Monetary and Financial Policies (Y 3.N21/16) was established originally as a statutory body by the Bretton Woods Agreements Act, approved July 31, 1945, and was later defined in EO 10033 of February 8, 1949. The council was reestablished as the National Advisory Council on International Monetary and Financial Policies by EO 11269 of February 14, 1966. Its annual report, *International Finance* (Y 3.N21/16:1) includes an account of U.S. participation in the International Monetary Fund and multilateral development banks during the year.

Peace Corps

The Peace Corps (PE 1) was established within the State Department (S 19) by EO 10924 of March 1, 1961, and continued by the Peace Corps Act of 1961 (75 Stat. 612) and EO 11041 of August 6, 1962. It was transferred to ACTION by Reorganization Plan No. 1 of 1971, effective July 1, 1971 (AA 4). It was made an independent agency in the executive branch by Title VI of the International Security and Development Cooperation Act of 1981 (95 Stat. 1540). The Peace Corps consists of a Washington, D.C., headquarters; three regional recruitment centers supporting sixteen area offices; and overseas operations in more than sixty countries. Thousands of volunteers serve throughout Latin America, Africa, the Near East, and the Pacific working primarily in the areas of agriculture/rural development, small business assistance, health, and education.

United States Arms Control and Disarmament Agency

The United States Arms Control and Disarmament Agency (ACDA) (AC 1) was established by an act of September 26, 1961 (75 Stat. 631). The ACDA conducts studies and provides advice relating to arms control and disarmament policy formulation; prepares for and manages U.S. participation in international negotiations in the arms control and disarmament field; and prepares for, operates, or, as needed, directs U.S. participation in international control systems that may result from arms control and disarmament activities. The ACDA annually publishes *Documents on Disarmament* (AC 1.11/2) and *World Military Expenditures and Arms Transfers* (AC 1.16).

United States Information Agency

The United States Information Agency (USIA) (IA 1) was established by Reorganization Plan No. 8 of 1953, effective August 1, 1953, pursuant to EO 10477 of August 1, 1953. It was abolished by Reorganization Plan No. 2 of 1977, pursuant to EO 12048 of March 27, 1978, and its functions transferred to the International Communication Agency (ICA 1), effective April 1, 1978. The name was changed back to United States Information Agency by an act of August 24, 1982 (97 Stat. 291). The basic legislative authorities for USIA activities are the United States Information and Cultural Exchange Act of 1948 (62 Stat. 2), which authorizes the dissemination abroad of information about the United States, and the Mutual Educational and Cultural Exchange Act of 1961 (75 Stat. 527), which authorizes educational and cultural exchanges between the United States and other countries as well as participation in international affairs and exhibitions abroad. USIA operates the Voice of America, which produces and broadcasts radio programs in English and 42 foreign languages for overseas audiences. It maintains 206 posts in 127 countries overseas. One of the better known periodicals issued by USIA is the bimonthly *Problems of Communism* (IA 1.8), which provides background information and scholarly analyses on various aspects of world communism.

United States International Development Cooperation Agency

The United States International Development Cooperation Agency (IDCA) was established by Reorganization Plan No. 2 of 1979, effective October 1, 1979, to be a focal point within the U.S. government for economic matters affecting U.S. relations with developing countries. IDCA includes the Agency for International Development, the Trade and Development Program, and the Overseas Private Investment Corporation. IDCA has lead budget and policy responsibility for the United Nations (U.N.) and the Organization of American States (OAS) development programs. IDCA shares responsibility with the Department of the Treasury for U.S. participation in the multilateral development banks (the World Bank Group and regional development banks) and with the Department of Agriculture for the Food for Peace Program (Public Law 480).

The Agency for International Development (AID) (S 18) was established by State Department Delegation of Authority 104 of November 3, 1961, as an agency within the Department of State pursuant to EO 10973 of November 3, 1961. It was transferred by Reorganization Plan No. 2 of 1979 and continued as an agency in IDCA by IDCA Delegation of Authority 1 of October 1, 1979.[25] AID directs U.S. foreign and economic assistance operations in more than sixty countries primarily under authority of the Foreign Assistance Act of 1961, as amended (75 Stat. 424), and the Agricultural Trade Development and Assistance Act of 1954, as amended (66 Stat. 1691).

The Overseas Private Investment Corporation (OPIC) (OP 1) was established as an independent agency by an act of December 30, 1969 (83 Stat. 805). OPIC offers U.S. investors assistance in finding investment opportunities in over 100 developing countries and provides insurance to protect their investments as well as loans and loan guarantees to help finance their projects.[26]

Other Independent Agencies, Corporations, Committees, Etc.

This final category includes other independent agencies, corporations, committees, commissions, and boards that do not fall into any of the categories above.

ACTION

ACTION (AA 1) was created as an independent agency under provisions of Reorganization Plan No. 1 of 1971, effective July 1, 1971, and EO 11603 of June 30, 1971, with legislative authority provided by the Domestic Volunteer Service Act of 1973, as amended (87 Stat. 394). ACTION includes Volunteers in Service to America (VISTA), the Foster Grandparent Program (FGP), the Retired Senior Volunteer Program (RSVP), the Senior Companion Program (SCP), the Volunteer Management Support Program (VMSP), the Demonstration Grant Program, the Mini-Grant Program, the Technical Assistance Program, and State Office of Voluntarism Program. ACTION consists of a Washington, D.C., headquarters and nine regional offices supporting forty-five individual state offices and Puerto Rico. ACTION is the principal agency in the federal government for administering volunteer service programs.

Administrative Conference of the United States

The Administrative Conference of the United States (Y 3.Ad6) was established as a permanent independent agency by the Administrative Conference Act of 1964. The statutory provisions prescribing the organization and activities of the conference are based in part upon the experience of two temporary conferences called by the president in 1953 and 1961, each of which operated for eighteen months. The conference consists of a chairman, a ten-member council, and membership. The membership is composed of forty-four high-level officials from thirty-seven departments and agencies and thirty-six private sector lawyers, university faculty, and other specialists in law and government. The membership is divided into six committees covering adjudication, administration, governmental processes, judicial review, regulation, and rulemaking. The entire membership meets at least once (but usually twice) in plenary session (the "Assembly") each year to consider recommendations of the committees. *Recommendations and Reports of the Administrative Conference* appear in Title 1, part 305, of the *Code of Federal Regulations* and are also published separately (Y 3.Ad6:9). A seminal publication issued by the conference is *A Guide to Federal Agency Rulemaking*, 2nd edition (1991) (Y 3.Ad6:8R86/991).

Advisory Commission on Intergovernmental Relations

The Advisory Commission on Intergovernmental Relations (Y 3.Ad9/8) was established by an act of September 24, 1959 (73 Stat. 703), as amended by an act of November 2, 1966 (80 Stat. 1162). The commission is one of the best sources for scholarly commentary on federalism. In addition, it publishes *A Catalog of Federal Grant-in-Aid Programs to State and Local Governments* (Y 3.Ad9/8:20).

American Battle Monuments Commission

The American Battle Monuments Commission (Y 3.Am3) was created by an act of March 4, 1923 (42 Stat. 1509). The commission is responsible for designing, constructing, and maintaining permanent federal military cemeteries and memorials on foreign soil, as well as certain memorials on U.S. soil. The commission has three regional offices. The European Office in Garches, France, administers cemeteries in France, England, and the Benelux countries. The Mediterranean Office in Rome, Italy, administers cemeteries in Italy and Tunisia. The Manila Office administers cemeteries in the Philippines.[27]

Appalachian Regional Commission

The Appalachian Regional Commission (Y 3.Ap4/2) was established by the Appalachian Regional Development Act of 1965 (79 Stat. 5) to develop plans for and coordinate the comprehensive programs for regional economic development authorized by the act. The commission consists of the governors of the thirteen-state Appalachian region (which includes parts of Alabama, Georgia, Kentucky, Maryland, Mississippi, New York, North Carolina, Ohio, Pennsylvania, South Carolina, Tennessee, Virginia, and all of West Virginia), a permanent federal co-chairperson, and a state co-chairperson who serves a one-year term. The commission publishes an *Annual Report* (Y 3.Ap4/2:1) and the journal *Appalachia* (Y 3.Ap4/2:9-2).

Commission on Civil Rights

The Commission on Civil Rights (CR 1) was created by the Civil Rights Act of 1957 (71 Stat. 634) and reestablished by the United States Commission on Civil Rights Act of 1983 (97 Stat. 1301). The commission holds public hearings and collects and studies information on discrimination or denials of equal protection of the laws either because of race, color, religion, sex, age, handicap, or national origin or in the administration of justice. The commission makes findings of fact and submits recommendations to the president and the Congress, but has no enforcement authority. The commission irregularly publishes *Catalog of Publications* (CR 1.9).

Federal Election Commission

The Federal Election Commission (FEC) (Y 3.El2/3) is an independent agency established by section 309 of the Federal Election Campaign Act Amendments of 1974 (88 Stat. 1280). It administers and enforces the Federal Election Campaign Act of 1971, as amended, and the Revenue Act, which are contained in Titles 2 and 26 of the *United States Code*. These laws provide for the public funding of presidential elections, public disclosure of financial activities of political committees involved in federal elections, and limitations and prohibitions on contributions and expenditures made to influence federal elections.

National Commission on Libraries and Information Science

The National Commission on Libraries and Information Science (Y 3.L61) was established by an act of July 20, 1970 (Public Law 91-345; 84 Stat. 440). Its activities are prominently discussed in the professional literature.

Panama Canal Commission

The Panama Canal Commission (Y 3.P19/2) was established as an independent agency by the Panama Canal Act of 1979 (93 Stat. 452), effective October 1, 1979, to carry out the responsibilities of the United States with respect to the Panama Canal Treaty of 1977. Under the treaty, the commission manages, operates, and maintains the canal, its complementary works, installations, and equipment and provides for the orderly transit of vessels through the canal. It will perform these functions until the treaty terminates on December 31, 1999, at which time the Republic of Panama will assume full responsibility for the canal. Its *Annual Report* (Y 3.P19/2:1) provides statistical data on traffic through the canal.

President's Committee on
Employment of the Handicapped

The President's Committee on Employment of the Handicapped (PrEx 1.10) was established by EO 10994 of February 14, 1962, superseding the President's Committee on Employment of the Physically Handicapped. The latter was established by EO 10640 of October 10, 1955, continuing the committee established by act of July 11, 1949 (63 Stat. 409).

Many of these "quasi-official agencies" are required by statute to submit an annual or fiscal year report to Congress. The list of agencies required to do so is issued annually as a House document later incorporated into the United States Congressional Serial Set. Each entity is listed with its required statutory authority and expected date of report. One example serves to illustrate:

NATIONAL COMMISSION ON LIBRARIES AND INFORMATION SCIENCE

Report of activities...Pub.L. 91-345, § 5(a) (7). Annually by Jan. 31[28]

NOTES

[1]"When Programs Don't Fit Anywhere in the Cabinet, This Is Where They Go," *The Washington Post*, December 18, 1978, p. A10.

[2]William H. Jones, "Commerce—A Post without Pizzazz," *The Washington Post*, October 5, 1979, p. E1.

[3]U.S. Department of Commerce (DOC), Office of the Secretary, *From Lighthouses to Laserbeams: A History of the U.S. Department of Commerce, 1913-1988* (Washington, DC: GPO, 1988), pp. 35-67. Pages 27-31 provide a chronology of the most significant organizational changes, including transfers to and from the department. On pages 72-79 are brief biographies and portraits of the secretaries of commerce from 1913 to 1988.

[4]The genealogy of the various agencies within the Department of Commerce may be constructed from the tables and agency entries in John L. Andriot, *Guide to U.S. Government Publications* (McLean, VA: Documents Index).

[5]DOC, *From Lighthouses to Laserbeams*, p. 56.

[6]DOC, *From Lighthouses to Laserbeams*, pp. 62-63.

[7]See *Administrative Notes*, 11 (November 30, 1990): 2; *Administrative Notes*, 13 (April 15, 1992): 6.

[8]*Price List 36*, Winter 1992, pp. 24, 39.

[9]SuDocs classification author symbol FS 5 was continued in use from 1953 to 1969, when symbol HE 5 was adopted.

[10]For the period 1972-1975 the Office of Education's publications continued to be assigned to the HE 5 SuDocs class.

[11]From 1972 to 1975 SuDocs class HE 18 was used for the National Institute of Education.

[12]From 1972 to 1975 publications of the National Center for Education Statistics were assigned to the HE 5 SuDocs class.

[13]Agencies formerly in the Health Resources Administration that were not assigned to the new Health Resources and Services Administration retained their SuDocs class numbers. This included the National Center for Health Statistics, which was placed under the Centers for Disease Control.

[14]*Morbidity and Mortality Weekly Report* (MMWR) is a world-famous scientific journal. Equally important is the *MMWR CDC Surveillance Summaries*, issued quarterly (HE 20.7009/2).

[15]Fewer than two pages are devoted to a summary of Housing and Urban Development (HUD) depository classes in a current edition of the *List of Classes*, and no HUD periodicals are found in a current edition of *Price List 36*.

[16]The *List of Classes*, revised September 1991, gives *Key Officers of Foreign Service Posts* a SuDocs class notation of S 1.40/5, whereas the winter 1992 edition of *Price List 36* provides a notation of S 1.40/2:Of2.

[17]"Supplemental Foreign Relations Authorization Act of 1990," S. Rep. 101-334, June 18, 1990 (Washington, DC: GPO, 1990), p. 15. See also 105 Stat. 685-691 (October 28, 1991).

[18]*Chronicle of Higher Education*, April 4, 1990, pp. A6, A12.

[19]A related series, *Documents on Disarmament* (AC 1.11/2), has been issued annually by the U.S. Arms Control and Disarmament Agency since 1961. These are compilations of basic documents on arms control, disarmament, and related matters that were issued during the year from U.S. and foreign sources. The 1960 edition was published by the State Department (S 1.117:960) as was a historical volume, *Documents on Disarmament, 1945-1959*, in two parts (S 1.2:D63/2).

[20]SuDocs has assigned to Central Intelligence Agency (CIA) publications PrEx 3 class numbers, which is the author symbol for the National Security Council. However, CIA is an independent agency within the executive branch and not part of either the National Security Council or the Executive Office of the President.

[21]SuDocs classification author symbol GS was reused for the General Services Administration.

[22]Functions concerning publication of the *United States Statutes at Large* and slip laws were transferred from the Department of State by Reorganization Plan No. 20 of 1950.

[23]Functions of numbering, editing, and distribution of proclamations and executive orders (EOs) were transferred from the Department of State by EO 7298 of February 18, 1935.

[24]Despite the change in name in 1975 from U.S. Tariff Commission to U.S. International Trade Commission, GPO continued to use SuDocs class notation TC 1 for the renamed agency until November 1981, when it adopted the ITC 1 class stem.

[25]GPO continues to use class number S 18 for Agency for International Development publications despite its change in status effective October 1, 1979.

[26]GPO continues to use class OP 1 for Overseas Private Investment Corporation publications despite its change in status in 1979.

[27]See also Joe Morehead, "The Devil's Best Century: Reflections on Our National Cemeteries," in *Essays on Public Documents and Government Policies* (New York: Haworth, 1986), pp. 217-27.

[28]This publication in slip form, titled *Reports to Be Made to Congress*, is issued annually (Y 1.1/7).

9

Publications of the Judiciary

INTRODUCTION

Patterns of access to legal information resources have remained largely consistent over time owing in part to the doctrine of stare decisis, the concept that attributes great weight to legal precedent, and perhaps in part to the conservative nature of the legal profession. However, some reputable online, CD-ROM, and other electronic services that facilitate improved and faster access to judicial materials are covered at appropriate points in the text.

Although this chapter could concentrate solely on those source materials that are government publications in the strict sense, it would leave an enormous gap in the reader's awareness. A reading of this chapter will, therefore, reveal the extent to which commercial sources play a pivotal role in legal research, a role necessitated by the early privatization of legal publishing. And, although the chapter will not prepare the reader for law librarianship, it is intended to provide an overview of basic tools required to conduct informed preliminary research in legal materials whether they are governmentally or commercially published. An awareness of options and of alternate or parallel sources is essential because many libraries incorporate their legal tools into the government publications collection or house governmentally published editions side by side with their commercial counterparts. First, though, some background on the branch that spawns this literature is in order.

THE THIRD BRANCH

The judiciary occupies a more subdued although certainly no less important role in the balance of powers; it is characteristically called the third branch, and its activities frequently follow on the heels of action by the congressional and executive branches. In teaching students whose backgrounds are somewhat remote from the legal process, it is at times difficult to convey how extensively federal policy relies on a constant give-and-take among the branches and is an amalgam of congressional enactment, administrative rulemaking, and judicial decision.

The judicial branch of the federal establishment forms a pyramid. At the bottom of that pyramid stand the U.S. district, or trial, courts. There are over ninety district courts including the District of Columbia, Guam, the Virgin

Islands, and the Northern Mariana Islands. On the next level are the U.S. circuit courts of appeals, which number twelve, and the U.S. court of appeals for the federal circuit. The latter is a subject court that receives cases from certain special courts and from various administrative agencies and independent entities. The other appellate courts are geographical.

In addition, special courts have been established by Congress from time to time to deal with particular types of cases. Among these are the U.S. tax court, court of international trade, claims court, and court of veterans appeals. The last was established by the Veterans' Judicial Review Act of 1988 (PL 100-687) and reviews decisions of the Board of Veterans' Appeals. Another special court is the U.S. court of military appeals, which receives and reviews decisions of the army, navy-marine corps, air force, and coast guard courts of military review.

The fact that Congress has empowered certain executive branch and independent agencies with quasi-judicial powers complicates the court structure. The decisions rendered by the tribunals of these administrative units, if appealed, may be reviewed by the district courts in some instances or may go directly to the courts of appeals.[1] A fuller explanation of the federal court system is found in a useful brochure issued by the Administrative Office of the United States Courts titled *The United States Courts: Their Jurisdiction and Work* (Ju 10.2:C83), revised periodically. Also of value is the current edition of *The United States Government Manual* (AE 2.108/2). The business of most of the federal courts is discussed in the Administrative Office's *Annual Report of the Director* (Ju 10.1).

There are also, of course, state courts that have general, unlimited power to decide almost every type of case, subject only to the limitations of state law. The courts located in every town and county are the tribunals with which citizens most often have contact (although the degree to which cases of these lesser courts are available in published form varies from jurisdiction to jurisdiction). The federal courts, on the other hand, have power to decide only those cases in which the Constitution gives them authority. Article III, Section 1, of the Constitution states that "the judicial Power of the United States, shall be vested in one supreme Court, and in such inferior Courts as the Congress may from time to time ordain and establish." Thus, the only indispensable court is the Supreme Court, and the Congress has indeed from time to time established and abolished various other federal courts. For more extensive background, see Erwin Surrency, *History of the Federal Courts* (New York: Oceana, 1987). An award-winning videotape package, *Understanding the Courts* (Chicago: American Bar Association), is also available to explain the U.S. court system.

The independence of the judicial branch is assured by the Constitution, even though federal judges are appointed by the president with the advice and consent of the Senate. It is important to understand that federal courts are mandated to exercise judicial powers and to perform judicial work, although the courts' decisions do have the force of law. Although high school civics teaches that courts cannot be called upon to exercise legislative power, the fact is that "judge-made" law is commonplace where constitutional interpretation is ambiguous or where provisions of statutes are ambiguous or unconstitutional. Typically one cannot determine the meaning of statutes without referring to the cases that construe them.

According to the U.S. Constitution, federal judges hold their positions "during good Behaviour" and can be removed from office against their will only by impeachment. Independence is further insured by compensation that "shall not be diminished during their Continuance in Office"—that is, neither a president nor the Congress can reduce the salary of a federal magistrate. An essential tool for the study of this and other parts of the Constitution is *Constitution of the United States of America: Analysis and Interpretation* (Y 1.1/3:99-16), prepared by the Congressional Research Service and published in a 2308-page volume. Title 2, *United States Code*, section 168, requires biennial updating of this publication, which is done via a pocket supplement (the 1990 supplement was issued, for instance, as S. Doc. 101-36 in 1991) and mandates a completely new edition every ten years. Each section of the Constitution is heavily annotated with citations and narrative on those court cases and other documentary sources that have construed that section.

Although independence and a concomitant ideal of integrity theoretically characterize the federal judiciary, selection is largely a political process. By tradition, senators of the president's party have the prerogative of naming persons for federal judgeships within their states. Judicial appointment is a powerful patronage lever for an incumbent president. On the U.S. Supreme Court level, questions regarding a judge's qualifications, background, and views are often best discovered by reading—in addition to opinions or other writings by the candidate—the transcript of the nominations hearings held before the Senate Judiciary Committee and distributed by the Government Printing Office (GPO). Beguiled by the televising of these hearings, members of this committee have often transformed this crucial part of the nominating process into disingenuous political theater.

REFERENCE AND RESEARCH AIDS

The scope of legal reference and bibliography is vast and seemingly complex. But the bibliographic apparatus adheres to a logic and elegance of symmetry not evident in other areas of government publications. Indeed, the list of sources is so specific and unique that library schools often offer a separate course in legal bibliography, and law schools require students to acquire a certain degree of sophistication in the use of source material. What follows is intended merely to introduce the reader to some salient materials supportive of federal case law. As noted earlier, the nature of publications in this field is such that a host of commercial material surrounds and amplifies a relatively small number of official government publications.

Basic Research Guides

A mastery of the legal literature begins with recognizing various types of tools: basic guides, legal citation forms, encyclopedias, dictionaries, directories, periodical indexes, digests, annotated law reports, looseleaf services, citators, popular name tables, and statistical sources. Many of these forms are familiar; a few, less so.

An abundance of useful guides is currently available. Morris L. Cohen, *Legal Research in a Nutshell*, 4th ed. (St. Paul, MN: West Publishing Co., 1985), affords a concise introduction to legal bibliography, and his *How to Find the Law*, 9th ed. (St. Paul, MN: West Publishing Co., 1989), is far more extensive.

J. Myron Jacobstein and Roy M. Mersky, *Fundamentals of Legal Research*, 5th ed. (Westbury, NY: Foundation Press, 1990), is even more detailed and a classic in the field. A paperbound abridgment of *Fundamentals* by the same authors serves as an excellent text for law librarianship.[2] Another updated classic is Julius J. Marke and Richard Sloane, *Legal Research and Law Library Management*, rev. ed. (New York: Law Journal Seminar Press, 1990). Miles O. Price et al., 4th ed. *Effective Legal Research* (Boston: Little Brown and Company, 1979), is very detailed and still serves a reference function for U.S. and foreign legal sources. Librarians as well as library school and law students will find John Corbin, *Find the Law in the Library: A Guide to Legal Research* (Chicago: American Library Association, 1989), and Christina L. Kunz, *The Process of Legal Research*, 2d ed. (Boston: Little, Brown, 1989), useful for the case studies approach they employ.

Other guides include Bernard D. Reams et al., *American Legal Literature: A Guide to Selected Legal Resources* (Littleton, CO: Libraries Unlimited, 1985), and Kent C. Olson and Robert C. Berring, *Practical Approaches to Legal Research* (New York: Haworth Press, 1988). More popularized guides are Stephen Elias, *Legal Research: How to Find and Understand the Law*, 2d ed. (Berkeley, CA: Nolo Press, 1986), and Al Coco, *Introduction to Legal Research: A Layperson's Guide to Finding the Law* (Washington, DC: Want Publishing Company, 1985). The novice researcher will find it useful to peruse several of these guides because authors make their points in various ways, some more useful than others to the lay individual. Nolo Press/Legal Star Communications also offers a two-and-one-half-hour videotape and manual, *Legal Research Made Easy: A Roadmap through the Law Library Maze*, and various law schools are beginning to use hypertext to introduce students to legal research.

Legal Citation Forms

Legal citation practice tends to be concise, and knowing how to cite and, obviously, how to interpret a legal reference are essential to providing reference service. For nonlegal writing, the many formats provided in Diane Garner and Diane Smith, *The Complete Guide to Citing Government Documents* (Bethesda, MD: Congressional Information Service, 1984), may be sufficient for official government editions. Citation form is thoroughly discussed in Jacobstein and Mersky's *Fundamentals of Legal Research*, chapter 24, and an extensive table of abbreviations forms their Appendix A. Citation rules and examples and tables of abbreviations are also found in Price et al., *Effective Legal Research*, chapter 32 and Appendix III, and in various law dictionaries and other citation manuals. Important sources include *The Bluebook: A Uniform System of Citation* (15th edition, 1991), published by the Harvard Law Review Association and commonly known as the "Bluebook," and its primary competitor, *The University of Chicago Manual of Legal Citation* (Lawyers Co-operative/Bancroft-Whitney, 1989), known as the "Maroon Book."

Consistency in legal citation is essential, and the increasing popularity of online searching and citation form-check programs such as JuriSoft's CiteRite II (Mead Data Central) build upon such consistency. Yet, as Jacobstein and Mersky suggest, "the electronic advantage of speed and accuracy is undermined by legal writers' inability to develop consistent citation formats."[3]

Encyclopedias

Two general legal encyclopedias dominate the field and provide topical coverage of the law in narrative form. *American Jurisprudence Second* (Am.Jur.2d) and *Corpus Juris Secundum* (C.J.S.) form part of the secondary literature. The former is published by Lawyers Cooperative Publishing (Rochester, New York); the latter is issued by West Publishing Company (St. Paul, Minnesota). As becomes evident, these two publishers are responsible for many of the sources mentioned in this chapter. Hereafter they are referred to as LCP and West, respectively.

Both Am.Jur.2d and C.J.S. are multivolume works arranged alphabetically by topic, with general indexes plus an index in each volume. Footnotes in C.J.S. purport to cite virtually all reported cases, whereas Am.Jur.2d cites selected decisions in its footnotes. Both are supplemented by annual pocket parts and replacement volumes. Each cites to its own related publications.

Am.Jur.2d and C.J.S. differ in certain features. For example, Am.Jur.2d has a table of statutes absent from C.J.S. Neither encyclopedia has a table of cases. C.J.S. provides definitions of words and phrases and legal maxims interfiled alphabetically with the narrative topics and in each volume preceding the index. Am.Jur.2d provides definitions only through the general index. On balance, however, their similarities outweigh their differences.

An encyclopedia that fits more into the traditional sense of an encyclopedia and may more commonly be found in smaller public and academic libraries is the twelve-volume *Guide to American Law* (West, 1983-1985), which has been updated by a 1987 annual yearbook and annual supplements. Also available is Robert J. Janosik's three-volume *Encyclopedia of the American Judicial System* (New York: Charles Scribner's Sons, 1987).

Dictionaries

It is difficult to provide even basic legal reference without an idea of the meaning of terms such as *headnotes, amicus curiae, certiorari*, etc., so access to a good legal dictionary is essential. Law dictionaries vary in size and purpose. Standard one-volume dictionaries include *Black's Law Dictionary*, 6th ed. (West, 1990); Ballentine, *Law Dictionary with Pronunciations*, 3d ed. (LCP, 1969); and B. Garner, *Dictionary of Modern Legal Usage* (New York: Oxford University Press, 1987). Law dictionaries provide precise definitions of words, phrases, and maxims and furnish citations to authority. The multivolume *Words and Phrases* (West) reprints definitions used in reported cases as culled from headnotes (statements prepared in concise summary form) or from the various units of the *National Reporter System*.

Directories

The most comprehensive legal directory is the multivolume *Martindale-Hubbell Law Directory* (Summit, NJ: Martindale-Hubbell). Published annually, it lists virtually all lawyers admitted to the bar, providing typical directory information and a "confidential" rating approximating each lawyer's legal ability;

contains law digests of states and foreign countries; provides information on U.S. copyright, patent, and trademark law; and includes uniform model acts and codes such as the Uniform Commercial Code. The list of foreign embassies and legations in Washington, D.C., and of U.S. embassies, legations, and consulates worldwide may prove useful in the absence of the Department of State's own publications. It is available in paper or on CD-ROM and online via LEXIS.

The U.S. Administrative Office of the Courts publishes the *United States Court Directory* (Ju 10.17) semiannually, providing names, mailing addresses, and telephone and FTS numbers for U.S. court judges and for librarians of those courts. Several other directories include the *Judicial Staff Directory*, 4th ed. (Mount Vernon, VA: Staff Directories, Ltd., 1989); the *Federal Legal Directory* (Phoenix, AZ: Oryx, 1990); and Want Publishing Company's *Federal-State Court Directory* (Washington, DC: Want Publishing, 1986).

Biographical directories also exist, the two most extensive being the Bicentennial Committee of the Judicial Conference of the United States' *Judges of the United States*, 2d ed. (1983) (Ju 10.2:J89/4/983, 1983), which covers 1780-1982, and *Biographical Dictionary of the Federal Judiciary, 1789-1974* (Detroit, MI: Gale Research Company, 1976).

Legal Periodical Literature

Although many legal periodicals are published by law schools or bar associations, a few are published by the government or other groups. The legal article is important as an aid to lawyers, judges, and others who need to understand an increasingly complex body of primary source material. The judiciary often cites this secondary literature in court cases; conversely, the articles make extensive reference to cases and statutes.

Most directly germane to the actual work of the courts are *The Third Branch* (Ju 10.3/2) and the *Daily Journal of the U.S. Supreme Court*, which gives a full account of the Court's proceedings, texts of decisions and orders (although not the opinions themselves), a list of the justices present on the bench that day, announcements of the chief justice, and names of counsel admitted to the bar. It was issued at one time as SuDocs Ju 6.5, but the GPO no longer distributes this; the title may, however, be found in the commercial *United States Law Week*.

Major law-related journals published by the federal government include the *Air Force Law Review* (D 302.9), *Army Lawyer* (D 101.22:27-50), the *FBI Law Enforcement Bulletin* (J 1.14/8), *Federal Probation* (Ju 10.8), *Military Law Review* (D 101.22:27-100), the *Journal of Legal Studies* (D 305.21/2), and *The Reporter* (D 302.11). Indexing for these is provided by the *Index to U.S. Government Periodicals*, discussed in greater detail in chapter 13. However, researchers and librarians should be aware of an array of other commercially published indexes to the legal literature.

Current Law Index (CLI) and *Legal Resources Index* (LRI), both of which began publication in 1980, are products of the Information Access Corporation of Menlo Park, California. CLI covers over 800 law and law-related periodicals and appears in print form monthly with quarterly and annual cumulations. Articles are accessed by author and subject. Book reviews are entered under the author and title of the book, and a table of cases and statutes lists all substantive cases or statutes cited in the articles.

LRI is the electronic equivalent of CLI, except that it goes beyond to include several legal newspapers and some specialty publications. LRI is available online via BRS(LAWS), as Dialog File 150, and through LEXIS and WESTLAW (vendors discussed at the end of this chapter). LRI's CD-ROM version, known as LegalTrac, has the unusual feature of providing letter grades, such as A, B, or C, for books reviewed.

Still more recent is *Legal Information Management Index* (Newton Highlands, MA: Fox Information Consultants, 1984-), which is of special appeal to law librarians needing access to topics such as legal research and bibliography, government publications, and reference problems. It indexes approximately 125 periodicals.

The H. W. Wilson Company's *Index to Legal Periodicals* (ILP) has been the standard guide since 1908.[4] It covers over 550 periodicals and related items, such as a selection of yearbooks, proceedings of annual institutes, and annual reviews of a particular topic or in a given field, published in the United States, Canada, Great Britain, Ireland, Australia, and New Zealand. Issued monthly with quarterly, annual, and multiyear cumulations, ILP is organized by interfiled subjects and authors and features a "Table of Cases," a "Table of Statutes," and a "Book Review Index." In the *Index to Legal Periodicals*, as well as others such as LRI and CLI, these tables of cases and statutes commented on provide the most direct access to primary government publications of interest to the documents professional. The following excerpt from the April 1990 *Index to Legal Periodicals* shows, for instance, that in the case of the United States versus the PLO, which case appeared at page 1456 and following of the *Federal Supplement*, volume 695, there were three related articles. Figure 9.1 (see page 292) shows this page from ILP.

The ILP is available in traditional print form; online through Wilsonline, LEXIS, and WESTLAW; and on CD-ROM. A corresponding *Thesaurus* was published in 1988.

A frequently overlooked but important tool is the quarterly *Index to Periodical Articles Related to Law* (Dobbs Ferry, NY: Glanville Publishers, 1958-), edited and compiled by Mersky and Jacobstein. It indexes English-language articles of a legal nature not covered by major legal index tools. As its editors point out, "Since legal subjects are assuming greater prominence in a variety of non-legal journals, this *Index* is particularly useful in locating timely articles on newly developing areas which often first appear in non-legal periodicals."[5] A four-volume cumulation covering 1958-1988 is available for retrospective searching.

Citators have been common in the legal field for many years; although they are most familiar to those searching case or statutory law, there also exists *Shepard's Law Review Citations* (1979, 1986, with supplements). Arrangement in this Shepard's tool is first by volume number and then page number for over 100 legal periodicals. It lists volume and page number of federal and state court reports and other law review articles that have cited an article that appears in the periodical. *Shepard's Federal Law Citations in Selected Law Reviews* (1985, with regular supplements) reverses the process. In this unit of Shepard's the cited matter includes the United States Constitution, *United States Code*, federal court rules, and the decisions of federal courts, whereas the citing sources are articles appearing in some twenty prominent law school reviews. Shepard's units and the concept of "Shepardizing" are discussed at greater length on pages 295-96.

(Text continues on page 293.)

Fig. 9.1. Page from Table of Cases, ILP

TABLE OF CASES 79

Smith Land & Improvement Corp. v. Celotex Corp., 851 F.2d 86
29 *Nat. Resources J.* 849-59 Summ '89
Societe Nationale Industrielle Aerospatiale v. United States Dist. Court for the S. Dist. of Iowa, 107 S. Ct. 2542
69 *B.U.L. Rev.* 1011-66 N '89
7 *Dick. J. Int'l L.* 65-93 Fall '88
Stanford v. Kentucky, 109 S. Ct. 2969
11 *Crim. Just. J.* 469-87 Spr '89
Starrels v. First Nat'l Bank, 870 F.2d 1168
45 *Bus. Law.* 469-510 F '90
State v. Bishop, 753 P.2d 439 (Utah)
1989 *Utah L. Rev.* 1013-45 '89
State v. DeMille, 756 P.2d 81 (Utah)
1989 *Utah L. Rev.* 969-89 '89
State; Ewing v., 745 P.2d 947 (Ariz.)
21 *Ariz. St. L.J.* 793-808 Fall '89
State v. Stewart, 763 P.2d 572 (Kan.)
23 *Akron L. Rev.* 89-104 Summ '89
State Farm Mut. Auto. Ins. Co.; Davenport v., 756 S.W.2d 678 (Tenn.)
19 *Mem. St. U.L. Rev.* 117-35 Fall '88
State Water Resources Control Bd.; Imperial Irrigation Dist. v., 231 Cal. Rptr. 283
19 *Golden Gate U.L. Rev.* 379-99 Summ '89
Stephens v. Avery, [1988] 2 All E.R. 477
53 *Mod. L. Rev.* 43-56 Ja '90
Stewart; State v., 763 P.2d 572 (Kan.)
23 *Akron L. Rev.* 89-104 Summ '89
Stockton Pregnancy Control Medical Clinic, Inc.; People v., 249 Cal. Rptr. 762
28 *J. Fam. L.* 146-52 '89/'90
Stotts; Memphis Fire Dep't v., 104 S. Ct. 2576
27 *Am. Bus. L.J.* 565-97 Wint '90
Suhail & Saud Bahwan Bldg. Materials LLC. (The 'Alev); Vantage Navigation Corp. v. [1989] 1 Lloyd's Rep. 138
53 *Mod. L. Rev.* 107-16 Ja '90
Sunny Slope Farms, Inc.; Roman v., 817 F.2d 116
21 *Rutgers L.J.* 197-212 Fall '89
Superior Court; Brown v., 751 P.2d 470 (Cal.)
21 *Ariz. St. L.J.* 809-31 Fall '89
Superior Court; Walker v., 763 P.2d 852 (Cal.)
1989 *Det. C.L. Rev.* 263-81 Spr '89

T

Tarkanian; NCAA v., 109 S. Ct. 454
21 *Ariz. St. L.J.* 621-61 Fall '89
17 *Pepperdine L. Rev.* 217-53 D '89
40 *Syracuse L. Rev.* 1123-44 '89
Taylor; Hanna Oil & Gas Co. v., 759 S.W.2d 563 (Ark.)
43 *Ark. L. Rev.* 201-15 '90
Technicolor, Inc.; Cede & Co. v., 542 A.2d 1182 (Del.)
14 *Del. J. Corp. L.* 999-1023 '89
Texas; Powell v., 742 S.W.2d 353 (Tex.)
11 *Crim. Just. J.* 449-67 Spr '89
Thornburgh; Michigan Citizens for an Independent Press v., 868 F.2d 1285
1989 *U. Ill. L. Rev.* 399-433 '89
Titan Landco Inc.; Bank of Montreal v., [1989] B.C.L.R.(2d) 114
68 *Can. B. Rev.* 797-802 D '89
Tito v. Waddell, [1977] Ch. 106
27 *Alta. L. Rev.* 354-72 '89
Treasure Salvors, Inc.; Florida Dep't of State v., 102 S. Ct. 3304
12 *Hous. J. Int'l L.* 143-58 Fall '89
Trident Center v. Connecticut Gen. Life Ins. Co., 847 F.2d 564
1989 *Utah L. Rev* 991-1011 '89

U

UAW v. Johnson Controls, Inc., 886 F.2d 871
103 *Harv. L. Rev.* 977-82 F '90
United States; Carpenter v., 108 S. Ct. 316
17 *Pepperdine L. Rev.* 185-215 D '89
United States; Kungys v., 108 S. Ct. 1537
3 *Geo. Immigr. L.J.* 387-401 Fall '89
United States; Mistretta v., 109 S. Ct. 647
39 *De Paul L. Rev.* 405-59 Wint '90
39 *De Paul L. Rev.* 299-319 Wint '90
United States; National Fed'n of Federal Employees v. 688 F. Supp. 671
3 *Admin. L.J.* 637-82 Wint '89/'90
United States v. Noriega, 683 F. Supp. 1373
4 *Conn. J. Int'l L.* 729-65 Spr/Summ '89
United States v. Owens, 848 F.2d 462
62 *Temp. L. Rev.* 1351-66 Wint '89
United States v. PLO, 695 F. Supp. 1456
13 *Hastings Int'l & Comp. L. Rev.* 25-70 Fall '89
12 *Hous. J. Int'l L.* 159-73 Fall '89
34 *Vill. L. Rev.* 1265-94 N '89
United States v. Salerno, 107 S. Ct. 2095
62 *Temp. L. Rev.* 1225-60 Wint '89
United States v. Smith, 851 F.2d 706
62 *Temp. L. Rev.* 1341-50 Wint '89
United States; UpJohn Co. v., 101 S. Ct. 677
19 *Mem. St. U.L. Rev.* 29-56 Fall '88
United States v. Whizco, 841 F.2d 147
5 *J. Min. L. & Pol'y.* 171-93 '89/'90
United States Army; Watkins v., 847 F.2d 1329
1989 *Det. C.L. Rev.* 243-61 Spr '89
United States Dist. Court for the S. Dist. of Iowa; Societe Nationale Industrielle Aerospatiale v., 107 S. Ct. 2542
69 *B.U.L. Rev.* 1011-66 N '89
7 *Dick. J. Int'l L.* 65-93 Fall '88
UpJohn Co. v. United States, 101 S. Ct. 677
19 *Mem. St. U.L. Rev.* 29-56 Fall '88

V

Van Houten; Longworth v., 538 A.2d 414 (N.J.)
21 *Rutgers L.J.* 213-26 Fall '89
Vantage Navigation Corp. v. Suhail & Saud Bahwan Bldg. Materials LLC. (The 'Alev), [1989] 1 Lloyd's Rep. 138
53 *Mod. L. Rev.* 107-16 Ja '90
Vault Corp. v. Quaid Software, Ltd., 847 F.2d 255
16 *Rutgers Computer & Tech. L.J.* 85-127 '90
Volkswagenwerk Aktiengesellschaft v. Schlunk, 108 S. Ct. 2104
12 *Loy. L.A. Int'l & Comp. L.J.* 317-40 D '89
Von Raab; National Treasury Employees Union v., 109 S. Ct. 1384
67 *Den. U.L. Rev.* 91-108 '90

W

Waddell; Tito v. [1977] Ch. 106
27 *Alta. L. Rev.* 354-72 '89
Wald; R. v., 65 A.L.R. (2d) 114
21 *Ottawa L. Rev.* 151-97 '89
Walker v. Superior Court, 763 P.2d 852 (Cal.)
1989 *Det. C.L. Rev.* 263-81 Spr '89
Wards Cove Packing Co. v. Atonio, 109 S. Ct. 2115
41 *Lab. L.J.* 102-7 F '90
18 *Real Est. L.J.* 307-42 Spr '90
Watkins v. United States Army, 847 F.2d 1329
1989 *Det. C.L. Rev.* 243-61 Spr '89
Webster v. Reproductive Health Servs., 109 S. Ct. 3040
62 *N.Y. St. B.J.* 55-6+ F '90
50 *Rev. Col. Ab. P.R.* 29-40 Jl/S '89
West Berkshire Health Auth.; F. v., [1989] 2 All E.R. 545
53 *Mod. L. Rev.* 91-106 Ja '90
White v. Secretary of State for the Env't, [1989] 15 E.G. 193
1989 *Conv. & Prop. Law (n.s.)* 403-11 N/D '89
Whizco; United States v., 841 F.2d 147
5 *J. Min. L. & Pol'y.* 171-93 '89/'90
Wilder v. Bernstein, 848 F.2d 1338
28 *J. Fam. L.* 152-8 '89/'90
Wood Pulp Judgment, [1988] 4 Comm. Mkt. L.R. 90
19 *Ga J. Int'l & Comp. L.* 149-73 Spr '89
Worsham v. Pilot Oil Corp., 728 S.W.2d 19 (Tenn.)
19 *Mem. St. U.L. Rev* 109-15 Fall '88

Y

Youngblood; Arizona v., 109 S. Ct. 333
5 *Touro L. Rev.* 309-25 Spr '89

Z

Zaluzna; Australian Safeway Stores Pty. Ltd. v., [1987] 162 C.L.R. 479
15 *Monash U.L. Rev.* 69-94 Je '89

Digests

Digests are important tools for conducting legal research, and no chapter on the subject would be complete without mention of them. The many types of digests include those covering specific states or types of courts, those covering multiple jurisdictions, and those covering federal courts. To understand the significance of a digest, one must realize that case reporters are chronologically arranged. The digest's main function is to rearrange all cases within the covered jurisdiction by broad topics. Cases are not reprinted; only abstracts, or "digests," are provided. Accompanying a digest are a separate table of cases and a Descriptive-Word Index that allows the user to work from a very specific topic to the broader one under which like cases on points of law are abstracted. Thus, ANIMALS is a topic and #47 is the key number representing the subheading "running at large."

Anyone who needs to work with court opinions of the various states would do well to read one of the basic research guides cited earlier to develop an understanding of the *National Reporter System*, the various components of which print cases from all jurisdictions; the *American Digest System*, which provides abstracts of those decisions in subject arrangement; and the Key Number System. The Key Number System, described by West as a "permanent, or fixed, number, given to a specific point of case law," was developed by the West Publishing Company to classify all cases under any of more than 435 appropriate legal concepts.[6] As our emphasis in this chapter is on materials related to the federal courts, the most important tools in this category include two competing digests for U.S. Supreme Court decisions and one multi-title set encompassing all of the federal courts.

The *U.S. Supreme Court Digest* (West) abstracts all decisions of the highest court and uses the West Key Number System. A competitor series is LCP's *Digest of United States Supreme Court Reports, Lawyers' Edition*, in twenty-two volumes. Regardless of which set is used, it is vital that the researcher check pocket supplements for later case material. Anyone planning to do legal research will find it standard practice to look for supplementation of legal tools. If the item is not a looseleaf service, supplementation is often accomplished with annual pocket parts, which continue to cumulate until it is necessary to republish the entire volume to accommodate all the changes, and/or by paper supplements, which libraries normally file with the basic set.

Encompassing digests of decisions from the federal district and appellate courts as well as from the U.S. Supreme Court and special federal courts is the West series that begins with the *Federal Digest*, covering all cases prior to 1939. This work is followed by the *Modern Federal Practice Digest* (1939-1960); the *Federal Practice Digest, 2d* (1961-1975); the *Federal Practice Digest, 3d* (1976-date); and the *Federal Practice Digest, 4th*, which begins in 1989 despite the fact that the 3d edition is not yet closed. Digests also exist for the special federal courts; however, mastery in the use of the above digests should be readily transferable.

Annotated Law Reports

Speed of issuance, ease of use, enhanced indexing, and editorial comment all add to the attractiveness of some of the value-added commercial products. One such product, generally requested simply as the A.L.R., is the *American Law Reports*. It is comprised of a selective number of court decisions. Published by LCP, this series consists of decisions that, in the opinion of the editors, are of general interest to the legal profession. A.L.R. is important

> not for the decisions it reports [which can be found in official reporters or in units of West's *National Reporter System*] but for the editorial service that follows each reported decision, or what the publishers call "Annotations." These are encyclopedic essays or memoranda on the significant legal topics from each case selected for publication in the *American Law Reports*.[7]

Stated another way, cases chosen for "Annotation" are either those that lend themselves "to an exhaustive treatment of an important subdivision of the law of a major topic" or those that treat "limited areas of the law which are not covered at all or are covered insufficiently in other law books."[8] Written by experts in the field, "Annotations" present an organized commentary on previously reported like decisions, and they range in length from one or two pages to over three hundred pages.

The *American Law Reports* are published in the following series: first (A.L.R.), covering 1919-1948; second (A.L.R.2d), for 1948-1965; third (A.L.R.3d), for 1965-1980; fourth (A.L.R.4th), for 1980 to date; and federal (A.L.R.Fed), which covers 1969 to date. A.L.R.Fed includes only leading decisions of the federal courts, followed by an annotation as described above.

Subject access to the A.L.R. Annotations series (A.L.R.2d, 3d, 4th, and Fed) is now offered by a five-volume *Index to Annotations*. Only the A.L.R. need now be accessed by the *Quick Index*. The five-volume index lacks a table of cases, but it is better indexed and collateral Annotations are provided.

Also available beginning in 1989 is the two-volume *Shepard's Citations for Annotations: A Compilation of Citations to Annotations and to Decisions of the United States Supreme Court, Lower Federal Courts and State Courts*, which enables the user to Shepardize every case cited in A.L.R.3d, 4th, and Fed and in L.Ed.2d since 1965 without going to the separate citators for each jurisdiction. It is the only Shepard's unit that lists Annotations as *both* citing and cited references.

Looseleaf Services

According to Jacobstein and Mersky, it was the growth of administrative agencies within the executive branch and the increasing complexity, inaccessibility, and volume of administrative rules and decisions that fostered the growth of privately published looseleaf services, or "reporters."[9] Government publications departments may at times subscribe to several of these services to augment existing official editions; to increase speed and convenience of access to important statutes, regulations, and cases; and to provide patrons with the value-enhanced editorial and explanatory notes and indexing these publications offer. Numerous looseleaf services are prepared for the legal community on specific topics, from accounting to taxation. The major publishers of these services are the Bureau of National Affairs (BNA) (Washington, D.C.), Commerce Clearing House (Chicago), and Prentice-Hall (Englewood Cliffs, New Jersey).

In addition to the immediacy of access that these looseleaf services provide, subscribers usually receive a "package" format consisting of the full text or digests of federal and state statutes, court decisions, agency rulings, administrative regulations, Attorney General opinions, and other relevant documentation; editorial explanations and abstracts; and up-to-date indexing by subject and case name as well as other finding aids.

Looseleaf services also generally cut across jurisdictional boundaries and provide laws or court decisions on a subject from among the various states and the federal government. One of the most commonly used looseleaf services for locating federal cases is the Bureau of National Affairs' *The United States Law Week*. Published since 1933, this source is divided into two binders, one housing U.S. Supreme Court cases and the other for that small percent of lower court cases, statutes, and agency rulings that establish precedent or involve new interpretations.

An example of a topical looseleaf service containing numerous government publications in reformatted fashion is BNA's *Media Law Reporter—Decisions*. This compendium provides coverage of all U.S. Supreme Court decisions as well as other important federal and state court decisions in the field of media law.

Shepard's Citations

Because the law is a dynamic process, the legal researcher must stay abreast of what acts or cases are valid and may properly be cited as authority. Citators provide current information on valid authority, and the most complete set of books and services for determining this is known as *Shepard's Citations* (Colorado Springs, CO: Shepard's/McGraw-Hill).

The word *Shepardizing* is used in legal parlance to describe the procedure whereby the applicability of cases, statutes, and other documents as authority is determined. Some Shepard's tools were referred to earlier. In addition, a set of *Shepard's Citations* is available for every set of court reports, such as *Shepard's New Jersey Citations, Shepard's Pacific Reporter Citations*, etc. The most important titles in the Shepard's series for research in federal case law are the *Federal Citations*, which is a compilation of citations to federal courts of appeals and district court cases, and the *United States Citations*, which covers decisions of the U.S. Supreme Court and statutes enacted by Congress as well as the U.S. Constitution, treaties, court rules, and citations to patents, trademarks, and copyrights. Other major Shepard's units for researching at the federal level include, for instance, the company's *Federal Rules Citations, United States Patents and Trademarks Citations, Federal Tax Citations, Federal Labor Law Citations, Federal Case Names Citator,* and *United States Supreme Court Case Names Citator*.

In Shepard's terminology, the word *citation* typically signifies a reference in a later authority to an earlier authority. The earlier authority is known as the "cited" case, statute, etc., and the later authority is referred to as the "citing" case, statute, etc. Anyone somewhat familiar with the various indexes, such as *SSCI—Social Science Citation Index*, published by the Institute for Scientific Information (Philadelphia) will recognize the concept. However, where SSCI cites only to the first page of the cited reference, Shepard's units cite to the exact page within a cited source. Through the appropriate Shepard's units, one can determine whether a decision has been reversed by a higher court, a statute repealed, a regulation held unconstitutional, a treaty amended, and so on. A Shepard's citator may also be used to locate parallel citations, to find law review articles relevant to the case, and to obtain a quick overview of the judicial history of the case. No narrative or text is provided with a Shepard's citator, however.

Figure 9.2 shows a typical page from *Shepard's United States Citations: Cases*. Users of any citator must become thoroughly familiar with the abbreviations. For instance, a lowercase "s" simply means the case is the same one; yet an uppercase "S" signifies that the item has been superseded, representing an important change in status of a regulation or a statute, etc. A 22-minute instructional video, *Introduction to Shepardizing* (1988) is available, as well as the booklet *How to Use Shepard's Citations*.

Shepard's Citations are available online through LEXIS and WESTLAW as well as in print versions. Each version has distinct advantages and disadvantages.[10]

Popular Name Listings

In addition to citators, Shepard's also publishes *Shepard's Acts and Cases by Popular Names, Federal and State*, which is a useful aid to anyone searching for cases or statutes when only the common name is known. For instance, it will show that the formal citation for the Endangered Species Act of December 23, 1973, is PL 93-205, 87 Stat. 884, *United States Code* 1982 Title 16, sec. 1531 et seq.; or that the Chambers-Hiss case sequence may be found at 185 F2d 822, 340 US 948, 95 LE 683, 71 SC 148, etc.

Other Sources of the Law

The bibliographic structure of U.S. law also encompasses court rules and procedures, opinions of the attorneys general, treatises and texts, restatements of the law, uniform laws, model codes, form books, and others. For these and other legal tools, the reader is advised to consult one of the basic texts noted earlier in this chapter. An essential source for tracking down information on many of the texts, treatises, periodicals, audio- and videocassettes, software, online databases, and microforms available is *Law Books and Serials in Print* (New York: Bowker Legal Reference Publishing, 1990).

(Text continues on page 298.)

Fig. 9.2. Page from *Shepard's United States Citations: Cases*

Vol. 443 — UNITED STATES SUPREME COURT REPORTS

Column 1

Vol. 443
758FS¹183
758FS²184
– 1 –
Cir. 5
758FS¹408
– 31 –
Cir. 3
758FS¹291
– 47 –
j59USLW
[4340
jUSDk
89-1632
Cir. 1
758FS¹95
Pa
397PaS305
Utah
808P2d146
104LE1056n
– 55 –
Cir. 5
758FS¹406
– 76 –
Cir. D.C.
928F2d1163
Cir. 11
j Dk 11
90-7078
– 97 –
Fla
576So2d846
– 111 –
Kan
248Kan477
– 137 –
Cir. 1
f759FS¹961
Cir. 3
758FS291
Cir. 5
928F2d700
758FS¹1156
Minn
465NW689
– 157 –
Kan
248Kan476
– 256 –
Cir. 8
Dk 8
89-1253
d Dk 8
89-2625
– 307 –
Cir. D.C.
928F2d¹1178
Cir. 1
928F2d9
928F2d¹1244
Cir. 2
928F2d577
928F2d¹577
928F2d¹1361

Column 2

401SE548
401SE551
402SE715
Cir. 4
402SE717
402SE720
402SE722
402SE725
402SE730
402SE734
Dk 6
402SE742
402SE748
402SE797
403SE38
403SE39
403SE59
403SE84
403SE439
Ill
208IIA236
208IIA768
568NE763
568NE845
569NE34
569NE210
569NE611
Iowa
467NW585
Kan
248Kan400
La
807P2d1302
260Ga771
260Ga776
260Ga781
260Ga783
260Ga785
260Ga792
260Ga797
260Ga808
260Ga809
260Ga815
260Ga817
198GaA339
198GaA352
198GaA358
198GaA362
198GaA369
198GaA372
198GaA381
198GaA404
198GaA415
198GaA417
198GaA425
198GaA426
198GaA433
198GaA438
198GaA450
198GaA458
198GaA478
198GaA497
198GaA506
198GaA514
198GaA516
198GaA519
198GaA520
198GaA524
198GaA530
198GaA842
198GaA844
198GaA870
198GaA875
198GaA882
198GaA887
198GaA891

Column 3

f759FS²1038
Cir. 4
f Dk 4
89-6686
Cir. 6
Dk 6
89-5606
Dk 6
90-5715
Dk 6
f927F2d¹1366
928F2d¹736
928F2d¹1457
Cir. 7
f929F2d¹309
929F2d351
Cir. 10
Dk 10
90-3125
Dk 10
90-6202
759FS¹1557
Cir. 11
928F2d¹1060
929F2d¹1550
32MJ151
Ga
260Ga...
574So2d337
574So2d446
574So2d453
574So2d475
576So2d524
576So2d1007
576So2d1060
576So2d1101
577So2d765
577So2d769
577So2d801
577So2d818
577So2d1124
577So2d1197
Mass
30MaA491
567NE958
Nev
808P2d4
NY
568NE1191
567NYS2d
[386
Ohio
59OS3d84
Ore
311Ore242
SD
466NW843
466NW846
Tenn
805SW778
806SW207
806SW542
806SW788
Tex
805SW806
806SW322
806SW878
Va
11VaA6
Wash
60WAp724

Column 4

60WAp862
806P2d1256
808P2d177
Wis
467NW563
Mass
– 368 –
Alk
807P2d1089
Pa
398PaS515
588A2d526
– 545 –
j59USLW
[4302
jUSDk
89-7024
Cir. 5
f Dk 5
929F2d¹1069
f929F2d1071
NJ
588A2d839
– 622 –
Cir. 9
j906F2d418
– 658 –
Cir. 7
758FS1270
Cir. 9
Dk 9
90-35448
– 912 –
Case 5
NY
162NYAD
[407
Case 6
La
576So2d1003
– 915 –
Case 1
Cir. 8
Dk 8
89-1253
Vol. 444
– 1 –
Cir. 10
759FS¹1557
– 11 –
Cir. 9
Dk 9
90-70418
– 37 –
Cir. 10
Dk 10
89-3152
– 51 –
NJ
588A2d1301

Column 5

– 85 –
Cir. 2
928F2d¹606
Ill
569NE596
410Mas241
NY
164NYAD
164NYAD
[458
[459
Va
241Va151
104LE1071n
– 111 –
Cir. D.C.
759FS891
Cir. 1
758FS83
Cir. 2
134FRD43
758FS¹1068
134FRD¹106
Cir. 5
759FS¹1214
Cir. 11
Dk 11
90-3502
– 164 –
929F2d134
ClCt
22ClC695
– 212 –
Cir. 3
927F2d1288
f927F2d1292
f927F2d¹1292
j927F2d1308
– 232 –
Cir. 9
929F2d¹498
– 277 –
Cir. 2
f758FS881
Cir. 5
Dk 5
91-1137
Cir. 7
928F2d¹778
– 286 –
Cir. 3
759FS¹266
Cir. 7
e929F2d353
759FS442
759FS¹474
Cir. 10
758FS¹661
Ill
208IIA438
La
576So2d984
NC
403SE603
Pa
398PaS612

Column 6

– 320 –
Cir. 7
759FS¹442
– 394 –
Cir. 10
Dk 10
90-1077
NY
148NYM444
– 555 –
928F2d184
– 572 –
Cir. D.C.
928F2d²419
– 672 –
Cir. 9
929F2d1440
Ohio
567NE256
– 803 –
Mich
466NW355
– 825 –
La
574So2d481
– 826 –
Case 3
Cir. 9
Dk 9
89-35233
Case 4
Cir. 9
928F2d826
– 827 –
Conn
218Ct245
– 829 –
Cir. 7
759FS479
– 831 –
Cir. 11
928F2d1066
– 832 –
Case 1
Cir. 11
927F2d1535
– 834 –
Cir. 1
760FS16
– 838 –
Cir. 8
759FS571
– 840 –
Cir. 10
j928F2d936
929F2d559

Column 7

– 841 –
Cir. 1
928F2d482
– 842 –
Cir. 5
929F2d179
– 848 –
Conn
218Ct245
f – 849 –
Case 6
Mass
567NE910
– 852 –
Case 8
Cir. 2
758FS187
– 860 –
Case 7
Cir. 4
Dk 4
90-5667
– 861 –
Cir. 10
929F2d1457
j929F2d1464
– 867 –
Ala
577So2d513
– 870 –
Cir. 11
928F2d1053
– 879 –
ECA
928F2d1141
– 881 –
Case 1
Mass
30MaA573
567NE902
568NE1149
NM
808P2d46
– 883 –
Fla
574So2d244
– 885 –
Fla
574So2d75
– 890 –
Case 1
Cir. 10
759FS1557
Kan
248Kan400
807P2d1302
Mass
567NE958
Nev
808P2d4

Column 8

Ore
311Ore242
– 893 –
Conn
588A2d650
– 902 –
Case 11
Cir. 8
Dk 8
90-1046
– 932 –
Case 6
Cir. 6
Dk 6
90-1665
– 935 –
Case 7
Conn
218Ct375
218Ct456
587A2d1056
– 937 –
Case 7
Cir. 4
Dk 4
90-1823
Nebr
465NW735
Case 10
Mass
410Mas86
– 941 –
Md
588A2d1220
– 946 –
Case 4
NY
162NYAD
[602
162NYAD
[949
162NYAD
[954
– 959 –
Cir. 10
929F2d1518
– 963 –
Cir. D.C.
929F2d740
– 968 –
Ore
311Ore248
– 969 –
Case 9
NY
162NYAD
[610
– 980 –
Case 10
Cir. 2
758FS888

THE FEDERAL COURT SYSTEM

In addition to developing an understanding of legal terminology—which can be gained from the law dictionaries and legal guides previously cited—an understanding of judicial pathways is essential to conduct legal research effectively. In fact, for the most basic of reference questions, such as, "Do you have *Baker* v. *Carr*?" some question negotiation may be required. Just as the librarian who is asked, "Do you have the Education for All Handicapped Children Act?" must in turn ask, "Would you like the act as it originally appeared in 1975, or do you want to see the text as it now stands?" certain clarifications may be in order when dealing with judicial inquiries.

The most basic question that usually needs addressing—assuming the librarian does not recognize *Baker* v. *Carr* as a landmark U.S. Supreme Court case— is that of jurisdiction: "Do you know what court decided the case?" Or, the question, "Do you have a case citation?" may need raising. It is not infrequent that someone asking for a case already has the needed reference in hand but has no idea of the meaning or relevance of the numbers and abbreviations and will therefore fail to offer this information until some well-phrased, courteous probing ensues.

As far as jurisdiction is concerned, the questioner may or may not be knowledgeable. If jurisdiction is unknown, a search must then proceed through the broadest available tables of cases in either print or online form. In locating cases, it is good to be aware, too, that as a case progresses to the appellate level, a reversal in the plaintiff-defendant name may occur. Most case tables do, however, provide case names in reverse order as an aid to research.

One should also understand that although a few important decisions of the district courts may be appealed directly to the Supreme Court, the appellate process generally rises hierarchically from district court to court of appeals and then to the Supreme Court. The courts of appeals review decisions of the district courts within their circuits and also some of the actions of the independent regulatory agencies. This structure serves a twofold purpose. First, the Supreme Court and the courts of appeals can correct errors made in the decisions of the trial courts. Second, these appellate courts can assure uniformity of decision by reviewing cases in which two or more lower courts have reached different results.

Lower court judges are required to follow the precedents established by the Supreme Court, but the system is not a monolithic unit in which, like the military chain of command, orders flow from the top. District and circuit judges have wide latitude in determining the lineaments of Supreme Court decisions. Those at the lower levels often take a different point of view toward legal disputes from that of the members of the High Court. And, as few of the thousands of cases adjudicated reach the Supreme Court, the judges of the lower federal courts are actually important policy makers. The federal judiciary, like the legislative and executive branches, reflects in its judgments the shifting and variegated interests of the body politic.

As previously suggested, the bibliographic apparatus created and maintained by commercial publishers such as West and LCP is necessary in large measure because of the doctrine of stare decisis, which "states that when a court has formulated a principle of law as applicable to a given set of facts, it will follow that principle and apply it in future cases where the facts are substantially the same."[11] From this construct, it follows that an attorney must have access to the latest cases in order to advise his or her client correctly. Commercial publishing of case law is geared to prompt reporting, not only of the opinions and decisions of courts but also of the indexes and other finding aids. The process is crucial to effective legal deliberation.

Decisions relied upon as precedent are usually those of appellate courts. Consequently, availability of published decisions increases in ascending order of the federal court hierarchy. Whereas only selected decisions of district courts are readily available, virtually all written and per curiam (literally "by the court") decisions of the appellate courts and the Supreme Court are reported either in their official edition or commercially. However, in recent years, the courts of appeals have increasingly rendered decisions without published opinions. These are noted in *Federal Reporter, Second Series* in tabular form by title (plaintiff-defendant order) referencing docket number, date, disposition (affirmed, reversed, petition for review denied, etc.), and a citation to or geographical abbreviation of the lower court from which the case was appealed.

Federal court reports can be placed within the context of West's National Reporter System, a network of reporters that includes the opinions of state, federal, and special courts. For state reports there exists within the National Reporter System a series of seven regional reporters, such as the Atlantic Reporter, that cover the opinions of several adjacent states and several separate units that cover the courts of New York, California, and Illinois. The federal courts and the special courts are covered in West's National Reporter System as follows.

District and Appellate Courts

During most of the nineteenth century, decisions of the U.S. district courts and courts of appeals were published in a number of separate series cited by the names of their official reporters. This "nominative" reporting, which caused bibliographic confusion, was rectified by the publication of a multivolume series known as *Federal Cases* (West). *Federal Cases*, covering 1789-1879, is arranged alphabetically by name of case and numbered consecutively. Some 18,000 lower federal court decisions are reported in this series.

For the years 1880 to the present, three units of West's National Reporter System must be consulted. There are currently no official government editions of these major federal court cases.

Federal Reporter

The *Federal Reporter* consists of two series. The first series, designated simply as F., comprises 300 volumes; the second series, cited as F.2d, began anew with volume 1 and is now over 900 volumes in length. The current series is the primary report channel for cases at the appellate court level, although, over time, first and second series have reported not only appellate, but also district cases and cases of selected special courts, some of which have since been abolished.[12]

Federal Supplement

The *Federal Supplement*, abbreviated variously as F.Supp., F.Sup., and FS, connects with volume 60 of the *Federal Reporter, Second Series*, and reports decisions of the district courts since 1932 as well as decisions of other courts.[13] Federal district court decisions, however, are published only selectively. Some may also be located using looseleaf services in a particular topical area or, as is often the case, by contacting the clerk of the appropriate court. Cases in both the *Federal Reporter* and the *Federal Supplement* may be accessed by using the appropriate West *Federal Practice Digest* (see page 293 for variant titles). The appropriate unit of Shepard's to match these court reports is *Shepard's Federal Citations*.

It should be observed here that opinions of the bankruptcy judges, who are actually judicial officers of the district courts, and reprints of the bankruptcy decisions of the U.S. Courts of Appeal and of the Supreme Court are contained in a separate series called *West's Bankruptcy Reporter* (1980-). On the other hand, opinions and decisions that involve the Federal Rules of Civil Procedure and the Federal Rules of Criminal Procedure are reported in West's *Federal Rules Decisions*, which first appears as an advance sheet followed by a bound volume. Periodically, the bound volumes also contain a cumulative index to articles about the federal courts and court procedure.

Special Courts

At present there are six special courts, plus two courts of local jurisdiction for the District of Columbia. These courts include the U.S. Claims Court, U.S. Court of International Trade, U.S. Court of Military Appeals, U.S. Tax Court, the Temporary Emergency Court of Appeals of the United States, and the U.S. Court of Veterans Appeals. *The United States Government Manual* provides a concise description of each court's background, constitution, and jurisdiction.

As noted at the beginning of this chapter, Congress from time to time has created these and other special courts to deal with particular types of cases. Appeals from the decisions of these courts may ultimately be reviewed in the Supreme Court.

Although the official district and appellate court reports have been discontinued by the government, the GPO still publishes reports from some of the special courts. An example of a special court reporter available to depository libraries is *Reports of the Tax Court* (Ju 11.7). Such reports, however, are far better covered in looseleaf topical reporters such as CCH's *Tax Court Reports, Tax Court Memorandum Decisions*, and *U.S. Tax Cases* and other comparable looseleafs issued by Prentice Hall and the Bureau of National Affairs, because of the greater currency and value-added enhancements of the private services.

Other official editions include *Cases Decided in United States Court of Appeals for the Federal Circuit* (Ju 7.5/2), *U.S. Court of International Trade Reports* (Ju 9.5/2), and the individual opinions of the U.S. Tax Court (Ju 11.7/a2). To keep up with report series currently being distributed by GPO, the GPO *List of Classes* (GP 3.24) is the best source to check. John L. Andriot's *Guide to U.S. Government Publications* is also a valuable aid for sorting out the various titles of report series.

No official edition is distributed for decisions of the U.S. Court of Military Appeals and the courts of military review for the army, navy-marine corps, air force, and coast guard. Instead, West has published the *Military Justice Reporter* since 1927. Other West reporters for the special courts include *United States Claims Court Reporter, Bankruptcy Reporter,* and *Veterans Appeals Reporter.*

For current awareness, one can consult *West's Federal Case News*, which, although not a reporter, is a weekly summary of cases decided in the Supreme Court, courts of appeals, district courts, and the several special courts. Each summary provides the essential points of cases, the name of the case, the court and name of the judge deciding the case, and the filing date and docket number of the case.

The Supreme Court

The U.S. Supreme Court consists of nine justices, one of whom is designated chief justice, who are appointed for life by the president with the advice and consent of the Senate. The Court's term extends from the first Monday in October until late June or, sometimes, early July. Popular opinion holds that the Supreme Court is an ultimate court of appeals for all, a bulwark of freedom to which every citizen can press his or her claim under federal law or the Constitution. Perceptions of the Court do vary, however. Of two books published on the Court during the same year, one author titled his *The Least Dangerous Branch*; another called his *Storm Center*.[14]

In actual fact, the Supreme Court is quite limited in its jurisdiction. It hears disputes between states, disputes between a state and the federal government, cases in which a federal court or the highest court of a state has held a statute unconstitutional, and a very few other categories. Moreover, it has discretionary power to decline to hear a large number of appeals.[15] Indeed, the Court "actually hears only a minute proportion of the cases brought to federal and state courts. Even within the federal court system, the Court hears fewer than 1 percent of the cases handled by the district courts."[16] Yet the cases that it does hear are those of great importance and interest, and the decisions of this tribunal are legally and politically of momentous consequence. Its rules and orders appear regularly as *Rules of the Supreme Court of the United States* (Ju 6.9).

The ongoing work of the Court may be followed through the *Daily Journal of the United States Supreme Court*, cited earlier on page 290. Subscribers to *United States Law Week* will find the information reproduced there under the section "Supreme Court Proceedings." The American Bar Association (ABA) also publishes *Preview of United States Supreme Court Cases*, issues of which cover each case orally argued before the Court, including the facts of the controversy, background and significance of the case, arguments of the parties, and the amici briefs.

Probably the most consequential undertaking of the Supreme Court as it relates to researchers, and librarians is dubbed Project Hermes, after the messenger of the Greek gods. As described by the *New York Times*, the "computerized transmission of decisions could end an archaic system that now finds law firm employees and others waiting in line at the Court day after day trying to

get one of the few printed copies of opinions that the Court makes available."
The same article notes that

> twenty years ago, the Supreme Court building did not even have a
> copying machine. Until the late 1970's, opinions were written on type-
> writers and printed by the Government Printing Office. In 1981, the
> Court installed an Atex, Inc. computer system with terminals in all the
> Justices' chambers, and began doing its own printing.[17]

Under the project, thirteen information-oriented organizations, including
the GPO, were selected to participate in the Court's experimental plan for releasing its opinions in electronic format. By the summer of 1990, some university
libraries had already succeeded in downloading a decision utilizing BITNET or
Internet computer link-ups to one of these thirteen, a consortium of Case
Western University, the National Public Telecomputing Network, and the Inter-
university Communication Council (EDUCOM). In early 1991, the full text of
Supreme Court opinions became available to *all* depository libraries within
12 hours of their release by the Court.[18]

Three basic, parallel series also contain full-text decisions of the Supreme
Court in traditional print form. A description of these editions follows.

United States Reports

The official GPO edition of Supreme Court reports is issued in three stages.
In order of appearance, they are as follows:

1. Slip opinions (Ju 6.8/b) are printed individually when rendered by the
    High Court. Information includes the docket number, date of argu-
    ment, date of decision, and a syllabus prepared by the Reporter of Deci-
    sions for the convenience of the reader. Figure 9.3 shows a typical slip
    opinion.

2. *Official Reports of the Supreme Court: Preliminary Print* (Ju 6.8/a) are
    issued in paperbound form and generally cover a two- or three-week
    period. They contain an index and cumulative table of cases reported.
    The pagination of the preliminary prints is the same as that which will
    appear in the bound volumes. Figure 9.4 (see page 304) shows the first
    page of a case published in an official *Preliminary Print*.

3. *United States Reports* (Ju 6.8) is the bound, permanent edition of the
    decisions. Once the bound volume is received, libraries may discard the
    individual opinions and the preliminary prints. The bound version con-
    tains a table of cases reported, a table of statutes cited, and a topical
    index. As with the material included in the preliminary prints, the
    United States Reports include per curiam decisions, orders, and
    chamber opinions as well as the full text of decisions. This official edi-
    tion is commonly cited simply as "U.S." The astute student needing to

(Text continues on page 305.)

Fig. 9.3. Slip opinion, *United States Reports*

SUPREME COURT OF THE UNITED STATES

No. 90–615

RAFAEL PERETZ, PETITIONER *v.* UNITED STATES

ON WRIT OF CERTIORARI TO THE UNITED STATES COURT OF
APPEALS FOR THE SECOND CIRCUIT

[June 27, 1991]

JUSTICE STEVENS delivered the opinion of the Court.

The Federal Magistrates Act grants district courts authority to assign magistrates certain described functions as well as "such additional duties as are not inconsistent with the Constitution and laws of the United States."[1] In *Gomez* v. *United States*, 490 U. S. 858 (1989), we held that those "additional duties" do not encompass the selection of a jury in a felony trial without the defendant's consent. In this case, we consider whether the defendant's consent warrants a different result.

I

Petitioner and a codefendant were charged with importing four kilograms of heroin. At a pretrial conference attended by both petitioner and his counsel, the District Judge asked if there was "[a]ny objection to picking the jury before a magistrate?" App. 2. Petitioner's counsel responded: "I would love the opportunity." *Ibid.* Immediately before the jury selection commenced, the Magistrate asked for, and received, assurances from counsel for petitioner and from counsel for his codefendant that she had their clients' consent to proceed with the jury selection.[2] She then proceeded to

---

[1] Pub. L. 90–578, 82 Stat. 1108, as amended, 28 U. S. C. § 636(b)(3).

[2] "THE COURT: Mr. Breitbart, I have the consent of your client to proceed with the jury selection?

"MR. BREITBART: Yes, your Honor.

Fig. 9.4. Page from official *Preliminary Print*

GULFSTREAM AEROSPACE CORP. *v.* MAYACAMAS CORP.   271

Syllabus

GULFSTREAM AEROSPACE CORP. *v.* MAYACAMAS CORP.

CERTIORARI TO THE UNITED STATES COURT OF APPEALS FOR THE NINTH CIRCUIT

No. 86–1329.   Argued December 7, 1987—Decided March 22, 1988

Petitioner sued respondent in state court for breach of contract. Respondent did not remove the action to federal court, but, one month later, filed a diversity action against petitioner in the Federal District Court for breach of the same contract. The District Court denied petitioner's motion to stay or dismiss the action before it, finding that the facts of the case fell short of those necessary to justify the requested discontinuance under *Colorado River Water Conservation Dist.* v. *United States*, 424 U. S. 800, which held that, in "exceptional" circumstances, a district court may stay or dismiss an action because of the pendency of similar state-court litigation. The Court of Appeals dismissed petitioner's appeal for lack of jurisdiction, holding that neither 28 U. S. C. § 1291—which provides for appeals from "final decisions" of the district courts—nor § 1292(a)(1)—which authorizes appeals from interlocutory orders granting or denying injunctions—allowed an immediate appeal from the District Court's order. The court also declined to treat petitioner's notice of appeal as an application for a writ of mandamus under the All Writs Act.

Held:

1. A district court order denying a motion to stay or dismiss an action when a similar suit is pending in state court is not immediately appealable under § 1291 or § 1292(a)(1).   Pp. 275–288.

(a) Since the order in question does not end the litigation but ensures that it will continue in the District Court, it is not appealable under § 1291. The order does not fall within the collateral-order exception to § 1291, since it fails to satisfy the exception's "conclusiveness" requirement in that it is inherently tentative and not made with the expectation that it will be the final word on the subject addressed. Given both the nature of the factors to be considered under *Colorado River* and the natural tendency of courts to attempt to eliminate matters that need not be decided from their dockets, a district court usually will expect to revisit and reassess an order denying a stay in light of events occurring in the normal course of litigation.   Pp. 275–278.

photocopy a case will often choose this version, which can be copied two pages per 8-1/2"-by-11" sheet. The printed official versions of the *United States Reports* have a time lag, however. The preliminary prints run about two years behind date of decisions; the bound volumes are about three years behind.

United States Supreme Court Reports, Lawyers' Edition

Published by LCP and cited as L.Ed. or L.Ed.2d, depending on series, this commercial version of Supreme Court reports is issued first in Advance Reports, published twice monthly. The page numbering is identical with that which will appear in the bound volumes. Advance Reports contain a very readable "Current Awareness Commentary," a cumulative table of cases and statutes, and an index. Case summaries and headnotes, which are classified to the *Digest of the United States Supreme Court Reports, Lawyers' Edition*, precede the text of each opinion. Figure 9.5 (see pages 306 and 307) shows two pages from an L.Ed.2d Advance Report showing the value-added library and annotation references.

As the number of cases accumulate, bound volumes are issued to supersede the Advance Reports. As with the official edition, opinions are arranged in chronological order within each volume. This edition is popularly sought after for the annotations it provides and for the summaries of briefs of counsel. Bound volumes have pocket supplementation that includes a "Citation Service," a "Later Case Service," and "Court Corrections."

Supreme Court Reporter

Cited as S.Ct., this special unit of West's *National Reporter System* contains the typical features of West's topic and key number classification system in addition to the cases themselves. Headnotes referencing topic and key number are classified to the *American Digest System*. Features of the advance sheets, issued biweekly, and the bound volumes include tables of cases, statutes construed, federal rules of civil and criminal procedure, ABA standards for criminal justice, dispositions, words and phrases, key number digest, and judicial highlights (synopses of current state and federal cases of special interest). Figure 9.6 (see page 308) shows a per curiam decision published in an advance sheet of West's *Supreme Court Reporter*.

Method of Citing

Citations to court cases may be found in numerous ways, such as through newspaper articles (usually case name at best), journal articles, notes of decisions located in volumes of annotated codes, and more systematic search routes. In the official edition of *United States Reports*, in law reviews, and in scholarly

(Text continues on page 309.)

Fig. 9.5. Pages from L.Ed.2d Advance Report

MISSOURI, et al., Petitioners

v

KALIMA JENKINS, by her friend, KAMAU AGYEI, et al.

491 US —, 105 L Ed 2d 229, 109 S Ct —

[No. 88-64]

Argued February 21, 1989. Decided June 19, 1989.

Decision: Under 42 USCS § 1988, enhancement of attorneys' fee award against state to compensate for payment delay held not to violate Eleventh Amendment, and market-rate paralegal and law clerk compensation held proper.

SUMMARY

After the United States District Court for the Western District of Missouri granted various remedies in a school desegregation suit against the state of Missouri and the Kansas City Missouri School District, a local attorney and the NAACP Legal Defense and Educational Fund (LDF), both of which had represented the plaintiff class in the litigation for several years, requested attorneys' fees under the Civil Rights Attorney's Fees Awards Act of 1976 (42 USCS § 1988), which authorizes a reasonable attorney's fee award to the prevailing party, other than the United States, in any action under certain civil rights statutes. In granting the award, the District Court, in order to take account of the delay in payment of attorneys' fees, calculated the hourly rates for the local attorney and his associates who worked on the case, and for the LDF attorneys who worked on the case, by using current market rates, rather than those applicable at the time the services were rendered. In calculating, as part of the award, the fees for the law clerks, paralegals, and recent law school graduates who were employed by the local attorney and the LDF to work on the case, the District Court also used current market rates to compensate for the delay in payment. The United States Court of Appeals for the Eighth Circuit affirmed the District Court's decision in all respects (838 F2d 260).

On certiorari, the United States Supreme Court affirmed. In an opinion by BRENNAN, J., joined by WHITE, BLACKMUN, STEVENS, and KENNEDY, JJ., and joined as to point 2 below by O'CONNOR and SCALIA, JJ., it was held that (1)

229

Fig. 9.5. *(continued)*

MISSOURI v JENKINS
105 L Ed 2d 229

HEADNOTES

Classified to U.S. Supreme Court Digest, Lawyers' Edition

Civil Rights § 79; Costs and Fees § 33; States, Territories, and Possessions § 88; Statutes §§ 102, 103 — 42 USCS § 1988 — enhancement of attorneys'

fee award against state — Eleventh Amendment

1a-1f. The Federal Constitution's Eleventh Amendment, which constrains actions for damages payable

---

TOTAL CLIENT-SERVICE LIBRARY® REFERENCES

7 Am Jur 2d, Attorneys at Law §§ 277 et seq.; 15 Am Jur 2d, Civil Rights § 278; 20 Am Jur 2d, Costs §§ 74, 78, 79

6 Federal Procedure, L Ed, Civil Rights §§ 11:89, 11:106-11:109

2 Am Jur Proof of Facts 233, Attorneys' Fees

1 Am Jur Trials 93, Setting the Fee

USCS, Constitution, Amendment 11; 42 USCS § 1988

US L Ed Digest, Civil Rights § 79; Costs and Fees § 33; States, Territories, and Possessions § 93

Index to Annotations, Attorneys' Fees; Civil Rights Attorney's Fees Awards Act; Eleventh Amendment; States

VERALEX®: Cases and annotations referred to herein can be further researched through the VERALEX electronic retrieval system's two services, **Auto-Cite®** and **SHOWME®**. Use Auto-Cite to check citations for form, parallel references, prior and later history, and annotation references. Use SHOWME to display the full text of cases and annotations.

ANNOTATION REFERENCES

Supreme Court's views as to awards of attorneys' fees in federal civil rights cases. 87 L Ed 2d 713.

Supreme Court's views as to requisites for award of attorneys' fees. 77 L Ed 2d 1540.

Supreme Court's construction of Eleventh Amendment restricting federal judicial power to entertain suits against a state. 50 L Ed 2d 928.

Award of attorneys' fees to pro se litigant under 42 USCS § 1988. 82 ALR Fed 800.

Recovery of additional attorney fees for time spent establishing original entitlement to attorney fees under 42 USCS § 1988. 69 ALR Fed 712.

Construction and application of Civil Rights Attorney's Fees Awards Act of 1976 (amending 42 USCS § 1988), providing that court may allow prevailing party, other than United States, reasonable attorney's fee in certain civil rights actions. 43 ALR Fed 243.

Fig. 9.6. Page from *Supreme Court Reporter* advance sheet

596   111 SUPREME COURT REPORTER

In re Michael SINDRAM.

No. 90–6051.

Decided Jan. 7, 1991.

Petitioner sought extraordinary writ and requested permission to proceed in forma pauperis. The Supreme Court held that petitioner's request that Court consider same claims that petitioner had presented in over a dozen prior petitions was frivolous and abusive.

Motion for leave to proceed in forma pauperis denied.

Justice Marshall filed dissenting opinion in which Justices Blackmun and Stevens joined.

Justice Blackmun filed dissenting opinion in which Justice Marshall joined.

1. **Federal Courts** ⚖444

Granting of extraordinary writ is, in itself, extraordinary.

2. **Federal Courts** ⚖444

Petitioner who sought writ compelling state appellate court to expedite considera-

tion of his appeal so that speeding ticket could be expunged from his driving record was not entitled to in forma pauperis status; petitioner's request that Supreme Court consider same claims that he had presented in over a dozen prior petitions was frivolous and abusive. 28 U.S.C.A. § 1651; U.S.Sup.Ct.Rule 39, 28 U.S.C.A.

PER CURIAM.

Pro se petitioner Michael Sindram seeks an extraordinary writ pursuant to 28 U.S.C. § 1651 and requests permission to proceed *in forma pauperis* under this Court's Rule 39. This is petitioner's twenty-fourth filing before this Court in the October 1990 Term alone. Pursuant to our decision in *In re McDonald*, 489 U.S. 180, 109 S.Ct. 993, 103 L.Ed.2d 158 (1989), we deny the motion for leave to proceed *in forma pauperis.*

Petitioner is no stranger to this Court. In the last three years, he has filed 42 separate petitions and motions, including 20 petitions for certiorari, 15 petitions for rehearing, and 2 petitions for extraordinary writs.[1] Without recorded dissent, the

---

1. *See Sindram v. Reading,* No. 87–5734, *cert. denied* 484 U.S. 1013, 108 S.Ct. 716, 98 L.Ed.2d 666 (1988); motion to file late petition for rehearing denied 488 U.S. 935, 109 S.Ct. 331, 102 L.Ed.2d 348 (1988); *Sindram v. W & W Associates,* No. 87–6689, cert. denied, 486 U.S. 1024, 108 S.Ct. 1999, 100 L.Ed.2d 230 (1988); *Sindram v. Taylor,* No. 88–5386, cert. denied, 488 U.S. 911, 109 S.Ct. 266, 102 L.Ed.2d 254 (1988), rehearing denied, 488 U.S. 987, 109 S.Ct. 546, 102 L.Ed.2d 575 (1988); *Sindram v. Maryland,* No. 89–5039, cert. denied, 498 U.S. ——, 110 S.Ct. 165, 107 L.Ed.2d 122 (1989); *In re Sindram,* No. 88–6538, petition for writ of habeas corpus denied 489 U.S. 1064, 109 S.Ct. 1358, 103 L.Ed.2d 826 (1989); *Sindram v. Ahalt,* No. 89–6755, cert. denied, 494 U.S. ——, 110 S.Ct. 1824, 108 L.Ed.2d 953 (1990); *Sindram v. Consumer Protection Comm'n.,* No. 89–7266, cert. denied, 496 U.S. ——, 110 S.Ct. 3222, 110 L.Ed.2d 669 (1990), rehearing denied, 497 U.S. ——, 111 S.Ct. 9, 111 L.Ed.2d 824 (1990); *Sindram v. N. Richard Kimmel Prop.,* No. 89–7847, cert. denied, 498 U.S. ——, 111 S.Ct. 123, 112 L.Ed.2d 92 (1990), rehearing denied, 496 U.S. ——, 111 S.Ct. 446, —— L.Ed.2d —— (1990); *Sindram v. WSSC,* No. 89–7848, cert. denied, 498 U.S. ——,

111 S.Ct. 124, 112 L.Ed.2d 92 (1990), rehearing denied, 498 U.S. ——, 111 S.Ct. 446, —— L.Ed.2d —— (1990); *Sindram v. Garabedi,* No. 90–5335, cert. denied, 498 U.S. ——, 111 S.Ct. 194, 112 L.Ed.2d 156 (1990), rehearing denied, 498 U.S. ——, 111 S.Ct. 448, —— L.Ed.2d —— (1990); *Sindram v. Steuben Cty.,* No. 90–5351, cert. denied, 498 U.S. ——, 111 S.Ct. 197, 112 L.Ed.2d 159 (1990), rehearing denied, 498 U.S. ——, 111 S.Ct. 448, —— L.Ed.2d —— (1990); *Sindram v. Abrams,* No. 90–5373, cert. denied, 498 U.S. ——, 111 S.Ct. 199, 112 L.Ed.2d 161 (1990), rehearing denied, 498 U.S. ——, 111 S.Ct. 448, —— L.Ed.2d —— (1990); *Sindram v. Nissan Motor Corp.,* No. 90–5374, cert. denied, 498 U.S. ——, 111 S.Ct. 234, 112 L.Ed.2d 194 (1990), rehearing denied, 498 U.S. ——, 111 S.Ct. 449, —— L.Ed.2d —— (1990); *Sindram v. Ryan,* No. 90–5410, cert. denied, 498 U.S. ——, 111 S.Ct. 261, 112 L.Ed.2d 218 (1990), rehearing denied, 498 U.S. ——, 111 S.Ct. 449, —— L.Ed.2d —— (1990); *Sindram v. Sweeney,* No. 90–5456, cert. denied, 498 U.S. ——, 111 S.Ct. 264, 112 L.Ed.2d 221 (1990), rehearing denied, 498 U.S. ——, 111 S.Ct. 449, —— L.Ed.2d —— (1990); *Sindram v. Wallin,* 90–5577, cert. denied, 498 U.S. ——, 111 S.Ct. 356, 112 L.Ed.2d 320 (1990), rehearing

journals, one finds parallel references to U.S. Supreme Court decisions written as follows:

> *Lassiter* v. *Department of Social Services*, 452 U.S. 18, 68 L.Ed.2d 640, 101 S.Ct. 2153 (1981)

The sequence is volume, reporter, page, and, finally, year. As noted earlier, U.S. refers to the official *United States Reports*, L.Ed.2d stands for the identical case published in *United States Supreme Court Reports, Lawyers' Edition, Second Series*, and S.Ct. represents the same case published in West's *Supreme Court Reporter*.

The first ninety volumes of the *United States Reports* are cited using the names of their reporters. Early nominative reporting is characterized as follows:

Name of Reporter	U.S. Reports	Years Covered
Dallas	v.1-4 U.S.	1789-1800
Cranch	v.5-13 U.S.	1801-1815
Wheaton	v.14-25 U.S.	1816-1827
Peters	v.26-41 U.S.	1828-1842
Howard	v.42-65 U.S.	1843-1860
Black	v.66-67 U.S.	1861-1862
Wallace	v.68-90 U.S.	1863-1874

Thus, a citation to an early report would be phrased as follows:

> *Marbury* v. *Madison*, 5 U.S. (1 Cranch) 137, 2 L.Ed. 60 (1803)

Because the first ninety volumes, from official reporters Dallas through Wallace, were later numbered consecutively, the conversion table shown above can be used to determine that, for example, Cranch's reports, in nine volumes, were renumbered volumes 5-13, and *Marbury* may be read either in the official edition or in the *Lawyers' Edition* (first series).[19]

Other Sources and Access Points

Additional tools are also available that either reprint Supreme Court cases or provide additional information and access. Among some of the more important are *The United States Law Week*, the *United States Supreme Court Bulletin*, a Shepard's citator, and several other items of which researchers of Supreme Court decisions ought to be aware.

Published by the Bureau of National Affairs (BNA), *The United States Law Week* (U.S.L.W.), as noted earlier, is a looseleaf weekly law reporter that consists of two sections. The Supreme Court section provides the full text of selected Supreme Court opinions mailed the same day as rendered. It also features the Court's journal of proceedings; cases docketed with subject matter summaries; and a table of cases, case status report, and topical indexing that cumulate. U.S.L.W. also has a "General Law Section" featuring summaries of legal developments, analyses of the week's leading cases, selected new court decisions, the text of selected federal statutes, and a topical index.

The *United States Supreme Court Bulletin*, published by Commerce Clearing House (CCH), is a looseleaf service that sends facsimile reprints of Supreme Court opinions to subscribers. It also features a statement of actions taken by the Court for the preceding week, Court rules, a summary of cases docketed, a table of cases, highlights of recently docketed cases and those awaiting decisions, and the usual detailed subject indexing.

The most appropriate unit of Shepard's is *United States Citations: Case Edition*, which provides citations to the citing cases under the official *United States Reports*, the *Lawyers' Edition*, and the *Supreme Court Reporter*. Shepard's is organized in separate sections including a base volume and bound supplements, which are further supplemented regularly by paper additions. The sections covering the two commercial editions provide parallel references in parentheses from their citations only to the official edition. Another useful source is Shepard's *United States Supreme Court Case Names Citator*, which is a master index to all reported court decisions handed down in that court since 1900 and lists case names alphabetically by both the plaintiff's and defendant's names. The 1987 edition is updated by supplements.

It is not unusual for students of the law to inquire about decisions rendered by specific justices. Although computerized systems make such information readily available, libraries without online access may find useful Linda A. Blanford's *Supreme Court of the United States, 1789-1980: An Index to Opinions Arranged by Justice* (Millwood, NY: Kraus International Publications, 1983; 2 vols.).

It should also be noted that some researchers will seek oral arguments and briefs. The oral arguments, in which counsel for each party attempts to persuade the justices of the merits of their case, are available back to 1953-1954 and as an ongoing subscription from CIS. A *Landmark Briefs and Oral Arguments* series is also sold by University Publications of America (Bethesda, Maryland). Briefs, which are written statements prepared by attorneys arguing a case that contain summaries of the facts, discussion of pertinent laws, and an argument as to how the laws apply to the facts supporting counsel's position, are also available through commercial publishers.

COMPUTER-ASSISTED LEGAL RESEARCH

Electronic access to many of the sources discussed in this chapter is available in both online and, increasingly, CD-ROM form. Although presenting many of the same advantages of speed, specificity of access, and ease of manipulation as other databases, these sources also present some of the same dilemmas. Just as librarians and researchers who have dealt with some of the major microform packages such as ERIC or the Readex or CIS collections will recognize, these databases represent treasure troves of source material generally unanalyzed through traditional card catalogs or online public catalogs. Particularly with the online databases in the legal field, the contents of each are also prone to sudden variation as the database vendor renegotiates its contracts and adds or eliminates information. Reviewing and understanding the databases' contents and scope at any given time is essential when conducting a search.

Computerized legal research generally begins with either a known citation or, to make the most efficient use of the technology, a carefully formulated search question. A computerized search may also be of immense value when only a tidbit of information is known. As one writer suggests though, "Once the researcher has refined the question or search query to the point that it is retrieving relevant cases, the system can print out a list of case citations, which can be used to find the cases on the shelves of a law library—in reporter volumes."[20] Although most electronic services are full text, probably few researchers would rely solely on online viewing, on- or offline printing, or downloading of the complete documents needed.

In recent years, the growth of the online industry and the entry of new companies into the legal publishing field have generated a practical as well as an interesting academic debate over who actually owns what in the commercially published legal volumes that, over the years, have acquired official status in most court systems. Although it seems an accepted notion that any annotation and interpretative material are entitled to copyright, and clear that the judicial decision itself may *not* be copyrighted, the debate is primarily over the proprietary nature of those embellishments such as page numbering that legal publishers have added to make their particular version usable. The controversy came to a head when Mead Data Central "sought to include the West page numbers in its Lexis computerized data base, making it possible to cite the West volumes without having to buy them."[21]

A variety of journals in the field attest to the significance of computerized legal information systems. Several journals in the legal field—*Computer/Law Journal* (v. 1, 1978-), *Rutgers Computer and Technology Law Journal* (v. 1, 1970, title varies), and *Law/Technology*, a continuation of *Law and Computer Technology* (v. 1, 1968-)—are devoted solely to the topic. Issues of *Law Library Journal* (v. 1, 1908-) and *Legal Reference Services Quarterly* (v. 1, 1981-) frequently carry articles related to online systems, and *High Technology Law Journal* (v. 1, 1986-) has published articles on the emerging applications of artificial intelligence and expert systems in law and legal research.

In addition to Project Hermes' electronic delivery of Supreme Court opinions, these and many other cases, statutes, administrative rulings, and a growing mass of secondary materials are offered through other online sources. The primary vendors in the field are Mead Data Central (Dayton, Ohio), with its LEXIS system, and West Publishing Company, with WESTLAW. A brief review of the composition of each follows.

LEXIS

LEXIS provides full-text, interactive commercial online retrieval for a wide range of materials. The database is divided into "libraries" that are made up of files. Files are further subdivided into documents, such as a specific case, section of a statute, or subsection of an administrative regulation. Currently, there are five basic "libraries" within LEXIS. GENFED provides general federal judicial, statutory, and regulatory information; STATES provides comparable information at the state level. The other libraries are LEXREF, which accesses legal reference tools including secondary ones such as directories and legal periodical indexes; LAWREV for law reviews; and ALR for the *American Law Reports* series. LEXIS also includes a service called AutoCite, produced by LCP and Veralex Corporation, that enables a searcher to verify a case's name, current validity, and prior and subsequent history and to locate parallel references.

Federal files include Supreme Court decisions with full text from 1925 to the present, courts of appeals cases from 1938, district court cases from 1960, court of claims cases from 1960, the current *United States Code*, the current *Code of Federal Regulations*, and the *Federal Register* from July 1980. Other files include the Internal Revenue Service (IRS) *Cumulative Bulletin*, Supreme Court briefs (the full text of all briefs submitted to the High Court for cases scheduled for oral argument, beginning with the October 1979 term), legislative histories (public laws and House, Senate, and conference reports for the 1954 *Code* and amendments thereto), the *Federal Reserve Bulletin*, and many more.

To learn about searching in LEXIS, Mead Data Central makes available *Learning LEXIS: A Handbook for Modern Legal Research* (1990).

WESTLAW

WESTLAW is West Publishing Company's computer-assisted legal research system. It, too, is interactive, which means that queries may be modified as frequently as desired to broaden or narrow the scope of a search. It contains bibliographic data and full-text materials that are found in print form in West's various reporter series as well as in other documentation. WESTLAW is composed of databases, analogous to the "libraries" in LEXIS, and files. A quarterly *WESTLAW Database List* apprises users on which databases are available in the system. WESTLAW also provides a service called InstaCite, a counterpart to LEXIS's AutoCite.

WESTLAW's federal databases include the "*U.S. Code, Code of Federal Regulations*, the *Federal Register*, and Full-Text Plus coverage of the U.S. Supreme Court from 1790 to date, Courts of Appeals from 1891 to date and U.S. District Courts from 1789 to date. Also included are *West's Bankruptcy Reporter* and *West's Military Justice Reporter.*"[22] Full-Text Plus "means that cases are checked for accuracy and up-to-date information (correct citations and parallel citations); and the full text of court opinions is enhanced with editorially prepared synopses and headnotes."[23] Also available through WESTLAW is a wide range of topical databases including cases, statutes, regulations, administrative decisions, articles, and commentary. Through WESTLAW gateways it is possible to access other legal and nonlegal databases.

Anyone planning to acquire or search the system would do well to read the *WESTLAW Introductory Guide to Legal Research* and the *WESTLAW Reference Manual* (3d ed., 1989) to understand its full capabilities. In addition to the print WESTLAW manuals, a very useful disk self-tutorial called WESTrain II contains ten modules including ones on retrieving a specific document, browsing retrieved documents, and searching parts of cases.

West has begun to offer selected databases on CD-ROM as well. Four topical libraries have initially been made available. These include Bankruptcy, Civil Practice, Government Contracts, and Federal Taxation. A CD-ROM somewhat comparable to its online federal database would appeal more, however, to larger general academic and public libraries in which WESTLAW itself has not developed strong roots.

For anyone inclined to pursue further details of LEXIS or WESTLAW, Robert J. Nissenbaum has prepared an excellent critical analysis and overview, with illustrations, for *Fundamentals of Legal Research.*[24] Numerous articles are also available in the professional literature.[25]

Other Online Systems

Other computer-assisted legal systems have also been developed but are not necessarily available to the general public. The JURIS system, developed by the Department of Justice in the 1970s, is a full-text system. According to early accounts, it holds two basic types of data files: (1) federal statutory and case law and (2) the "work product" of the Justice Department, consisting of briefs, memoranda, policy directives, procedural manuals, and other materials generated by the attorneys in Justice in their day-to-day work routines.[26]

In 1989, law libraries also gained access to OCLC's Legal Electronic Network and Database (LEGEND). Through LEGEND, one can gain access to the bibliographic records, combined locations, serial holdings, and loan policies of about 500 law libraries that participate in the OCLC database without the requirement of subscribing to full OCLC coverage.

THE ACQUISITION OF LEGAL MATERIALS

It should be obvious at this point that only a limited number of those materials necessary to conduct legal research are available through the Superintendent of Documents or other official channels. The preponderance of legal tools are sold commercially by a small number of legal publishers, cited throughout this text. Older materials, of course, retain their value due to the role of precedent; libraries needing to replace or enhance their collections may, however, find it difficult to obtain print back files of important titles through normal commercial channels. For this reason, microform editions often become essential purchases.

The earlier cited *Law Books and Serials in Print* includes items available in microform and appears to replace Henry P. Tseng's *Complete Guide to Legal Materials in Microform*, last supplemented through 1982 (Columbus, OH: AMCO International). However, another source important to the acquisition of historical materials is the Law Library Microform Consortium (LLMC). This consortium is a self-governing, nonprofit corporation organized in 1977 by the law schools of the University of Hawaii and Wayne State University; it markets microfiche products directly to participating institutions. It also offers its publications for sale through established commercial law book dealers on a commission basis. Authorized dealers include William S. Hein and Company (Buffalo, New York) and Fred B. Rothman and Company (Hackensack, New Jersey).

The acquisition of a collection of legal materials appropriate to basic research can be a costly venture, particularly as such a paucity of governmentally published editions is available for purchase. Librarians need to carefully assess which tools are essential in their specific environment; conduct critical evaluations of commercial counterparts of those official editions that are available; and determine to what degree they are willing to provide enhanced speed of receipt, convenience, and value-added products by selecting privately published versions. Of course, as has been seen throughout this chapter, in many instances no alternative exists but to purchase commercially. When making commercial purchases of legal materials, selectors also need to decide whether they will stay within the boundaries of one commercial legal system by buying only sister publications or whether the situation warrants variation in the products acquired. The benefits, as well as the shortcomings, of online systems also require careful attention, particularly because the contents of online products tend to change and because legal research is predicated upon historical precedent.

SUMMARY

The year 1990 marked the 200th anniversary of the first meeting of the Supreme Court. The High Court was the last branch of government to assume its tasks, almost eleven months after the House of Representatives convened. Article III of the Constitution is the soul of brevity, within a document that is nothing if not succinct. The 1st Congress found few guidelines for the creation of the Supreme Court and the lower federal courts; the delegates to the Constitutional Convention "had been far more specific in their design of the [Congress] and the authority of the President." The framers agreed "on the structure of the House and Senate and created a new kind of national executive, but it left for the First Congress the difficult choices concerning the Federal Courts."[27] Hence, the Congress enacted the landmark piece of legislation popularly known as the Judiciary Act of 1789 (1 Stat. 73).

Over these two centuries, the judiciary has assumed immense powers. Judicial review by the courts of the Bill of Rights gives U.S. society its stability and resiliency. As a member of Congress has observed, the courts have

> found a way to protect the discrete and insular minorities from the tyranny of the majority. It is this role which led [the judiciary] to gain the respect of the American people. If the legislative branch finds itself swayed by the political passions of the era, the [judiciary] must rise to protect the people who find solace in no other quarter.[28]

By and large, the protection of the rights of the less empowered members of society is the essence of the third branch's mandate under the Constitution.

NOTES

[1]For a helpful guide, see V. Maclay, "Selected Sources of United States Agency Decisions," *Government Publications Review*, 15 (May/June 1989): 271-301.

[2]The abridgment is titled *Legal Research Illustrated*, 5th ed. (1990), and has an assignment supplement keyed to both editions. Foundation Press is the publisher.

[3]J. Myron Jacobstein and Roy M. Mersky, *Fundamentals of Legal Research*, 5th ed. (Westbury, NY: Foundation Press, 1990), p. 554.

[4]Prior to 1908, one must use the six-volume *Jones-Chipman Index to Legal Periodicals*. Jacobstein and Mersky, *Fundamentals of Legal Research*, p. 333.

[5]Cited in Jacobstein and Mersky, *Fundamentals of Legal Research*, p. 345.

[6]*West's Law Finder: A Legal Research Manual*, 1989, p. 11.

[7]Jacobstein and Mersky, *Fundamentals of Legal Research*, p. 114.

[8]Miles O. Price et al., *Effective Legal Research*, 4th ed. (Boston: Little, Brown and Company, 1979), pp. 172-73.

[9]Jacobstein and Mersky, *Fundamentals of Legal Research*, p. 266.

[10]For further information, see, for instance, Cole, "Shepardizing: A Comparison of the Printed Citators and the On-Line Shepardizing Services," *Legal Reference Services Quarterly*, 7 (Summer/Fall/Winter 1987): 261-70.

[11]Jacobstein and Mersky, *Fundamentals of Legal Research*, p. xli.

[12]According to the *Guide to American Law*, vol. 5, p. 211, the *Federal Reporter* also carries cases from the U.S. courts of appeals and the former U.S. Court of Customs and Patent Appeals for the years beginning with 1932; from the U.S. Emergency Court of Appeals for 1942 to 1961 and the U.S. Temporary Emergency Court of Appeals for 1972 to the present; and from the former U.S. Court of Claims for 1960 to the fall of 1982, after which it became the U.S. Claims Court.

[13]The *Federal Supplement* also contains decisions of the U.S. Court of Claims from 1932 to 1960 and of the U.S. Customs Court from 1949 to 1980. In 1969 it began carrying rulings of the Judicial Panel on Multidistrict Litigation. *Guide to American Law*, p. 217.

[14]Alexander M. Bickel, *The Least Dangerous Branch*, 2d ed. (New Haven, CT: Yale University Press, 1986), and David M. O'Brien, *Storm Center* (New York: Norton, 1986). A second edition of the latter work was published in 1990.

[15]Public Law (PL) 100-352 (102 Stat. 662) of June 27, 1988, gave the Supreme Court even greater discretion in selecting the cases it will review. The legislation follows a pattern established by Congress to help relieve the increasing caseload burden on the Court. Indeed, in the October 1989-June 1990 term, the Court heard about 15 percent fewer cases than it had the previous term.

[16]Lawrence Baum, *The Supreme Court* (Washington, DC: Congressional Quarterly Press, 1981), p. 12.

[17]"Supreme Court to Transmit Decisions by Computer," *The New York Times*, December 19, 1989, p. A24.

[18]The February 15, 1991, issue of *Administrative Notes* advised depositories to refer to the newsletter's volume 11, no. 24, for instructions on accessing Project Hermes through the Government Printing Office's electronic bulletin board.

[19]West's *Supreme Court Reporter* did not begin its series until the October term of 1882.

[20]William P. Statsky, *Legal Research and Writing: Some Starting Points*, 3d ed. (St. Paul, MN: West, 1986), p. 152.

[21]"Progress Spawns Question: Who Owns the Law?" *The New York Times*, February 16, 1990, p. B7.

[22]*West's Law Finder*, p. 31.

[23]*West's Law Finder*, p. 30. West also has an Insta-Cite that connects with *Shepard's Citations* and provides prior and later direct case histories for federal cases.

[24]Jacobstein and Mersky, *Fundamentals of Legal Research*, ch. 22, "Computer-Assisted Legal Research and Microtext," pp. 441-61.

[25]For several reviews, see Dabney, "The Curse of Thamus: An Analysis of Full-Text Legal Document Retrieval," *Law Library Journal*, 78 (Winter 1986): 5-40, and subsequent issues; Coco, "Full-Text vs. Full-Text Plus Editorial Additions: Comparative Retrieval Effectiveness of the LEXIS and WESTLAW Systems," *Legal Reference Services Quarterly*, 4 (Summer 1984): 27-37; and Shapiro, "Which Is Better, Lexis or Westlaw?" *California Lawyer* (January/February 1988): 56 + .

[26]James E. Hambleton, "JURIS: Legal Information in the Department of Justice," *Law Library Journal*, 69 (May 1976): 199.

[27]*Congressional Record*, daily edition, February 1, 1990, p. H196.

[28]*Congressional Record*, daily edition, February 1, 1990, p. H198.

10

Statistical Sources

INTRODUCTION

The breadth and depth of the U.S. government's statistics gathering enterprise has no equal; likewise, the timeliness and relevance of the government's data often mean that these statistics are the best available on myriad topics. The statistical system of the federal government is decentralized. Numerous agencies gather various kinds of data and report these data for the use of both the private sector and the government itself. Congressional hearings also generate a wealth of data on a wide array of issues high on the national agenda. Statistics help measure the quality of life; provide the basis for modifications in union contracts, child support, and Social Security payments; determine where the United States stands in relation to other countries; and address a host of other economic, social, and scientific matters. A striking example of the significance accorded one statistic alone, the Consumer Price Index (CPI), is noted in the Office of Technology Assessment's *Statistical Needs for a Changing U.S. Economy: Background Paper* (Y 3.T22/2:2ST2/2, 1989, p. 3):

> Constructed as an indicator of inflation, the CPI has a direct effect on nearly every citizen in the United States. At least 8.5 million workers are covered by collective bargaining contracts that link wage rates to changes in the CPI. The payments made to 38 million Social Security beneficiaries, 3.5 million retired military and civil service employees and survivors, 20 million food stamp recipients, and 23 million children who eat lunch at school are also linked to the CPI by law.

Improving the quality of federal statistics is a topic of frequent concern among professional data users, and a number of articles and reports in the late 1980s expressed concern that that decade had been marked by a deterioration in statistical quality.[1] Initiatives in 1991, in fact, led to improved funding for the Bureau of the Census and the Bureau of Labor Statistics, two major statistics-gathering agencies. In addition, the President's Council of Economic Advisors proposed an Economics Statistics Initiative that recommends improvements in seven broad areas and calls for spending $230 million over a five-year period to enhance the quality of federal economic statistics.[2] However, concepts must constantly be refined, statistics collecting methods updated, and redundancies among agencies' data collection programs evaluated. Although the economist or historian doing time series analyses would find life much simpler if statistical tables remained constant over time, maintenance of the status quo must often take a back seat to current requirements. Keeping up with changes in statistical procedures and tools can itself be a time-consuming affair. The 1990 edition of the annual *Statistical Programs of the United States Government* (PrEx 2.10/3) contains information on over seventy agencies that have annual budgets of at least $500,000 for statistical activities.

Volumes have been written about the federal statistical system. This chapter is intended to identify and explain some important, basic statistical sources. It also tries to provide the beginning researcher with a starting point for understanding our national censuses and with an explanation of the process and sources involved in creating another complex statistical undertaking, the federal budget.

GUIDES TO THE LITERATURE

Two highly readable guides to using government statistics offer help to the novice searcher. Jean L. Sears and Marilyn K. Moody's *Using Government Publications* (Phoenix, AZ: Oryx Press, 1986) devotes several chapters to statistical searches, covering topics from foreign trade, to defense and military statistics, to projections. Judith Schiek Robinson's *Tapping the Government Grapevine* (Phoenix, AZ: Oryx Press, 1988) concentrates most of chapter 12 on census products.

Various books published by Libraries Unlimited focus on significant sources of federal statistical and demographic data and offer brief annotations especially useful from the reference or collection development standpoint. Included are LeRoy C. Schwarzkopf's *Government Reference Serials* (1988), his *Government Reference Books 88/89* (1990), and William G. Bailey's *Guide to Popular U.S. Government Publications* (1990). Discovering what governmental agency (or other Washington-based organization) is responsible for data collection on a given topic might be accomplished through use of Congressional Quarterly's (CQ) annual *Washington Information Directory*.

Examples of some specialized guides to aid the more sophisticated researcher include Norman Frumkin's *Guide to Economic Indicators* (Armonk, NY: M. E. Sharpe, 1990), and William Evinger's *Federal Statistical Databases: A Comprehensive Catalog of Current Machine-Readable and Online Files* (Phoenix, AZ: Oryx Press, 1988), which supersedes the Commerce Department's 1981 *Directory of Federal Statistical Data Files*. Where extensive work is warranted, librarians and researchers may also want to contact the library of the appropriate agency. Those who have access to the Inter-University Consortium for Political and Social Research (ICPSR) (Ann Arbor, MI) may consult ICPSR's annual *Guide to Programs and Services*. The seasoned research learns that data not readily identifiable through basic sources often turn up in more elusive places and may already have been manipulated to fit the specific need.

PROFESSIONAL ORGANIZATIONS

In recent years, professional organizations have played an increasingly important role in lobbying the government regarding its information gathering and data dissemination functions. Two such organizations are the Association of Public Data Users (APDU) and the Council of Professional Associations on Federal Statistics (COPAFS).

APDU sponsors an annual conference that focuses on federal data programs and publishes the *APDU Newsletter*, useful for the quick glimpse it provides into new programs and publications. Originally created in 1975 "to save money in the acquisition and use of public data on computer tape," APDU, based in Princeton, New Jersey, has evolved into an organization that also attempts to increase its members' knowledge of new sources of information while at the same time affecting the awareness of federal agencies regarding the needs of data users.[3]

COPAFS, located in Alexandria, Virginia, has broad concerns regarding the federal statistical system and is composed of other groups such as the American Political Science Association, the Association for Vital Records and Health Statistics, and APDU. The January/March 1990 *News from COPAFS*, for instance, presented an informative analysis of recommendations emerging from the Working Group on Improving the Quality of Economic Statistics, a group established by President George Bush in 1989, and reported extensively on hearings held by the Joint Economic Committee on the state of the federal statistical system.

A third organization that merits attention because of its early emphasis on using machine-readable data archives is the International Association for Social Science Information Service and Technology (IASSIST), located in Ottawa, Canada. It publishes the *IASSIST Quarterly*. Librarians and researchers should recognize these organizations as alternative sources both for information regarding new statistical products and services and for evaluative studies on the federal statistical system.

MAJOR INDEXES AND GUIDES

The single best index to federal statistical publications is the *American Statistics Index* (ASI), published since 1973 by the Bethesda, Maryland-based Congressional Information Service (CIS). The comprehensiveness and quality of ASI place it in a category by itself. ASI indexes and provides abstracts for statistical publications of the executive branch, Congress, the judiciary, and other federal entities. It is issued monthly with quarterly cumulated indexes, followed by the ASI/*Annual Supplement* consisting of a cumulated, bound index volume correlated to a separately bound volume of the abstracts. Index cumulations also are available for intervals covering 1974-1979, 1980-1984, and 1985-1988. An initial three-volume set published in 1974, titled ASI *Annual & Retrospective Edition*, provides indexing and abstracting on a selective basis for publications issued from the early 1960s to January 1974. The ASI database may also be accessed online through Dialog (File 102) or through the *CIS Statistical Masterfile on CD-ROM*. The *Statistical Masterfile* affords the user access not only to the entire contents of ASI but also to CIS's *Statistical Reference Index* and its *Index to*

International Statistics. Its powerful search capability allows for boolean logic, wildcard adjacency, and free-text searching.

Figure 10.1 shows a sample abstract from ASI. Exhaustive indexing is provided by subjects, names (personal and corporate), categories (demographic and

Fig. 10.1. Sample abstract from ASI

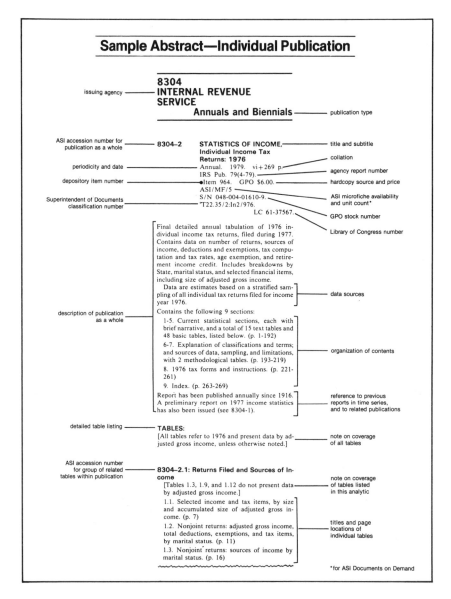

geographic), publication titles, and agency report numbers. References are to abstract numbers, from which full bibliographic information and specific content information can be determined. Library users can proceed directly from the abstract to (1) a library's collection, whether it be a paper/microfiche depository collection using the Superintendent of Documents (SuDocs) number provided; (2) the Readex collection of depository or nondepository microprint or fiche using the *Monthly Catalog* year and entry number (or SuDocs number for later years); or (3) CIS's own microfiche collection, which is available for purchase. CIS also offers a CIS & ASI Documents on Demand service that provides almost any publication abstracted on an individual order basis. Prices depend on the number of pages reproduced and on whether the publication is requested in paper copy or microfiche. An outstanding feature of ASI is the in-depth abstracting given to government periodicals that contain statistical information. The same applies to congressional hearings, which often unveil newly collected statistical data either in the text of the hearing or as an appendix to it.

A number of other guides exist that will at least steer the user in the direction of needed statistical sources. *Statistics Sources*, 14th ed. (Detroit, MI: Gale Research, 1991, 2 vols.), edited by Jacqueline O'Brien and Steve Wasserman, remains a standard for all types of statistics but concentrates heavily on U.S. federal data. Although lacking SuDocs numbers for sources cited, it does provide names and telephone numbers of key federal statistical personnel and identifies major federal government statistical files available in machine-readable format. John L. Andriot's *Guide to U.S. Government Statistics*, 5th ed. (McLean, VA: Documents Index, 1990/1991), may be a slightly more affordable tool for libraries interested solely in public data and offers the advantage of tracing title changes and providing SuDocs numbers. Also available is William Evinger's *Federal Statistical Source: Where to Find Agency Experts and Personnel* (Phoenix, AZ: Oryx Press, 1991). Issued by the government through twenty-six editions (1935-1979) as the *Federal Statistical Directory*, this title was privatized and is now in its twenty-ninth edition. Still another option is Allison Ondrasik's *Data Map* (Phoenix, AZ: Oryx Press, 1983-), published annually beginning in 1988. In the introduction to the 1990 edition the author claims to "provide the most frugal coverage of the widest possible variety of social, political, economic, technical, and other data" for sixteen selected, key federal sources. A fifth alternative is Juri Stratford and Jean Slemmons Stratford's *Guide to Statistical Materials Produced by Government and Associations in the United States* (Alexandria, VA: Chadwyck-Healey, 1987).

BASIC STATISTICAL COMPENDIA

If a first tier of core statistical sources were to be selected, it would surely include the *Statistical Abstract of the United States* (C 3.134). Published annually since 1878, the *Stat Abstract* as it is popularly called is the basic "summary of statistics on the social, political, and economic organization of the United States," according to its own preface. Data are selected from many statistical series, both governmental and private. The tabular data may be used either by themselves to answer questions or to serve as a guide to more detailed information. This latter function is accomplished by the introductory text to each section; by the "source notes" that refer the user to the issuing entity, where more comprehensive information may be found; and by appendixes that contain a "Guide to Sources of Statistics" and "Guide to State Statistical Abstracts."

Each edition adds, drops, or refines features of the *Stat Abstract*, but the contents, divided into sections, typically cover over thirty broad areas, from population, vital statistics, education, and the labor force to energy, science, transportation, and comparative international data. Among the many recent additions are statistics on religious congregations, school enrollment projections by state, deaths from AIDS, household pet ownership, child care arrangements, employee drug testing, and home equity loans. A special feature introduced in 1990 provides data on the growth of computer technology in the office environment, and with 1991 increased statistical coverage comes from the quinquennial economic and agricultural censuses. Given its scope and valuable source notes, the *Statistical Abstract* is a government publication that may safely be called indispensable.

Several major tools are considered supplements to the *Stat Abstract* and offer starting points for many reference questions. *Historical Statistics of the United States, Colonial Times to 1970* (C 3.134/2:H62/789-970) contains over 12,500 time series, largely annual, on U.S. social, economic, political, and geographic development from 1610. Well over 1,000 pages, this massive two-volume compilation includes source notes for additional information, definitions of terms, a descriptive text, and a detailed subject index. An appendix in the annual *Stat Abstract* serves as an index to *Stat Abstract* tables that continue *Historical Statistics* tables. The Census Bureau is compiling an official supplement to cover 1940-1990. The bureau also plans to add new series that began in the postwar period and that link to tables in the *Stat Abstract*.

Whereas the *Stat Abstract* and its companion *Historical Statistics* focus on the national arena, two other sources emphasize smaller geographic areas. The 1991 edition of the *State and Metropolitan Area Data Book* (SMADB) (C 3.134/5) is the fourth in a series that began in 1979 and presents data not only for the United States as a whole but also for each state and each Metropolitan Statistical Area (MSA). Important geographic concepts such as the MSA, the Primary Metropolitan Statistical Area (PMSA), and the Consolidated Metropolitan Statistical Area (CMSA), and changes from the earlier Standard Metropolitan Statistical Area (SMSA) are detailed in the section on geographic codes and concepts.[4] Suggested uses for the SMADB include locating areas that are growing the fastest or that have the most college graduates or highest median family income and determining which areas receive the largest amounts of federal contracts.

The *County and City Data Book* (C 3.134/2), its last quinquennial edition issued in 1988, reaches to the smaller geographic level and presents 203 statistical data items for each county in the United States, 134 data items for 952 incorporated cities having 25,000 inhabitants or more, and several data items for unincorporated areas. In addition, information for census divisions and regions, states, and federal administrative regions is provided. Both the *County and City Data Book* and the *State and Metropolitan Area Data Book* are available on diskette; the former is also offered on computer tape and on CD-ROM, and excerpts are available online through CENDATA; and the SMADB has a related County Statistics File on tape.

Because of its extensive reporting on national data needed by businesses, economists, and all types of planners, another source high on the priority list is the *Economic Report of the President* (Pr 41.9; also issued in a congressional edition). The *Economic Report* reviews in narrative form national economic trends and developments; examines economic policy and problems; and presents, through over 100 tables, many of which provide annual historical data, statistics on national income and expenditures, prices, corporate profits and finances, and numerous other economic indicators. A wide array of agency-specific or subject-specific statistical compendia also exists, a representation of which is discussed further later in this chapter.

KEY STATISTICS-PRODUCING AGENCIES AND THEIR PRODUCTS

As the contents of any issue of *American Statistics Index* demonstrate, numerous agencies generate statistics related to their own programs. In addition, several large agencies have as their primary function the collection and dissemination of data for their own publishing programs and those of other federal entities. These are called general-purpose statistical agencies, and among them are the Bureau of the Census, which conducts surveys for departments such as the Department of Housing and Urban Development as well as for itself, and the Bureau of Labor Statistics. Both agencies are examined in detail below. However, although methods of collecting data remain substantially unchanged, it is important to note several technological advances for disseminating information.

Although the status quo prevails in some instances, these new methods of delivering census and other statistical data files emerged through the 1980s and into the 1990s. These changes have prompted librarians and others to lobby actively to have depository libraries included as recipients of the new technologies and to reassess their role in the information pipeline. CD-ROM products and online access via commercial vendors and electronic bulletin boards have opened up a variety of options for the receipt of data; at the same time, librarians have been sent scrambling for the equipment needed to utilize these technologies and are struggling to obtain the training and expertise required to be effective researchers or intermediaries. Two important developments are represented by the Economic Bulletin Board and the National Trade Data Bank.

Economic Bulletin Board

A database especially relevant to the statistical data spawned by both the Census Bureau and the Bureau of Labor Statistics (BLS) is the Commerce Department's Economic Bulletin Board (EBB). EBB opened for service in 1985 and is available on a subscription basis through the National Technical Information Service. EBB delivers to its users a wide range of data released not only from the Census Bureau and BLS, but also from the Federal Reserve Board, the Bureau of Economic Analysis, the International Trade Administration, the Department of the Treasury, the Department of Energy, and the U.S. Special Trade Representative. It is designed to serve as a one-stop source for current economic information, and it includes materials such as the *Daily Statement of the Treasury* (T 63.113/2-2) and the *Trade Opportunities Bulletin* (TOPS), a file previously available to libraries in a published version.

As of September 1990, there were over 2,000 subscribers to the EBB and about 90 new subscribers were being added each month.[5] In the second half of 1990, 100 depository libraries around the United States began participating in a pilot project that extended the service to them and their patrons. The pilot project, one of several that the Government Printing Office (GPO) launched, was considered a critical test of depository libraries' ability to integrate electronic technology into their service component.

Subscribers to EBB receive three types of service. Users may read bulletins, download files, and send messages to or receive messages from the bulletin board. Bulletins provide general economic news, a calendar of release dates for economic indicators, contacts within the various economic statistical agencies, and instructions in the use of the bulletin board; the bulletins may be printed out. Files, on the other hand, are generally larger than bulletins, include the major economic press releases, and are more appropriate to downloading. A typical use of EBB would be for a librarian to check the schedule of release dates in the bulletin section for the frequently requested Consumer Price Index (CPI), download the CPI file on the day of release each month, and then print out a copy for general information, as the data usually are available within minutes of its official release, are far more detailed than the next day's report in *The New York Times* and other newspapers, and appear far in advance of their eventual inclusion in the monthly *CPI Detailed Report* (L 2.38/3). Use of the Economic Bulletin Board does, however, require practice, and it is not amenable to patron searching.

National Trade Data Bank

Whereas the Economic Bulletin Board takes advantage of online technology, the National Trade Data Bank: The Export Connection® (NTDB) (C 1.88) utilizes CD-ROM, a laser technology that permits one 12-centimeter plastic disk to store as much data as would be contained on 1,500 floppy disks. The NTDB is a product of the Department of Commerce and incorporates data from fourteen different agencies, including the Census Bureau and the Bureau of Labor Statistics. It was established under the Omnibus Trade and Competitiveness Act of 1988 to provide "reasonable public access, including electronic access" to an export promotion data system and an international economic data system. The first production CD-ROM was issued in October 1990, and depository librarians selecting the disk soon thereafter learned to understand its uses and parameters.[6]

Statistical files in the NTDB include data from the CIA's *Handbook of Economic Statistics* (PrEx 3.10/7-5), the government's International Energy Database, and the Bureau of Economic Analysis's report on pollution abatement and control expenditures. In addition to the statistical series on the disk, the NTDB also contains several full-text files including the *World Fact Book* (PrEx 3.15), *A Basic Guide to Exporting* (C 61.8:Ex7/3/986), *Understanding United States Foreign Trade Data* (C 61.2:F76/5), and the *U.S. Industrial Outlook* (C 61.34). Articles from the biweekly *Business America* (C 61.18) have also appeared. The disk, updated monthly, also contains a Foreign Traders Index, which is a directory of companies and organizations in other countries with an interest in dealing with U.S. companies. Users may initiate a search by selecting either a BROWSE or a ROMWARE program and either a source (one of the fourteen agencies that supply data), a general topic, an NTDB information program (such as international labor statistics), a subject (title keyword), or an item identification code. Files may be printed or downloaded, and some may require the use of a wide-carriage printer.

Bureau of the Census

Of all the vast statistics-generating federal machinery, that of the Census Bureau is best known. Census publications are the core of a library's collection of statistical data, and the data may be required by anyone from the most sophisticated researcher to the parent who, high school student in tow, asked ever so seriously to see the "consensus on demagoguery." The bureau's primary function is to collect, process, compile, and disseminate statistical data for the use of other government agencies, groups in the private sector, and the general public. It publishes more statistics than other agencies do, covers a wider range of subjects, and serves a greater variety of needs. Moreover, Article I, Section 2, of the Constitution, construed by the one-person, one-vote principle established by the U.S. Supreme Court, requires congressional redistricting based upon population shifts recorded in the decennial census.[7] In *Wesberry* v. *Sanders*, 376 U.S. 1, 11 L.Ed.2d 481, 84 S.Ct. 526 (February 17, 1964), the High Court held that as nearly as practicable one person's vote should be worth as much as another's. Later that year, in *Reynolds* v. *Sims*, 366 U.S. 533, 12 L.Ed.2d 506, 84 S.Ct. 1362 (June 15, 1964), the Court ruled that state legislative districts must be as nearly of equal population as practicable. The two decisions in theory were supposed to eliminate or reduce dramatically the pernicious practice of gerrymandering. In a number of subsequent decisions involving apportionment disputes between 1966 and 1972, the Court followed the precedents set in *Wesberry* and *Reynolds*. However, the practice of gerrymandering continues as blatantly as ever.

The first census was taken in 1790, and the process has been repeated each succeeding decade. In 1902 the Bureau of the Census was established as a permanent office (32 Stat. 51). By laws codified in Title 13 of the *United States Code* and by virtue of Article I, Section 2, of the Constitution, the bureau is enjoined to take a census of population every ten years. Furthermore, as a result of legislation passed by Congress in 1976, the Census Bureau was authorized to conduct a mid-decade census beginning in 1985 and every ten years thereafter, although none materialized for lack of congressional funding. A chronology of major census events appears in the bicentennial issue of *Census and You* (C 3.238:25/8, August 1990, pp. 6-8).

Although media attention tends to focus on the decennial census of population and housing (discussed later), other, lesser known censuses are taken on a five-year schedule. These quinquennial censuses include agriculture, governments, and the "economic censuses" comprised of retail trade, wholesale trade, service industries, construction industries, manufactures, mineral industries, and transportation. Beginning with the 1987 agricultural and economic censuses, the Commerce Department started producing the results on CD-ROM. Since 1977, the bureau has also collected statistics on outlying areas, enterprise statistics, minority-owned business enterprises, and women-owned businesses.[8]

The 17-minute videotape *An Introduction to the 1987 Economic Censuses*, produced in March 1989, traces the economic censuses back to 1810, when questions on manufactures were first asked; examines census concepts such as the Standard Industrial Classification (SIC) system; and gives an excellent overview of the content of these censuses.

In addition, the bureau conducts various U.S. and foreign censuses and surveys in its international research and foreign trade programs. Anyone intending to export or import goods will want to become familiar with the wide array of export/import data collected and published as well as with the classification systems needed to interpret the data. A major revamping of the Commerce Department's classification schedules and series occurred in 1988 and is explained in the *Census Catalog and Guide.* Another useful videotape is *Understanding and Using the HS-Based Schedule B, 1988 Edition*, which explains the Harmonized Commodity Description and Coding System (HS) designed to make U.S. data more comparable to trade data produced by other countries. An awareness of HS is essential to anyone attempting to navigate through trade statistics from 1989 forward. By 1990 the Census Bureau had also begun to distribute the *U.S. Exports of Merchandise* and the *U.S. Imports of Merchandise* series (C 3.278) to depositories on compact disk.

From just this brief glimpse, it is apparent that the Census Bureau is a complex agency. The bureau's overall programs are well summarized in *Census Bureau Programs and Products* in its *Factfinder for the Nation* (May 1990; C 3.252:18). Lest anyone think that only the Census Bureau conducts censuses, however, consider the 1991 census of trumpeter swans conducted by the U.S. Fish and Wildlife Service!

Because users need information far more frequently than on a decennial or quinquennial schedule, the bureau also conducts intercensal activities on a continual basis. Certain reports may be issued annually, quarterly, or monthly; special censuses, such as those requested by local governments, and other surveys and studies also update and supplement the major five- and ten-year counts.

Basic Bibliographic Sources

The *Census Catalog and Guide* (C 3.163/3), published annually, provides information about selected products that became available to the public during the reported year. Organized by census subjects, the *Census Catalog* provides bibliographic data, abstracts, and ordering information for all formats in which the bureau produces material. Access to the contents of the *Census Catalog* is through subject, title, and series indexes. In addition to the current year's *Census Catalog*, a basic collection for research purposes should include several other items. The *Bureau of the Census Catalog of Publications, 1790-1972* (C 3.163/3: 790-972) is a large volume that provides a comprehensive historical bibliography of sources issued by the bureau covering these years. This volume combines the previously issued *Catalog of United States Census Publications, 1790-1945*, prepared by Henry J. Dubester, chief of the Census Library Project, Library of Congress, with the *Bureau of the Census Catalog of Publications, 1946-1972*, which is a compilation of data published in the annual issues of the *Bureau of the Census Catalogs* from 1946 to 1972. From 1972 to 1979, annual, non-cumulative catalogs must still be consulted. Information for 1980 through 1988 is contained in the 1989 *Census Catalog and Guide.* The 1991 *Census Catalog* covers the bureau's products from mid-1988 through 1990, plus early 1990 census releases.

The *Monthly Product Announcement* (C 3.163/7) serves as a supplement to the current *Census Catalog;* even newer information may be accessed through the *Daily List* on CENDATA, which is discussed later. *Census and You* (C 3.238), a monthly newsletter issued by the bureau, keeps users informed about current censuses and surveys; products and programs, including computer tape and online files and other unpublished data sources; seminars and conferences the bureau conducts periodically; contact sources for specific bureau activities and products; and statistical products available from other federal agencies. Periodically the bureau also revises its *Telephone Contacts* list (C 3.238/5), which provides census helplines and other valuable telephone numbers that enable the user to speak directly to someone familiar with specific files and projects.

The *Factfinder for the Nation* (C 3.252) cited earlier is a set of topical brochures published irregularly that describe the range of census materials available on a given subject. Titles in this numbered series include *Data for Small Communities* (no. 22), *Construction Statistics* (no. 9), and *Reference Sources* (no. 5).

Other sources particularly helpful in understanding and maneuvering within the bureau's complex of products include the *Subject Index to Current Population Reports* (C 3.186:P-23/144), *Guide to the 1987 Census of Agriculture and Related Statistics* (C 3.6/2:Ag8/2/987), *Guide to the 1987 Economic Censuses and Related Statistics* (C 3.253:Ec87-R-2), and *Guide to Foreign Trade Statistics: 1983* (C 3.6/2:E70/983) and its supplement, *Summary of Changes in Foreign Trade Data Products for 1988.*

One commercial product is Suzanne Schulze's three-volume *Population Information* series (Phoenix, AZ: Oryx Press).[9] Perhaps the best known complementary commercial endeavor is the annual series *Guides to 1990 U.S. Decennial Census Publications* (Bethesda, MD: Congressional Information Service). The first of the *Guides,* issued in March 1992, consists of five separate indexes and microfiche reproductions of the census reports. This initial *Guide* covers all 1990 census publications that have been issued by the bureau in 1990 and 1991, as well as important background reports on census methodology and policy published by the Commerce Department, the Congress, and the General Accounting Office. Subsequent annual printed guides and microfiche texts will be published in March 1993, 1994, and 1995. Essentially, the *Guides* are republished annual cumulations of ASI abstracts and indexes but only those covering the 1990 census; the text on microfiche is a standard feature of the dual-media package offered by CIS for all its products.

Slater Hall Information Products (SHIP), a Washington, D.C.-based company, is releasing a number of CD-ROM data series under the rubric "Census Plus." Included are *SHIP County-City Plus,* an update of the Census Bureau's *County and City Data Book* with new figures from the 1990 census and the 1987 economic censuses. 1990 census population data for smaller municipalities as well as state and national figures are incorporated in this enhanced database. Data in greater detail are contained in the *SHIP County and City Compendium,* in which the *County-City Plus* information is included with county and metropolitan area data from the bureau's most current county statistics tapes. Also provided are personal income and earnings and employment by industry annual data, commencing with 1969 figures. Both of these CD-ROM products are updated annually.

Census Format and Availability

In addition to the conventional printed reports, census data are also available in microform and computer tape and increasingly are offered online, on diskette, CD-ROM, and data maps. Whereas printed information is available from GPO, other formats such as computer tapes, compact disks, diskettes, microfiche, and technical documentation are obtained by contacting the Data User Services Division, Customer Services, Bureau of the Census, Washington, DC 20233. Customer Services also makes available deposit accounts for the convenience of data users; these accounts permit the ordering of materials from either their Publications or their Electronic Media, Microfiche and Other Products sections without requiring that a check be sent each time an order is placed.

A new method for delivering selected census information was developed by the Census Bureau when it began providing information online through its CENDATA program. A significant aspect of CENDATA, which is offered through Dialog (File 580) or through CompuServe, is the ready access it provides to a substantial amount of data for anyone, home users included, equipped with a personal computer and a modem. Although the casual user most likely will continue to utilize library resources, increasingly, sophisticated researchers are simply dialing up needed information through local terminals. A list of the reports included in CENDATA may be found in the bureau's *Census Catalog and Guide*.

A 1989 study by Sandra Rowland, statistician for the bureau's 21st Century Staff, stresses the importance of the role that intermediaries, especially depository libraries, the State Data Centers, and private vendors, play in disseminating data as well as in conveying user needs to the bureau.[10] Indeed, many Census Bureau series are available to depository libraries in printed form, but some items (such as the Women-Owned Businesses series) are available on microfiche only. With the 1990 census, data are increasingly available on CD-ROM.

In addition to the federal depositories, the bureau also maintains 129 Census Depository Libraries. In 1950 the bureau initiated its own depository system, and at its height over 400 libraries participated. With enactment of the Depository Library Act of 1962 a large number of these libraries joined the Title 44 depository program. Moreover, the bureau no longer adds new member libraries. The 129 libraries designated are required to select the Censuses of Population and Housing for their individual state. They have the option to select a variety of other census information found, for example, in the quinquennial censuses. A list of Census Depository Libraries, arranged by state, is found in *Administrative Notes*, vol. 10 (June 15, 1989), pages 15-20. Because some of these libraries directly administered by the Census Bureau are also Title 44 depositories, confusion can arise over which agency is providing which materials. The information in *Administrative Notes* (pp. 1, 14) clarifies this distinction.

Other sources for census materials include the bureau's State Data Center Program, the National Clearinghouse for Census Data Services, Census Bureau Regional Information Services, and Department of Commerce District Offices.[11]

Personal Data Searching

Although statistics are the focus of this chapter, another use of the census ought not to be overlooked. A seasoned reference professional knows to probe further when asked, "Where is your census of 1870?" Although statistics from the printed reports distributed to libraries may be the object, the query may just as likely be coming from an individual seeking the raw census schedules for genealogical tracing. By law, individual records from the federal population censuses are confidential for seventy-two years. Population census schedules from 1790 through 1920 are available to the public on 35mm positive microfilm at the National Archives and its regional centers or for purchase from the National Archives Trust Fund. Most of the 1890 schedules, however, were destroyed by fire in 1921, and records of the 1920 census opened to the public in 1992.

Researchers looking for specific names in the 1790 census should consult the publication *Heads of Families at the First Census of the United States Taken in the Year 1790* (C 3.11). Special Soundex indexes that show the page and line number on the appropriate census schedules are available for 1880, 1900, 1910, and 1920. In the intradecennial years, particularly during the nineteenth century, a number of state and territorial censuses were also taken. These are described in Henry J. Dubester's *State Censuses: An Annotated Bibliography of Censuses Taken after the Year 1790, by States and Territories of the United States*. An appendix in that volume provides information on the location of existing records. The *Factfinder for the Nation* CFF No. 2, *Availability of Census Records about Individuals*, provides further information regarding the availability of census records pertaining to persons.

The Census Bureau also maintains a staff of employees at Pittsburg, Kansas, whose function is to search the census files from 1900 to date and to provide at nominal cost personal data from census records to individuals who lack other documents of birth or citizenship. The transcripts that may be obtained are used for various purposes—to qualify for old-age assistance, to get a job, to obtain naturalization papers, to get a passport, to establish a claim to an inheritance, to get an insurance policy, or to trace ancestry. The transcripts generally show age at the time the census was taken (not date of birth), sex, relationship to the householder, and, where requested, race. Applications may be mailed directly to the Personal Census Services Branch, 1600 North Walnut Street, Pittsburg, KS 66762. Although one should comfortably be able to assume that data collected in modern times via computer are safe for future generations, concern has arisen over the impact of computer technology on the preservation of the collected material. The problem has been studied by the Government Operations Subcommittee on Government Information, Justice, and Agriculture. Alarming aspects of the technology were also reported in the press.[12]

Alternative Sources of
Census Publications

Retrospective editions of census materials in a microformat have been published by a number of private companies. Congressional Information Service, Inc. (CIS) (Bethesda, Maryland), offers a collection of census reports and serials exclusive of decennial materials covering the period 1820-1967. The collection is divided into two parts. Part 1, 1820-1945, is based on Henry J. Dubester's *Catalog of United States Census Publications, 1790-1945*. Part 2, 1946-1967, is based on the *Bureau of the Census Catalog of Publications, 1946-1972*. Both parts are divided into sections representing specific censuses (agriculture, foreign trade, transportation, etc.) and may be purchased by individual sections. Part 1 contains about 2,500 reports on 5,934 fiche, and Part 2 contains approximately 400 reports, for which there are 4,226 fiche and 181 reels of microfilm for Section III (foreign trade) only. CIS produced a companion guide to these non-decennial publications based on the Census Bureau's catalogs covering those years. Moreover, Congressional Information Service sells a comprehensive microfiche file, drawn from its ASI Microfiche Library, of the decennial censuses 1970-1980 available as a single collection or in three separate parts: population, housing, or population and housing. Research Publications, Inc. (Woodbridge, Connecticut), also sells decennial census publications on 35mm positive microfilm.

A full reprint edition of the first ten U.S. Census Reports (1790 to 1880) is available from Norman Ross Publishing, Inc. (New York City). Out-of-print dealers such as Q. M. Dabney (Box 42026, Washington, DC 20015) also provide a source for acquisition of selected census volumes in hard copy.

1990 – THE CENSUS BICENTENNIAL

Preparations for a new decennial census begin early, often well before the last volume of the preceding decennial is distributed. Concern over the escalating cost of conducting the census and over ensuring accuracy of the count prompted the General Accounting Office study *A $4 Billion Census in 1990?* (GA 1.13:GGD-82-13) as early as 1982. In March 1986 the Census Bureau sent out its *1990 Census Products Issues* in an effort to encourage comments and raise issues preliminary to the 1990 Products Meetings that were held around the country that spring; and, by 1988, dress rehearsals for the bicentennial census were underway.[13] The staging of a decennial census is no small feat, and the characters are plentiful. Newspapers and pertinent journals such as *American Demographics* carry numerous census-related articles; even Garry Trudeau, in his *Doonesbury* comic strip, and other cartoonists have used the census as grist for the mill.[14]

The census of population is the oldest of the censuses taken, and it has been enumerated every ten years since 1790. The first census of housing was taken in 1940, although counts of "dwelling houses" were obtained in earlier censuses of population. Beginning in 1940, a housing census has been taken every ten years in conjunction with the population count. Today published reports and electronic products covering both results refer to the combined census of population and housing. The census questionnaire is subject to change with each new decade, and changes usually reflect the political climate and social realities of the time. This is evidenced in the 1990 special census that attempted to count the "homeless" (see below).

In the census taken April 1, 1990, households received either a "short form" consisting of fourteen basic questions or a "long form" requiring the respondent to answer over forty-five additional questions. All households, whether they received the short or the long form, were asked the same basic questions, which are known as the 100-Percent Component. 100-Percent population items surveyed were household relationship, age, race, sex, marital status, and Hispanic origin. Housing questions addressed the number of units in the structure, number of rooms in the unit, tenure, value of the home (or monthly rent paid), congregate housing, and vacancy characteristics. About one in six housing units received the long form, from which sample social, economic, and housing data were gathered.[15] A capsule view of the major report series and the machine-readable products scheduled for release appears in the Census Bureau's brief *Introduction to 1990 Census Products* and is shown as figure 10.2 (see pages 332, 333, and 334). In many of the series there is one report for each state plus a U.S. summary report; in others, there may be one report for each metropolitan area. Still other reports are released by topic rather than by geographic area. Selected 1990 census statistics are also included in CENDATA. The first 1990 data available were those commonly referred to as the Public Law 94-171 or redistricting file, because it contains information that states need for apportionment purposes. An excellent overview is contained in *1990 Census of Population and Housing Tabulation and Publication Program* (C 3.2:T11/2; July 1989), which discusses dissemination media, data, map, and custom products and also summarizes the differences between 1980 and 1990 products.

Although CD-ROM will not replace the printed reports, the Census Bureau is placing on compact disk additional data such as the Summary Tape Files (STF), files to which depository libraries did not previously have ready access. The printed reports are derived from the STFs. Although one author called distribution of the census through new technologies "democratization" of the data, ease of access for the casual user has yet to be seen, as librarians and other users struggle with unfriendly software.[16] However, one may assume that these technical difficulties will gradually be ironed out and that the laser-disk technology may indeed attract new users in smaller units of government, in public interest groups, and in small businesses, users who were overwhelmed by the computer tape files of the 1970 and 1980 censuses because the tapes required larger computers to process the data. It is clear that the public now has a wide variety of formats from which to gain access to recent data. For example, EXTRACT is public domain software designed to interact with census dBase files to create subsets of data from census CD-ROM databases to be printed or saved to disk. EXTRACT is intended only to perform these transfer functions.

Maps are also an important component of the decennial census. A researcher wishing to study a given area will normally want to consult the appropriate tract or block map corresponding to the tract or block report to ascertain the boundaries of a given area. Census tracts are areas of roughly 2,500 to 8,000 population having relatively homogeneous economic status and living conditions. Tract boundaries are established cooperatively by local statistical area committees in conjunction with the Census Bureau. Blocks, as the name suggests, represent the smallest geographic area for which data are tabulated. For 1990, tract maps are available from the GPO; block maps, unlike in the 1980s, must be purchased directly from the Census Bureau.

(Text continues on page 335.)

Fig. 10.2. Sample 1990 census products

CENSUS '90 U.S. Department Of Commerce BUREAU OF THE CENSUS

Introduction to
1990 Census Products

Subject Items Included in the 1990 Census of Population and Housing

Population	*Housing*
100–Percent Component*	
Household relationship	Number of units in structure
Sex	Number of rooms in unit
Race	Tenure (owned or rented)
Age	Value of home or monthly rent paid
Marital status	Congregate housing (meals included in rent)
Hispanic origin	Vacancy characteristics

Sample Component*

Social characteristics:

Place of birth, citizenship and year of entry to the United States

Education (enrollment and attainment)

Ancestry

Migration (residence in 1985)

Language spoken at home

Veteran status

Disability

Fertility

Year moved into residence

Number of bedrooms

Plumbing and kitchen facilities

Telephone in unit

Vehicles available

Heating fuel

Source of water and method of sewage disposal

Year structure built

Condominium status

Farm residence

Shelter costs, including utilities

Economic characteristics:

Labor force

Place of work and journey to work

Year last worked

Occupation, industry, and class of worker

Work experience in 1989

Income in 1989

Data from the 1990 Decennial Census will serve decision-makers into the 21st century. We've designed a variety of products to fit your data needs. This brochure is an introductory guide to the reports, machine-readable products, and other products of the 1990 census.

If you need more information, contact one of our regional offices, a State data center, or the Census Bureau's Data User Services Division, Customer Services, Washington, DC 20233 (301/763-4100).

* Note: The 100–percent component subject items appear on the short and long forms and are collected from all persons and housing units.   The sample component subject items appear only on the long form or sample questionnaire and are collected from a sample of approximately one in six housing units.

Fig. 10.2. *(continued)*

Major Report Series From the 1990 Census

Population

1990 CP–1 **General Population Characteristics.** (One per State and U.S. Summary) This report series provides detailed statistics on age, sex, race, Hispanic origin, marital status, and household relationship characteristics. Data are presented for States, counties, places of 1,000 or more inhabitants, minor civil divisions (MCDs) of 1,000 or more inhabitants in selected States, State parts of American Indian areas, Alaska Native areas, and summary geographic areas. (There are similar reports for American Indian areas and Alaska Native areas, metropolitan areas (MAs), and urbanized areas (UAs).

1990 CP–2 **Social and Economic Characteristics.** (One per State and U.S. Summary) These reports provide data focusing on population subjects such as income, education, and occupation. Data collected on a sample basis are shown for States (including summaries such as urban and rural), counties, places of 2,500 or more inhabitants, MCDs of 2,500 or more inhabitants in selected States, the State portion of American Indian areas, and Alaska Native areas. (Similar reports show data for American Indian areas and Alaska Native areas, MAs, and UAs.)

Housing

1990 CH–1 **General Housing Characteristics.** (One per State and U.S. Summary) These reports provide detailed statistics on units in structure, tenure, value and rent, number of rooms, and vacancy characteristics. Data are presented for States, counties, places of 1,000 or more inhabitants, MCDs of 1,000 or more inhabitants in selected States, State parts of American Indian areas, Alaska Native areas, and summary geographic areas. (Similar reports present data for American Indian areas and Alaska Native areas, MAs, and UAs.)

1990 CH–2 **Detailed Housing Characteristics.** (One per State and U.S. Summary) This report series provides data on housing subjects such as year structure built, number of bedrooms, plumbing and kitchen facilities, telephone, vehicles available, source of water, sewage disposal, and shelter costs. This report series contains data collected on a sample basis and presents totals for States (including summaries such as urban and rural), counties, places of 2,500 or more inhabitants, MCDs of 2,500 or more inhabitants in selected States, and the State portion of American Indian areas, and Alaska Native areas. (Similar reports present data for American Indian areas and Alaska Native areas, MAs, and UAs.)

Population and Housing

1990 CPH–1 **Summary Population and Housing Characteristics.** (One per State and U.S. Summary) This report series provides total population and housing unit counts as well as summary statistics on age, sex, race, Hispanic origin, household relationship, units in structure, value and rent, number of rooms, tenure, and vacancy characteristics. Data are shown for States, local governments, and American Indian and Alaska Native areas.

1990 CPH–2 **Population and Housing Unit Counts.** (One per State and U.S. Summary) Data on total population and housing unit counts for 1990 and previous decennial censuses are shown for States, counties, MCDs/CCDs, places, State component parts of MAs and UAs, and summary geographic areas.

1990 CPH–3 **Population and Housing Characteristics for Census Tracts and Block Numbering Areas.** (One for each MA and one for each State covering the non-MA balance) Data on most 1990 census subjects are shown for census tracts in MAs, and census tracts or BNAs in the remaining (non-MA) portions of each State. Some tables provide data only on 100–percent subjects, others on sample tabulations.

1990 CPH–4 **Population and Housing Characteristics for Congressional Districts of the 103rd Congress.** (One per State and the District of Columbia) These reports show population and housing data for Congressional Districts as well as counties, places of 10,000 or more inhabitants, and MCDs of 10,000 or more inhabitants in selected States within each Congressional District.

1990 CPH–5 **Summary Social, Economic, and Housing Characteristics.** (One per State and U.S. Summary) This report series, a companion volume to CPH-1, provides data on the sample subjects for local governments, including American Indian and Alaska Native areas.

Fig. 10.2. *(continued)*

1990 Census Machine–Readable Products

Summary Tape Files (STFs)

STFs provide 1990 census data in a series of computer tapes. There may be only one reel of tape for a small State like Vermont, but several tapes for a larger State like California. Each STF has three files or more (shown by a letter suffix attached to the STF number). The files differ in the types of geographic detail tabulated. Files A and B are released State–by–State, each with a somewhat different geographic hierarchy. File C is a United States summary file that follows the release of all the State files. Some STFs provide additional geographic variations. For example, STF 1D presents data for Congressional Districts of the 103rd Congress. The census data in the printed reports, on microfiche, and on laser discs are derived from the tables on the computer tapes. Here are the census tapes available to the public:

STF 1. These STFs include 100–percent population and housing unit counts and characteristics similar in subject content to the 1980 STF 1 but with expanded detail. Data are provided down to the block–group level (File A), block level (File B), and for the United States, regions, divisions, States (including summaries such as urban and rural), counties, MAs, and American Indian and Alaska Native areas.

STF 2. These STFs contain 100–percent population and housing characteristics similar to the 1980 STF 2. These files show more subject detail than STF 1. Each file of the STF 2 includes records for the total population and iterations for race and Hispanic–origin groups. These records also are available separately from the total population records. STF 2 provides data down to the level of census tracts and BNAs.

STF 3. These STFs include sample population and housing characteristics similar in subject content to the 1980 STF 3 but with expanded detail. File A provides data for States and their subareas in hierarchical sequence down to the block group level. File B offers data summarized for 5–digit ZIP Codes.

STF 4. These STFs contain sample population and housing characteristics similar in content to 1980 STF 4. These files show more subject detail than STF 3. Each file of STF 4 includes records for the total population and iterations for race and Hispanic–origin groups. These records also are available separately from the total population records. STF 4 provides data down to the census tract/BNA level.

Other 1990 Census Computer Files

Public Law 94–171 Counts (Redistricting Data File). This data file presents the counts designed and formatted for use in legislative redistricting. The counts, for areas as small as blocks, census tracts, and voting districts, include totals for population, race groups, persons of Hispanic origin, population 18 years and over, and housing units.

Public–Use Microdata Samples (PUMS). These files present a sample of long–form household records for large geographic areas. Each housing unit sample record presents essentially all the census data collected about each person in the household plus the housing unit's characteristics. Geographic information that might tend to identify an individual or a housing unit is not contained on the file. Microdata files enable users to prepare customized tabulations and cross tabulations of virtually any item on the census questionnaire. There are two sets of public–use microdata files: A 1–percent and a 5–percent sample.

Census/Equal Employment Opportunity (EEO) Special File. This file provides 1990 census sample data with particular relevance to EEO and affirmative action uses. This computer file contains two tabulations: one with detailed occupation data by age and the other with educational attainment by age. Both sets of data are cross tabulated by sex, Hispanic origin and race.

Topologically Integrated Geographic Encoding and Referencing (TIGER) System. Extracts from the TIGER File, the automated geographic data base used by the Census Bureau for producing 1990 census maps, are available to the public in several formats. One extract of selected geographic and cartographic information is called the TIGER/Line™ Files. The TIGER/Line™ Files contain, for each feature (e.g., the various individual segments that make up roads, railroads, rivers) information such as geographic area codes, latitude/longitude coordinates of features and boundaries, and the name and type of each feature. The TIGER/Line™ Files also furnish address ranges and associated ZIP Codes for each side of street segments for the densely settled urban core of MAs (approximately the same areas covered by the 1980 GBF/DIME Files). The TIGER/Line™ Files are available on computer tape and CD–ROM.

Other Media

CD–ROM (Compact Disk–Read Only Memory). A single compact laser disk, a new data storage medium, can hold the contents of approximately 1,500 flexible diskettes, or four high density tapes. For the 1990 census, the Public Law 94–171 Counts File and STFs 1A, 1B (extract), 1C, 3A, 3B, and 3C are available on CD–ROM.

Microfiche. As in the 1980 census, microfiche of STFs 1A and 3A (data down to block groups) are available. Block data extracted from STF 1B also are available in this medium.

Online. Selected items and excerpts from the 1990 census reports are available on the Census Bureau's online system, CENDATA.

The TIGER System

Although geography is the foundation of census activities, it has always been the least reliable component of data evaluation. Over the decades the Geography Division of the Census Bureau prepared traditional enumerator assignment maps, and field workers relied on direct observation to assign each household to the correct geographic location. These methods were prepared in separate complex clerical operations by hundreds of workers who, inevitably, made different errors on each product.

The TIGER system went a long way toward eliminating these problems. An acronym for Topologically Integrated Geographic Encoding and Referencing, TIGER is not a map itself. Rather, it is a "digital data base that allows a user to topologically integrate map features with other data (demographic, economic, etc.) by means of suitable applications software." The TIGER extracts "contain exclusively a digital description of geographic areas—including political and statistical area boundaries and codes, latitude/longitude coordinates, feature names and types, and, mostly in metropolitan areas, address ranges."[17] Thus, for the first time, TIGER permits consistency in the geographic products it is capable of generating.

Depository libraries selecting TIGER/Line CD-ROM products noted their first announcement on Shipping List 91-0036E. These microdata were previously available only on magnetic tape. The Library Programs Service did not distribute paper copies of documentation because the Census Bureau places documentation directly on the compact disks in a README file, subdirectory "Document." Paper copies of the documentation, however, may be purchased from Customer Services. Moreover, the applications software to access the digitized data on the TIGER/Line disks is sold through commercial vendors. The bureau's Customer Services will provide a list of firms that have indicated they have the appropriate software. Figure 10.3 (see page 336) shows a decision tree for TIGER/Line file users.

Counting the Homeless

On the nights of March 20-21, 1990, the Census Bureau conducted "shelter and street night" (S-Night) operation, a separate count of the "homeless" population. The shelter count included pre-identified hotels, motels, emergency shelters, and shelters for abused women. Street enumeration included people visible to census takers in pre-identified open street and public locations. Selected S-Night tabulations are included in STF 1A, which was released state by state. These data are found under the heading "Group Quarters." A subdivision of that topic, "Other Persons in Group Quarters," includes tabulations for "emergency shelters for homeless" and "visible in street locations," thus comprising the two major components of this special shelter and street count.

Because the number of homeless is a controversial and emotional issue, the official results came under criticism by advocacy groups for this segment of the population. Moreover, the General Accounting Office (GAO), in testimony before the Senate, found weaknesses in the S-Night methodology that vitiated

(Text continues on page 337.)

Fig. 10.3. TIGER/Line decision tree

Decision Tree for Potential TIGER/Line File Users

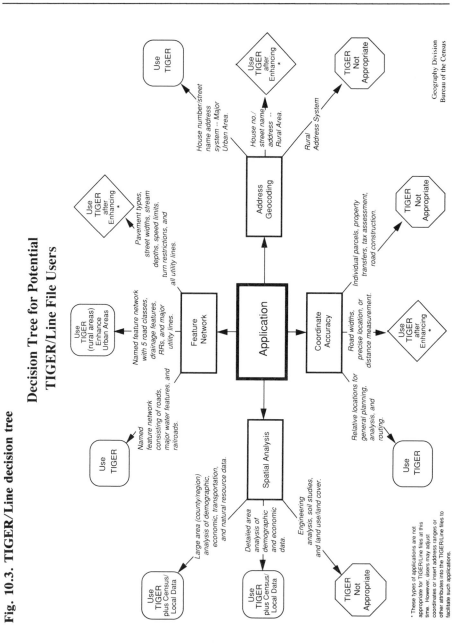

Geography Division
Bureau of the Census

data quality ("Counting the Homeless: Limitations of 1990 Census Results and Methodology," GAO/T-GGD-91-29, May 9, 1991, p. 2). Both the Census Bureau and the GAO acknowledged that a count of this population can never be wholly accurate because a portion of the homeless remains elusive. GAO officials surmised that the intense media attention given to S-Night contributed to unrealistic expectations about the scope of the Census Bureau's effort and the degree to which the enumeration would produce an accurate count of the homeless. To emphasize S-Night methodological inadequacies, a later GAO study concluded that data gathered on March 20-21 can be of only limited value in meeting needs for information on the number of homeless and their characteristics (GAO/GGD-92-1, December 30, 1991).

Disregarding the Undercount

Despite the bureau's planning activities (see figure 10.4, page 338), the initial mail response rate was disappointingly low. Accordingly, July 1, 1990, marked another phase of the count. Enumerators took to the streets, faced with the task of locating an estimated 37 million households that, for one reason or another, had not responded to the census questionnaires that most households received during the last week of March 1990. Yet even the enumerators' efforts in their post-April 1 activities fell short of a complete count. Analyses by bureau officials and outside "experts" led to the conclusion that the 1990 census failed to ferret out some 4 to 5 million persons, a disproportionate number of them African-Americans, Native Americans, and Hispanics.

Revised estimated figures based on a post-enumeration sample survey of 165,000 households increased the national count to 253,978,000, as contrasted with the "official" April 1, 1990, count of 248,709,873. Nevertheless, the secretary of commerce, on July 15, 1991, announced his decision not to adjust the final figures to correct the undercount. Anticipating an undercount even before April 1, 1991, several cities and states filed suit to force the bureau to adjust the official figures to reflect an expected undercount. If the 1980s serve as exemplary, court skirmishes may occupy the judiciary for the remainder of the 1990s. The courts could, for example, order the Census Bureau to provide state legislatures with revised data collected and extrapolated to a national corrected upward figure. And court rulings favorable to the plaintiffs could substantially alter redistricting for state legislators and for Congress. Moreover, because of the constitutional question involved, controversies could reach the Supreme Court.

A lengthy statement by the secretary of commerce detailing his reasons against adjustment was published in *Census and You*, vol. 26 (August 1991), pages 1-4.

Before the end of 1991, the Census Bureau had begun to release the final TIGER/Line compact disks state by state and the first printed reports. Concerning the former, all of the state files are contained on forty-four CDs. Most states are available on one CD-ROM but in some instances more than one state are stacked onto a single CD-ROM. Conversely, a few states required more than one disk. For example, Maine, Massachusetts, New Hampshire, and Vermont together required but one CD. California required three disks and Texas required

(Text continues on page 339.)

Fig. 10.4. 1990 census content planning

CONTENT PLANNING PATH FOR THE 1990 CENSUS

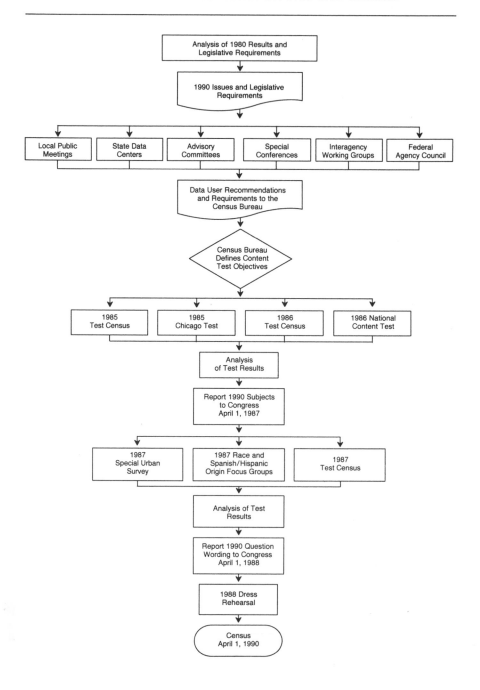

four. The first printed series from the 1990 census was the *Summary Population and Housing Characteristics*, Series CPH-1. On a state-by-state distribution pattern, these reports provide total population and housing unit counts as well as summary data on age, sex, race, Hispanic origin, household relationship, units in structure, value and rent, number of rooms, tenure, and vacancy characteristics for local governments, including American Indian and Alaska Native areas.

State Data Center Program

The State Data Center (SDC) Program was initiated by the Census Bureau in 1978 to improve access to the many statistical products available from the agency. The bureau furnishes products, training in data access and use, technical assistance, and consultation to the states, which, in turn, disseminate the products and provide assistance in their use to county and local governments as well as to nonprofit organizations and private profit-making businesses. As an example of their functioning, some SDCs encouraged and assisted municipalities' participation in the bureau's Local Review Program, designed to help improve the accuracy of the 1990 count to help ensure that those local areas would receive their fair share of state and federal funds that are distributed based on results of the decennial census.[18]

The organization of each SDC varies from state to state but generally includes a major state executive or planning agency, a major state university, and the state library. Similarly, the structure of the individual state programs varies, but in all cases consists of a primary agency and several affiliates. These serve as the principal service, delivery, and coordinating units. An updated list of SDCs, with over 1,400 affiliated offices throughout the nation including addresses and telephone numbers, is published in the 1991 *Census Catalog and Guide*.

Data Processing Centers

A number of Summary Tape Processing Centers in the private and public sectors process Census Bureau machine-readable data for users by creating their own computer software packages and establishing their own cost structure for services. Obtaining data from one of these organizations may be no more expensive than buying the products from the Census Bureau. Moreover, Processing Centers, which are user-oriented, may provide information more specifically related to the user's needs.

Centers are not franchised, established, or supported by the bureau. They have developed through local initiatives and respond to needs recognized by their organizers. They are located in state agencies, special laboratories, market research organizations, and universities. Cooperative ventures are common, wherein organization members of a data user group employ their collective purchasing power to acquire machine-readable copies of bureau surveys and censuses, write files to meet the needs of members, and make the files available at a reduced cost. In the higher education enterprise, notable programs are well established at Princeton University (working in conjunction with Rutgers University), at the University of Florida Libraries, and at other university centers, and they have been capably serving census data users both within and without the academic community.

Moreover, private industry cooperates with the Census Bureau to disseminate its products and services. For example, the National Planning Data Corporation of Ithaca, New York, rescued a 1980 census program that the bureau was forced to cancel because of budgetary problems. The firm paid the bureau $250,000 to tabulate 1980 census data for the nation's five-digit zip code areas. The corporation distributed the zip code data through a consortium of data users that included retailers, direct mailing organizations, private data firms, an insurance company, a publisher, and a university, and these institutions aided the corporation in funding the project.

Intercensal Publishing Patterns

The several decennial and quinquennial censuses are supplemented and updated by various annual surveys, current reports, and other studies. They are available from the bureau's Customer Services or from GPO as noted in *Monthly Product Announcement* and the annual *Census Catalog and Guide* in the various formats described above. Depository libraries, too, participate in this process through item selection.

A few examples of intercensal publishing illustrate the way in which the Census Bureau accomplishes its mission between major censuses. The series noted below are issued on a periodic or irregular basis, offered to depository libraries under various item numbers, and sold through the Superintendent of Documents.

Current Population Reports (C 3.186) are continuing, up-to-date statistics on population counts, characteristics, and other special studies. Separate series include Population Characteristics (P-20), Special Studies (P-23), Population Estimates and Projections (P-25), Farm Population (P-27), and Consumer Income (P-60). The Current Population Reports series represents valuable data for libraries. A special index for this series is issued irregularly within the P-23 sequence, which contains infrequently published reports on methods, concepts, and specialized data.

Current Housing Reports (C 3.215) provides data on various housing characteristics. Included are H-111, *Housing Vacancies* (quarterly with an annual issue); H-130, *Market Absorption of Apartments* (quarterly); and H-170, *American Housing Survey* (AHS). Prior to 1984, the AHS was called the *Annual Housing Survey*. The name change occurred when the national sample (AHS-N) was no longer conducted annually. AHS is now conducted biennially in odd-numbered years. It is designed to provide current information on the size and composition of the housing inventory, the characteristics of its occupants, indicators of housing and neighborhood quality, and characteristics of recent movers. Microdata from the AHS are available on computer tape and on CD-ROM.

Construction Reports consists of data compiled into various series covering all areas of construction. Included in this series are *Housing Starts* (C 3.215/2), a C20 monthly; the quarterly C21 *New Residential Construction in Selected Standard Metropolitan Statistical Areas*; the monthly C22 *Housing Completions*; and several other C-series reports.

Current Business Reports (C 3.138) consists of the following series: *Monthly Retail Trade Sales and Inventories* (C 3.138/3); *Annual Retail Trade* (C 3.138/3-2); and an *Annual Survey* (C 3.138/3-4). The series cover estimated and actual dollar sales volume of all retail establishments by type of business. Although the statistical series listed above may seem highly specialized, it is important to understand that these data are a significant reflection of the U.S. economy and are highly important to many in the business world.

Another important title, *County Business Patterns* (C 3.204/3), a popular source for the local entrepreneur, presents annual information on employment; number and employment size of establishments; and payrolls by two-, three-, and four-digit levels of the Standard Industrial Classification (SIC) for states and counties. The series includes a separate report for the United States, each state, Puerto Rico, and the District of Columbia. Anyone interested, for example, in establishing a local brewery or bakery would likely want to consult the latest *County Business Patterns* issue for the state to get an idea of what already exists in the area. A depository CD-ROM version (C 3.204/4) is available, too. The data by county and by industry are also available on computer tape or diskette from the bureau's Customer Services and excerpts are online in CENDATA.

Census Summary

The foregoing is but a small indication of the indefatigable activities of the Census Bureau as they are reflected in the production and distribution of data in printed form, microfiche, computer tape, diskette, CD-ROM, online information, and maps. And although the publications are listed in the *Monthly Catalog* and its *Periodicals Supplement* to a degree, the most appropriate method of keeping abreast of Census Bureau materials and services is by perusing current awareness sources such as *Census and You, Monthly Product Announcement, Factfinder for the Nation* series, and the accessing capabilities of the *American Statistics Index.*

How developing technologies may transform these products in the next century, the rate of absorption of new technology by federal depository libraries, and trends in the use of census data were addressed in *Use of Census Bureau Data in GPO Depository Libraries: Future Issues and Trends*, a study prepared for the bureau's 21st Century Decennial Census Planning Staff.[19]

BUREAU OF LABOR STATISTICS

Another large, general-purpose statistical agency is the Bureau of Labor Statistics (BLS), Department of Labor. The BLS, like the Bureau of the Census, has regional offices around the country that can at times provide help on inquiries. Its annual *Major Programs, Bureau of Labor Statistics* (L 2.125), offers a good overview of the work of this agency. The BLS generates a multitude of data on such crucial aspects of the economy as wholesale prices, consumer prices, unemployment, work stoppages, occupations, productivity and costs, and union wages and benefits. These figures appear in press releases, many of which become immediately available on the Economic Bulletin Board and later, in monthly, quarterly, or annual publications; most are available to depository libraries or by subscription. And when figures are released on a specific indicator, these data are accorded swift and solemn treatment by the news media. Some examples of BLS publications serve to indicate their importance and sociopolitical volatility.

Employment and Earnings (L 2.41/2) provides monthly data on employment, hours, earnings, and labor turnover for the nation as a whole, for individual states, and for more than 200 local areas. An annual *Supplement* is also produced (L 2.41/2-2). The headline news in the monthly is the *rate* of unemployment, a percentage showing that portion of the labor force actively seeking work but unable to find it. The present formula for measuring unemployment is but one of several measures devised by BLS statisticians. Unemployment figures are determined by results of the Current Population Survey for the eleven most populous states and two areas (New York City and the Los Angeles-Long Beach metropolitan area) and from data gathered by state employment security agencies for the remaining 39 states, the District of Columbia, and over 5,000 additional areas.[20]

CPI Detailed Report (L 2.38/3), a monthly, measures the price change of a constant market basket of goods and services over a period of time. The data are used to measure retail price changes affecting the purchasing power of the dollar, which is to say the rate of inflation or deflation. During periods of rising prices, it is an index of inflation and is used to measure the success or failure of government economic policy. Like employment figures, the Consumer Price Index (CPI) is the object of media attention. The CPI began during World War I (it was then called the cost-of-living index, a term still used by the media) as a way of determining a fair wage scale for the shipbuilding industry, and it has undergone several major revisions in methodology since then. Each revision has been called an "improvement" by the BLS. Despite these improvements, the determination of the index population and the categories of goods measured remain controversial and are the subjects of many scholarly analyses. As suggested earlier in this chapter, much is at stake in the construction of the CPI. Millions of workers are covered by collective bargaining contracts that provide for increases in wage rates based on increases in the CPI. Various federal statutes mandate adjustments in wages and benefits as the CPI rises or falls. And the CPI affects the official definition of poverty, which is the basis of eligibility in numerous health and welfare programs at the federal, state, and local government levels.

Producer Price Indexes (L 2.61), a companion periodical to the *CPI Detailed Report*, was formerly called the *Wholesale Price Index* and later the *Producer Prices and Price Indexes*. It shows monthly price movements at the primary market level, including statistical tables of summary indexes for groups of products and for most commodities. Fluctuations in producer prices foreshadow CPI rates and are closely watched and analyzed by government, business, and the media.

The *Monthly Labor Review* (L 2.6) covers most BLS series and carries articles on employment, the labor force, wages, prices, productivity, unit labor costs, collective bargaining, worker satisfaction, social indicators, and foreign labor developments. Indexed in many indexing and abstracting services, it is perhaps the most respected government periodical extant.

Current Wage Developments (L 2.44) is a monthly account of wage and benefit changes resulting from collective bargaining settlements and unilateral management decisions. It includes the appropriate statistical tables and special reports on wage trends.

The *Occupational Outlook Quarterly* (L 2.70/4) contains articles on new occupations, training opportunities, salary trends, career counseling programs, and the like. It updates occupational information between editions of the well-known *Occupational Outlook Handbook* (L 2.3/4), a biennial publication. The *Occupational Outlook Handbook* is an example of one of the many recurring titles that the Labor Bureau produces within its BLS Bulletin series (L 2.3) but that have in recent years been assigned unique SuDocs stems. Other examples of this change include the important Area Wage Survey series, now done annually by state and classed as L 2.121. Also produced within the BLS Bulletin series are two important compendia for historical time series, *Employment and Earnings Statistics for the United States, 1904-[date]*, and *Employment and Earnings Statistics for States and Areas, 1939-[date]*, both of which have periodically revised supplements that receive a different Bulletin number with each revision.

Probably the most generally useful compendium within the Bulletin series is the *Handbook of Labor Statistics* (L 2.3/5). Produced since 1924, the handbook is revised periodically and is a treasure trove of statistical data on all types of labor-related topics, from work stoppages to consumer expenditures to occupational related injuries. Tables start at the earliest date from which continuous and reliable statistics were available.

The foregoing briefly presents a selection of important and regularly requested sources that emanate from the Bureau of Labor Statistics. For other titles, John L. Andriot's *Guide to U.S. Government Publications*, the *List of Classes* (GP 3.24), or the *Publications of the U.S. Department of Labor* (L 1.34/6) should be consulted.

OTHER STATISTICAL COMPENDIA

When Appendix A of the Minimum Standards for Depository Libraries was adopted by the Depository Library Council in 1976, twenty-one titles appeared on the Basic Collection List. Of these twenty-one, eight titles were strictly statistical in nature, and of those eight, seven are still published and are covered in this chapter. The eighth, the *Congressional District Data Book*, has been replaced by other series. Beyond these, however, and beyond those other statistical titles mentioned under the Bureau of the Census and the Bureau of Labor Statistics, many important statistical titles abound that emanate from other agencies. Although the temptation to provide a litany here of favorite statistical sources is avoided, a brief sample is provided to illustrate the wide range of offerings the government makes available to the public.

From the Department of Agriculture, established in 1862, one can obtain statistical reports ranging from data on food consumption to wildfires to the number of cranberries produced. Each subagency publishes its own needed series, of which there are literally hundreds. The publication best able to bring much of the data together is *Agricultural Statistics* (A 1.47), published annually since 1936. It picks up where the former Statistical Section of the well-known but now subject-oriented *Yearbook of Agriculture* (A 1.10) left off. Some of its 700-plus tables include information for an 18-year time span.

Representative of the many statistical series issued by the Department of Education (created in 1979 following the breakup of the Department of Health, Education, and Welfare) is the *Digest of Educational Statistics* (ED 1.326), which comes from the department's Office of Educational Research and Improvement. Since the *Digest*'s first appearance in 1962, its SuDocs number has evolved from HE 5.98 to HE 19.315 to ED 1.113 to its current ED 1.326, illustrating the organizational changes to which many government series are subjected. The *Digest*'s more than 350 tables are an excellent starting point for collecting data on foreign students enrolled in institutions of higher education in the United States, on the use of microcomputers in elementary and secondary schools, on Department of Agriculture obligations for child nutrition programs by state, on degrees conferred, on student attitudes, and on a host of other educational topics. Like the *Statistical Abstract*, the *Digest* provides source notes for both published and unpublished data generated either by government or by the private sector. And, despite this annual's relatively recent vintage — compared to *Agricultural Statistics* — one must not assume that the government began collecting the data reported only in 1962. Instead, the serious researcher must look beyond for clues — to the narrative portions of *Historical Statistics of the United States*, to the various guides by Andriot, to table source notes in earlier years of the *Statistical Abstract*, to the *Monthly Catalog*, and to the *Document Catalog*. Inevitably, many of the earlier statistics can be found in other sources.

Although its provenance and, therefore, its SuDocs number also varied over the years, the *Vital Statistics of the United States* (HE 20.6210) has been the standard source for detailed information on natality, mortality, marriage, and divorce since 1937. The annual volume on mortality, for instance, presents deaths from 72 selected causes for each state by 10-year age groups as well as selected data for urban places with populations of 10,000 or over. Heavily used at reference desks is the National Center for Health Statistics' booklet *Where to Write for Vital Records* (HE 20.6202:V83).

Whereas a search for annual data on specific crimes and arrests in a given geographic area may best be pursued using the Federal Bureau of Investigation's *Uniform Crime Reports for the United States* (J 1.14/7), the Justice Statistics Bureau's annual *Sourcebook of Criminal Justice Statistics* (J 29.9/6) provides a more general overview of law and society. Unlike the *Statistical Abstract* or *Digest of Educational Statistics*, however, the *Sourcebook*'s main function is "to bring together data from diverse sources for presentation as originally published, rather than to transform or recompute the original data." Most *Sourcebook* tables appear exactly as in the original source.

Statistical projections are important to planners in all fields, and the government includes them within some of its series. For instance, *Projections of the Voting Age of the Population* is a recurrent publication found within the *Current Population Reports* (C 3.186:P-25/). The *U.S. Industrial Outlook* (C 61.34) surveys industry trends and shows, for example, in its 1991 edition that demand for electronic information services will experience a high growth rate through 1995. The *Industrial Outlook* is available for sale through the Office of the Superintendent of Documents and on microfiche and machine-readable magnetic tape or diskette through the National Technical Information Service (NTIS).

Illustrative of a small, independent agency with limited publishing output but responsible for an important statistical compendium is the Arms Control and Disarmament Agency. Its *World Military Expenditures and Arms Transfers* (AC 1.16) complements various Defense Department annual compilations such as the *United States Military Posture, [Fiscal Year]* (D 5.19) and *Selected Manpower Statistics, [Fiscal Year]* (D 1.61/4). Although *World Military Expenditures* provides an eleven-year analysis of each country's armed forces as well as related economic data, it is interesting to note that the 1989 compilation, the latest available during the Gulf War of 1990-1991, indicated that military expenditure figures for Iraq were "not available" for 1986-1988, the last years posted.

The preceding represents but the tip of the iceberg. When it comes to a question of statistics, the safest tactic is to assume that the statistic needed is probably collected and that it is likely to be available somewhere within the government's vast information structure. A wide-reaching imagination helps, as does a search of ASI and other statistical reference tools; a call to the agency most likely to be involved in issuing the data, coupled with a little perseverance, will usually result in the needed information.

THE FEDERAL BUDGET AND RELATED STATISTICS

The federal budget process can be confusing because it is, necessarily, complex. The process has been subject to numerous changes over the years, and the nuances surrounding it can probably confound the most avid budget watcher. It is an ongoing process subject to the viscissitudes of war, natural disaster, and an ever-changing array of domestic needs as well as unanticipated fluctuations in revenues. Yet it is important to acquire at least a minimal degree of awareness of the overall process, from its development at the executive level, to the more open and elaborate congressional budget procedures, to an awareness of some of the sources available for determining actual outlays and for helping assess financial impacts. A basic understanding also aids in achieving a better grasp of why laws are not always implemented and why actual expenditures sometimes fall short of amounts authorized in enabling legislation.

Although learning the basics of the process may seem tedious at first, the reference librarian confronting a mass of students each given the assignment to track the flow of funds within an area of the student's choosing, will approach the challenge with a significantly greater degree of confidence in suggesting appropriate sources. It is not unusual for faculty, particularly those in social policy curricula, to ask students to seek out the funding background on a particular social program and to attempt to trace the flow of funds from federal to state to local levels.

Guides to Understanding the Budget Process

Some excellent sources exist that prepare the beginner and provide a much deeper explanation than this chapter attempts. Chapter 10 (pp. 161-221), "The Federal Budget Process," in Jerrold Zwirn's *Congressional Publications and Proceedings: Research on Legislation, Budgets, and Treaties* (Englewood, CO: Libraries Unlimited, 1988) is a meaty analysis of the entire budget context. It explains differences between terms such as *fiscal policy* and *monetary policy*, explains the various actors (the Federal Reserve Board, the Council of Economic Advisors, the congressional budget committees, etc.) in the process, annotates key types of documentation, and advises on where the pieces are indexed. A useful but more limited description may also be found in chapter 4 (pp. 91-99), "The Congressional Budget Process," in *Congress and Law-Making: Researching the Legislative Process*, 2d ed. (Santa Barbara, CA: ABC-CLIO, 1989) by Robert U. Goehlert and Fenton S. Martin. Jean L. Sears and Marilyn K. Moody, in their *Using Government Publications*, volume 2, provide a basic start for the uninitiated in chapter 21, "Budget Analysis" (pp. 179-85). Readers of any of the above guides should, however, be aware that the budget timetable is subject to frequent amendment. Title 2, section 631, of the *United States Code* (Y 1.2/5) provides the latest dates applicable to the congressional budget process.

Published since 1982, Stanley E. Collender's *Guide to the Federal Budget, FY[year]* is probably the best year-by-year analysis of budget development. The author also publishes a biweekly *Federal Budget Report* (Government Information Systems). Various Congressional Quarterly books are helpful, including Michael Nelson's *Guide to the Presidency* (June 1989) and John Cranford's *Budgeting for America*, 2d ed. (1989), especially chapter 3 (pp. 59-92), "Shaping Budget Policy," and Appendix A (pp. 195-202), "The Budget Process." Eric Hansen's "Introduction to the U.S. Congressional Budget Process," in *Government Publications Review*, vol. 16, no. 3 (1989), pages 219-37, is another point of departure.

In addition to the aforementioned privately published sources, the U.S. government offers some assistance. The General Accounting Office's *Terms Used in the Budgetary Process* (GA 1.2:B85/2/year) and *The Congressional Budget Process: A General Explanation* (Congress, House, Budget Committee, Y 4.B85/3:C76/6/986) are revised periodically. The latter's Senate counterpart, *The Congressional Budget Process: An Explanation* (Y 4.B85/2:S.Prt.100-89), is also available. Another related publication is the Senate Budget Committee's *Gramm-Rudman-Hollings and the Congressional Budget Process* (Y 4.B85/2:S.Prt.99-119, 1986). Useful subject bibliographies include *Budget of the United States Government and Economic Report of the President* (SB 204), *Congressional Budget Office Publications* (SB 282), *General Accounting Office Publications* (SB 250), and *National and World Economy* (SB 097).

Pertinent Legislation

Four pieces of legislation are primary to tracking the budget process historically. The Budget and Accounting Act of 1921 (42 Stat. 20) first conferred budget-making authority on the president; required the president to submit to Congress an annual budget detailing actual spending and revenues in the previous fiscal year, estimates for the year in progress, and proposals for the year ahead; and established the Bureau of the Budget (renamed the Office of Management and Budget in 1970).[21] The process appears to have remained basically stable until Congress, angered over the president's refusal to spend funds it had already appropriated, passed the 1974 Congressional Budget and Impoundment Control Act (PL 93-344; 88 Stat. 297), which requires congressional review of any presidential proposal to withhold the expenditure of enacted appropriations and allows Congress to override any proposed expenditure amendments. More recent legislation amending PL 93-344 that attempts to streamline the process is commonly referred to as G-R-H, or Gramm-Rudman-Hollings, the Balanced Budget and Emergency Deficit Control Act of 1985 (PL 99-177; 99 Stat. 1038). A subsequent revision, the Balanced Budget and Emergency Deficit Control Reaffirmation Act of 1987 (Gramm-Rudman II; PL 100-119; 101 Stat. 754), requires a balanced budget by 1993, although fallout from the budgetary consequences of the 1990-1991 Gulf War may result in changes in this expectation. Current budget procedure is governed by Title 2, *United States Code.*

The Process Itself—
A Simplified Overview

The budget document, which depositories normally receive in early February and which commands wide coverage in the press, is actually the president's proposal for spending for a given fiscal year. Since 1977, the fiscal year runs from October 1 through September 30. The executive budget bears the date of the calendar year in which it ends. Simply put, the development of the president's budget, which must be submitted to Congress no later than the first Monday after January 3 of each year, begins many months in advance of the January deadline. The main actors are the president; his staff, including the Council of Economic Advisors; heads of the various agencies and departments, especially the secretary of the treasury; and the head of the Office of Management and Budget (OMB), which relates to the Office of the President in much the same way that the Congressional Budget Office relates to Congress. As noted by Zwirn:

> The executive budget is a comprehensive statement through which the president expresses judgment about the relative merits of governmental activities in the context of a fiscal policy designed to stabilize the economy and meet special needs. It also provides Congress with an overall budget program that can be examined in parts, yet remain a general plan. Though it contains only estimates and recommendations, the executive budget offers an unusually favorable opportunity for the president to marshall support behind his programmatic preferences.[22]

In recent times the executive budget has appeared in multiple volumes. Beginning with the budget for fiscal year (FY) 1991, it was consolidated into one volume (PrEx 2.8:991). Regardless of number of volumes, the budget is voluminous. The director of the OMB remarked in "Green Eyeshades and the Cookie Monster," his introduction to FY 1991's 1,269 pages, that

> if anything were meant for viewing through proverbial green eyeshades, it would seem to be the Federal budget. The typeface is small. The text is tedious. Tables are seemingly endless. The sheer size of the budget makes it seem like a monster. It contains almost 190,000 accounts. At the rate of one per minute, eight hours per day, it would take over a year to reflect upon these![23]

In addition to the one-page "Budget Message of the President" and the "Director's Introduction to the New Budget," section one provides an extensive overview of key government programs and discusses the budget process itself (pp. 265-69, chap. VII.A, "Reforming the Budget Process") including recommendations for a biennial rather than annual budget process. Section two includes the "Detailed Budget Estimates," which previously formed the extensive appendix volume to the budget; a "Glossary of Budget Terms"; Historical Tables; other chapters; and the index. Although indexing of the budget is extensive, not every reference to minute programs (such as the Points of Light Initiative) is captured fully, and a search for full information may require close combing and an understanding of where the program falls within a broader context. For instance, nothing is indexed under "Libraries" specifically that would lead one to pertinent information under "Government Printing Office."

The budget document must next be shepherded through Congress under the timetable prescribed in Title 2, *United States Code*. Despite the timetable, however, the mandate to meet specific deadlines is often arrested by political realities, and a series of continuing resolutions have frequently been required to keep the federal establishment operating beyond September 30 at the previous year's level. In theory, though, Congress has from the first Monday after January 3 to September 30 to finalize its recommendations on the budget.

As described by Goehlert and Martin, the budget's movement through Congress is often a two-step, sometimes overlapping, process involving authorization and appropriations. Standing committees first *authorize* the allocation of funds for specific programs. They determine both the substance of the programs and which agencies are to be responsible for implementing them. Then, in what is known as the *appropriations* process, the House and Senate Appropriations Committees, with jurisdiction over specific departments and agencies, work out the programs' specific funding.[24] Each house also has a separate budget committee to assist in implementing budget procedures and monitoring congressional spending.

Emanating from the congressional deliberations is an array of publications that the researcher can best trace through the use of *CIS/Index*. Documentation will include hearings, reports, committee prints, and related materials. A search of the *American Statistics Index* will, however, turn up the relevant statistical sources. *Budget Information for the States*, published annually by the OMB, is one of the more useful compilations available for tracking state-by-state obligations and estimated data on the major federal formula grant programs to state and local governments. Although it is available by calling the OMB or, for recent years, in the ASI microfiche file, it unfortunately has escaped depository distribution. One particularly hefty product of the congressional budget process is the Senate's *Appropriations, Budget Estimates, Etc.*, which is published within the Senate Document series (Y 1.1/3) and which presents texts of appropriations legislation passed by Congress within a given session.

Certainly other sources of budget information exist, and the more sophisticated researcher may need to tap them. An example is Dialog file 589, DMS/FI Market Intelligence Reports, which now includes U.S. budget documents provided annually to the Department of Defense oversight committees of Congress (*Dialog Chronolog*, vol. 90 [November 1990]: 392). On the other hand, the researcher should also be aware that, as open as the budget process is, there are portions, referred to as the "black budget," about which very few in government know even the barest details and that are best explained and documented by Tom Weiner in *Blank Check: The Pentagon's Black Budget* (New York: Warner Books, 1990).

Again, as with other statistical areas, one must merely stretch the imagination to discover the wealth of sources available to the determined user. Most sources are distributed to depository libraries; however, as one can also see, there are increasingly sophisticated ways of extracting data, ways that may require more than minimal awareness and perseverance.

NOTES

[1]See, for instance, Katherine K. Wallman, *Losing Count: The Federal Statistical System* (Washington, DC: Population Reference Bureau, Population Trends and Public Policy no. 16, September 1988), and Jonathan Fuerbringer, "Accuracy in Short Supply in Flood of U.S. Statistics," *The New York Times*, October 30, 1989, pp. 1 + .

[2]"Initiative Proposed to Improve Statistics," *APDU Newsletter*, 15 (April 1991): 1 + .

[3]"Federal Data Users Form APDU," *Government Publications Review*, 2 (1975): 383.

[4]Revisions of geographic concepts and areas are generally announced in the *Federal Register*. In June 1992, the Office of Management and Budget is scheduled to "announce all the redefinitions of MSAs throughout the United States based on the population and commuting data obtained from the 1990 Census" (U.S. Office of Management and Budget, *Statistical Program of the United States Government, FY 1990*, p. 38).

[5]*Economic Bulletin Board Update*, September 1990, p. 1.

[6]Many helpful hints and reactions to new CD-ROM products have been shared by electronic mail subscribers over BITNET's GovDocs Listserv. For example, in addition to personally trying out the National Trade Data Bank, coauthor Mary Fetzer sought clues to its use from Arlene Hanerfeld's (University of North Carolina, Wilmington) December 11, 1990, Listserv memo written preliminary to an article planned for *The Docket, Newsletter of the North Carolina Documents Section of the NCLA*.

[7]*Wesberry* v. *Sanders*, 376 U.S. 1, 11 L.Ed.2d 481, 84 S.Ct. 526 (1964).

[8]Outlying areas include Puerto Rico, the U.S. Virgin Islands, Guam, and the Northern Mariana Islands.

[9]This set is composed of *Population Information in the Twentieth Century Census Volumes: 1950-1980* (1988), *Population Information in the Twentieth Century Census Volumes: 1900-1940* (1985), and *Population Information in Nineteenth Century Census Volumes* (1983).

[10]U.S. Census Bureau, *The Role of Intermediaries in the Interpretation and Dissemination of Census Data Now and in the Future*, paper distributed by the bureau, October 1989.

[11]U.S. Census Bureau, *Census Catalog and Guide 1990*, pp. 2-3.

[12]See *Taking a Byte Out of History: The Archival Preservation of Federal Computer Records* (H. Rep. 101-978; Y 1.1/8:101-978), November 6, 1990. See also "Decades of Computer Data at Risk of Vanishing," *Star Ledger* (Newark, NJ), January 2, 1991.

[13]U.S. Bureau of the Census, *1990 Census Products Issues*, March 1986, 22 pages.

[14]Garry Trudeau's syndicated series appeared in various newspapers, such as the *Star Ledger* (Newark, NJ), in the spring of 1990.

[15]James Gleick, "The Census: Why We Can't Count," *The New York Times Magazine*, July 15, 1990, pp. 22+.

[16]Felicity Barringer, "Census in the Age of Information Grows to Fill a Hunger It Created," *The New York Times*, January 2, 1990, pp. 1+. The "democratization" quote is attributed to Martha Farnsworth Riche, an *American Demographics* magazine economist.

[17]U.S. Bureau of the Census, *TIGER: The Coast-to-Coast Digital Map Data Base* (November 1990), p. 9.

[18]Vince Furmenec, "1990 Census Local Review," *Garden State Data News*, 38 (Winter 1989): 4.

[19]Charles R. McClure and Peter Hernon, *Use of Census Bureau Data in GPO Depository Libraries: Future Issues and Trends*, Final Report for United States Bureau of the Census 21st Century Decennial Census Planning Staff (Manlius, NY: Information Management Consultant Services, June 1990).

[20]Department of Labor, Bureau of Labor Statistics, *How the Government Measures Unemployment*, BLS Report 742 (September 1987), p. 9.

[21]*Congress A to Z: CQ's Ready Reference Encyclopedia* (Washington, DC: Congressional Quarterly, 1988), p. 43.

[22]Jerrold Zwirn, *Congressional Publications: A Research Guide to Legislation, Budgets, and Treaties* (Englewood, CO: Libraries Unlimited, 1988), p. 188.

[23]*Budget of the United States Government, Fiscal Year 1991* (Washington, DC: GPO, 1990), p. 7.

[24]Robert U. Goehlert and Fenton S. Martin, *Congress and Law-Making*, 2d ed. (Santa Barbara, CA: ABC-CLIO, 1989), p. 93.

11

Technical Report Literature and Related Research Sources

INTRODUCTION

Librarians and researchers alike tend to pride themselves on achieving a certain level of proficiency in the intricacies of legislative and executive finding aids. But when confronted with the need to locate a study that is government sponsored yet not found in the general and specialized sources we have thus far examined, the resultant frustration and perplexity may have a dispiriting effect on that initial burst of confidence.

It is important to understand that the depository library system, although it provides thousands of series, does not encompass all federal publishing. In the *Monthly Catalog* alone, entries lacking an item number and the "black dot," or bullet symbol (•), must be obtained by other than depository means. This chapter focuses upon certain categories of publications not normally accessed through the depository library system. These nonconventional sources are sometimes referred to as "gray" literature. One of the more prominent categories in this area is the technical report or translation.

Technical reports are generally issued as "non-GPO" publications by a wide variety of agencies and their contractors and are not subject to bibliographic control or distribution by the Government Printing Office (GPO). However, a small number of series are printed by GPO, usually through its central or regional procurement offices, cataloged in the Library Programs Service (LPS), and entered into the *Monthly Catalog*. Department of Energy (DOE) research results, which are primarily non-GPO, are distributed directly by DOE to depository libraries on microfiche under a special arrangement. The index, *Energy Research Abstracts* (ERA) (E 1.17), is a depository item and is sold by the Superintendent of Documents (SuDocs), but the vast majority of entries in ERA are neither cataloged by LPS nor entered into the *Monthly Catalog*. This pattern holds for many of the bibliographic and textual services discussed in the following pages.

A variety of characteristics help define technical reports. Generally they are detailed studies, written in part to satisfy a funding agency's accountability requirements, and designed to disseminate research findings in a timely manner. Report writing is guided by *American National Standard, Scientific and Technical Reports: Organization, Preparation, and Production.*[1] Although the earliest technical reports were probably those produced by the National Advisory Committee for Aeronautics (NACA) from 1915 forward, their development as a major means of communicating the results of research and development (R&D)

escalated with World War II and the establishment of the Office of Scientific Research and Development.[2] Originally a forum utilized primarily in scientific areas, the technical report has become increasingly important in the social sciences as well.

For various reasons, this vast body of federally sponsored technical report literature lies largely outside the depository program. Some may be classified; some may be reports that the various sponsoring agencies have simply neglected to distribute; others may fall within the provisions of Title 44 that exempt distribution under the depository program. Whatever the reasons, these publications reflect the federal commitment to R&D, a commitment made manifest by multitudes of contracts and grants awarded by federal agencies to corporations, universities, think tanks, specialized consultants, and professional organizations and societies. The volume of technical reports produced in any given year relies greatly on the degree of federal largesse for R&D.

As various authors have observed, the government invests heavily in the development of scientific and technical information (STI) but allocates little toward the transfer of this information. Thomas Pinelli and Madeline Henderson, for example, lament the absence of a coordinated government-wide policy for the distribution and bibliographic control of government technical reports; they claim that "in the absence of a national STI policy, dissemination practices and procedures have become decentralized and are largely determined by the various technical report-producing agencies."[3] Walter Blados underscores the need for a cohesive scientific and technical information (STINFO) program when he discusses the potential for waste in the U.S. Air Force's program.

> Current budget appropriation for national defense is about $41.5 billion, of which the Air Force receives about $13.2 billion. The scientific and engineering community has been accused of wasting from 10 to 50% of our resources simply because people are not receiving adequate and timely information. If this is true, this would mean that the Air Force alone was wasting from 1.3 to 6.6 billion dollars a year.[4]

It is therefore incumbent upon the skilled librarian or researcher to be able to recognize this genre and to become aware of the basic sources available for identifying and locating technical reports. Translations and declassified documents are also included in this chapter, as translations figure prominently in the technical report literature and as both represent often elusive types of documentation.

Citations to technical reports are often cloaked with acronyms for issuing agencies or with series of numbers prefixed with "codes" designating the originating agency. Clues that an item falls within the technical report category frequently emerge in the form of a contract or grant number or an accession or report series code. A basic tool for deciphering codes or for locating the prefix used by various agencies is the *Report Series Codes Dictionary*, 3d ed. (Detroit, MI: Gale Research Company, 1986). Most of the bibliographic tools generated by the report-producing agencies include indexes by contract/grant number and by accession/report series codes. For a chronological guide to many of the earlier indexes to the technical report literature, see Yuri Nakata's *From Press to People*.[5]

NATIONAL TECHNICAL INFORMATION SERVICE

Although many agencies disseminate technical reports, they distribute primarily those created as a result of their own R&D efforts. The National Technical Information Service (NTIS), on the other hand, produces little but is the primary conduit for technical reports in general. NTIS is a self-sustaining federal agency within the Department of Commerce. It was established in 1970 to simplify and improve access to data files and to scientific and technical reports produced by federal agencies and their contractors. Its genesis goes back to 1945, when the Publications Board was set up and charged with receiving all government-generated scientific and technical reports to determine what could be released to the public and to organize declassified information to permit improved access to researchers. Successors to the Publications Board included the Office of Technical Services (1946-1964) and NTIS's immediate predecessor, the Clearinghouse for Federal Scientific and Technical Information (1964-1970).

In its recent promotional literature, NTIS is described as *"the* source for U.S. and foreign government-sponsored R&D results, business information, and engineering solutions." It is also the lead agency in the exchange of international technical information, with approximately 35 percent of the NTIS collection coming from foreign sources. In fiscal year 1990, the agency added 60,000 new titles to its collection, of which 1,500 were from Japan and 20,000 were from other foreign countries. The NTIS collection is estimated at some 2 million items, all of which are available for sale in print, microform, audiovisual, or electronic format. Despite the magnitude of its collection, NTIS estimates that "more than one-third of Federal scientific and technical reports are never submitted."[6] The agency must rely on voluntary submission of source documents by the various agencies, many of which have their own outlets for disseminating their research results. The agency also manages the Federal Computer Products Center, which provides access to software, data files, and databases produced by federal agencies; the Federal Software Exchange Program, which handles intragovernmental distribution of software; and the Center for the Utilization of Federal Technology (CUFT), which runs the most active inventions licensing program in the U.S. government. With its directories and catalogs, CUFT links U.S. firms to federal laboratory contacts and technologies. An 8-minute video tour, *NTIS—The Competitive Edge* (PR-858, June 1989), is available as an introduction to current NTIS operations.

The NTIS Mandate

NTIS is an agency in transition. Despite controversy over the years regarding its proper role and function, and despite Reagan administration initiatives in the 1980s to privatize NTIS, it remains an agency of the federal government. It is governed by the provisions of Title 15, *United States Code*, sections 1151-1157, and by the National Technical Information Act of 1988 (PL 100-519; 15 U.S.C. 3701 et seq.). According to the latter, the agency's functions are to:

1. establish and maintain a permanent repository of nonclassified scientific, technical, and engineering information;

2. cooperate and coordinate its operations with other Government scientific, technical, and engineering information programs;

3. make selected bibliographic information products available in a timely manner to depository libraries as a part of the Depository Library Program of the Government Printing Office;

4. in conjunction with the private sector as appropriate, collect, translate into English, and disseminate unclassified foreign scientific, technical, and engineering information;

5. implement new methods or media for the dissemination of scientific, technical, and engineering information; and

6. carry out the functions and activities of the Secretary under the Act entitled "An Act to provide for the dissemination of technological, scientific, and engineering information to American business and industry, and for other purposes" enacted September 9, 1950, and the functions and activities of the Secretary performed through the National Technical Information Service as of the date of enactment of this Act under the Stevenson-Wydler Technology Innovation Act of 1980.

The National Technical Information Act also requires the submission of an annual report to Congress and establishes an Advisory Board of NTIS designed to "review the general policies and operations of the Service, including policies in connection with fees and charges for its services." As of spring 1991, recommendations for membership had been made to the secretary of commerce, but the board was not yet operational.[7] NTIS already had in place, however, a Library Liaison Network designed to strengthen communication and cooperation between the agency and the library community. The network includes representatives from many library associations, university and state library groups, and online users.

The pricing structure and nondepository status of many NTIS products have frequently been objects of debate and contention within the community of documents and special librarians. As an agency of the federal government dealing with so-called cooperative publications (44 U.S.C. 1903), NTIS consistently maintains that it is exempt from participation in the depository library program. The crucial provision is found at Title 15, *United States Code*, section 1153, which says in part:

The Secretary [of Commerce] is authorized ... to establish ... a schedule or schedules of reasonable fees or charges for services performed or for documents or other publications furnished under this chapter.

It is the policy of this chapter, to the fullest extent feasible and consistent with the objectives of this chapter, that each of the services and functions provided herein shall be self-sustaining or self-liquidating and that the general public shall not bear the cost of publications and other services which are for the special use and benefit of private groups and individuals; but nothing herein shall be construed to require the levying of fees or charges for services performed or publications furnished to any agency or instrumentality of the Federal Government, or for publications which are distributed pursuant to reciprocal arrangements for the exchange of information or which are otherwise issued primarily for the general benefit of the public.

In 1974 the Public Printer asked the Comptroller General of the United States to decide whether the Depository Library Act of 1962 is applicable to publications sold by NTIS. His ruling (Decision Number B-114829, June 27, 1975) was lengthy, but the last paragraph, which expressed his conclusions, was published in *Documents to the People* and supported the distribution of "certain serial publications (by NTIS); e.g., *Government Reports Announcements and Index* (GRA&I) and the *Government Reports Annual Index* (GRA), which are of widespread public interest, most especially to the library community."[8] The National Technical Information Act of 1988 subsequently reinforced the Comptroller General's decision in that it now mandates that NTIS "make selected bibliographic information products available in a timely manner to depository libraries."

The NTIS Bibliographic Database, established in 1964, includes all documents that have been received and processed by NTIS. Citations are merged on a two-week cycle to produce the NTIS Bibliographic Database update file, which is available to commercial online vendors. The file is also used to produce NTIS primary announcement publications (*Abstract Newsletters* and *Government Reports Announcements & Index*), as well as to designate reports that will be distributed automatically in the *Selected Research in Microfiche* (SRIM) service. The NTIS Bibliographic Database is available online from the following vendors: BRS Information Technologies, Data-Star, DIALOG Information Services, Pergamon ORBIT InfoLine, and STN International. Batch searching and Selective Dissemination of Information (SDI) service are also available from NERAC, Inc.

Citation elements in the NTIS Bibliographic Database include the following fields in the order indicated. Most (but not all) fields are found in both the online and the printed announcement services. The fields are NTIS order number (accession number), NTIS subject category codes, NTIS prices, corporate source, title, title note, personal author, report date, pagination, report number, contract or grant numbers, project and task numbers, monitor agency number, supplementary notes, availability statement, descriptors, identifiers, abstract, title annotation, and corporate source code. Each field is described in detail in the *NTIS Bibliographic Database Guide*.

The NTIS subject category codes are used primarily to sort reports for the subject arrangement in GRA&I and for the SRIM service. Two subject classification schemes have been used by NTIS and its predecessor organizations: the COSATI subject classification, consisting of 22 major subject fields (categories) with a further subdivision into 178 groups (subcategories), and the NTIS subject classification, consisting of 40 major categories with a further subdivision into 336 subcategories. Twenty-six of these categories are used to sort reports in the weekly *Abstract Newsletters*. Prices for reports are listed by code, with suffixes for PC (paper copy) and MF (microfiche). Previously amounts were listed, but the use of code was adopted to accommodate frequent price changes.

Descriptors are indexing terms or subject headings assigned by NTIS or the contributing agencies using controlled vocabulary or thesauri. Nearly complete citations (to included descriptors) are provided by Defense Technical Information Center (DTIC), Department of Energy/Office of Scientific and Technical Information (DOE/OSTI), and National Aeronautics and Space Administration/Scientific and Technical Information Facility (NASA/STIF), which results in a lack of uniformity in subject headings. Department of Defense (DoD) sponsored reports are indexed using *DDC Retrieval and Indexing Terminology Posting Terms with Hierarchy and KWOC* (AD-068500, May 1979); Department of Energy (DOE) reports are indexed using the *Energy Information Database: Subject Thesaurus* (DE84-010568, October 1981); and National Aeronautics and Space Administration (NASA) reports are indexed by NTIS using the *Thesaurus of Engineering and Scientific Terms* (TEST) (1969, available from the American Association of Engineering Societies). Identifiers are subject headings for which no adequate descriptors exist in the four thesauri mentioned.

Accordingly, the basic bibliographic tool of NTIS, *Government Reports Announcements & Index*, is available through the depository library system (C 51.9/3), as are a number of other key NTIS-produced items such as the *Directory of Federal Laboratory and Technology Resources* (C 51.19/2-2). But a large number of publications listed in GRA&I are excluded from depository distribution. Karen Sinkule and Marilyn Moody point out that agencies that distribute some technical reports through the depository system include the DOE, Environmental Protection Agency (EPA), Department of Transportation (DOT), NASA, and U.S. Geological Survey (USGS).[9] This has been accomplished largely by the cost-effective characteristics of microfiche distribution. It is safe to say, however, that the library community still is not satisfied with the pace of deposit. Also, although index tools such as NASA's *Scientific and Technical Aerospace Reports* (STAR) and the DOE's *Energy Research Abstracts* (ERA) do indicate those items included in the depository library program, many indexes do not. Librarians are advised to search their collections carefully for the presence of technical reports in various forms.

NTIS Products and Services

The basic NTIS Bibliographic Database on magnetic tape is the resource from which NTIS designs and produces a number of services and the bibliographic tools by which those services can be accessed. Key tools for staying abreast of NTIS's expanding role are its annual *Catalog of Products & Services* (PR-827; C 51.11/8) and the quarterly *NTIS NewsLine* (C 51.14). Following are some of the primary information packages from the agency.

Government Reports Announcements & Index

As already mentioned, the basic bibliographic tool for libraries and information centers is *Government Reports Announcements & Index*, a semimonthly indexing and abstracting service containing citations for all publications currently received by NTIS. Although sold through NTIS in various forms, GRA&I

(C 51.9/3) and its companion annual index (C 51.9/4) are available to depository libraries in paper copy.

Entries are arranged by NTIS's subject categories, among which are administration and management, behavior and society, business and economics, communication, health care, library and information sciences, and problem-solving information for state and local governments. Subcategories under, for instance, its behavior and society field are law, job training and career development, and social concerns. The preponderance of categories are in the scientific and technical fields. In 1970, NTIS developed its own subject scheme designed to provide useful sorting categories for both hard and soft sciences and to be used in conjunction with Committee on Scientific and Technical Information (COSATI) headings. An *NTIS Subject Classification (Past and Present)* (PB-270-575/4CBK, September 1977) is available for anyone who needs to know the changes that were made to the NTIS subject categories during their first six years. It includes a list of the academically and scientifically oriented COSATI headings, the NTIS-generated classification scheme, and a table for converting from COSATI to the NTIS categories.

The main entry section, "Reports Announcements," contains the basic bibliographic information, and each entry (which also bears a consecutive entry number) is arranged by subject category and subcategory. Within the latter the reports are organized alphanumerically by NTIS order number. Preceding these numerals is an "accession number prefix" that indicates the entity from which the report was received. Commonly used prefixes and the source agencies they signify include AD (Department of Defense), JPRS (Joint Publications Research Service), and N (National Aeronautics and Space Administration). Also frequently used is the prefix PB, an acronym for Publications Board, the predecessor agency of NTIS. The prefix has been continued despite reorganization and agency name changes. PB is employed to indicate reports entered by NTIS for other agencies. The accession number (rather than the entry number) is used by subscribers as an order number for the documents. Many libraries also use this unique accession number for filing the technical reports they acquire from NTIS. Figure 11.1 (see page 358) shows a portion of a main entry page from GRA&I.

GRA&I index entries are by keyword, personal author, corporate author, contract/grant number, and NTIS order/report number. The keyword index functions as a subject approach, and most keywords are selected from the controlled vocabularies of the Department of Defense, Department of Energy, NASA, or NTIS. Each index reference provides an entry or abstract number (in addition to the accession number); these consecutive numbers allow the user to move quickly from the various indexes to the main entry. NTIS began using these numbers in 1984.

Government Reports Annual Index is published in six hardbound volumes. Sections 1-2 contain the keyword index; section 3 is the personal author index. Section 4 is the corporate author index. Sections 5 and 6 comprise the contract/grant number index and the NTIS order/report number index.

Because GRA&I and its annual index lack a title approach, the agency publishes a separate microfiche, *NTIS Title Index*, that must be purchased. This is a cumulation of new publications merged quarterly on a two-year cycle. The *NTIS Title Index* is issued within two weeks after the closing of the last GRA&I for the quarter. An *NTIS Retrospective Title Index* covers July 1964 through December 1988 and includes over 1 million publications. These products each contain a keyword-out-of-context (KWOC) title index, an author index, and a report/accession number index.

Fig. 11.1. Main entry page from GRA&I

MANUFACTURING TECHNOLOGY

Engineering Materials

104,045
N90-26368/2/GAR PC **A04**/MF **A01**
Technische Hogeschool Delft (Netherlands). Faculty of Aerospace Engineering.
Blunt Notch Behaviour of Metal Laminates: Arall and Glare.
C. A. J. R. Vermeeren. Jan 90, 63p LR-617, ETN-90-97180

The use of stress concentration factor to describe blunt notch properties of ARALL is evaluated. The blunt notch theory for aluminum alloys is discussed. Results for ARALL laminates are discussed and a test series is proposed. The stress concentration factor value is based on the size and geometry of the notch. For aluminum almost no size effect is found. The size effect for ARALL laminates is investigated by using different specimen widths with the same stress concentration factor value. The failure mechanism for ARALL laminates is different for different fibers. GLARE showed static delamination for certain specimens with high fiber volume percentage. The delamination can level off the stress distribution in the prepreg layer and thus give higher blunt notch strength.

104,046
N90-28110/6/GAR PC **A03**/MF **A01**
Akron Univ., OH.
Creep and Creep Rupture of Strongly Reinforced Metallic Composites.
Final Report.
D. N. Robinson, W. K. Binienda, and M. Miti-kavuma. Aug 90, 23p NAS 1.26:185286, NASA-CR-185286
Contract NAG3-379

A creep and creep damage theory is presented for metallic composites with strong fibers. Application is to reinforced structures in which the fiber orientation may vary throughout but a distinct fiber direction can be identified locally (local transverse isotropy). The creep deformation model follows earlier work and is based on a flow potential function that depends on invariants reflecting stress and the material symmetry. As the focus is on the interaction of creep and damage, primary creep is ignored. The creep rupture model is an extension of continuum damage mechanics and includes an isochronous damage function that depends on invariants specifying the local maximum transverse tension and the maximum longitudinal shear stress. It is posited that at high temperature and low stress, appropriate to engineering practice, these stress components damage the fiber/matrix interface through diffusion controlled void growth, eventually causing creep rupture. Experiments are outlined for characterizing a composite through creep rupture tests under transverse tension and longitudinal shear. Application is made to a thin-walled pressure vessel with reinforcing fibers at an arbitrary helical angle. The results illustrate the usefulness of the model as a means of achieving optimal designs of composite structures where creep and creep rupture are life limiting.

104,047
N90-28114/8/GAR PC **A03**/MF **A01**
National Aeronautics and Space Administration, Hampton, VA. Langley Research Center.
Damage Tolerance of Woven Graphite-Epoxy Buffer Strip Panels.
J. M. Kennedy. Aug 90, 42p NAS 1.15:102702, NASA-TM-102702

Graphite-epoxy panels with S glass buffer strips were tested in tension and shear to measure their residual strengths with crack-like damage. The buffer strips were regularly spaced narrow strips of continuous S glass. Panels were made with a uniweave graphite cloth where the S glass buffer material was woven directly into the cloth. Panels were made with different width and thickness buffer strips. The panels were loaded to failure while remote strain, strain at the end of the slit, and crack opening displacement were monitoring. The notched region and nearby buffer strips were radiographed periodically to reveal crack growth and damage. Except for panels with short slits, the buffer strips arrested the propagating crack. The strength (or failing strain) of the panels was significantly higher than the strength of all-graphite panels with the same length slit. Panels with wide, thick buffer strips were stronger than panels with thin, narrow buffer strips. A shear-lag model predicted the failing strength of tension panels with wide buffer strips accurately, but over-estimated the strength of the shear panels and the tension panels with narrow buffer strips.

Joining

104,048
DE90008971/GAR PC **A03**/MF **A01**
EG and G Rocky Flats, Inc., Golden, CO.
Penetration in GTA welding.
C. R. Heiple, and P. Burgardt. 1990, 17p RFP-4390, CONF-901008-1
Contract AC04-76DP03533
Fall meeting of the Minerals, Metals and Materials Society on physical metallurgy and materials in conjunction with materials week and the material applications and services exposition, Detroit, MI (USA), 7-11 Oct 1990. Sponsored by Department of Energy, Washington, DC.
Portions of this document are illegible in microfiche products.

The size and shape of the weld bead produced in GTA welding depends on the magnitude and distribution of the energy incident on the workpiece surfaces as well as the dissipation of that energy in the workpiece. The input energy is largely controllable through the welding parameters selected, however the dissipation of that energy in the workpiece is less subject to control. Changes in energy dissipation can produce large changes in weld shape or penetration. Heat transport away from the weld pool is almost entirely by conduction, but heat transport in the weld pool is more complicated. Heat conduction through the liquid is an important component, but heat transport by convection (mass transport) is often the dominant mechanism. Convective heat transport is directional and changes the weld pool shape from that produced by conduction alone. Surface tension gradients are often the dominant forces driving fluid flow in GTA weld pools. These gradients are sensitive functions of weld pool chemistry and the energy input distribution to the weld. Experimental and theoretical work conducted primarily in the past decade has greatly enhanced our understanding of weld pool fluid flow, the forces which drive it, and its effects on weld pool shape. This work is reviewed here. While less common, changes in energy dissipation through the unmelted portion of the workpiece can also affect fusion zone shape or penetration. These effects are also described. 41 refs., 9 figs.

104,049
MIC-90-00175/GAR PC **E07**/MF **E01**
Canada Centre for Mineral and Energy Technology, Ottawa (Ontario).
Determination of stress intensity factors for weld toe defects, phase III: Final report.
R. Bell. c1988, 85p
Contract CANMET-OST85-00428

Report describing modifications to the fatigue crack growth prediction program and comparison of the prediction results to experimental test results for welded T plate joints produced in the Canadian offshore steels research program. The report also describes the implementation of a variable amplitude loading capability in the fatigue life prediction program, including the European common load sequence data to produce a realistic load history, and the miner summation procedure to calculating cumulative damage. A 2-dimensional finite element analysis to determine the stress distribution near the weld toe of T plates for a range of thicknesses and weld toe radii ranging from 0.2-10.0 mm is given, as well as a method of developing a procedure to obtaining SIFs at the weld toe of pipe-to-plate joint using 3D finite element methods. The report concludes with details of the attendance of the principal investigator at Canada-ECSC progress meetings.

104,050
N90-25358/4/GAR PC **A03**/MF **A01**
Valtion Teknillinen Tutkimuskeskus, Espoo (Finland).
Inspection of Welds with Eddy Current.
K. Lahdenpera. cOct 89, 37p VTT-RR-644, ISBN-951-38-3606-1
In Finnish; English Summary.

The application of eddy current inspection to the testing of welds in ferritic steel structures is studied. All artificial EDM notches exceeding 6 mn were found. More than half of 3 mn notches were found. Eddy current method was used to detect and evaluate natural defects. All specimens were tested with magnetic particle method. Results from eddy current and magnetic particle inspection are compared. With long cracks (10 mm) the results were comparable. With shorter cracks the magnetic particle method was more sensitive than eddy current method.

104,051
N90-28095/9/GAR PC **A03**/MF **A01**
Thiokol Chemical Corp., Brigham City, UT.
Nylon and Teflon Scribe Effect on NBR to Chemlok 233 and NBR to NBR Bond Interfaces.
Final Report.
S. K. Jensen. Jun 90, 20p NAS 1.26:184004, TWR-60832, NASA-CR-184004
Contract NAS8-30490

A study was requested by Manufacturing Engineering to determine what effects marking with nylon (6/6) and Teflon scribes may have on subsequent bonding. Witness panel bond specimens were fabricated by the development lab to test both acrylonitrile butadiene rubber (NBR) to Chemlok and NBR to NBR after controlled exposure. The nylon rod used as a scribe tool demonstrates virtually no bond deterioration when used to scribe lines on either the Chemlok to NBR surfaces or the NBR to NBR interface. Lab test results indicate that the nylon rod-exposed samples produce tensile and peel values very similar to the control samples and the Teflon exposed samples produce tensile and peel values much lower than the control samples. Visual observation of the failure surfaces of the tested samples shows that Teflon scribing produces an obvious contamination to the surface and the nylon produces no effect. Photographs of test samples are provided. It is concluded that Teflon stock used as a scribe tool on a Chemlok 233 to NBR surface or an NBR to NBR surface has a detrimental effect on the bond integrity on either of these bond interfaces. Therefore, it is recommended that the nylon rod continue to be used where a scribe line is required in the redesigned solid rocket motor segment insulation layup operations. The use of Teflon scribes should not be considered.

104,052
TIB/B90-82037/GAR PC **E11**
Gesamthochschule Kassel (Germany, F.R.). Fachbereich 15 - Maschinenbau.
Vibrationsschweissen von Polymerwerkstoffen. Prozess, Struktur, Eigenschaften. (Vibration welding of polymer materials. Process, microstructure, properties).
Diss. (Dr.-Ing).
A.K.H. Schlarb. 1989, 141p Rept no. ISBN 3-88122-512-9
In German.

Welding experiments with a fully-instrumented vibration welding machine show that the vibration process itself can be divided into three phases. The on-line measured parameters, the microstructure and the mechanical behavior of the welds depend on the phase that is reached during welding. Reaching phase V3, microstructure and properties are determined primarily by the weld pressure in that phase and the pressure in the following cooling phase. Welds with high mechanical properties are built up from a typical multilayer structure. They can be produced only if the welding pressure in the stationary phase is low and the pressure in the cooling phase is not changed. The parameters in the first two phases do not affect weld quality. Therefore the welding procedure can be modified. The reason for different weld qualities is deformation processes in the molten layer. This processes can be quantified simply by the maximum elongation rate in the stationary phase of vibration. For high quality welds with multilayer structure, the elongation flow rate must not exceed a critical value. The results can be transferred from polypropylene to other polymers. Fracture mechanics tests show that the long-term behavior can be extrapolated from short-term tests. (orig./MM). (Copyright (c) 1990 by FIZ. Citation no. 90:082037.)

Manufacturing, Planning, Processing & Control

104,053
DE90017023/GAR PC **A03**/MF **A01**
Oak Ridge National Lab., TN.
Electroplating corners.
L. J. Gray. Feb 90, 11p CONF-9007161-1
Contract AC05-84OR21400
BETECH '90, Newark, DE (USA), 10-12 Jul 1990. Sponsored by Department of Energy, Washington, DC.

Keyword Authority Sources

Controlled language terms used by NTIS to index reports are taken from different authority lists. The authorized keywords are listed hierarchically in special publications called thesauri. Major thesauri are used as an authorized source for all keywords for a particular agency or report series; minor thesauri are used to assist analysts in vocabulary control for free language terms selected by NTIS to express concepts or terminology not covered by the major thesauri. DoD-sponsored reports are indexed using the *DDC Retrieval and Indexing Terminology Posting Terms with Hierarchy and KWOC* thesaurus. DOE employs the *Energy Information Data Base: Subject Thesaurus*; NASA uses the two-volume authority *NASA Thesaurus, Volume 1: Hierarchical Listing, Volume 2: Access Vocabulary*, and supplement. Citations from these three agencies are indexed directly by these agencies, and NTIS indexes all other citations. Because searching the NTIS database using controlled subject terms can, therefore, be difficult, NTIS has also developed its own micro-thesauri in the areas of computer sciences, energy, environment, health care, and social sciences and business to integrate hierarchically the vocabulary from relevant thesauri. Thesauri in use by NTIS and its contributing agencies are available for sale from NTIS or from the appropriate entity and are listed in the *NTIS Bibliographic Database Guide*, separate versions of which have been prepared depending upon which vendor's database is being used.

Electronic Services

The NTIS Bibliographic Database is available online from BRS, Canada Institute Scientific & Technical Information (CISTI), Data-Star (Wayne, Pennsylvania), DIALOG, ORBIT, and STN International (Columbus, Ohio). Moreover, the database is available on CD-ROM via DIALOG, OCLC, and Silver-Platter. These vendors, with addresses and telephone numbers, are published in the service's *1991 Catalog of Products & Services*.

NTIS *Published Searches*

NTIS *Published Searches* are annotated bibliographies containing full bibliographic citations developed by information specialists in subject areas most frequently requested by NTIS customers. Each *Published Search* provides up to 100 or more summaries of completed research results from both the U.S. government and sources worldwide. NTIS searches not only its own database but also twenty-three other databases such as Conference Papers Index and the U.S. Patent Bibliographic Database in compiling these. Each *Published Search* is a "bound" print version of a computerized online search, and purchasers may be notified by mail as updates become available. The *1990 Published Search Master Catalog* (PR-186/827; C 51.13/2-2) lists over 3,000 available bibliographies.

Selected Research in Microfiche

SRIM is an acronym for *Selected Research in Microfiche*, a twice monthly service that provides full-text microfiche copies of U.S. and foreign government research reports from over 400 subject categories from which the customer may select. *SRIM Index*, tailored to one's particular SRIM profile, is published quarterly and cumulates into an annual index. Available to subscribers in paper copy or microfiche, the *SRIM Index* is accessed by subject, personal author, title, contract or grant number, accession or report number, or corporate author. As the volume of NTIS reports generally precludes libraries from collecting the material comprehensively, subscription to a SRIM service often enables libraries to obtain those titles most likely to be needed by their clientele and to reduce the number of on-demand orders they might otherwise need to place.

Tech Notes

Tech Notes (C 51.17/12) digests monthly the latest applied technology developed by federal agencies and their contractors. Each monthly issue contains more than 100 fact sheets, arranged by subject, that provide information on a backup report and a contact address or telephone number for an agency technology transfer office or laboratory scientist or engineer. Subscribers receive a free copy of the annual *Federal Laboratory Technology Catalog*.

Abstract Newsletters

Abstract Newsletters, formerly called *Weekly Government Abstracts*, are summaries of current research in 26 categories of interest. The various newsletters include *Behavior and Society, Energy, Physics, Chemistry*, and *Library & Information Sciences*. A yearly index is available for each newsletter. Although *Abstract Newsletters* are not available through depository distribution, they are bibliographically noted in the *Periodicals Supplement* to the *Monthly Catalog*.

FEDRIP Database

When the Smithsonian Science Information Exchange (SSIE) ceased operation in October 1980, NTIS assumed responsibility for SSIE's research-in-progress database. The Federal Research in Progress (FEDRIP) Database summarizes over 140,000 U.S. government-funded research projects currently in progress, making it possible for investigators to ascertain developments in specific areas before technical reports or journal articles are available. FEDRIP focuses on health, the physical and life sciences, agriculture, and engineering. The database entries include project title, starting date, principal investigator, performing and sponsoring organization, and a detailed abstract. Designed for individuals and organizations seeking new technologies and collaborative opportunities with the federal government, universities, and the private sector, FEDRIP is available on Knowledge Express Data Systems, a service of the Technology Resources Company. The company's proprietary software system, which is menu-driven, eliminates the need for extensive training and complex command language and offers exclusive features such as Hyperword and Relevancy Searching.

FEDRIP is also available online via DIALOG files 265 and 266 and in offline batch processing from NERAC, Inc.

Other Database Services

In addition to its master Bibliographic Database on magnetic tape and the FEDRIP Database, NTIS leases databases such as the Agricultural Online Access (AGRICOLA) Database prepared by the Department of Agriculture and the army's Cold Regions Database. NTIS also offers subscriptions and standing orders to other agencies' data files and software. These are generally very costly and highly specific files such as the Drug Enforcement Administration's Pharmacy Extract File or the Federal Reserve Board's Call and Income Report. For a list of items available, consult NTIS's *Subscription Data Files and Software on Tape and Diskette* (PR-481, December 1990) and the agency's *CenterLine* newsletter.

Summary

Considerable attention has been paid here to NTIS because it provides a significant amount of federal material not elsewhere available, and librarians need to be aware of its services. Confusing the situation, however, is the fact that NTIS also sells selected items available through the GPO and through other channels as well. Examples of recent sources available through NTIS but also in GPO's depository program include the *U.S. Industrial Outlook* (C 61.34), the *Standard Industrial Classification Manual* (PrEx 2.6/2:In27/987), and *The World Factbook* (PrEx 3.15). NTIS also offers several subscription items that are available through either GPO or other agencies. Examples are the Department of State's *Dispatch* (S 1.3/5) and the *International Energy Statistical Review* (PrEx 3.14). Although these purchase options may be of special assistance to foreign buyers, they may confuse the novice searcher, and they indicate that comparative shopping may be in order.

Over the years, librarians have bemoaned what appear to be confusing policies in the decentralized and somewhat chaotic structure that exists for distributing the results of federal scientific and technical information. Recent recommendations have encouraged greater cooperation, especially between GPO and NTIS. Certainly differences exist between the two agencies. For instance, the average sales volume is about 10 copies per title for NTIS's stock of 2 million document titles, whereas GPO's SuDocs averages sales of 2,000 copies per title out of its more limited inventory of the estimated 20,000 titles it judges to have sales potential.[10] Also, NTIS is within the executive branch, whereas the GPO is in the legislative branch. Nevertheless, there is cooperation whereby GPO may disseminate NTIS publications through GPO bookstores and NTIS may sell out-of-print GPO sales items.

DEFENSE TECHNICAL INFORMATION CENTER

The Defense Technical Information Center (DTIC) is the central unit within the DoD for acquiring, storing, retrieving, and disseminating scientific and technical information to support the management and conduct of DoD research, development, and engineering programs. DTIC is an entity within the Defense Logistics Agency. By arrangement with NTIS, DTIC provides cataloging information and copies of unclassified DoD reports that are announced in GRA&I and made available to the public. Moreover, DTIC disseminates *classified* technical reports to qualified defense organizations, their contractors, and other government agencies that meet the eligibility criteria. Kurt Molholm et al. indicate that there are about 4,000 registered users and that about 30,000 "RDT&E technical reports ... are added to DTIC's extensive document collection" of over 1.5 million publications annually. Within its five classification categories, an estimated 50 percent of the collection falls into the "unclassified and unlimited [distribution]" category.[11] The NTIS order number assigned to DoD technical reports carries an AD prefix, a holdover from the old Armed Services Technical Information Agency (ASTIA) document designation.

According to Allan Kuhn, DTIC, while continuing to fill its traditional mission to acquire, store, retrieve, and disseminate technical information, is "also involved in developing services such as gateways and user interfaces to diverse information sources."[12] DTIC's automated Defense RDT&E On-Line System (DROLS) is searchable online or by request to DTIC. Classified and limited technical reports were announced in the center's *Technical Abstract Bulletin* (TAB), but the title was assigned a "confidential" security classification in 1967, and in 1971 that security designation was placed on the indexes to TAB. TAB subsequently ceased publication and was replaced in 1987 by the monthly *Technical Reports Announcements Circular* (TRAC), which was discontinued in 1989. Detailed information about DTIC products and services is found in the *Handbook for Users of the Defense Technical Information Center* (DLAH 4185.8).

DEPARTMENT OF ENERGY

The Office of Scientific and Technical Information of the Department of Energy (DOE/OSTI), located in Oak Ridge, Tennessee, collects, organizes, and disseminates the results of DOE's research and development activities and combines these reports with related domestic and foreign energy information. It maintains the Energy Data Base (EDB), which contains abstracts of results published worldwide covering all aspects of energy research as well as basic scientific studies in physics, chemistry, biology, and engineering carried out in support of energy- or nuclear-related research. EDB is available online via DIALOG and STN International and on lease (to domestic customers only) from NTIS. The portion of the database covering a current year is available through the OSTI Integrated Technical Information System. Detailed information on DOE/OSTI products and services is found in *Scientific and Technical Information Products from U.S. Department of Energy Office of Scientific and Technical Information* (DOE/TIC-11631) and *DOE Technical Information Center — Its Products and Services* (TID-4660).

Energy Research Abstracts (ERA) is classed in E 1.17, sold by the Superintendent of Documents, and available to depository libraries. ERA is a monthly indexing/abstracting service that provides coverage of all scientific and technical reports, journal articles, conference papers and proceedings, books, patents, theses, and monographs originated by DOE, its laboratories, energy centers, and contractors. ERA also includes energy information reports produced by other federal and state government organizations, foreign governments, and domestic and foreign universities and research centers. Entries are arranged under the DOE subject classification system and include report number, title, personal author(s), corporate author, journal citation, date of publication, contract/grant number, availability, and abstract. Each issue contains corporate author, personal author, subject, contract number, and report number indexes.

In 1982 DOE/OSTI entered into an agreement with GPO under which GPO would distribute to depository libraries on *microfiche only* a series of Contractor Reports and Publications. Distribution began in 1983 under forty categories (such as coal and coal products, petroleum, natural gas, and fusion energy) each governed by a different depository item number (0430-M-01 through 0430-M-40). The categories correspond to the main subject divisions used in ERA. These reports are not cataloged by the Library Programs Service (LPS) or entered individually by title in the *Monthly Catalog*; rather, access to their contents is through *Energy Research Abstracts*. Figure 11.2 (see page 364) shows a sample entry from *Energy Research Abstracts*.

A companion indexing/abstracting service, *Energy Abstracts for Policy Analysis* (E 1.11), was a monthly service limited primarily to nontechnical articles or reports on the analysis and evaluation of energy research and public policy. Its contents included congressional publications, department and agency reports, regional commission studies, reports of state and local governments, periodicals, conference proceedings, and monographs. Unfortunately, this reference source was discontinued, announcement of its demise appearing in the "Discontinued Periodicals" section of the 1991 *Periodicals Supplement* to the *Monthly Catalog*.

NATIONAL AERONAUTICS AND SPACE ADMINISTRATION

The Scientific and Technical Information Branch of the National Aeronautics and Space Administration (NASA) publishes a semimonthly abstract journal titled *Scientific and Technical Aerospace Reports* (STAR) (NAS 1.9/4). STAR announces the unclassified report literature related to aeronautics, space, and supporting disciplines. It includes NASA, NASA contractor, and NASA grant reports; reports by other federal agencies, foreign and domestic institutions, universities, and private firms; NASA-owned patents; and dissertations and theses. STAR is categorized by ten major subject divisions divided into seventy-six specific subject categories and one general category/division. Major divisions include astronautics, chemistry and materials, life sciences, and social sciences. Each issue contains indexes by subject, personal author, corporate source, contract number, and report/accession number that cumulate into an annual bound index (NAS 1.9/5). Figure 11.3 (see page 365) shows a sample entry from STAR.

(Text continues on page 365.)

Fig. 11.2. Sample entry from ERA

Energy Research Abstracts: Sample Entry

● ABSTRACTS IN *ENERGY RESEARCH ABSTRACTS*

The principal elements of abstract entries for a typical research and development report and a typical technical journal article are illustrated below.

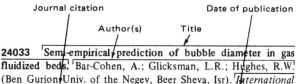

Report number   Date of publication   Contract number

Availability   Author(s)   Title   Corporate

24582 (LA–8830-MS) Nucleonic analysis of the ETF neutral-beam-injector-duct and vacuum-pumping-duct shields. Urban, W.T.; Seed, T.J.; Dudziak, D.J. (Los Alamos Scientific Lab., NM (USA)). May 1981. Contract W-7405-ENG-36. 82p. NTIS, PC A05/MF A01. Order Number DE81023986.

Abstract

A nucleonic analysis of the Engineering Test Facility neutral-beam-injector-duct and vacuum-pumping-duct shields has been made using a hybrid Monte Carlo/discrete-ordinates method. This method used Monte Carlo to determine internal and external boundary surface sources for subsequent discrete-ordinates calculations of the neutron and gamma-ray transport through the shields. Confidence was provided in both the hybrid method and the results obtained through a comparison with three-dimensional Monte Carlo results.

Journal citation   Date of publication

Author(s)   Title

24033 Semi-empirical prediction of bubble diameter in gas fluidized beds. Bar-Cohen, A.; Glicksman, L.R.; Hughes, R.W. (Ben Gurion Univ. of the Negev, Beer Sheva, Isr). *International Journal of Multiphase Flow;* 7: No. 1, 101-113 (Feb 1981).

Abstract

Theoretical expressions for bubble diameter in both small and large particle fluidized beds are derived by the application of two phase theory and gas flow continuity. Comparison with experimental data suggests that the numerical and analytical solution of these expressions, combined with empirical bubble frequency relations, can provide an accurate prediction of bubble size and its parametric trends. 25 refs.

Fig. 11.3. Sample entry from STAR

Scientific and Technical Aerospace Reports: Sample Entry

TYPICAL CITATION AND ABSTRACT

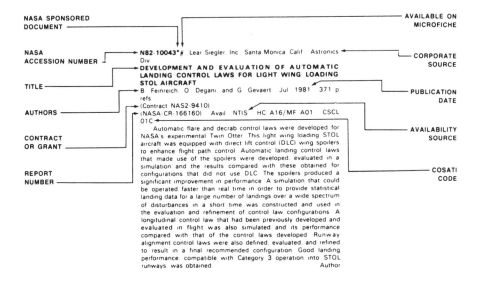

NASA SPONSORED DOCUMENT

NASA ACCESSION NUMBER

TITLE

AUTHORS

CONTRACT OR GRANT

REPORT NUMBER

AVAILABLE ON MICROFICHE

CORPORATE SOURCE

PUBLICATION DATE

AVAILABILITY SOURCE

COSATI CODE

N82-10043*# Lear Siegler, Inc. Santa Monica, Calif. Astronics Div

DEVELOPMENT AND EVALUATION OF AUTOMATIC LANDING CONTROL LAWS FOR LIGHT WING LOADING STOL AIRCRAFT

B. Feinreich, O. Degani, and G. Gevaert Jul 1981 371 p refs

(Contract NAS2-9410)

(NASA-CR-166160) Avail NTIS HC A16/MF A01 CSCL 01C

Automatic flare and decrab control laws were developed for NASA's experimental Twin Otter. This light wing loading STOL aircraft was equipped with direct lift control (DLC) wing spoilers to enhance flight path control. Automatic landing control laws that made use of the spoilers were developed, evaluated in a simulation and the results compared with these obtained for configurations that did not use DLC. The spoilers produced a significant improvement in performance. A simulation that could be operated faster than real time in order to provide statistical landing data for a large number of landings over a wide spectrum of disturbances in a short time was constructed and used in the evaluation and refinement of control law configurations. A longitudinal control law that had been previously developed and evaluated in flight was also simulated and its performance compared with that of the control laws developed. Runway alignment control laws were also defined, evaluated, and refined to result in a final recommended configuration. Good landing performance, compatible with Category 3 operation into STOL runways, was obtained.   Author

NASA also publishes *Limited Scientific and Technical Aerospace Reports* (LSTAR), which announces classified and limited-distribution reports. Like classified DTIC information, these publications are available only to designated users. NASA also sponsors publication of a semimonthly, privately published, document announcement journal, *International Aerospace Abstracts* (IAA), whose entries complement but rarely duplicate the entries in STAR. LSTAR and IAA are not distributed to depository institutions.

NASA's master database is called NASA RECON (REmote CONtrol). It is neither leased by NTIS nor available to the public from commercial vendors. Available to registered users only, NASA RECON's data files include STAR, LSTAR, IAA, unannounced documents of limited importance, NASA Research and Technology Operating Plan Summary (RTOPS), NASA Contracts Data File, NASA Tech Briefs, and the NASA library collection.

The *NASA Thesaurus* (NAS 1.21:7050) is issued irregularly as a two-volume set; volume 1 provides a hierarchical listing and volume 2 consists of a controlled vocabulary. *The NASA Scientific and Technical Information System and How to Use It* describes the agency's information products and services, and this guide is available free from the NASA Scientific and Technical Information Facility.

NASA CD-ROM Products

Among the CD-ROM products generated by NASA are the Space Science Sampler series, a two-disk set called Voyagers to the Outer Planets, and a disk containing color imagery called the West Coast Time Series, volume I. The last contains gridded and navigated images of near-surface pigment concentration and cloud covers for the eastern Pacific Ocean "derived from measurements by the Coastal Zone Color Scanner (CZCS) on board the Nimbus-7 satellite."[13]

Duplication of Information

NASA, DOE, and DoD account for most of the technical reports in the NTIS Bibliographic Database and, as we have observed, the majority of the reports announced in GRA&I are not available to depository libraries. But so vast is the bibliographic net cast by NTIS that over 600 federal units, state and local government agencies, foreign government sources, and private sector firms contribute to the service. The result is information overload and duplication of bibliographic material. A number of publications are indexed not only in GRA&I but also in STAR, ERA, *Inis Atomindex* (published by the International Atomic Energy Agency, an international governmental organization [IGO] within the United Nations system), and the *Monthly Catalog*. Like the multiplicity of information in congressional and presidential sources, duplication ultimately benefits the user, who may not know precisely what index or database to search.

EDUCATIONAL RESOURCES INFORMATION CENTER

The Educational Resources Information Center (ERIC), a nationwide information network, is a unit of the Educational Research and Improvement Office within the U.S. Department of Education. Established in 1966, its purpose is to acquire, index, and disseminate timely education-related materials for the use of teachers, administrators, researchers, students, and other interested persons. This is accomplished by a central coordinating staff in Washington, D.C., plus sixteen full and three adjunct clearinghouses located at universities or professional organizations across the country. Each clearinghouse is responsible for a particular subject area of education and for collecting all relevant unpublished, noncopyrightable material of value on that topic. Examples of clearinghouse areas include rural education and small schools; adult, career, and vocational education; reading and communication skills; and information resources. The clearinghouse for the last area, known as ERIC/IR, is located at Syracuse University in Syracuse, New York, and is sponsored by the university's School of Information Studies and School of Education. Today, the ERIC database, the world's largest source of educational information, contains abstracts of over 7,000 documents and journal articles.

ACCESS ERIC

In 1989, ACCESS ERIC, a comprehensive outreach and dissemination program for the entire ERIC system, was established. ACCESS ERIC includes reference staff trained to answer questions about the system and maintains its own databases of organizations that provide computerized searches of the ERIC database, of resource centers and other organizations that provide information in education-related areas, and of education-related conferences. ACCESS ERIC sells publications produced from these smaller databases and, by 1990, had begun to offer these reference and referral databases online to anyone with a personal computer, modem, communications software, and telephone line through GTE Education Services (Irving, Texas). ACCESS ERIC, located in Rockville, Maryland, has a toll-free number (1-800)USE-ERIC) for assistance on other new services such as Compact ERIC and ERIC SchoolDisc, intended to provide the full-text, compact disk versions of 2,000 to 3,000 documents and journal articles of special interest to teachers and administrators. It also provides gratis copies of *A Pocket Guide to ERIC, All about ERIC,* and *Directory of ERIC Information Service Providers* (all revised in 1991); and *The ERIC Review* (ED 1.331:), published three times a year.

Bibliographic Tools

Two major indexing/abstracting services provide the bibliographic control of educational materials screened by the clearinghouses and accepted into the ERIC database. *Resources in Education* (RIE) announces "document" literature, and *Current Index to Journals in Education* (CIJE) covers the "journal" literature. Both tools are available in paper version for manual searching, and the major link between them is their use of a common indexing vocabulary, established by the *Thesaurus of ERIC Descriptors.* RIE and CIJE are also available as an integrated service online and on CD-ROM. Online access is available through DIALOG Information Services, through BRS, and through ORBIT. The popular CD-ROM format may be obtained from DIALOG, SilverPlatter, and OCLC. As with online versions, search procedures vary, and the individual vendors should be consulted for search idiosyncrasies.

Resources in Education

Resources in Education, a monthly abstract journal, is sold through the Superintendent of Documents and is distributed to depositories (ED 1.310). It consists of a main entry section composed of "résumés" arranged in clearinghouse/accession order number and indexes. The indexes are by subject, author, institution, publication type (book, dissertation, report, audiovisual material, etc.), and clearinghouse number/ED number cross-references.

A sample résumé from RIE appears in figure 11.4 (see page 368), and a page from RIE's main entry section is shown in figure 11.5 (see page 369). Preceding the bibliographic citation above each abstract are two alphanumeric codes. The

(Text continues on page 370.)

Fig. 11.4. Sample résumé from RIE

SAMPLE RESUME

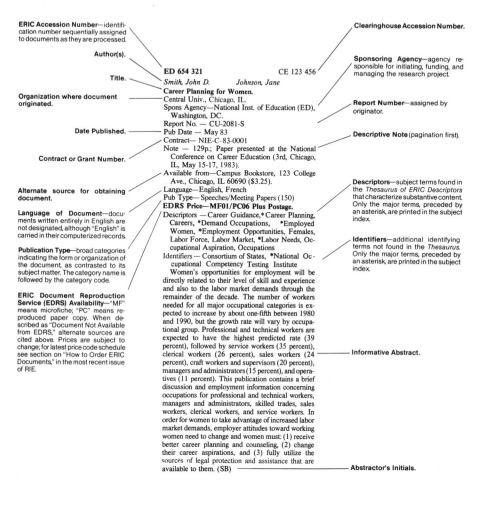

ERIC Accession Number—identification number sequentially assigned to documents as they are processed.

Author(s).

Title.

Organization where document originated.

Date Published.

Contract or Grant Number.

Alternate source for obtaining document.

Language of Document—documents written entirely in English are not designated, although "English" is carried in their computerized records.

Publication Type—broad categories indicating the form or organization of the document, as contrasted to its subject matter. The category name is followed by the category code.

ERIC Document Reproduction Service (EDRS) Availability—"MF" means microfiche; "PC" means reproduced paper copy. When described as "Document Not Available from EDRS," alternate sources are cited above. Prices are subject to change; for latest price code schedule see section on "How to Order ERIC Documents," in the most recent issue of RIE.

Clearinghouse Accession Number.

Sponsoring Agency—agency responsible for initiating, funding, and managing the research project.

Report Number—assigned by originator.

Descriptive Note (pagination first).

Descriptors—subject terms found in the *Thesaurus of ERIC Descriptors* that characterize substantive content. Only the major terms, preceded by an asterisk, are printed in the subject index.

Identifiers—additional identifying terms not found in the *Thesaurus*. Only the major terms, preceded by an asterisk, are printed in the subject index.

Informative Abstract.

Abstractor's Initials.

ED 654 321   CE 123 456
Smith, John D.   *Johnson, Jane*
Career Planning for Women.
Central Univ., Chicago, IL.
Spons Agency—National Inst. of Education (ED), Washington, DC.
Report No. — CU-2081-S
Pub Date — May 83
Contract— NIE-C-83-0001
Note — 129p.; Paper presented at the National Conference on Career Education (3rd, Chicago, IL, May 15-17, 1983).
Available from—Campus Bookstore, 123 College Ave., Chicago, IL 60690 ($3.25).
Language—English, French
Pub Type— Speeches/Meeting Papers (150)
EDRS Price—MF01/PC06 Plus Postage.
Descriptors — Career Guidance,* Career Planning, Careers, *Demand Occupations, *Employed Women, *Employment Opportunities, Females, Labor Force, Labor Market, *Labor Needs, Occupational Aspiration, Occupations
Identifiers — Consortium of States, *National Occupational Competency Testing Institute
Women's opportunities for employment will be directly related to their level of skill and experience and also to the labor market demands through the remainder of the decade. The number of workers needed for all major occupational categories is expected to increase by about one-fifth between 1980 and 1990, but the growth rate will vary by occupational group. Professional and technical workers are expected to have the highest predicted rate (39 percent), followed by service workers (35 percent), clerical workers (26 percent), sales workers (24 percent), craft workers and supervisors (20 percent), managers and administrators (15 percent), and operatives (11 percent). This publication contains a brief discussion and employment information concerning occupations for professional and technical workers, managers and administrators, skilled trades, sales workers, clerical workers, and service workers. In order for women to take advantage of increased labor market demands, employer attitudes toward working women need to change and women must: (1) receive better career planning and counseling, (2) change their career aspirations, and (3) fully utilize the sources of legal protection and assistance that are available to them. (SB)

Fig. 11.5. Page from "Document Resumes," RIE

Document Resumes

The document resumes in this section are arranged in numerical order by ED number, and also alphanumerically by Clearinghouse prefix and Clearinghouse accession number.

As explained in the Introduction, each Clearinghouse focuses on a specific aspect of education. The reader who is interested in one of these major aspects (e.g., Reading) may, however, find pertinent resumes among the entries of virtually any Clearinghouse, dependent on the orientation of the document. For this reason, it is important to consult the Subject Index if a comprehensive search is desired.

The following is a list of Clearinghouse prefixes and names used in this Section, together with the page on which each Clearinghouse's entries begin:

AA

ED 275 804   AA 001 157
Resources in Education (RIE). Volume 22, Number 4.
Educational Resources Information Center (ED), Washington, DC.; ORI, Inc., Bethesda, Md. Information Systems Div.
Spons Agency—Office of Educational Research and Improvement (ED), Washington, DC.
Pub Date—Apr 87
Available from—Superintendent of Documents, U.S. Government Printing Office, Washington, DC 20402. On annual subscription, $56.00 (Domestic), $70.00 (Foreign).
Pub Type— Reference Materials - Bibliographies (131) — Collected Works - Serials (022)
EDRS Price - MF03 Plus Postage. PC Not Available from EDRS.
Descriptors—*Abstracts, Catalogs, Education, *Educational Resources, *Indexes, Resource Materials
Identifiers—*Resources in Education
Resources in Education (RIE) is a monthly abstract journal that announces (catalogs, indexes, abstracts) documents of interest to the educational community (including researchers, teachers, students, school board members, school administrators, counselors, etc.). Each issue announces approximately 1,100 documents and provides indexes by Subject, Personal Author, Institution, Publication Type, and ERIC Clearinghouse Number. This special Computer Output Microfiche (COM) edition is prepared directly from the ERIC magnetic tape database prior to publication of the printed journal and therefore is lacking the cover and other regular introductory and advertising matter contained in the printed journal. The COM edition contains only the first three of the five indexes in the printed edition. The first accession in each issue of RIE is the issue itself. In this way, the monthly microfiche collection for each issue is immediately preceded by a microfiche index to that collection. This practice began with the RIE issue for May 1979. (CRW/WTB)

CE

ED 275 805   CE 043 515
Brodel, Rainer And Others
Continuing Training as a Means of Preventing Unemployment. A Comparative Study of Denmark, the Netherlands, the Republic of Ireland, the United Kingdom and the Federal Republic of Germany.

Free Univ. of Berlin (West Germany).
Spons Agency—European Centre for the Development of Vocational Training, Berlin (West Germany).
Pub Date—82
Note—285p.
Pub Type— Reports - Research (143)
EDRS Price - MF01/PC12 Plus Postage.
Descriptors—Adult Education, Adult Vocational Education, Comparative Analysis, *Continuing Education, *Developed Nations, Foreign Countries, *Labor Market, *Prevention, *Unemployment, *Vocational Education
Identifiers—Denmark, Ireland, Netherlands, United Kingdom, West Germany
This study is a preliminary phase in an attempt to illustrate the link between the labor market and continuing vocational training. It not only compares developments in Denmark, the Netherlands, the Republic of Ireland, the United Kingdom, and the Federal Republic of Germany, but also makes a systematic analysis of the theoretical approaches underlying the courses of action adopted by these countries. The first chapter in Part I introduces the problems of unemployment and their analytical dimensions. Chapter 2 defines the concept of preventive continuing training in a theoretical framework. Chapter 3 focuses on functions of preventive continuing training at a time of socioeconomic change. Three ideal phases of labor market policy are described: reactive, active, and integrative. Part II contains case reports on the five countries studied. The topics generally discussed in these case reports are: labor market development, institutional structures of continuing training, and the preventive approach. Part III is an attempt to compare the five continuing training systems and their preventive effects. A five-page general bibliography and an eight-page bibliography of literature on the five countries are included. (YLB)

ED 275 806   CE 043 516
Harrison, Jeremy
Planning Vocational Preparation Initiatives for Unemployed Young People. A Handbook Based on the Experiences and Views of a Group of Practitioners, Policy-Makers and Funders from Seven Member States of the European Community.
European Centre for the Development of Vocational Training. Berlin (West Germany).
Report No.—ISBN-92-825-2402-7
Pub Date—82
Note—143p.
Pub Type— Guides - Non-Classroom (055)
EDRS Price - MF01/PC06 Plus Postage.
Descriptors—Basic Skills, Developed Nations, Educational Planning, Education Work Relationship, *Employment Programs, Foreign Countries,

Guides, Job Skills, Postsecondary Education, *Program Development, Secondary Education, Unemployment, *Vocational Education, Work Experience Programs, *Youth Employment, *Youth Programs
This handbook is intended for use as a tool in planning vocational preparation initiatives for young people. Chapter 1 contains an introduction to the handbook, a glossary, a section describing a practical approach to vocational preparation, and a guide to using the handbook. Chapter 2 is a diagram of a planning framework. Chapters 3 through 7 concentrate on the five elements of planning: objectives, design, action, evaluation, and future developments. The focuses of the chapter on objectives are the scope of vocational preparation, potential participants/trainees, educational/training priorities, relationship to the labor market, and relationship to local political, educational, social, and community initiatives. Chapter 4 on design considers organizational structures and staffing, funding and resources, and activities. Chapter 5 on action discusses setting up administrative and management systems; selection, induction, and training of staff; and selecting participants. Chapter 6 proposes a means of providing self-evaluation. The three components of this approach to evaluation are addressed: description, assessment, and judgment of value. In Chapter 7 on future developments the focus is on planning for change prompted by changed circumstances or the initiative's evolution. Lists of readings, of publications of the European Centre for the Development of Vocational Training, and of useful addresses are appended. (YLB)

ED 275 807   CE 045 053
Boyd, Joshua
Pre-Service Training for Volunteer Teachers of Adult ESL Learners: How to Facilitate Communicative Competence in the Classroom.
Pub Date—Oct 86
Note—27p.; Paper presented at the Annual Conference of the American Association for Adult and Continuing Education (Hollywood, FL, October 22-26, 1986),
Pub Type— Speeches/Meeting Papers (150) — Reports - Descriptive (141) — Guides - Classroom - Teacher (052)
EDRS Price - MF01/PC02 Plus Postage.
Descriptors—Adult Education, *Communicative Competence (Languages), *English (Second Language), *Second Language Instruction, Second Language Learning, *Teaching Methods, *Verbal Communication
The English as a Second Language (ESL) method variously described as communicative methodology, communicative approach, or Communicative Language Teaching refers to a focus on the use of language to communicate. A communicative ap-

ED followed by six digits is the more important, as it represents the permanent accession number assigned by the central processing staff and allows the user to locate a document in the ERIC collections, which many libraries have purchased in microfiche. A small percent of ED citations have double parallel strokes or slashes following them, signifying that the document is not available from the ERIC Document Reproduction Service (EDRS) and is not, therefore, in the fiche collection. However, a closer look at the bibliographic reference should yield an alternative source for obtaining the document cited. Libraries may, of course, have some of these items elsewhere in their collections. The alphanumeric designation opposite the ED number is merely the temporary accession number assigned by staff at one of the sixteen clearinghouses.

Subject indexing of ERIC materials is guided by the *Thesaurus of ERIC Descriptors*, discussed below. The institution and publication type indexes also warrant further elaboration. The former, in much the same manner as the corporate author indexes in GRA&I, shows the various institutions or agencies responsible for initiating, funding, or managing a project and can be extremely useful for a number of reasons. It can help one identify the specific types of research being done within various universities, think tanks, agencies, etc. Even IGOs such as UNESCO may sometimes be found among the institutions listed, and it may come as a surprise that the ERIC collection is so wide-ranging that it may, therefore, include the actual selected documents from some IGOs. The publication type index, on the other hand, is ideal for helping one narrow the vast number of materials in the ERIC database down, for instance, to teaching guides, to legal/legislative/regulatory materials, or to tests and evaluation instruments. Cumulative indexes to the ERIC collection from 1966 to the present are described under the section titled "Other ERIC Products and Services."

Other features of RIE include thesaurus additions and changes, ordering information, and a current list of ERIC clearinghouses. Semiannual indexes covering January/June and July/December are available for sale or on deposit.

On July 19, 1982, GPO Survey 82-16 accompanying Depository Shipping List No. 17,246 offered depository libraries the opportunity to select *Education Documents Announced in RIE* (ED 1.310/2). The annotation for this category conveyed the impression that *all* the documents listed in RIE would be made available on microfiche. The September 1982 issue of *Administrative Notes* apologized for this inaccuracy, stating that "only those publications printed by the National Institute of Education or otherwise federally funded will be distributed to depository libraries. Thus you will not receive all of the documents announced in RIE. Under Title 44, section 1903, GPO is only authorized to distribute Government publications." Unfortunately, even this putative clarification was misleading. It remained for ERIC officials to provide the correct information.

The fact is that *Education Documents Announced in RIE* comprises somewhat less than 10 percent of ERIC's total announcements. The 100 or so documents per issue of RIE obtained from ERIC by GPO for the microfiche shipments represent *only* those Department of Education prepared or sponsored documents that have been issued by the entity *and* that have met ERIC selection criteria. They do not necessarily represent the total departmental output. Presumably libraries that acquire the full ERIC collection would not select this smaller subset of material available on deposit.

Current Index to Journals in Education

Current Index to Journals in Education (CIJE) is a monthly guide to periodical literature in education and related subjects. Articles published in almost 800 education journals, including many library-oriented periodicals, are indexed and abstracted by the same ERIC clearinghouses. The main entry section of CIJE includes full bibliographic information and an "annotation" or abstract of the article, followed by indexes for subjects, authors, and journal contents. Figure 11.6 shows a page from a main entry section of CIJE.

Fig. 11.6. Main entry page from CIJE

46 / EJ 421 597 / Higher Education (HE)   MAIN ENTRY SECTION (CIJE Jun 91)

EJ 421 597   HE 527 844
Assessing Competency to Address Ethical Issues in Medicine. Cohen, Robert; And Others *Academic Medicine;* v66 n1 p14-15 Jan 1991 (Reprint: UMI)
Descriptors: Higher Education; *Medical Education; Professional Education; *Ethics; *Medical Students; *Student Evaluation; *Foreign Medical Graduates; Clinical Experience; Evaluation Criteria; Evaluation Methods; Test Validity; Test Reliability
Identifiers: *University of Toronto (Canada); *Objective Structured Clinical Examination
A study evaluated the feasibility of an objective structured clinical examination to assess the competence of foreign medical school graduates, clinical clerks, and interns to address clinical ethical situations. The University of Toronto's experience with the measure found it useful but in need of improvement. (MSE)

EJ 421 598   HE 527 845
Medical Knowledge Bases. Miller, Randolph A.; Giuse, Nunzia B. *Academic Medicine;* v66 n1 p15-17 Jan 1991 (Reprint: UMI)
Descriptors: Higher Education; *Medical Education; Professional Education; *Databases; *Computer Oriented Programs; Computer Uses in Education; College Faculty; Teacher Role; *Epistemology; *Information Utilization
Few commercially available, successful computer-based tools exist in medical informatics. Faculty expertise can be included in computer-based medical information systems. Computers allow dynamic recombination of knowledge to answer questions unanswerable with print textbooks. Such systems can also create stronger ties between academic and clinical practice. (MSE)

EJ 421 599   HE 527 846
The Validity of Lecturer Ratings by Students and Trained Observers. Albanese, Mark A. *Academic Medicine;* v66 n1 p26-28 Jan 1991 (Reprint: UMI)
Descriptors: Higher Education; *Medical Education; Professional Education; *Validity; *Student Evaluation of Teacher Performance; *Faculty Evaluation; Medical School Faculty; *Interrater Reliability; *Teacher Characteristics
A study compared student and trained observer ratings of 15 high-rated and 15 low-rated lecturers in a multi-instructor medical course to identify distinguishing delivery characteristics. Student ratings were stable over three years; trained observers discriminated between students' highest- and lowest-rated lecturers. Voice presentation was the characteristic discriminating most effectively. (MSE)

EJ 421 600   HE 527 847
Comparing Students' Feedback about Clinical Instruction with Their Performances. Anderson, David C.; And Others *Academic Medicine;* v66 n1 p29-34 Jan 1991 (Reprint: UMI)
Descriptors: Higher Education; *Medical Education; Professional Education; *Student Evaluation of Teacher Performance; *Academic Achievement; Comparative Analysis; *Clinical Teaching (Health Professions); Medical Students; Test Validity; Test Reliability; Neurology; *Teacher Effectiveness
Identifiers: *University of Minnesota Minneapolis; *Objective Structured Clinical Examination
A study sought to correlate University of Minnesota, Minneapolis clinical medical students' performances in neurology on an objective structured clinical examination with previously and independently collected student feedback on teaching. Student evaluation of instruction was found to accurately reflect more effective teaching occurring at one of four hospitals. (Author/MSE)

EJ 421 601   HE 527 848
Learning to Care for the Dying: A Survey of Medical Schools and a Model Course. Mermann, Alan C.; And Others *Academic Medicine;* v66 n1 p35-38 Jan 1991 (Reprint: UMI)
Descriptors: Higher Education; *Medical Education; Professional Education; *Death; National Surveys; *Medical Schools; Course

Descriptors: Higher Education; *Medical Education; Professional Education; National Surveys; *Medical Schools; *Legal Responsibility; *Physicians; *Course Content; *Curriculum Design
A survey of 120 medical schools found 61 percent have curricula on professional liability. Many indicated students' training has been compromised or jeopardized by physicians' concerns about medicolegal issues, and many had students named in malpractice suits. Findings suggest issues of professional liability have significantly affected undergraduate medical education. (Author/MSE)

EJ 421 603   HE 527 850
Why Medical Students Choose Primary Care Careers. Kassler, William J.; And Others *Academic Medicine;* v66 n1 p41-43 Jan 1991 (Reprint: UMI)
Descriptors: Higher Education; Medical Education; Professional Education; *Career Choice; *Medical Students; *Primary Health Care; *Student Characteristics; *Decision Making; *Physician Patient Relationship
Identifiers: *Ambulatory Health Care
A study of factors influencing medical students to choose primary care careers, in contrast with high-technology careers, found students attracted by opportunity to provide direct care, ambulatory care, continuity of care, and involvement in psychosocial aspects of care. Age, race, gender, marital status, and some attitudes were not influential. (Author/MSE)

EJ 421 604   HE 527 851
Comparing Physicians' Specialty Interests upon Entering Medical School with Their Eventual Practice Specialties. Carline, Jan D.; Greer, Thomas *Academic Medicine;* v66 n1 p44-46 Jan 1991 (Reprint: UMI)
Descriptors: Higher Education; Medical Education; Professional Education; *Specialization; *Student Attitudes; *Attitude Change; *Career Choice; *Medical Students
Identifiers: *University of Washington
University of Washington medical school graduates' (n=519) practice specialties were compared with the one or more indicated earlier as possible choices. Nearly 70 percent remained stable, double the proportion when stability is based on a single choice at medical school entry, suggesting students consider several possibilities and choose one of them. (Author/MSE)

EJ 421 605   HE 527 852
Differences in Residency Performances and Specialty Choices between Graduates of Three- and Four-Year Curricula. Gunzburger, L. K.; And Others *Academic Medicine;* v66 n1 p47-48 Jan 1991 (Reprint: UMI)
Descriptors: Higher Education; *Graduate Medical Education; Professional Education; Graduate Medical Students; *Career Choice; *Specialization; *Program Length; Graduate Surveys; Comparative Analysis; *Academic Achievement
Identifiers: *Loyola University of Chicago IL
Using an 18-item form, residency program directors rated residency performance of graduates (n=401) of a 3- and a 4-year medical school program at Loyola University of Chicago. Three-year program graduates showed less strength in background medical knowledge and experience using research data. The only marked differences were in surgery and medicine residencies. (Author/MSE)

EJ 421 606   HE 527 853
Investigating Whether Medical Students' Intolerance of Ambiguity Is Associated with Their Specialty Selections. DeForge, Bruce R.; Sobal, Jeffery *Academic Medicine;* v66 n1 p49-51 Jan 1991 (Reprint: UMI)
Descriptors: Higher Education; *Medical Education; Professional Education; *Medical Students; *Ambiguity; *Student Attitudes; *Specialization; *Career Choice; Longitudinal Studies

Descriptors: Higher Education; *Medical Education; Professional Education; Graduate Students; *Medical Schools; *Academic Achievement; *Extracurricular Activities; Student Participation; College Admission; *Nontraditional Students
Identifiers: *Brown University RI
Of 123 matriculants to the Brown University medical program in 1987-88 and 1988-89, more than one-third had taken traditional premedical course requirements after graduating from college. Academic performance, self-reports of preparation, or involvement in extracurricular activities in this group were comparable to that of traditional premedical students in the first two years. (Author/MSE)

EJ 421 608   HE 527 855
Characteristics of Effective Clinical Teachers of Ambulatory Care Medicine. Irby, David M.; And Others *Academic Medicine;* v66 n1 p54-55 Jan 1991 (Reprint: UMI)
Descriptors: Higher Education; *Medical Education; Professional Education; *Clinical Teaching (Health Professions); *Teacher Effectiveness; *Teacher Characteristics; *Medical School Faculty; School Surveys; Medical Students; Graduate Medical Students
Identifiers: *Ambulatory Health Care; *University of Washington
A 1988 survey of 122 senior medical students and 60 residents at the University of Washington indicated the most important characteristics of ambulatory care teachers were active involvement of learners, promotion of learner autonomy, and demonstration of patient care skills. Environmental factors were not influential. (Author/MSE)

EJ 421 609   HE 527 856
An Assessment of 15 Years' Experience in Using Videotape Review in a Family Practice Residency. Premi, John *Academic Medicine;* v66 n1 p56-57 Jan 1991 (Reprint: UMI)
Descriptors: Higher Education; *Medical Education; Professional Education; *Videotape Recordings; Instructional Effectiveness; *Family Practice (Medicine); *Physician Patient Relationship; *Interpersonal Competence; Classroom Techniques
Identifiers: *McMaster University (Canada)
The use of videotape recordings of resident-patient encounters for review of medical situations and issues is discussed. Practices at McMaster University (Ontario) are described, and two examples in which the recordings helped students develop objectivity are presented. It is proposed that the method is useful and feasible. (Author/MSE)

EJ 421 610   HE 527 857
Highest-Paid Administrators; 1990-91 Salaries of Administrators Are up by 5.4%; Fact File: Median Salaries of College and University Administrators, 1990-91. Leatherman, Courtney *Chronicle of Higher Education;* v37 n19 pA1,13-15 Jan 23 1991 (Reprint: UMI)
Descriptors: Higher Education; *Administrators; College Administration; *Salary Wage Differentials; Trend Analysis; *Deans; *College Presidents; *Inflation (Economics); Futures (of Society); National Surveys; Institutional Characteristics; *Economic Change
Salary increases for college and university administrators slightly outpaced last year's inflation rate, similar to the increase for professionals outside higher education. Analysts feel higher education is trying to be more competitive, but expect the trend to reverse as the economy worsens. Average salaries are charted for position and institution type. (MSE)

EJ 421 611   HE 527 858
Colleges' Failure to Tackle Pressing Academic Problems in 1980's Laid to Lack of Collaboration by Professors and Administrators. Leatherman, Courtney *Chronicle of Higher Education:* v37 n19

CIJE is produced and distributed in paper copy by Oryx Press. In 1989 it was temporarily discontinued as a depository item because of microfiche contract problems. However, the difficulties were resolved and, according to the June 15, 1991, issue of *Administrative Notes*, the microfilming process is on schedule and "running smoothly."[14]

Although the annotations found in CIJE bear EJ accession numbers, they, unlike their RIE counterparts bearing ED numbers, function only within the source itself and do not represent materials available in a microfiche collection. CIJE users must obtain the full journal citation and seek out the original journal itself. Copies of many of the articles included are also available from University Microfilms International, Ann Arbor, Michigan, when indicated by the words "(Reprint: UMI)" in the main entry section.

Thesaurus of ERIC Descriptors

The *Thesaurus of ERIC Descriptors*, twelfth edition, was published in a clothbound edition by Oryx Press in 1990. In addition, it was distributed through GPO on microfiche (ED 1.310/3) to depository libraries. The thesaurus contains a controlled vocabulary of education terms called "descriptors" that conform to the major terms used in the subject indexes of both RIE and CIJE. Subjects can be located through a main "Alphabetical Descriptor Display," which provides a variety of information including scope notes; narrower, broader, and related terms; and terms no longer valid. The "Rotated Descriptor Display" groups related terms in an alphabetical index; the "Hierarchical Display" provides "generic trees" for each descriptor; and "Descriptor Groups" serves as a table of contents for the thesaurus. The thesaurus is kept current by the section in both RIE and CIJE called "Thesaurus Additions and Changes" until a new revision of the basic thesaurus is published.

Duplication of Information

Citations to ERIC documents appear in various sources, and a number of studies have sought to determine the extent of duplication. Studies found that there was a 25 percent overlap in the journals regularly scanned and indexed in CIJE and *Psychological Abstracts*, and a much greater duplication was found "between CIJE and *Education Index* ... though CIJE covers about three times the number of journals as does *Education Index*." The overlap between RIE and *Dissertation Abstracts* was approximately 4 percent.[15] Until 1990, a few documents in RIE were also found in GRA&I, but since then the ED numbers have been eliminated from the NTIS database. Even in earlier years, duplication between RIE and GRA&I appears to have been "numerically insignificant."[16]

Other ERIC Products and Services

Most documents announced in RIE may be purchased from the ERIC Document Reproduction Service (EDRS) in Springfield, Virginia, in paper copy or microfiche. Each issue of RIE contains an order form that gives the current unit price schedules for paper copy and microfiche. ERIC documents may also be ordered online through the vendors. In addition, more than 800 libraries and resource centers worldwide subscribe to the ERIC microfiche collection.[17] *Directory of ERIC Microfiche Collections*, revised periodically, lists subscribers to the collections alphabetically by state and name of institution.

EDRS also produces and sells special microfiche products that include cumulative subject, institution, author, and descriptor/identifier usage report indexes from 1966 to date. The last is a concise cumulative index containing in four separate lists all the terms used in each publication with the ED or EJ numbers for the documents or articles to which they were assigned. The fiche provides the only published access to minor identifiers.

In addition to collecting the literature of education for announcement in RIE and CIJE, the ERIC clearinghouses analyze and synthesize information into research reviews, bibliographies, state-of-the-art studies, and interpretive studies on topics of interest to users. Called *Information Analysis Products* (IAPs), these studies are usually available directly from the appropriate clearinghouse. When announced in RIE, they are available in paper copy or microfiche from EDRS. Periodically, ERIC prepares bibliographies of its IAPs, and these are assigned an accession number and abstracted in RIE. A 1991 *Catalog of ERIC Clearinghouse Publications* lists about 500 such publications. The GPO also distributes a publication entitled *The Best of ERIC* (ED 1.323).

AGENCY FOR INTERNATIONAL DEVELOPMENT

Another source of report literature is A.I.D. Research and Development Abstracts (ARDA) (S 18.47, v. 1, 1973-), published quarterly by the Department of State's Agency for International Development (AID). AID provides economic assistance to help people in developing countries develop their human and economic resources, increase their human and productive capacities, and improve the quality of life as well as promote the economic and political stability of friendly nations. Programs such as Food for Peace, International Disaster Assistance, and Women in Development fall within AID's purview.

ARDA's target audience, therefore, is AID staff worldwide, as well as key government, academic, research, and other significant public and private sector institutions in developing countries. The abstracts of AID-funded research studies are divided into twelve broad categories such as agriculture, general development, private enterprise, and human settlements and are indexed by subject, geographic area, author, institution, and document number (expressed as a PN number, e.g., PN-AAX-235).

Although some libraries have received ARDA for years through mailing list arrangements or via subscription, the tool has been offered to depository libraries since 1982 but only in microfiche, thereby limiting its visibility and use. Full text of ARDA documents may be ordered in either paper or microfiche directly from the agency; however, a thorough search of library resources is advisable prior to placing orders. Occasional reports cited may be depository items, even though the bibliographic citations make no reference to the SuDocs number or to depository libraries. Other reports may already be in a library's collection, having been obtained through a co-sponsoring international agency such as the World Bank or through some other route.

GOVERNMENT TRANSLATIONS

A 1991 *New York Times* article provides the grist for a potential reference inquiry. It says:

> The Soviet fighter pilot said to have shot down a Korean Air Lines jumbo jet in 1983 insists that he had no idea it was a civilian airliner and that he still thinks "it was a spy plane."
> The remarks of the pilot, Lieut. Col. Gennadi Osipovich, were the highlights of an unusual series of 17 articles published this year by the Soviet Government newspaper Izvestia, translations of which were made by United States Government agencies.[18]

Some awareness of possible starting points for pursuing an inquiry to see these translations is therefore important. Translations of the Foreign Broadcast Information Service (FBIS) and its Joint Publications Research Service (JPRS) offer likely points of departure.

Foreign Broadcast Information Service

Standard sources such as the *United States Government Manual* omit descriptions of the Foreign Broadcast Information Service, leaving one to search secondary sources for a better understanding of the workings of this office, which operates under the auspices of the Central Intelligence Agency (CIA). According to one *New York Times* reporter,

> Each day, thousands of quiet sleuths employed by the C.I.A. spend their days listening to foreign radio broadcasts at American installations abroad. They also monitor foreign press reports and, when they can hear well enough, television.
> The choicest items are transmitted to a central office in Rosslyn, Va. where the agency publishes them each weekday in eight daily reports.[19]

The article goes on to suggest that the CIA's monitoring agency is similar to other news-gathering organizations except that it ignores sports and comics and operates on a low-profile basis and that, until 1970, reporters quoting from FBIS sources were prohibited from citing the service as their source.

The FBIS was established in 1941, when the demand for information from enemy sources was pressing, as the Foreign Broadcast Monitoring Service; in 1946 its functions were transferred to the Central Intelligence Agency. It recorded, translated, analyzed, and reported to other government agencies broadcasts from foreign countries. These translations were made available under the title *Daily Report, Foreign Radio Broadcasts*. Until 1946, reports were issued by the U.S. Federal Communications Service, and from January 1946 to February 21,

1947, they were issued by the Latin American, European, and Far Eastern Sections of the FBIS in separate sections. Beginning with January 24, 1947, the reports were combined into one unrestricted "white cover" series. Some libraries will have these backfiles, which are available for purchase from the Library of Congress's Photoduplication Department.[20]

A rare official glimpse of the agency, one done by using excerpts of historically significant broadcasts intercepted and translated, was published by the agency in 1971 under the title *FBIS in Retrospect: 30 Years of the Foreign Broadcast Information Service* (PrEx 7.2:R31). Today, the daily reports produced by the FBIS are available in a variety of ways and are widely cited. It is not uncommon to find them cited in or appended to congressional materials, and they are generously used in academic courses on international relations and area studies.[21] One author claims that the "FBIS reports probably come as close as any reasonably accessible source to being a transparent medium accurately conveying overseas reaction to the news"[22]; another touts reading the reports "like spinning the dial on a car radio that picks up the entire world."[23]

FBIS's Daily Report series (PrEx 7.10) are now issued to depository libraries on microfiche in separate editions covering East Asia, East Europe, Latin America, Near East and South Asia, Africa (Sub-Sahara), China, former Soviet Union, and West Europe. Events of the 1990s precipitated a new series in 1991, Soviet Union: Republic Affairs. The reports feature daily news accounts, commentaries, and government statements from foreign broadcasts, press agency transmissions, newspapers, and periodicals published within the previous 48 to 72 hours. As an example, the *Daily Report-Soviet Union* for October 23, 1990 (FBIS-SOV-90-205), contained numerous reports including "PRAVDA Explains Soviet Position on Gulf Crisis" [21 Oct.]; "Iraqi 'Anxiety' over Soviet-U.S. Ties Noted" [Soviet TV]; and "Bovin Views Ties with Korea, China, Japan" [IZVESTIYA, 11 Oct.]. Although a six-month delay in receipt of the depository fiche is not unusual, some libraries that subscribe to the paper edition of the dailies indicate receipt within two weeks or less.[24] NTIS sells the paper edition; it also sells a microfiche edition that has a one-month production delay from issuance of the printed version. NewsBank, Inc. (New Canaan, Connecticut), also produces a microfiche edition concurrent with indexes.

Little of what the FBIS produces is analyzed by the *Monthly Catalog*, although the FBIS series are identified in the *Periodicals Supplement*. Although government distribution of the *Daily Report* has been ongoing for years, and although each issue is preceded by a contents page, access by anyone lacking the specific date of an event to be researched was difficult until NewsBank began indexing the reports. Beginning with indexing for China in 1975 and for the former Soviet Union in 1977, NewsBank subsequently expanded its indexing to cover all areas. Anyone seeking local reporting on the Tiananmen Square incident of 1989, for instance, would find several reports listed under "China, People's Republic—National Affairs—education—students" in the June 1990 *Index to the Foreign Broadcast Information Service Daily Reports—China*. NewsBank currently produces monthly paper indexes and annual cumulations for each of the individual areas, with coverage of most editions retrospective to 1975, as well as a CD-ROM index that combines all regions with coverage retrospective to 1983.

Joint Publications Research Service

Also operating under the aegis of the FBIS is the Joint Publications Research Service (JPRS). Founded in 1957 to serve as an interagency clearinghouse for U.S. agencies needing translations, JPRS is the largest source of English translations in the world. Information in the JPRS translations originates from non-English-language newspapers, speeches, journals, and some broadcasts emanating from foreign countries. There are many series within the JPRS translations; as an example, the JPRS Report China for June 26, 1990 (JPRS-CAR-90-046), contained about seventy translations. Among them were "Social Demand Brought under Control in First Quarter" [XINHUA]; "March's Export of Cereals, Oils, Food" [China Daily 14 Jun.]; and "TOEFL Craze Sweeps Qinghua University" [DAXUESHENG No. 5]. Coverage includes the sciences and technology as well as the social sciences. As with the FBIS Daily Report series, the JPRS reports are also distributed to depository libraries on microfiche. To the consternation of many librarians, classification numbers have varied over time, thereby creating filing dilemmas; currently they are assigned a PrEx 7.13 designation.

The *Monthly Catalog* provides limited access to the JPRS reports as well, and commercial access to this material has had a spotty history.[25] Since 1974, however, U-M-I, a Bell and Howell Company, has provided access through *TRANSDEX*. Issued in monthly paper editions and cumulated annually on microfiche, *TRANSDEX* uses an uncontrolled vocabulary and keyword indexing that picks up geographic areas as well as subjects. It is supplemented by a personal name index and a publications list that can be scanned by series and their contents.

The JPRS also prepares and sells through NTIS a weekly synthesis of foreign and domestic political developments covering many countries, under the title *Trends. Trends* was distributed to depository libraries as *Trends in Communist Media* (PrEx 7.12) until 1981. However, it does not appear as a depository item selection in the September 1991 edition of the *List of Classes.*

DECLASSIFIED GOVERNMENT DOCUMENTS

As the seasoned historical researcher is well aware, a search through the standard indexes such as the *Monthly Catalog* and the various CIS index products may yield sources that represent but the tip of the iceberg. As a result of Executive Order (EO) 11652, signed by President Richard Nixon in 1972, thousands of post-World War II documents originally classified as Top Secret, Secret, or Confidential were declassified under the mandatory review provision of that order. Carrollton Press, Inc. (Washington, D.C.), subsequently began to acquire, index, abstract, and make these declassified items available to the public. It published the *Declassified Documents Retrospective Collection* (2 vols. in 3, 1976-1977) and the *Declassified Documents Quarterly Catalog* (vol. 1, 1975-) and made corresponding microfiche collections available for purchase.

Found within the collections are many nontraditional items ranging from one-page telegrams, correspondence, and unevaluated field reports to extensive background studies, detailed minutes of cabinet-level meetings, and situation reports. Entries provide information on the classification level that had been assigned to the piece, the date of publication, and the date each was declassified. A better sense of what *Declassified Documents* contains may be gained when one knows what was excluded from the source. Intentional exclusions were

(1) documents which were declassified automatically in bulk following expiration of the 30 year rule, (2) documents which already have been given wide public dissemination (such as parts of the "Pentagon Papers," documents included in *Foreign Relations of the U.S.*, and research reports indexed and published on microfiche by NTIS, AEC, or NASA), and (3) documents which we believe to be of marginal interest to anyone other than the requestor [foreword to vol. 1, no. 1, January/March 1975].

Since 1986, Research Publications, Inc. (Woodbridge, Connecticut), has produced the *Declassified Documents Catalog* bimonthly. Indexes are cumulated annually, and a corresponding microfiche collection continues to complement the indexes and brief abstracts. Arrangement of the abstracts is alphabetical by issuing agency. Neither the catalog nor its contents on fiche are available on deposit but must be privately purchased. Subjects are broad and heavily geared to country names, however, and the user is required to search extensively to locate detail. In the January-February 1991 issue, for example, under "Brazil — Politics and government," one must wade through all seventeen abstracts cited to determine the relevance of any one to a specific inquiry. Figure 11.7 (see page 378) shows a page from the catalog.

Over the years, many other documents, especially those of a foreign policy nature, have been made available to the public through the National Security Archive (NSA), a Washington, D.C.-based foundation that functions as a repository for materials released under the Freedom of Information Act (FOIA). The National Security Archive has microfilmed numerous sets of topically oriented documents obtained in this manner and sells the collections to libraries. Examples of documentation collected and made available through FOIA requests by the NSA and others include *The Cuban Missile Crisis 1962* and *The U.S. Intelligence Community 1947-1989*. Both are microfiche collections of previously classified documentation from various federal agencies and are available with corresponding indexes or guides from Chadwyck-Healey (Alexandria, Virginia).

The historical researcher can pursue many avenues when seeking access to documents that may have been at one time classified or elusive and that, when pieced together, reflect policy decisions made at the highest level of government. Much of this material has been collected, indexed, and made available by private publishers rather than through the government itself. Although many depository libraries may have collections of materials that reflect current, popular needs, generally one must turn to the larger research collections to tap these materials because these resources require substantial commitments of funds, staff, and space. Even the resources of a long-established regional depository collection may pale when held against those libraries that have supplemented their collections with the many privately published historical materials now available. Although a detailed examination of these sources goes beyond the intent of this text, it behooves the serious researcher to investigate the catalogs of some of the

(Text continues on page 379.)

Fig. 11.7. Page from *Declassified Documents Catalog*

State Department (continued)

Iraq (continued)

A.   [Reports of disturbances in Baghdad exaggerated; reaction to Nuri Said's appointment as Prime Minister mixed.] Am Cons Basra, Airgram A-8. Jan. 12, 1949. 2 p. CONFIDENTIAL.

B.   Iraq: Political Review, January 22, 1948 [Prime Minister Nuri Said takes stand against opponents; pressure for war in Palestine is relieved; dissident foreign Arab papers are banned; student demonstrations are broken up.] Am Emb Baghdad, Airgram A-27. Jan. 22, 1949. 3 p. CONFIDENTIAL.

C.   [Description of Communist and Independence Party demonstration in honor of Baghdad's "Martyrs".] Am Cons Basra, Airgram A-14. Jan. 26, 1949. 2 p. CONFIDENTIAL.

D.   [Situation in Basra: police arresting "Communist" agitators; economy slumping.] Am Cons Basra, Airgram A-19. Feb. 2, 1949. 1 p. CONFIDENTIAL.

E.   Iraq: Political Review, February 14, 1949 [Prime Minister Nuri Said answers critics of government policy on: British recognition of Israel; arrests of political opponents; handling of Palestine War]. Am Emb Baghdad, Airgram A-58. Feb. 14, 1949. 4 p. RESTRICTED.

F.   Notes on Current Events and Opinions in Iraq [reaction to US and British recognition of Israel; possibility of incorporation of Arab Palestine into Transjordan; possible approval of union with Syria (Greater Syria Plan)]. Am Emb Baghdad, Airgram A-60. Feb. 14, 1949. 2 p. RESTRICTED.

G.   [Executions of Communists Yousif Salman Yousif and Hussain Mohammed El-Shabibi; economic outlook.] Am Cons Basra, Airgram A-26. Feb. 16, 1949. 2 p. CONFIDENTIAL.

H.   Prime Minister Nuri As Said Talks Frankly to Parliament about Iraq's Economic and Political Difficulties. Am Emb Baghdad, Airgram A-78. Feb. 25, 1949. 2 p. RESTRICTED.

I.   [Situation in Basra: Communist arrests; struggling economy.] Am Cons Basra, Airgram A-32. Mar. 3, 1949. 2 p. CONFIDENTIAL.

major microform publishers for additional materials. A search of publisher catalogs reveals research-level collections such as *Confidential U.S. State Department Central Files — China* for various twentieth-century periods or *Official Conversations and Meetings of Dean Acheson (1949-1953)* (University Publications of America), *Post-War Foreign Policy Planning* (CIS), and *The FBI File on the House Committee on Un-American Activities* (HUAC) (Scholarly Resources).

INTELLECTUAL PROPERTY

According to legal historian Lawrence M. Friedman, the formal source of federal control over patents and copyrights is found in Article 1, Section 8, Clause 8, of the Constitution, which gives Congress the power to "promote the progress of science and useful arts, by securing for limited times to authors and inventors the exclusive right to their respective writings and discoveries." Trademark law, "relatively undeveloped before the 19th century," is grounded in the so-called Commerce Clause of the Constitution (Article 1, Section 8, Clause 3), which gives Congress the authority "to regulate commerce ... among the several states." The unwieldy body of statutes, administrative laws and regulations, and case law comprising the textual and bibliographic apparatus of patents, trademarks, and copyright comes under the rubric "intellectual property."[26]

Patents

A patent for an invention "is a grant of a property right by the Government to the inventor (or his heirs or assigns)" administered by the Patent and Trademark Office (PTO) of the Department of Commerce. The patent grant "extends throughout the United States and its territories and possessions" and has a term of "17 years from the date the patent is granted, subject to the payment of maintenance fees." The first patent law was enacted April 10, 1790 (1 Stat. 109). The law now in effect is codified in Title 35 of the *United States Code*.[27] The first patent granted by the colonies was awarded to Samuel Winslow in 1641 by Massachusetts "for a new method of extracting salt," and the first patent granted by the federal government was issued to Samuel Hopkins of Vermont on July 31, 1790, for "a process of making potash and pearl ashes."[28] The current regulations of the PTO are promulgated in Chapter I of Title 37, *Code of Federal Regulations*.

The awarding of patents has been a process of dramatic acceleration. By 1836, 9,957 patents had been issued. "Between 1836 and 1890, 431,541 were granted."[29] On March 19, 1991, the *five millionth* patent was awarded to the University of Florida, where a microbiologist combined the traits of two bacteria into a genetically engineered form that can recycle agricultural waste, yard trash, and newspapers into ethanol.

Those of us who assisted library patrons in conducting a patent search in the pre-electronic days were obliged to direct the inventor in a sequence of steps involving the *Index to the U.S. Patent Classification* (C 21.5/2), an annual that provides the class and subclass designations; the *Manual of Classification* (C 21.12) if the *Index* failed to reveal the precise field of search; *Classification Definitions* (C 21.3/2), if necessary, which defines the scope embraced by each of the classes and subclasses; and a *Microfilm List* that provided individual patent numbers under the "original classification" (OR) as well as a cross-reference listing of more numbers for related classifications. Our intrepid searcher then had to update this information by bridging the gap between the latest cumulation of the *Microfilm List* and the latest annual *Index* for additional numbers in the desired class/subclass notations. Moreover, to update the *Index,* all weekly issues of the *Official Gazette of the United States Patent and Trademark Office: Patents* (C 21.5) had to be consulted. This weekly series of abstracts of current patents awarded is known by the short title *Official Gazette: Patents* (POG) and is arranged by class/subclass designations. The patron, now armed with dozens or perhaps hundreds of individual patent numbers, was obliged to examine at least the POG abstract to determine whether his or her invention was sufficiently different from all other like patents previously awarded to make the "claims" of novelty upon which a grant of ownership is assigned.[30]

Thus, whether it be a novel type of mousetrap (class/subclass 43-58 +) or a genetically engineered mouse (Patent No. 4,736,866, "Transgenic Non-Human Mammals," announced in the April 12, 1988, issue of POG), the searcher must fulfill the criteria set forth in the appropriate provisions of Title 35 of the *United States Code* as construed by the courts or else become, alas, an inventor *manqué.*

This simplified explanation of a complex bibliographic process has been amplified elsewhere, especially in a series of 1991 and 1992 issues of *Documents to the People.*[31] A large number of depository institutions subscribe to the *Official Gazette: Patents,* and almost seventy Patent Depository Libraries (PDLs) house the complete patent specifications. A collection of the full patents is located in the Search Room of the Scientific Library of PTO (Arlington, Virginia), where the public may search and examine patents granted since 1836. The scope of the designated PDLs varies from library to library, ranging from patents of only recent years to all or most of the patents issued since 1790. These collections are organized in patent number sequence and are available for public use free of charge. PTO's Search Room, however, arranges patents in the class/subclass scheme and in addition "contains a set of United States patents arranged in numerical order and a complete set of the *Official Gazette.*[32]

CASSIS

The Classification and Search Support System (CASSIS), developed by the PTO, is available online at all Patent Depository Libraries. In 1987 CASSIS/CD-ROM was developed at PTO to reduce the cost of the online service and eventually replace it. The replacement of the online system with the compact disk is expected to provide annualized savings to the PTO of over $300,000. Moreover, the relatively low-cost, fixed-cost CD-ROM product has allowed the Patent and Trademark Office to expand coverage of Patent Depository Libraries to regions of the United States in which there are no PDLs. CASSIS/CD-ROM has been available to all PDLs since January 1989, "offering patent researchers an indexing tool of superior power and sophistication to the online service, and a system much more capable of meeting a searcher's needs at the 'point of use.'"[33]

CASSIS/CD-ROM is available by subscription to libraries and information centers not designated as PDLs on a bimonthly schedule. Users who do not understand the intricacies of the patent classification system will have difficulty with the product, but once a user has mastered the system, or at least gained familiarity with the search strategies required to proceed logically from class/sub-class to patent number, he or she will find the CD-ROM far friendlier than either the online version or the tedious manual procedures. Accompanying the disks are the *CASSIS/CD-ROM User's Manual* and a "shorter, more concise *CASSIS/ CLSF User's Guide*," which is "more useful as a quick reference guide than the longer *User's Manual.*[34]

APS—Automated Patent Search

APS—Automated Patent Search, another CD-ROM product developed by MicroPatent (New Haven, Connecticut), contains "the text of U.S. patent claims (ClaimSearch), the full text of U.S. patents (FullText), and the drawings for all U.S. patents (PatentImage)." Like CASSIS/CD-ROM, APS uses Dataware (Cambridge, Massachusetts) search and display software. Updated monthly, APS contains more information than CASSIS and is more timely. However, APS "is housed on five compact discs that cannot be searched in a single procedure (even on five CD drives)." APS documentation and installation instructions "are easy to comprehend" and the manual accompanying the software is "noticeably easier to use than its overly descriptive CASSIS counterpart." However, patent coverage begins in 1973 "with limited data to 1969." As one reviewer noted, as vendors such as SilverPlatter, Research Publications, and others are "entering the patent CD market, MicroPatent's use of Dataware software may give them an edge among buyers who also purchase PTO products."[35]

Other Electronic Sources

Several vendors provide various types of patent information, among them DIALOG, BRS, and LEXIS. BRS Information Technologies carries PATDATA, which includes detailed information and abstracts for all utility patents issued since 1971 and all reissue patents since July 1, 1975. Coverage is updated weekly. LEXIS, a Mead Data Central source, contains a number of "libraries" and "files" on patents. For example, LEXPAT includes the full text of design, plant, and utility patents since 1975; patent numbers with classification; the Manual of Classification; its index; and combined plant, utility, and design files. In addi-tion, the PTO allows public access to CASSIS online and on CD-ROM for searching at its headquarters in Arlington, Virginia, and these electronic products comprise all the necessary bibliographic finding aids available in print formats.

Reference Text

The beginner would do well to consult Susan B. Ardis, *An Introduction to U.S. Patent Searching: The Process* (Englewood, CO: Libraries Unlimited, 1991). This basic primer contains a variety of types of search strategies that users might employ, with sample searches illustrating mistakes that can be made as well as successful strategies. The text includes a glossary and thirty-four appendixes containing samples of the basic types of patents, search screens from computerized databases, relevant provisions of Title 35 of the *United States Code*, a list of Patent Depository Libraries, and other useful exhibits. The author, on page 77 of her book, provides a list of twenty-one electronic patent databases, referencing dates of coverage, number of patents in each database, and name of vendor. Rounding out this source is an index providing access to its contents by name, title, and subject.

Selected PTO Publications

In addition to the publications mentioned above, the Patent and Trademark Office issues publications in support of patents and the process of securing this property right. *Attorneys and Agents Registered to Practice before the U.S. Patent Office* (C 21.9/2) is a listing of patent attorneys and agents arranged alphabetically and geographically. But attorneys and agents are as close to the user as the Yellow Pages of one's local telephone directory. The *Manual of Patent Examining Procedure* (C 21.15) serves primarily as a detailed reference source on patent examining practice and procedure for patent examiners and is issued in looseleaf format. It is announced in *Price List 36* as a SuDocs subscription item. *Basic Facts about Patents* is a small brochure, revised periodically, that answers in nontechnical language questions frequently asked by prospective applicants. Sections include "Types of Patents" (utility, design, plant), components of a patent application, a definition of the "Disclosure Document Program," and a list of Patent Depository Libraries.

International Patent Classification

Concordance: United States Patent Classification to International Patent Classification (C 21.14/2) consists of parallel tables and is revised periodically. For example, inventions such as the jack-in-the-box constitute a field of search that includes United States class 46 and various subclasses. Patent 3,691,675 (September 19, 1972) was awarded for a "Jack-in-the-Box Sounder" equipped with a bellows extending between the pop-up figure and the box so that the bellows expands when the figure emerges from the box. An air-operated sounder provides a distinctive noise when the air is expelled through a passageway. This momentous invention was given, *inter alia*, a 46/118 class/subclass designation, described in the *Manual of Classification* as "Amusement Devices, Toys. Figure Toys. Combined. With Sound. Movable Figure." The *Concordance* shows that particular U.S. class is equivalent to international class A63h 13/16, with a descriptive breakdown as follows: "Human Necessities (A). Sports; games, amusements (63). Toys (h). Toy figures with self-moving parts, with or without movement of the toy as a whole (13/00). Boxes from which figures jump (13/16)." Patent classification schemes are, beyond doubt, quite complex.

Patent Law

If patent examiners reject the claims of applicants, they may first appeal to the Board of Patent Appeals and Interferences, an administrative tribunal with quasi-judicial powers within the PTO. And if the board's decision is adverse to applicants, they may carry their appeal further to the Court of Appeals for the Federal Circuit or file civil action against the agency in the U.S. District Court for the District of Columbia.

As the number of patents granted increased over the decades, so did the volume of patent litigation. In recent times, the courts, "keenly aware that a patent could be used to stifle competition," have tried "to restrict the patent to genuine novelty, to individual skill," as a reaction to the increasing phenomenon of "corporate mass production of small improvements."[36] The Supreme Court has attempted to clarify words such as *new* ("never known before"), *useful* ("operative" — that is, having and accomplishing a purpose), and *inventive* ("something beyond the skill of an ordinary skilled person in the field of the idea.")[37] Court cases involving patent infringement are found in *Federal Supplement, Federal Reporter, 2d Series*, and the West and Lawyers Cooperative Publishing Company editions of *United States [Supreme Court] Reports. United States Patents Quarterly* and *Patent, Trademark & Copyright Journal* are both weeklies published by the Bureau of National Affairs (BNA). LEXIS and WESTLAW provide online access to *United States Law Week Daily Edition* and BNA's *Patent, Trademark & Copyright Law Daily*. LEXIS's PATCOP library carries a large number of jurisdictions, as do WESTLAW's online databases.

Patents: Benefit or Obstacle?

Patents have generally been considered inducements to economic growth, but as with other incentive systems (such as corporate franchises and land grants), "public opinion was of two minds about it. The original law no doubt had in mind the small inventor, working through the night in his study or laboratory. There were [and still are] such people," but they constitute a "minority of American inventors; and in general, they were precisely those who could not bear the costs of patent litigation, or fight off the patent pirates."[38]

This ambivalence about the desirability of the system itself is reflected in comments made before the Senate Judiciary Committee by Dr. Fritz Machlup in 1958; the point is as true today as it was over three decades ago.

> No economist, on the basis of present knowledge, could possibly state with certainty that the patent system ... confers a net benefit or a net loss upon society.... If we did not have a patent system, it would be irresponsible, on the basis of our present knowledge of its economic consequences, to recommend instituting one. But since we have had a patent system for a long time, it would be irresponsible, on the basis of present knowledge, to recommend abolishing it.[39]

Figure 11.8 shows a drawing of a battery-powered electric tractor, issued as Patent No. 4,662,472 (May 5, 1987). Its U.S. classification designation in original classification (OR) is 180/235; its international classification is B60K 17/30. In the full patent specification, the inventors articulated twenty-eight claims and included five "Drawing Figures."[40] When this patent was published in POG, only the basic bibliographic data, the abstract, and one drawing were provided.

Fig. 11.8. Drawing from full patent specification

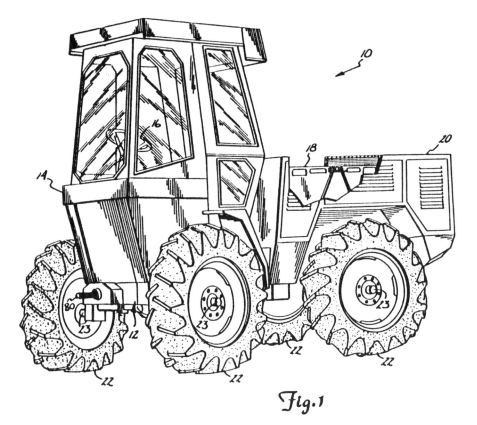

U.S. Patent   May 5, 1987   Sheet 1 of 4   4,662,472

𝓕𝓲𝓰.1

Trademarks

The federal registration of trademarks is governed by Title 15, *United States Code*, section 1051 et seq.; regulations promulgated in 37 CFR Part 2; administrative rulings; the *Trademark Manual of Examining Procedure*; and a body of case law that has construed the code and the regulations. Registered trademarks are of six main categories: design only, word and design, stylized letters and word, block letters and word, word only, and sound only. To these types an olfactory category has been added, for in 1991 the PTO ruled that a smell can be trademarked.[41]

When used to identify a service, a trademark (TM) can be called a service mark (SM), although the word *trademark* is typically used as the generic term to include service marks. Normally a trademark for goods appears on the product or on its packaging, whereas a service mark (such as American Express or Planned Parenthood) is commonly used in advertising to identify the owner's services. Moreover, a trademark and a trade name are similar but technically not the same. The former, when duly registered by the PTO, provides the registrant with the same legal protection against infringement granted to a patentee. The symbol ® on a product indicates that the PTO has issued the registrant formal notification of acceptance, subject initially to an appeal in opposition. If no party or parties come forth to challenge the mark within thirty days of PTO approval, the registration becomes active and its owner has in effect a legal contract.[42]

Similar to patented and copyrighted materials, a registered mark signifies ownership and all the commercial and legal benefits that may derive by virtue of ownership. However, unlike copyrighted and patented works, trademark rights can last indefinitely as long as the mark continues to be used in commerce. The term of federal trademark registration is ten years, with ten-year renewal terms, on into the future.

There are over one million active, expired, abandoned, or cancelled trademarks, and one sees those currently in use so often that they appear to be ubiquitous. There are the golden arches of McDonald's, the CBS eye, the Jolly Green Giant, the Hallmark crown, the Gerber baby, Mister Donut, the circle "W" of Westinghouse Electric Corporation, the imposing figure of Colonel Sanders, and hundreds of thousands more. Less obvious, perhaps, are all the words or phrases without an accompanying design or symbol. Simply look in kitchen and bathroom cabinets, for starters, and you will find multitudes of brand names with the familiar ® denoting official PTO approval. When a word or phrase is a registered mark, the search for that verbal designation is not difficult. However, the search for nonverbal characteristics becomes more difficult, requiring skill and experience. Unlike the patent search, few individuals conduct their own trademark searches, especially if a complex design has been drafted for approval.

The most complete record of all active and inactive registrations and pending applications is maintained by the PTO's "trademark search library" in Arlington, Virginia. The applicant, however, "may hire a private search company or law firm to perform a search if a search is desired before filing an application."[43] As for patent attorneys and agents, the Yellow Pages of the telephone directory are a source. One may also contact local bar associations for lists of attorneys specializing in trademark law and procedure or consult *Martindale-Hubbell's Law Directory*, now available on CD-ROM as well as in print.

TRADEMARKSCAN—DIALOGLINK

A number of firms that conduct trademark searches for a fee employ a commercial online database called TRADEMARKSCAN-FEDERAL.[44] If the registration number is known, the database retrieves both the "trademark information and design" in "less than five minutes." Thomson & Thomson, a trademark and copyright research firm, added designs to text on TRADEMARK-SCAN-FEDERAL in January 1988. "Simultaneously, DIALOG developed DIALOGLINK, version 1.20, a powerful and easy-to-use software to receive and display images online from mainframe computers." However, the database's "main weakness is its inability to provide a tool to *search* for design elements." The research firm is developing "design code searches" and they will be made available to users of TRADEMARKSCAN-FEDERAL. The applicant must supply a clear and precise written description of the mark. "This description is defined as the Design Phrase (PH =) field" and "is the weak link in the system because it does not have a controlled vocabulary, and because only about 30 percent of the records with a design have a design phrase." When the design phrase is "far-fetched," it is difficult for the searcher to "match the description" in order "to be able to retrieve the image."[45] As a General Accounting Office study remarked, the classification process is interpretive and to some extent subjective. And if a design is classified inappropriately, users have trouble retrieving it from the database when doing searches of designs that contain similar elements.[46]

The Hershey Kiss

In her informative article on TRADEMARKSCAN and DIALOGLINK, N. J. Thompson shows a figure of a downloaded design-only mark of the well-known chocolate delicacy, the Hershey "Kiss," first registered in 1924. The unrevealing design phrase reads, "Plume extending out of wrapper."[47] Yet that is presumed to be the singular distinguishing element, a duplication of which would imply infringement. Thus, the descriptive quality of the design phrase is crucial to an accurate trademark search in this category. Today the words *Hershey's Kisses* are followed by the symbol ®.

T-Search

A computer-based search and retrieval system for trademarks has been operational at the PTO since 1986. The major goal in developing T-Search was to provide users "with the capability to conduct a trademark search as fast or faster than manual searches of the paper files." Acting upon complaints about the quality of this online service, a House Judiciary Subcommittee directed the General Accounting Office (GAO) to investigate and analyze the T-Search operation. In preparing its report, GAO interviewed "PTO trademark and automation officials, several PTO examining attorneys, some public users of the system, and officials of the United States Trademark Association, which represents trademark attorneys and many trademark owners." Like PTO patent examiners, the examining attorneys for trademarks are responsible for determining whether a mark may be registered. Both examining attorneys and other users complained that search time using T-Search took too long for design queries, and they were "greatly concerned about inaccuracies in the system's data base." Interviewees told of "numerous data errors—such as misspelled words, missing data, or data entered into the wrong data fields."

Another serious complaint involved the design coding done by PTO staff. "Design coding is the process of assigning index numbers to trademarks in order to classify them according to the various design elements that make up the trademark, such as geometric shapes, objects in nature, or depictions of animals and people."[48] Out of this process a mark is assigned to one or more numbered classes, corresponding to a U.S. and an international class schedule. The Hershey Kiss, for example, is assigned U.S. class 46 (Foods and Ingredients of Foods) and International class 30 (Staple Foods). Within those classes are a number of subdivisions, such as coffee, tea, cocoa, sugar, rice, tapioca, biscuits, honey, treacle, pepper, vinegar, sauces, and confectionery. The last, of course, would be the specific subdivision to which the Hershey Kiss belongs. But in contrast to the class/subclass scheme devised for patents, trademarks do not carry a subclass notation. Moreover, as the GAO report notes, "a personified ear of corn wearing a sombrero and playing a guitar ... is coded under several design categories, such as plants representing people; playing musical instruments; husked ears of corn; sombrero; and guitars, banjos, ukuleles."[49] The ingenuity of artists and draftspeople in concocting designs is admirable, but it taxes an inadequate classification system when one is searching designs that may contain similar elements.

In addition, GAO found that "the design codes are not always revised to reflect modifications made to a trademark design during the application review and approval process. Consequently, coding representing the original rejected design—rather than the modified and approved design—remains in the T-Search data base."[50] The result of these defects is slow search time. Some users stated that design searches have taken anywhere from 20 to 45 minutes to complete. Several have gone back to searching the files manually, but Trademark Association officials averred "that the condition of the paper files was always poor and has been getting worse." PTO officials told the GAO that they "are considering placing trademark data on compact disks" and "making T-Search available for text searches through standard personal computers." Although this would speed search and retrieval of textual material, users still would "not be able to get design images on their computer screens." PTO's long-range plan is to replace T-Search with a better automated system "by the mid-1990s in order to improve trademark automation."[51] At this time it appears that TRADEMARKSCAN is a more reliable online product. Because Patent and Trademark Office examining attorneys are graded on the number of marks they can identify for registration and classify correctly, they are understandably irritated when the shortcomings of T-Search and the inherent difficulties of manual searching oblige them to work overtime to meet their quotas.[52]

Selected Publications

Basic Facts about Trademarks (C 21.2:T67/4), revised periodically, contains brief, nontechnical information about trademarks, including the legal advantages of registration, trademark notices, the registration process, statutory grounds for refusal (which include categories that "may be registrable on the *Supplemental Register*"), how to fill out an application, and foreign applicants.[53] The *Trademark Manual of Examining Procedure* (C 21.14/2:T67), issued in looseleaf format, is written for trademark examiners in the PTO, trademark applicants, and attorneys and representatives of applicants. The *Trademark Manual* is a detailed explication of the practices and procedures in the registration process. The *Index of Trademarks* (C 21.5/3) is published annually and contains an alphabetical list of registrants, registration numbers, dates published, classification of goods for which registered, and administrative decisions published during the calendar year. The *Official Gazette of the United States Patent and Trademark Office: Trademarks*, like its companion periodical for patents, is a weekly known by its short title *Official Gazette: Trademarks* (TMOG). Classed in C 21.5/4, TMOG contains an illustration of each trademark published for opposition, a list of trademarks registered, the classified list, an index of registrants, PTO notices, and other information relevant to searchers. POG and TMOG constitute two of the most formidable serials in the capacious federal publishing inventory.

These and related in-print titles on both patents and trademarks are announced in *Subject Bibliography No. 21*, revised periodically.

Trademark Law

Trademark disputes follow the pattern described for patent litigation. "Once the Examining Attorney approves the mark" and it is published in TMOG, any "other party then has 30 days to oppose the registration ... or request an extension of time to oppose." Oppositions are held before the Trademark Trial and Appeal Board, an administrative tribunal in the PTO. If that board's ruling is unfavorable to the party or parties opposing the mark, action may be taken in a federal court of original jurisdiction with the possibility of appellate action.[54]

Trademark law expanded dramatically in the late nineteenth and twentieth centuries. As Friedman noted, "The first injunction in a trademark case was granted in 1844" and "from this acorn grew a mighty oak." In a mass production economy where numerous goods and services almost identical except for package and name competed zealously for consumers' dollars, trademark litigation began to flourish. Lawsuits were "acrimonious" and "relatively frequent," and trademark cases record "the activity of many jackals of commerce who tried to make off with values that inhered in another man's product."[55]

Blatant infringement of a trademark is an obvious case under law, but some cases may appear to the general public as frivolous or downright ludicrous. For example, Mead Data Central, owner of the LEXIS trademark for its computerized legal research services, brought action in 1988 against the Toyota Motor Corporation, which had announced in August 1987 that it planned to name a new line of luxury cars Lexus. The U.S. District Court (S.D.N.Y.) ruled in Mead Data's favor under the tight statutory language of New York's "antidilution" law (McKinney's General Business Law, Section 368-d). On appeal, however, the U.S. Court of Appeals for the Second Circuit reversed and vacated without a published opinion.[56] Mead Data Central might have reasoned that if the Lexus line of cars turned out to be lemons, the public would somehow entertain the notion that LEXIS was an inferior product. This homophonic dispute is by no means bizarre or unusual in trademark litigation, such is the assiduity with which companies guard their symbolic assets of commerce.[57] In his written opinion, the district court judge noted that the "law of trademarks and unfair competition in this country has traditionally been based on the law of fraud or deceit."[58] One is reminded of the couplet penned by the eminent British jurist Sir Edward, Lord Coke (1552-1634):

Ask thou, why in such swelling volumes law do flow?
The cause is in the need; fraud in the world doth grow.[59]

Copyright

Copyright and its privileges are conferred upon authors by virtue of Article 1, Section 8, Clause 8, of the Constitution, regulations promulgated in Title 37, Chapter II, of the *Code of Federal Regulations*; Title 17 of the *United States Code*; and court cases construing provisions of the *U.S. Code* and the regulations pursuant to statutory authority. The Copyright Act of October 19, 1976 (90 Stat. 2541), became effective January 1, 1978, and represented a major revision of copyright law.

The first copyright act of 1790 (1 Stat. 124) granted an author "sole right and liberty of printing, reprinting, publishing and vending" a "map, chart, book or books" for fourteen years, renewable for one additional fourteen-year term. Authors had to deposit a printed copy of their work with the clerk of the federal court in their district before publication, and another copy had to be delivered "within six months to the secretary of state as well. In 1831, the original term was extended to 28 years," and by this time the act "covered musical compositions, designs, engravings, and etchings" in addition to maps, charts, and books. In 1856 the copyright statute "was amended to include dramatic productions; in 1865, to cover photographs and negatives."[60] Various amendments added categories of "original works of authorship" until the Copyright Act of 1909 (35 Stat. 1075) effected significant changes in the law. The 1909 act, as amended in 1947, proved woefully inadequate to accommodate the technological advances of recent decades. But the act of 1976 is extremely complex, and court cases construing its provisions represent an ongoing effort, especially concerning the pace of electronic publishing developments.

Exclusive Rights

Section 106 of the act of 1976 empowers the owner of copyright to do and authorize any of the following:

1. reproduce the copyrighted work in copies or phonorecords

2. prepare derivative works based upon the copyrighted work

3. distribute copies or phonorecords of the copyrighted work to the public by sale or other transfer of ownership, or by rental, lease, or lending

4. perform the copyrighted work publicly, in the case of literary, musical, dramatic, and choreographic works, pantomimes, and motion pictures and other audiovisual works

5. display the copyrighted work publicly, in the case of literary, musical, dramatic, and choreographic works, pantomimes, and pictorial, graphic, or sculptural works, including the individual images of a motion picture or other audiovisual work

Published Copyright Information

The Copyright Office, a unit within the Library of Congress, issues several series that serve different purposes. Numbered *Circulars* include application forms, registration information, Copyright Office services, licensing, mandatory deposit procedures, and the like. *Circular 2*, "Publications on Copyright," is revised from time to time; much of the information that follows is excerpted from this particular circular.

NTIS makes available on microfiche or in paper copy a large number of specific studies on copyright issues, copyright law revision reports and hearings, reports of the Register of Copyrights required by the 1976 Copyright Act, and related publications. The Library of Congress Photoduplication Service offers subscribers microfilm and electrostatic prints of compilations such as *Musical Compositions 1891-1977* and *A Compilation of the Regulations Concerning Copyright, 1874-1956.*

Copyright Office issuances classified by the Superintendent of Documents include *Decisions of the United States Courts Involving Copyright* (LC 3.3/3), an annual containing substantially all copyright cases since 1909, as well as many involving related topics, that have been decided by the federal and state courts; the *Annual Report of the Register of Copyrights* (LC 3.1) on microfiche; a *Compendium of Copyright Office Practices* (LC 3.11), now issued as "Compendium II"; and the fourth series of the well-known *Catalog of Copyright Entries* (LC 3.6/6). This massive compilation lists all copyright registrations made by the office, including entries for both published and unpublished works. Since 1979 (beginning with the fourth series, volume 2) the *Catalog of Copyright Entries* (CCE) is available to depository libraries on microfiche only. CCE consists of eight parts: (1) Nondramatic Literary Works; (2) Serials and Periodicals; (3) Performing Arts; (4) Motion Pictures; (5) Visual Arts; (6) Maps; (7) Sound Recordings; and (8) Renewals. All index entries (author, title, claimant) and related cross-references are arranged in a single alphabetical sequence. International Standard Bibliographic Description (ISBD) format is used in the descriptive portion of the entries, which includes available ISBNs and ISSNs. Basic copyright information is given in a statement following each descriptive entry.[61] Other copyright titles are listed in *Subject Bibliography No. 126*, revised irregularly.

Computers and Copyright

An exception to the Computer Software Rental Amendments Act of 1990 (Title VIII, section 802, of PL 101-650) allows lending by nonprofit libraries for nonprofit purposes without the permission of the copyright owner, but requires libraries to affix a warning of copyright to the package containing the computer program. Section 802 also provides an exemption for the transfer of possession of a lawfully made copy of a computer program by a nonprofit educational institution to another nonprofit educational institution or to faculty, staff, and students. These transfers, however, do not require a specific copyright warning.

Both the library and education exemptions are applicable only to copies of software acquired after December 1, 1990, and remain in force through October 1, 1997. Notice of the requirement covering nonprofit libraries to attach the standard warning was published in 56 *Federal Register* 7811-12, February 26, 1991. Copyright Office *Circular 21*, "Reproduction of Copyrighted Works by Educators and Librarians," revised periodically, provides for guidance a "Model District Policy on Software Copyright."[62]

Copyright Royalty Tribunal

The Copyright Act of 1976 also created the Copyright Royalty Tribunal (17 U.S.C. 801), whose regulations are promulgated in 37 CFR, Chapter III. The tribunal makes determinations concerning the adjustment of copyright royalty rates for records, jukeboxes, and certain cable TV transmissions. It also renders decisions concerning terms and rates of royalty payments for the use by public broadcasting stations of published nondramatic compositions and pictorial, graphic, and sculptural works. Factors involved in tribunal decisions include existing economic conditions, the impact on copyright owners and users and the industry involved, and the availability of creative works to the public. Like the Board of Patent Appeals and the Trademark Trial and Appeal Board, the Copyright Royalty Tribunal is authorized to adjudicate cases of controversy among claimants regarding the distribution of royalty fees.

Copyright Law

Court decisions based on copyright statutes reflect in their arcane language and subtle nuances the complexity of the legislative provisions case law is called upon to interpret. Indeed, this fundamental question of ownership seems to have perplexed jurists since the nineteenth century. In *Folsom* v. *Marsh* (1841), Justice Joseph Story averred that "patents and copyrights approach, nearer than any other class of cases, ... what may be called the metaphysics of the law, where the distinctions are, or at least may be, very subtle and refined, and, sometimes, almost evanescent."[63] The legal battleground, exacerbated by information published in electronic formats, has included in recent years authors, publishers, biographers, and other aggrieved parties. A small sample of cases construing provisions of the Copyright Act of 1976 follows.

West v. *Mead Data Central.* In June 1985, Mead Data Central (MDC), which owns and operates LEXIS online services, announced a plan to include "star pagination" in the text of its court reports by October of that year. The West Publishing Company filed suit, claiming that MDC's intention "constitutes an appropriation of West's comprehensive arrangement of case reports in violation of" the 1976 Copyright Act. West was granted a preliminary injunction "to enjoin MDC's alleged infringement." A U.S. district court granted West's motion for preliminary injunction, based "upon its determination that West would be able to show that its copyright arrangement included the numbering of pages in each volume."[64] MDC appealed, but the Court of Appeals for the Eighth Circuit upheld the lower court's decision. The appellate court ruled that (1) West's particular arrangement of legal decisions was entitled to copyright protection, (2) MDC's use of pagination from West's National Reporter System would infringe its copyright in arrangement, (3) West would suffer irreparable harm from MDC's infringing action, and (4) West was entitled to preliminary injunction against MDC's use of page numbers.[65] In 1987 MDC's petition for writ of certiorari was denied by the Supreme Court.[66] In this instance West convinced the courts that its numbering system ("star pagination") was within the boundaries of the "fair use doctrine" fundamental to copyright law and thus fell within the intent of the Copyright Act of 1976. After the High Court denied certiorari and before a trial on the merits commenced, the two companies reached an out-of-court settlement "whereby Mead will compensate West for a license to use West's case report arrangement in the National Reporter System."[67]

"Fair use" as a legal doctrine was originally judge-made in an effort to balance the economic incentives to creators of copyrighted works and the dissemination of those works to the public. "It has been held that the fair use codification by Congress [in the act of 1976] was not intended to depart from court-created principles and use factors developed in case law to determine fair use defense."[68] These factors are set forth in Section 107 of the Copyright Act of 1976 and explicated in the House and Senate reports in the legislative history of the act.[69]

Other Copyright Cases. Reclusive author J. D. Salinger brought suit against the Random House publishing company and biographer Ian Hamilton, seeking preliminary injunction barring publication of Hamilton's biography of Salinger on grounds that the biographer used Salinger's *unpublished letters* (which were available for perusal at collections in university libraries) to others without permission. Moreover, an appellate court held that Hamilton could not even describe the correspondence in such a way that it caught the spirit of Salinger's style of writing. A sufficient number of "infringing" quotations and paraphrases in the manuscript of the biography (which a friend of Salinger's had surreptitiously sent to him in that form) resulted in a construction of the Copyright Act that, needless to say, had a chilling effect on publishers and biographers. Copyright law permits reasonable use of limited portions of published works to be quoted, but such "fair use" is severely restricted for unpublished materials.[70]

The Supreme Court in a 1991 decision held that names, towns, and telephone numbers taken from a telephone utility's local white pages and reproduced for publication in an area-wide phone directory by a different publisher "were uncopyrightable facts" that did not even constitute a "modicum of creativity." Justice Sandra Day O'Connor, who delivered the opinion of the Court, noted that Title 17, *United States Code*, section 102(a) extends copyright to "original works of authorship" and that section 102(b) avers that "there can be no copyright in facts."[71] Curiously, both the district and appellate courts held that the white pages of telephone directories are copyrightable, based upon a "sweat of the brow" or "industrious collection" test. But Justice O'Connor disdained that misinterpretation of copyright law, stating that "there is nothing remotely creative about arranging names alphabetically in a white pages directory. It is an age-old practice, firmly rooted in tradition and so commonplace that it has come to be expected as a matter of course."[72] Unfortunately, most cases that reach the Supreme Court are not so unequivocal as this decision (despite the lower courts' constructions in this instance), and copyright interpretation by the judiciary will probably continue to be a thicket of confusing and conflicting precedents in disparate jurisdictions.

Copyright Subterfuge

Section 105 of the act of 1976 states that "copyright protection under this Title is not available for any work of the United States Government, but the United States Government is not precluded from receiving and holding copyrights transferred to it by assignment, bequest, or otherwise." Section 101 defines a *work* as that "prepared by an officer or employee of the [government] as part of that person's official duties." However, the House Judiciary Committee's report on S.22, the Senate version of the bill that became the Copyright Act, stated that

> a more difficult and far-reaching problem is whether the definition should be broadened to prohibit copyright in works prepared under U.S. government contract or grant. As the bill is written, the Government agency concerned could determine in each case whether to allow an independent contractor or grantee to secure copyright in works prepared in whole or in part with the use of Government funds.

The committee report went on to say that "the bill deliberately avoids making any sort of outright, unqualified prohibition against copyright in works prepared under Government contract or grant" and that there may be instances in which copyright should not be granted and other conditions where "denial of a copyright would be unfair or would hamper the production and publication of important works."[73]

Critics of these provisions allege that the interpretation of intent has permitted "the manipulation of public opinion via privately published books secretly funded into existence by government agencies, typically under arrangements enabling the agencies to control the contents of works ostensibly authored by independent writers." Chief offenders, it is claimed, have been the CIA and the U.S. Information Agency, but "other arms of the executive branch, including the State and Defense Departments, have also spawned propagandistic books with the benefit of 'copyright protection' artifice." Morris B. Schnapper argues that copyright law "was never designed to afford camouflage 'cover' for surreptitious government publishing ventures," but owing to "freewheeling interpretations" of Sections 101 and 105, "literally thousands of government-funded books have ... entered the marketplace in the guise of free enterprise products." The degree to which this has taken place, according to Schnapper, "may be less relevant than the fact that the American people remain unaware that a large number of books ... have polluted, perhaps poisoned, the marketplace of ideas and library bookshelves." The framers of the Constitution authorized copyright to "promote the progress of science and useful arts," but the "ambiguous provisions of the present statute ... have in effect been construed to sanction" public property "exploited through private property mechanisms."[74]

GAO DOCUMENTATION

Established by the Budget and Accounting Act of 1921 (96 Stat. 887) as an independent agency, the General Accounting Office (GAO) was not recognized as a unit within the Congress until 1945. Over the years, the Congress has expanded GAO's audit authority, added new responsibilities and duties, and taken steps to increase the agency's ability to act independently. Its chief officer, the Comptroller General of the United States, serves for a fifteen-year term. This long tenure secures for GAO a degree of independence from both the executive branch and the Congress, for GAO includes other congressional agencies in its audits and investigations.

Today the GAO assists the Congress, its committees, and its individual members in carrying out their legislative and oversight responsibilities; performs legal, accounting, auditing, and claims settlement functions with respect to federal government programs and operations; and makes recommendations designed to provide for more effective government operation. According to Joseph Pois, the types of reports generated by discharging the above functions can be divided into three categories:

> [R]eports to the Congress; reports to Congressional committees, sub-committees and individual Members of Congress; and reports to agency officials. The reports to Congress ... are regarded as the keystone of the total reporting system since they are the medium through which the Comptroller General reports to the Congress as a body.

Moreover, the "discretion that characterizes the transmittal of reports to Congress affords the Comptroller General a certain sanction in his dealings with agencies since officials are ordinarily hesitant about having Congress apprised as to shortcomings alleged by the Comptroller General." Internal GAO procedures mandate that "individual reports to the Congress should be prepared if one or more of the following purposes would be served: comply with a specific statutory requirement; call attention to important matters requiring or warranting action by the Congress; communicate useful information on important matters of interest to the Congress."[75]

Despite the fact that GAO reports of incompetence and chicanery are trumpeted by the media, it is probably safe to say that the GAO is one of the lesser known entities of the federal establishment. Indeed, the agency produces "hundreds of reports and decisions as well as testimony before Congress that deal with an enormous variety of facets of American government and society,"[76] yet "few people have heard of the General Accounting Office. Few know what it does. Fewer still know that it is an arm of the United States Congress."[77]

GAO Information Sources

A monthly index titled *Reports and Testimony* (GA 1.16/3) consists of a number of annotated titles arranged under broad topics — such as energy, information management, national defense, and veterans affairs — and includes mimeographed transcripts of testimony by GAO officials before congressional committees. An annual *Index of Reports and Testimony: Fiscal Year [yr.]*

(GA 1.16/3-2) is organized similarly but lacks the annotations found in the monthly reports and testimony schedule. Neither index has detailed subject, title, or author indexes, but the monthly issues are relatively easy to browse. The first copy of each report announced in both monthly and annual indexes is available free by writing to the U.S. General Accounting Office, P.O. Box 6015, Gaithersburg, MD 20877.

Other GAO publications include *Decisions of the Comptroller General of the United States*, including testimonies and reviews (GA 1.5/2) and the same series issued irregularly (GA 1.5/a-2). These publications were formerly distributed to depository libraries in paper format. In 1991, LPS announced that the two series would be made available on microfiche only, because the Library Programs Service "cannot use appropriated funds to reproduce materials not procured through the Government Printing Office" under the provisions of Title 44, *United States Code*, section 1903. The *Reports to Congress by the Comptroller General of the United States* (GA 1.13), known by its short title *GAO Reports*, is also shipped to depository libraries in a microfiche-only format. During 1985-1987, "GAO inadvertently dropped LPS from its distribution list for *GAO Reports*, resulting in gaps in depository holdings." LPS notified depository institutions to "identify the missing issues" so that the service can try to obtain GAO's fiche to duplicate and distribute the missing *Reports*.[78] *The GAO Review*, a quarterly, was replaced by *The G.A.O. Journal* (GA 1.15/2). Like the Library of Congress, the General Accounting Office has its own field printing facility. Other GAO series are announced in *Subject Bibliography No. 250*.

The *Index to U.S. Government Periodicals* (IUSGP) has a subject heading for General Accounting Office. Through IUSGP the researcher can locate articles about the agency and its activities in federal government periodicals such as *Program Manager, Air Force Law Review, Army Lawyer, Census and You*, and *Nuclear Safety*. The *Public Affairs Information Service Bulletin* (PAIS) provides entries for books and articles about GAO as well as GAO publications. *Business Periodicals Index* covers GAO information, as does *ABC Political Science Abstracts*, in its journal contents section. In addition, many listings under GAO are found in *CIS/Index* and *American Statistics Index*.

Audits and Investigations

As noted above, the GAO is generous in supplying copies of its reports to institutions and individuals. Under its audit authority, the agency has been given a broad mandate to investigate all matters related to the receipt, disbursement, and application of public funds. Several organizational units within GAO divide the tasks assigned to them by congressional committees, subcommittees, and individual members of Congress, and these "divisions" have names and corresponding acronyms. For example, several reports on the 1990 census have been issued by the General Government Division (GGD); reports on Medicare, rural hospitals, and health insurance are published under the auspices of the Human Resources Division (HRD); and studies on computer security, automated systems, and public access to federal electronic databases are the provenance of the Information Management and Technology Division (IMTEC).

GAO Legislative Histories

Since its creation in 1921, the GAO has compiled and maintained legislative histories of public laws to assist the agency and its divisions in their duties. REMAC/Information on Demand, Inc., a private company located in McLean, Virginia, sells the legislative histories compiled by GAO in full text on microfiche or in paper format. Included in this package are bills in all their parliamentary forms, including amendments; committee reports; debates and general remarks from the *Congressional Record*, hearings, and related congressional materials; and, if applicable, the history of related measures. Subscribers can purchase the retrospective files from the 67th through the 96th Congresses, individual collections for a Congress, specific laws and associated amendments to enacted legislation, or compilations on particular subjects or impacted federal agencies. Moreover, individual "on-demand" orders can be placed for specific laws or portions of materials relating to the legislative process, such as debates, hearings, or reports.

GPO and GAO

The Government Printing Office and the activities of the Superintendent of Documents have been the focus of GAO investigative and research reports over the years.[79] In late 1990, at the request of the Joint Committee on Printing "for a general management review of the printing and procurement operations of the Government Printing Office," GAO issued a report wherein GPO's operations were characterized by

> (1) costly, sometimes wasteful in-house production that relies on out-dated equipment and does not focus on efficiency or quality; (2) a procurement system that lacks necessary and readily available performance information and continues to award contracts to poorly performing contractors; (3) poor communications with customers and poor systems for tracking and resolving customer complaints; and (4) weak accountability.

When GAO solicited comments from the Government Printing Office on these allegations in a draft of the report, "GPO generally concurred with GAO's recommendations" but stated that "it did not believe its operational deficiencies were attributable to its monopoly-like status. It said the problems [articulated] in the report were managerial and not structural or systemic in nature."[80]

GAO reports provide comprehensive scope, authoritative analysis, and importance to a variety of users; therefore, librarians should make every effort to ensure that these reports are not underutilized, an unfortunate but apt adjective that applies to many other information sources discussed in this chapter. Figure 11.9 shows a standard abstract from a 1991 issue of the monthly GAO *Reports and Testimony*. Figure 11.10 shows the title page of GAO testimony concerning an incident that received wide media attention in 1991 (GAO/T-IMTEC-92-5, November 20, 1991).

Fig. 11.9. Page from GAO *Reports and Testimony*

Counting the Homeless: Limitations of 1990 Census Results and Methodology, by L. Nye Stevens, Director of Government Business Operations
Issues, before the Subcommittee on Government Information and Regulation, Senate Committee on Governmental Affairs, and before the Subcommittee on Census and Population, House Committee on Post Office
and Civil Service. GAO/T-GGD-91-29, May 9 (15 pages).

GAO testified on the Census Bureau's 1990 Shelter and Street Night Enumeration, which was designed to count people who might otherwise
have been missed by the census. The census and S-Night were not
designed to, and did not, provide a complete count of the nation's homeless. The Bureau consistently has warned data users that the decennial
census is not the appropriate vehicle for determining the extent of
homelessness. In past reports, GAO has discussed efforts that extend well
beyond the census that need to been done to estimate the number of
homeless. As a result of methodological and operational weaknesses,
however, the Bureau added fewer people to the census count through
S-Night than it probably could have if it had aggressively pursued the
daytime method early in the decade. S-Night is an example of what has
been one of GAO's major concerns for several years: that the late census
planning and the failure to fully consider and evaluate alternatives that
characterized the 1990 census must be avoided for the 2000 census.

Fig. 11.10. Title page from GAO testimony

GAO	Testimony
	Before the Subcommittee on Government Information and Regulation, Committee on Governmental Affairs, United States Senate

---

For Release
on Delivery
Expected at
1:00 p.m. EST
Wednesday,
November 20, 1991

COMPUTER
SECURITY

Hackers Penetrate DOD
Computer Systems

Statement of
Jack L. Brock, Jr., Director
Government Information and Financial Management
Information Management and Technology Division

DOCUMENTS EXPEDITING PROJECT

The government's Depository Library Program represents but one, albeit major, method of acquiring U.S. federal government publications. Many libraries, especially larger academic and public, avail themselves of various acquisition routes. Common alternatives include (1) receipt of materials through mailing lists maintained by many agencies, particularly for newsletters, annual reports, and publication lists; (2) individual orders to GPO or vendors such as Bernan for separate pieces needed as duplicates for functions such as class reserves and other heavy demand or "hot" items; (3) selection from exchange lists not only from other depositories but also from special libraries that periodically weed their collections and offer some of the more difficult-to-acquire fugitive pieces; (4) purchase of reprints or historical microform sets from commercial firms; (5) acquisition of older documents from out-of-print dealers and groups such as the Universal Serials and Book Exchange[81] and the National Archives and Records Service;[82] (6) subscription for current materials to private publishers such as Readex and CIS; (7) outright gifts; and (8) participation in the Documents Expediting Project of the Library of Congress.

Some of the above collecting alternatives are addressed elsewhere in this text. Because of its rather unique nature, however, the Documents Expediting Project, or Doc Ex, warrants special attention. Begun in 1946 and operating out of the LC's Exchange and Gift Division since 1968, Doc Ex was originally designed to procure and distribute war documents and other publications not available through the GPO. According to its own brochure, it also "made available a large number of mimeographed reports and documents procured by the Library of Congress Mission in Europe."[83] Over the years, Doc Ex also became the primary distributor of congressional committee prints until the GPO began to include them more consistently in the Depository Library Program. Today Doc Ex distributes to participating libraries many elusive titles not designated as depository and not available by purchase from the GPO or from the issuing agency. Items distributed range from the Research Report series of the U.S. Army Research Institute for the Behavioral and Social Sciences, to the Bureau of Mines' Mineral Industry Survey series, to the *Amtrak System Train Timetables*.

As of 1990, Doc Ex had 132 regular subscribers, each of whom pay between $500 and $750 per year for the service. Although libraries may request that materials from specified agencies not be included in their distribution package, recipients do not get to select as they do under the Depository Library Program. A library's receipts are based on a priority ranking determined by the annual fee each has chosen to pay and on the length of time the library has been in the program. During FY 1990, Doc Ex distributed 3,252 titles and 360,286 pieces, which their central location in Washington, D.C., and their well-developed connections with federal agencies allow them to acquire for libraries. Doc Ex also offers a separate subscription service in which 329 libraries participate for the Central Intelligence Agency's various reference aids.[84]

The Documents Expediting Project also offers several special features that enhance the attractiveness of participation. Regular subscribers may submit requests for individual current or retrospective government publications, which Doc Ex staff can often supply from the project's extensive collection or through agency contacts. It is often an excellent source of replacements for missing issues of periodicals. Subscribers visiting the Library of Congress are also permitted to browse the Doc Ex collection and directly select needed materials on their own want lists.

SUMMARY

One major characteristic shared by these disparate sources of information is that the individual titles within series or categories often are not listed in the *Monthly Catalog* or available to Title 44 depository libraries. The extent to which technical reports, for example, continue to be the primary vehicle for rapid transmission of federal R&D may depend in part on the government's use of electronic technologies. If the electronic journal becomes a popular alternative for swift reporting of research in progress and final documents, the importance of the print or microfiche report may decline. Of concern to libraries and their users are equitable access to the new technologies and preservation of various electronic versions. In his formulation of federal information dissemination policy, Fred Wood challenges Congress to review existing statutory language "to determine what actions are needed to ensure that legislative intent is carried out in an electronic environment and whether any adjustments in legislative objectives or in legislation are needed."[85]

NOTES

[1]American National Standards Institute (ANSI), *American National Standard, Scientific and Technical Reports: Organization, Preparation, and Production*, ANSI Z39.18-1987 (New York: ANSI, 1987).

[2]Thomas E. Pinelli and Madeline M. Henderson, "Access to Federal Scientific and Technical Information through U.S. Government Technical Reports," in *U.S. Scientific and Technical Information (STI) Policies: Views and Perspectives*, Charles R. McClure and Peter Hernon, eds. (Norwood, NJ: Ablex, 1989), p. 113.

[3]Pinelli and Henderson, "Access to Federal Scientific and Technical Information," p. 128.

[4]Walter R. Blados, "U.S. Air Force Scientific and Technical Information Program—The STINFO Program," *Government Information Quarterly*, 8 (1991): 136.

[5]Yuri Nakata, *From Press to People* (Chicago: American Library Association, 1979). See chapter 7, Table 2, pp. 100-104.

[6]U.S. Technology Assessment Office, *Informing the Nation: Federal Information Dissemination in an Electronic Age* (Washington, DC: GPO, October 1988), p. 109.

[7]Joseph F. Caponio, *The NTIS Library Liaison Letter*, 91-1 (February 1991), as received via GovDoc-L from Tim Byrne, GODORT liaison to NTIS, March 15, 1991.

[8]*Documents to the People* (DttP), 3 (November 1975): 41.

[9]Karen A. Sinkule and Marilyn K. Moody, "Technical Reports of the U.S. Government," *Microform Review*, 17 (December 1988): 263-64.

[10]U.S. Technology Assessment Office, *Informing the Nation*, p. 119.

[11]Kurt N. Molholm, Betty L. Fox, Paul M. Klinefelter, Ellen V. McCauley, and William M. Thompson, "The Defense Technical Information Center: Acquiring Information and Imparting Knowledge," *Government Information Quarterly*, 5 (1988): 327, 331.

[12]Allan D. Kuhn, "Defense Technical Information Center (DTIC): Its Role in the USAF Scientific and Technical Information Program," *Government Information Quarterly*, 8 (1991): 205.

[13]Jerry McFaul, "Uncle Sam Offers a Wide Variety of CD-ROM Titles," *CD-ROM EndUser* (September 1989): 24.

[14]*Administrative Notes*, 12 (June 15, 1991): 5.

[15]Katherine Clay, "Searching ERIC on DIALOG: The Times They Are a'Changing," *Database*, 2 (September 1979): 47-48. See also Jane Caldwell and Celia Ellingson, "A Comparison of Overlap: ERIC and Psychological Abstracts," *Database*, 2 (June 1979): 62-67.

[16]J. C. Meredith, "NTIS Update: A Critical Review of Services," *Government Publications Review*, 1 (1974): 346.

[17]Lynn Barnett, "ERIC's Indexing and Retrieval: 1990 Update," *ERIC Thesaurus of Descriptors*, 12th ed. (Phoenix, AZ: Oryx Press, 1990), p. x.

[18]Richard Witkin, "Soviet Pilot Insists Downed Korean Jet Was Spy Plane," *The New York Times* (international), May 15, 1991, p. 12.

[19]Lynn Rosellini, "Inside Line on the Overseas Action," *The New York Times*, October 8, 1982, p. A26.

[20]U.S. Library of Congress, *U.S. Foreign Broadcast Information Service*, Photoduplication Department Ref. C-206, August 1973.

[21]Examples are *Intermediate-Range Nuclear Forces Treaty and the Conventional Balance in Europe*, S. Prt. 100-94 (Y 4.Ar5/3:S. Prt. 100-94); and *Proposed General Capital Increase for the World Bank*, Committee Serial No. 100-62 (Y 4.B22/1:100-62), 1988.

[22]John Merrill, "Bringing the World to the Classroom: Using the FBIS Reports in the Int'l Politics Course," *NEWS for Teachers of Political Science* (Fall 1984).

[23]Alan Tonelson, "Media Verite," *Atlantic*, 261 (February 1988): 35.

[24]Based on messages received over the GovDoc-L through BITNET from Barbie Smith, University of Virginia, and Carolyn Kohler, University of Iowa, March 7, 1991.

[25]David Y. Allen, "Buried Treasure: The Translations of the Joint Publications Research Service [JPRS]," *Government Publications Review*, 9 (March-April 1982): 91. Allen's article provides a good beginning for understanding the indexing of JPRS reports. See also Rita Lucas and George Caldwell, "Joint Publications Research Service Translations,"

College and Research Libraries, 25 (March 1964): 103-10; and Bruce Morton, "JPRS and FBIS Translations: Polycentrism at the Reference Desk," *Reference Services Review*, 11 (Spring 1983): 99-110.

[26]Lawrence M. Friedman, *A History of American Law*, 2d ed. (New York: Simon & Schuster, 1985), pp. 255-57.

[27]U.S. Patent and Trademark Office, *General Information Concerning Patents: 1790-1990, 200th Anniversary, U.S. Patent System* (Washington, DC: GPO, 1989), pp. 2-3.

[28]Joseph N. Kane, *The Pocket Book of Famous First Facts* (New York: Pocket Books, 1970), p. 341.

[29]Friedman, *History of American Law*, pp. 256, 435.

[30]Joe Morehead, "Of Mousetraps and Men: Patent Searching in Libraries," *The Serials Librarian*, 2 (Fall 1977): 5-11.

[31]Timothy Lee Wherry, "Patent Searching for Librarians," *Documents to the People* (DttP), 19 (March 1991): 39-41; DttP, 19 (June 1991): 88, 90. See also Judith Schiek Robinson, *Tapping the Government Grapevine: The User-Friendly Guide to U.S. Government Information Sources* (Phoenix, AZ: Oryx Press, 1988), pp. 56-65.

[32]Patent and Trademark Office, *General Information Concerning Patents*, p. 9. This brochure has a list of Patent Depository Libraries organized alphabetically by state and within state by name of library.

[33]See John H. Sulzer's comprehensive and informative review of CASSIS/CD-ROM in *Government Publications Review*, 18 (1991): 83-87.

[34]Sulzer, *Government Publications Review*, p. 87.

[35]See Duncan M. Aldrich's equally thorough and instructive review of APS in *Government Publications Review*, 18 (1991): 87-89.

[36]Friedman, *History of American Law*, p. 437.

[37]Kay Ollerenshaw, "How to Perform a Patent Search: A Step by Step Guide for the Inventor," *Law Library Journal*, 73 (Winter 1980): 1.

[38]Friedman, *History of American Law*, p. 436.

[39]Morehead, "Of Mousetraps and Men," p. 11.

[40]Claims are the "operative part of the patent. Novelty and patentability are judged by the claims, and, when a patent is granted, questions of infringement are judged by the courts on the basis of the claims" (Patent and Trademark Office, *General Information Concerning Patents*, p. 15).

[41]*Time*, March 18, 1991, p. 27.

[42]U.S. Patent and Trademark Office, *Basic Facts about Trademarks* (Washington, DC: GPO, November 1989), pp. 1-2.

[43]Patent and Trademark Office, *Basic Facts about Trademarks*, p. 4.

[44]File 226 on DIALOG and via WESTLAW. See N. J. Thompson, "DIALOGLINK and TRADEMARK-SCAN-FEDERAL: Pioneers in Online Images," *Online* (May 1989): 16.

[45]Thompson, "DIALOGLINK and TRADEMARKSCAN-FEDERAL," pp. 16, 19.

[46]*Trademark Automation: Information on System Problems and Planned Improvements* (GAO/IMTEC-91-1), October 1990, p. 5.

[47]Thompson, "DIALOGLINK and TRADEMARKSCAN-FEDERAL," figure 3, p. 18.

[48]*Trademark Automation*, pp. 1, 2, 5.

[49]*Trademark Automation*, p. 5.

[50]*Trademark Automation*, pp. 5, 6.

[51]*Trademark Automation*, pp. 3, 4, 6, 7, 8.

[52]*Trademark Automation*, p. 4.

[53]Patent and Trademark Office, *Basic Facts about Trademarks*, pp. 3-4.

[54]Patent and Trademark Office, *Basic Facts about Trademarks*, p. 2.

[55]Friedman, *History of American Law*, pp. 437-38.

[56]*Mead Data Central, Inc.* v. *Toyota Motor Sales, U.S.A., Inc.*, 702 F.Supp. 1031, 1033 (1988); 875 F.2d 308 (1989).

[57]*The Random House Dictionary of the English Language*, 2d ed. (unabridged), defines a homophone as "a word pronounced the same as another but differing in meaning, whether spelled the same way or not, as *heir* and *air*."

[58]702 F.Supp. 1041. (See note 56.)

[59]Lord Coke, Twyne Case, 3 Coke 80, 1 Sm.L.Cas. 1.

[60]Friedman, *History of American Law*, pp. 256-57, 437.

[61]U.S. Copyright Office, *Circular 2* ("Publications on Copyright"), November 1988, *passim*.

[62]U.S. Copyright Office, *Circular 21* ("Reproduction of Copyrighted Works by Educators and Librarians"), May 1988, pp. 26-27.

[63]*Folsom* v. *Marsh*, 9 Fed.Cas. 342 (No. 4901), 2 Story 100 (1841).

[64]*West Publishing Co.* v. *Mead Data Central, Inc.*, 616 F.Supp. 1571, 1575, 1579 (1985).

[65]799 F.2d 1219 (1986). (See note 64.)

[66]107 S.Ct. 962 (1987). (See note 64.) See also Robert A. Gorman, "Opinion on Legal-Research Services Raises Major Computer-Age Issues," *National Law Journal*, 9 (July 20, 1987): 40-41; Linda Greenhouse, "Progress Spawns Question: Who Owns the Law?" *The New York Times*, February 16, 1990, p. B7.

[67]*Noter Up*, no. 4 (1987 ed.) (December 1988): 10.

[68]Steven H. Gifis, *Law Dictionary*, 2d ed. (New York: Barron's, 1984), pp. 178-79.

[69]H. Rep. 94-1476, pp. 65-74, and S. Rep. 94-473, pp. 61-67, contain a discussion of Section 107.

[70]*Jerome D. Salinger* v. *Random House, Inc.*, 650 F.Supp. 413, was reversed and remanded in 811 F.2d 90 (January 29, 1987). The appellate court granted a rehearing but reached the same conclusion that the "biography, in its present form, infringes Salinger's copyright in his letters" (818 F.2d 252, 253 [May 4, 1987]). Hamilton had to rewrite his biography, *In Search of J. D. Salinger* (New York: Random House, 1988), but it was more of a diatribe against the court's construction of the law than a solid biographical portrait.

[71]*Feist Publications, Inc.* v. *Rural Telephone Service Company, Inc.*, 111 S.Ct. 1282, 1285 (March 27, 1991).

[72]*Feist Publications*, pp. 1295-97.

[73]H. Rep. 94-1476, p. 59.

[74]Morris B. Schnapper, "Copyright Camouflage—Its Role in Governmental Manipulation of Public Opinion," *Government Information Quarterly*, 2 (1985): 127, 129. See also drea Simon, "A Constitutional Analysis of Copyrighting Government-Commissioned Works," *Columbia Law Review*, 84 (March 1984): 425-66.

[75]Joseph Pois, *Watchdog on the Potomac: A Study of the Comptroller General of the United States* (Washington, DC: University Press of America, 1979), p. 206.

[76]Frederick C. Mosher, *The GAO: The Quest for Accountability in American Government* (Boulder, CO: Westview Press, 1979), p. 2.

[77]William Proxmire, foreword to Richard E. Brown, *The GAO: Untapped Source of Congressional Power* (Knoxville: University of Tennessee Press, 1970), p. v.

[78]*Administrative Notes*, 12 (May 15, 1991): 19.

[79]For example, see *The Government Printing Office Can More Effectively Manage Its General Sales Program* (GAO/AFMD-84-20), November 16, 1983; *Depository Librarians'*

Views on GPO's Administration of the Depository Library Program (GAO/AFMD-84-50), April 9, 1984; and *Government Printing Office's Depository Library Program* (GAO/AFMD-85-19), December 17, 1984.

[80]U.S. General Accounting Office, *Government Printing Office: Monopoly-Like Status Contributes to Inefficiency and Ineffectiveness* (GAO/GGD-90-107), September 26, 1990, pp. 2-3, 8.

[81]The Universal Serials and Book Exchange (USBE) revived its operations in Cleveland, Ohio, in 1991. Member libraries may purchase any serial held by USBE for a flat rate of $7 per bibliographic issue. See "Serials News," *The Serials Librarian*, 20 (1991): 133.

[82]U.S. National Archives and Records Administration, *Looking for an Out-of-Print U.S. Government Publication?* (NARA General Information Leaflet 28; AE 1.113:28/990), rev. 1990.

[83]U.S. Library of Congress, Exchange and Gift Division, Document Expediting Project, *Brochure*, April 1981.

[84]Statistics for 1990 were received in a telephone interview with Mr. Bloxum of the Documents Expediting Project, May 16, 1991.

[85]Fred B. Wood, "Title 44 and Federal Government Information Dissemination—A Technology and Policy Challenge for Congress," *Government Publications Review*, 17 (January/February 1990): 5.

12

Geographical Information Sources

INTRODUCTION

According to William Katz, geographical sources "may be subdivided into three large categories: maps and atlases, gazetteers, and guidebooks."[1] The last include a number of brochures issued by the Forest Service, the Bureau of Reclamation, the Fish and Wildlife Service, the Bureau of Land Management, and the National Park Service containing information on camping, picnicking, hiking, fishing, skiing, and other activities. These titles are announced in *Subject Bibliography No. 17*, "Recreational and Outdoor Activities," and usually include maps and geographic names. The *American Guide Series*, produced during the 1930s by the Federal Writers' Project of the defunct Works Progress Administration, includes over 150 volumes, some of which are still in print. Frequently reprinted and issued by numerous publishers, the *American Guide Series* still is useful and is distinguished by its detailed contents and style of writing.[2] This chapter focuses on publishing and distribution activities with regard to federal mapping, charting, geodesy, surveying, and gazetteer endeavors.

Millions of maps and charts have been and continue to be distributed to depository libraries. Within the government are entities that produce maps but do not issue or sell them as well as agencies that both produce and sell their cartographic products. Task forces over the years have recommended that a single civilian unit be established to coordinate these diffuse activities.[3] Advances in technology have improved the quality and accuracy of cartography. The activities of the National Cartographic Information Center and the inclusion of major mapmaking agencies in the Title 44 depository library program have enhanced the distribution and availability of these products, but the single-agency concept so highly recommended by study groups remains unconsummated.

BASIC GUIDE

Mary Lynette Larsgaard, *Map Librarianship: An Introduction* (Littleton, CO: Libraries Unlimited, 1987), is a thoroughly revised and updated version of the author's 1978 edition. There are chapters on selection and acquisition, classification employing the Library of Congress "G" schedule, cataloging, storage, care and repair, reference services, public relations, and education. The book includes a bibliography arranged by subject and author. Competently discussed are the significant changes that have occurred since the 1978 edition: *AACR2*, the applications of computer cartography, OCLC, the establishment of several map societies, and the inclusion of the major map-producing agency products in the Title 44 depository library system. Appendixes include a machine-readable cataloging workform and a recommended syllabus for a course in map librarianship. Virtually all aspects of cartographic practices and procedures are included in this indispensable guide.

FEDERAL CARTOGRAPHIC ACTIVITIES

Cartography is defined as "the production of maps, including construction of projections, design, compilation, drafting, and reproduction."[4] This enterprise is

> one of the oldest activities of the United States Government. Recognizing the need for large scale maps based on field surveys, the Continental Congress in 1775 authorized General George Washington to appoint a Geographer of the Army. The corps of surveyors that compiled sketch maps of terrain, prepared plan maps of military posts, and laid out routes for troop movements was the predecessor for permanent mapping agencies with both military and civil functions.[5]

According to Charles Seavey, "Maps are probably among the most valuable and least understood government publications available today. Yet, the government agencies of the world (national, state, and local) account for over 80% of all maps published in a given year."[6]

National Mapping Policy

The U.S. Geological Survey (USGS) is the principal federal agency responsible for implementing the nation's mapping program, which is decentralized and requires coordination among many mapping agencies, both federal and state. USGS receives funds from states to help prepare maps of their areas. The federal government matches state contributions and allots priorities to those areas where both governments require new or revised maps. USGS also enters into cost-sharing programs with other federal entities in support of joint mapping requirements.[7]

The establishment of National Map Accuracy Standards and the issuance of Office of Management and Budget (OMB) Circular A-16 represent milestones in the development of a national mapping program. On June 10, 1941, the first official set of U.S. National Map Accuracy Standards was released following a meeting arranged by OMB. The standards provide for horizontal and vertical accuracies and define how each map is to be marked to show compliance with the standards. USGS maintains the standards and prepares and distributes a series of topographic instructions to its map production centers and to other federal, state, and private mapping organizations. The instructions furnish information on contour intervals, triangulation standards and datum, bench marks, map revision, map lettering and marginal data, symbols, projections, color separations, reference systems, boundaries, geographic names, and many other subjects.[8]

In 1953 OMB issued Circular A-16, "Coordination of Surveying and Mapping Activities." The circular and its May 1967 revision describe the responsibilities of federal agencies with respect to coordinating surveying and mapping activities. The Interior Department, the parent agency of USGS, is assigned responsibility for topographic mapping, *The National Atlas of the United States* (I 19.2:N21a), and the operation of a Map Information Office. Every year the USGS asks each agency to prepare a statement of mapping requirements for new and revised maps in three orders of priority. When all priorities have been received, USGS assigns the scheduling of mapping for the following year. *The National Atlas* was published in 1970. Lack of funding has precluded an updated version, but it still is useful and was the first official atlas the nation produced. To circumvent the lack of monies to produce a new edition of *The National Atlas*, individual maps (I 19.111/a) are issued to depository libraries that update portions of the atlas, but these "separates" are patently less useful than would be a replacement of *The National Atlas* with a new edition. The National Ocean Service of the Commerce Department was assigned responsibility for collecting control data for the National Networks of Geodetic Control and for preparing separate status maps showing horizontal control (latitude and longitude) and vertical control (elevation) of first- and second-order classification. Each year status maps are prepared by June 15 for planned activities and by September 15 for accomplished work. The Office of the Geographer within the State Department is responsible for ensuring that all cartographic representations of international boundaries, other than those of the United States with Canada and Mexico, are consistent and conform to U.S. foreign policy.[9]

Major Mapping and Charting Agencies

Although a number of agencies produce maps for various purposes, the leading producers of maps and charts are the Geological Survey, the Defense Mapping Agency (DMA), and the National Ocean Service (NOS), formerly called the National Ocean Survey.

National Ocean Service

The National Ocean Service is the principal federal agency for producing and distributing nautical charts and maps. The NOS Charting Program consists of creating harbor charts for navigation and anchorage in small waterways, coast charts for coastal navigation inside the offshore reefs and shoals, general charts for navigation well offshore, sailing charts for planning and navigation between distant coastal ports, and international charts (standard small scale) produced in cooperation with the International Hydrographic Organization program for charts covering the world's oceans.

A major series produced by NOS is the *Nautical Chart Catalogs* (C 55.418: no.). Issued as index maps showing which nautical charts are available, *Catalog 1* covers the Atlantic and Gulf coasts, including Puerto Rico and the Virgin Islands.

Catalog 2 includes the Pacific Coast and Hawaii, Guam, and Samoa. *Catalog 3* covers Alaska and the Aleutian Islands. *Catalog 4* comprises the Great Lakes and adjacent waterways. *Catalog 5* consists of bathymetric and fishing maps including topographic/bathymetric maps. Moreover, NOS generates *Instrument Approach Procedure Charts* (C 55.411); *Airport Obstruction Charts* (C 55.411/3); *Standard Terminal Arrival Charts* (C 55.416/3); *Helicopter Charts* for cities such as New York, Los Angeles, Washington, D.C., and Chicago (C 55.146/12-no.); *World Aeronautical Charts* (C 55.416/13); and other important series.

NOS and Title 44 Depository Libraries. The National Ocean Service had its own separate map depository program by which it distributed most of its nautical and aeronautical charts to selected designated libraries. However, in the late 1970s it closed its depository program to new applicants and in the mid-1980s was forced to reduce the number of charts distributed due to budgetary constraints. Throughout the 1980s, the Government Printing Office (GPO) and NOS staff met to negotiate a merger. In December 1987, NOS provided the Library Programs Service (LPS) with samples of maps and charts, which were classified and item number assigned, and distribution was initiated in 1989 under the Title 44 depository system. LPS advised depository libraries selecting NOS items that the service "distributes approximately 500 charts and over 200 other publications annually," of which many "are revised at various intervals, e.g., every 28 days, every 56 days, semi-annually, etc. It is crucial," LPS noted, "that the superseded maps and charts be discarded upon reaching the expiration date and that they not be used for navigation purposes."[10]

Satellite Imagery. The National Ocean Service is a subagency within the National Oceanic and Atmospheric Administration (NOAA), which has been funding a private corporation called EOSAT that processes and distributes remote sensing imagery from the LANDSAT satellites. During the 1980s, the Reagan administration was niggardly in providing adequate funds for this operation, and EOSAT has experienced "difficulty in staying financially solvent over its several years of existence." As a consequence, purchasers of this imagery "have experienced considerable price increases, causing major budget impacts for libraries" specializing in this information. "Items costing in the range of $8 to $12 from the government now sell for $80 to $150, while the price for the computer tapes from which the imagery is generated has jumped from $300 to $3,000."[11]

According to LPS, satellite image maps appear in depository shipments within many other map series or groups. These maps carry the USGS alphanumeric notation of the different series but have an SI symbol within that numbering. The satellite image maps are found in the U.S. 1:100,000 scale series (I 19.110) and the topographic maps, with the 1:250,000 scale (I 19.98). The new satellite version is the main map, and the older topographic map on the recto is provided for the sake of comparison by users.

Defense Mapping Agency

In 1972 the mapping operations of the army, navy, and air force were combined into the Defense Mapping Agency (DMA), which produces topographic, nautical, and aeronautical maps and charts needed by the military services for defense purposes. Most maps produced by DMA are of foreign areas and are available to the public and depository libraries only if the international agreements under which they are produced allow their distribution. The DMA depository program had its origins in the Army Map Service (AMS) depository system, which began following World War II. In the early 1940s the army found it did not have large-scale maps of areas expected to be theaters of military operations. It received help from the academic community and other map collections in supplying not only maps but also geographers and cartographers. By war's end the army found itself with a large number of maps, both captured and army-produced. Partly out of gratitude to the academic community and partly out of a desire to dispose of the maps, the AMS established a depository program that eventually enrolled 245 designated libraries. Most of the materials were maps distributed during the immediate postwar years. Revisions were not usually supplied.

The AMS program became the DMA depository program, but few shipments were made in the 1970s.[12] In 1982 DMA joined with the Geological Survey to participate in the Title 44 depository program, and DMA discontinued its own depository arrangements.[13] In addition to being provided to depository institutions, the world nautical and aeronautical charts generated by DMA are sold to the public by the National Ocean Service, and DMA's topographic maps, gazetteers, and other publications are sold by the Geological Survey.

Among the items available to depository libraries in the DMA mapping and charting series are JNC-Jet and GNC-Global Navigation Charts (D 5.354); Series 1308 Mid-East Briefing Maps (D 5.355); Omega, Loran C, and Display Plotting Charts (D 5.356); and sundry others. The *Catalog of Maps, Charts, and Related Products, Part 2, Hydrographic Products*, used to be distributed to depository libraries in ten separate series. These were consolidated into one volume, published annually, titled *Catalog of Maps, Charts, and Related Products, Part 2, Hydrographic Products, Volume 1, Nautical Charts and Publications* [United States and Canada] (D 5.351/2:1/). Updates to this consolidated catalog are published in the *Quarterly Bulletin* (D 5.351/2-2) and the weekly *Notice to Mariners* (D 5.315) as appropriate.[14]

United States Geological Survey

As noted above, the USGS is the premier civilian mapping agency in the federal establishment. It produces some 10,000 separate topographic and thematic maps annually. Many thematic maps are included in its book publications, such as bulletins (I 19.3), circulars (I 19.4/2), water supply papers (I 19.13), and professional papers (I 19.16). A pamphlet published by USGS's National Mapping Program titled *Catalog of Maps* (I 19.2) briefly describes and illustrates the following types of maps: Antarctic, photoimage, geologic, hydrologic, land use, maps of the planets and moons, *National Atlas* separates (mentioned above), and special maps.

Geologic maps are also published as folded sheets in envelopes in the following series: geologic quadrangle maps (GQ series, I 19.88); miscellaneous field studies maps (MF series, I 19.113); mineral investigations resource maps (MR series, I 19.90); oil and gas investigations maps (OM series, I 19.93); oil and gas investigations charts (OC series, I 19.92); coal investigations maps (C series, I 19.85); geophysical investigations maps (GP series, I 19.87); and miscellaneous investigations series maps (I series, I 19.91). In addition, USGS prepares multicolor geologic maps in cooperation with many states, but the majority of states have geological agencies that also prepare their own maps.

USGS's State Map series in 1990 were subsumed into one class stem (I 19.102), but there is no U.S. Summary for this series. It has been noted that "many map depositories do not file maps by SuDocs [Superintendent of Documents] number. Maps sheets are interfiled alphabetically by state and quadrangle." For example, for the state of Pennsylvania, its planimetric (SP) map, scale 1:500,000 (500), is now classed in I 19.102:40076-C8-SP-500-00; its topographic (ST) map, scale 1:500,000 (500), is classified as I 19.102:40076-C8-ST-500-00; its shaded relief (SR) map, scale 1:500,000 (500), is given the notation I 19.102:40076-C8-SR-500-00; and its planimetric (SP) map, scale 1:1,000,000 (01M), is classed in I 19.102:40076-C8-SP-01M-00.[15]

By agreement in 1990 between USGS and the Circum-Pacific Council for Energy and Mineral Resources, USGS began publishing the council's remaining map project series. The first map issued under the agreement was *Natural Hazards Map of the Circum-Pacific Region, Pacific Basin Sheet* (I 19.91/2: CP-35), which was shipped on USGS map shipping list #90-49 (August 27, 1990). Previously published titles of this project are available from the American Association of Petroleum Geologists, Box 979, Tulsa, OK 74101.[16]

USGS Topographic Maps. Topographic maps are the best known and most widely used USGS series. A topographic map is defined as a "line-and-symbol representation of natural and selected man-made features of a part of the Earth's surface plotted to a definite scale. A distinguishing characteristic of a topographic map is the portrayal of the shape and elevation of the terrain by contour lines."[17] Another characteristic of topographic maps is their use of color and symbols to represent features. Water features are blue, human-made objects are black, built-up areas are red, the color green distinguishes wooded areas from clearings, and contour lines are brown. Some maps also contain symbols (pictographs) resembling the objects they represent.

Of the several topographic series, perhaps the most used is the 7.5-minute, 1:24,000 scale, where 1 inch represents 2,000 feet. These quadrangle maps cover 7.5 minutes of longitude and of latitude on each side. Approximately 55,000 maps are needed to show the continental United States and Hawaii. For Alaska, 15-minute quadrangle maps at a scale of 1:63,600 are standard. The complete Alaska series consists of some 2,920 sheets. Some parts of the United States are covered by 15-minute maps published in cooperation with DMA at a scale of 1:50,000 with contour intervals in meters.

The best way to access USGS maps, particularly topographic maps, is through the indexes prepared by the agency. The *Index to Topographic and Other Map Coverage* (I 19.41/6-3) is prepared for every state, the District of Columbia, outlying areas, and a U.S. summary. A companion publication, *Catalog of Topographic and Other Published Maps* (I 19.41/6-2), is organized similarly.

Each *Catalog* contains lists of dealers for topographic maps and USGS depository libraries for each state. New and revised topographic maps are announced in the monthly *New Publications of the Geological Survey* (I 19.14/4), but they are *not* listed in the annual cumulation *Publications of the Geological Survey* (I 19.14).

National Cartographic Information Center. The National Cartographic Information Center (NCIC) was established by USGS in 1974 to serve as the central source of information for all federal, state, local, and private-sector cartographic and geographic data. It accepts orders for the full range of maps, map byproducts, and other cartographic information produced by the Geological Survey, including millions of aerial photos and space images. For other materials, NCIC provides ordering information from the appropriate agency. Located at the USGS National Center in Reston, Virginia, NCIC also has regional offices in Alaska, California, Colorado, Mississippi, and Missouri. In addition, cooperative agreements have been made with many state governments to operate NCIC-affiliated offices.

Electronic Products. USGS has produced "several prototype discs containing a variety of earth science information." The GLORIA disk contains "sonar-scanned imagery from the Gulf of Mexico sea floor ..., the result of a cooperative effort between the USGS, NOAA, and NASA." NCIC has produced a CD-ROM containing "over 2.3 million records which serve as the master index to over 12 million frames of photography available either from the USGS or private companies." Known as the Aerial Photography Summary Record System (APSRS), the disk is "being placed in all of the Earth Science Information Centers around the world." *Selected Water Resources Abstracts* (SWRA) contains "thousands of abstracts from hydrologic scientific papers" worldwide. Free to government affiliates of USGS, it is online from DIALOG and on CD-ROM from the National Information Services Corporation (Baltimore, Maryland) and from OCLC; it is also available for lease through the National Technical Information Service (NTIS). An Aeronautical Data Sampler (ADS) to support "both airborne cockpit displays and air traffic control requirements" has been produced on CD-ROM by the National Ocean Service. Information on these products and other activities is summarized by Jerry McFaul in the September 1989 issue of *CD-ROM EndUser*, pages 20-26.

Multimedia publishing of mapping information is illustrated by the CIA's annual issuing of *The World Factbook* (PrEx 3.15). The 1990 edition provides current geographic, economic, and demographic facts about the countries and geographic areas of the world, and the appendixes include a list of geographic names. In addition, the 1990 *Factbook* has color maps by continent of all the world's countries as well as a map showing the time zones of the world. This publication is available in print format to depository libraries and is for sale through NTIS. It is also available on microcomputer diskettes, magnetic tape, and CD-ROM.

National Map Library Depository Program

In 1982 the chairperson of the Joint Committee on Printing (JCP) announced the beginning of a program that would incorporate the several map-making agencies into the Title 44 depository system.[18] The first participants were the USGS and the Defense Mapping Agency. However, Ken Rockwell asserts that this program could be jeopardized by Interior Department efforts "to privatize the mapmaking activities of the U.S. Geological Survey."[19]

For depository libraries, the LPS periodically revises Section 7 of the *Federal Depository Library Manual*, which has a list of maps and atlases easier to use than the *List of Classes*. Maps may be mailed to either the "depository of record" or to an alternate address, which can be established for USGS and DMA products. The "depository of record" has the option to house the maps and charts in the documents collection or in a designated map library.[20] Addresses and telephone numbers for USGS and DMA shipments never received or damaged in transit to depository institutions are listed in *Administrative Notes*, vol. 11 (March 31, 1991), page 6.

Other Map-Producing Agencies

Charts, atlases, and maps available to depository libraries are issued by a number of agencies in addition to the NOS, DMA, and USGS. A selective list would include the Forest Service (A 13.28), which publishes maps of the national forests it administers; the soil survey maps of the Soil Conservation Service (A 57.38); navigation charts of various rivers from the Army Corps of Engineers (D 103.66); surface management status and surface and minerals management status maps of the Land Management Bureau (I 53.11/4); maps and atlases of the Central Intelligence Agency (PrEx 3.10/4); and many more. Transmittal 2 revising and updating Section 7 of the *Federal Depository Library Manual* was published in *Administrative Notes*, vol. 10 (August 21, 1989), pages 8-15. The list is arranged by depository item number referencing the item title/issuing agency and SuDocs class notation.

The Geographic Information System (GIS) applications of the Census Bureau's TIGER files have revolutionized geography. For the 1990 decennial census, the bureau consulted private-sector GIS experts and joined forces with the USGS to develop a "single, integrated geographic data base for the entire Nation." USGS's role in this coordinated effort consisted of scanning or manually digitizing its most current 1:100,000-scale maps covering the country's land area. USGS supplied the Census Bureau with computer tape files containing digital descriptions of water and transportation features as well as major power lines and pipelines; the bureau in turn merged these data into a seamless map database. The result was an acceleration of map production and a dramatic demonstration of the manifold advantages of computer mapping.[21]

When TIGER was first launched in 1983 to automate the mapping and other geographic activities required to support the bureau's censuses and surveys, many potential users were under a misconception that the database was *itself* a map that could be loaded into a computer and that, with a simple command, various geographical features such as street maps would be displayed. In fact, TIGER is a "digital data base that allows a user to topologically integrate map features with other data ... by means of suitable applications software.... The Census Bureau does not provide the software; it must be developed or purchased from a software developer." However, the bureau does provide "a list of software vendors upon request."[22]

GAZETTEERS

A gazetteer is a geographical dictionary or index containing geographical names and descriptions arranged alphabetically. The United States Board on Geographic Names (BGN) is the federal agency responsible for establishing official names for use throughout the federal government. Its purpose is to resolve name problems and to eliminate duplication of effort by agencies responsible for the production of maps and other publications that use geographic names. Its membership consists of representatives of several federal units who are appointed for a two-year term, and it has developed principles, policies, and procedures governing the use of both domestic and foreign geographic names as well as underseas and extraterrestrial feature names.

With respect to domestic names, the board's policy is to recognize present-day local usage or preferences when possible. To implement this policy, BGN maintains close cooperation with state geographic boards, state and local governments, and the general public. When confusing duplication of local names exists or when a local name is derogatory to a particular person, race, or religion, BGN may disapprove such names and seek alternate local names for the features. In instances where local usage is ambiguous or weak, well-established documented names and names with historical significance are given strong consideration. Moreover, BGN has a policy of disapproving new domestic geographical names that commemorate or may be construed to commemorate living persons. Any person or organization, public or private, may make inquiries or request BGN to render formal decisions on proposed new names, proposed name changes, or names that are in conflict.

Decisions on Geographic Names

Decisions on Geographic Names in the United States (I 33.5/2) bears the subtitle *Decision List* followed by the year of issuance. It was published on a quarterly schedule until *Decision List* 8904 (October-December 1989), which carried the following notice: "This will be the last quarterly publication. Starting in 1990 the *Decision List* will be published once a year." The current annual issues follow the format of the earlier quarterly serials. The contents are organized alphabetically by state and within state alphabetically by name. Entries define the spellings and applications of the names for use on maps and other publications of federal agencies. Unapproved variant names, spellings, or applications are listed following the word "Not"; these may include former names or spellings no longer used, names derived by the application of policies other than those approved by BGN, misspellings, and names misapplied to all or part of the subject feature. For example, "Dipping Vat Reservoir" (Arizona) is "Not: Merlyn Lake, Merlyn Reservoir, Merlyn Tank."[23]

In each entry coordinates are given for the mouth of a stream, canyon, or gulch; the foot of a glacier; the center of a bay, lake, island, or populated place; the dam of a reservoir; the summit of a mountain, peak, or hill; the tip of a point of land; and each end of a linear feature such as a range, ridge, canal, or channel. The information following the coordinates supplies the name of a USGS topographic map or National Ocean Service chart on which the features can be located. If the feature is on more than one map or chart, the map cited is the one on which the primary coordinate is located, such as the mouth of a linear feature or the center of an areal feature. And if a populated place is incorporated under the laws of its state, its legal designation (city, town, borough, village), as of the date of the decision, is specified in parentheses. A populated place without such a designation is not incorporated. Figure 12.1 shows a page from *Decision List 1990*, which contains names approved by BGN during that year.

Fig. 12.1. Page from *Decision List 1990*

NORTH CAROLINA

Edinburgh: populated place, elevation 76 m (250 ft.), 5.6 km (3.5 mi.) NE of Wagram; Hoke Co., North Carolina; 34°54'22" N, 79°18'37" W; USGS map - Wagram 1:24,000; Not: Edenburg.

Gap Branch: stream, 3.7 km (2.3 mi.) long, heads at 34°02'26" N, 78°07'37" W, flows W to Middle Swamp, 3.2 km (2 mi.) SW of Bolivia; Brunswick Co., North Carolina; 34°02'33" N, 78°09'43" W; USGS map - Bolivia 1:24,000; Not: Half Hell Branch.

Half Hell Swamp: stream, 3.8 km (2.4 mi.) long, heads at 34°00'53" N, 78°06'26" W, flows WSW to River Swamp, 0.8 km (0.5 mi.) SE of Suburb and 7.2 km (4.5 mi.) S of Bolivia; Brunswick Co., North Carolina; 34°00'29" N, 78°08'35" W; USGS map - Bolivia 1:24,000; Not: River Swamp.

Jackson Hamlet: populated place, 146 m (480 ft.) elevation, 5.4 km (3.4 mi.) NW of Aberdeen; Moore Co., North Carolina; 35°10'00" N, 79°28'30" W; USGS map - Southern Pines 1:62,500; Not: Jackson, Vine Vista.

Jobes Creek: stream, 5.6 km (3.5 mi.) long, heads at 35°07'43" N, 79°43'47" W, flows SW to Little Mountain Creek 4.8 km (3 mi.) N of Ellerbe; Richmond Co., North Carolina; 35°06'49" N, 79°45'56" W; USGS map - Ellerbe 1:24,000; Not: Jobs Creek, Little Mountain Creek.

Pleasure Island: island, 19.3 km (12 mi.) long, extends S from Carolina Beach Inlet, between the Atlantic Ocean and the Cape Fear River; includes towns of Carolina Beach, Wilmington Beach and Kure Beach; New Hanover and Brunswick Cos., North Carolina; 34°04'45" N, 77°52'35" W [N end], 33°55'18" N, 77°56'28" W [S end]; USGS map - Carolina Beach 1:24,000.

River Swamp: stream, 11 km (6.8 mi.) long, heads at 33°58'29" N, 78°07'11" W, flows NW to Lockwoods Folly River, 4.8 km (3 mi.) SW of Bolivia; Brunswick Co., North Carolina; 34°02'02" N, 78°10'59" W; USGS map - Bolivia 1:24,000; Not: Midway Branch.

OHIO

Amolsch Ditch: canal, 6.9 km (4.3 mi.) long, heads at 42°37'20" N, 83°29'01" W, trends NE to Driftmeyer Ditch, 2.9 km (1.8 mi.) S of Harbor View; Lucas Co., Ohio; sec 26, T 9 S, R 8 E, First Principal Mer.; 41°40'12" N, 83°26'54" W; USGS map - Oregon 1:24.000; Not Amlosch Ditch.

Grape Island: island 0.64 km (0.4 mi.) long, in the Maumee River 0.8 km (0.5 mi.) E of Maumee and W of Ewing Island; Lucas Co., Ohio; 41°33'58" N, 83°38'34" W; USGS map - Maumee 1:24,000.

Latcha: populated place, 6.4 km (4 mi.) SE of Walbridge; Wood Co., Ohio; 3 secs 22, 23, 26, and 27, T 7 N, R 12 E, First Principal Mer.; 41°32'39" N, 83°27'13" W; USGS map - Walbridge 1:24,000; Not: Latchie.

Sautter Ditch: canal, 7.2 km (4.5 mi.) long, heads at 41°37'49" N, 83°22'04" W, trends NE 1.9 km (1.2 mi.) then N to Maumee Bay, 1.6 km (1 mi.) E of the community of Niles Beach; Lucas Co., Ohio; sec 21, T 9 S, R 9 E, First Principal Mer.; 41°41'20" N, 83°21'07" W; USGS map - Reno Beach 1:24,000; Not: Anderson Ditch.

OKLAHOMA

Battle Creek: stream, 3.5 km (2.2 mi.) long, heads at 36°00'11"N, 95°22'29"W, flows SE to North Bay in Fort Gibson Lake, 3.2 km (2 mi.) NE of Wagoner; stream is the site of a Civil War skirmish in which black Union soldiers were killed; Wagoner Co., Oklahoma; sec 1, T 17 N, R 18 E, Indian Mer.; 35°59'03"N, 95°20'56"W; USGS map - Wagoner East 1:24,000; Not: Nigger Creek.

The National Gazetteer of the United States of America

The National Gazetteer of the United States of America (I 19.16:1200-State) is an ambitious cooperative venture of the Geological Survey and the Board on Geographic Names. It is derived from the National Geographic Names Data Base, part of a computerized Geographic Names Information System (GNIS) developed by the National Mapping Division of USGS. The GNIS database contains information for about two million names used throughout the United States, its territories, and outlying areas. The system can furnish alphabetical and special listings in the form of bound reports, magnetic tapes, and microfiche to meet the special needs of a wide variety of users in government, education, business, and industry. Information about available services and costs of GNIS may be obtained from the Chief, Branch of Geographic Names, USGS, 523 National Center, Reston, VA 22092.

Issued in the Geological Survey's Professional Papers series, the *National Gazetteer* formerly was available to depository libraries under Item 0624 along with other scientific reports in that series. A number of libraries became dissatisfied with that arrangement; some were interested only in obtaining the *National Gazetteer*, and others needed the various *Professional Papers* but did not wish to select the *Gazetteer*. Accordingly, LPS split off *Professional Paper 1200* from the rest of the Professional Papers series and created an individual item number. Now, under Item 0624-A-01, depository libraries are receiving the state *Gazetteers* as they are issued, and Item 0624 is used to receive all other numbered *Professional Papers*.[24] In the SuDocs class system, the identifying and unique "book number" is the abbreviation for the state. Thus, *The National Gazetteer of the United States of America—Arizona 1986* is assigned the notation I 19.16:1200-AZ; the *Gazetteer* for North Dakota (1990), I 19.16:1200-ND; and so on.

Each state's gazetteer lists in alphabetical order geographic names, excluding the names of railroads, streets, and roads, found on various maps, charts, and other published documents. The names are followed by seven categories of information in separate columns on the gazetteer pages, including primary reference names and variant names or spellings for the same features; the kinds of features or places to which the names apply (these terms, such as *stream, ridge, park*, etc., are defined in the glossary); a status column in which names are classed according to their use or official status as determined by the Board on Geographic Names; name of the county in which the entity is located; geographic coordinates; coordinates for the source of streams, valleys, and arroyos; elevation; and the name of the map on which the place or feature is located.

The maps themselves reproduced in each gazetteer do not show all names owing to various cartographic limitations, but column 8 ("Map") is a handy cross-reference to the USGS topographic quadrangle areas. Reproduced maps include not only current information but also eighteenth- and nineteenth-century maps, useful sources for historical and genealogical research.

National Gazetteers have been issued for only a few states as of 1991. Among early issuances were New Jersey (1982, with a minor revision in 1983), Delaware (1983), Kansas (1984), Arizona (1986), Indiana (1988), South Dakota (1989), North Dakota (1990), Massachusetts (1990), Florida (1990), and Alabama (1990). Volumes will, of course, be revised periodically, and current geographic name information supplementing the volumes is found in the annual *Decision List*.

Naming or renaming places and features often engenders impassioned debate. For example, a creek nearby a small Pennsylvania town "far back in the depths of local history" had been christened Booze Ditch. The abstemious denizens of the town petitioned the Board on Geographic Names, which granted a change to Coles Creek.[25] Another anecdote concerns a federal official who was verifying map names and came upon a discrepancy. "It seemed that local residents had changed the name of one area from 'Whorehouse Meadow' to 'Naughty Girl Meadow' without notifying the Board." The euphemism, however, was granted and now appears on all current USGS maps.[26]

DMA Gazetteers

The Defense Mapping Agency produces and distributes foreign gazetteers as part of its overall mission of supporting foreign-area scientific studies for the federal government. Even though different agencies may have been responsible for the content of the DMA gazetteer series, they have been assigned the DMA SuDocs notation D 5.319. In 1990 the Library Programs Service, in reviewing DMA's *Public Sales Catalog*, discovered that the agency had not sent a number of gazetteers to depository libraries. When LPS notified the Defense Mapping Agency of this discrepancy, the agency filled the request and also provided LPS with one copy of nearly every gazetteer listed in its catalog. In turn, LPS converted these volumes to microfiche and made a "one-time special distribution" of the fiche. At one time the Board on Geographic Names was the provenance of gazetteers covering a single country or a group of countries, and these were issued under now discontinued SuDocs notation I 33.8. Consequently, some libraries "may discover duplicates in their collections when comparing SuDocs class stems D 5.319 and I 33.8."[27] The DMA gazetteers series is still based on the work of linguists, geographers, and cartographers, and wherever possible the compilation is carried out with the cooperation of the concerned country. With German reunification, the upheavals in Eastern Europe, and the dissolution of the former Union of Soviet Socialist Republics, name changes have occurred with unusual alacrity. During 1990 and 1991 officials of the Defense Mapping Agency met with greater frequency to assign new names to countries and cities, with the approval of the Department of State and the country involved.

The Romance of Names

Geographic names evoke an almost numinous response in the souls of those who love language. In Stephen Vincent Benét's celebrated poem "American Names" (1927), the author expresses his preference for domestic names while acknowledging the enchanted connotations of names foreign:

I have fallen in love with American names,
The sharp names that never get fat,
The snakeskin-titles of mining-claims,
The plumed war-bonnet of Medicine Hat,
Tucson and Deadwood and Lost Mule Flat....

I shall not rest quiet in Montparnasse.
I shall not lie easy at Winchelsea.
You may bury my body in Sussex grass,
You may bury my tongue at Champmedy.
I shall not be there. I shall rise and pass.
Bury my heart at Wounded Knee.[28]

NOTES

[1]William A. Katz, *Introduction to Reference Work, Volume I: Basic Information Sources*, 5th ed. (New York: McGraw-Hill, 1987), p. 320.

[2]The Works Progress Administration (WPA) was established by Executive Order (EO) 7034 (May 6, 1935). Its name was changed to the Work Projects Administration by Reorganization Plan No. 1 of 1939 and placed under the Federal Works Agency, which was abolished June 30, 1949 (63 Stat. 380).

[3]For example, see National Research Council, *Federal Surveying and Mapping: An Organizational Review* (Washington, DC: National Academy Press, 1981), pp. 1-2.

[4]*The Random House Dictionary of the English Language*, 2d ed., unabridged (New York: Random House, 1987), p. 320.

[5]Ken Rockwell, "Privatization of U.S. Geological Survey Topographic Maps: A Survey," *Government Publications Review*, 17 (1990): 200.

[6]Charles A. Seavey, "Collection Development for Government Map Collections," *Government Publications Review*, 8A (1981): 17.

[7]Gary W. North, "Maps for the Nation: The Current Federal Mapping Establishment," *Government Publications Review*, 10 (1983): 345-47.

[8]North, "Maps for the Nation," pp. 347-48.

[9]North, "Maps for the Nation," pp. 348-49.

[10]*Administrative Notes*, 9 (February 1988): 21.

[11]Rockwell, "Privatization," p. 206.

[12]Those few shipments included scarcely any topographic maps and consisted mainly of aeronautical and nautical charts (Seavey, "Collection Development"), pp. 19-20.

[13]North, "Maps for the Nation," p. 352.

[14]*Administrative Notes*, 11 (September 30, 1990): 6.

[15]*Administrative Notes*, 11 (September 30, 1990): 7.

[16]*Administrative Notes*, 11 (September 30, 1990): 6.

[17]Theodore D. Steger, *Topographic Maps* (Washington, DC: GPO, 1986), p. 3.

[18]North, "Maps for the Nation," p. 355.

[19]Rockwell, "Privatization," p. 199.

[20]*Administrative Notes*, 10 (August 21, 1989): 7.

[21]Bureau of the Census, *TIGER: The Coast-to-Coast Digital Map Data Base*, November 1990, pp. 2, 5.

[22]Census, *TIGER*, p. 9.

[23]United States Board on Geographic Names, *Decisions on Geographic Names in the United States: Decision List 1990* (Washington, DC: Department of the Interior, 1990), p. 3.

[24]*Administrative Notes*, 10 (May 15, 1989): 5.

[25]Robert Froman, "Who Puts the Names on Maps?" *Science Digest*, 27 (April 1950): 77.

[26]Mark Wexler, "The Naming (and Misnaming) of America," *National Wildlife*, 16 (August-September 1978): 16.

[27]*Administrative Notes*, 12 (January 30, 1991): 2.

[28]Benét's famous poem is published in many anthologies, including F. O. Matthiessen (comp.), *Oxford Book of American Verse* (New York: Oxford University Press, 1950).

13

Government Periodicals and Serials

INTRODUCTION

It has been observed that four out of five federal documents are serial in character.[1] In fact, the Superintendent of Documents (SuDocs) classification system reflects, to a large extent, the serial nature of government publishing. These reasons, as well as the complexity of, the substantial reference value of, and the detailed record-keeping attendant upon government serials, lead us to devote a separate chapter to these sources. Periodicals are addressed independent of other government serials.

GOVERNMENT PERIODICALS

Although government periodicals cannot be fully discussed outside the broader context of government serials, they nevertheless warrant a section of their own. A noteworthy feature of these periodicals is the degree to which many of them constitute publications of significant reference value. Definition of a government periodical can vary; the one currently in use by the Government Printing Office (GPO) in its *Periodicals Supplement* to the *Monthly Catalog* is that of a serial publication issued three or more times each year.

The exact number of government periodicals is difficult to determine, and figures can change with the vicissitudes of administrations and budgets. A 1982 Office of Management and Budget (OMB) report to the Senate Appropriations Committee on Administrative Expenses pegged total spending on periodicals and pamphlets by the Department of Defense (DoD) at about $30 million for fiscal year (FY) 1982.[2] The recent trend, however, has been toward fewer government periodicals and serials, due in part to the Reagan administration's somewhat successful efforts to eliminate unnecessary and expensive periodicals.[3] Nevertheless, 1,475 are still listed in the 1991 *Periodicals Supplement*.

Identifying and Acquiring
U.S. Government Periodicals

The most commonly available sources for identifying and acquiring the better known federal government periodicals are GPO's own *Price List 36*, titled *Government Periodicals and Subscription Services*; *Publications Reference File* (PRF); and the annual *Periodicals Supplement* to the *Monthly Catalog*.

Price List 36 (GP 3.9:36), a holdover title from the series that is now called *Subject Bibliographies*, is revised and issued on a quarterly basis and is available free from the Superintendent of Documents. It is a title listing of regularly issued dailies, weeklies, monthlies, and quarterlies, as well as of subscription services and irregular subscriptions, available directly through the GPO. The Winter 1992 edition, for example, provided forty-seven pages of annotated entries for such items and alerted the reader to 3 new subscriptions, 4 title changes, and 8 discontinued titles, and to a handful of price increases. *Price List 36* (PL-36) provides stock number, SuDocs number, and complete ordering information. It contains a subject index as well as a detailed "Agency Index" that serves as a table of contents, and the bullet symbol (•) is used to distinguish subscription services from dated periodicals. In lieu of PL-36, subscribers may want to identify and order from information available in the *Publications Reference File*, discussed in chapter 2. If PRF is used on DIALOG (File 166), orders can be placed directly via DIALORDER.

Unlike PL-36, which is limited to subscriptions available through GPO, the *Periodicals Supplement* to the *Monthly Catalog* lists many non-GPO titles available directly through other government agencies as well as GPO sales items. The *Periodicals Supplement*, now issued annually as the first issue of the year, provides full OCLC entries for the titles listed. Besides containing collective records for serial publications issued three or more times each year, it also provides indexing by author, title, subject, series/report number, stock number, and title keyword.

Anyone wishing to search historically should be aware that the *Monthly Catalog* began its special treatment of periodicals, periodic releases, serials, and statistical statements semiannually with the July 1945 issue. Beginning in July 1950, the lists were separately published as appendixes to the January and July issues, and in 1953 these appendixes were moved to the February and August editions of the *Monthly Catalog*. From February 1962 through 1976, the periodicals appeared as a supplement to the February issue. They were subsequently listed in the separate *Serials Supplement* from 1977-1984, which from 1985 on is titled the *Periodicals Supplement*.

Prices of government periodicals increased drastically in many instances over the last twenty-one years. A few periodicals retained moderate pricing. For instance, *Aging* (HE 23.3015) went from only $2.00 in 1970 to $6.50 in 1992; *Occupational Outlook Quarterly* (L 2.70/4), from $1.50 to $6.50; and the *Social Security Bulletin* (HE 3.3), from $4.00 to $21.00. Others, however, soared in cost. Major price increases included equally essential journals, such as the *Monthly Catalog* (GP 3.8), which went from $7.00 to $199.00; the *Federal Register* (AE 2.106), from $25.00 to $425.00; and the *Weekly Compilation of Presidential Documents* (AE 2.109), from $9.00 to $96.00.

For libraries with a need to obtain miscellaneous titles or replace issues of federal periodicals, various options may be considered. Libraries that participate in the Library of Congress's Documents Expediting Project (discussed in chapter 11) may be able to locate needed issues through this excellent service. Those who have a Documents on Demand account with CIS, Inc., can obtain microfiche copies of selected articles if they are statistical in nature. A third possibility is to use the revived Universal Serials and Book Exchange (Cleveland, Ohio) service. Beginning with the 1982 volumes of the *Index to U.S. Government Periodicals*, journals indexed therein and having a "periodical sequence number" following the year in the main entry are also available in Infodata's *Current U.S. Government Periodicals on Microfiche* service. Out-of-print dealers offer additional options; see Susan L. Dow, "A Selective Directory of Government Document Dealers, Jobbers and Subscription Agents," in *The Serials Librarian*, vol. 14 (1988), pages 157-86.

Reviews of Federal Government Periodicals

Federal government periodicals are not widely reviewed, although some sources can be suggested. William Katz's *Magazines for Libraries*, 6th ed. (New York: R. R. Bowker, 1989), reviews about fifty basic titles, and LeRoy C. Schwarzkopf's *Government Reference Serials* (Englewood, CO: Libraries Unlimited, 1988) addresses considerably more. Another route for finding reviews is to locate the Serials Review Index found in *Serials Review*. It identifies by journal title in which of the 175 journals scanned by the editor a review has appeared. Most review citations for government periodicals are to *Government Publications Review*, however.

Access to Government Periodical Literature

The story of access to the periodical literature of the U.S. government is punctuated by various problems and short-term solutions. Locating appropriate indexing has been a major problem to be dealt with shortly, but, for some libraries, simply identifying which government journals and newsletters are held may be a serious problem. Although a library's regular journal holdings generally show up in its online catalog or union list of serials, one must raise the question of how many U.S. government titles owned by a library actually appear in the library's standard listings. Even those libraries that have made a conscious effort to provide mainstreaming for government titles may still be ignoring a significant number.

Of particular concern are the many federal periodicals that libraries have but that may be owned only in a microformat. It is easy to forget, for instance, that from 1953 forward, when the Readex Corporation began to make available non-depository collections of the material listed in the *Monthly Catalog*, it included many of the non-depository periodicals as well. Similarly, some libraries that purchased the depository microformat set 1956+ will have the same dilemma. Few libraries are likely to have taken the time to include these periodicals in their standard lists. Instead, they rely on the resourcefulness of librarians servicing the collection to remember these potential sources. Aware of this resource, Margaret Rich compiled the *Index to U.S. Government Serials (1956-1960)* (New York, 1975) as published by Readex in her effort to promote better access. Rich included title; issuing agency; frequency; SuDocs number; and, for depository materials, the item number. She also produced the *Title Index to U.S. Government Serials 1953-1955* (New York, 1978), with supplements for the periods 1961-1970 (1979), 1971-1975 (1982), and 1976-1980 (1987).

Another potential holdings gap is with the many federal statistically oriented periodicals that appear within the *American Statistics Index* (ASI) (discussed in chapter 10). CIS, Inc., publishes a list of the periodical titles received and reviewed for inclusion at the front of each issue of ASI. Its practices in abstracting periodicals are commented on in the separate *ASI User Guide* (1991) reprinted from the 1990 ASI annual. Again, it is unlikely that many libraries have implemented a systematic way of entering all the titles covered, especially those that are non-depository, in their union lists or online catalogs.

A tool still useful for identifying federal periodicals is volume IV of *Checklist '76*, titled *U.S. Government Serial Titles 1789-1976*. This 611-page volume includes an annotated alphabetical list of current and discontinued titles in the Serial Card File of the U.S. Superintendent of Documents' Public Documents Library 1789-1970 plus a supplemental listing for 1971-1976. Each citation, according to the compilers, is "at least as complete as the entries in the *Monthly Catalog* and often provides more information."[4] Along with John L. Andriot's *Guide to U.S. Government Publications* (McLean, VA: Documents Index, 1973-), these two commercial guides significantly aid in the search for information on the history of various government journals.

Reference Value of Government Journals

Many government periodicals offer useful information of a relatively common nature, a few examples of which are provided; yet another group provides high-value, current information that warrants their placement among other reference tools.

The popular bimonthly *Children Today* (HE 23.12) published by the Office of Human Development Services, Department of Health and Human Services, reports on federal, state, and local services regarding children and child health and welfare. Each issue generally carries a half-dozen or so signed articles on topics such as vestibular disorders or children's rights and ends with a book review section. *Occupational Outlook Quarterly* (L 2.70/4) is advertised in *Price List 36* as a periodical to help young people, employment planners, and guidance counselors keep abreast of current occupational and employment developments between editions of the *Occupational Outlook Handbook* (L 2.3/4). The magazine is written in nontechnical language, with color illustrations, articles on new occupations, training opportunities, salary trends, career counseling programs, and the results of new studies from its provenance, the Bureau of Labor Statistics.

Typical of a lesser known, newsletter-type publication that worked its way into depository distribution after having been supplied primarily through mailing lists and, to libraries, through the Documents Expediting Project is the monthly

Third Branch: A Bulletin of the Federal Courts (Ju 10.3/2), which serves as an information conduit for judges and other court personnel. It is probably of little consequence whether a library owning these titles keeps them in a separate documents collection or in a reference area or interfiles them among its commercially produced issues of *Fortune, Public Opinion Quarterly,* and *Scientific American.*

On the other hand, there exist a significant number of government periodicals that a reference service must have in close proximity to its staff. Apart from obvious government reference titles such as the *Monthly Catalog, Resources in Education,* and *Government Reports Announcements & Index,* many carry statistical data or other information of such current and utilitarian nature that shelving them at any great distance from a reference point would significantly hinder the expeditious dissemination of information. Among these are titles such as *Dispatch* (formerly *Department of State Bulletin*), *Monthly Labor Review, Social Security Bulletin,* and *Survey of Current Business.*

When the *Department of State Bulletin* (S 1.3) issued its fiftieth anniversary issue (July 1989), it lauded itself as the only official monthly record of national foreign policy published by any country in the world. Yet by 1990, budget cuts (funding information is sometimes available in a periodical's masthead) had threatened the very existence of the journal and became the topic of an intense letter-writing campaign among librarians to salvage the venerable publication. Private-sector takeover seemed likely. The journal's reference value lies in that it was sometimes the easiest or first place to locate official information. The journal was full of statements issued by the Department of State itself or by the president, excerpts of news conferences and interviews, communiques, proclamations, texts of occasional United Nations and Organization of American States resolutions, updated profiles of countries, press releases, announcements of new department publications such as the *Foreign Relations of the United States* series, and reports on current actions on multilateral and bilateral treaties. The *Bulletin* has since been replaced by the weekly *Dispatch* (S 1.3/5), which "provides a diverse compilation of major speeches, congressional testimony, policy statements, fact sheets, and other foreign policy information from the State Department." The full text of *Dispatch,* as well as other information, is online via the Computer Information Delivery Service (CIDS).

The *Monthly Labor Review* (L 2.6), a major organ of the Bureau of Labor Statistics, is packed with timely articles about collective bargaining, labor and the Supreme Court, family spending, and budgets. In fact, some are so popular that, as with the *Occupational Outlook Quarterly,* reprints of individual articles are often made available. The *Review's* regular columns report on significant decisions in labor cases, major agreements expiring in the next month, developments in industrial relations, and new books and articles in the field. Important as this all is, it is the "Current Labor Statistics" section of over fifty tables updated monthly that make this journal a tool of major reference caliber. Replete with data on the labor force, prices, productivity, labor compensation, collective bargaining, illness, and injury, this long-running journal picks up, in part, where the latest annual *Handbook of Labor Statistics* (L 2.3/5) leaves off. It provides researchers with the monthly or quarterly statistics they often need to do their spreadsheet calculations, develop time series, analyze trends, and develop projections.

Another journal of critical importance to the economic community is the Bureau of Economic Analysis's monthly *Survey of Current Business* (C 59.11), which now incorporates cyclical indicators from the defunct *Business Conditions Digest*. In addition to information on trends in industry, the business situation, and business outlook, it is the source of the latest national income and product account tables, information on input-output accounts of the U.S. economy, and data on federal fiscal programs. The January 1991 issue of the *Survey* (pp. 44-56) also included a helpful "User's Guide to BEA [Bureau of Economic Analysis] Information." As with the *Monthly Labor Review*, however, it is the substantial "Current Business Statistics" section that generates the essential reference component of this publication. The *Survey* is supplemented periodically by a historical volume titled *National Income and Product Accounts of the United States* (C 59.11/4:In2), the latest of which spans 1929-1982, and by the biennial *Business Statistics* (C 59.11/3). Both supplements are worthy candidates for any reference collection.

In the social welfare field, no journal probably holds greater prominence than the *Social Security Bulletin* (HE 3.3). Regular features of this mouthpiece of the Social Security Administration include "Social Security in Review," a section in which federal poverty income guidelines based on size of family unit may appear, and notes on research grant summaries or abstracts of articles from other professional journals. Articles often present well-documented time series and analyses of both public and private social welfare expenditures from 1965 onward. The primary reference segment of the *Social Security Bulletin* is "Current Operating Statistics," a section of monthly or quarterly tables revealing current and sometimes historical data on topics such as Medicare benefits, income maintenance programs, and black lung benefits. An annual *Statistical Supplement* (HE 3.3/3) represents another tool of significant reference value that provides similar social data for 1955 onward.

Many other government periodicals—*Economic Indicators* (Y 4.Ec7:Ec7), *Current Population Reports* (C 3.186), *CPI Detailed Report* (L 2.38/3), and others far too numerous to mention—fall into this category of quasi-reference sources and require careful scrutiny before being relegated to distant periodical shelves.

Indexing of Government Periodicals

Various studies in the 1970s and 1980s either lamented the paucity of indexing for federal government journals or commented on new efforts at indexing them. Historically, little indexing was done, although some articles were analyzed by the *Document Catalog* (1893-1940). Also, occasional articles from periodicals and other serial publications were individually cataloged over the years and may appear as separate titles in the *Cumulative Title Index to U.S. Public Documents 1789-1976*, according to its compilers. They suggest, however, that most analyses of this kind ceased in the 1950s, even though some indexing continued for separates, offprints, and reprints of articles.[5]

A sampling of recent issues of some of the better known and commonly held periodical indexes demonstrates the minimal coverage still accorded government journals. *PAIS International* covers several, indexing twenty-six in 1991 (although of the twenty-six, nine were Federal Reserve Board publications); *Readers' Guide* indexed only six; and the Infotrac Academic Library Edition on CD-ROM covered eighteen titles.

Two sources that represented major breakthroughs in the 1970s are the *Index to U.S. Government Periodicals* (IUSGP) (Chicago: Infodata International, Inc.) and the *American Statistics Index* (referred to in detail in chapter 10).

The quarterly IUSGP successfully provides author and subject access to about 170 federal government journals, many of which are depository items. A sample page appears as figure 13.1. IUSGP has also become available online

Fig. 13.1. Page from IUSGP

INDEX TO U.S. GOVERNMENT PERIODICALS

LEE, A. James

Evaluation of the maximum allowable cost program. A. James Lee and others, ref, tab Health Care Fin Rev 4 3 71-82 Mr **83-237**

LEE, Christopher L.

Guardian on station. il Nav Av News 24-27 My-Je **83-073**

LEE, Dave

It's getting better all the time: La Maddalena. il All Hands 799 28-30 Ag **83-010**

LEE, Elaine C.

Cytogenetic studies of human breast cancer lines: MCF-7 and derived variant sublines. Jacqueline Whang-Peng and others, il, ref, tab, gr J Nat Cancer Inst 71 4 687-695 O **83-060**

LEE, Elisa T.

Inefficacy of Sc Corynebacterium parvum in stage I malignant melanoma: preliminary results of a single-institution pilot study. J. Lee Murray and others, ref, tab Cancer Treat Rep 67 2 191-192 F **83-176**

LEE, G.

Distinctive biochemical pattern associated with resistance of hepatocytes in hepatocyte nodules during liver carcinogenesis. L. Eriksson and others, ref, tab Env Health Persp 49 171-174 Mr **83-037**

LEE, Hugh James

Mass spectrometry: weighing one molecule at a time. il News & Feat Nih 8-9 Ap **82-300**

Researchers discover bombesin, a polypeptide, to diagnose tumors. Aubin Tyler and Hugh James Lee, il News & Feat Nih 10 Ap **82-300**

LEE, J. E.

How to increase electrical power to ships and save money. gr Nav Civ Eng 22 4 14 Wint **83-077**

LEE, James M.

"Anytime, any place". il MAC Flyer 30 5 4-7 My **83-063**

C-5: the first 15 years. il MAC Flyer 30 6 3-5 Je **83-063**

LEE, John M.

Effect of peptides on morphine-induced tolerance and physical dependence. Ronald F. Ritzmann and others, ref, gr Psychopharm Bul 19 3 321-324 **83-091**

LEE, Martin R.

Funding environmental protection. ch, tab Cong Res Serv Rev 4 4 19-21 Ap **83-314**

LEE, Rex E.

Act of State Doctrine: foreign expropriations. Rex E. Lee and Davis R. Robinson, Dept Sta Bul 83 2070 70 Ja **83-029**

LEE, Richard E., Jr.

Physiological adaptations of antarctic terrestrial arthropods. Richard E. Lee, Jr. and John G. Baust, il, ref Antar Jour US 17 5 193-195 spec iss **82-012**

LEE, Robert E. (1807-1870)

Diversity of leadership. Kenneth J. Campbell, ref Air Univ Rev 34 6 102-106 S-O **83-008**

Logistics of the Gettysburg campaign. Gilbert S. Harper, III, il, mp Army Logis 15 4 29-33 Jl-Ag **83-016**

LEE, Rose

Does upward mobility work? Spotlight 1 5 1+ F **83-247**

LEE, Sung M.

Physics at Yonsei University, Korea. Sci Bul Onr 8 2 28-32 Ap-Je **83-287**

LEE, W.

Air chemistry monitoring. Elmer Robinson and W. Lee, Antar Jour US 18 3 14 S **83-012**

LEE-FELDSTEIN, Anna

Arsenic and respiratory cancer in humans: follow-up of copper smelter employees in Montana. ref, tab J Nat Cancer Inst 70 4 601-609 Ap **83-060**

LEEK, Steve L.

Survival and homing of juvenile coho salmon, Oncorhynchus kisutch, transported by barge. George T. McCabe, Jr. and others, mp, ref, tab Fish Bul 81 2 412-415 Ap **83-050**

LEEK, Thomas

55 years of silence. 'On the Roof Gang'. il All Hands 801 34-39 O **83-010**

LeFEBVRE, Rachel Belenker

Handling a tax problem. il, ch Sold Sup J 10 1 42-44 Ja-F **83-301**

LEFEVRE, P. A.

Initiation/promotion versus complete carcinogenicity in the rodent liver. John Ashby and others, ref, tab, gr Env Health Persp 50 339-346 Ap **83-037**

LEFFINGWELL, Sanford S.

Mortality from brain tumor and other causes in a cohort of petrochemical workers. Richard J. Waxweiler and others, ref, tab, gr J Nat Cancer Inst 70 1 75-81 Ja **83-060**

LEFLER, Melissa M.

Misawa: Navy divers assist in recovery of F-84 thunderjet at NAF Misawa, Japan. il Faceplate 13 4 12-15 Wint **82-121**

LEGAL aid

Attorneys' fees and expenses under the Equal Access to Justice Act. James A. Hughes, Jr., ref Army Law 27-50-130 1-12 O **83-015**

Family law. Army Law 27-50-129 31 S **83-015**

Individual Retirement Accounts. Army Law 27-50-129 30 S **83-015**

Legal assistance items. See issues of Army Law **83-015**

Legal assistance items. John F. Joyce and others, Army Law 27-50-131 33-34 N **83-015**

National Agriculture Legal Fund formed. Soil & Water Cons N 3 12 8 Mr **83-254**

Sale of personal residence previously rented. Army Law 27-50-129 30-31 S **83-015**

Service of process on government officials made easy: recent changes to the federal rules of civil procedure. Calvin M. Lederer and Thomas R. Folk, ref Army Law 27-50-125 23-28 My **83-015**

Theory of the case instruction. Vincent S. Green and Mary C. Hutton, ref Advocate 15 3 149-156 My-Je **83-240**

Victim and witness assistance: new state laws and the system's response. ref Bul/Bur Just Stat 1-8 My **83-302**

U.S. Armed Forces

American Bar Association/Young Lawyers Division military service lawyers committee meeting. Bruce E. Kasold, Army Law 27-50-125 36-37 My **83-015**

Annual compilation of policy letters of the Judge Advocate General 1982. Army Law 27-50-122 1-8 F **83-015**

Army labor counselor program. Army Law 27-50-124 22-27 Ap **83-015**

Driver license compact. Army Law 27-50-127 32 Jl **83-015**

Garnishment—military pay. Army Law 27-50-127 32 Jl **83-015**

Impact of Section 1034 of the Internal Revenue Code of 1954 on the decision to sell or rent a principal residence when a service member is reassigned. Murray B. Baxter, ref Army Law 27-50-130 12-24 O **83-015**

Legal clerks. Russell Strand, il Sold Sup J 10 3 57-58 My-Je **83-301**

Nonsupport. ref Army Law 27-50-128 46-49 Ag **83-015**

Only things certain are death and . . . state taxation of military income. Michael E. Schneider, ref Army Law 27-50-123 27-30 Mr **83-015**

Some survivor benefit plan benefits may now be included in the gross estate. Army Law 27-50-123 33 Mr **83-015**

Where there's a will, it's your way. Keith Schneider, il Soldiers 38 8 46-48 Ag **83-100**

LEGAL education

American Bar Association/Young Lawyers Divisin mid-year convention. Bruce E. Kasold, Army Law 27-50-127 27-28 Jl **83-015**

Annual compilation of policy letters of the Judge Advocate General 1982. Army Law 27-50-122 1-8 F **83-015**

Bar membership and continuing legal education requirements. tab Army Law 27-50-121 31-33 Ja **83-015**

FOIA focus: Maj. Michael E. Schneider. por Foia Update 4 3 7 Sum **83-306**

Justice offers new training course. il Foia Update 3 2 6 Mr **82-306**

Status of the legal adviser to the Armed Forces: his functions and powers. Dov Shefi, ref Mil Law Rev 100 119-134 Spr **83-067**

Theory and practice: some suggestions for the law of war trainer. H. Wayne Elliot, ref Army Law 27-50-127 1-18 Jl **83-015**

LEGAL immunity

Admissibility of illegally obtained evidence: American and foreign approaches compared. Stephen J. Kaczynski, ref Mil Law Rev 101 83-166 Sum **83-067**

Community service: a developing concept. Thomas P. Brennan and Leonard Mason, ref Fed Prob 47 2 49-57 Je **83-047**

Constitutional torts and military effectiveness: a proposed alternative to the Feres doctrine. Howard L. Donaldson, ref Air F Law Rev 23 2 171-207 **82-83-130**

Due process immunities in military law. Michael J. Hoover, il Reporter 12 1 2-9 F **83-242**

Individual status and individual rights under the NATO status of forces agreement and the supplementary agreement with Germany. David S. Gordon, ref Mil Law Rev 100 49-98 Spr **83-067**

Iranian hostages crisis: international law & United States policy. James P. Terry, ref JAG Jour 32 1 31-79 Sum **82-059**

Procurement and presentation of evidence in courts-martial: compulsory process and confrontation. Francis A. Gilligan and Frederic I. Lederer, ref Mil Law Rev 101 1-82 Sum **83-067**

State taxation contractors—a view after United States v. New Mexico. Craig E. Hodge, ref Air F Law Rev 23 1 104-128 **82-83-130**

LEGAL immunity (cont)

Tort liability of military officers: an initial examination of Chappell. Don Zillman, ref Army Law 27-50-128 29-37 Ag **83-015**

Use of compelled testimony in military administrative proceedings. Thomas R. Folk, ref Army Law 27-50-128 1-13 Ag **83-015**

LEGAL profession

Advice of counsel. Nav Civ Eng 23 2 26 Sum **83-077**

American Bar Association/Young Lawyers Divisin mid-year convention. Bruce E. Kasold, Army Law 27-50-127 27-28 Jl **83-015**

American Bar Association/Young Lawyers Division annual convention. Bruce E. Kasold, Army Law 27-50-121 29-30 Ja **83-015**

American Bar Association/Young Lawyers Division military service lawyers committee meeting. Bruce E. Kasold, Army Law 27-50-125 36-37 My **83-015**

Annual compilation of policy letters of the Judge Advocate General 1982. Army Law 27-50-122 1-8 F **83-015**

AO 1982-63: Check-off system used by law partnership to solicit funds to its PAC. FEC Rec 9 3 5 Mr **83-225**

Area defense counsel credibility. Bernard E. Donahue, il, ref Reporter 11 4 113-115 Ag **82-242**

Attorney work-product protection. Foia Update 4 3 6 Sum **83-306**

Bar membership and continuing legal education requirements. tab Army Law 27-50-121 31-33 Ja **83-015**

Client perjury: a guide for military defense counsel. Lawrence A. Gaydos, ref Army Law 27-50-129 13-22 S **83-015**

Commander and the defense counsel. Stephen J. Kaczynski, il Infantry 73 6 23-27 N-D **83-312**

Conflict of interest: a free meal may be your most expensive one. Thaddeus J. Rozanski, C Guard Eng Dig 22 219 3-7 Sum **83-284**

Dangling participles, hanging prepositions, and other high crimes against the English language. Richard P. Laverdure, ref Army Law 27-50-121 25-29 Ja **83-015**

Discovery—foundation for due process. Larry R. Dean, ref Army Law 27-50-125 13-18 My **83-015**

Effective assistance of counsel. John A. Schaefer, ref Army Law 27-50-130 25-37 O **83-015**

Exemption 5 upheld in Grolier. Foia Update 4 3 1-2 Sum **83-306**

General Counsel reflects on government experience. Charles A. Moore, Monitor 3 7 3+ Ap 4 **83-304**

Goode response seven years later. Richard A. Morgan, ref Reporter 12 2 32-40 Ap **83-242**

If it's legal, is it moral? Michael McKown, il Sold Sup J 9 1 14-16 Ja-F **82-301**

In memoriam: Charles Lowman Decker. por Mil Law Rev 100 2-3 Spr **83-067**

Judge advocate shares his views on leadership. Edward J. Murphy, Air Univ Rev 34 3 47-49 Mr-Ap **83-008**

Judiciary: caveat. See issues of Reporter **83-242**

Meaning of being part of the "corps". Richard J. Bednar, Army Law 27-50-123 1-2 Mr **83-015**

Medical law and risk management. Reporter 11 6 187-188 D **82-242**

NIMH briefs "ambassadors" to Europe. il Adamha N 9 13 3 Jl 22 **83-299**

Obtaining military publications of interest to the Judge Advocate. Army Law 27-50-124 16-18 Ap **83-015**

Part I: guilty plea checklist. ref Advocate 15 1 5-74 Ja-F **83-240**

Power struggles in the child abuse field. Elizabeth Davoren, il, ref Child Today 12 6 14-16 N-D **83-022**

Professional ethics and criminal justice: standards for the prosecution and defense functions. Robert B. Slocum, il, ref Reporter 12 3 62-70 Je **83-242**

Professional responsibility opinion: cases 82-3, 82-4. ref Army Law 27-50-128 37-40 Ag **83-015**

Quick reference guide to medical law topics. Jeffrey L. Grundtisch, tab Med Serv Dig 34 2 13-16 Mr-Ap **83-229**

Recovery agenda for the mid-1980's. Charles R. Lucy, Reporter 11 5 139-143 O **82-242**

Reports on the 76th annual meeting of the American Association of Law Libraries. Marie-Louise H. Bernal and others, Lib Cong Inf Bul 42 47 402-406 N 21 **83-062**

Reserve participation in appellate practice. Army Law 27-50-124 19 Ap **83-015**

Side bar. See issues of Advocate **83-240**

SJA as the commander's lawyer: a realistic proposal. Lawrence A. Gaydos, ref Army Law 27-50-128 14-22 Ag **83-015**

Soldier-lawyers serve time with the Corps. Margaret McBride, il Eng Update 7 12 7 D **83-294**

Standard for admitting scientific evidence: a critique from the perspective of juror psychology. Edward J. Imwinkelried, ref Mil Law Rev 100 99-118 Spr **83-067**

Supreme Court reviews hiring, promotion policies of law firms. Wom & Work np S-O **83-135**

Targeting federal resources on recidivists: an empirical view. Brian Forst and others, ref Fed Prob 47 2 10-20 Je **83-047** through BRS (GOVT), BRS/BRKTHRU, and BRS/After Dark, as well as on CD-ROM through WILSONDISC. During the late 1980s, publication lags developed with IUSGP, and it has fallen behind as much as almost four years. Unfortunately, this time lag diminishes the usefulness of an otherwise notable contribution to the bibliographic control of federal government periodical literature.

With the indexing of many statistically oriented periodicals through the *American Statistics Index*, significantly improved access accrued to this segment of the journal literature as well.

An index easily forgotten because of its specialized nature that provides subject access to over seventy English-language military and aeronautical periodicals is the quarterly *Air University Library Index to Military Periodicals* (Maxwell Air Force Base, AL: Air University Library), issued under variant titles since 1949. At least twenty-five of the journals indexed are government publications.

At this point, one might observe that an important feature of the *Periodicals Supplement* to the *Monthly Catalog* is that it tells the user where government periodicals are indexed. Each main entry contains "Indexed by" information citing indexing sources such as IUSGP, ASI, and others.

Government Journal of the Future

Rapidly changing technologies are having an impact on government periodicals of the 1990s. The advent of electronic bulletin boards in the late 1980s signaled changes in the availability of some government journals. One of the first journals to cease publication in paper and to become available only in electronic format was *TOPS: Trade Opportunities Bulletin*. This important Department of Commerce tool was transferred to the Economic Bulletin Board (EBB), available to libraries and others through the National Technical Information Service (NTIS). The disappearance of *TOPS* in a print version gave pause to librarians in particular. Many of the government's economic indicators, commonly dispensed to the public in other printed journals, are also available via EBB. Might some of these other journals also disappear? At this writing, one can only caution that trends of this nature warrant close observation.

Another popular government newsletter, although continuing to be available in print format, has been searchable in full text online (DIALOG Files 194-195) for a while. Issued every weekday by the Commerce Department, the *Commerce Business Daily* (C 1.76) alerts firms interested in bidding on government purchases, purchasing surplus property, or seeking subcontracts from prime contractors of existing opportunities.

Depository librarians already know that one way to keep track of official changes in government serials is to observe the "Whatever Happened to ...???" column in *Administrative Notes*. At the same time, news regarding the publication status of some other major government journals and their possible demise began spreading rapidly in the 1990s as librarians subscribing to the Government Documents Round Table's (GODORT's) Listserv (accessed by the code GOVDOC-L@SUVM.BITNET) began exchanging rapidfire information (and, sometimes, misinformation) and taking quick action on journals such as the *Department of State Bulletin, Business Conditions Digest,* and NASA's *Scientific and Technical Aerospace Reports* (NAS 1.9/4). The status of numerous government periodicals appeared in jeopardy, and the ready availability of information traditionally contained in them became a cause of concern.

GOVERNMENT SERIALS AND SUBSCRIPTION SERVICES

The government newsletter or periodical is only one, albeit important, component in the larger picture of the government serial. Therefore, it seems fitting to focus attention on additional types of serials. The term *serial* has been variously and extensively defined, but for the purpose of this chapter, it includes those irregular or regular issuances of the federal government such as titles in series; annual, biennial, monthly, and quarterly reports; looseleaf and legal services; and the previously discussed periodicals.

Federal Serials

Serial publications are normally items held together by a common thread. They could be the annual reports of any agency, regular series such as the monthly or quarterly subseries within the *Current Industrial Reports* (C 3.158), or the irregularly issued items within the U.S. Geological Survey's Professional Paper (I 19.16) series or the Library of Congress's *Network Planning Papers* (LC 30.24). Some samples of different serial types may provide the best aid to a basic understanding of this complex genre.

Some serials, such as the *Annual Report* (TD 1.1) of the Transportation Department, retain a consistent title year after year, whereas other annual publications, such as the *Yearbook of Agriculture*, take on a unique title each year. For instance, the 1990 *Yearbook* is titled *Americans in Agriculture: Portraits in Diversity* (A 1.10:990). Irregular serials, many of which are numbered series, also often bear individual titles, and libraries are faced with perplexing dilemmas over whether to record such items simply by overall serial title and number and rely on printed index sources to ferret out specifics or to analyze each unique title in the series. A simple numbered series might be the National Institute on Alcohol and Alcoholism's Alcohol Alert (HE 20.8322) series, in which, for example, number 2 is *Alcohol and Aging*, number 4 is *Alcohol and Cognition*, and number 7 is *Alcohol Use and Abuse: Where Do the Numbers Come From?*

An example of a more complex series is the Bulletin series issued since 1913 by the Bureau of Labor Statistics (BLS). Until recently certain popular, heavily demanded titles resided within the Bulletin series and all bulletins fell under the L 2.3 SuDocs designation. One had to dig within the larger series to locate important recurring titles because each year of the title was assigned a different bulletin number. This meant complex record development, especially for research libraries shelving by SuDocs and for whom being able to deliver quickly on a patron request for historical editions of, for instance, the *Handbook of Labor Statistics*, is of critical importance to good service. Now the *Handbook* (L 2.3/5) and other major titles such as the *Industry Wage Surveys* (L 2.3/3) and *Occupational Outlook Handbook* (L 2.3/4) have been accorded the individual SuDocs stems indicated in parentheses. Of course, BLS still assigns a bulletin number.

Looseleaf and Subscription Services

Looseleaf services are another essential part of any major collection of government publications and are counted among serial publications. Again, there are various types, and if nothing else were to distinguish government publications from the rest of the library, looseleaf services surely do. This is not to say that looseleaf services do not exist among the commercial sources of publications; it is simply that such a sheer volume of them exists among government publications. And their complexity occupies extensive processing and filing time in any collection.

Typical of the looseleaf services is the important *Catalog of Federal Domestic Assistance* (PrEx 2.20), which advises on all government grants available; explains eligibility and filing requirements; and indicates uses and restrictions, regulations, guidelines, program accomplishments, information contacts, and so forth. It is subject to constant change, hence the looseleaf nature of the service. The *Catalog* is also available online through FAPERS, offered by the General Services Administration, as well as in an easier to use but less comprehensive commercial edition titled *Government Assistance Almanac*.[6]

Serving a more specialized audience is the looseleaf *Federal Travel Regulations*. Consisting of a basic manual and supplementary material, the *Regulations* administer federal civilian employee entitlements and allowances for per diem, transportation, and relocation. These rules are promulgated by the General Services Administration under the provisions of Title 5 *United States Code*, section 57, and are classed in GS 1.6/8-2 as a Bulletins series. They are announced in *Price List 36* (PL-36) and are available to depository libraries.

One of the most complex looseleaf issuances is the *Federal Personnel Manual* (PM 1.14/2). The basic manual provides information on the general policies and requirements in the several program areas of personnel management and is divided into a number of supplements ranging from Personnel Data Standards (PM 1.14/3:292-1) to Life Insurance (PM 1.14/3:870-1). Similarly, *Federal Aviation Regulations* is divided into over thirty numbered Parts covering airworthiness standards, ultralight vehicles, airport aid program, etc. These *Regulations* are also available in subscription form as announced in PL-36 and on deposit. Looseleaf services typically arrive punched for a three-ring binder and require constant updating as new pages are received replacing superseded information.

In administering a collection, it becomes evident that some services are accompanied by transmittal sheets that clearly state which pages are to be removed and which inserted into the basic manual. These duties can be relegated to competent clerical personnel. On the other hand, some extensive and complex services are accompanied by confusing transmittals that require the effort of an experienced staff member. The receipt of looseleaf pages for which no basic volume was ever sent, or sets of insert pages received out of sequence, has perplexed many a documents professional and required valuable time to resolve. Likewise, rectifying a once improperly filed looseleaf service can be the filer's nightmare. Some librarians, frustrated by the experienced staffing and time required to maintain these services properly, have resorted to hiring outside filing service agencies that are available in some areas of the country.

Legal services are also considered here under the general rubric of serials. The legal services may have slightly different patterns of updating—often the addition of pocket parts or the substitution of cumulated editions—to distinguish them. As with other looseleaf services, they require care and accuracy in filing lest one confuse the naive user or provoke the hurried attorney with inadequately updated source material. The *United States Reports* (Ju 6.8), discussed further in chapter 9, represents a fairly straightforward service in which initial slip decisions are superseded by advance sheets (eagerly awaited by law review staffs so they can give proper official citations to Supreme Court cases), which are subsequently superseded by the final bound volume. The advent of electronic publishing such as Project Hermes may eventually mitigate some of the filing requirements, but most libraries will still need to cope with them.

Bibliographic Control of
Government Serials

Control of the serial literature of the federal government has always been a challenge. International Standard Serial Numbers (ISSNs), an eight-digit number consisting of seven digits as a unique title number plus a check digit, were first assigned to government serials in the late 1970s, when the National Serials Data Program (NSDP), in cooperation with Cornell University, began assigning key titles and ISSNs to these publications. It was at this point that the *Monthly Catalog* began its introduction of a separate *Serials Supplement.*

Various attempts have been made to bring these materials under improved control, with probably the most extensive effort resulting in volume IV of the five-volume *Checklist of United States Public Documents, 1789-1976*, titled *U.S. Government Serial Titles 1789-1976* (mentioned earlier in this chapter). Two useful more recent sources are LeRoy C. Schwarzkopf, *Government Reference Serials* (Englewood, CO: Libraries Unlimited, 1988), an annotated bibliographic guide to about 600 items primarily depository in nature, which now forms a companion guide to the publisher's *Government Reference Books*; and Priscilla C. Geahigan and Robert F. Rose, *Business Serials of the U.S. Government*, 2d ed. (Chicago: American Library Association, 1988). Of continuing substantial value for tracing a serial's history is John L. Andriot, *Guide to U.S. Government Publications*, previously cited.

Issues of *The Serials Librarian* (New York: Haworth Press) as well as other library journals need to be consulted to keep up with frequent changes in government serials. GPO's own *Administrative Notes* forms an important source of information for those responsible for record keeping. For others more involved with the acquisition of government serials, *The Bowker Annual Library and Book Trade Almanac* keeps track of prices of document serials. The 1991 edition, although showing that prices for government serials rose less on the average than those for other categories of serials, cites an increase from an average cost of $62.88 in 1977 to $101.45 in 1990.[7]

In its comprehensive list of the types of serials, the Fall 1983 issue of *The Serials Librarian* carried categories that subsume government publications, regardless of format. Among those listed were administrative reports, annuals, bibliographies, bulletins, catalogs, directories, financial statements, guidebooks, handbooks, indexing and abstracting services, journals, law reports, laws and statutes, lists, looseleaf services, monographic series, newsletters, patents, periodicals, standards, statistics, technical reports, and yearbooks.[8] As noted, these forms require accurate record keeping and contain significant and often timely information.

NOTES

[1]Andrew D. Osborn, *Serial Publications: Their Place and Treatment in Libraries*, 3d ed. (Chicago: American Library Association, 1980), p. 39.

[2]Office of Management and Budget, *Report to the Senate Appropriations Committee on Administrative Expenses* (Washington, DC: GPO, March 1982), p. 11. Total fiscal year (FY) 1982 spending on periodicals and pamphlets was an estimated $138 million.

[3]"Federal Audiovisual Aids and Publications," Statement by the President, April 20, 1981, in *Weekly Compilation of Presidential Documents*, 17 (April 27, 1981): 447.

[4]*Checklist of United States Public Documents 1789-1976*, 5 vols. (Arlington, VA: United States Historical Documents Institute, 1972, 1978), p. v.

[5]*Cumulative Title Index to United States Public Documents 1789-1976*, 16 vols. (Washington, DC: United States Historical Documents Institute, 1979-1982), p. vii.

[6]J. Robert Dumouchel, *Government Assistance Almanac, 1990-1991*, 4th ed. (Detroit, MI: Omnigraphics, 1990). "The ALMANAC reduces the information in the federal catalog's approximately 2000 pages [including the 'Update'] to the essentials needed by most persons seeking federal assistance" (p. 1).

[7]*The Bowker Annual Library and Book Trade Almanac*, 36th ed. (New York: R. R. Bowker, 1991), p. 402.

[8]"Appendix I: Definition of a Serial and Types of Serials," *Serials Librarian*, 8 (Fall 1983): 99-100.

Appendix:
GODORT's "Principles on
Government Information"

The following is a list of eleven principles set forth by the Government Documents Round Table of the American Library Association (ALA/GODORT). They present GODORT's position on the collection, dissemination, and management of government information. While some of the principles and background statements may relate directly to United States federal information and the U.S. Depository Library Program, the principles and statements are meant to be more broadly applicable to all types of governmental information, be it city, county, state/province, regional, national, or international (or any of the many derivations or combinations thereof).

1. **Access to government information is a public right that must not be restricted by administrative barriers, geography, ability to pay, or format.**

    An informed citizenry is a prerequisite to maintaining the social contract between the established government and those governed by it. The people who constitute nations, states, or localities require unimpeded access to information to continually assess and evaluate their governments. Government must accept the responsibility to provide to its citizens unrestricted access to public information on government activities. This responsibility includes providing information regardless of geographical location or mobility of those who require it. Information must be made available to the public without impediment through deliberate policies, charging fees which intentionally or unintentionally limit access by those unable to pay, or by limiting access through the use of format(s) which are not equally accessible to all citizens.

2. **The government has a responsibility to collect and disseminate information to the public.**

    The free flow of information between the government and the public which it serves is essential to maintaining an informed citizenry. The public's right to know about governmental operations and functions is essential in holding government accountable to its citizenry. To facilitate accountability, it is the government's responsibility to collect information on its policies, programs, debates, deliberations, and legislative or executive activities, and to disseminate this information to the public.

431

3. **Government information, including information in electronic form, should be disseminated in a manner and format that promotes its usefulness to the public.**

Because many different social and commercial decisions depend on information generated by governments, it is vital that governments issue information in formats that promote access to and enhancement of the usefulness of government information. Public access to government information must not be thwarted by costs nor by special knowledge required to use the media in which government information is maintained. In managing information resources, governments must always consider the dual responsibility of maintaining public information in formats that are useful both to government agencies and to the public. Furthermore, information collected by the government must be consistent in content so as to facilitate geographic and/or chronological extrapolations, and be in formats which make it easily accessible to the public.

4. **Depository library programs must be preserved to provide equitable, no-fee access to government information for all citizens.**

Depository library programs are effective means for providing wide dispersal of and free public access to government information. As joint ventures between government and libraries, depository library programs are based on the principle that government information is a public resource that must be freely available to the people regardless of their location. The imposition of fees by libraries or by governments to access government information   would undermine the basic principle of free access to this rich public resource. Furthermore, user fees would deny access to government information by those unable to pay the fees. This would foster the creation of an information poor and an information elite. The introduction of such a convention should be abhorrent to governments dedicated to principle of equal opportunity.

5. **Cost of collecting, collating, storing, and disseminating government information should be supported by appropriation of public funds.**

The collection, collation, storage, and dissemination of public information are integral responsibilities of government. Government must allocate adequate financial resources from publicly appropriated funds to meet these responsibility. The government cannot abrogate this obligation to ensure that government information is freely and equitably available to the public.

6. **The role of private publishers should complement government responsibilities in the collection, storage, and dissemination of public Information. Private sector involvement does not relieve the government of its information responsibilities.**

Access to government information is essential to the maintenance of a responsible government, the health and well-being of society, and the continued economic growth and development of the nation. The obligation to guarantee full public access to valuable government information resources rests with the government. While the participation of the private sector in the collection, storage, and dissemination of government information may be significant, this involvement does not relieve the government of its fundamental information responsibilities. Government must guarantee widespread, free, and equitable access to public information, regardless of whether the information is produced and disseminated by the government or through the services of the private sector. In its contracts with the private sector, government must carefully assess whether factors such as corporate stability, continuity of service, proprietary control, or fees required to assure profitability will impede public access to the product.

7. **Government information policy must insure the integrity of public Information. This policy should be determined by the chosen representatives of the people.**

Just as the government has a responsibility to collect and disseminate information to the public, the government must also guarantee that information collected by the government is presented to the public in its entirety, without editing or omissions which may change content or interpretation. This policy is intended to ensure the integrity of the information collected. Furthermore, policy affecting the collection and dissemination of government information must come under the review and approval of the elected representatives of the citizenry.

8. **It is essential to safeguard the right of the government information user to privacy and confidentiality.**

It is essential to protect the individual's right to privacy, therefore confidentiality must be maintained in all transactions wherein individuals access government information, whether through libraries, government agencies, or private vendors. Any mechanism that might identify users must be prohibited, except in instances where proper legal procedures are employed.

9. Government has an obligation to archive and preserve public information, regardless of format.

Most information generated by government serves as the official public record of government. Government, as an agent of the people, has the responsibility to preserve public information, regardless of format, as official record. To fulfill this responsibility, government must examine preservation technologies and adopt those which will best preserve government information. Archived government information, regardless of format, must be readily accessible to the public, except for information which would violate the right of privacy or endanger national security.

10. Government has a responsibility to provide comprehensive catalog of all public information and services.

Government information is a public resource collected at public expense. A comprehensive catalog describing all government information and information services, regardless of their format, is necessary to ensure that the public has the knowledge of and access to this resource. The absence of such a catalog is, in effect, a barrier to public access to government information. The catalog must provide sufficient information by which individuals seeking government information can identify and access it. Furthermore, access to this comprehensive catalog must be widely available and in formats that ensure all people have the opportunity to utilize it.

11. Copyright should not be applied to government information.

Copyright of government information would impede public access to that information. The underlying intent of copyright is to protect the intellectual property rights of private authors. However, property rights of government information reside with the people; therefore, copyright should not apply to information produced by government.

Title/Series Index

Personal Name Index

451

Subject Index

Marcive, 39, 66, 101
Marine Corps, United States, 183, 236-37
Maritime Administration, 258-59
Marsh, Folsom v., 391
Mathias, Charles McC., 21, 72
McCormick, Thomas J., 69-70
Mead Data Central, 281, 288, 311, 312, 388, 391-92
Mead Data Central, West v., 391-92
MEDLARS, 245-46
Memorial addresses, 164-65
Merchant Marine, 258
Metropolitan Statistical Areas, 322, 349(n)
Microform products
  distributed to depository libraries, 55, 69-72, 121
  dual format distribution to depository libraries, 55, 70, 71-72
  silver halide versus diazo, 71
  as substitute for hard copy in depository libraries, 68
MicroPatent, 381
Micropublishing Advisory Committee, 69
Military review courts, 286, 301
Minerals Management Service, 248-49
Mines, Bureau of, 249-50
Minority Business Development Agency, 230
Minority Business Development Centers, 230
Monthly Catalog
  audiovisual materials in, 86
  automated versions, 39, 66, 100-101
  commercial indexes, 95, 99
  features of bibliographic records, 94-95
  format, 90, 94
  full-text editions of entries, 99
  history, 89-90
  indexes, 90
  Online Computer Library Center participation, 37, 90
  production of, 37, 39
  sample entries, 96-98(fig.)
  searching, 94-95
  Serial Set supplement, 92, 93(fig.), 150, 154(fig.)
Museum Services, Institute of, 269

NASA RECON, 365
National Advisory Committee for Aeronautics, 351
National Advisory Council on International Monetary and Financial Policies, 277

National Aeronautics and Space Administration, 14, 22, 265
  CD-ROM products, 366
  NASA RECON database, 365
  publications, 363, 365
  technical reports, 356, 366
  thesauri, 356, 359, 365
National Agricultural Library, 224-25
National Agricultural Statistics Service, 226
National Archives, 266, 329
National Archives, Office of the, 266
National Archives and Records Administration, 85, 103, 266-67
National Archives and Records Service, 14, 398
National Archives Trust Fund, 329
National Association of Government Communicators, 13
National Audiovisual Center, 85-86
National Bureau of Standards, 230
National Cartographic Information Center, 411
National Center for Education Statistics, 238, 239
National Center for Health Statistics, 244, 344
National Center for Toxicological Research, 244
National Center on Child Abuse and Neglect, 241
National Clearinghouse for Census Data Services, 328
National Commission on Libraries and Information Science, xxviii, xxx, 281
National Convention of Disabled American Veterans, 147
National Credit Union Administration, 276-77
National Defense University, 233
National Encampment proceedings, 147
National Endowment for the Arts, 269
National Endowment for the Humanities, 269
National Foundation on the Arts and Humanities, 268-69
National Geographic Names Data Base, 415
National Highway Traffic Safety Administration, 258
National Historical Publications and Records Commission, 179, 267
National Information Services Corporation, 411
National Institute of Mental Health, 243